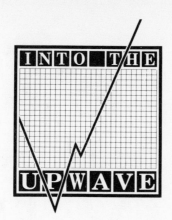

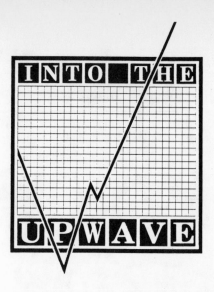

INTO THE UPWAVE

HOW TO PROSPER
FROM SLUMP TO BOOM

Robert Beckman

MILESTONE PUBLICATIONS

By the same author:
THE DOWNWAVE
SUPERTIMING
THE ELLIOT WAVE PRINCIPLE AS APPLIED TO THE UK STOCK MARKET
SHARE PRICE ANALYSIS

Published by
Milestone Publications
62 Murray Road,
Horndean, Portsmouth, Hants PO8 9JL

First edition 1988
Second edition 1988

British Library Cataloguing in Publication Data

Beckman, Robert
  Into the upwave : how to prosper from
  slump to boom.
  1. Economic history——1971-
  I. Title
  330.9   HC59

  ISBN 1 85265 110 5

Design   Brian Iles
Index   Anne Coles

Typeset by Barbara James Typesetting, Hayling Island, Hampshire
Printed and bound in Great Britain by Richard Clay, Chichester, Sussex.

CONTENTS

ILLUSTRATIONS

To my wife Penelope,
the best cure for recession, depression,
inflation, stagflation, hyper-inflation. . .
or whatever other catastrophe anyone
could ever possibly conceive.

ACKNOWLEDGEMENTS

I would first like to acknowledge Professor William Garrett, who first introduced me to the work of Josef Schumpeter and F.A. Hayek, from whom I first began to learn precisely how the world really worked. Second, I am grateful to James Dines, for his remarkable insight into the human aspect of economic behaviour. It was through the writing of James Dines that I truly began to appreciate the role of political self-interest in the economic free-for-all that has landed us where we are today. Finally, I must acknowledge George Soros for broadening my thinking. His brilliance has all but taken the fun out of economic forecasting!

Above all, I wish to thank those who played key roles in the production of this book. If it were not for the constant encouragement of Nicholas Pine, my publisher, there would certainly have been no book. If it were not for the tireless efforts of Bob Finigan, whose contributions have been well beyond that of an editor, the book would be far, far less readable than it is. . . and probably a lot less accurate. Betty Stabler was instrumental in the editing and typing of part of the manuscripts, which only someone with considerable courage would have dared attempt — given my less than intelligible typing. She also assisted in the irksome task of compiling obscure paragraphs and articles that have appeared in the various issues of *Investors Bulletin* that I have written over the years.

And, of course, I must acknowledge the contribution of governments the world over, without whose mindless meddling, rhetoric and propaganda, this book would not be mandatory reading for all.

INTRODUCTION

Pavlov, in his experiments with animals, demonstrated that one of the most certain methods of breaking down the stability of a dog is to give a trained but anxious animal a random series of positive and negative conditioned stimuli. The result initially will produce uncontrollable neurotic excitement which will ultimately lead to hysterical submissive behaviour.

"You will, of course, have heard of Pavlov, the Russian medical psychologist?" asks one of the KGB agents of the hero in Alistair MacLean's espionage novel *The Secret Ways*. The agent then pauses pensively before the prisoners from whom he intends to obtain classified information. Then adds:

"With the combination of the very advanced developments we have made in Pavlov's physiological techniques and certain psychological processes that will become apparent to you in the course of time, we can achieve quite incredible results. We can break any human being who has ever lived. . . and break him so that never a scar shows. With the exception of the incurably insane, who are already broken, there are no exceptions. Your stiff-upper-lipped Englishman of fiction. . . and, for all I know, fact. . . will break eventually like everyone else; the efforts of the Americans to train their servicemen to resist what the world so crudely calls brainwashing. . . let us call it rather a reintegration of personality. . . are as pathetic as they are hopeless. We broke Cardinal Mindszenty in eighty-four hours: we can break anyone."

Several years ago, around the time of the U-2 episode which was the basis of an international incident between the Soviet Union and the United States, Dr. William Sargent, of the Department of Psychological Medicine at St. Thomas's Hospital, accused the Communists of using Pavlovian tactics as part of a "psychological warfare scheme." In the rantings and utterances of Nikita Khrushchev at the time of the Paris Summit Conference, Dr Sargent claims that signals were applied to the free-world citizenry with such skill and subtlety "that some of the British and American press and public alike became temporarily just as suggestible as did Pavlov's dogs." In MacLean's spy tale, the purpose of heightening the intended victim's suggestibility is made clear. The subject is reduced to a soporific state where the extraction of information is facilitated. . . and, as MacLean's KGB devil states,

"We will add what we please to your minds, and that, for you, will also be the truth!"

Perhaps, unknowingly, it would appear that politicians and spokesmen of American industry were exposing the free-world citizenry to a similar phenomenon during the years 1979-1983, as a result of the strenuous attempts that were made to produce "forecast-feedback" among businessmen and the electorate in the United States at about that time. Attempting to achieve forecast-feedback is the technique by which vested interest organisations will produce a positive forecast in the hope that if enough people believe in the forecast, the forecast will come true.

In other words, if an economic recovery is forecast, the intention is that in preparing for and anticipating this recovery, the recovery will be induced.

The global economy entered a recession during the fourth quarter of 1979. The consensus forecast was that the recession would be short and shallow leading to a recovery during the second half of 1980. Businessmen began increasing their inventories in anticipation of the recovery, while members of the public assumed they would be able to coast right through the recession without dismay. The recovery never took place. Inventories remained on the shelf. Businessmen began going bankrupt. The fourth quarter of 1980 saw the recession biting deeper.

At the beginning of 1981 the consensus forecast agreed the recession had lasted longer, and caused more destruction, than originally anticipated. But it was unanimously accepted that the recessionary forces had just about spent their force, and an economic recovery was likely to be underway by the spring of 1981. Once again, businessmen began increasing their borrowings, boosting their inventories and generally making preparations compatible with the upsurge in demand that was promised. The fourth quarter of 1981 arrived, and once again the high hopes were shattered. The economic recovery, which all had agreed upon for 1981, had proved to be just as elusive as it had in 1980. The number of corporate bankruptcies mounted. The number of businessmen and individuals who were willing to believe an economic recovery was around the corner shrank.

You can fool all the people some of the time, and some of the people all of the time. The future of many political appointments rests upon this credo. I'm not saying that politicians all get together and say to each other, "what cock-and-bull story can we make up to convince people an economic recovery is on the way?" I feel their motives are far less sinister and are, indeed, well meaning in most cases. Since 1979, the authorities have wanted very badly to convince themselves that an economic recovery is on the way. They succeeded in doing just that. . . convincing themselves very badly. In early 1981, the self-delusions began anew. The consensus forecast called for an economic recovery during the spring of 1982.

During the course of the first three quarters of 1983, there were pockets of strength in a few of the economic aggregates of the US economy. But they were in no way commensurate with the type of economic activity seen during the recovery phases of the 1950s, 1960s and 1970s. There was also strong evidence to suggest that the modicum of economic improvement which had developed would soon peter out. In the meantime, the world's capital markets began behaving like an elevator with a lunatic at the controls, implying that the participants had reached the state of "hysterical and submissive behaviour" observed in Pavlov's dogs.

Are we to assume from the evidence that the authorities (or their behind-the-scenes manipulators) had begun dallying in the markets in order to make capitalistic hay of the findings of Dr Pavlov? The possibility cannot be ruled out.

Attempting to manipulate markets in an effort to convince a sceptical electorate that all is well is certainly not a new trick. Richard Witney, president of the New York Stock Exchange, tried it in 1929 when he confidently strolled across the trading floor buying stocks in an effort to convince the madding crowd that there was no need for alarm.

That exercise may have allayed the fears of a few in the shorter term. But it was ultimately futile in the longer term. Such has been the experience with similar manipulative endeavours throughout history. The inexorable economic forces that permeate the world economy are far too great for any man, or group of men, to manipulate for any appreciable period.

Besides, there will always be those who will refuse to join the herd; often with such determination that friends and colleagues alike will merely conclude that they have a perverse nature. *This*, it will be assumed, is why they charge in as enthusiastic buyers after a severe price decline, but show signs of extreme anxiety after a long period of rising prices and rampant speculation. Such, I must confess, is my inclination. It is one which has developed over the past 30 years. Not, I would claim, through sheer perversity, but because I learned very early on in my investment career to ignore what others on Wall Street were saying about the Market, and take my own decision as to *what the Market itself was trying to tell me.*

One event which stands out in my mind occurred during the 1960s stock market boom in America.

For several years I shared a desk with Charlie Meyer, one of Wall Street's old-timers. He had been around during the Wall Street crash, and had witnessed the events leading up to it. Charlie was an instinctive stock market operator. He would gauge the investment climate by the tempo of speculative activity. Without balance sheets and other popular investment aids, he managed to acquire several million dollars just by watching the prices as they travelled across the New York Stock Exchange ticker-tape, and by monitoring the expressions of greed and fear on the faces of his fellow investors.

One day, Charlie spun around in his chair, slapped me on the back and said, "Beckman! Too many dummies are getting rich. I'm getting the hell out." Charlie telephoned the firm's floor broker on the New York Exchange, and sold every investment he had within the hour. That was two days before shares peaked and began tumbling. Charlie reckoned the stock market craze had turned to insanity, and that share prices had reached a level beyond any realistic measure of value.

G.F. Warren and F.A. Pearson in *The Prices Series* wrote of the dislocations which followed that legendary collapse on Wall Street in 1929:

> "Economic changes, drastic in character, occurred with such rapidity that it was difficult for the human mind to forsee them or even to grasp the significance of the changes after they occur."

In the spring of 1983, I was putting the finishing touches to my book, *The Downwave*. It was clear that the world was no longer moving towards the crest of a wave of prosperity. Now, after three decades, that phase has ended. Henceforth we would be moving into a period where the world as we knew it would be turned upside down. We were due for one of those "economic changes, drastic in character". I also realised that many would not only find it difficult to grasp, but that they would do their best neither to hear, nor see, nor sense that any change was taking place at all.

Absurd, you may say, since the forces that shape our destiny (and our individual fortunes) must involve change.

Yet, in spite of the certainty of change, most individuals are essentially conservative, fearing change more than anything else. Most of us spend our lives in a futile effort to halt the passage of time. Most people expect and wish to continue to plod on, clinging to the paths that are familiar to them. It would not be unreasonable to assume that in a bustling and dynamic society such as the United States, people would prefer change. Yet, this is not so. Most changes are generally regarded as regrettable.

Any sane man must truly reconcile himself to the undeniable fact: change is inevitable. The problem is, there is no consensus as to the direction of change. Few people feel any competency in deciding the direction that change will take. We are told that history will repeat itself, that the changes that have gone before will happen again. George Santayana tells us that if we cannot learn from history we are condemned to repeat it. The only thing we can really learn from history is that nobody really ever learns anything from history. The lessons of the past are often denied.

We resort to planning our lives as if the future involved nothing more than a straight line projection of the past until death do us part. We demand higher salaries because we think prices will continue to go up. We have been brainwashed by successive governments into believing that a steadily increasing standard of living is our inalienable right. So we continue to seek higher wages to pay for higher prices which we think will go on rising forever, because they have gone up for as long as we can remember.

Along with this inalienable right to a steady increase in our living standards, we also believe we are entitled to our own homes. It is part of the system. Maybe the best part. Over the past couple of years we've seen the rise in house prices slow and actually fall in some places. We assume this temporary, because we have been programmed to believe that house prices will always rise. It might be a tighter pinch nowadays to meet those higher mortgage repayments, but buying a house has always been a good investment. There is really no reason to doubt that it wouldn't always be a good investment. We are undeterred by the recent sluggishness of prices. We will buy a house as soon as we can, or move into a bigger and better one.

As businessmen, we have learned to live with inflation. By and large, inflation has been our friend. Interest rates may be high, but as long as we have inflation we will also be able to pass those borrowing costs on to our customers in next year's price increase. If we borrow now to expand, the money we pay back will be worth less than the money we are borrowing. Inflation is not really such a bad deal. The last thing a businessman wants is empty shelves when his customers come into the shop to buy. He will keep those shelves full, no matter what the cost of borrowing. Inflation will always be around to bail him out. After all, it always has been. . . hasn't it?

As consumers, we are determined to live within our means even if we have to borrow to do it! A recent advertising campaign featured the slogan, "Now you can borrow all you need to get completely out of debt". The last thing in the world we want to do is save. We see how inflation has ravaged our life insurance policies. Twenty years ago when we took out a $10,000 endowment policy, we thought $10,000 would see us clear through our retirement. Now we see that $10,000 barely provides the down payment on our vacation home. No, we are certainly not going to get caught in that trap again. We should at least be capable of demonstrating the conditioned response of Pavlov's dog.

Live today, pay tomorrow. Why not? The government will see to it that we don't starve. The unions will protect our jobs. Inflation will protect our businesses. Over the past few years we have learned to keep up with inflation. Some of us have learned how to beat inflation by buying gold, property and other things that have risen in value faster than the rate of inflation. Now that we have learned to handle the problem, the rest of our lives should be serene.

While change is accepted, it is inconceivable that life as we perceive it in the future should be subject to any dramatic change. Our elders spoke of the Great Depression and falling prices. To us, that was just a freak, a one-off social phenomenon that could never happen again. Our programming instructs us that government has learned a great deal since the bad old days. Nothing like that could ever happen in our society. It never has since the dawn of creation. . . which we believe began just after World War II.

Most people are aware that inflation had accelerated at an alarming rate. A frightening rate. But that was only temporary. We now see that inflation is coming down again. It is assumed that the economy will soon return to normal and life will be just the same as it always was. Persistent inflation will disappear along with any other economic discomfort we can conceive. We've had a recession, but that recession has enabled the government to bring down the rate of inflation. Large numbers of people have lost their jobs in the process; but we still have our jobs, our businesses. The other guy losing his job, or going bankrupt, is a small price to pay for having our lives returned to the state to which we've become accustomed. All in all, there may be temporary dislocations to our life-style, but we are confident that government will be able to solve these problems. . . if not this government, another government. Pavlov lives!

If I were to describe the attitude of the American people during the early 1980s as one of self-satisfied complacency, shared by the majority of the people, I don't think I would be too far off the mark. Adults behave like children and children behave like adults, but this is progress. Government has gone into business, while business has gone into government. This is also progress. This is also considered to represent social progress. Uncle Sam has turned the country over to his Big Brother. Everybody loves Ronnie! Anyone who challenges this complacency is coded at best as a radical, at worst a lunatic.

Yet, this complacency must be challenged. The well-being of vast multitudes depend on it. We are now entering a social/political/economic environment of immense and dynamic change. Only a handful of people alive today are able to remotely recollect the nature of such changes. For most of you, the vast changes that are now taking place are totally unrecognised; to many, they will be without precedent. To those whose perspective goes beyond recent history, what is about to happen has happened before.

Changes in our environment which lie beyond the experience of four or five decades are in the course of development. What we are about to relive happened during only two decades in six. Personal life-styles are about to be reversed, and the precedents which served us so well during the past few decades will be of no use at all. As I will demonstrate, we are now embarking upon a period where the political, social, cultural and economic structures which we all know so well will be turned upside down. Our personal well-being will rely solely upon adapting to this much-changed social structure. The savers, the cautious, the prudent, the frugal, all who have been penalised during the past four decades, are about to be rewarded. The spenders, the profligates, the borrowers, the gamblers and the speculators, who have been rewarded over the past four decades, could soon be faced with the most horrifying experience of their lives.

Very few people will have opened their eyes to the changes that have already taken place since the platform began to rock in the latter part of 1983. Even fewer will be prepared for the changes that still lie ahead.

A large number will be unwilling or unable to accept that such changes could occur. It is a known fact that dynamic changes in our economic and social structure occur because most people never prepare for them, continuing in the future to make the same mistakes they've made in the past. In the following pages I will try to broaden the horizon of the reader by demonstrating the nature of the likely changes in the life-style of every person on this planet, while providing the empirical evidence to support the likelihood of the changes that I foresee. Secondly, I will try to help my readers develop a program, and life-style, which is compatible with the alterations that are likely to take place in our social and financial structure.

I am not forecasting either apocalypse or disaster in the years that lie ahead. I am doing nothing more than anticipating change. Those who are unable to adapt to these changes may suffer. Those who are willing and able to make the adjustments will flourish, and many find they are about to enter the most rewarding period of their lives.

Chapter One

THE DOWNWAVE REVISITED

The more extensive a man's knowledge of what has been done, the greater will be his power of knowing what to do.

Benjamin Disraeli

Eager in pursuit of the knowledge that is essential for any young man embarking on a career as a professional economist, I went through the standard University training then available in the 1950s. There (as I thought) I learned all there was to learn about the technique — as well as the *mystique* — of economics. By the early 1960s, I had been set loose to pursue my chosen career, in the course of which I believed I would undoubtedly make a signal contribution to the elimination of those economic ills which had periodically assailed us since the start of the Industrial Revolution.

It was not merely that I had faith in my ability. It was also that most of my contemporaries felt the same. We were utterly convinced that *our* generation was better equipped than any before to undertake the task. For one thing, we had such a mass of data, such an accumulation of wisdom, that for the first time since the Industrial Revolution we could ensure steady growth without summoning up those twin evils, Boom and Bust. For another, we at last understood how a national economy *really* worked; no need, therefore, to rely any longer on some wild theory, thought up in sheer desperation. We clearly *knew* the answers. We understood everything there was about economic relations. What's more, we had the micro-economic "models" with which to demonstrate their validity; not merely to academics and fellow-practitioners, either! But to anyone of reasonable intelligence, which naturally included national leaders and central bankers.

Moreover, at the Bretton Woods conference in 1944, the leading allied statesmen (and their economic advisors) had created two institutions which would ensure that international finance and international relations would henceforth be kept on an even keel. We — like our Professors — believed devoutly in the International Monetary Fund and the World Bank. To us they were more than mere symbols. They were the new tools for a New Age; tools with which skilled and dedicated international officials would maintain the World Economy in a safe and healthy condition. In short, the IMF and World Bank would be the economic and financial counterpart of the United Nations Assembly and the Security Council rolled into one.

The moment of truth came in the run-up — or run-down — to the 1972/75 recession. Professor James Morell of the Henley Institute had predicted that the FT 30 Share Index would undoubtedly reach the 700 level. I believed that too. In the event, in January 1975, we saw the FT 30 Share Index down to 146, with shares having lost 78% of their value. After that came the worst recession the world had known since the 1930s.

There was for me the consolation that no economist anywhere had been able to anticipate the return of recession. Certainly few if any realised the extent of the dislocation that a 78% fall in share values would bring for everyone, but particularly for the genuine entrepreneur.

As a professional money man, I could not afford to be caught out like that again. I realised I could no longer rely on the post-war "models" which we had built. I decided the only thing was to go back to fundamentals, and try to see whether some of the earlier economic "models" might prove helpful. Above all I wanted to look again at the work of those who had been right, for example, about the 1920s. That meant studying the work of men like A.C. Pigou, Professor W.L. Crum and another Harvard professor, Joseph Schumpeter. Schumpeter had combined the findings of three cyclical economists, Kitchin, Juglar and (a man we shall meet again before long) Kondratieff.

I realised that their economic models did not rely on the easy assumption that inflation was necessarily linked to prosperity. I looked closely at the structure of the longer cycles, because anyone who was prepared to study them should be able to read off the advance warning signals they contained.

By August 1974, I had studied the Long Wave cycles, as I shall recount later. I was therefore able to write in my publication, *Investors Bulletin:*

" — assuming that commodity prices have peaked this year, we would expect a trough in the stock market cycle between late 1974 and mid-1975 leading to a secondary recovery which will ultimately lead to another great depression, likely to begin in the early 1980s — *but not likely to materialise this decade."*

At the nadir of January '75, most of the City was mourning the death of the capitalist system, predicting that we were now in a bear market that would last for the forseeable future — if not longer! I, however, was able to confirm in my *Investors Bulletin* that we were about to see an extremely vigorous bull market running for the period of secondary prosperity which I had already forecast. This time I was right! The stock market hit bottom in January '75. It was bang on schedule. So was the final recovery phase. The FT 30 was making 600 by May '81, just as I forecast.

Already, though, in one of my regular broadcasts on LBC, in January 1979, I stated categorically that we should soon be entering a deep recession, far deeper than that of '73 to '75. What's more, it would end by plunging the world into a depression as deep, painful and ugly as that of the 1930s.

By the following year, 1980, I decided that one thing I *had* to do was to put my work into book form; which is how *The Downwave,* subtitled *Surviving the Second Great Depression,* and published in 1983, came to be written.

In the five years that have passed since publication of *The Downwave,* more and more evidence has come to light to confirm my first impression that we should again be forced to relive the experience of the 1930s. Nor was I alone in that view.

In June 1974, Professor Geoffrey Barraclough, the historian, implied (in a piece he wrote for the *New York Review of Books)* that a steep lunge into a depression could be expected around 1979. In the *Wall Street Journal,* in October 1974, Alfred L. Malabre Jr, was predicting a deep secondary slump in the early 1980s. Shuman and Rosenau expected the plunge to come about 1981.

Walter W. Rostow, author of the *The World Economy* saw the price explosion of 1973 as analogous to that of 1919-1920. Therefore, he warned, expect a crash in 1983!

Even as I finished each chapter of *The Downwave,* I found that wherever I looked, there were disturbing parallels between the events of the early 1980s — and those which had followed all previous long-wave peaks from the 18th century through to the 1930s. Day by day, I was witnessing the same decline in capital investment and employment; the same levelling out of labour productivity; the same reduction in innovation.

Anyone who cared to, could see that some of the developments were frighteningly similar to those which took place in the early 1820s, 1870s and 1920s; and during the latter part of the 18th century, when interest rates rose to historic heights, as investment opportunities diminished and heavy debts were incurred.

Joseph (Joe) Granville, probably the most controversial stock market analyst on Wall Street, wrote in 1985, in his book *The Warning,* that there were almost three hundred parallels between the state of the markets in the early 1980s and the way they had been behaving in 1929. He wrote:

"When I saw precisely the same market signals being flashed in 1983 as had appeared in 1929 — (I saw) Wall Street was about to make the same mistakes all over again, stressing the economy and corporate earnings when the market would not be listening to those things."

Granville's conclusion was that:

"the evidence of gloom was so overwhelming that I put myself on record in speeches and interviews, saying we had entered a bear market in the spring of 1983 which would lead to a major market crash."

So — I was not alone!

From some of the things readers of *The Downwave* have said or written to me, they have clearly misunderstood why I quoted that famous remark of George Santayana, namely that those who cannot *learn* from history are condemmed to *repeat* it. Some concluded that I meant to say, "History repeats itself." Others thought I was going even further, and suggesting that history imposes a dominating influence on all but the strongest-minded of us — from which there is little chance of escape. I was not taking that narrow, determinist view. Nor, I suggest, was Santayana. I do believe, however, that those who will not *learn* from the experience of others are likely to go on repeating their mistakes *ad infinitum*.

I also believe that there is great danger in taking too extreme a view of history; either dismissing history as "bunk", or believing that we are so closely bound to the past that our lives are little more than a cosmic action replay. Perhaps the main advantage of taking a balanced view is that history can help us to avoid being bowled over by too great a surprise, when something we never dreamed of occurs on our territory.

It is also helpful to realise that most of the things that happen again and again do so for a perfectly sound, logical reason, which has nothing to do with "history repeating itself." It is rather than in science (which often means little more than *in nature*), a particular sequence of operations, under similar given circumstances, will invariably produce the same result. For example: take a 45 gallon container of water, and a funnel, and try to pour it into a 40 gallon tank. You can conduct the experiment as often as you like — today, next week, and in 10 years time. But the rest of us can quite safely bet every penny we possess that you will not succeed. However, that in itself does not justify your, or anyone else's claiming that "History is repeating itself." Because it's nothing whatsoever to so with history!

This also applies to stock cycles, trade cycles or any other cyclical economic phenomena. There are perfectly sound and logical reasons — social, political and economic — for these regularly spaced, cyclical upwaves and downwaves, which occur throughout the capitalist (or quasi-capitalist) system.

What, you may wonder, entitles us to make that claim? Firstly, there is evidence of their existence for several centuries. Secondly, we can, in every case, point to the real-world events — and technical market factors — which trigger off a change from a rising to a falling trend. The waves have been more marked, and of longer duration, throughout the 200 years since the start of the Industrial Revolution. Moreover, try as we may, we have never been able to eliminate these cycles; not even with the increasing sophistication of specialist civil servants, or the willingness of governments to work together. They have persisted despite the existence of international advisory and regulatory bodies like GATT or the IMF, the World Bank, OECD, the Group of Five, the International Bank for Reconstruction and Development or the Bank of International Settlements.

But if these great waves are really uncontrollable, why do so many people — including academics who should know better — dismiss them as, at best, "too esoteric", or at worst, "merely the excuse given by economists and politicians who have fallen down on the job"?

One answer is that the individual span of human life is so short that certain regular, cyclical events — comparable to the re-appearance of Haley's Comet, or a total eclipse of the Sun — will occur no more than once or twice in a lifetime. Moreover, when they do, the individual concerned may be too ignorant — or preoccupied — to grasp half the things that are happening. Let alone appreciate their significance.

Let's face it: we prefer to ignore signals warning of war, depression, inflation, or mass unemployment. We insist that it is "nothing to do with us". It's a task for our elected representatives — or our self-appointed leaders. Let THEM take care of it! Once we have abdicated responsibility, and placed the burden on broader backs than ours, we feel we can safely return to our proper task of "living our own lives". A cardinal self-deception.

It's easy enough for those of us who live, and work, in the cosy South-East corner of Britain to take the attitude — "**** you, Jack — I'm all right". It had not been *quite* so easy in Wales, or Scotland or most places North of Watford in 1986. Still, what they get up to is "THEIR business: not ours!"

Similar sentiments were expressed by the fortunate souls who lived in New York or Chigaco in the 1930s, comparatively untouched by the Depression.

Should we see cracks appearing, signs that the downside drift is spreading, that we too could be caught up in something rather nasty, there is still one final line of defence. We can adopt the beautifully modulated, impeccably genteel approach adopted by those who are neither so Great — nor Good — as they once were.

"Of course," we'll say, "things like that DID happen. . . once. In the far off 1920s. Or the even-further-off 1780s. But our leaders (and our sages) know far too much to let it happen ever again." Common sense should tell us — though it probably doesn't — that if our leaders failed in those simple days of yore, they are not likely to be any more successful under today's daunting conditions. In reality they are likely to do rather worse; whether it's trying to halt the downward price spiral, defusing the labour situation, moderating the effects of unemployment, or isolating our own small economy from the effects of a world-wide swing to protectionism, which ultimately means the collapse of our strongest markets.

To be fair, countless attempts have been made to produce a social and economic order, free from corruption, injustice, and out-dated dogma. That has been the task of both national and world-leaders: the latter being distinguished mainly by their ability to command an undue share of Boob-Tube time, which is far more valuable today than mere column inches. But even they have been unable to turn the tide, once it is flowing against them — though they continue to try, and we applaud them when they do. After all, we must miss no opportunity to underline the fact that the responsibility is *theirs,* not *ours.*

Naturally, the opposition will seize on the latest failure as the cue to pile all the blame on their rivals in office. We shall probably applaud them for that too! But by now, after 200 years of recurrent waves of inflation — of deflation — we should have learned that when disaster strikes (or good times return), it is no more a case of "history repeating itself", than it is the "fault" of a particular administration, or ideology. Moreover, we should realise by now that these upswings and downswings occur at such regular intervals that they are for all intents and purposes unavoidable. How, in all conscience, would we feel about a Trinity House pilot who said, "Sorry, I can't guide you down the channel until they have done something about the tides!"?

Most scientists, economists, forecasters and Heads of State are reluctant to admit that they will never control these powerful cyclical forces. Although, strangely enough, they are not too proud to admit that they will never control the tides. They seem quite content merely to harness a small part of their energy. Why, therefore, should any government worthy of the name be unable to treat these cyclical wave forces in the same way? It is clear that few of them even try. They are too busy pointing to the difficulties, explaining away their failure.

Most of the excuses make little or no sense; particularly when the same authorities are prepared from time to time to launch some wild experiment. True, we know that those whom the Gods would destroy, they first make mad. But mad at whose expense?

Many people believe that men, and women, seek office to serve their fellow creatures. The sad truth is that all too often winning or holding office is seen as as end in itself. That is why, once the election is safely behind them, they start campaigning for the next. As though their mere presence was a boon to mankind!

Nor are the general run of the population any more successful, or realistic, when it comes to handling their individual and civic responsibilites. In primitive societies, there is no benign government to ensure that a man's family will have food, warmth and shelter. Yet, hard though their lives may be, they are less vulnerable to sudden shocks and commonplace disaster than we in our sophisticated, Western society. When times are hard for us, and the system collapses, we are not only deprived of our comfortable shelter: we also lack the will and the know-how to build another. Again, we maintain, looking after *us* is a task for *them*.

Sadly, the readiness with which we shuffle off responsibility, leaving the initiative to others means that when *they* fall, we go down with them. Nowhere is that more true than in the financial marketplace, as we shall find. Nor does all that computer "magic" really help. Sound judgement, which we so often lack, cannot be replaced by bigger and smarter silicon chips. It may sound a bleak prospect for mankind. But that is what the speeded-up scenario of modern life offers: greater rewards, but infinitely greater penalties. Many more options, but fewer safe ones.

So what may we depend on?

We are safe in believing that for us the sun will rise and set once every twenty-four hours. No harm will come to us if — like Neanderthal Man — we build our daily lives around that assumption. We may also trust Maynard Keynes when he declared that "in the long run" we are all dead. But we are undoubtedly heading for trouble the moment we go out on a limb, in the belief that something which has happened for the greater part of our lives, will *always* happen.

Luckily, however, those Upwaves and Downwaves we shall be studying together *are* here to stay. In one sense, they will provide to some degree a progressive structure, which in turn will refine our faculties, sharpen our wits, enabling us to plan more practically. At the same time we will soon learn the amplitude, intensity and timing of these trends are not timetables. What is more they will seem very different to different people. For the measure of these forces will depend very largely on individual perception.

Think how the rich man perceives his wealth; or the poor man his poverty! And then, without warning, reverse their roles. Whenever this happens in real life (and it happens not all that infrequently), the absolutes of wealth and poverty do not change; but the new-rich man's, and the new-poor man's perception will.

If we are prepared to learn to identify, and then anticipate, the strength of the oncoming economic waves, we can start to ride them as a beach-boy rides the surf. In so doing we shall come to sense the way the Long Wave system operates. Then we shall be in a position to take a cool, rational decision, rather than merely react to what appears to be a jumble of random and unconnected occurences.

The same aims that led me to settle down to write *The Downwave* have persuaded me to carry the story and the argument forward — *Into The Upwave.* Since it follows on from where my earlier book left off, you may find it helpful to keep your copy of *The Downwave* by you, to refer to from time to time.

In one important respect, there has been a major change in the state of technology since the early 1980s. In *The Downwave* I wrote:

> "While many marvel at the wonders of the silicon chip, genetic engineering and bio-technology, none of the recent developments actually involves new technologies, merely an extension of existing ones."

That is something I would not say today: as I shall explain in the closing pages of this book. But the immediate aim of *Into The Upwave* is not to give you the benefit of my discoveries — or to show off the depths of my research. It is rather to say *"Do not be led into a sterile, passive acquiescence by those who assure you that there is nothing you can do to save yourself. . . during the Downwave."* That is quite untrue. There is much you can do. Nor is it true that the era of technological innovation is over. The *old* era certainly is. Now — towards the end of the 1980s — the new era of innovation will arrive, in readiness for the next Upwave.

Before we get there, we shall experience many of the bad things we thought we had left behind with the Great Depression of the 1930s. A period of acute crisis will lead to an unexpected panic, a state of mind which — by definition — implies irrationality. Panic which has struck from time to time, all down the ages, is rooted in human emotion. It descends like a bolt from the blue, paralysing the will as it strikes. Instead of seeking a rational way of dealing with the oncoming depression, most people will simply try to escape. Many will leave their homes to seek solace where they may; others will dump their investments without reason or compunction. The panic, which represents the nadir of the crisis, cannot be anticipated in any statistical, systematic fashion. Being mainly a form of psychological and moral collapse, it can happen at any time during a severe crisis: a crisis of the kind we are about to experience.

But we must not be misled by terms! Henry Vansittart was the first to use the term "panic" to describe the business slowdown of 1793. Karl Marx preferred "crisis". President Herbert Hoover, who presided in the USA over the chaos of the 1930s, believed that a softer term was necessary. He talked of "depression". When President Franklin D. Roosevelt was persuaded that the malaise in the economy was likely to remain for a long time, he acted on the principle that it was wrong to speak of rope in the house of a man about to be hanged. Or depression when the Great Depression was all around! Since then a series of dubious euphemisms have been employed: "business contractions", "periods of stagflation", "inflession", "extended seasonal slumps" and "rolling adjustments".

But when I talk of depression, I mean the long-term evil of the 1930s; the same kind of depression described in detail in *The Downwave*. It is important to realise that unlike a crisis or a panic, a depression does not materialise overnight. As I wrote in *The Downwave*.

> "A depression begins slowly in vulnerable areas and gradually spreads. It does not reach everything, even at its nadir. Many businesses will go bankrupt. Many banks will fail. Many individuals will suffer severe hardships, but not all. Neither the United States nor the rest of the industrialised West will disappear into oblivion, never to recover."

It is too easy to fall into the error of thinking that when depression struck in the United States, it left nothing behind but hoards of people on relief lines and "hunger marches". It was not so; any more than it was when depression struck Britain.

Here too were "hunger marchers", covering hundreds of miles in broken boots, on blistered feet, to display their plight — and that of their fellow workers — to the people, and the Westminster politicians. Bands of unemployed Welsh miners stood in the gutters, singing for half-pennies; but above all begging to be allowed to work. In contrast to these industrial ghosts from the silent foundries and the idle mills, were the thousands who had taken a job in one of the well lit, modern factories which were springing up across the once open farmland of the Home Counties.

Even in the United States, where 25% of the workforce were unemployed, some 75% were still in jobs. And since the prices of goods and services continued to fall (as they will in a depression) those in a job were getting a *de facto* increase in their wage-packet each and every week, without once having to ask the boss for it!

Many times when I have written, or broadcast, or lectured to the public on the prospect which I believe now lies ahead, I have been accused of being a cynic. Only a cynic could present such a scenario, they tell me; and in such a cold blooded manner. My way of using the sharp, neat. . . sometimes flippant phrase, to hammer home my message has also been criticised. The answer to that is self-evident. When people begin complaining, you can be sure you have got your message across. And that is my first object: to spread the word. So I'll happily plead guilty to that particular charge.

As to my being a cynic! Definitely not. What's more I can prove it. A cynic is a man. . . or woman. . . who believes in absolutely nothing. (Which in itself is a considerable intellectual feat.) But I DO believe in something. I believe in the therapeutic quality of pure cynicism. . . administered in suitably small doses. *Ergo:* I cannot be a cynic.

That's not just a diversion: because questions of personal philosophy kept cropping up all the time I was writing both *The Downwave* and *Into The Upwave.* For example, some would say that it is immoral to write a book like *Into The Upwave* which could make some readers sufficiently aware of what's ahead for them to escape the worst of the depression, while others — equally worthy in every respect — will go quietly under. Do I deny that I am my brother's (and my sister's) keeper? I do not. That is why I hope that those who get the message will do better than merely survive. I would like them to turn the depression to their advantage. Plenty did so in the 1930s: and there was nothing immoral about that!

What would be highly immoral in my book (no pun intended) would be for me to pretend that I see a greater virtue in suffering than in success. What I would consider immoral is to be in a position to pass on soundly based information and advice which others could use to advantage, and not do so. As I put it in one of my public lectures recently, "When the frightened crowds are hammering on the locked doors of their neighbourhood bank crying, 'Why did no one tell us what it would be like?', then at least I shall be able to say, 'I did.' "

Time now, I think, to take a closer look as what the Long Wave theories really imply.

From Stock Cycle To Long Wave

The identification of "stock cycles" or "trade cycles" of varying duration is not new. Their existence, in one form or another, has been known — or suspected — for a long time. Indeed, in his book on *Sterling*, from the

FOUR LONG WAVE CYCLES 1780 - 2000

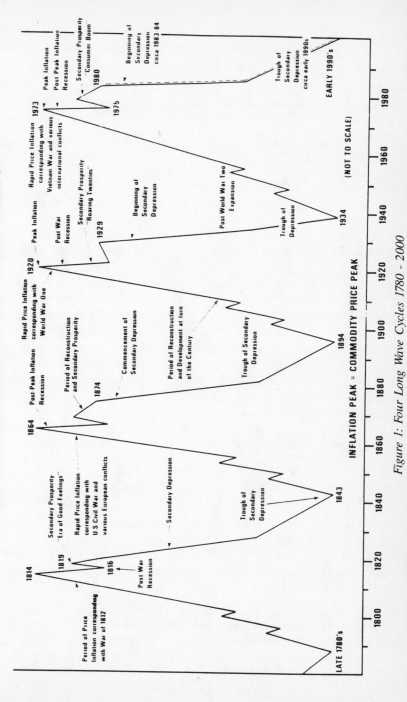

Figure 1: *Four Long Wave Cycles 1780 - 2000*

13th to the 20th century, Douglas Jay (one-time Financial Secretary to the Treasury and Fellow of All Souls) points out that:

> "short-term cycles of two or three years' duration, connected with accumulation and then dispersal of stocks, had been familiar before the 19th century. But as the 19th century wore on, and both the banking system and large-scale industrial investment developed rapidly, the older short-term 'stock cycle' came to be superseded by a longer nine to ten year fairly regular cycle that became clearly apparent first in Britain, but gradually grew international in its scope."

In early times, it was necessary to rely mainly on price movements, and changes in the London bank rate. More accurate, or relevant, figures did not exist. By the latter part of the 19th century, however, "trade union unemployment percentages (helped) to fill in the picture."

Some economists tried to find strictly non-economic explanations for the different kinds of cycle. For example, A.C. Pigou concluded that an up-cycle or a down-cycle occurred when the business community was gripped by alternating fits or optimism and pessimism. Others, says Douglas Jay, put them down to "fits of profiteering, to excessive speculation, to price rings, or (perhaps nearer the mark) mismanagement of the currency."

The depression of the 1880s was attributed by the *bi-metallists* to the failure to use a silver standard as well as a gold standard. The Commission set up in 1866 to look into the depression was unable to agree.

A satisfactory explanation may have proved elusive, but there was ample evidence that after the Industrial Revolution, which came towards the end of the 18th century, regular waves of prosperity and adversity began first to affect Britain and then all the industrialised nations, regardless of their economic theory or political creed.

Moreover the importance of these waves was being recognised. Indeed, from the mid-nineteenth century until 1914, writes Jay:

> "Although Britain and many other countries enjoyed a huge expansion of output and international trade. . . the wobble inflicted on them a major loss of output and therefore a reduction in living standards, as compared with what they might have been enjoying if all available productive capacity had been fully used."

For one thing, employment could be affected. From 1850 to 1914, unemployment varied between 2% and 11%. But for two or three years out of every decade it climbed to between 5% and 11%. Furthermore:

> " . . . the value of the pound sterling was influenced. . . by another longer term, and in some ways more curious, cycle. From 1820 to about 1850-51 the trend of sterling prices (and world prices) was downwards. After 1850 the trend changed, and the general level of prices tended to rise till the boom of 1873-4. . . the recessions were relatively mild and the upswing of prices stronger. From 1873-4 till 1895-6 the process was again reversed, and sterling prices gradually fell to their lowest point of the century."

What was happening became much clearer as the 19th century wore on. But *why* it was happening remained a mystery.

The great price rise of the 16th century had been attributed by some economists to the huge flow of silver and gold from the Americas. After 1846, gold production from California and Australia increased seven-fold. Again prices rose. It was argued by some that the increased supply of the precious metal lowered its value in terms of other goods. With the pound tied to gold, sterling's purchasing power too was bound to suffer.

By the 1870s, it was just as reasonably argued that the output of goods was now sufficient to balance fresh supplies of gold — which, in any case, were no longer on the same scale. So gold's, and therefore sterling's purchasing power recovered.

But this still did little to explain why a boom should end so suddenly; or why an economy — in the depths of depression — should equally unexpectedly begin to pick up once more. But for many there was (and, for some of us, there still *is*) an even greater mystery: why these upward and downward swings (which we shall call the Upwave and the Downwave) *should* seem to be governed by these inexplicable rhythmic forces.

Look again at what Douglas Jay had to say about that middle period running from 1850 to 1873-4.

During those 25 years, he argues, whenever prices rose, they rose more strongly, and the recurrent recessions became noticeably more shallow. That is what experience has conditioned us to expect during the Upwave. In the Downwave, the opposite should occur; namely, shallower price rises, and deeper, more lasting recessions.

The profile of the characteristic Long Wave is now beginning to emerge. The Upwave leads to a peak of activity. A check to the Upwave is followed by a limited recession. After the recovery, comes a period of Secondary Prosperity. The upswings will no longer be so strong; and the limited recessions will be deeper and more prolonged. Eventually — and usually with very little warning — the "bubble" bursts, and the economy plunges headlong into depression.

There are several points to be stressed here. Firstly, each Long Wave (measured from the beginning of the Upwave to the collapse into depression) will usually last some 50 to 60 years. The first 25 to 30 years will be spent in an Upwave. This, it should be noted, is never a smooth climb, like a ski-lift ascending. There are bound to be checks and set-backs on the way — just as there are in the classical bull market of rising share markets.

So long as the Upwave lasts, the trend is upward towards the peak. The recession which must follow is deeper and more lasting than any that has occurred on the way up. The Secondary Prosperity phase may last between 8 and 10 years, before the final bursting of the bubble, and the steep dive into depression. This last phase can last anything from 20 to 25 years. During this phase, there will be moments when the fall will be halted, with frequent recoveries. Indeed, more time will be spent rising than falling: though the falls will be deeper, and rises less strong. Nevertheless, this is the dangerous phase for the inexperienced, and for those who are eager to believe that the worst is over; that the Market has bottomed out. There will be no further doubting the direction once the Downwave sets in.

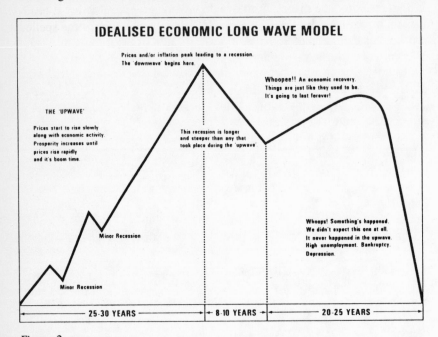

Figure 2

A High Propensity for Panic

It took until the 1920s before a Soviet economist, one Nikolai Dimitriyevitch Kondratyev first launched his Long Wave Theory, in German, in the *Archiv fuer Socialwissenschaft und Sozialpolitik.*

In fact it was Karl Marx who had been the first to tread this particular path. The works of Pravus, Van Gelderen and De Wolff were all inspired by the business cycle of Marx. He had hoped, and believed, that he had discovered the mechanism by which capitalism would ultimately destroy itself. Disappointed when it became clear that this was not likely, Marx dropped the whole idea.

Kondratieff (as he is usually referred to) was a Russian agricultural economist. Still in his 20s, he became Minister of Food in Alexander Kerensky's provisional Government in May 1917. Three years later, he founded the Conjuncture Institute, which he directed for the next 8 years.

While most economists of his time were still concerned with cycles of three, five and fifteen years' duration, Kondratieff identified a much longer term business cycle. He had spent some 10 years studying the rhythmic sequences of economic activity for the previous 130 years, and formulating his hypothesis — that a new upswing caused by the dynamics of the capital system was inevitable; that it had occurred twice since the beginning of the 18th century and would probably occur again in the 1930s. Thus he was challenging the theory Karl Marx failed to prove, and doing so head-on. In 1926, under the title *Die Langen Wellen der Konjunktur*, he spelled out his discovery; and, some would say, sealed his fate:

"The upswing in the first long wave embraces the period from 1789 to 1814, i.e. 25 years; its decline begins in 1814 and ends in 1849, a period of 35 years. The cycle is therfore completed in 60 years. The rise in the second wave begins in 1849 and ends in 1873, lasting 24 years. The decline of the second wave begins in 1873 and ends in 1896, a period of 23 years. The length of the second wave is 47 years. The upward movement of the third wave begins in 1896 and ends in 1920, its duration 24 years. The decline of the wave, according to all data, begins in 1920."

In 1928, Kondratieff fell from favour, and lost his post. Solzhenitsyn writes of him in his *Gulag Archipelago,* telling how Kondratieff was sent without trial to Siberia, where he suffered solitary confinement, became ill and died. His alleged "crime" was being the instigator of an illegal "Working Peasants Party". His mistake was that he had come up with economic developments which the regime regarded as heretical and dangerous to the State.

The price cycles peaked, as Kondratieff had predicted, in 1920. The Downwave that followed lasted 20 years and involved the Great Depression. But Kondratieff did not live to enjoy his success.

For many, Kondratieff's hypothesis may seem strange, calling for an act of blind faith. But, whether or not it is accepted, it is simple and logical. It should certainly not be beyond the grasp of the reasonably intelligent, and interested observer.

That, for a long time, is what I believed. Recent experience, however, has taught me otherwise! After giving numerous lectures and seminars all over the country, at which the participants discussed the ideas set out in my book, *The Downwave,* I have come to the conclusion that I was probably wrong to expect too many to understand the Long Wave theory right away. Comparatively few of those who have read my book, or bother to attend my courses are willing to suspend judgement long enough to take in what our everyday experience should be telling us. In any case, their depth of ignorance about the most elementary aspects of the economy are disturbing. They are disturbing because those who will not bother to prepare for what lies ahead are liable to become self-selected victims of the Depression.

A short time ago, I was giving a lecture in York. As the audience was dispersing, two elderly ladies came up to the stand where *The Downwave,* and my other books, *The Elliott Wave Principle, Share Price Analysis* and *Supertiming* were on display. "Tell me, " asked one of the ladies, "Is that man a prophet or a charlatan?" My wife, who came with me to the lecture, overheard this. Wondering, as wives will, what dreaded heresy I might have been uttering, she enquired what had given them that impression.

"Well," replied one of the ladies, "he did say that even the shares that we buy from our broker could fall in price." "Yes," chimed in her companion, "that's *exactly* what he told us. He said that even *good* shares could lose us money."

At this point my wife admitted that it was, indeed, likely that I had told them that. After all, it was something every investor took for granted. But not these two ladies, apparently.

They were silent for a moment, Then one of them gathered up her papers and, in a firm, Miss Marple-ish kind of voice said, "Come along, my dear. We'd better telephone Mr X first thing tomorrow morning, and tell him to sell *all* our shares. . . before they can do anything of the kind."

That little encounter served to reinforce *my* worst fear: namely that those who shrink from the moment of truth, will not be equipped to act wisely (or even rationally) once they are unable to go on pretending that nothing has changed. This is the true moment of danger for such folk.

The initial reaction of many people is to throw up their hands in desperation, declaring bravely that they will stand firm. After all, what else *can* they do? Throughout their lives, say, they have known nothing but a period of rising prices. Their earliest memories will be of their elders telling them, "Always borrow as much as you can. In that way you will have the use of your purchase right away, and when it comes to paying, you will be paying in pounds (or dollars or whatever) which will be worth less and less in terms of goods and services as each month passes. So the longer the credit terms, the cheaper the goods will really be."

Mind you, the odds are that the period of rising prices will have almost run its course before the entire population have learned that lesson. So we may expect it to take just as long — if not longer — to adjust their thinking to the new situation of *falling* prices.

That learning-lag is one of the reasons why, after 200 years, we (and our leaders) have not yet learned to react in time. It is barely within the bounds of possibility that common-sense and an open-minded attitude will be so common that the average man or woman's irrational resistance to change will vanish. Thus, theoretically, it is impossible to foresee a time when the intensity of the hitherto uncontrollable, cyclical forces will be moderated. But we may be confident that if so-called "experts" — those in government and the prophets elsewhere — were prepared to respond with the right policies, they would still fail to make it in time.

It is difficult to judge with any meaningful degree of accuracy what stage of any cycle has been reached: whether the phase of Secondary Prosperity is likely to be prolonged; when the present shallow recession will be over; or whether this is the terminal decline that leads to the plunge into long-term depression. As Malcolm S. Forbes put it:

"Only if you think the depression is now beginning could you say that the recession has now ended."

What of the individual businessmen, entrepreneurs or investors who have succeeded up to now in avoiding the need to recognise that something they have never met before is going on? The odds are that, after the first brave gesture, a determination to stand firm, doubts will begin to creep in. I saw this with people who were prepared to believe that in 1983 or '84 I might be right — that we *might* be entering the Downwave. As the months passed, they began to wonder why they were not witnessing the sensational collapse they thought I had predicted. Where were the waters gushing from the rock? Where the burning bush?

They may have held out for months, or perhaps even a year, in the course of which it had looked as though the Downwave had started. There have in fact been sound reasons why the decline I wrote of in *The Downwave* was delayed. It has been difficult, if not impossible, to make some of my correspondents realise that we are dealing with a trend of some 50 to 60 years in duration. We cannot expect it to "turn up on time" like a commuter train. Even those who were kept in touch with events, week by week — like the subscribers to my *Investors Bulletin,* found it difficult not to wonder where that Downwave had got to.

I suspect that many of those who claimed to be losing their patience, were beginning to lose their nerve. They wanted, they needed, they craved ACTION. Unfortunately those who act before the time is ripe, tend to lose the game.

So we had individual men and women, who had managed to stay the course, suddenly looking around for a way out. *Who* was it (they would ask themselves) who came up with that "magic formula"? Was it the bank manager, or the brother-in-law's friend in the City? One morning, after days of fretting, the uncertainty will become too much. "Never mind who *said* that it was a good thing. . . SOMEONE did: so I'll DO it!" At last. . . thank goodness! ACTION!

Ironic, when you come to think of it, that those who lack the courage to face facts, can risk everything they possess on sudden *macho* impulse. After all, "a chap OUGHT to be able to make up his mind. . . be decisive. . . if he's a REAL man." Thus an enterprise may be launched. Or a fortune made. More often it will be lost!

The media bear their share of responsibility in this matter. They too get tired of the same old story: but even *more* tired of the same old non-story. No harm done, so long as we remember that they are there to sell newspapers in order to attract advertising revenue. Radio and TV, whether commercial or in the public service, seek to "sell" their own network. A broker exists to buy and sell on commission; the bank manager is rarely averse to selling the odd insurance policy, or a selection of unit-trusts on the same basis. But just because *they* have their problems, it is no reason for applying *their* criteria to *our* judgements.

My continuing hope is that by showing the What, the How, and the Why of the changes that have already taken place, I can help at least a handful of my readers to learn to read what the Market is saying. I would also like them to remember what that multi-billionaire extraordinaire, Bernard Baruch wrote in his introduction to a re- publication of the hundred-year-study by Charles Mackay, called *Extraordinary Popular Delusions and the Madness of Crowds:*

> "All economic movements, by their very nature, are motivated by crowd psychology. Graphs and business ratios are of course, indispensable in our groping efforts to find dependable rules to guide us in our present world of alarms."

But Baruch could never see "a brilliant economic thesis expounding. . . the mathematics of price movements" without recalling Schillers's dictum:

> "Anyone taken as an individual, is tolerably reasonable and sensible — as a member of a crowd, he only becomes a blockhead."

Blockheads were as plentiful in the 18th century as they are today. Hence the literally devastating success of the "The South Sea Bubble" in England, or "The Mississippi Bubble" in France. These were not private disasters, like the Clarence Hatry affair in the 1920s. Indeed, the South Sea Company was recommended by no less a person than the Chancellor of the Exchequer, who thought that the Company would be such a success that he would be able to wipe out the National Debt. The shares in John Law's Mississippi Company were linked to the French currency. In both cases, however, the "bubbles" burst.

Although the South Sea Company collapsed in 1720, its effect was still felt — as we shall see later — for two whole generations. By this time we find the start of the first Upwave noted by Kondratieff. Figure 1 shows Kondratieffs's three distinct repetitions of the Long Wave tendency from 1780 to 2000.

Chapter Two

THE SIRENS' SONG RESUNG

Great economic and social forces flow with a tidal sweep over communities that are only half conscious of that which is befalling them.

John, Viscount Morley

It is not inconceivable that Trappist monks, those from the far regions of Tibet, or isolated individuals on this planet who have been hiding under a rock for the past 5 or 6 years, may not have read my original book *The Downwave.* With this in mind, it would appear that a review of the original Long Wave thesis would not go amiss.

The Long Wave theory is based on the concept that there is strong interaction between political developments, social developments, wars and the long-term ebb and flow of economic forces, all coming to a peak at intervals of approximately 50 years.

In his original work Kondratieff produced charts (Figures 3 and 4) showing the overall long term pattern of Commodity Prices for the USA, England and France between 1780 and the 1920s. In the shorter term the peaks and troughs are irregular. But the overall longer term pattern is astonishingly coincident. So is the long term trend of Government Securities in England and France.

The chart (Figure 5), reproduced with the kind permission of *The Economist,* exemplifies the Long Wave cycle in an even more striking manner, The study published in 1926 dealt with the period between the late 1700s and the early 1920s. *The Economist* chart goes further and covers a period of 300 years. The main point illustrated here is that the British economy has undergone a prolonged period of rising prices and strong business expansion similar to that preceding the South African (Boer) War, 50 years earlier; similar, in fact, to six Long Wave cycles in UK history.

Kondratieff did not have all the data *The Economist* was able to use. But an integral part of his thesis was the existence of a common characteristic around each of the peaks in the form of a War. War, he suggested, brings both rising social tensions and culmination of the inflation occurring over two previous decades.

Looking backwards, there was the Great War in 1914, and before that, the American Civil War of 1865, which had its repercussions in England in the form of failures due to US railroad stock financing. Then we come to the peak year of inflation in the UK in 1872, at the time of US reparations.

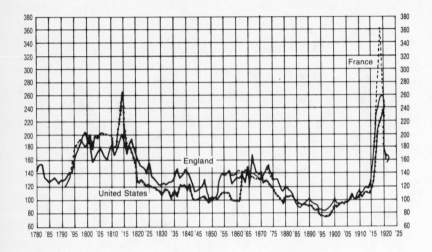

Figure 3: Index numbers of commodity prices (1901-10 = 100)

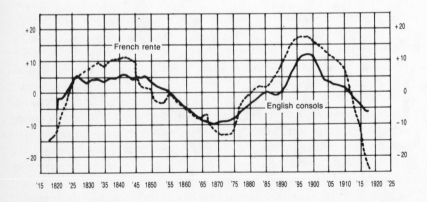

Figure 4: This chart shows the comparable long term trend of Government securities in England and France. Clearly the 1970s would represent an important pivotal point with regard to Government issues.

SOURCE: N.D. Kondratieff, The Long Waves of Economic Life

The entire exercise seemed to Long Wave adherents to be a repetition of the 1813 terminal cycle point during the Napoleonic Wars, which was coincident with the War between the UK and America, 1812-1814. Turning to the US, a similar conformation can be seen. Peaks in the US business cycle were practically coincident in 1814, 1865 and 1920.

A detailed study of those dates, and the course of history during those years, brings out quite clearly the main points of the Long Wave cyclical theory. First, following a War there tends to be a primary peak "recession", usually quite sharp and severe. That is followed by strong business recovery, against a long period of price deflation which would have begun after the "primary peak" of expansion. This price deflation probably continues throughout the business recovery. Being mild in the early stages, however, it does not impede business recovery. Social attitudes improve, and there is usually a more peaceful coexistence between management and labour, as people by now try to free themselves from previous tensions.

In Figure 6, we have a chart which appeared in the August 1972 issue of *The Media General Financial Weekly*. The Long Wave has been superimposed on the US Wholesale Price Index from 1780 to the year 2000. There is a marked similarity between the timing of peaks in the US Wholesale Prices and that of inflationary peaks since the Cromwellian period.

Before considering the Long Wave cycle in relation to the current period (i.e. beyond the mid-way point of the 1980s), let us look in detail at the first three Long Wave periods. The fact that the United States, England and Western Europe still had primarily agricultural economies does not make the progress of the First Long Wave cycle any less significant. This is an extremely important point to keep in your mind.

The First Cycle 1783-1843

Due to the lack of reliable data, it is difficult to include the period before the 1780s as part of the Long Wave economic *schema*. The decade from 1750 was a time of great economic activity in England, with the full impact of the Industrial Revolution beginning to make its mark. Employment was abundant, and thanks to the far reaching improvements brought in during the earlier Agricultural Revolution, food was plentiful and cheap. For consumers — the vast majority of whom still lived in, and depended on, the countryside — the years between 1730 and 1750 were especially favourable. Wheat cost less than it had done for 150 years, meat was half the price it had been five years earlier. Rabbits were there for the taking, and in normal years all staple foods were cheap, on top of which the poacher was ever active, despite the harsh game laws and savage penalties.

The general tendency to mechanise and substitute machines for human skill and effort, brought drastic changes to the traditional life-style. Until the invention of Thomas High's "Spinning Jenny" in 1764 and Sir Richard

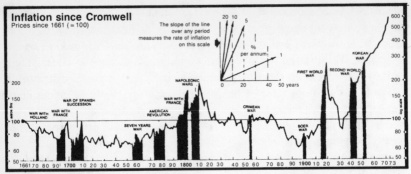

Figure 5: Inflation since Cromwell   SOURCE: The Economist

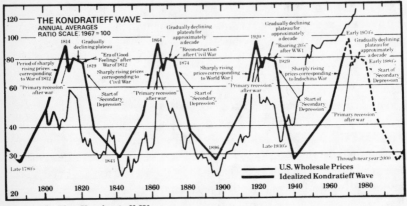

Figure 6: The Kondratieff Wave
SOURCE: The Media General Financial Weekly, *August 1972*

Arkwright's first water-powered spinning mill in 1769, hundreds of thousands of cottage workers had been needed to keep the textile industry in yarn. Machines increased productivity by 1,000 per cent. Cottagers lost their livelihood, and the market was flooded with cheap yarn. The production explosion in textiles was characteristic of the growth period of the cycle, when mining, metal work and machine manufacture underwent similar changes. As a result of soaring demand, coal production increased fivefold; pig iron production tenfold.

The quickening pace of industrialisation reduced the cost of many manufactured articles such as cotton and soap, then available to the workers in abundance. This, of course, is the way things are *supposed* to be.

The years leading up to the middle of the century typified the growth phase of the Long Wave cycle, which contains all the symptoms that usually lead to the depression within the Downwave portion of the long term up-and-down cycle. There was the steady shift of labour and capital from the land and non-mechanised crafts to the new industries with their promise of high profits. Since progress was neither equal nor simultaneous, there were dislocations in the system. Some areas had production surpluses, while others lacked the required capacity. Though every effort was made to improve, and build new highways, the limited power of the horse kept transportation slow. Moreover many of the manufactured goods were now too heavy for overland transportation, so were transferred to the canals and rivers. These in turn could be even slower, causing serious bottle-necks in distribution.

But all good things must end! After generations of stability, prices began to rise around 1750. The Upwave, which probably ended around 1760, was accompanied in its closing stages by heavy speculation in commodities, especially sugar. As I wrote in *The Downwave*:

> "In Holland, heavy speculation in sugar was being financed by *Wisselruitji* in Amsterdam, involving a chain of accommodation bills. In addition there was a speculative mania involving the East India Company, fuelled by credit advanced by the Bank of Amsterdam. In England there was a speculative boom in housing, turnpikes and canals. . . The speculative orgy reached a crescendo in the early part of 1763. Sugar prices peaked, then wobbled, then fell. The East India Company collapsed. A host of English companies heavily involved in the Dutch East India Company tumbled after it."

The consequences for England were what might have been expected. There was an end to the boom in construction, housing, turnpikes and canals. The Ayr Bank, which had financed many developments, came toppling down, bringing down with it a host of smaller provincial banks. Thousands of investors in England and Europe lost their savings. Three years later came a severe recession. About 200 years later came the collapse of Britain's second line banking system — the so called "fringe" banks! The long term forces have lost none of their potency, as we'll discover.

In 1783 the current boom collapsed in yet another crisis. Raw material prices fell, and European economists were severely squeezed. Wheat, the backbone of the still largely agricultural economy, was especially hard hit. Needless to say, the embryonic American economy bore the full brunt of the international collapse. By the last decade of the century, war and catastrophic harvests, on top of monetary inflation, exposed many families to poverty and famine — unthinkable at any earlier time in the generally prosperous 18th century.

However, from the moment the depression of the 1780s hit bottom in '83, we see the first observable Upwave portion of the Long Term cycle. Slowly the European economies began to pick up. By 1787 prosperity had returned, and was to remain through to 1793, growing all the time. Innovations in the cotton industry and canal construction were partly responsible. There were other minor features like the cautious introduction of the steam engine. In '93 came the war between Britain and France; the gradually rising level of prices turned into an explosive upsurge. A further sharp price escalation took place between 1798 and 1801, and yet again after the Napoleonic Wars.

As I pointed out in *The Downwave*, prices rose between 1789 and 1814 by 25%. They rose slowly at first, gathering momentum with the increase in business activity. After the Anglo-French War, however, the increase exploded. According to the "Gayer Index of Domestic and Imported Prices" (the standard inflation index covering the period) the price index rose from a pre-war trough of 88.0 (in 1792) to 107.9 in six years. By 1801, it had climbed no less than 61 points, continuing until it reached its peak of 168.9 in 1813. Prices on the Gayer Index rose in the 30 years between 1783 and 1813 by 92%. Nevertheless, prices did not go straight up. The years 1799, 1805, 1810 and 1814 were all years in which prices peaked. The intervening years saw no dramatic falls, merely an easing back. Then, after 1814, the turning point was reached. Prices began to head downwards.

Seen through the eyes of Long Wave cycle exponents, the First Cycle included all the social, political and military elements identified in the basic theory. There was war: the War of 1812. There was a period of unusually excessive social tension. And, in addition to the major conflict, civil wars were raging the world over. There were rebellions too against the Napoleonic regime, as well as a series of revolutions to liberate Latin America.

There were also unsustainable prices. By 1814, raw material costs and economic activity approached a level which — in hindsight — could not possibly be held. There was a sharp drop in prices, and deep recession from 1814 to 1815. This gave way to a *minor* post-war boom between 1815 and '16, but it never matched the level of activity in the two previous years. Over in the United States, the boom centred on expansion of the New England textile industry.

The rise of American cotton had all the characteristics that fuel a speculative boom. It was also to have a global impact. It awoke a massive overseas sales drive in England, until exports to Europe and the United States far exceeded all possibilities of resale. Then the boom ended. It had to. Again, depression was waiting around the corner. As it had before — as it will again, so long as Man retains the nature of the original beast. Technologically, we may have come a long way. But anthropologically, we've made little progress.

From 1816 to 1819 there was an export frenzy in Britain; but by 1819 a collapse in commodity markets set off a fresh crisis.

In the United States trouble arose from mismanagement inside the Second Bank of the United States. Having failed in its attempt to check inflation, the Bank decided in 1818 on a policy of contraction. It therefore called in pledges from a number of under-capitalised provincial state banks. This led to the collapse of the Second Bank, which took a number of smaller banks with it. Public outcry against the Bank brought a Congressional investigation which uncovered evidence not only of mismanagement, but of dishonest dealing. The result was a movement to repeal the Bank's charter. Bad as it seemed, the collapse of the fragile financial facade was more of a token than a cause of what followed.

The problems of the Second Bank had transformed public confidence into fear, leading to the rapidly spreading distress characteristic of a depression.

Prices fell. Business bankruptcies multiplied. Unemployment rose. By the following year, 1819, the price of wheat took a sharp fall. Cotton sales collapsed, so did land sales. Six years later, the depression was universal, bringing down the value of stocks and bonds invested in canals, along with that of South American government and mining bonds. Britain's exports plunged.

The final straw in Britain was the Baring crisis in 1825, when — as one of the chronicles of the era put it:

"A panic seized upon the public such as had never been witnessed before".

The panic of 1825 was a precursor to the depression of the 1830s. Once again, depression was to lag ten years behind the panic which ended the Upwave. By 1830, there was an outbreak of wild speculation in the new and spreading railroads. As so often, the speculators got their timing badly wrong. Even before the end of that year, the economy had gone into a tail spin. The Long Wave cycle was alive and well! Moreover it was indisputably in control.

The Second Cycle 1843-1896

A new wave began in 1843, sixty years after the trough of the 1783 depression. Survivors from the worldwide depression of the 1830s and '40s began building anew. One by one, in Europe and elsewhere, sections of the world economy began to recover. Industrial production picked up. The volume of world trade expanded, and the price of wheat took a huge jump. Between 1852 and '54, a surge in raw material prices mirrored what had happened between 1798 and 1801. For the second time, inflation was rising again, just as people had grown accustomed to falling prices, having known nothing else for 35 years. Between 1852 and 1854, prices increased by 33%. This, in fact, was the worst period of the inflation. For these two years accounted for more than 90% of the overall price rise between 1849 and 1873.

The recession of 1854-1855 did not take the calamitous proportions of a true depression; partly because the South was less affected. It fell to the approaching Civil War to subject the country as a whole to consequences of inflation. . . economic and social. The subsequent collapse in raw material prices spread deflation and depression throughout the country. Just as the Napoleonic Wars had been responsible for an unsustainable upsurge in prices, so were the American Civil War and the conflict against Russia in the Crimea.

At this stage it may be worth while noting that the two wars referred to were not necessarily the cause of the dislocations within the Long Wave cycle. These tend to be the combined effect of a number of factors within the Long Term Wave *schema*; factors which in themselves are actually the product of our personal behaviour patterns. In the case of the Crimean War, there was big power rivalry in the Levant, disguised as concern for the care of the Holy Places. The behaviour of the powers engaged in the struggle was plain to see, even at the time. With the American Civil War, the issue leading to the South's secession from the Union was one of race and colour; specifically revolving around Lincoln's move to free the slaves.

It is worth noting that there are two quite distinct kinds of wars; those which come at the beginning of the Upwave portion of a Long Wave cycle and those which come at the end. War at the beginning lands on an economy with unused resources, deflated prices, reduced debts and reasonably low interest rates. The increased production and new demand for war goods assists the subsequent business recovery of the Upwave. Wars that come at the end of the Upwave within a Long Wave cycle have a negative impact. Inflated debt, high prices and interest rates, under-capacity and full employment tend to accentuate the inbuilt distorions of an expansion which has run out of control. War in these circumstances can only add to the underlying forces which terminate the Upwave portion of the Long Term cycle.

The crisis of 1809-1810, it was said, had *whispered* to those capable of hearing that all was not well. But the Panic of '57 spoke in a louder voice. It positively *shouted* that the situation was out of hand, even before the final peak in economic activity in 1864. It was a further illustration of the fact that a *crash* is a *loud cry* for the benefit of the financially hard of hearing.

In 1854, after the speculative boom in railway stocks had been halted by a sharp decline in prices, the *New York Herald Tribune* predicted the imminent approach of a crisis; one, it declared, that would end the current "Fitful Spasmodic System" of American business. During the following winter, business stagnated and unemployment exploded. There was considerable distress and popular unrest.

The speculative mania had snowballed in the early 1850s, finding expression in the railway bonanza, new gold discoveries, speculation in wheat and other commodities. It was finally halted by the Commercial Crisis of 1857-1858, which set the stage for a series of world-wide panics. After the Civil War, the entire international financial structure seemed to break apart at the seams.

On August 24th 1857, the New York branch of the Ohio Life Insurance and Trust Company suspended payments. Two days later the *Herald Tribune* returned to its earlier theme, predicting that the financial difficulties now beginning were bound to acquire the proportions of a major crisis. Two months later, England was in the grip of panic which spread, in the following year, to Europe. By 1863, France had become a major victim.

Heavy speculation in shipping and companies led to the financial crisis of 1864, which originated in France, spread to Italy and moved across to Britain. Between 1860 and 1864, bank collapses took on horrendous proportions; and the prevailing recession was judged to be worse than anything since the depression of the 1840s. One of the worst panics arose from the collapse of the Overend Gurney Company in May 1866. It led to a crash on the stock market in London, which spread to America, France, Italy, Germany and the Austro-Hungarian Empire.

The whole period threw up a dozen examples which tended to support the Long Wave theorists' contention that a panic often marks the first stage in the transition from boom and expansion to contraction and depression. These were the characteristics of the Downwave, as I pointed out in my book of that title:

> "Panics figured prominently in the America of the 19th century. It was an age of individual and virtually unregulated enterprise. There was little by way of means for stabilisation and prevention through advance, concerted and united action."

During the Second Cycle, panic struck hard in the middle of 1884. Prices of shares and commodities alike fell rapidly, accentuating the shift from speculation to an orgy of selling. Banks, caught up in the panic, reacted by contracting their loans and withdrawing funds from the very volatile call market. Money shortages developed, driving some to substitute devices, adding to the psychological uncertainties of the time. Accompanying the panic phase there was a progressive decline in the price of most goods and services, affecting every kind of property. . . including residential property, the final Eldorado in the Britain of the 1980s. In the 1880s, in the drab working quarters of the cities, distress, hunger and deprivation were rife. They spread outwards and downwards from New York until they affected the poor in every small town and city.

Not only in America, but in virtually every corner of Western industrialised civilisation, the system appeared unable to sustain itself. A series of panics began in Germany in 1873. Within a few months, they had spread to England and the United States. Economic activity contracted steadily on a global basis throughout the 1880s and 1890s. Prices fell. Hardships mounted. For the third time since the late 18th century, the world was sliding into a deep depression, comparable only to that of the 1840s and 1780s — something most people believed could never happen again.

Even without the benefit of hindsight, one thing was becoming clear — that the financial crisis contains deep roots reaching out through the entire international financial structure. This is particularly so in the final stages of an Upwave. Therefore, it is not surprising that these roots ran unusually deep in 1864. Charles P. Kindleberger, in his book *Manias, Panics and Crashes* (1978) brings to life the disturbing experience of one Parisian banker:

> "Alfred André, a Parisian banker with major interests in Egypt, spent an 'exhausting week' in London looking after the interests of his firm at the time of the Overend Gurney crisis. He returned to Paris on May 17th, having concluded that the finance companies were ruined and that business was paralysed in Italy, Prussia, Austria and Russia, with France standing pretty well, but only momentarily. The speculative mania that led up to the series of financial crises involved heavy speculation in cotton and shipping companies in France, England and Italy."

The second Long Wave that began in 1843 was completed in 1896. It had lasted just under fifty-four years. Fifty-four years *again*! Two repetitions might be dismissed as mere coincidence. But what if there were a third? At the time it seemed most unlikely. But *suppose* there were!

Keynes and the Kondratieff Threat

Some years ago, Paul Samuelson, a neo-Keynsian (who was my Professor) met Milton Friedman, the arch-Monetarist (who was not).

Said Paul Samuelson, "I've heard everything you say. . . but you must be wrong."

"I can understand why you disagree with me," replied Milton Friedman, "but why do you say I *must* be wrong?"

"Well!", answered Paul Samuelson, "unless *you're* wrong, I must be. And that is just *not* possible."

How well can one imagine a similar dialogue taking place if Nikolai Dimitryevitch Kondratieff and John Maynard Keynes had ever chanced to meet.

That is because (as I pointed out in my weekly publication, *Investors Bulletin*, 2 Aug 1974), neo-Keynsians consider that the short business cycle lasts no more than a few years from peak to trough.

By using the fiduciary priming pump and Government interference and "fine-tuning", Keynsians claim to be able to reduce the burden of the trough in the business cycle; either by smoothing out the erratic cyclical fluctuations, or by eliminating them altogether. Therefore, I argued:

"An admission of cyclical continuity in the form of the Kondratieff cycle would spell nothing short of absolute disaster for the Keynsians. In effect this would mean that all Keynsian economics has achieved would be short term stabilisation allowing longer term distortions to accumulate."

If the Long Wave adherents are right, their theory has extremely harsh implications for the real world, as opposed to Academia! We might expect to find the number of secondary business cycle corrections, eliminated since 1935, suppressed and stored within the Upwave of the current cycle — unlike the irregular pattern preceding the Napoleonic War, but similar to the pattern preceding the first World War. In that case, we could now be due for a super-cyclical correction of horrifying proportions. I also pointed out in August 1984 that the 1920s provide an example of the type of prosperity that can follow an inflationary peak. The period after the US Civil War and the Overend Gurney crisis in 1866 was similar. From 1867 to 1873 the price of UK Industrial Ordinary Shares rose by over 50%. Unemployment fell from 6% to 0.2%. UK foreign trade was booming, as was UK Industrial production, while credit expanded briefly. Go back to the Napoleonic Wars, and the peak inflation that produced a similar trend was evident.

The record tells us that the three longest and worst depressions in Europe since the end of the 18th century came about 8-10 years after the Long Wave peak, each lasting 4 to 5 years respectively. Following the depression, general price deflation remained for another 15 years, until the final trough of the long cycle was reached. Those periods of depression came in 1825, 1873 and 1929. It can been seen from the *Economist* chart that a major inflationary peak occurred around 1920, *the terminal point of the expansion that led up to the peak.* We then entered a decade of mild deflation (compatible with the Long Wave three decade thesis) before the 1930s brought a decade of severe deflation. This, the doctrine tells us, is the factor normally associated with the middle decade of a major downswing in the cycle. Before we turn our attention to what could well prove to be the fourth Long Wave cycle, there is still the period between the late Victorian age and the start of the Second World War.

The Third Cycle 1896-1940

Professor Jay W. Forrester shed considerable light on the technological sequence of the Long Wave patterns of economic life in an article in the MIT publication, *Technology Review,* in 1978. He is well known among economists and Treasury officials for his computerised econometric model of the US economy called the *Systems Dynamic National Model.* One of the points in Forrester's theory is that technological developments, coming at the right time, can act as a spur to the Long Term period of prosperity that follows a depression. There are almost always sound and potentially rewarding developments on the drawing board during the Downwave of a Long Wave cycle. But during that phase businessmen are cautious. They are depressed. Above all they are unwilling to take on anything of a speculative nature, let alone invest money in it. So all these splendid innovations remain there on the shelf. . . assuming that they have managed to get that far!

Once the entrepreneur is convinced that we are heading for an Upwave, it's a totally different situation. New technological developments are taken down and dusted off. They are tested and modified. More money, time and management effort are spent on them. Some will fall by the way, but the best will be launched. They will be promoted. Once accepted they become the harbingers of the foundation of the Upwave, a phase that can last 20 or 30 years.

So long as the innovations embodying the new technology serve a useful *economic* purpose, they will continue to act as a spur and a stimulant. But sooner or later a point will be reached in the cycle when existing technology has to be replaced by something recognised as more up-to-date. . . Otherwise the spur of one generation becomes a liability for the next.

Today, says Colin Clive, Chairman (1986) of the British Venture Capital Association, all those concerned with launching a company in the high-tech sector must be prepared to see their product overtaken, and discarded, in as little as 5 years. So it's necessary to achieve virtually an instant acceleration. . . from 0 to 80, so to speak. . . and from a standing start!

This was not so with the Third Cycle, at the turn of the century. Each advance was just as important then as are those of today. But by contemporary standards, the Victorian scientists and technologists alike were still inching their way forward from the Known to the Partially Known. It remained a largely mechanical world in which steel and diamonds were the symbol of strength and durability, and steam and the newly harnessed electric current were the common forms of motive power. Better performance was the aim, rather than a "breakthrough". Men and women in 1896 still only *talked* of flying. Children and visionaries alone were free to dream of flying to the moon.

Railway developments in the 1840s were the chief reason (especially in Britain) for citing the start of the Second Cycle, along with the trough of the depression. The outstanding feature of the Third Cycle was the gradual introduction of electricity which came just as business was emerging from what came to be known to posterity as the *Great* Depression. 1897 is generally held to be the pivotal year, marking the end of one era and the beginning of the next.

The early years of the new century brought tremendous innovations from the production of electricity and the expansion of the American automobile industry. The creation of assembly lines and the standardisation of parts were but two examples. England was still a backward area so far as engineering, and particularly chemical and electrical engineering, were concerned. Hence the influx of entrepreneurs from the continent.

The Kaiser's drive to build the world's most powerful navy — and the British response — gave great impetus to metal and associated industries. The British navy's move from coal to oil for its newer ships gave an added importance to an already fast developing oil industry, and to the Persian Gulf. Oil exploration and the production of asphalt and cement for the new bridges and highways boosted business. The United States began the advance which was to make it the leading industrial nation in the world.

All was set fair until the Great War, which took raw material prices, wages and consumer prices (which were inching up steadily) and sent them screaming up like a rocket. In England, the wages paid to women workers in the munition factories were held up as a hideous example of what could happen to the economy and society in modern war.

The war was no sooner over than the escalation of prices, which had occurred three times already over the previous 150 years, returned with even greater ferocity. But not immediately. The Cunliffe Committee, which had been set up to plan for the post-war economy, recommended in August 1918 that the state should live within its income, reduce the note issue, repay a large part of the government securities held by the banks — and pay for them from revenue!

The economy reacted immediately after the Armistice on 11th November 1918 with a sharp fall in prices, which lasted until March 1919. Thereafter prices began to pick up. In the thirteen months to April 1920, a speculative boom developed with prices rising 50%. In November 1919, the authorities raised Bank Rate to 6%, and two months later began to cut the size of the note issue. In April 1920, Bank Rate was raised to the crisis rate of 7%. Suddenly, violently, the collapse set in.

Raw material prices suddenly crashed. Hundreds of small British investors went bankrupt. . . some from speculating in Argentinian companies of dubious merit. The collapse in commodities was the precursor to the depression of 1920-1922. Unemployment was rife. It rose from 2.4% in 1920 to 15% in 1921 and 1922 — that meant a total of around 2 million workless. The Government was trying to make the transition from a wartime economy to a more normal, peacetime regime. Its deflationary measures between 1919 and 1920, designed to moderate the price rise without bringing on a deep recession, were in the event too drastic. Moreover they were kept on for too long. The 7% bank rate was still in place until April 1921, by which time unemployment was 15%. It was more than the fragile economy could stand.

In the United States, by contrast, the depression was relatively short. But it was more serious elsewhere. In Germany, in a unique monetary context, the collapse became the hyper-inflation horror of 1923. It does not matter whether a loaf of bread costs a penny or one thousand dollars. The main thing is to be able to lay hands on that penny. . . or that one thousand dollars. The same applied in Germany where a loaf of bread cost 30 billion marks. The trouble was that very few people had 30 billion marks. Maybe they *could* somehow have managed to rake together 25 billion. But, in the circumstances, 25 billion wouldn't help.

There was a reasonable recovery after 1922, at least on the surface. But recovery was not helped by government changes. The first Labour Government under Ramsay MacDonald took office during this critical period. In 1923, there was an inconclusive election, after which Stanley Baldwin turned down the premiership. In January 1924, MacDonald agreed to head a minority Labour Government. But it was not to last long. On October 25th in the same year, four days before the General Election, the press published the so-called *Zinoviev* letter. This was the text of a letter allegedly sent by Gregori Zinoviev, a leading Bolshevik and a prominent figure in the Third International, to British Communists urging them to promote revolution. MacDonald and the Labour Party lost the election. They were replaced by a Conservative administration with Baldwin as Premier and Churchill as Chancellor.

Their economic and financial thinking was governed by the ideas of the 17th century philosopher, John Locke. Locke, who was also a commissioner on the Board of Trade, was very much a "sound money" man. Depreciation of the currency was anathema to Locke. He denounced one proposal to issue new money at a depreciated rate on the grounds that it would:

"deprive great numbers of blameless men of a fifth of their estates beyond the relief of Chancery. . ."

In his book, *Sterling,* Douglas Jay describes what was happening in the early '20s in the environs of Westminster and Whitehall:

"The post-war downward slide of the British economy ended in 1922. But it was followed by stagnation, not recovery. The Bank and Treasury regarded the lull as an opportunity, not for restoring high production and employment, but for enforcing the whole Cunliffe Committee medicine and returning once again to the full gospel of John Locke, the pre-war gold standard and the mystical price of £3.17s.10½d. for an ounce of gold. By 1924 the rise in living costs compared with 1913 was 78 per cent and in average money wages 94 per cent. To this extent the pound had depreciated in terms of goods and services."

In the latter part of 1924, American prices were rising and the market rate of exchange moved up to $4.70. The new Government decided to act, albeit inadvisedly. The bank rate was raised to 5% in February 1925, and in the April Budget the Chancellor announced the return to the Gold Standard at the old rate. This was the £3.17s10½d which Locke had declared to be the proper value of Sterling. By now that sum was the equivalent of £4.86. The gap between the market rate and the rate decreed by Government may not seem much to us today. But at the time it was a fateful decision, says Douglas Jay:

"It probably did more long-term damage to Britain as an economic power than any decision taken by a twentieth-century British Government until the 1970s. . . To those of us who have known the 1970s and 1980s with their wildly fluctuating exchange rates, an overvaluation of the pound (which had fallen further) by 10% may not sound very alarming. But it was enough in 1925-6 to throw the whole precarious British coal industry, then employing nearly one million men, into deficit."

The bare facts of the Great Wall Street Crash, on 24th and 29th October, 1929, and Britain's decision to leave the Gold Standard two years later need little elaboration here. But it is instructive to see how the affair looked at the time. For example, F.W. Pethick-Lawrence MP brought out the kind of book on the flight from the Gold Standard which today would be one of those all-but-instant paperbacks. In 1931, it came out as one of Victor Gollancz's lightning publications between strawberry-coloured hard covers. In many ways it brings home quite forcibly some of the differences between events of our own time and those of the early 1930s. Older readers may find it difficult to realise that the events of that dreadful summer took place more than half-a-century ago!

In a style which seems quaint to us, Mr Pethick-Lawrence is described on the flyleaf as "Sometime Fellow of Trinity College, Cambridge and late Financial Secretary to the Treasury". His book, called *This Gold Crisis* was prepared with commendable speed, going to press before "the repercussions of the fateful decision of September 21st have taken full effect." He began by describing the state of bewilderment in which the public found itself:

> "I doubt whether there has ever been a time when the intelligent man in the street has felt more mystified. All the rules and maxims which he learned in childhood, all the commonplaces and commonsenses which he has picked up in his journey through life seem to be working out in the opposite way to that which he has been led to expect."

The trouble in 1930 and 1931 originated within the banking community rather than on the stock market. In May 1931 there was pressure on the German and Austrian banks which they could not withstand. Lower world prices had raised the value of money debts, while shrinking the funds on which the debtors were relying. In other words, the move from an inflationary to a deflationary environment left many people baffled, and even more people deeper in debt, with little hope of paying their way out. The "wiseacres" had told them, "Be a debtor, and let your *creditors* worry when they realise that each payment you make is worth progressively less in real terms." Now this convenient doctrine was no longer valid.

It was moreover a crazy world in many respects. The rule had been maintained, "Germany must pay", but by now Germany was suffering from a crippling level of unemployment. To enable Germany to meet its formal obligations, reparations had been financed by short-term borrowing, much of it from the United States. Suddenly this could not go on. It was far too similar to the position over sovereign debt in the 1980s for us to adopt a superior attitude towards those who struggled to observe the form, knowing they were powerless to do so in other than a risible pantomime fashion. Mr Pethick-Lawrence made that point in *This Gold Crisis*.

> "It is easy to understand that if a nation is beaten in war and compelled to pay a big sum annually to the victors, her people will have to work extra hard. . . But whoever would have thought that 15 or 20% of the adults of the beaten nation would have no work to do, and that the victors would be so embarrassed by receiving the money that they would try to scheme out some way of remitting it without looking ridiculous."

The final blow fell when Austria's oldest bank, *Credit-Anstalt* was faced with losses which exceeded its entire capital. After failing to get help from the French, the Austrians turned to London. So did the Germans. The Governor of the Bank of England, Montagu Norman came to the rescue of the Austrians with an advance of £4½ million. The French were furious and joined sterling's attackers, selling pounds with unconcealed vigour. Governor Norman told the Government that to restore confidence, drastic budget economies would have to be made. Premier MacDonald and his Chancellor Snowdon were bewildered by it all, and thoroughly at sea. They did what Montagu Norman demanded. In August most of MacDonald's Labour cabinet resigned, and a National Government took their place. Understandably this did not restore public — or international — confidence. The pound's gold parity was suspended on 21st September (Pethick-Lawrence's day of "fateful decision"). In truth it was not "suspended" but given up.

Some of the panics of the 1930s led to political cries of international dimensions. A suicide on 3rd January 1934 began the panic. It was the only escape left to one Serge Stavisky, a company promoter of Russian origin, accused of uttering fraudulent bonds. On the face of it, another dead swindler! But official investigations uncovered widespread corruption in French Government circles, with Ministers and Deputies giving Stavisky protection. Communists, Right Wing and Royalist groups all exploited the scandal. After serious rioting in Paris on 6th, 7th and 9th of February, a general strike followed. The Republic was saved from the worst only by the establishment of a broad coalition government which excluded any of the tainted men.

Enter John Maynard Keynes! Crudely, his theory was that economic recovery could be induced by Government spending. President Roosevelt's "New Deal" was based on Keynsian doctrine. So were the policies of the British administration during the tail end of the depression of the 1930s. Once again, came a major upheaval. After little more than 20 years, Britain and the majority of her former allies faced war with Germany.

Britain had not been so badly hit as many countries, and neo-Keynsians would claim that this was largely thanks to a Government which, from 1936 onwards, did not hesitate to intervene in a number of ways to wake up the economy. One of the major symbols of the Government's acceptance of the new expansionist doctrine was the broadcast in which J. Maynard Keynes explained his "Accumulator" theory to the "ordinary listener". The benefits of the Government's giving money — and orders — to firms in the capital goods industries were plain to see. By stimulating activity among the capital goods firms, but specifically among the aircraft manufacturers and armaments firms, two purposes would be served. Re-armament would be speeded on its way, and a boost would be given to the under-employed economy as a whole.

In addition to their purchases of energy and raw materials, the favoured firms would help to boost the order books of the building trade and electricians, as well as giving direct employment to tens of thousands of men and women, whether on the shop floor, in the drawing office, the canteen or the transport pool. A fair proportion of each weekly wage packet would then find its way into the shops, the pubs, the cinemas. The shopkeepers and their families, the publicans and the usherettes would also spend a fair proportion of their weekly wage. So — hopefully — every pound put in by the Government would go on circulating for quite a while. Thus the effect of that first capital injection would be cumulative.

And it all appeared to happen like magic in many parts of the country, as one witness of those days recalls:

"For months I'd walked past this battered old corrugated iron shed off the Eccleshall Road, in Sheffield. I heard this economist fellow Keynes say his piece. Frankly I was very impressed. Next morning the *Sheffield Telegraph* was full of re-armament and what it would mean for all of us. Coming back dinnertime, I heard banging from inside this old shed. I thought they were going to take it down. But no. . . when I passed by next morning the whole place was shaking and vibrating, and the three old machines inside were stamping out spoons and forks for the Army. Couple of days later one of the lads working there told me he'd been "out" (of a job), and skint for two and a half years. That's what re-armament meant off the Eccleshall Road."

Long Wave cycle enthusiasts would argue that it wasn't the expansionist doctrines of John Maynard Keynes that did the trick, and produced the recovery of the 1940s. It was actually the infrastructure of the long-term economic cycle that permitted the successful application of J. Maynard Keynes's doctrine. Had he attempted the same type of economic stimulus during 1931 or 1932, in the same manner as the Hoover administration, it would have got nowhere. It was the natural economic forces bearing down on the global economy which allowed Keynsian expansionist theory to be applied effectively. It wasn't the theory itself that wrought the transformation.

More relevantly, the application of the new-Keynsian doctrine during the 1970s and '80s has been seen to be totally ineffective.

It was not merely manufacturing industry that suffered in the 1930s, affecting what used to be called the "working class." The middle-classes were often hard hit when stock markets around the world plummeted. On Wall Street the Dow Jones Industrial Ordinary Share Index lost 90% of its value. The Great Wall Street Crash is history that has already been written. England was not hit quite so hard. In London, the stock market came down, but did not reach its low point until the second year of the World War. The "new" Financial Times Ordinary Share Index (the FT 30), had been set up on July 1st 1935 (Base 100). It hit its all-time low of 49.4, as share values halved on June 26th 1940, the day after the cessation of hostilities between France, Germany and Italy.

Not all forms of investment suffered so badly as Equities. Gold, for example, did well. So did fixed interest securities, including "Gilts". Indeed, the Government Securities Index (Base 100, October 15th 1926) peaked on January 9th at a record 127.4.

The 1920s and '30s Revisited

Once again, depression had come after a long lag following the crash; though it was not until the USA entered the Second World War in 1941 that the depression reached a meaningful trough. By that time Britain had been caught up in the abnormalities of another wartime economy; a period which, in many ways, must be viewed as starting with the re-armament programme after 1936.

Now we have come to the point where we must consider the likelihood that the Fourth Cycle (1940-1994) has already reached the Downwave, which I explored in my book in 1983.

Once again, we come up against the hard fact that a depression is one thing, but the *perception* of what a depression entails is something else; especially for those who have never lived through one. In *The Sunday Times,* in June '86, one correspondent called me the "Boris Karloff" of the City. It was said that I got my "kicks" from frightening the life out of people — rather like the Fat Boy in Pickwick. The truth, I more than suspect, is that people dislike mentioning certain things. Depression is one of them, death is another.

The '30s were called "the Devil's Decade." And with some justification. For many in the United States, who felt they had made something of their lives, it brought a hand-to-mouth existence. After the closure of the banks. . . an emergency measure in March 1933, shopkeepers toured the streets looking for a newspaper boy, or an apple vendor, who would sell them change for paper money. The going rate for a dollar bill at one stage was 8 cents! Workers with cheques in their pockets which couldn't be cashed, fainted on the job for lack of food. Thousands suffered from hunger and cold. I know. I was there. But we survived.

Much of the horror people feel at even talking of depression — and which paralyses them when it comes to taking action — can be laid at the door of the movies, like Steinbeck's "Grapes of Wrath", or — in England — Greenwood's "Love on the Dole". Like the song "Brother, Can You Spare a Dime", they are moving and sound authentic, but they were heavily larded with propaganda at the time.

It is a pity that so many people are so afraid that they will cling to their truly frightening fantasies rather than risk an encounter with reality. Which, logic tells us, cannot be any worse. Indeed, Shakespeare may have been right when, through his characters, he reassures us that "present fears are less than horrible imagining".

Frankly, I am *not* afraid. Not of depression. I was raised in the middle of one. But there's something else; something I'd like to repeat from *The Downwave:*

"During the 1930s, 25% of the workforce may have been unemployed. But that meant 75% of the workforce was employed. Falling prices brought an effective wage rise with every fall in price.

"There were several boom industries during the 1930s depression. The film industry was at its height. The Stork Club and the Copacabana were packed every night. . . More self-made millionaires came from the ruins of the 1930s than from any other time over the past fifty years."

If the Long Wave cycle *is* repeating itself. . . here and now. . . the unprepared will suffer. But those who are bold enough to anticipate events, and plan accordingly, could find the next few years offering them the opportunity of a lifetime. *Indeed, there may be rewards at your very fingertips that exceed your wildest dreams of avarice.*

Chapter Three

PARADOXES, PARADOXES, PARADOXES

People who talk about gradually inflating might as well talk about firing a gun off gradually.

Bernard Baruch

You could say that a *little bit* of inflation is like *a little bit of pregnancy.* It just keeps growing. But, to those who had struggled through the Depression of the 1930s, it was difficult to see inflation, as such, as anything to be feared. Many economists, however, recognised that the danger existed. John Maynard Keynes, who had persuaded governments that public expenditure was the way to conquer unemployment, was one of them. A fact that is often overlooked.

In London he published his views in *The Times* newspaper, just as Edmund Burke had published *his* thoughts on the role of the Parliamentary representative. Keynes further developed his thoughts in a booklet called *How to Pay for the War,* published in New York in 1940. He had seen the way war-workers' wages rose in the 1914-18 War. He had seen fortunes made by the so-called "profiteers". He did not wish to see either again. Basic necessities, like rent, food and clothing should be provided at stable prices. This should help to moderate wage claims. In order to keep aggregate demand, and the supply of goods available, more or less in equilibrium, his prescription was the removal of purchasing power:

". . . the only way to escape from (inflation) is to withdraw from the market an adequate proportion of consumers' purchasing power, so there is no longer an irresistible force impelling prices upward."

The levy on wages, salaries and profits, as Keynes saw it, would be returned, with interest, once peace came. In his testimony before the House Banking and Currency Committee, in Washington on 19th September 1941 — shortly before Pearl Harbour — Bernard Baruch also drew on his Great War experience:

"I think you have first to put a ceiling over the whole price structure including wages, rents and farm prices."

In *Review of Economic Statistics* (May 1941), a young economist observed that "the best remembered lesson" of America's experience in the Great War had concerned. . . Inflation! Whatever the state of feeling about the present war, he wrote, "any sort of poll would show a grim determination to defeat inflation." That paper was written by J.K. Galbraith, who urged that the ultimate weapon against inflation should be on measures "to crack the increase or reduce the volume of spending in the economy as a whole. More than twenty years later, in his book called *Money*, Galbraith reminded his readers that there was little to choose between a period of depression and one of inflation from the individual's view:

> "Inflation causes discomfort and frustration for many. Unemployment causes acute suffering for a lesser number."

Unfortunately, there was no certain way of knowing which caused the most pain. What it boils down to is that it doesn't matter whether the loaf of bread costs $1,000 or a bent penny! What *does* matter is whether or not you can lay your hands on the $1,000, or that equally important bent penny.

On a regional or national scale, the 1930s had brought deflation and depression, which destroyed the international order — leading each nation to seek its own salvation, regardless of the damage to others. Yet Galbraith warned against anyone's imagining the past could ever be safely buried:

> "It has equally been the lesson of the late sixties and early seventies that inflation too destroys international order. Those who express or imply a preference between inflation and depression are making a fool's choice. Policy must always be against whichever one has."

Reading those lines, there are many who will fold their hands contentedly. "You see," they'll be saying. "It's a job for them. . . for the politicians, the policy makers." Alas, that proverbial "tangled web" is never more tightly woven than when we set out to deceive ourselves; the most common conceit being to imagine that the individual — or the individual government, can beat inflation — any more than they can ward off depression.

J. Maynard Keynes is too often blamed for encouraging politicians to think they *can*. That is mistaken and unfair. Had Keynes not died in 1946, he would certainly have warned them against treating the policies he had recommended for the specific task of easing the Depression of the 1930s as a panacea. But he was dead; and as so often when the Master goes, the self-appointed disciples apply his teaching with such zeal, and such a lack of discrimination, that they turn a living and valuable body of doctrine into mere dogma. In this case they did so, with such dedication and insensitivity, that they undoubtedly fuelled the fires of inflation which were to blaze with alarming ferocity between 1939 and 1974.

Ironically they fell into the same error as those hard-faced men whom Keynes had so severely castigated after the First World War. These were the so-called "practical" men, who were in fact the unwitting prisoners of some long outmoded philosophy.

To speak so disparagingly, and so openly, about the bulldozer attitude of some of the more active neo-Keynsians will, I appreciate, be seen as a mark of arrogance. *(That Beckman's at it again!)* Above all, I realise that it is utterly beyond the pale to infer — let alone state categorically — that governments are as powerless as individuals when it comes to dealing with global economic forces.

For centuries governments have tried to control the tides. . . or, perhaps, have tried to convince us that they *could* control the tides. Like gamblers they have advanced all kinds of theories, devised all kinds of systems. The Law of Averages, however, applies to governments as well as anyone, or anything, else. So, every now and again, they have managed by some happy chance to back the right number. When that happens, they will forget that they have been the table's most consistent losers. All past failures forgotten, they will turn to their friends, crying, "You see! That proves our system works!"

What we're saying is that whether we are dealing with the economic policy of Keynes, Friedman, Ricardo, Schumpeter, or what-have-you, it was not in fact the policies themselves that stimulated economic recovery (or thwarted economic expansion). It was rather the underlying forces in the economy that allowed those policies to work.

At times, those who are sufficiently ruthless have a good chance of achieving their aim. Unquestionably, Mussolini *did* make the trains run on time. Hitler conquered unemployment. But at what cost?

You can say that by 1986, the second Thatcher Government had, indeed, brought inflation down. Or at least it looked as though they'd done so. The cost of that 7 year operation can be readily assessed by reference to the state of the real economy. True, the large rise in VAT from 8% to 15% in 1979 lifted retail prices and stimulated bigger wage claims. The higher prices cut general demand. Mainly as a result of this, writes Douglas Jay, "the rise in retail prices shot up from an annual rate of 8 per cent in early 1979 to 21 per cent in 1980." By the time I came to write *The Downwave* in 1982, it was already possible to get an idea of the cost of the new Government's experiment by looking at the state of the real economy.

Most striking of all was the jump in unemployment in terms of the United States' definition of unemployment, which includes both the registered and unregistered workless. Figure 7 shows the rapid growth in unemployment in Great Britain in the decade between 1972 and '82. It will be seen that the figure for GB is far in advance of that in Canada, France, West Germany, Japan or the United States. The validity of the excuse that unemployment has been rising everywhere — implying "Great Britain is no worse" — may be judged from the chart.

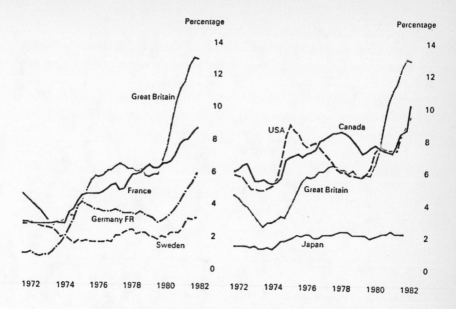

Figure 7: Unemployment rates adjusted to US concepts — international comparison
SOURCE: Bureau of Labor Statistics, US Dept. of Labor (1983).
Reproduced with the permission of the Controller of HMSO

Two points should be noted here: the rates have been adjusted to the US concept of unemployment, rather than that of Great Britain. Nevertheless, by 1981, the GB's 12.5% (however approximate that figure may be) was well above the runners-up, Canada and the USA with 8.4% and 8.3% respectively. Yet in 1980, only West Germany, Japan and Sweden had lower rates than Great Britain.

Figure 8 carries us on to the beginning of 1985. This time the OECD concept has been applied. This conforms as closely as possible to the guidelines of the International Labour Organisation (ILO). The total Labour force is taken to include civilian employees, professional and conscripted members of the armed forces, the self-employed, unpaid family workers and the unemployed. The unemployed embrace all those who are of working age, without work, available and seeking employment for pay or profit. This is a wider definition that in the UK which, when the 1986 Survey was published, comprised "People claiming benefit. . . at Unemployment Benefit Offices on the day of the monthly count. . . able and willing to do any suitable work." The UK concept of the unemployment rate is expressed as a percentage of "the latest available. . . estimates of all employees in employment *plus* the unemployed."

This time the figures cover the United Kingdom, rather than merely Great Britain. Except for the two laggards of Europe, Belgium and Spain, the

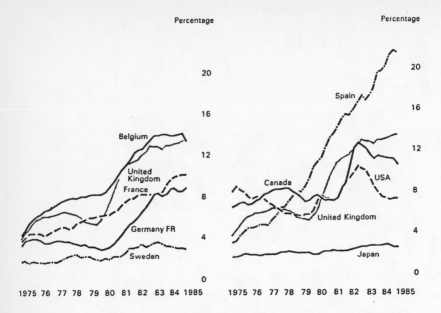

Figure 8: Unemployment rates adjusted to OECD concepts — international comparison   *SOURCE:* Main Economic Indicators and Quarterly Labour Force Statistics, *OECD (1986). Reproduced with kind permission of the Controller of HMSO*

UK leads. By now the most significant UK development is the relative levels of unemployment by regions (Figure 9). Within some regions there are also large variations. For example, the rate in Scotland in September 1985 ranged from 25.9% (Irvine Travel To Work area) to 5.7% (Shetlands).

The chart showing the likelihood of becoming, or ceasing to become unemployed (Figure 10) merits close study, but comment would be superfluous.

Those who were so determined to question the validity of *The Downwave* thesis, after my book had been published, may well have been blinded by the economic statistics still being bandied about during the rapid, all-round deterioration in the spring and summer of 1986. It should have been impossible for anyone of normal intelligence, with a reasonably open mind, to ignore. But all credit to the Central Statistical Office. They were not fooled for one minute!

The same well-balanced source shows the effects of tax and inflation on the real disposable earnings of the "family man", between 1975 and 1984 (Figure 11). It is instructive to see how little effect the much vaunted tax changes of successive governments have had on the overall Income Tax (plus National Insurance) "take". Even more striking is the real impact of inflation. Although incomes have been rising since 1945, the 1980s still

Unemployment rates[1]: by region

Percentages

	1976	1979	1983	1984
STANDARD REGIONS				
North	7.2	8.3 [2]	17.9	18.3
Yorkshire and Humberside	5.3	5.4	14.1	14.4
East Midlands	4.5	4.4	11.8	12.2
East Anglia	4.7	4.2	10.3	10.1
South East	4.0	3.4	9.3	9.5
South West	6.2	5.4	11.2	11.4
West Midlands	5.5	5.2	15.7	15.3
North West	6.7	6.5	15.8	15.9
England	5.1	4.8	12.3	12.4
Wales	7.1	7.3	16.0	16.3
Scotland	6.7	7.4	14.9	15.1
Great Britain	5.4	5.2	12.7	12.9
Northern Ireland	9.5	10.7	20.2	20.9
United Kingdom	5.5	5.3	12.9	13.1

1. Annual averages of claimants (including school leavers).
2. Comparison is affected by the 1983 Budget provisions.

Figure 9: Unemployment rates': by region
SOURCE: Department of Employment (1986).
Reproduced with the permission of the Controller of HMSO

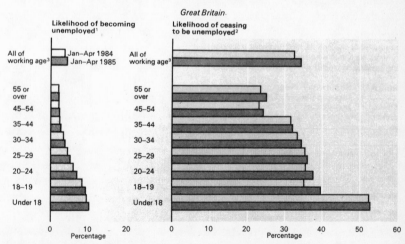

Figure 10: Likelihood of becoming or ceasing to be unemployed: by age, 1984 and 1985　　　*SOURCE: Department of Employment (1986).*
Reproduced with the permission of the Controller of HMSO

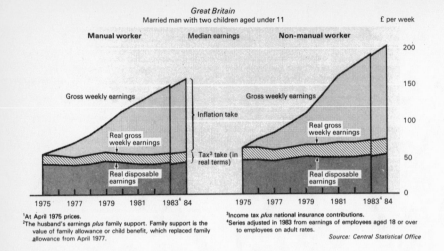

Great Britain
Married man with two children aged under 11   £ per week

Manual worker   Median earnings   **Non-manual worker**

¹At April 1975 prices.
²The husband's earnings *plus* family support. Family support is the
value of family allowance or child benefit, which replaced family
allowance from April 1977.

³Income tax *plus* national insurance contributions.
⁴Series adjusted in 1983 from earnings of employees aged 18 or over
to employees on adult rates.

Source: Central Statistical Office

*Figure 11: The effects of income tax, national insurance contributions, and inflation
on the real¹ disposable earnings of men*

SOURCE: Central Statistical Office. 1986.
Reproduced with the permission of the Controller of HMSO

found the economy "swaying uncertainly", as Douglas Jay put it, "between
excessive unemployment and excessive price inflation, without any clear
method of resolving the deadlock being yet agreed or apparent."

There are many who still regret that governments (and even splendid bodies
like the IMF and GATT) have proved powerless against the undertow of
the Long Wave cycle. There are others who have grown just as weary of
always being disappointed by the way "They" manage things. For those
still on the road to disillusion, I have one piece of advice. That is not to
abandon *hope*, but merely to shed all those high-minded preconceptions.
I say, try to live life like life is meant to be lived on Planet Earth. Governments
never have, and never will succeed in controlling the immense potential
of world economic currents, which have been surging around the globe from
ancient times.

Accepting that a complete solution should not be expected from any
government, we can try to get a little closer to the action. Perhaps we may
even come to grips with economic reality. First, though, we have to recognise
the thread that links all economic trends. That thread is Monetary Policy.
After that, our aims must be realistic. We must also accept our limitations.
We must appreciate that to know the cause of a malady may help. It will,
for instance, help us understand how the patient feels. But understanding,
determination and generous supply of the proven remedy still cannot
guarantee a cure.

Again, in talking of Monetary Policy — which implies taking monetary measures — it is imperative to distinguish between *monetary* policy and *monetarist* policy: the doctrine associated with Professor Milton Friedman and his followers. It used to be held that excessive *investment* was responsible for booms and inflationary pressures. The case was well argued by authorities like Friedrich von Hayek, Roy Harrod and Sir John Hicks. Milton Friedman, on the other hand, puts the blame on an excessive quantity of *money*. This is the doctrine supposedly adopted by the first Thatcher administration. More recently, however, Professor Friedman has accused Westminster and Whitehall of only flirting with monetarism. In fact you could say he disowned them.

It would be wrong to assume that there is nothing governments can do. Experience, as well as commonsense tell us there *are* measures which any but totally *laissez faire* government can — and must —take to protect the "players". But first, they must stop trying to change the rules. Or, as tends to happen in G5 and IMF circles — keep asking other better players not to try so hard. That is the ploy the US Treasury Secretary, James Baker was trying with the West Germans and the Japanese throughout the summer of 1986. After several frustrating weeks, the Group of Seven (France, the UK, Italy, Canada and the three "game-players") met ahead of the IMF Meeting. Phrases such as "constructive debate" and "broad consensus" were thrown around. But nothing of substance emerged. Angus MacMillan of Shearson Lehman Brothers, Messel's London Metal Research Unit spoke for quite a few market men at the sharp end of the economy:

> "Offering little more than chummy rhetoric as a panacea is not what international economic co-operation should be about. . . However, the inability of governments to learn at all once they have set their minds on a limited number of policy objectives is currently evident in the UK. The government's preoccupation with monetary aggregates and the control of inflation has left the *real economy* in a parlous state."

However, L. Peter Cogan spelled out the possible, positive aspects of discreet intervention. (He was assuming a slightly greater sense of realism on the part of the Authorities.) His book was called *The Rhythmic Cycles of Optimism and Pessimism:*

> "Monetary and fiscal policies do not appear to be the primary causes of the business cycle, but appear to modify the amplitude and, to some extent, the timing for better or worse, depending upon the correctness, liquidity and ingenuity of lenders, borrowers, and spenders. It would appear that 1929 — 1932 would have been a major turning point regardless of who had been (the US) President."

L. Peter Cogan could write that in 1969, without fear or favour. It was more than 35 years after the event. But had he written anything of the sort in the late '30s or early '40s, he would have been the subject of an instant and bitter attack for daring to express such views. Were the great 18th century philosophers of freedom alive today, I fear that some of them would be telling us: "I would fight to the death to defend your right to hold that view, but only so long as you promise to be discreet, and make clear that it's *Strictly Off the Record.''*

That may sound rather exaggerated, but I can assure you it is not! I have more than once experienced the *flak* you receive when you speak out of turn. It was certainly so in 1983 when *The Downwave* was published, which carried the same kind of "outrageous" views that I express, week by week, in my *Investors Bulletin.* For I am not talking merely of the past two or three years.

My first major prediction on the UK stock market was way back in 1968. This was just after the FT 30 Share Index had reached 520 that August. By the end of '68, it seemed to be heading back towards 520 again. My prediction was that the FT 30 *might* rise to 520, but it wouldn't rise much higher. What's more, I said, any rise would lead to a peak, and be the precursor to a long term cyclical bear market. It was one that would see the FT dropping to 300. At that time, most of the market mob were bullish. It was *totally impossible,* they told me, for the index to go that low. Why, if it DID fall to 300, there would be panic on the streets, with massive unemployment to follow. . . culminating in social disorder and utter chaos!

I tried to explain that nothing like that would happen. The fall would be accepted quite calmly. To start with, not many people in the country would be all that affected by the movement of share prices. But since the mob were Bulls at the time, and I was a Bear, I became a ready target for their scorn. I've been a target ever since.

The big problem with veering away from the path of the mob is that if you're in a herd and you veer to the left when the mob moves to the right, you run the risk of being trampled to death.

In 1983 my publisher and I had imagined that *The Downwave* was just the kind of book that the newspapers (and especially the quality Sundays) would see as "shock-horror" material. Therefore, they should be FIGHTING each other to serialise it. In the event. . . no offers. In many quarters, a chilled response. From others, silence.

What had I done? Was I scaremongering when I said firmly, and clearly, that we should wave a last goodbye to the overheated conditions which had made the 1970s a speculator's paradise? Certainly, the economy had been no great shakes when I sat down to write my book in 1982. Certainly few pundits were prepared to award Chancellor Howe the Cup for First Class Economic Management. (At best, he might have expected a small rosette, to encourage him to do better next time.)

Or was it blasphemy, perhaps, to predict. . . when the owner-occupier cult was going great guns, that residential property was riding for a fall?

Eventually, by talking to friends in Fleet Street (and especially to others who were no friends of mine) I began to realise what I had done; what heinous crime I had committed. It was far worse than "prophesying doom and gloom" or "talking down" house prices. What I had written in my book about the all-powerful Long Wave cycles, and the puny attempts by successive governments to resist them, had been interpreted as an attack on the *First Lady of the Falklands.* To men of the Media, apparently, I was dismissed as a crass, insensitive Alien from Another Place — well, that's how Wall Street can seem in the narrow alleyways around Throgmorton Street. Everyone knows what an unscrupulous lot the Americans are! Look how they reacted over what "the average decent chap" recognised as the well-deserved chastisement of the cowardly and despicable Argies!

My particular "crime", I realise now, had been to forget how much the columnists, the Anchor Men and the Camera Crews of All Nations felt they owed to their *Iron Lady.* She had made it possible to write of, talk of and above all shoot unlimited footage of a real, live "local" war. . . with all the trimmings from Top Ministerial Resignations, through Inadequate Radar Cover and Inflammable Aluminium Warships to Military Blunders and Old-Fashioned Acts of Heroism, which put names like Goose Green among the Great Battle Honours of the Past, from Balaclava and Rorke's Drift to Dunkirk and the Falaise Gap.

To some of the Patriots of El Vino's, my conduct could not have been more deplorable had I mingled with the admiring crowds in a Downing Street still echoing with that memorable cry, *Rejoice Rejoice!,* planning to break cover, dash past the policemen and scrawl the Most Obscene Message Possible across the Front Door of No 10.

Governments Are Impotent. . . OK?

Shortly after the publication of my book, I was asked to give a lecture to a property group in London. During the course of my lecture, I mentioned in passing that before the Falklands War, Margaret Thatcher was one of the most unpopular Prime Ministers in British history. The reaction I had from the crowd was actually violent. They began banging their glasses on the table, shouting and ya-hooing. All I did was mention an historical fact. But so incensed and inflamed were they by the Jingoism aroused by the Falklands Campaign, that they were completely oblivious to reality. They wanted to tear something — or someone — apart. This is the way the Mob frequently react when history doesn't happen to please them.

Taking up that thread on which our fortunes hang, you may have noticed that the Long Wave cycle ideology treats the period of rising prices and inflationary prosperity as the Upwave period of the cycle. But that is not the same as saying that rising prices are the *cause* of the Upwave. They are, rather, the effects of underlying forces which can be traced to *the actions of politicians.* They, in turn, reflect the demands of the electorate. Or — to be just a little cynical — the demands of the electorate after the politicians have had a chance to "get at them". Mind you, there is not a great deal of logic in the relationship between what the electorate genuinely tell their politicians and the path those politicians ultimately choose to follow.

The vast majority of the inhabitants of the United Kingdom would like a return to cheap food. Those who know about it are bitter that the London daily price of sugar is most times well below the European Community price. Plain men and women are angered by butter mountains. They are angry when they learn that these are being reduced by selling butter cheap to the Eastern bloc. But their representatives at Westminster, and in the European Parliament, persist in what looks to them very much like "feather-bedding" the farmers.

For the French and other EEC members, the farming community represents a sizeable bloc of votes. Many of them can truly be described as traditional peasant stock. Here the only "peasants" we ever see are performing in some pageant or dance festival in national costume. Nor is there a massive bloc of agricultural votes in the UK any longer. Nevertheless, both the CBI and the TUC-affiliated trades unions would be delighted if they felt they could wield the same clout in the Lobbies and Committee Rooms at Westminster as that powerful employers' organisation which goes by the manifestly inappropriate title of *The National Farmers Union*.

It is probably worth recalling, for the benefit of those who regard Britain's adoption of the CAP (Common Agricultural Policy) as the Dawn of Time, that the strength of the farming Lobby, which has kept alive the myth of the agricultural vote, was recognised and operative well before Britain agreed to raise food prices every year from 1973 to 1976; in line with the protectionist, dear-food regime of CAP.

Right away from matters of business and the economy, the British Parliament has steadfastly continued to resist the nationwide, grass-roots clamour for the return of Capital Punishment. On this subject, MPs of every political persuasion can be relied on, when challenged, to reply that in line with Burke's inspired view of the role of the Parliamentarian, they are the people's "representatives", not their "delegates".

By and large, therefore, when it comes to economic and social matters, it is probably not too harsh to demand that the politicians answer for their own misdeeds and omissions; and to take with a pinch of salt the excuse, "It's what the electorate demand of us."

Nor are the great British public themselves entirely free from *newspeak* and *double-think*. Those who have gone canvassing at election time will know that one of the outstanding characteristics of the GBP is their unwillingness to hurt anybody; not even rival politicians and their supporters. Thus, without in any way meaning to deceive, many worthy householders will pledge their vote to whichever canvassers happen to come along, and in whatever order they turn up!

Sincere as their protest may be about that dangerous new road, those insanitary old school lavatories, they may at the same time be embarrassingly co-operative. So when the candidates' supporters stammer out the routine, lame excuses the constituency agent told them to offer, the householder can be relied on, often enough, to spring to their rescue and finish their sentences for them!

I don't know if you ever saw Robert Redford in the movie, *The Candidate*. In one scene, he is in his tiny office, with a friend. In comes the slick and suave campaign manager. Redford's friend asks, "What are you doing here?" The man in the sharp suit says, "I'm in Politics."

Scornfully, the candidate's friend says, "Politics is bullshit." "You're RIGHT!" replies the campaign manager. "I always wondered what it was." Old Sigmund Freud knew precisely what "humour" was: a way of saying aloud what we would hate to be caught thinking.

All this polite, deliberate avoidance of the truth, if not, indeed, evasion — which goes on on all sides — makes for an apparently harmonious relationship between the leaders and the led. It is, in truth, a most unhealthy (and at times potentially dangerous) practice, degrading to the relationship. That is because it is a relationship involving *collusion* rather than co-operation. What is presented as a consensus, achieved through a mutually respectful exchange leading to understanding, is too often a facade. Behind the shallow front both parties figure as victims, in the sense that neither ever quite appreciates what has really taken place.

Whatever the explanation, one thing is clear: it all makes T. Rowe Price's assessment of what the mob will (or will not) tolerate seem somewhat unreal:

"The masses (he claims) will not support any government in the near future that puts the control of inflation ahead of full employment and continued prosperity."

Isn't this the course on which the first Thatcher Government embarked in the summer of 1979? And was it *only* the Falklands factor which returned the same party, with the same policies on offer in '83?

My book refuted the effect of any such policies. It can now be readily seen how, in our politically dominated environment, any book half as outspoken as *The Downwave* would have to be rejected out of hand. Books like that make people think. Thought can challenge the most firmly held beliefs. Worse, thought can destroy faith. Obviously, from the first page, I was not in support of government. . . any government.

Returning to Price's comment, a great deal depends on the way the question. . . *would you support?* is put.

Any reasonably proficient public opinion pollster could translate T. Rowe Price's thesis into the form of two questions. One to invite a firm "No", the other a hesitant "Yes". The first question would be worded as follows:

Could you or your family go on supporting a Government which arbitrarily decided that controlling inflation was so important that it would risk sacrificing jobs like YOURS, and/or that of your family's breadwinner, merely to safeguard Company profits and protect City interests?

Does not such a question *command* a firm "No?" But suppose it were changed around a little, to read:

Both the Prime Minister and President Reagan have said that Inflation is Public Enemy No 1. Could you be relied on, therefore:

(a) *To support their endeavours to the best of your ability, in order to reduce inflation for the sake of a healthy economy, for yourself and your family, and the next generation; and, in so doing, safeguard British industry and protect Britain's vital "invisible" income from the City (banking, insurance, shipping etc.) against the threat of unfair foreign competition?*

OR

(b) *Would you join those who criticise the Prime Minister and her Cabinet, on the grounds that the standard of living, and certain people's job prospects might suffer in the short term, regardless of the very real threat of foreign competition?*

What answers might we expect here? (I suggest you try it out on colleagues, neighbours and friends.)

In order to plan our lives, we must be in a position to anticipate the future. There is no possibility of doing anything of the sort unless we understand the present. If our understanding of the present is confused by rhetoric, and befogged by preconceptions, there is no chance whatsoever of planning our lives, or anticipating the future. The underlying theme of my book, *The Downwave,* is the basic need for economic truth and reality, avoiding propaganda and vested interests. Quite clearly this was not the way to win popularity during the '83 Election year.

The point in introducing those two examples of the currently popular forked-tongue technique may now be clear. It is to stress, and to warn that what so often appears as a "straight" question, merely seeking information, is anything but! The great majority of us —when we think about it — spend a fair slice of every day ducking and dodging a barrage of persuasive pseudo-questions or arguments weighted with sly inferences and seductive half-truths. Nor is it confined to the office, factory, pub or club. In the home too, television and radio supplement the daily dose of print-indoctrination.

It is clear that our deeply rooted aversion to "rocking the boat" or "giving offence" renders us ever willing victims. We end up accepting without question what those who have the means to act tell us is the thing they should be doing on our behalf. When argument fails, the Jack- or Jill-in-Office only has to fall back on the old gambit of declaring, hand-on-heart, "There is no alternative!" Reflect for a moment, and you will see what nonsense it is. There must *always* be an alternative: even though it be no more than refraining from action.

During the course of the many lectures I have been giving since the publication of the book, I've tried to explain to the audience that it's not my mission to convince them of anything whatsoever. I'm not prepared to debate my views. Not because of my overweening arrogance, but because I can see that no constructive purpose can possibly be served. I try to get my audience to understand I'm there for one purpose only: to open the doors of perception for them. . . just a little bit wider. If they like what lies behind those doors (or even if they don't *like* what they see, but at least find something useful) they are free to adopt whatever they discover behind those doors. On the other hand, if they *don't* like what they see, they need only slam the door, and walk away. In no time, they will have forgotten all about it! I shall certainly not be offended. For at least they have been willing to be exposed for an hour or so to another point of view.

The Inflation Bogy

Nowhere is there a greater urge to take cover from new ideas (or uncomfortable thoughts) than when inflation looms. Unlike depression, people will at least talk about it, pouring out everything that others told them about it. But. . . try getting them to tell you what *they* know and *believe*! You are unlikely to get very far on that tack. Certainly the opinions they offer will tend to be a jumble of half-digested hearsay. But why should the ordinary man or women in the home, or the office, bear the blame, when those who *should* know better, (and many of those who *do* know better) go on hedging and trying to persuade you there is nothing in it. . . instead of coming clean?

Let's not do that! Let's go straight for it. That means asking three basic questions as a first step:

What is inflation?
What causes it?
How can it be got rid of?

Understanding the answers to these questions is vital in planning the future. From the period of the 1940s to the mid-1970s, inflation had been with us. It was not, at that time, unreasonable to assume that inflation must have become a permanent feature of life. True, it had been with us for close on 30 years. It was not surprising, therefore, that when I suggested back in 1974 that inflation was not forever, it was seen as another of "Beckman's outlandish heresies." As you discover more about inflation, you will grasp the underlying theme of *The Downwave,* and appreciate why inflation *cannot* be a permanent feature.

The next question, in all logic, must be: *if inflation is not a permanent feature of life,* what then? Before we pursue that one, let's deal with inflation itself.

I have already inferred that if you were to ask your colleagues, neighbours and friends to give you their views on inflation, they would do so. Unlike depression, inflation is a subject most of us feel we *ought* to be able to talk about. So it is unlikely that anyone would have nothing to say. Again, the response you received would, as we have seen, depend very much on

the way you phrased your question. But the odds are that you would be
told three things:

(a)   That inflation means "rising prices".
(b)   That this, or that, individual or group is to blame.
(c)   But that inflation, like the poor, is always with us.

The first answer is simply not true; and the next two tend to show the
extent of the confusion that prevails. If we really believe that some one
or other is to blame, then it implies that something *could* (and *should)* be
done about it. On the other hand, if inflation is inescapable, why blame
anyone?

The truth is, *no* government can eliminate inflation. It can tinker with
the economic mechanism to minimise the impact. By tinkering with a
mechanism it does not understand, it will often enough make matters worse.
People can be surprisingly tolerant. Or are they merely passive? Whatever
the answer, some will tell you, "Maybe it wasn't always like this, but that's
how it is today. So we'd better learn how to live with it." Pure self-delusion!
Others will say they don't understand why ". . . you all keep on about the
'evils of inflation'. It's been great for me and my business." There you
have the truly *Grand Delusion!*

I find that the perception of inflation entertained by readers of *The
Downwave* and my weekly *Investors Bulletin* differs widely, according to
individual temperament and circumstances. The same applies to the many
hundreds of people whom I have met, face to face, at the countless seminars
and public lectures I have given since publication of the book.

But that still leaves in the air the two key questions which must be
answered before we can begin to seek an effective remedy or remedies.
Those questions are:

What is inflation?
What role does it play in the Long Wave cycle?

Towards a Definition

A good, adequate definition should theoretically enable us to recognise the
inflationary Unicorn, even though we may never have come face to face
with him. But clear, simple definitions belong to the glib world of
grammarians, whose main tool is hindsight. Most market men are rather
like the proverbial keeper at the London Zoo, who would be hard to put
to it to "define" a giraffe, but knows better than anyone (except, possibly,
another giraffe) exactly what it needs.

Inflation is too complex a phenomenon to be summed up in three lines
in a dictionary of economic terms. It was John Maynard Keynes who said

not one man in one thousand can fully understand — or protect himself against — inflation. Unfortunately too many people think it can be neatly pigeon-holed. Perhaps because they feel they have an inalienable right to instant knowledge and effortless enlightenment. Effortless enlightenment happens to be the very plague of our economic existence! With inflation, they'll be unlucky. For two hundred years or so, if the truth be told, the very smartest of governments have not coped all that cleverly. However, this is not to be wondered at when they consistently ignore history — which would at least spare them the embarrassment of being surprised.

There is no reason, or excuse, for anyone in authority to be unaware of the shifting, transitory nature of inflation. The evidence is all there, as I pointed out in the American edition of *The Downwave:*

> "Rising prices are certainly not a permanent part of the economic system, wheat prices from 1295 to 1980 show that clearly. Long waves of economic life ebbed and flowed well before the first observable wave began in 1798."

Some governments, however, are determined to ignore history, preferring to put their faith in the power of rhetoric. "Inflation is public Enemy No. One", they cry — as though that solved the problem once and for all. Or they offer some spurious message of mock-assurance: "We shall control inflation." A promise they must know they are unlikely to fulfil. But they fear that unless they go on making promises — however threadbare — they are selling the pass to the other side, and throwing away the next election. Some governments live like that: planning the next campaign the moment the ballot boxes have been put away. Fear is the prevailing emotion when a government finds itself caught up in a wave of inflation. I wrote:

> "Americans thought an inflation rate of 10 per cent astronomical, but in the mid-1970s Britain was cited as a nation on the brink of becoming a 'Banana republic', with inflation up to 28%. . . (The) fear that something horrible will happen if inflation is not conquered and obliterated leads us into the same trap as other governments in other countries during periods of high inflation."

One "trap" is to imagine that inflation appears quite suddenly, springing from recent and shallow roots. Thus we may expect to deal with it effectively, provided the remedy is applied without delay. Given this belief, it is usual to blame "the last Government" or "the last Chancellor" for their "obvious" mistakes. Students of the Long Wave cycle have discovered that inflation is not shallow rooted like an annual weed. It is more like convolvulus or ground elder. It is deeply rooted, and is the result of policies implemented many years earlier by men whose names are all but forgotten. They may appear in a footnote to their time, but rarely on the main page.

It is clear — vary the metaphor — that it is too late merely to stamp on the smoking fuse. The clock governing the time of detonation was set ticking long before the first smell of powder attracted anyone's attention to the bomb.

To be specific, the train for the price explosion between 1939 and 1974 was laid during the Great Depression, when unemployment during the 1930s took over from inflation as the major threat. True, the German experience of hyper-inflation in the 1920s was horrifying. But the Great Depression made the more lasting impression on the policy makers of the time. Indeed, by the beginning of the 1940s, as J.K. Galbraith sees it, the problems of inflation were all but forgotten.

On 20th November 1923, the German hyper-inflation had ended. It came quite abruptly. "Perhaps", wrote Galbraith in his book, *Money*, ". . .it ended simply because it could not go on".

On that day in November, the old currency, Reichmarks were exchanged for Rentenmarks at the rate of One Rentenmark for each trillion (or 1,000 billion) Reichmarks. Galbraith sees it as a face-saving expedient, and something of a fraud:

> "The new Rentenmark was declared to be backed by a first mortgage on all the land and other physical assets of the Reich. . . (but) any German seeking to exercise rights of foreclosure on German property with his Rentenmarks would have been thought mentally unstable. . . Nevertheless it worked."

Shortly afterwards unemployment, which had been low during the hyper-inflation, returned. By Christmas 1923, more than 25% of all trades union members were without jobs; during 1924, after a swift recovery, unemployment fell to 6.4% of the total labour force. In 1925, it had shrunk to 3.3%. By 1927, Germany's national income had reached its pre-war level with low unemployment. By December 1931, however, more than 16% of the total work force were unemployed. Here the German authorities fell into another well-worn trap: their understandable but exaggerated fear of inflation. J.K. Galbraith comments:

> "We have noticed. . . that the strongest action is taken against inflation when it is least needed. . . with one-sixth of the total German labour force out of work, the government of Heinrich Brüning decreed a reduction of from 10 to 15 per cent in most wages. . . also a reduction in industrial prices of 10 per cent, a similar reduction in rents, railway fares, rail freight charges and charges for municipal services. . . Unemployment benefits were also reduced. . . In the following year unemployment rose to one-fifth of the German labour force, and in the next year came Hitler."

In *The Face of the Third Reich,* Joachim Fest reminds us that already by 1934, 49% of public expenditure was invested in the armaments industry. By 1938, it had risen to 79%. In the United States, in 1929 unemployment reached 1.6 million, or 3.2% of the labour force. By 1932, it was up to 12.1 million, or just under 25% of the working population. Military spending in the States brought the unemployment rate down to 14.6% in 1940. In

1941, the year of Pearl Harbour, the rate was down to 9.9%. As already pointed out, the way to climb out of depression — even the Great Depression — was the Keynsian way, whereby economic recovery had to be induced by government spending. Keynes was not blind to the dangers of inflation. But he thought its effects could be mitigated so long as government cut social spending once the economy picked up again.

What he did not foresee, or perhaps turned a blind eye to, was that once a politician commits himself to buying votes by promising a "chicken in every pot", there can be no turning back.

There was a great deal of self-satisfaction among neo-Keynsian circles in London and Washington. The *Economic Report of the President, 1968* is indicative of the mood:

> "Fiscal and monetary policies have not been perfectly executed nor perfectly coordinated in the past few years. . . (But) our actions have been consistently in the right direction, if not always perfectly timed nor in precisely the right degree."

The Anatomy of Inflation

As stated already, inflation does not just mean rising prices. Nor do falling prices necessarily signal deflation. The price of a particular commodity may rise because demand has risen and supply cannot keep up. Not at the moment, at any rate. Prices can rise or fall because tastes have changed, or because near substitutes have shot up in price, or are just not available.

Prices at the London tea auctions, say, can shoot up because Indian and Sri Lankan consumers are drinking more at home leaving less tea for export. But the rise in price of tea can perfectly well coincide with a fall in the Retail Price Index (RPI), generally regarded as a crude measure of inflation. In addition to price rises for those very obvious reasons, tastes may change.

Sales of ice cream will tend to fall off under blizzard conditions; as will sales of lager and open-toed sandals in a wet summer. Those, however, are just temporary hitches; and anyway, ice cream and lager can both be kept on ice until demand revives. Naturally, tastes can be manipulated to some extent by advertising, the hard sell, or a change in the climate. For example, lightweight rather than heavyweight suits may be demanded, because they are "the thing" for the Young Man on his Way. Or it may simply be that the firm's American customers are tending to shift from the cooler New England climate to the warmer Southern States. Higher prices may also be charged because of a rise in manufacturing or transportation costs.

Sometimes, though, demand may fall quite sharply, and quite suddenly, leaving the suppliers — whether makers, wholesalers or retailers — with unwanted stocks. When the US Government delayed its move to require car exhaust systems to contain a platinum wire filter to take out the noxious element in the gaseous products of the internal combustion engine, it did no good for the price of platinum. The square-bottomed "frock coat" went almost instantly out of fashion when a certain North London dentist, Dr Crippen, appeared so attired in the dock on a charge of murder. The reaction, we are told by those who can remember that era, was almost instantaneous — as though someone, somewhere had sternly forbidden the wearing of the frock coat.

Yet, time and again, when the objective is a narrow, and apparently simple one, we will each of us tend to approach our task in a way which is dictated more by our upbringing and way of thinking, than the way an outsider would expect a "professional" to tackle it.

Most of us, I imagine, have heard the story (in one form or another) of the managers on a cinema circuit, who are told by the owners of the chain to sell more soft drinks. The first manager, an Ivy League graduate and a traditionalist, orders a whole range of colourful but discreet glass slides to be projected in the breaks between the movies. The second man, young, thrusting and eager, fresh from MIT, decides to go for subliminal advertising: flashing the words *Thirst* and "Cool, cool Cola" on to the screen — at moments of high drama — for a matter of mere micro-seconds. The third manager, who had never been to Business School. . . or even college, turns up the heating!

You can say that in many parts of Britain it still costs no more than £60 per square foot, or thereabouts, to build a new house to a reasonable standard, including central heating and fully fitted kitchen and bathroom. Differences in the final price can arise from the cost of the land, or the taste — or status-premium which the vendor can screw out of the purchaser. It may be a combination of the two. Have we not heard sales talk of that kind? This introduces a further range of possible ways of solving what may look from the ouside like a perfectly straightforward case; one in which "anyone" would know how to react. "You *could* go for a perfectly *beautiful* home on the other side of the Lake, sir. . . or madam, But our homes *this* side have a certain. . . *je ne sais quoi!* And besides, the *other side* would just not be right for *you*!"

Little wonder that location, and the social connotations of the choice made, are so important in the UK at the moment. What is more, with prices sagging (if not actually falling throughout most of the country) property "of the right kind" and "in the right area" has been shooting up in price, at the same time that inflation was falling lower and lower. It is a case of the "right (or the *wrong)* side of the tracks" with a vengeance, and in no way dictated by the trend in inflation. However, insofar as the high cost of the delectable home is not entirely absorbed by the purchase, it must make some impact on the economy as a whole — since it is impossible to conceive of a situation in which the tastes, routine purchases, entrepreneurial and investment activities of any man or woman can fail to impact on others.

Only a few years ago, it was fashionable to complain that much of the investment flowing into property should have been going into industry. They blamed the Government's campaign of encouragement to would-be owner-occupiers, claiming that mortgage relief was causing further distortions of the investment flow. Was this not a case, then, in which Government *was* intervening successfully — even if it did upset the critics?

A moment's recollection of what actually goes on in the real world will show that so-called "inducements" by the authorities, whether tax concessions or lower interest rates, may well reinforce (or speed up) the decision of a firm to invest in new plant, expand existing premises, or launch a new product. But it must already have made up its mind that it wants to go in that direction. After all, the plan has been devised because there are sound *business reasons* for so acting. An adverse tax position may deter, so may extremely high real interest rates. But a reduction in either can be no more than an invitation to the waltz. There is no way to guarantee that the guests will accept. Therefore, would people have poured money into property, had they not believed they could do better than in any other sector?

Now we are getting close to appreciating the true nature of inflation, and the dangers associated with it. We must have gathered by now that it is the product of a number of factors including the tastes, routine purchases, entrepreneurial and investment activities *of every man and women*. What makes inflation more than merely a run of rising prices, due to an imbalance between the amount of goods and services available and the amount of money in circulation?

To adopt Douglas Jay's definition — probably the briefest on record: it's "a general rise in prices caused by the expansion of the currency beyond the point needed for full use of real resources."

One further point should be made here. It will be crucial when we come to examine the way the Government has reacted over the past 7 years to the need to curb inflation. There are two kinds of inflation — cost inflation and demand inflation. Without going any further into the subject, it would seem likely that the way to cure one form of inflation must also be the way to make the other worse. Indeed, that is one of the reasons why inflation has been curbed, but at so high a cost in terms of the real economy.

An understanding of inflation is the central theme of *The Downwave* because an understanding of inflation leads to the discovery that it is not a permanent aspect of our way of life. Once we recognise that inflation can — and, indeed, must — have its end, and when we see that it is even now in the process of ending (and in some areas has already done so), then the thesis of *The Downwave* becomes to that extent more relevant. The proofs that we have seen since the book was published in 1983 also become much more evident. When the book first came out, the deflationary forces were already building, but less plainly than now. Since 1983, we have seen the collapse of energy prices, the collapse of farm produce prices, and of the market for most metals. Even the most successful commodity agreement of all time, the International Tin Agreement, has come to grief. We have seen how the market decline has affected certain states of America, driving them down into depression. As the farmland states were hit, banks there began to fail.

The energy-based states slid into depression. The banks, once so eager to make large and loosely secured loans to the oil and associated industries began to fail. Agricultural land and domestic property values in the USA plummeted, as the deflationary forces swept like a tornado through the affected areas. It would be inconceivable to imagine that the deflationary forces, which have been developing since the publication of my book, will be confined to a few localities in a handful of unlucky states. What we are seeing now, as I predicted back in '83, is a global phenomemon. In the UK, we certainly have our problems too. As recently as the late summer of 1986, the fortunes of oil-rich Aberdeen collapsed: jobs were slashed, property values fell by 40% or so.

Nor were the nations gathered at the Annual Meeting of the IMF and World Bank (or the Group of Five meeting which preceded it) to produce anything more substantial than rhetoric. The G5 initiative to drive down the exchange rate of the dollar in '85 succeeded because the Market was already moving in that direction. Within months, however, it had gone too far, certainly for the Japanese. Treasury Secretary Baker was driven to appealing to Tokyo and Bonn to do what the archetypal cricket-playing, public-school, Edwardian Englishman would have termed "the decent thing". Yet, despite a fall in inflation as well as in oil prices, there was no great upsurge in economic activity in the industrialised nations; though the oil-producing states were already reacting (as might have been expected) by cutting imports to match their falling revenues.

What is essential is that *anything which occurs elsewhere in the world may not necessarily move the American economy, but anything that happens to the American economy will be magnified and translated the world over*. There is another thing we would be wise to recognise, before the Downwave, already with us, deepens into depression. It is that the difference between the American economy and European economies is nothing more than one of visibility.

Sadly, in a way, those "gloomy", "fleshcreeping" forecasts in my earlier book are already being vindicated across the world. So far as this country is concerned, I am no longer alone in my much repeated (and bitterly resented) forecasts of an end to the UK property boom! Within a matter of weeks, the chairman of a leading High Street bank and the Governor of the Bank of England both warned of the dangers of excessive optimism on the part of property speculators, and the apparently irresponsible loan policies of certain building societies.

Chapter Four

TULIPOMANIA 1980s STYLE:
RESIDENTIAL PROPERTY

*. . .we do not predict a collapse in house prices. If the Halifax had any
such concern, we would feel it our duty to warn existing and new borrowers.*
The Halifax Building Society (*The Times,* 30 Sept '86)

In *The Downwave,* I recounted the story of *Tulipomania,* a speculative craze
that swept Holland during the 17th century. Somebody, somewhere got the
idea that investing in tulips was the best thing since the discovery of the
wheel. The mania reached a *crescendo* with Dutch people selling their
livestock, farms, homes and all they possessed simply to invest in the precious
bulbs. Like all bubbles, the Tulip Bubble burst. It brought the Dutch economy
to its knees, resulting in a political upheaval and widespread deprivation
which was to last for many years to come.

What tulips were to the Dutch economy in the 17th century; what the
US stock market was to the US economy in 1929. . . is what the residential
property market became to the British economy in the 1980s.

September 30th 1986 could well be a date to remember; and not only
for the Halifax Building Society. You'll soon see why. But first, let me take
you back to April 22nd 1983. That was the date when the *Financial Weekly*
carried a review of *The Downwave,* headlined *Economics and an eye for
debauchery.* "According to Bob Beckman's new book," wrote the reviewer,
"what we should all be doing is going out and counting the bare breasts
in Soho strip joints, personally testing out promiscuity levels, and measuring
the lengths of women's skirts."

I wonder how many who read that went off to buy their copy of *The
Downwave* before the Vice Squad raided the bookshops! Had they done so,
they would have been disappointed. However. . . back to the reviewer:

"Permissiveness is one of the most accurate barometers for the economy.
When things are getting naughtier, you can be sure the economy is on a
long upwave."

Cute! What I had pointed out (on Page 42. . . in case you'd like to take another look) was that:

> "The central characteristic of the final stages of the upwave is the consumer mentality. During the upwave of the 18th and 19th centuries, the West rejected two kinds of authority: the authority of the king to tell us what to do, and the authority of the church to tell us how to think. . . Fashion, music, literature, theatre and dance all fall under the influence of the upwave. . . the repressive status of the traditional religions, which can cope with the social *mores* of the early stages of the upwave, are incompatible with the freedoms required during the later stages of the upwave."

The increasing desire to shed social *mores* and rid ourselves of constraint had its influence on literature and the theatre in Britain in the 60s. Remember *Oh Calcutta* or *Hair?* With their unfamiliar full frontal nudity on stage, they were the hit shows of the 1960s. Twenty years later, it is difficult to imagine the sensation generated by those shows, or by some of the trends in women's fashion at the time.

But this is not new. Since the 14th century fashion trends have been linked inextricably to inflation. The Ladies of the Court displayed various amounts of decolletage with tightly-laced corsets and elaborate hairstyles. In the 15th century, when the going was tougher, the rule was minimum exposure. Necklines were high, the feminine form well covered and corsets loosely tied. Back went fashion in the following century to free display, until the decline among the wealthier nations in Tudor times saw the bosom covered up once more, and the female form disguised. Elizabethan prosperity led to further unveiling. So did the changes in American colonial life, with the Puritan maid 'out', and the Restoration beauty 'in'. Following the French Revolution, women's fashions were light and near-transparent. Then, during the bad years after 1814, legs and bosoms disappeared again until the upwave of the 1840s to '60s. The downwave at the end of the 19th century brought hemlines so low that skirts had to be lifted if M' lady was to walk at all.

During the period of prosperity at the turn of the present century, erotic capital achieved its grandest exploitation in history by revealing the feminine form. But not for too long, as I wrote:

> "During the downwave of the 1930s, ladies covered up again. . . Our recent prosperity brought the hemline up to the crotch, the neckline down to the waistline. Bras were discarded, and nipple erections were outlined under outer garments. Some young women were having their pubic hair tinted and permed for purposes best left to the imagination."

You can see how the reviewer got round to his Soho strip joints! However, he did pick up two basic points, as I hoped every reader would. The first was that these Long Wave cycles have been identifiable for more than 200 years. Although you'd think by now we would "have the sense to prepare". . .

we never do. Certainly, I'd say that those who ignore the social factor, and treat the Long Wave cyclical swings in fashion, entertainment and popular morality as "information of indifferent quality" deserve what they get. Still, I was delighted to see that the reviewer had managed to pick up the even more basic point I'd been trying to make on the way:

> ". . . the secondary depression of the 1980s will bring excruciatingly high unemployment, massive bankruptcies through industry, a collapse in capital markets, a sustained decline in property values and a great deal of hardship for many people."

Well, well! And he added, no doubt sarcastically:

> "If you believe Bob Beckman, sell your house and your equities, buy Treasury bills and government and corporate bonds. Don't leave your money in the building society and stay out of index linked investments."

In case you haven't got the message yet, what the reviewer had been attempting to do was detract from the credibility of the message in *The Downwave* by being cute. In 1988, it doesn't sound that cute any longer. Not so far as domestic property is concerned!

Bricks Without Mortar

"Bricks without mortar" is how one property man of long experience recently described the housing market in the summer of 1986. "It looks good, it feels good. And so long as everyone says, 'How nice! How durable', as they stroll past. . . on their way to raise another loan. . . then fine! But try leaning too hard against the end wall. . . or start getting worried about the level of borrowing. . . and the odds are the whole impressive edifice of mortarless brick will come crashing down like the walls of Jericho."

Property. . . even domestic property. . . has come tumbling down too often (both literally and metaphorically), and at roughly the same stage of the economic cycle, to dismiss what has happened as mere co-incidence. We shall see this as we examine the record. We shall also see that the style, numbers and standard of housing (using the term broadly) are important elements in the structure and quality of a modern society.

During the second-line banking crisis of the 1970s, we saw the implosion of commercial property, which at the time was a market where the participants believed prices would rise in perpetuity. In Britain today, the most important, potentially sensitive end of the market is that of the owner occupier. Here we are dealing with a growing slice of the population as the 1983 Report on Social Trends reveals (Figure 12). The role and importance of commercial property in the market of the early 1970s, has been assumed by the owner occupier in the 1980s.

| | *Great Britain* | | | *Millions and percentages* | | |
| | *Millions* | | | *Percentages* | | |
	1961	*1971*	*1981*	*1961*	*1971*	*1981*
TENURE OF HOUSEHOLDS IN PERMANENT ACCOMMODATION						
Owner-occupied	6.5	8.7	10.8	40	48	56
Rented from local authority/ new town	4.1	5.5	6.0	25	30	31
Rented privately	5.5	3.9	2.5	34	21	13
HOUSEHOLDS IN NON-PERMANENT ACCOMMODATION	0.1	0.1	0.1	—	—	—
ALL HOUSEHOLDS	16.2	18.2	19.5	100	100	100

Figure 12: Households: by tenure
  SOURCE: Population Census 1961, 1971, and 1981. *Office of Population
  Censuses and Surveys: General Register Office (Scotland), 1983.
  Reproduced with permission of the Controller HMSO*

It must be said that the term owner-occupier contains a strong element
of hope: hope that in 20, 25 years (or less) the occupier will be the *de jure*
owner. In the meantime, he (and increasingly she) is in reality no more
than a mortgagee. Official statistics show that by 1981, just about a quarter
of all households owned their home outright. But this, like so many easy-
to-swallow averages, makes better sense when broken down. The figure was
40% for households where the head-of-house was retired, or otherwise
"economically inactive". But 86% of semi-skilled manual and personal
service heads of household had a mortgage. Lest anyone should say, "That
class of person would," be advised! Households headed by professionals,
employers and managers showed a 62% mortgage count! Of the group
comprising unskilled, manual heads of household, only 16% had a mortgage.
Most of the remainder were presumed to be renting their homes. If they
were fortunate enough, it would be from a local council or new town
authority.

In the following five years of the Thatcher administration, to the middle
of 1986, it was reckoned that the right-to-buy legislation covering council
tenants, combined with mortgage tax relief for buyers, had helped to swell
the ranks of the hopeful mortgagee. But there were obviously other factors.
For one thing, the growth of home ownership in Britain had by then been
elevated to a cult; encouraged by Government, and facilitated by the open
handedness of building societies, high street banks and other institutions.

The level of mainly mortgage-backed, "owner" -occupation in Great Britain
stood at 40% in 1961. It was 48% by '71. By 1981, the third year of the
first Thatcher administration, the comparable figure was 56%. Now, five

years later, the figure has been standing around 64% in England, and 62% in the UK as a whole. It may not sound all that impressive, until you recall that in 1914, no more than one home in ten was owner occupied; and then by the "better off".

This change, which has brought the near extinction of the private landlord, has been accompanied more recently by a slowdown in council building, a fall in the funds available for housing associations and an acceleration in the sale of heavily discounted council properties. In 1987, the Government began to consider ways of encouraging the building of homes to rent.

An Englishman's Home

The spread of owner-occupancy has its roots in the social history of Great Britain since the last century; a history more complex than most people imagine. Apart from the impact of two World Wars, and new technology, the changes in the social structure have been as far reaching and complex as any other change in the everyday life of the country. The big development of the middle-class suburbs began in earnest when the railways reached out to the quiet, far-off villages in and around the big cities. Even when the movement was well under way, London was still a neat, tight City, where a high proportion of the residents had been born, or raised, in the surrounding countryside. Many of the young men who were to work and save, and become the speculative builders of the 1920s and '30s had arrived on foot from the neighbouring counties before the outbreak of war in 1914.

They had come to seek their fortune; and they were determined to find it. These were the working-class equivalent of the Welsh linen drapers, who were to build their Oxford Street stores; the publishing Macmillans, no more than one generation away from the proud but humble croft; or Sir Ernest Barker, the distinguished political philosopher, whose family had been village craftsmen. When these young bricklayers and carpenters had trudged the last mile down the lanes towards the capital, they still carried proudly the mark of their trade, the "brickie's" hod and trowel, and the "chippie's" set of chisels and saws, well-greased and swathed in sacking.

Before the First World War, some local authorities had begun to build the early "council dwellings". There was a small "estate" at the foot of Barnet Hill, not all that far from the farmland around Hendon, where the pupils of the Graeme White flying school were still hedge-hopping across the fields, which later were to become Hendon Aerodrome. Similar developments were being contemplated elsewhere. In recent years, until the tower blocks in inner London began to block the view, it was possible to stand on the heights of Kenwood or Crystal Palace, and see clearly (especially after a bout of summer rain) the curving line of slate roofs which marked — broadly speaking — the outer limits of London before the 1920s.

Although Birmingham and Manchester, Liverpool, Cardiff and Glasgow were beginning to spread, London was still considered to be the leading Metropolitan City. But Charles Furth, who watched the successful launch of middle-class suburbia, wrote in his study of *Life Since 1900,* that all this new building had:

". . . drained off the comparatively well-to-do, leaving the old buildings, in the town centres, to be filled by those with less to spend. The outward movement was carried by the electric tram, which, together with electric light, was a late Victorian legacy. . . (But) London lagged behind the general movement, and until 1905 the City and West End still depended on horse-drawn omnibuses, so that to come to the capital from Manchester or Liverpool was to go back to Victorian world, although London had its first Tube as early as 1890."

Life in London was certainly not easy for the poor, especially the "respectable poor". C.F.G. Masterman in his book, *The Condition of England* described the dwelling of a typical working-class family in the early 1900s:

". . . the small four-or five-roomed cottage, containing on the ground floor a front parlour, a kitchen, and a scullery built as an addition to the main part of the house; and on the upper floor the bedrooms. . . (with a view of) that enormous acreage of chimney pots and tiny tumbled cottages. . . the desperate efforts made by a race reared in village communities to maintain in the urban aggregation some semblance of a home."

Eighty years later, many of those "tumbled cottages" have survived. Where it is still a working class area, most of the cottages will have been bulldozed to make way for council houses and municipal tower blocks. However, if the area has "come up in the world", the former workmen's cottages will almost certainly have been "gentrified". In which case, they will be advertised in estate agents' windows in Chelsea or Fulham, Richmond or Hampstead as "fully modernised", and priced at anything from £180,000 upwards. In Chelsea and Mayfair, it is possible to buy a mews "cottage" at a price which would secure a reasonably good small farm in the South or South-West. Gentrification is a strange process. It has as strong an attraction for the so-called-*Yuppies,* the young, upwardly mobile, as it had twenty years and more ago for their parents. Then, Lambeth and Stockwell were especially favoured. Now Brixton had joined the list; and was already doing so within 12 months of the latest riots. Fashion has always been an important factor in the property market. So has social status. In the Middle Ages, after the Black Death had killed off whole villages, City merchants and other worthies began looking around for suitable "estates" whose purchase would raise them — socially speaking — above their fellow Freemen. It was the fashion.

We know from the 1911 census that the population of Great Britain was around 40.8 millions. The figure for Ireland, which was still ruled from Westminster, had fallen slightly. It was a little more than 4 millions. By 1981, the population of Great Britain and Northern Ireland had reached 56 millions; representing an increase of almost one third, with higher living standards, and even higher expectations. More significant than the size of the population in 1914, was the fact that the birthrate was declining. The excess of births over deaths was down to 9.8 per thousand. By 1918, when the Great War ended, it had fallen to 0.4. The brief "baby boom" after the Armistice was matched by the spread of contraception. In the inter-war years, the annual increase in population was to be halved from the pre-war 1% to around 0.5%. Not only was the large Victorian family a thing of the past, but the post-war years would see the emergence of an older population. Both factors would have their impact on the demand for housing in the brief period between the wars.

There was also the economic aspect to be considered. The average weekly wage in 1914 had been just over £1.10s (thirty-shillings). It was insufficient for a working class family, given the steady rise in the price of everyday necessities. So there could be no question of their even considering to buy their own home. There was a housing boom at the turn of the century, but it had been based on houses built expressly for letting. Retired shopkeepers and builders, small businessmen and local bank officials believed fervently in the virtues of "bricks and mortar". They were easily persuaded that a row or two of houses would be the best form of investment.

Somewhere between 7 and 8 million families rented their homes, or bits of houses, from private landlords. It is perhaps surprising to discover that as late as 1961, some 5.5 million were still in privately rented property. 20 years later, by '81, the figure had halved to 2.5 million. That included tenants of housing associations, as well as those in tied accommodation. Otherwise, rented property was mainly at the top of the market (beyond the reach of rent controls), or in the gift of local councils and New Town authorities.

Other events were taking place in the early 1900s which were to have a direct impact on society after the Second World War, thereby helping to establish the profile of the present day property market. In 1900, the year before Queen Victoria's death, the Labour Representation Committee was established; and from the committee would spring the Labour Party. And from the Labour Party would come a whole flood of property legislation. Trade Union membership in 1913 totalled some 4 million. It was 6.5 million by 1918, and 8.5 million in 1920. Although the Suffragettes were to steal the headlines immediately before the Great War, the so-called *Women's Movement* had been active since the 1820s. Then there was a Royal Commission into the Poor Law, convened by a Conservative Government in 1905. It is something of a shock to learn from Mr John Davy, head of the Poor Law Division, how the poor were regarded. In the workhouse, he explained:

> ". . . you have got to find work which anybody can do, and which nearly everybody dislikes doing. . . the unemployed man must stand by his accidents; he must suffer for the general good of the body politic."

By 1908 a pension of 5 shillings a week was being provided for those past work and without means. That, as we can see from the average wage in 1914, was not enough to keep the unfortunate recipient above starvation level. The first Labour Exchanges were also set up in 1908. A National Insurance Act came three years later in 1911, calling for contributions from employers and workers. Experimental unemployment insurance was provided for a few trades. But it was not until 1920 that the majority of wage-earners were allowed to subscribe. Even then, domestic and agricultural workers, civil servants and those working on the still privately owned railways were excluded. They were judged to have an adequate security of tenure! By 1929, but not before, the Poor Law Guardians were abolished, and the relief of destitution became the duty of the local authority. Strange to think *that* was more than ten years after what many regarded as the "dawn" of the modern world — Captain Alcock and Lieutenant Brown's successful flight across the Atlantic. It is even more remarkable when you consider that the 1920s were when the United States in general, and Wall Street in particular, were enjoying an unprecedented level of prosperity — at least until Wall Street collapsed! What seems "only yesterday" in some respects may truly have belonged to "another age".

The building boom of the early 1900s slowly began to reduce overcrowding. Chiozza Money in his book *Riches and Poverty* pointed out that almost half the national income ended up in the pockets of one-ninth of the population. Booth's and Rowntree's researches disclosed that nearly one third of the population could not afford enough to eat. Yet it was not until the big strikes of 1911 and 1912 that the large general unions (as opposed to the craft unions) started to organise the great mass of the unskilled workers, demanding better conditions.

For some reason, this period of English (and American) history tends to get overlooked; even though it is still within the living memory of some. One reason no doubt is that for so many the Great War blotted out all else. The increasingly active trades unions and the Women's Movement had an importance which war memories have tended to minimise. Taking into account the overcrowding and the foul slums, near-starvation, and the inadequate care provided for the sick, it is little wonder that the horrific conditions in the trenches did not seem so intolerable as they would have done to the sons and grandsons who fought in the Second World War.

Here again, the fact that we are talking of another world, must make it virtually impossible for the young working class of today to believe that those alert and talkative 90 year old ex-soldiers, who appear on TV to talk about "their" war, are real. Or that the "Blighty" they talk about so lovingly could have been that land of poverty, inequality and injustice. Such is the measure of social change over the past 75 years.

Not that the Armistice on November 11th 1918 changed very much. By the time the peace treaty was signed at Versailles, on 28th June 1919, the mood of jubilation had faded. Fear of unemployment had prompted the authorities to introduce a plan to release "key" men from the Services first of all. These were skilled workers whose return to the bench would help to get things going, and create jobs for the less skilled. This was a bad move in one respect: these key men tended to be tradesmen who had been the last to be called. Many had never seen a shot fired in anger. This led to great resentment, and helped to incite mutinies at the Dover and Folkestone transit camps. On one occasion, a mob stormed Epsom Police Station, and lives were lost at Kinmel Park. The patient "Tommy" had stood firm throughout and never more firmly than at Passchendaele. There a man who slipped on a duck-board could drown in the mud. Discipline had held in 1917 when France's front line troops had mutinied; and the French generals had, in one instance, ordered the artillery to shell the mutineers. But, now the fighting was over, it was going too far to allow the "lads" who'd had it so "cushy" to get away with it again.

Winston Churchill, who was made War Minister in January 1919, at once introduced a fairer system. Serving men would be released according to age and length of service. Those wounded three or more times would be released at once. But it was too late to prevent a mutiny in Calais. Two divisions of front line troops were brought in to surround and disarm a number of line-of-communications and supply troops. On Feburary 8th, Churchill was summoned to the War Office. 3,000 soldiers, who had just enjoyed home leave, refused to return to France. Churchill has told how he remained in his room at the War Office, and from the window watched the huge iron gates being closed by the Life Guards. Although he could not see them, he learned afterwards that the Grenadier Guards advanced slowly from one side, bayonets fixed, and the Household Cavalry advanced from the other. There could have been bloodshed. But fortunately, the 3,000-strong leave party came to their senses, and allowed themselves to be shepherded back across the Park to Wellington barracks. There, instead of being arrested and charged — perhaps with mutiny, they were given a good breakfast, and despatched quietly to France.

That same year saw strikes which broke all records. In 1912, some 40.9 million working days had been lost; more than ever before. Then when the two-year boom ended in 1920, back came unemployment. But there was now a more determined mood after the war. So many things, they had said, would be different "after the war". But were they? The man in the street was resolved that no worker's pay should be allowed to fall to the starvation levels of 1914. Nor would families any longer tolerate the overcrowded conditions of "before the war". "The war" was a turning point. There could be no going back.

One of the promises the Government had given was to build "homes for heroes". Christopher Addison, Minister of Health, ordered local authorities to start. On completion, these houses would be let at controlled rents at the 1914 level. Government was to give local authorities a subsidy to cover any costs which exceeded a 1 penny rate. Unhappily, the 1920-22 recession depressed the housing market to such an extent that by early 1921 Addison was forced to pay £910 for a house which could have been built a year or two earlier at £385. Writes A.J.P. Taylor in his book *"English History — 1914-1945"*:

"There was an outcry against this waste of public money. In March 1921

Christopher Addison left the Ministry of Health. For a few months he was minister without portfolio and was then driven from office altogether."

That year saw the return of hard times; and, with them, more strikes. Days lost through industrial disputes rose to a new record of 85.9 million. From 1920 to '22 a sharp fall in building land, building costs and building materials was accompanied by a 50% fall in the cost of housing. From 1922 to '26, the year of the General Strike, both building costs and house prices rose. It was only in 1924 that a respectable rate of building took place. In 1927, the Wheatley Act came into force and the State began to play a major role in housing.

Following the Great Depression, living standards in all but the worst affected areas tended to rise. Charles Furth bears witness to the greater interest the ordinary family were able to take in their surroundings:

"Between 1913 and 1937 the employed worker increased his outlay on clothes by about a half, but he spent two and a quarter times as much on his home. By 1939, most were in dwellings built after 1920, while working class families generally occupied 19th century buildings. By 1939. . . gross overcrowding was past, except in the East End of London, on Tyneside and in Scotland."

Men like Sir Ebenezer Howard and Sir Raymond Unwin had made a considerable contribution to the cause of planning in the early 1900s. The standard of the average housing estate was improved. As Arthur Marwick wrote in his Pan Special, *The Explosion of British Society,* in the 1930s:

"Such houses as were built were reasonably well designed and situated in fairly well planned estates, laid out, however, according to a rigid class segregation. Ribbon development along the main highways was open to criticism on even broader grounds, and the many mannerisms of the domestic builder were to find an effective satirist in Osbert Lancaster: this was the age of 'Stockbrokers' Tudor' and 'By-pass Variegated.' "

In 1935, a group of 150 or so prominent people, including parliamentarians from all parties — and members of most the arts and learned professions — published what they called "An Essay in Political Agreement". It was titled, *The Next Five Years.* They included Professor Lascelles Abercrombie, Sir Norman Angell, Professor Ernest Barker, John Bromley (a former chairman of the TUC), the Rt. Hon. H.A.L. Fisher, Warden of New College, Oxford, Professor Julian Huxley, Professor C.E.M. Joad, Viscountess Rhondda, Commander Stephen King-Hall, Dame Sybil Thorndike, H.G. Wells, and three well-known Parliamentary figures — Miss Eleanor Rathbone, Isaac Foot and Harold Macmillan. They called for powerful, effective Planning Authorities, to curb "ribbon building" along the exits from towns, and protect areas of natural beauty from anarchic building:

"Even as we write, irreparable damage is being done. . . no one who has travelled through the newly built-up areas, especially around London, can help feeling that ruinous and permanent damage both of the country and the town is being inflicted by this thoughtless spawning of little house-boxes, mile after mile. . . "

It could have made a great deal of difference to the housing market in London and the South East today if their warnings had been heeded. Their observations on the new suburbs and the location of industry were published 12 months before the Jarrow Crusade:

"While the middle-class town-dweller has been moved out into new suburbs, industry has also been growing in what were recently country districts; in particular. . . in southern England and at the expense, frequently, of the old industrial areas of the North. . . the industrialist may locate his industry wherever he pleases; but the plant and the population of Jarrow, North Shields, or Wallsend cannot be relocated except to a very limited extent and with enormous loss and suffering."

Harold Macmillan (then disapproved of by many fellow Conservatives as a young Conservative "progressive") had already accepted the argument for planning and controls. Nor was it for "idealistic reasons", as he explained in 1933, in his book *Reconstruction*. It was rather that the "old mechanism" which had served well while Britain's markets were expanding, was no longer adequate when "the tendency is in the opposite direction". Macmillan and Clifford Allen, of the Independent Labour Party, (who was to become Lord Allen of Hurtwood) are generally recognised as the inspiration, and the "brains" behind the Inter-Party group which produced *The Next Five Years*.

There we have the background to the explosion in house-building that began in the 1930s. It produced more and better accommodation, and at an unprecedented rate. To that extent it could be called a boom. But it was not a boom that led to an escalation in house prices. In fact, both labour and raw material costs declined; and increasing competition kept profit margins far narrower than many builders would have liked. One new element was the broad acceptance of the need for planning, with the Town and Country Planning Act of 1935 drawing together the earlier legislation of 1909, '25 and '29. Although it was an important step, less than 5% of the nation's land would be under planning control before 1939.

Slum clearance, prompted in most of our major cities by the Blitz began well before the outbreak of war in 1939. A particularly zealous local authority in Sheffield spent so much on clearing slums that it had virtually no money left for rebuilding. A vast acreage, less than a mile from the City Hall, was reduced to rubble. There much of it remained until well into the 1950s. The younger generation were generally convinced that it "must have happened during the war". There was much talk, and much enthusiasm for "better conditions" in London. Yet, by 1937, says Charles Furth, in almost 20 metropolitan boroughs north of the Thames, "only 10 per cent of working-class families claimed so much as a share in a bathroom."

Latter day critics of pre-1939 housing policy tend to blame the speculative builders for "ribbon development" which stretched for miles each side of our main roads. The truth of the matter was that this was what most couples wanted: a place of their own, with a garden back and front and a view of the green countryside. The link with the country, severed by their parents or grand parents, still coloured their choice. Small towns like Harrow grew until they joined up with the erstwhile villages around them. Those who could afford it could go off into Hertfordshire or Buckinghamshire. They could go as far as Penn or Beaconsfield, Amersham or Aylesbury. To the south there were Orpington or Petts Wood, Epsom or Crawley. (As yet no threat of a New Town being established there!) The more adventurous could follow in the footsteps of the Edwardian pioneers, and add their small villa or bungalow to the narrow fringe surrounding one of the "quainter" towns in Surrey. Oxted, for example, could boast its own Barn Theatre, and fast trains to London. It was also the home of a famous lady 'cellist, who was recorded in her own garden, playing to the nightingales, who obligingly joined in.

For those who could just scrape together enough to put down the deposit, the choice was not that wide. It often meant putting yourself in the hands of one "jerrybuilder" or another. After all, the cost of a season ticket, and the occasional shopping trip on a cheap day ticket, had to be taken into the family's calculations. Close to one million houses were built in the 1920s, most of them by speculative builders. That term has become one of opprobrium in some quarters, but it would only be fair to say that by no means all speculative builders were "jerrybuilders". It only meant that they were prepared to put up a row, or a street of houses, and then wait for someone to come along and buy them.

The more expensive homes in the inter-war years in Britain cost on average between £600 and £2,000. A worker earning £5 a week had an above average income. £3 was closer to what most employees were getting. Lodgings with full board would cost something around £1.10.0 or £2.0.0 a week at the outside. So to buy even a £600 house (though there *were* cheaper ones) could put a strain on the family budget, when a down payment of £125 "would secure." Although house ownership increased from the 10% level of 1914, it had reached no more than 20% by the time the National Government took office after the gold standard "crisis" of '31.

One third of all houses built in 1931 cost less than £600. By 1939, that was true of 50% of the new houses. Second hand properties sold even cheaper, at between £400 and £500. By now low interest rates on top of official encouragement brought the building societies into their own. The building rate in the late 1930s had risen to between 300,000 and 350,000. That was double the figure reached in the 1920s. At the lower end of the market, house purchase became easier than ever before. In return for a guarantee from the builder, building societies were prepared to raise their mortgage limit from 75% to 95% of the purchase price. This meant that a £25 deposit would "secure" a £500 home.

So clerks and better-paid blue-collar workers could hope to buy a place of their own on a wage of £4 a week. At one stage, the price of one type of house was reduced from £500 to £480. It could then be bought for £40 down, and 13s6d a week over 20 years! Nevertheless, in the mid-1930s some two thirds of all families still lived in rented property. But, increasingly, the wish to have "a home of one's own" grew stronger year by year. That is to say until the Munich crisis of 1938, when gas masks were issued, and all thoughts of settling down and living a "normal family life" came to an abrupt end.

The Dawn of a New Era. . . 1939-45 and Beyond

The war in 1939 led to a complete upheaval for many hundreds of thousands of families. It brought hardship, tragedy, bereavement. But, by taking young families and school children, as well as servicemen and women, far from their home environment, it also gave them a chance to see how others lived; how different *their* own lives might be. This was especially true for those who went to Australia, Canada, South Africa or the United States. It did more than broaden their outlook. For many it was to awaken their ambition; and to make them resolve that — once the war was over — "things would be different this time round." It produced a sense of solidarity among all who had served; a solidarity which transcended politics. Horizons were opening up. Expectations, which before the war would have been pushed aside as "foolish", "over-ambitious" or simply "not for people like us", now seemed within reach.

In 1946, there were indications that the Welfare Services had recognised the change in outlook. They appreciated how important higher housing standards would be when the troops returned and families were reunited. For example, at one of the huge, impersonal, military transit camps in Alexandria, there stood (close to the camp cinema) one of the Ministry's new "pre-fabricated dwellings". A humble pre-fab! Only then there was nothing *humble* about it. True, it would not be long before its many disadvantages would come to light in the cold, damp climate of Britain. But in Alex, it towered above the surrounding tent-lines, a bright, shining symbol of the conditions the "lads" could expect to find "this time round".

In 1939, when the barrage balloons went up all over Britain, there were no more than 3 million or so owner-occupiers: a bare 25% of all families. By 1947, the number had risen by less than half-a-million. It does not seem much today, but millions of pounds worth of war damage work had still to be carried out. Materials were short, and so was civilian labour. There were building controls, and a flourishing black market. When young ex-service couples talked of finding "a place of their own", they usually meant a couple of rooms to rent. Though for tens of thousands a bed-sitter was all they could afford. There were council flats and houses: there were also waiting lists. There were privately owned flats. But landlords and their agents tended to demand "key-money" or a couple of hundred for the "furniture". The Citizens Advice Bureaux were there to give advice. But advice was about the only commodity that was *not* in short supply.

For servicemen and women, there was paid "release" leave, and many had back-pay to spend. But "civvy street" soon palled. Everything seemed to cost so much! In many ways, it was worse than being "back there". For one thing, a solitary life and routine were not what you were accustomed to. Instead of having to keep the Commander or the Sergeant-Major off your back, you now had an army of local civil servants to deal with, at the Food Office and "the Labour". Many of them were wartime "temporaries", who were hanging on. The end of the "emergency" meant the end of their jobs. They had rather enjoyed the way they were able to throw their weight about. They did not take kindly to the returning servicemen and women, particularly those who tried "standing up for their rights". It was, "Watch It!. . . there's no war on now, soldier!" But there *was* food rationing, with sweets and tinned foods "on points". Nor could you roll up at the QM stores or Slops (if you were in the navy) and change a shirt, a pair of boots and a couple of pairs of socks. Before you bought a thing, you had to have coupons. No one ever had enough. You also had to register with the "Labour". If you were wise — and lucky — you got a job before your leave expired. Then you would still be "in uniform" and free to choose. If you were without a job when your leave ran out, you were just another "civvie", and liable to be "directed" into employment.

For many people, the first five years of so after the War were years of difficulty and frustration. The decision to mount the Festival of Britain in 1951 seemed somewhat premature. What *was* there to be "festive" about? But when the vast, colourful show was launched on London's South Bank, in the summer of 1951, it became an even more powerful symbol of hope than that the pre-fab in the Alexandria Transit Camp. The vision which the Festival evoked was of a peaceful, and compassionate society; a society in which design, colour and music would enrich the lives of all. It saw Beauty and Science in partnership. In every way it was the very antithesis of Aldous Huxley's sterile *Brave New World*, or George Orwell's nightmare parodies of human existence, *Animal Farm* and *1984*.

It would have seemed incredible then, but in ten years home ownership would grow by 3.02 million to 7.04 million. That was more than double the 1939 figure, and represented the biggest ever percentage rise to date. Today, some 25 years on, more than 64% are nominally home owners. Some believe that the peak has been reached. Does that necessarily mean that the era of rising prices must soon be over?

It is difficult to plot the course of the housing market in the UK until recent times. It is easier in the United States. As I pointed out in the US edition of *The Downwave, residential property during the 1970s and 1980s has ceased to be regarded as primarily a place for people to live in.*

Homes have become gambling tokens, and residential property has taken on all the characteristics of an historical speculative bubble. Purchasing a property for its investment potential based on future assumption is speculation. As such, house prices are likely to respond to the same mechanisms as any other medium, once the bubble stage has been reached. A decline of as much as 80 per cent of the peak values achieved in certain classes of houses would therefore not be inconceivable in the period that lies ahead.

The Global Housing Roller Coaster

Most people harbour the illusion that the price of their homes can only go up. . . never down. A reporter for the London *Times* says, "House prices always move up, step by step, reaching a plateau, then moving higher." Professor Irving Fisher of Harvard University said the same thing about the American stock market in 1929. The idea is no less fallacious when applied to housing, than when it is applied to the stock market. Not only do house prices move up and down quite vigorously, but in the past they have fallen much faster than they have risen. The trends in house prices are less visible than those of the stock markets, commodity markets, gold, silver and the like, because we don't have an index or a daily price monitor to watch. Trends in house prices move slowly, and ponderously, over long periods of time before the collapse becomes ostentatiously obvious.

A collapse in house prices is certainly not rare, or unusual. Crashes in residential property values have been plundering speculators, property developers and home owners for centuries. The somewhat elusive trend in house prices seems to have an eighteen-year rhythm, involving major peaks at fifty- to sixty-year intervals. Actually, residential property prices move in tandem with the long wave of economic life to a more exacting degree than any other capital market. Severe price declines occur about once in every fifty years in different places around the globe, conforming to the peak in the overall price cycle as seen since the late 18th century The subdominant eighteen-year rhythm in real estate activity is linked to corresponding rhythms in new building and the marriage rate, which also succumbs to major peaks in activity about every fifty to sixty years. This provides further evidence to justify the validity of the long wave of economic behaviour. We may hazard a postulate that man's mating instinct and man's building instinct may be aboriginally associated in his being, just as they extend down the scale to the nesting of birds, and the periodic abandonment and rehousing of the hermit crab in his shell.

As far back as the 18th century, which is about as far as available statistics on the subject of residential land prices and building construction can be obtained, we can see traces of the recurrent rhythm in real estate activity at work. In 1934, H. A. Shannon published the results of research carried out on the number of bricks produced in England and Wales during the period 1785 through 1849. It was the fact that bricks were taxed at the time, and records kept, that made the research possible. Warren and Pearson, soon afterwards, interpolated population data, adjusting brick production per capita during the same period. The result was further vindication of both the sixteen to nineteen-year rhythm of activity and the over-riding fifty-to sixty-year rhythm revealing the parallel between housing activity and our long waves of economic behaviour.

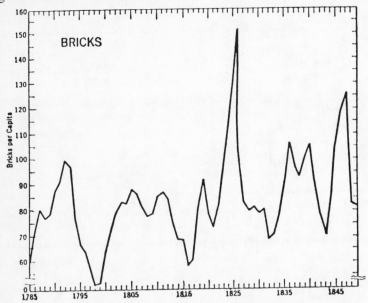

Figure 13: Bricks produced per capita in England and Wales 1785-1849
SOURCE: The Price Series by G.F. Warren and F.A. Pearson.
Reprinted by permission of Chapman and Hall, Ltd.

If we assemble the somewhat fragmental data from various international sources, the records suggest a deep depression in residential property in the United States, and elsewhere, at around the turn of the century, when the terminal juncture of the third Downwave was reaching its nadir. It is likely that house prices edged marginally higher during the early part of the 20th century, and then embarked upon a thrilling and explosive rise following World War I. They peaked at just about the time of the 1920-1922 recession. From 1920 to 1922, the combination of a sharp fall in construction, land and building material costs resulting from global deflation would certainly have affected the price of residential housing. Building costs in Britain for example, had fallen by 50 per cent. In France

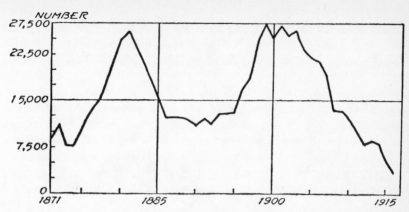

Figure 14: New houses built in the Metropolitan Police District of London 1871-1916
SOURCE: The Prices Series *by G.F. Warren and F.A. Pearson.*
Reprinted by permission of Chapman and Hall, Ltd.

and Germany, building costs were down 28 per cent and 37 per cent respectively.

Most individuals believe that residential property prices will always rise, because land and construction costs may seem like an unprecedented occurrence. There have been many wild fluctuations in construction costs in the United States, and elsewhere, throughout history. Between 1941 and 1944 the construction costs for houses in the United States dropped by 12 per cent. Between 1937 and 1939 costs fell by 8.5 per cent. The periods 1891, 1895 and 1897-1899 all witnessed notable falls in construction costs. The same holds true for the periods 1901, 1903, 1904, 1911 and 1921. There was also a significant fall in construction costs from 1960 to 1962, and during 1970. The most severe drop in construction costs on record took place during the five years from 1929 through 1934. In the United States the cost of building a home plunged by 39 per cent during that period.

Land prices also fluctuate with the same degree of volatility. Between 1890 and 1920, the average cost of one acre of residential land in the United States rose from $747 to $1,507. Beginning in 1920, residential land prices began to slide and continued to slide for twenty years, reaching a trough in 1940 at $798 per acre. There was a rise in land prices from 1940 through 1950 when the average price per acre in constant dollars reached $1,061. While consumer prices in the United States trebled between 1890 and 1950, and the population of the country grew by two-and-a-half times, land prices increased only slightly.

Another variable in the house-price equation over the years is the relative cost of land to the total cost of the home. In 1890 the cost of the land accounted for nearly 40 per cent of the price of a single family home. The cost of construction amounted to 60 per cent. By 1953, that figure had changed appreciably. Construction costs amounted to 83 per cent of the price of the home. The share of the costs that was attributable to the price of the land had fallen to a mere 17 per cent. It has been demonstrated that both land prices and the cost of construction fluctuate widely over time. Neither can be said to offer the promise of support for house prices in the future. The aspect of land scarcity is certainly not a consideration in the United States.

During boom times, more people have more money and there is credit available. Demand for housing increases, as does the cost of materials and the level of building activity. When a crunch comes, demand for housing falls. The level of building activity also falls along with the demand for land and raw materials. During the period of expansion, builders who are late to develop are still able to make a profit on their unit costs, since the rise in the price of the house is usually faster than the rise in the cost of materials. However, when there is a contraction in demand and material costs fall, those who begin their developments later in the cycle are able to reduce the cost per unit as a result of lower unit costs of production. Those who were locked into high cost developments find they must then sell at a loss in order to compete with builders whose development costs are lower.

There is a distinct commonality in housing trends among the industrialised nations. While the extent of expansion and contraction differs from one nation to the next, over the past 200 years we saw that peaks and troughs in *residential housing* activity, which is directly related to *price* activity, have occurred in sequence without deviation among all of the major countries. More important, according to Dewey, a tendency for major global panics has come with us two to four years after the peaks in building activity. There was a peak in building activity in the United States in 1836. There was a major panic in 1837. There was a peak in building activity in several countries simultaneously in 1871. There was a global panic two years later in 1873. Construction peaked in Hamburg, Germany in 1890. The number of new houses built in London, England, peaked in 1890. Brick production peaked in the city of Glasgow, Scotland, in 1890. Real estate activity in the United States peaked in 1890. In 1893 there was a worldwide depression of immense proportions.

It must be recognised that over the past fifty years there have been significant structural changes in the residential housing market. As such, residential housing is a much more potent capital market than it has been at any time during the past 200 years. Widespread home ownership in the United States, and elsewhere, is essentially a product of the last three decades; just as widespread shared ownership was a product of the 1920s.

The trend in the UK and most of Europe is similar to that in the United States. In Britain, during the 1920s, despite the revival in house building, only the exceptionally highly paid worker could hope to buy his home.

It is difficult to ascertain precisely how the Great Depression affected house prices. There is strong evidence to suggest that prices fell sharply, but attempts at constructing actual house price indices have been notoriously unreliable. A good deal of the fall in house prices during the Great Depression of the 1930s took place over the relatively short period between 1930 and 1933. Much of the fall can be attributed to cheaper labour, and the fall in raw material prices. Records for house prices in the United States are suspect for that period.

The fall in UK house prices during the 1930s could not really be described as a collapse, even though many people had lost their homes for nonpayment of mortgages. Since there was never really a boom in house prices to start with, there was no exalted plateau from which house prices could fall. The fall was merely that of a normal cyclical decline. Today it is not the commercial builder who is assuming the risk of the mania in housing, but the individual.

What a reading of history shows us is that whole nations, like individuals, have their whims and peculiarities, their seasons of excitement and recklessness. What we can see also is that these periods of excitement and recklessness conform to a long-term rhythm of a fifty-to sixty-year periodicity, involving the commingling of many social, economic and cultural communities. Millions of people become simultaneously impressed with one delusion, and run after it till their attention is caught by some new folly, more captivating than the first. While the past two decades have brought about a worldwide boom in housing, in the United States we have what can only be described as a housing mania. This involves the same characteristics as the bubbles that have been described throughout history. Conventional wisdom says that about one-quarter of the family income should be spent on housing. In 1971, 17.6 per cent of the average family income was being used to service monthly mortgage repayments. By 1981, 45.6 per cent of the median annual family income of the average American was being used to service the Urban Development. In 1970, half the families in America were able to afford a medium-priced new house. By 1980, the figure of 50 per cent had fallen to 13 per cent. By 1981, the figure had fallen to 5 per cent. *In other words, 95 per cent of American families were unable to afford a medium priced home in 1981.* Increasingly, many Americans had to rely on a second income to help meet mortgage repayments. Sometimes that second income would require not only two people working, but one of them taking a second job to meet these mortgage repayments.

Anatomy of a Housing Crash

Over the past few hundred years, there have probably been more booms and busts in residential property in the United States than in any other country. Four times, prices of homes have sky-rocketed — during the 1830s, 1880s, 1920s and 1970s. By the time I produced the American edition of *The Downwave,* three out of four of those booms had collapsed. They led to a fall in prices of up to 50% according to John Wesley English, in his book, *The Coming Property Crash*. The fourth crash, said English, was yet to come.

In the depression of 1819-22, pauperism became a serious problem for the very first time in American history. In New York, soup kitchens were established; in Cincinnati, people made for the backwoods to raise food. Even the propertied class suffered. Many properties had outstanding debts which could be liquidated only by forced Sheriffs' sales at auction. This, not surpisingly, depressed the price of the other properties, pushing them down even further. A commitee of the Pennsylvania Senate reported that there were 14,537 auctions for debt within the State. In New York State, the value of real and personal property declined from $315m in 1818 to $256m two years later. In Pennsylvania, land that had fetched $150 an acre in 1815, fell to just $35 by 1819.

In 1835, journalist Harriet Martineau wrote that it seemed "as if the commercial credit of New York could withstand any shock short of an earthquake." New York had demonstrated its strength the way it recovered from "the great fire" earlier that year. Two years later, the whole nation. . . and not just New York — was knocked sideways by the sheer impact of a Chicago real estate crash that followed another speculative boom. Again the propertied classes were hard hit. Land in Chicago, sold for $11,000 an acre in 1836, failed to fetch $100 by 1840. Twelve months later, what had begun as a severe, but localised, crash in Chicago developed into a national calamity.

Forty years after the Chicago disaster came the California real estate bubble. Theodore Van Dyke penned its epitaph in *Millionaires of a Day,* published in 1890:

> "We were a lot of very ordinary toads whirled up by a cyclone until we thought we were eagles sailing with our own wings in the topmost of heaven".

Speculators in Los Angeles and San Diego drove up the price of land from around $200 an acre in 1885 to nearly $10,000 by the summer of '86. By then it was possible to borrow 75% of the cost price. In retrospect, it is clear that price was unimportant, since everyone *knew* that prices would go on rising until they reached their *real* value; the same illusion that was being entertained a century later! Eventually illusion took its toll — in this case, the ruin of thousands of people. By the end of 1889, values had fallen by 75%.

The meanest-ever plunge in property values in the United States undoubtedly came after the collapse of the Florida land boom of the mid-1920s. The first of the newcomers were farmers and retired folk who had been attracted by the semi-tropical climate and the sandy beaches. As the State prospered, so did the real-estate business. The dollars poured in. So did the speculators. They seemed to have a hypnotic influence on the grim-visaged Florida bankers, who threw caution to the winds. The loans on their books all but doubled in a year. It was mostly margin play — a dangerous game at any time — with buyers putting down no more than 10% of the purchase price, hoping to sell at a profit before the contract ran out and time came to pay. Huge paper fortunes were made this way. According to Miami's city records, one plot had sold for $1,500 in 1914. Twelve years later, in 1926, it was resold for $1.5 million.

That autumn two hurricanes struck. They did massive damage to property, but much more to prices. Even then *The Wall Street Journal* was confidently reassuring its readers that the boom would continue. But it didn't. It was not until the 1960s that Florida real-estate regained its 1925-1926 price levels.

But what went wrong? Land was still a scarce commodity. As one rip-off merchant used to tell his victims, "Land is something they just don't make no more!" That is also true of Chinese Porcelain, Georgian Silver or French Post-Impressionists. But the bottom has fallen out of those markets often enough!

Most people will understand what has happened if they go into a saleroom and find that a splendid piece of porcelain, identical with one sold for £3,000 a week ago, has failed to reach the reserve price of say, £1,200. Porcelain, they'll agree, can be a bit of a gamble. But tell them (an actual case in October 1986) that an average three-up, two-down "semi" in Manchester, valued at £20,000 six months earlier, could not find a buyer at £8,000! They will not merely tell *you* you're talking rubbish. The odds are they'll become angry. Especially if they themselves are paying off a large mortgage.

For quite a few in that position, the potential threat to their pocket is felt less than the blow to their pride. Some may say they cannot understand, merely to save face. But many amateur speculators genuinely find it difficult to understand that no object will be accepted as a "store of value" unless other people believe it is. People may readily accept this as applied to pictures or whatever. But they may still insist that "it MUST be wrong" to apply the same yard-stick to property. How CAN the market have "gone so crazy"? *"Everyone knows* (they'll tell you,) *that 'bricks and mortar' have always been a sound investment."*

You may point out that by the last quarter of 1986, average national prices were being supported by land and property in and around the capital, and in the South East generally. But you are still unlikely to convince them. "If 'bricks-and-mortar' are not 'safe' ", you may be asked, "what on earth is?" The short answer is the brutal one: *nothing* is safe — not 100%. Market men and economists accept this freely, and without emotion. That is because neither will agree to argue about "intrinsic value". . . if there is such a thing! "Value" is a word which has its place in the vocabulary of moralists and salesmen. When economists talk of *price,* it is not "the asking price", or the "fair price". It is the price (in terms of money, goods or services) at which someone is willing to effect an exchange.

Even economists must accept, however, that buying or selling a house (or even just thinking about it) arouses more violent and irrational emotions than anything else — except perhaps a divorce. Those who are looking for a first-time buy within their means, will wax indignant over the way prices keep running ahead of them — forever *just* out of reach. They may well have good reason for feeling bitter. But let them become owners, and the tune changes. How "unfair" that prices in the neighbourhood are"sticking". "Three months ago," they tell you, "we could have sold this house for another £25,000. . . easily!" Outraged pride has nothing on frustrated greed. Should the market have "collapsed" —meaning that they may have sustained a loss — then "Cousin, we've been robbed!"

The conviction that it "ought" to be possible to live in a house virtually rent-free for twenty-years, and still walk away at the end with a sizeable profit, may not be challenged lightly. Sadly, this merely means that thousands more people will be quite unprepared when the blow falls. But who's to warn them? Few politicians would dare to. No one who earns commissions from property transactions would be such a fool. You don't geld a stallion that's likely to win the Derby! Frankly, I get the feeling that many of the people who have read *The Downwave,* or heard me on radio, see me as the devil incarnate. Have I not gone so far as to suggest that property prices *ought* to fall?

I trust that when those same people come along to my lectures, or learn to read between the lines in their newspapers, they will gradually realise that I bear neither horns nor tail. And it's not just a trick of the light. This is important to me. Because I have always felt that those who DO know the score, have a duty to pass on the facts to those who — for fear, pride or some other inadequate reason — still keep their eyes tightly closed.

Not that it means they stay safely indoors. On the contrary! Those who are loudest in their denunciation of the markets for their "capriciousness", are the very same folk who will sally forth — clad in a borrowed cloak of righteousness — to assume risks and obligations *which would make a seasoned professional's blood run cold.*

It is always possible to suggest gently that people should treat a house or apartment as an amenity — like that Ferrari they've always dreamed of owning. But take that line, and you'll only get a withering look. *"Can you deny that over the past ten years or so property has been the best possible form of investment. . . producing a tax-free capital gain?"* Naturally — so long as you value the friendship — you will not point out that they must have been saying something rather similar in good old unshakeable, shock-proof New York in 1835. Or in San Diego in 1885. Or in Miami shortly before they hoisted the storm cones in 1926.

It's also what an awful lot of people were saying when I wrote *The Downwave* in 1983. They were still saying it when I started to write its successor *Into The Upwave* in the summer of 1986. But by then, I fancy, some of them already suspected — if they didn't admit it openly — that house prices wouldn't go on climbing for ever. But until they could discover a satisfactory explanation, one they could live with, they would continue to keep their eyes on the ground immediately in front.

Mind you, by the early autumn of 1986, it was getting more and more difficult to hold that posture. According to the country's biggest building society, the Halifax, the annual rate of increase in house prices in the UK had slowed from 13.6% in August to 12.8% in September. But this was only an average for the whole country, and therefore an almost meaningless figure. This is clear from a glance at a handful of comparative prices in different regions. The table published in *The Observer* on 28th September, was based on figures from the Nationwide Building Society (Figure 15). The differences are striking.

The big gap is between house prices in the North and South, which one wag in the City called "the Watford gap". Prices were rising at an annualised rate around 20% in London and its immediate surroundings. In the North, in the first quarter of 1986, the figure was 1%. In the second quarter they rose by 5%. But why? Nationwide's statistical expert could only say, "We just can't explain it."

To get a close-up view of the London market, we talked to a leading West End estate agent, whose firm also covers commercial and agricultural property. He saw no reason to wonder why prices had surged as they have over the last couple of years. In part, it had been in anticipation of the City's Big Bang.

Average prices (£)

Area	Semi-detached	Detached	*All
Yorks & Humberside	26,870	45,260	27,080
Northern	29,150	NA	27,800
N. Ireland	24,820	37,370	27,930
Wales	29,140	35,260	28,950
North-West	29,180	50,530	29,140
E. Midlands	27,220	40,630	30,410
W. Midlands	28,950	46,080	30,650
Scotland	38,010	42,630	33,170
E. Anglia	36,190	55,600	39,710
South-West	38,980	56,020	39,710
Outer South-East	42,390	64,640	45,810
Greater London	67,470	89,770	56,210
Outer Metropolitan	56,950	85,320	56,280

*Includes flats, maisonettes and bungalows. Semi-detached and detached prices relate to older properties.

Figure 15: House prices nationwide

SOURCE: *Nationwide Building Society 1986*

Foreigners have been coming to London and the South-East and paying high prices for properties. The erstwhile owners have then moved on, paying over-the-odds elsewhere. Moreover, a large number of people have made a great deal of money in the run up to Big Bang. This affects the top of the market:

> "The top depends on people making large capital sums; and it doesn't matter where those capital sums are made. . . maybe in Timbuktoo. Englishmen in general have had this feeling that they like to buy property. So when fortunes are made, and it's been so right down the ages, money comes back and gets ploughed into property. And that's a lot to do with what keeps up the top end of the market. Of course, a lot of the sort of houses that make big money are houses that aren't built any more. As the money gets distributed round a greater number of people, more people are able to buy this sort of house, and competition for houses at the top certainly has been tending to grow, forcing the price of those houses up. And I don't, at this moment, see that slackening."

But what about the bottom of the market where, outside London and the South, prices are slowing down, if not actually falling?

> "As it happens, the bottom end has become a lot more popular because it's easy to borrow. And first time buyers are encouraged to go out and borrow as much as possible, and buy a house. And so it goes on through the chain. . .

> "I am concerned about the level of lending compared to income and the risks that people seem to be happy to take, which I consider in many cases to be more than they probably should be. And this, if we're not careful, could be a recipe for problems."

A Question of Timing

Several people have asked me recently why — if the housing market proved so resilient to the Great Depression in the 1930s — should it not remain so again? Firstly, house prices *did* decline in the 1930s, even though they may not have collapsed. Secondly, the reason that the Great Depression did not bring about a collapse in house prices was because it was a *different type of housing boom*. It was essentially a *building* boom, with thousands of new houses being built. But there was never a *price* boom, in the sense of an over-valuation calling for self-correction. Both raw material and labour costs fell. Some builders were operating on a sufficiently large scale for them to enjoy appreciable economies of scale. What is more, they could afford a good foreman, and a clerk-of-works to achieve a high standard of site-management.

Nevertheless, it is true we are entering a World Depression, but that's where the likeness ends. On the one hand, more mobile equipment is used on site today — cranes, bulldozers, dump trucks, trench diggers, pneumatic drills and the like. Many builders will erect a temporary roof of plastic sheets to avoid being held up by the weather. On the other hand, building regulations and planning controls are much tighter. Money is far more expensive, and wage costs in 1988 were racing well ahead of inflation. But, as we saw in the case of Florida, when you operate in Boom-town it matters very little what things cost, so long as inflation is still out front, to guarantee a quick profit. In the favoured South-East, London is the most favoured spot of all. Here, unlike the 1930s, we *do* have an overblown market. Prices — as we have seen — have risen astronomically. There would in any case be a need for self-correction, even without the approaching Depression.

In some ways Britain is becoming more like the United States. An increasing number are putting a nervous toe in the water and buying their first shares. But they have still a long way to go. Property, however, is a different story. People are plunging head-first into the home market, taking on huge commitments.

The epicentre of the latest price storm appears to lie within the 8.5 square miles of the London Docks. In 1981, the London Docklands Development Corporation (LDDC) sold the batch of land for housing at £33,000 an acre. In 1986, a prime site on the waterfront was fetching slightly under £4m an acre. With more than 9,000 houses on their way to completion, prices all but doubled during 1984-86. In the commercial and industrial sector, City rents were running out at £40 per square foot, and between £20 and £25 in Fleet Street and the West End. But in Dockland they were as low as £15. However, land sold for commercial development shot up from around £75,000 per acre in 1981 to £2m five years later.

By November 1986, the LDDC had committed no less than £300m. By the same date, private interests had put up some £1.5 billions! Developers and contractors like Heron, Mowlem and Regalian were among the first to arrive. But, in 1986, City property interests began to join the land rush. Many asked where all this would lead. To a change of emphasis over the whole London market? In which case, what would happen to prices in the areas North and West of Knightsbridge? Would they hold their price? What of the "gentrified" zones South of the river — in Kennington, Lambeth and Stockwell? What would happen to the sudden interest shown in Brixton, and beyond?

It is possible that Dockland could provide the urban equivalent of the greenfield sites that Belgravia, Mayfair and St Marylebone were offering the developer at the end of 18th century, and into the 19th. It was just feasible that London's Dockland could reinforce the trend set by the Merseyside rescue plan, spreading to the vast acreage of derelict and sub-standard property in the rest of London — as well as in other inner city areas. Thus the explosion — in terms of money and activity — might represent the start of a solid and lasting phase of development. But, in view of past experience, we have to consider an alternative scenario: that the whole Dockland venture will end up by becoming no more than the hard core of yet another massive extravaganza, in which speculative gain remains the main objective. In the end, as history shows, such schemes will often develop a manic phase before they over-heat and finish in a costly burn-out.

In Britain we have seen it time after time. Take the Railway Boom of the 1840s, which ended with an almighty crash. The United States had already been launched into a phase of railway speculation, which had began in the 1830s. By 1854, the boom in railway stocks was halted by a sharp decline in prices. The *New York Herald Tribune* was busy predicting that the impending crisis would put paid to the current "Fitful Spasmodic System of American Business". Not surprisingly, it did nothing of the sort: too many people were expecting it. Another 19 years were to pass before the crunch came in '73, when financial commentators pointed out *the risk of crisis from the perilous debt structure in the US banking system.* Financial speculation in the railways and homesteading were blamed. Then, as I wrote in the US edition of *The Downwave:*

> "the New York Warehouse Company failed. Five days later, Kenyon Cox and Company failed. Rumours spread quickly that several other large companies were in dire straits. On September 17, 1873, the US stock market collapsed and there was pandemonium on the New York Stock Exchange. The year ended with over 5,000 business failures, with liabilities a staggering $228,500,000."

The significance of this episode, and the reason I refer to it in the context of today's property market, is that *there was nothing wrong with railway development in itself. The Iron Horse did more to open up the whole North American sub-continent than all of Custer's cavalry.* In a broader context, you may have noticed that natural disasters have been responsible for far fewer market crashes than the over-enthusiastic "honest Joe" who has been taken in, taken over, and used by the out-and-out speculator. Very often the "speculator" is no more than a conventional, moderate banker or fund manager who gets the bit between his teeth and cannot be stopped. . . or stop himself. That is what happened in many instances during Britain's Property Boom (and Crash) in the 1970s.

That collapse is highly relevant in the context of our inflated domestic property market. The fundamentals of that period are mirrored in events today, even though the earlier crash involved mainly industrial and commercial property. A certain number of private property empires were threatened as well, with the result that the Receiver gave many hundreds of tenants a chance they would not otherwise have had to become long lease-holders of flats they had previously rented.

Other large landlords, who had avoided being caught up in the property scandals — like the Church Commissioners, for example — were later to sell large numbers of mansion blocks and flats in converted properties. This was partly prompted by the Rent Acts, and the low margins they enjoyed, and certainly speeded the demise of the privately rented sector. It was possible by then to persuade building societies in England and Wales to grant mortgages on conventional mansion blocks, or new "luxury" apartments. It was to be some time before they were generally prepared to lend on flats in conversions.

One lesson that the 1970s affair should have taught us is that it takes no more than a good tug at one of the table-legs to bring down the most artistically constructed house of cards. Another is that the collapse of the 1970s did not start with property. It began because of certain financial market needs linked to changes in government policy. In 1954, building licenses had been abolished. After a while, as John Plender points out in his book, *That's the Way the Money Goes:*

> "(The) institutions began to realise that they had turned a whole generation of property men into millionaires. From 1959 onwards they started to demand shares and options on shares in the property companies which they financed with mortgages and loans. By this time, however, the first boom was close to its peak. Most insurance companies over-paid for the equity they acquired in entrepreneurial property companies. . . By the time the second post-war property boom started in the late 1960s, the insurance companies and pension funds had discovered that property was a sound investment in its own right."

"Security, marketability and a potential for a rising income", says Plender, made property an "ideal asset". In the 1970s, property served as a substitute for index-linked government stock which successive administrations refused to issue. However, it was not the institutions but the bankers who mainly fuelled the second great post-war property boom: the lethal one! Banks, which knew little about the market, were too ready to accept a chartered surveyor's valuation without question. The danger, says Plender, was:

> ". . . that blind faith in the wisdom of the valuer will leave the British banking system vulnerable to collapse if property investment bubbles over into speculation. This is precisely what happened in the early 1970s."

The fundamental weakness lay in the standard practice whereby surveyors put a value on a building *by reference to comparable recent transactions in the open market. . .* as well as taking into account the position, scope for rental growth, the terms of the lease and the state of the structure. But suppose there had been relatively few "comparable transactions"? In that case the chartered surveyor would still have to hazard a guess at a property's value. This is not so very different from what happens in the market today.

The speculative orgy of the early 1970s was also the result of the distinct change in the thinking of certain sections of the Conservative Party. Crucial in this development was the Conservative Party think-in at Selsdon. The "ideal Conservative" which emerged from that gathering was dubbed the "Selsdon Man". He was seen as the archetypal figure, embodying all the virtues of his Party. Labour's Harold Wilson told the Greater London Party, at a Rally in Camden Town on February 24th, that the Selsdon Man was designing a society for the ruthless and the pushing. His message to the rest of the population, said Wilson, was ". . . you are out on your own."

The chronology of the crash, which most people have forgotten, is detailed by Jerry Coakley and Laurence Harris in their book, *The City of Capital*. It was started, in their view, with the operations of the financial institutions

— for reasons similar to those Plender gave. In particular, they single out the secondary banks, which had more experience of hire-purchase, stock market dealing or straight money-lending than basic banking. They were frequently headed:

> ". . . by men like Jim Slater, whizz-kids who seemed to typify the new conservatism of Mr Heath and Selsden (sic) Man, that collapsed in the crash: the 1974 crisis directly or indirectly hit at the most blue-blooded firms. . . The. . . crisis had repercussions on some houses as late as June 1982, when one of the City's top stockbroking firms, Carr Sebag with roots going back 177 years, collapsed, partly because (according to the *Financial Times* of 5 June 1982) it was finding it difficult to escape the stigma of having enjoyed a close relationship with Slater Walker, the most spectacular failure of 1973-75."

By December, the Bank of England had been forced to organise a bankers' "Lifeboat" to prevent a worse collapse, reaching right down to the High Street banks. While there is little doubt that the National Westminster Bank was in no real danger, it was nevertheless a blow to confidence generally when it began to be whispered that Nat West might have difficulty in meeting its obligations. The less visible origins of the crisis were two-fold, as Coakley and Harris saw it: first there was:

> "the implementation of the policies christened "Competition and Credit Control" (CCC) combined with the dash for growth of Edward Heath's Tory administration. CCC sought to encourage competition between banks by heralding an end to credit ceilings. . . (that) in this expansionary environment precipitated an enormous leap in bank lending."

Margaret Reid wrote, in *The Secondary Banking Crisis 1973-75,* that it was the Bank of England which originally came up with the CCC idea, which was foisted on to Chancellor Barber at a private dinner in January 1971. The point was that, ever since the Second World War, the Treasury had kept a "ceiling" on the loans that commercial banks might make to private borrowers. This had limited the natural urge of banks to lend more to make a bigger profit. Although the ceilings were to be removed, the Governor, Lord O'Brien, in the *Bank of England Quarterly Bulletin* (June 1971), appeared confident that CCC should not lead to a free for all:

> "What we have in mind is a system under which the allocation of credit is primarily determined by its cost."

The safety-mechanism, in other words, rested on the same ideas of "market forces" and "competition" on which Sir Keith Joseph and Margaret Thatcher were later to base policy. There was a further, technical factor which changed the climate — the change in the liquidity ratio of the banks from 12.5% to 28%, albeit on a slightly different definition.

At this point, the secondary banks came on to the scene, producing a greater overall effect than most of the City could possibly have anticipated. There were some fully recognised "secondary" establishments already. They were normally referred to as "Other British banks", and included associates and subsidiaries of both UK merchant banks and clearing banks. They were joined, after the passage of the 1967 Companies Act, by a new species of secondary bank, the so-called "Section 123 companies." These houses relied for their newly-enhanced status on a judgement given by Lord Denning in 1966, in *United Dominions Trust v. Kirkwood*. His Lordship had ruled that the court recognised the UDT as a bank, and not a money-lender. His judgement was incorporated into Section 123 of the new Companies Act — hence the name. By 1973, there were 133 Section 123 companies.

The secondary banks as a whole were financed mainly by borrowing from the City. In addition, a handful of the country's biggest banks and insurance companies owned almost 25% of the equity of some of the leading secondary banks. Once the property game started, the big names joined in. In his book *Sterling,* Douglas Jay called it a "scramble" in which:

> "Companies with well known names such as Slater Walker Securities, First National Finance Corporation, and London and County Securities, not to mention the Crown Agents, were far from being alone."

In passing, we may compare what happened fifteen years and more ago with the situation in domestic property in the 1980s. In the course of 1986, banks and insurance companies stepped up their activities in the home loans business. The building societies were preparing to join the banking community as soon as the Building Societies Act came into force; and a number of foreign institutions entered the home loans business. By autumn 1986, some of the biggest Building Societies had started borrowing on the Euromarket. Moreover, banks, building societies and insurance companies dipped even deeper into the bran tub, by buying up a large number of estate agency chains.

It is worth noting the extent to which the growth in bank credit, between August 1971 and December 1973, acted like a first-stage rocket. Before the first "burn-out", sterling bank advances had increased by more than two-and-a-half times. More critically, say Coakley and Harris:

> ". . . the bulk of the increased lending went to finance. . . property companies (increase of 519 per cent) and other financial companies. . . lending for speculative purposes fuelled the 1971-73 property boom during which average property prices increased by one-quarter in both 1972 and 1973. . . The collapse was heralded by an increase in what was then the City's key interest rate. . . in November 1972, by a tough Autumn mini-Budget, and by a looming confrontation between the Tories and the miners. Worst hit were the secondary banks. . . The collapse of the property market followed in spring 1974 when prices of commercial property dropped to between three-quarters and a half of their former value, and this collapse of their assets combined with the higher cost of their debts to produce a pincer movement of military precision."

As early as 1972, the Heath Government's plan to speed its "dash for growth" by increasing industrial investment already appeared in danger of frustration. Far too much money was going into financial and property companies. The Bank of England said so — publicly! Since controls had gone under the Government's CCC plan, there was nothing left but exhortation, John Plender maintains that the authorities had no hope of regaining control before an almighty crash took place. And for a reason which makes the whole unhappy business seem alarmingly inevitable:

> "Those banks that exercised restraint could not help financing the less restrained lenders via the impersonal mechanism of the money market. Secondary banks. . . took the spare cash that others were putting into the market, and recycled it in ever increasing amounts to the property men.

> "A more fundamental reason for the banks' headlong plunge into property was that they could think of nothing else to do in the face of the most serious inflation since the First World War. . . Insurance companies and pension funds were no less prone to this attitude than bankers."

The end came in the way we have come to expect since the Wall Street Crash of 1929. As Douglas Jay tells the story, it was another Classic Event:

> ". . . a point was reached in the later months of 1973 when property values had risen so far in sterling terms that not enough people believed they would rise further. So those who had bought for a rise began to sell, and some of those who had sold at a loss could not repay the money they had borrowed. In July 1973 the Bank of England's minimum lending rate (as bank rate was then called) had been raised to the crisis level of 11.5% in a rather desperate effort to check speculation. . . This naturally tended to lower property values and make borrowing more difficult. And so at 9 a.m. on 19 December 1973 a series of secret crisis meetings started at the Bank of England. . . and lasted till 3 a.m. the following morning."

This still didn't quite do the trick. An equally secret meeting of *all* the City banks had to be called on Friday 21st. By afternoon — success! The "Lifeboat" had been safely launched.

How close are we to a replay of the 1970s crisis? That is a question many people would like answered. But, somehow, they shrink from asking openly. Let *us* examine the pros and cons, and some of the key factors.

First — there is the ability of the would-be house buyer to pay. So far as disposable incomes go, we have seen a reversal of the redistribution achieved by wartime taxation, as well as the policies of post-war Labour Governments. The policies of the 1940s and '50s were very much in line with the prevailing mood of egalitarianism, which influenced many younger people, regardless of their political beliefs.

Looking back, it is surprising how effective the 1940s game of Beggar Your Rich Neighbour was. Historian, Arthur Marwick reminds us in his book, *The Explosion of British Society* (already referred to) that the Excess

Profits Tax was 60% in 1939, and 100% in 1940. In 1938, as many as 7,000 people had incomes of more than £6,000. By 1947-48 the figure had fallen to 70. There was always a touch of the punitive in the quest for a more "just" income and tax structures. This has, as I say, been reversed: and with a vengeance. Some would claim that though most have forgotten the existence of the Selsdon Man, he still walks the land, exacting retribution.

Go to the top income bracket, and we find that the 60% ceiling on income tax has brought a considerable benefit at the secondary, or investment stage. Thanks to Bernard Baruch's Eighth Wonder, compound interest, the initial net gains have been increased and consolidated. In *The Sunday Times* (October 16 1986), Ivon Fallon wrote that he had just been forced to raise his estimate of the number of City millionaires in 1985-6. A few weeks earlier he had assumed that around 20 people probably qualified. Then, more recently, a merchant banker assured him that he and 4 of his colleagues accounted for 25% of the figure he was quoting. So, Fallon concluded, "I reckon it must be 200."

For the sizeable minority of those who still have a place — if a less spectacular one — in the higher income brackets, prime property is, in a social sense, a "must." In many circles, prestige is established, maintained and indissolubly linked with the ownership of property. For those on lower branches of the national income tree, a great deal must depend on what happens to employment.

Lord Young, Employment Minister, claimed that the September 1986 figures showed an "encouraging" fall in the underlying jobless rate. The next month was even more "encouraging". We shall be examining the whole question of unemployment in due course. But at this stage it may be of interest to compare the level of unemployment we have in the UK today with that in Britain and Germany during the Great Depression.

In January 1933, unemployment in Britain peaked at just under 3 million. Within seven months it had fallen to 2.5 million. By 1936, it was no more than 1.6 million. In Germany, on November 20th 1923, the introduction of the Rentenmark brought the Great Inflation to an end. Employment collapsed. Christmas saw more than a quarter of all trade union members without a job. Throughout 1924, the unemployment averaged 6.4% of the total labour force. By March 1925, it was down to 3.3%. The striking thing is the speed with which the blight was overcome in both countries. They provide a disturbing contrast with today's UK total of more than 3 million. Especially when "long-term unemployment" means being without a job for months or years, rather than weeks and months.

Equally disturbing is the present level of debt. Again this is something we shall be returning to.

Killed By Kindness

There was a time in Britain when it was difficult for a man to get a mortgage, and virtually impossible for a single woman. One ex-model, who became a fashion editor, dress designer and manufacturer had great difficulty in getting a mortgage to buy the flat in which she was already a sitting tenant. Her quest ended only when her *son* (who had far less money than her) was accepted as guarantor.

Today, it is a very different story. The family which once would have been driven to buy a caravan because the Jones's next door had one, now compete in terms of 3-bed, 4-bed, detatched or semi-, one or two bathrooms, single or double garage. Rarely will they be modest in their requirements. Not with the family man's best friend, the bank or building society telling them, "Don't skimp yourself. Go for a NEW house. . . a really LARGE one. You'll get a bigger mortgage that way." And though, naturally, no self-respecting building society or bank employee would say such a thing outright, our future owner-occupier would gain the impression that were he to ask for a *slightly* bigger mortgage than he needed, he'd be in a position to buy that brand new Volvo, or Rover — which would go so well with those electronically operated garage doors! What's more, so far as the bank or whoever was granting the mortgage was concerned, it would be a case of "No questions asked!" Where else could you get a long-term loan so cheap? Nowhere, when Plastic Cards set you back well over 25%.

The fact that so many people were seduced into joining the Big Spend has produced the heavy weight of borrowed money: bank money or building society money. To this must be added the vast sums already owing to members of the Finance Houses Association. Government figures for August 1986 showed spending on credit growing at four times the rate of inflation. Infolink, a leading credit information agency, showed in October 1986 that applications for credit in August were 6% higher than in the same month a year before. That had been the highest August figure on record. Infolink's director-general attributed the rise to new car registrations, buoyant retail sales and increased activity in house buying. The amount advanced by retailers, finance houses and card companies alone totalled £2.68 billion. To think that at one time people used to worry that they might fall sick, or lose their job while they were still buying that 3-piece suite! Today they owe so much, there's little point in worrying. The fact that there are no free lunches, and someone pays in the end is not something they wish to consider. Dreams are one thing — they may be remembered or forgotten at will. But nightmares are to be shaken off at the moment of waking.

That is one of the main articles of faith in the Creed of the 1980s: *What we do not care to think about, does not exist.* A fall in house prices is unthinkable. The fact that we may have borrowed money that we will never ever be able to pay back in our lifetime is also unthinkable. The consequences are equally unthinkable.

A more aggressive attitude will often be taken by the amateur speculator who has done well in the past. He treats any suggestion that prices *could* fall as some form of evil propaganda. It reminds me of Mark Twain, who once said that the worst thing that could possibly happen to any man was to *win* on his first trip to the racetrack.

Our amateur speculator will continue to pay up to the hilt for a bigger and better property, regardless of the mortgage load he will have to carry. "Inflation will soon sort THAT one out," he will say defiantly. You may suggest to him that it could be a little risky to rely so much on inflation, when most governments and central banks are doing their best to bring it down. (You realise you had better not mention economic cycles. These, he has told you more than once, are "bunkum". . . like astrology.) His utterly disgusted response is predictable! Change tack, and remind him that Deflation exists; and his face will light up! "Of *course* it does. . . but NOT so far as property is concerned! Can you point to a time when property has ever REALLY fallen in value?" Suggest he consults history, or reads what's already happening elsewhere, and he'll be consumed with indignation. "I'm talking about THIS country. Frankly. . . I can't understand why you are *always* trying to talk property down."

Even when no one is seeking to gain an advantage — or even a quick profit — professional men, like solicitors and accountants, find some clients maddening. After the lawyer has finally got everything in place, the client — all of a sudden — gives every sign of having forgotten his initial instructions.

"A couple of years ago", said a partner in a leading firm of Huddersfield accountants, "one of our oldest and most valued clients got on to us." It was shortly before the present Inheritance Tax was introduced. The old man wanted them to sort out his estate, so that when he died there would be "something left after the vultures had had their pick". Fortunately, from an accountant's point of view, "Old Benjamin" had a large family, and despite his great age, was in a fair state of health. Eventually, a cast-iron scheme was devised in accordance with his wishes. His quite sizeable estate would be divided up and disposed of within his lifetime, so as to reduce the tax that would have to be paid following his death. The accountant went up to the house where the family beneficiaries were all assembled. Over a glass of sherry, he proceeded to explain the plan.

When he finished, he turned to the family and asked what they thought of the plan, They said they were delighted. So did the old man. "That's first class, John, " he said. "just what I was hoping you'd do. It was a wise move the day *my* old father had the sense to ask *your* old father to take on our family's affairs." On that happy note they had a second glass of that very modest sherry, and went in to dinner.

A couple of days later, the old man rang the accountant in his office. This time, he sounded far from happy. "John," he said, in his all-too-familiar voice of disapproval, "I'll grant you did a gradely job for t'family. But so far as I can see, lad, you've done b. . . . . all for me!"

While people, as we have seen, are unwilling to face facts, they are nevertheless prepared to go out on a very shaky limb in pursuit of their favourite fantasy. When it comes to property speculation these days, one thing is clear. Apart from winning a large prize on the pools, or premium bonds, there really is no other way — except by peddling drugs or robbing a bank — for an ambitious, conventional, middle-aged, middle-class male to "really make it". Rarely, though, can they come up with figures like those that the Yorkshire accountant came across the other day. Two brothers, who were business partners and clients of theirs in 1896, made a profit one year of no less than £96,000. Their tax bill came to £2,400! Even then they grumbled!

There is no question about it: when it comes to handling family affairs or property matters, otherwise normal and well behaved people become both irrational and irresponsible. Take "gazumping", usually blamed on a greedy vendor. The vendor is not necessarily to blame, according to Tim Blenkin, director in York for Jackson Stops and Staff. In the *Financial Times* (27 Sept '86) he stated:

> "Of every dozen agreed sales which fall through before contract, we estimate that 11 abort through the actions — or inaction — of buyers, who can back out without cost or fear of retribution, and often on a whim."

One of the lamest excuses he had come across was when, after solicitors had been instructed, the prospective buyer cried off saying that the garden was "rather larger than we had realised."

The article also showed how quickly prices have been climbing:

> "Our vendor agreed terms for a sale at £58,000, where offers had been invited at over £56,000. After six weeks the buyer, who had produced the usual string of plausible excuses for delaying the contract, backed out. We reoffered the house at £60,000 and agreed terms at once, the difference being no more than representative of an improved market.'

A rate of increase of £2,000 in 42 days, and in terms of *the price actually agreed and paid!* Not that surprising you might say, when it took Knight Frank Rutley and Robert Bruce and Partners just under 12 days to sell Park House, one-time home of the late property and hotels magnate, Sir Maxwell Joseph. A European client of Beauchamp Estates had been looking for a house in the £1.5 to £2m range. Then, according to the FT, he saw this splendid 7-bedroomed mansion, set in half-an-acre of grounds in SW7. The price agreed was £4.5m. This made the Park House sale the second most expensive in London in 1986; coming, as it does, immediately after the Nuffield House Sale, where the asking price had started off at £8m.

The Chairman of one of the smaller building societies in North-East London agreed that it would be foolish to hide the fact that no form of investment was entirely free from downside risk. But he did make the point that the relationship between the rise in wages and salaries and in property prices has tended to remain fairly constant over the years. This does not necessarily have to apply, however, to properties like Park House or Nuffield House. They — like "pop" stars and best-selling authors — represent what an economist would call a "quasi-monopoly", a unique "property", another Frank Sinatra. But it is a term which is scarcely used any more. Possibly because there are so many claimants to such a title in the overheated atmosphere of one of the longest bull markets of history . Superlatives have always been used: today they are accepted at face value. There are many who would like to believe, and consequently have convinced themselves, that the experiences of Park House and Nuffield House are the norm. There are others whose objectives are more modest. They consider that a growth rate of 15% per annum in the price of housing is also the norm. But, if you spare a moment's thought, and do a few sums in simple arithmetic, it can at once be seen that a 15% norm it totally improbable. If the price of the average home in the London area were to grow at the rate of 15% per annum, it would not be long before we saw the average house price at half-a-million pounds. In the future that would mean one of two things: either inflation would be rampant, and what you buy for £50,000 today would cost you £500,000; or that mortgages on a £500,000 house would be impossible to obtain, because the mortgage lenders would have crowded out of the market every single profit-making enterprise.

Despite the quasi-monopoly argument, it is disturbing (if not frightening) to discover that some building societies have granted mortgages of more than 100%, relying (like our amateur gambler) on inflation to "put things right". By October 1986, *Blay's Mortgage Guide* was listing no less than 25 banks, building societies and insurance companies willing to grant 100% mortgages. Among the most "generous" were Century, offering with a maximum of £60,000, followed closely by Walthamstow, with a top limit of £59,000.

The grant of 100% mortgages upsets Dr John Doling, of Birmingham University's Centre for Urban Regional Studies. It was also one of the practices which prompted Barclays Bank's Chairman to call for greater restraint. It is to be noted, however, that on October 9th 1986, Barclays announced their intention of offering mortgages for second homes. To qualify, people would have to live in their second home "occasionally", and letting would have to be confined to "holidays". The top limit for both first and second homes will be £200,000.

In a matter of weeks, Robin Leigh-Pemberton, Governor of the Bank of England, had castigated the over generous lenders; and Sir Gordon Borrie, Director-General of the Office of Fair Trading, had warned those financial institutions which were "falling over themselves in their eagerness to offer credit" that if they did not live up to their responsibilities to help solve the problem they had created, they could well "face the prospect of government regulation that would force them to do so." Ian Stewart, Economic Secretary to the Treasury, added his warning at a meeting of Building Society officials at Eastbourne in October 1986:

"Although competition provides a healthy stimulus to business, it can also bring some extra risks. . . It has never been a sound commercial principle that a lender has to do as much as possible of the available business regardless of price or risk."

A construction analyst at stockbrokers Alexanders Laing and Cruickshank (as they then were), said at the time that if building societies had been quoted on the Stock Exchange during 1986, "their share prices could well have been depressed due to concern over increased competition, and the amount by which lending is outstripping the inflow of funds."

Turning to the new Building Societies Act, which was then about to come into force. Mr Stewart urged societies not to abuse the right to raise as much as 20% of their money from the wholesale market. The new sources should be seen:

". . . as providing a valuable degree of flexibility in the management of their funding and liquidity in volatile market conditions."

About the same time Michael Bridgeman, Chief Registrar for Friendly Societies, warned that competition between the societies for retail deposits had led to a "persistent upward drift in the average rates paid on shares as reported month by month to the registry." This in turn had led to upward pressure on mortgage rates. Nevertheless, the London building society chairman, already quoted, said — on the day before the Chancellor's 1986 Mansion House speech (which so disappointed the City) — that he was confident building societies had already heeded the warnings of the Registrar and the Governor of the Bank of England.

He also felt that the giant societies, as powerful financial institutions, were eager to expand their activities, and move into what had hitherto been regarded as banking territory. But small societies like his own were likely to maximise the advantage of their local knowledge — "as well as being known locally". He did not see every society wanting to break new ground, regardless of their size and standing. If they did, many would become no more than jacks-of-all-trades and master-of-none. Indeed, said the minister, Mr Stewart:

"I hope that many societies, particularly those with a local or regional base, will not be afraid to specialise, only exercising such additional powers as are sensibly related to their mainstream business."

All the same, it is not unreasonable to wonder how much can be done to set the matter right, or check over-borrowing, once the mortgage has been granted; especially when it is for 20 to 25 years.

Building societies in general were once again to feel the pinch when much of the £5.6 billion chasing the TSB share issue came from small investors. They, it was estimated, had drawn £1.5 billion from their building society deposits. Worse lay ahead. In November, 1986 — as the building societies well knew — the £6 billion British Gas flotation would be competing for the same small investors' funds. By then, with Big Bang over, others would be dipping their toes into the water. In the event, while over-subscribed, the British Gas issue did not live up to the euphoria created by the massively expensive advertising campaign.

It also transpired in 1986 that the old Post Office Bank, now called the National Giro Bank, was to join in. Announcing its intention of entering the housing market, it was disclosed that it had a fund of £100 million ready to hand out. In addition, it would be prepared — subject to a top limit — to lend as much as 95% of the value, or in some cases, of the actual purchase price of a property. This trend continued unabated into 1987.

Mortgages and Means

A London building society chairman said that in his experience there is a more or less fixed relationship between the rate of inflation in earnings, and that in property. We are, therefore, left with the question, "What happens when incomes stop rising?" Or rather fall? It must also be recognised, now that the Conservatives have been re-elected, that privatisation schemes will have financed what are perceived to be tax cuts. During their term ahead, the Conservative Government will seek further choice enterprises to sell to finance those tax cuts. Perhaps I should say "perceived" tax cuts, because what we have really seen are no tax *cuts* at all. All the two Conservative administrations achieved was to redistribute the tax burden. But the Government has preferred to employ the *newspeak* vocabulary, which fails to distinguish between the redistribution of tax and cuts.

From what is known of the policies which a future Labour, Liberal or SDP administration would bring in, it is not easy to see tax rates remaining as they are, let alone being cut. However, should direct taxes be cut, then indirect taxation contributions would almost certainly have to be raised. It was clear by 1987 that, with the Conservative Party safely in office for a third term, this was bound to happen sooner or later.

Much play is made with unemployment figures. Earlier we have seen how even the basis of calculation differs from that of either the United States or the EEC countries. On October 16th 1986, a few days after the end of the Conservative Party Conference, Lord Young, the then Minister for Employment, put the customary reassuring gloss on September's unemployment figures. 53,000 joined the ranks of the unemployed, of whom 3,333 were summer school leavers becoming eligible to claim benefit for the first time. On a seasonally adjusted basis, the "underlying jobless rate" showed a fall. Thereupon Lord Young claimed that the fall in the adjusted total, and a continuing rise in the number of vacancies "can only give encouragement to all concerned about the level of unemployment in the country." Many of these jobs have been part-time and for women.

On the basis for comparison introduced earlier in 1986, the adjusted jobless total represented 11.6% of the working population; the unadjusted, 12.1%. But on the old basis, the adjusted total would have represented 13% and the unadjusted, 13.5%. But how much "encouragement" should we allow ourselves to draw from the fact that the new way of counting the same number of heads looks a little better than the old? Perhaps it might be better to forget the unemployment figures, and concentrate instead *on the actual number of males finding full time work.*

In any case, how does the "encouragement" to be derived from the game the statisticians are still playing with their industrial figures stand up to the crude fact that productivity is failing to keep pace with the growth in average earnings. On the face of it, if average earnings are growing, and there is no let-up in the amount of debt which the public are willing to incur, there should be no less available to spend on white-goods, new cars, property or anything else. But the point so often overlooked is that not being "unemployed" is not necessarily the same as having a "real" job; one which will enable the holder to go on paying the rates, meeting the cost of upkeep, and having enough left over to pay off the mortgage. The repossession figures speak for themselves.

There are two reasons why, in this context, merely not being "unemployed" may mean very little. Firstly, there are the ever changing "schemes" for youths and others. They take the person concerned off the unemployment roll, but the take-home pay on such a scheme does not go very far towards the mortgage raised in easier times. Secondly, the proud statement made by the Department that 30,000 people took up self-employment in the three months to June 1986! This too can mean very little in terms of ability to pay off the mortgage. That is because new entrants to the ranks of the self-employed are rarely able to earn very much for the first couple of years — assuming that they manage to survive into 1988 or 1989.

Moreover, few newly self-employed are able to raise the working capital they will need without some form of loan. That means putting up some form of collateral. This usually means signing over any insurance policies or securities they hold, as well as the deeds of any property they own. If they are paying off a mortgage, this will greatly increase their burden — provided the building society, or bank, agrees. Some may be driven to taking out a second mortgage. Second mortgages, as we shall see later, should not be taken out except as a last resort. So the newly self-employed cannot be rated very highly in the ranks of those most likely to discharge their debt without problems. Indeed, with the high mortality rate in the early years of any small business, the entrepreneur can find himself in double jeopardy, if he sets out weighed down by a mortgage loan.

That leaves us with those in employment. They face two risks: one, that they will be made redundant because they have become an unjustifiable expense; or, two, that the firm that employs them will go under. Here we do not have to rely on guesswork. Or on the way statisticians handle government figures. Both Trade Idemnity and Dun and Bradstreet Ltd have plenty to tell us on that score.

Among the other things they do, Dun and Bradstreet keep a close eye on bankruptcies and company liquidations. But *their* figures are not the kind of deceptive "averages" which mean something to statisticians, but tend to deceive the lay person. Nor are they based on "opinions", like the CBI Surveys which tell us what their members "expect". Dun and Bradstreet's offerings are simple, honest-to-goodness numbers obtained by the process of counting heads. They do offer the odd average, but it is easy to see how — and where — they got it. They quickly spot a change in the trend.

In their report on the first three quarters of 1986, managing director, Keith Williams reported:

> "Regrettably, the volume of failures is on the increase again, after a short lived decline at the start of the year. Viewed as a percentage of the entire British business universe the failure rate at 1.1 per cent, is the same as it was in the first nine months of last year."

What were the *hard* numbers? To begin with, company liquidations totalled 10,573 and bankruptcies among firms, partnerships and individuals rose to 5,352. And the *hard numbers* for the comparable period of 1985 were 10,885 and 4,965 respectively. Equally important is the fact that the rate of failure varies considerably from area to area. Scotland saw a drop in company liquidations from 440 (1985) to 424 (1986). Wales showed a drop in total failures. In the Midlands, there was a drop in failures (including liquidations), but an increase in bankruptcies. Here the rise in bankruptcies was severe: 283 (1985) to 347 (1986). That was a rise of 22.6%. Not unexpectedly the North-West accounted for the second largest regional total of 2,147 failures. That made the North-West responsible for 13.2% of all UK failures.

But what about London and the South-East, where property was still booming —in marked contrast to some other regions? This, as you may by now have surmised, turned out to be the wild card in the pack. As, indeed, it was during the first 9 months of 1985. The 6,800 failures in 1986 represented approximately 41% of all UK business failures. Taken together with the North-West, it means that all the other regions put together accounted for less than half the failures.

Keith Williams pointed to one of the more disturbing aspects of the figures — the rise in bankruptcies, which were "all the more noticeable in occurring during a period when interest rates have dropped, which should have made life easier for the small businessman." When interest rates rose again in the week between the Conservative Party Conference and the Chancellor's 1986 Mansion House Speech (on 16th October), Dun and Bradstreet's immediate reaction was that higher interest rates would make it more difficult for those companies with large, regular debtors or a cash flow problem.

What was beginning to happen to both interest rates and inflation in October

1986 served to stress the underlying concern over the durability of the so-called "prosperity" underpinning the upper end of the property market in the London area and the South of England. Would it hold? And, if so, for how long into 1987-88 would it be possible for the "favoured" areas to avoid being affected by the fate of the "unfavoured"? Had they become two distinct markets, having no influence on each other? If so, could this be relied upon to cover the foreseeable future? Or was it merely one of the forms of suspended animation, while the economy, and the main players, waited to see what Big Bang and the international interest rate/exchange rate ploys would achieve? Certainly the rise in interest rates in October 1986 renewed concern over the rising real cost of a mortgage. Even were inflation to rise to 5%, it would still represent a *real* burden for the mortgagee.

Already society had begun to modify its behaviour to suit the property boom. Many who had too high a mortgage for them to enjoy more than a marginal benefit from mortgage tax relief persisted in managing their affairs unchanged. So long as they could pay the regular outgoings without feeling it, why not? The bulk of their capital could go — or remain — where it could grow tax-free. Even though that might be an anonymous foreign bank account!

Further down-market, many young couples continued in 1987 to stay unmarried for the sake of the two slices of mortgage tax relief. How many would be unable to meet their obligations if they were not relying on mortgage tax relief is frightening. Particularly when the upper limit of tax relief helped those at the lower end of the market; and it was the lower end of the market which would feel the bite of higher interest rates, and a return to inflation at 5% or more. The tax cut produced in the closing days of the second Thatcher administration merely reduced the effective benefit of the tax relief secured by the lower-end mortgages.

Given the uncertainty of the business climate, whichever way one looked, it seemed at best bizarre (and at worst irresponsible) for building societies, and others, to grant mortgages equal to four times annual salary.

So far as raising the necessary funds went, the smaller societies (our building society chairman thought) would remain in a difficult position as they competed for monies. They, unlike the giants, could not go to the Euromarket for cheaper money. This could well increase their exposure to competition, since some of the foreign banks could easily undercut their rates if they so wished. On the other hand, the small societies would be less tempted to become one-stop-shops, or move into the acquisition game, gobbling up small estate agents in their catchment area.

Bearing in mind the comparatively low level of achievement of many of the established estate agency "names" in the High Street, it was difficult to see why any bank, insurance company or building society, keen to make its mark in the property game should wish, in the first place, to become associated in the public's mind with a far from prestigious sector of the business, not that they were cheap. Indeed, for both banks and building societies, buying up these chains of agency branches was an expensive business. Time alone will tell whether it will have been worth it. Nevertheless, it would seem quite pointless to aim at "one-stop-shopping", if the staff have to conceal the fact that the client is in fact dealing with the Superlative Assurance Company, rather than "good old" Buggins, Buggins & Brown. . . as it still says over the shop.

Some people feel that the law should require that the identity of the true owner should be revealed. They argue that conflicts of interest can arise just as easily as in the stock market. If Government demands transparency in the City, how much more should it be required in the High Street, where the client was considering spending between £50,000 and £250,000 on a property in 1986, and even more in 1987.

But that's looking at only one column in the book. What of the demand side in October 1986? Stockbrokers L. Messel Co came up with one answer in their Quarterly Macro Economic Forecast:

> "A projected 40% increase in mortgage lending in 1986 indicates the exceptional nature of the current boom in housing finance. While growth rates of this magnitude cannot be repeated, rises of 8% in 1987 and 4% in 1988 suggest continued buoyancy over the next 18 months at least. . . (But) the long upswing in house building, which started in 1981, may end in 1988. Meanwhile, the rate of price increase, very high in 1986 and 1987, declines in 1988 as monetary growth falls to more acceptable levels."

Whichever way the industry may go in 1988, the primary role of any property-loan institution is still to attract short-term deposits and make long-term loans. Prudence would suggest that retaining the investor's deposits deserved more attention than it got until after the 1987 crash. It would prove quite impossible if the Dutch Auction going on at the end of the summer of 1986 returned; with National Savings holding their interest rates (when the general direction was down) and building societies having to out-bid each other to maintain the level of funds required to cover the huge mortgages they were still prepared to grant. Meanwhile it can safely be assumed that a succession of superficially attractive privatisation offers will be continuing to compete for the small investors' funds. While the N.E. London society chairman maintained an outward air of confidence in 1986 (the least to be expected from any chairman), he did concede that the societies themselves, and their clients, could be in a serious position — if not actually in trouble — were the loan/deposit balance to get out of control at any time in the future.

Many would-be home-owners no longer regard a mortgage as a debt. They see is as their inalienable right; as though a mortgage were a grant. Unfortunately, that is precisely what it is likely to end up as. The question arises, on whose shoulders will that bad debt fall? For every debt must in the end be repaid; and with interest! Where the debt falls on the community as a whole, it is in effect transformed from a debt into tax. It is unlikely, even with a poll tax, that debt will be evenly spread. So who will pay must depend on future fiscal policy. Local losses could at one time be assured to end up as a higher rate demand. But, for many years, so much local authority spending has now been funded by central government that increasingly it has been the tax payer, or the subscriber to National Insurance who has paid.

There is a marked similarity between massive losses which get passed on to "the government" and inflation. Both in reality end up as taxes on the individual. In the case of inflation, it reduces the purchasing power of every pound in everyone's pocket. Simple! And far less wasteful than any other system of taxation. It is, in effect, a poll tax that the public has not yet learned to make a fuss about. Indeed, by pressing for high wages, higher prices, the public are aiding the authorities. Unfortunately, too many of us have been taught, by constant repetition, that the mortgage is the golden way to home ownership. According to the current myth, spawned in Downing Street, the man (or woman) who is not an owner-occupier cannot possibly know the joys of "a real home", or the "quiet enjoyment" thereof. Therefore, let home ownership, like joy (and privatisation) be unconfined!

Here we come up against one of the biggest bugaboos, which is the manner in which self-delusion has replaced commonsense among many would-be home owners. In my office I had a young clerk who had been in this country for nine months. Her husband had held his current job for six months. Somehow the wife managed to get a 100% endowment mortgage. After it had been agreed, she discovered that they could not raise enough between them to pay either the legal fees or the first year's premium on the endowment policy. Eventually, and in desperation, she managed to get a second mortgage to cover legal costs and the first year's premium. But what happens next year? And suppose either he loses his job, or she gets pregnant? Or both! As it happens the relationship is quite a volatile one. According to the latest reports, the odds are on either, or both of them, seeking a divorce. Whatever the outcome on that level, the debt looms large.

The pernicious thing about a second mortgage is that in the event of default, the second mortgagor can apply to purchase the first mortgage from the bank or building society concerned. Thereafter the second mortgagor is likely to seek to obtain possession, so as to put the home on the market quickly to limit the loss. Once upon a time, few banks or building societies would permit a mortgagee to take out a second mortgage. It is not necessarily so today. Furthermore, it is worth bearing in mind that if a second mortgagor undertakes the unpopular task of foreclosing on the mortgage, he or she alone bears the odium. The original mortgagor's image remains bright and shining. Moreover, the disaster is not marked down as a statistic under the heading *Foreclosure By Banks or Building Societies.*

In urging the simplification of the mortgage structure in October 1986, the Law Commission recommended that there should be protection for mortgagees over interest rates. If the mortgage deed so states, the rate may be raised to any level! There was also a need, the Commission thought, to permit the cancellation of unacceptable conditions, and impose a limitation on losses if the lender sold. At the moment, the Commission warned, the development of the secondary mortgage market meant that no borrower would be wise to assume that the lender would always be a stable, reputable institution anxious to continue lending in the same market. As things stand, the selling on of mortgages clearly constitutes a hazard for the mortgagee. The question is, *can something be done?* For example, were an effort made to put a fixed ceiling on mortgage interest rates, we arrive back at the situation which caused the bankruptcies of all the Savings and Loan Institutions in America over the past few years.

I well remember, as a boy in New York in the 1940s, how different it all was. My parents' neighbours would throw an end-of-mortgage party when their mortgage was paid off and their home was free of debt. That was an occasion for great rejoicing in the United States, where home ownership was both rife and a coveted prize. Most Americans in those days would be anxious to pay off their mortgage as soon as possible; securing their release — as they said jokingly — from their ball and chain. They knew there could be no joy in home ownership if you were never entirely free from the threat of repossession. Britons have yet to experience the type of foreclosure common to the United States throughout the 1930s. But that painful and humiliating experience may not be all that far-off for far too many people. As, I fear, we shall see.

In Britain, over the past decade and more, the prospective home owner has been sheltered from the darker side of life as a mortgagee-occupier. Since the Thatcher administration took office, he or she has basked in the comforting glow of Cabinet approval. But while the euphoric phrases, and promises of better things, continue to pour forth, as they did at the 1986 Bournemouth Conservative Conference, the climate is changing.

In *The Downwave* I gave warning of the fragility of the current rise in property values. It has become even more fragile in the past five years. Nor is it the level of prices alone that is responsible. There is also the question what happens if, as many expect, the stock market crash of October 1987 makes it impossible for the most determined optimist to deny that we have entered a long-term bear market; and, moreover, that we are heading for a depression. Put together that fragility of prices and the increasing inability to pay, and we have two further reasons, apart from the overall influence of the Long Wave cycle, why a deep prolonged collapse in the property market must follow.

Already the figures have spoken. Repossessions in Britain rose by 54% in 11 years; from 10,870 in 1974 to 16,770 in 1985. The Social Trends Survey (1988) shows that the position has been getting worse. In 1984, the courts dealt with some 35,397 cases of home occupiers, threatened with orders for possession. Not that they should really be called *home owners,* or they would not have been in this plight! In 1985 the number of such cases rose to 42,555. Unofficial figures, quoted by *The Times* newspaper in September

1986, suggested that some 300,000 would-be owners were struggling along with serious mortgage arrears. Dr John Doling, of Birmingham University, has claimed that official figures from the building societies were misleading. He agreed with the estimate of 300,000 mortgagees in trouble. They represented no less than "5 per cent of the mortgage paying public."

It is difficult not to take the view that when Government bangs the drum, the financial sector, including the building societies, can scarcely be blamed for marching in step. Although some would say that it is up to the City — and all those who know what they are doing — to set an example to Government. For whatever their ideological tilt, recent administrations have tended to take on more and more responsibility, and issue more and more directives for the conduct of extremely technical matters. What is more, they have done so with a flourish and an air of infallibility to which few men of standing in the relevant professions would care to lay claim.

At the end of 1985 there were an estimated 7.5 to 8 million mortgaged dwellings. Year by year the number grows.

Robert Moffat, Assistant General Manager for marketing at the Nationwide, has said that their general rule is to extend a mortgage if people cannot meet their commitments in full. Since the average mortgage is for 25 years, it is possible to extend it to 35. It means, however, that a 30 year-old, who has problems in his, or her, first year can settle down to paying off the mortgage until retirement age. Past retirement age in the woman's case! What this means is that mortgagees are, *force majeur,* transformed into tenants. A further snag is that the DHSS will hand out supplementary benefit to cover interest payments, but not the capital repayments or life assurance payments. If the "problem" lasts for six months, it is likely that steps may be taken to secure possession.

The problem was best illustrated in all its complexity by the plight in which the so-called oil-rich city of Aberdeen found itself by September/October 1986. The alarm was sounded loud and clear. All was not well in at least one area of Great Britain. All was not well in at least one residential housing area. How many more are there? How many more. . . for whom the bell will toll?

The Alarm has Sounded. . . Only a Fool Argues with Fact

The alarm has been sounding loud and clear, ever since the oil price plummeted. It is true that the present house price peak scarcely compares with that of the 1970's. In 1973, for example, house prices on average were 50% higher than they had been a year earlier. In 1979, prices were 31% higher than in 1972. Notwithstanding the greater pace of advance in the 1970s, Patrick Foley, Lloyds Bank group economist, points out that house prices have been rising since the beginning of 1982, and by the summer of 1986 were higher than at any time since 1973. But not in that once oil-rich granite city of Aberdeen. A *Spectrum* feature in the London *Times* in September 1986 reported that "no fewer than 45 houses (were) up for sale (in Lee Crescent, North Aberdeen), or just over 1 in 10; the main reason is the oil slump which has hit Britain's premier oil town at a cost of 7,000 jobs." In all but the top housing sector, where there was some upwards movement in prices, the prospect looked poor with another 5,000 to 11,000 jobs at risk.

Nor was Aberdeen alone. A table was published in the *Financial Times* in October 1986, based on Halifax Building Society figures. John Edwards commented that while all houses had risen in price by 134.1% since 1983:

> " . . .there were signs of a general slowdown in quarterly increases. In all regions except Wales, house inflation during the third quarter rose more slowly compared with the rise in the second quarter."

There was a seasonal decline in demand, with mortgages running about 30% below the mid-summer peak.

Suppose other towns follow in Aberdeen's wake, and more and more mortgagees are unable to meet their obligations. Are the building societies and banks going to foreclose? Or could they be forced to accept the mortgagees as *de facto* tenants? A point put to the West End estate agent!

> "It's an interesting theory. . . because if the bank can't sell the house. . . and, anyway, I'm sure they don't like throwing people out on to the street. . . then maybe the only way they can do it is cut their losses and say, well. . . we've got an investment property! That is when, again, the Rent Acts might have to be changed. So that at least there is a lesser amount of protection for the tenant if that happened to be the way things go."

Since then, shared ownership has been introduced. Fortunate, indeed, since many Local Authorities could find it difficult, if not impossible, to carry out their statutory duty to re-house evicted families:

> ". . . some of these people are not possibly going to be able to pay the mortgages. Yet the local authority, which hasn't got the house, can't rehouse them. And I'm afraid it will take a lot of these cases before the thinking changes and suddenly we realise that maybe the housing stock has gone too much the wrong way. And there will have to be some middle grounds, some way of providing rented accommodation for people. . . in these circumstances."

Imagine the social upheaval, to say nothing of the political uproar, were otherwise impotent local authorities to try putting several hundred middle- and upper-middle class families into bed and breakfast accommodation; and merely because some London based Administrative Class Ostrich had failed to alert his (or her) Minister to the facts of life North of Watford.

Were the situation to reach such a pitch, it is to be hoped that sufficient notice would be taken of what was happening, and in time. Otherwise there will have to be one of those last-minute Whitehall brainstorming sessions, which could be relied on to come up with what looked like a slick, plausible solution. It might not solve anything. But it would be put into operation — with a suitable TV obligato. For whatever the Civil Service experts might say, it would carry the seal of approval issued by the Downing Street "kitchen-cabinet"; among whom the image makers appear to be outranking mere Departmental Ministers these days. It is a select band, whose motto is said to be, "If at first you don't succeed, at least put out a good story. Then get someone else to try it next time."

When we were looking at the last century — and as late as the 1960s in Britain — we were treating residential property as property to reside in. But, as we have seen, property has more and more been treated as an investment. Thus the key issues which once related to bricks-and-mortar now relate to debt.

That is the plain, unvarnished truth. Look at the decision to start trading PINCS (or Property Income Certificates) on the Stock Exchange in 1987. That shows how far we have gone in transmuting a home into a financial instrument. No longer do we think of amenity now, but of the possible re-sale value at some far off date. Although. . . beautiful thought! If inflation has been *really* kind to us, that date need not be quite so far off after all.

But, in the end (as the unhappy Dutch found out), a tulip is only a flower; and a house but merchandise. . . like a car, a washing machine. . . a tooth brush.

Those are the cold, hard facts, my friends. And only a fool ignores the facts.

Chapter Five

PRIVATISATION, BIG BANG &
THE SOUTH SEA BUBBLE

A notion prevails that the money market is something so impalpable that it can only be spoken of in very abstract words. . . (it) is as concrete and real as anything else.

Walter Bagehot

It is more than 100 years since Bagehot's standard work on the mysteries of the City appeared under the plain title *Lombard Street.* He dismissed the popular view that the financial world "can only be spoken of in very abstract words", and — therefore — that "books on it must always be exceedingly difficult." The money market, he insisted, "can be described in plain words. . . it is the writer's fault if what he says is not clear." Alas, despite Bagehot's endeavours, the mystique of the market place has carefully and consciously been shielded from prying eyes and enquiring minds, keeping the "ordinary" man or woman at arm's length. Brokers, academics and politicians have all tended to do it. That is, until quite recently.

Now, in the 1980s, under the two Thatcher administrations, they have become the focus of attention and the target for an unprecedented sales drive from every quarter. Wooed by building societies, banks, insurance companies and plastic card companies, we are urged to borrow, take out a mortgage or spend on credit. Unit trusts and investment trusts compete with the banks and building societies, urging us to invest. Time-share companies, franchisors, investment advisors, tip-sheet editors, and a whole army of less reputable operators swell the chorus. Above all, the Government has mounted a massive campaign, backed by a huge advertising budget, to persuade those "ordinary" men and women not only to take an intelligent interest in the stock market, but to go out and buy shares for themselves. Cutting their teeth, you might say, on the privatisation issues, and the semi-privatisation issue, TSB. Nor has the Crash of '87 cooled their ardour.

Writing just after the launch of British Telecom, the archetypal People's Share, financial journalist and former stockbroker Simon Rose published a "layman's guide to buying and selling stocks and shares". His book, *Fair Shares,* probably comes closer to the truth than most recent authors of similar volumes have done. The sale of British Telecom was estimated to have increased the number of Britons holding shares by around 50%, to three million. Shortly after the issue, a Gallup Poll found that "29% of all adults hoped to buy shares in the future." There were several points, however, which appeared to worry Mr Rose. The first was the manner in which BT shares had been promoted:

> "The media and the City, the one terrified of losing its advertising, the other of missing out on its massive commission revenues, somehow neglected to criticise the British Telecom launch for what is known as 'share-pushing'. . . Everyone in the City knows that the way British Telecom was sold would have been completely illegal if attempted by a private company, but it was in everyone's interest to keep quiet about it at the time."

The theory seems to have been that encouraging the financially unwashed to try their hand with the privatisation issues would enable them to learn something about the way that stock markets worked. But had the public managed to learn anything about the mystique of dabbling in shares? Were they any more conscious of the fact that investment in shares involves risk?

> "Lamentably. . . those first-time share buyers learned about as much of the workings of the stock market from the bumpf sent to them by British Telecom Share Information Office as they would have done about sheep-farming from listening to a recitation of Little Bo-Peep".

Having been told that something was "good for us", wrote Simon Rose, and told, moreover, "in that arrogant manner fairly typical of the 'Nanny' school of government", the plain message was that:

> ". . . we should simply accept it and not be naughty children and ask awkward questions. It was simply assumed that people would learn about the stock market from trial and error. Such a method of tuition is possible, but it can prove very expensive to the pupil."

Plain words, employed in a manner of which Walter Bagehot would surely have approved!

Bubbles, Bubbles, Toils and Troubles

If we are seriously seeking parallels with the present time, Bagehot would have told us to go back to the late 16th century. That was when private capital was being raised for the earliest of the British joint-stock companies. Alan Jenkins reminds us, in his book *The Stock Exchange Story,* that the period of transition between Tudor and Elizabethan times was very much like our own in some respects. Imports were rising; exports were falling. Something was needed to correct the imbalance. Spain was dominant in the newly discovered American continent; and Portugal was the only European power in India. The Dutch would soon be monopolising the products of the East Indies. The Reverend Richard Hakluyt, who was to interview most of the sea-captains returning from their voyages, tells us of the advice which the greatly respected voyager, Sebastian Cabot (who happened to be in the City), gave the London merchants. It was to fit out three ships to explore the all-but unknown land to the North East, in the hope of finding a North-East passage to Cathay (China). But, Hakluyt tells us:

". . . lest any private man should be too much oppressed or charged, a course was taken, that every man willing to be of the society, should disburse the portion of twenty and five pounds a piece: so that in a short time, by this means a sum of six thousand pounds being gathered, three ships were bought."

When the boy-King, Edward VI recommended one of his friends, Richard Chancellor to the merchants, they were — no doubt — still muttering about the high cost of provisioning three ships for eighteen months; to say nothing of fitting thin plates of lead over the lower part of the hull to ward off the "little (ocean) worms. . . which bore through the very stoutest oak." The King rebuked them gently. "While we are entrusting a mere trifle of money to the dice fortune, he will be exposing what is sweetest to man, his very life, to the remorseless sea." One may be certain, however, that not a few of the merchants — including the subscribers — will have made some remark to their Chief Clerk, on returing to their counting house, about these *adventurers*. "They may hang themselves if they wish. But if they do, I'll wager they'll be round here first, seeking a loan with which to buy the rope."

In May 1553, the *Mysterie and Companie of the Merchant Adventurers for the Discoverie of Regions, Dominions, Islands and places unknowne* despatched three vessels, the *Bona Esperanza,* of 120 tons, the *Edward Bonaventure,* 160 tons, and the 90 ton *Bona Confidentia.* Together they sailed via the Lofoten Islands to the Arctic Circle. Richard Chancellor, aboard the *Edward Bonaventure*, reached "a large gulf of about 100 miles wide". We would call it the Bay of Archangel. Helped by a party of Russian fishermen, they went ashore. There the headman of the village gave them hospitality, but he regretted that their Prince, one Ivan Vasalivich (later known as Ivan the Terrible) had forbidden them to buy any goods from foreigners, without consulting him first. Fortunately, writes Alan Jenkins:

"The local headman offered Chancellor safe conduct to Ivan, but secretly despatched a courier to the Czar, who, seeing it was a long way to Moscow (about 650 miles) and that they would need provisions en route, gave permission to trade with the English mariners."

The upshot was that they eventually reached Moscow. They had no idea what they would find there. For, although King Edward had two Tartar grooms in the royal stables, they were not very coherent. . . even when sober, says Jenkins. The grooms did say, though, that Moscow was more or less the same size as London. When Chancellor and his party arrived, they found Moscow to be "a city of fir-wood houses surrounded by city walls with an arsenal looked after by monks." They were left to kick their heels for almost two weeks before they were summoned to the Czar's presence:

> "Chancellor, without any change of countenance and with only a perfunctory bow, delivered a letter from Edward VI. . . and presented the Czar with a royal gift. Ivan, already ill and neurotic, badly wanted outlets to the West, and would one day offer Queen Elizabeth an alliance and even a half-hearted proposal of marriage. The outcome of all this. . . was a treaty giving freedom of trade to English ships."

The important thing about the Muscovy Company was not merely that it penetrated beyond the Caspian to Persia, Bokhara and Turkestan, but that its members were no longer trading on their own account or managing their own affairs. As Cabot had suggested, they contributed money or goods to the "joint-stock", leaving the management of the Company to a Governor, Deputy-Governor, and assistants. Later the assistants would be called Managers or Directors. With ownership divorced from management, and the capital divided into shares, the "equity" became freely transferable. Thus, concludes Jenkins, "the history of the Stock Exchange begins in the pack-ice of the White Sea." So too does the 300 year-old informal partnership (or is it a "love-hate" relationship?) between the State and the *entrepreneur*. Soon other similar companies would be set up: each holding a Royal Charter granting them privileges and monopolies in specified regions.

When the members of one of them, the Turkish company, realised that the route across Asia Minor was highly dangerous, they decided to set up a new Company to trade with India and the East Indies, where the Dutch had something of a stranglehold. The Company was called, *The Governor and Company of Merchants of London trading into the East Indies*. By 1717 the East India company, now a joint-stock enterprise, had been capitalised to the tune of £1,609,000.

Not only did the Dutch enjoy a near monopoly of trade with the Spice Islands in the East, they were also making a great success of the comparatively new stock market in Amsterdam. It is important not to imagine that these early financial markets were simple, or primitive. From what we know of the Amsterdam *bourse,* it bore a striking resemblance to the financial markets in the City of London today; as Joseph de la Vega makes clear in his *Confusion de Confusiones*. Published in 1688, it described a very sophisticated market, which offered facilities for options and futures trading, as well as an enticing range of highly speculative stocks, which might be bought on margin. Vega summed it up as:

> ". . . a quintessence of academic learning, and a paragon of fraudulence . . .It is a touchstone for the intelligent and a tombstone for the audacious, a treasury of usefulness and a source of disaster."

Bulls and Bears were already recognised as distinct species. Bulls, as Vega described them, were "like the giraffe. . . scared of nothing". Bears were ". . . completely ruled by fear, trepidation and nervousness. Rabbits become elephants, brawls in a tavern become rebellions, faint shadows appear to them as signs of chaos."

Vega's fascinating study was rescued and republished by the Baker Library, Harvard Graduate School of Business Administration in 1957. Thirty years later, Richard Lambert, one of the sharper pairs of eyes on the *Financial Times* regaled his readers with a wealth of quotations. When Joseph de la Vega settles down to advise the would-be investor of his day, the advice could well have been taken from the financial section of one of the heavyweight Sunday papers. For example:

"Take every gain without showing remorse about missed profits, because an eel may escape sooner than you think."

or

"The expectation of an event creates a much deeper impression upon the exchange than the event itself. When large dividends or rich imports are expected, shares will rise in price; but if the expectation becomes a reality, the shares often fall; for the joy over the favourable development and the jubilation over a lucky chance have abated in the meantime."

How long, I wondered, would the joy last over *our* prime example of a "favourable development", Big Bang; or Mr and Mrs Greedyman's "lucky chance". . . or lucky dip. . . which went by the name of privatisation? And was there anything more than a superficial likeness between 1987's market euphoria and the two major, speculative manias of the early 18th century: John Law's Louisiana and Mississippi swindles and the infamous South Sea Bubble? In the space of ten years, the creation of money by government decree was born. But the unfortunate circumstances of its birth were to bring down the whole financial system on both sides of the *Pas de Calais*.

Money, Credit and Calamity

John Law, son of a goldsmith, was in many ways a financial genius. Law was a Scot, like William Paterson, a member of the Merchant Taylors' Company who had persuaded King William III and the Government to accept his plan for a Bank of England established in 1694. Paterson had gained some renown as a writer on political and economic matters; and John Law was considered a man likely to make his mark in London. But he was forced to flee to Amsterdam after killing one Edward Wilson in a duel. In Holland, Law studied banking, returning to Scotland after 11 years. There he submitted his plan for a separate national bank for Scotland. Unlike William Paterson's, *his* plan was rejected. Partly, it was said, because Paterson had used his influence to kill it. For ten years, Law lived by gambling, making the huge sum of £100,000. He also went round various European capitals, in a vain attempt to secure support for his plan.

In the end, he persuaded France to allow him to set up the Banque Générale in Paris. He could now put into practice his theory of the nature and role of credit. Most of us would not quarrel with it today:

> "The workings of trade revolve wholly about money. . . the more you have, the more people you can keep employed. Credit will take the place of money and will have the same results."

In 1716, Law's Banque Générale was launched with a capital of six million *livres,* and permission to issue notes. These were payable on demand, and acceptable to the tax authorities. Over the next two years Law's bank prospered. Although the notes were backed neither by gold, nor silver (nor indeed by any other tangible asset), Law enjoyed the complete confidence of the French Government.

Across the Channel, some five years before Law established his bank in Paris, Robert Harley, first Earl of Oxford, became Chancellor of the Exchequer. At that time, England was in a far from happy state. It had gone through the two domestic revolutions of 1642-1649 and 1683-1689. 1689 saw the start of the wars with Louis XIV, which lasted 8 years. They were to cost £40 million. Five years of peace followed, then came the War of the Spanish Succession in 1702. Like all wars, it was expensive, and brought the issue of the National Debt to the fore. As Alan Jenkins tells the story:

> "Both Government and business men hoped that the war would end with a treaty under which trade with Spanish America might be opened. . . On 7th March 1711, Harley announced in Parliament his plan to discharge the National Debt by converting it into shares in a new joint-stock company. . . *The Governor and Company of Merchants of Great Britain, trading to the South Seas and other parts of America, and for encouraging the fishery.* The company was to be given a monopoly of trade to South America and the Pacific, in which holders of navy and ordnance bonds were offered stock with a guaranteed interest of 6% (for which the Government provided £586,000 a year)."

The climate at this period was one in which many people were looking for somewhere to place their money. During dangerous, bad times. . . which had lasted on and off for more than 40 years, they had bought land, given it to the goldsmiths for safe keeping, or simply buried it. That was what Samuel Pepys had done with his gold and more valuable possessions when he ran off to escape the Fire of London. Now that more settled times had returned, people were looking for a profitable investment. Amsterdam was still well ahead of London. A manual for money changers was issued by the Dutch Government in 1606. It showed that they were having to cope with no less than 505 gold and 341 silver coins. Within the Dutch Republic alone, there were 14 separate mints. It was a field-day for the counterfeiter. Adam

Smith tells us in *Wealth of Nations* that the solution was found — the establishment of a public bank in Amsterdam, under the "guarantee of the City". So far, Britain still had to rely on the goldsmiths. Most of those who had lent money to Charles II lost it! Two notable survivors, says Alan Jenkins, were Child's and Hoare's which eventually became private banks. But changes were on the way.

The settlement which followed the Glorious Revolution of 1689 established Parliament's right to tax and to borrow. So when the French War and inflation came together, the Government was driven to raising funds by one means or another. Charles Montague, Earl of Halifax, planned to raise £1 million on 99 year annuities. But when Paterson suggested a National Bank, his plan was chosen. On 1st June 1694 the lists were opened. They closed 12 days later, with the necessary capital fully subscribed. In return for a loan to the King of the £1.2 million raised (at 8%), the Bank received a Royal Charter. This gave it the right to issue notes, payable on demand, up to the same figure. Duties on wines, spirits and ships' tonnage provided the security for a perpetual fund of interest amounting to £100,000. The £1.2 million raised by subscription was a huge sum. It represented almost 25% of the year's national revenue.

The Bank was seen as a great success by all but the goldsmiths, who, at one blow, lost the virtual monopoly they had enjoyed as surrogate bankers. From now onwards, the Bank of England encouraged new enterprises to launch joint-stock companies which would attract funds from a public eager to invest. For their benefit, John Houghton, a Fellow of the Royal Society (who had published *A Collection of Letters for the Improvement of Husbandry and Trade*) wrote articles on *Joint Stocks and the various dealings therein, commonly called Stock Jobbing.*

Brokers were not limited to dealing in stocks. Indeed, they handled anything from gold to bread and fish. Nor were they considered to be members of a very reputable profession. Two years after the launch of the Bank of England, there was a slump; and a Commission was set up to "look after the Trade of England". It chose as its target the brokers and the "monied men" — or jobbers. It was brutal in its criticism:

> "The pernicious art of Stock-jobbing hath, of late, so perverted the end and design of Companies and Corporations, erected for the introducing or carrying on of manufactures, to the private profit of the first projectors, that the privileges granted to them have. . . (been used) to sell again with advantage, to ignorant men."

Some promoters had taken the opportunity of getting out while they could, leaving the company to be run by less skilful managers, or "men allured by the noise of great profit". One wonders how the Commission would have reacted today to the idea of an Unlisted Securities Market or dealings Over-the-Counter!

The Commission blamed the fact that some of the enterprises were not doing so well as they might have been on their tendency to give first priority to the successful manipulation of their shares on the market. Some basic industries, the Commissioners believed, might benefit from being brought under direct Government control. A similar view was to be expressed more than a generation later by Mr Gladstone with regard to the railways. Since family businesses tended to lose their energy by the third generation, he reasoned, should not the railways, established by Act of Parliament — but operated by private companies — be placed sooner or later under State control, in order to ensure their enterprise and efficiency?

John Houghton was one who defended the market men. Many of them "do abominate the least unjust action, and would not for the world have an ill-gotten penny among the rest of their estates." But he had to concede that some unscrupulous brokers were rigging the options market, by "the mystery of buying more than all." This technique, writes Alan Jenkins, was a principle which could be seen:

> ". . . at work in many doubtful share issues, many swindles which no amount of restriction and regulation can entirely avoid, right up to comparatively recent times. . . we shall find it in the South Sea Bubble, the Railway Mania, Horatio Bottomley, and Clarence Hatry"

Although an Act of 1697 sought to restrain "the number and ill practices of brokers and stock jobbers", imposing severe penalties on offenders, the malpractices continued. But, in the case of the South Sea Bubble, which was to collapse 20 years later, neither the Company nor the brokers could have created such an enormous Bubble on their own. It took the actions of the Government, and the gullibility of some very distinguished persons of the time: men like Sir Theodore Janssen, a Governor of the Bank of England, Dean Swift, and John Barter, a future Lord Mayor of London. The fact that Government not only sanctioned the scheme, but leading members of the administration bought shares in it, was enough for lesser mortals.

While the seeds of the 18th century version of People's Capitalism were being sown in England, ominous developments were afoot on the other side of the Channel. 1715 was the year King Louis XIV died, leaving the finances of his former kingdom in an appalling state. Expenditure outran revenue by 100%. The treasury was empty. So hopeless was the position that the Duc de Saint-Simon was even suggesting a declaration of national bankruptcy. The Regent, Philippe, Duc d'Orleans, was at a loss and incapable . But when John Law arrived on the scene the following year, Philippe recognised him as a man he had met some years earlier in a gambling house; and he remembered how impressed he had been by the Scotsman's perspicacity at the time. Saint-Simon wrote of Law in his *Memories* as "the kind of man who, without ever cheating, continually won at cards by the consummate art (that seemed incredible to me) of his methods of play".

Nevertheless, under an edict of May 2nd 1716, John Law and his brother were given permission to establish the Banque Générale in Paris, with a capital of 6 million *livres,* equivalent to around 250,000 English pounds. The bank was authorised to issue notes, which it did in the form of loans. The loans were largely made to the Government. At first things went well, and the public preferred Law's notes to the coin of the realm. Success in Paris led to the opening of further branches of the Banque Générale in Amiens, La Rochelle, Lyons, Orléans and Tours. Whatever the Duc de Saint-Simon had to say about this foreign card player, Law certainly helped to put the French economy back on its feet.

Two years later, still riding high, Law's bank became a publicly chartered company, the Banque Royale. Now he could issue bank notes, guaranteed by King Louis XV. . . a child of ten. Law also launched his Mississippi scheme. Starting with a merger between the Canada Company and the French Louisiana Company, the plan was to control all trading in the area of the Mississippi, to explore the large gold deposits which Louisiana was believed to possess in the lower subsoil. Early in the year 1719, the Mississippi Company (Compagnie d'Occident) was given exclusive trading rights in India, China and the South Seas. The next step for Law was the launch of this early conglomerate on to the market. As J.K. Galbraith tells us (in *Money):*

> "The jam of people seeking to buy the stock was dense; the din of the sale was deafening. . . The value of adjacent property rose sharply from the demand of people seeking to be close to the action. The shares rose phenomenally. . . Men who had invested a few thousands. . . were worth millions in a matter of a few weeks or months. Those who were so transformed were called *millionaires.''*

Meanwhile the Banque Royale continued to flourish. In the Spring of 1719, some 100 million *livres* in notes were outstanding. By the end of the year the figure had risen to 1,200 million. In essence, says Galbraith:

> "Law was lending notes of the Banque Royale to the government. . . which then passed them on. . . in payment of government debts or expenses. These notes were then used. . . to buy stock in the Mississippi Company, the proceeds. . . (going) to the government to. . . pay off creditors who then used the notes to buy more stock. . . and so it continued, each cycle being larger than the one before."

Law was ennobled, becoming the first Duc d'Arkansas. On January 5th 1720, he received the ultimate accolade: the Comptrollership General of France. He could scarcely hope to rise higher. John Law played his final master-stroke when he amalgamated the India Company with the Banque Royale. This time, he had gone too far. He had allowed his ambition to take him, and the whole structure he had built, to the very brink of collapse. Early that year, the Prince de Conti had become annoyed when he found he could not buy Law's stock at what he considered the "right" price. He reacted by sending a bundle of notes to the Banque Royale to be redeemed in hard currency. The "bundle" was big enough to require the despatch of three waggons to carry away the gold and silver coins!

The story leaked out. Others began exchanging Law's notes for metal, and then shipping the proceeds out of the country. Various manoeuvres were tried out in an attempt to restore confidence. They included, as Galbraith tells us:

> "the impressment of some thousand or more assorted mendicants from the Paris slums. . . equipped with shovels. . . (They) marched in small groups along the streets as though on their way to Louisiana to mine the gold."

When they were still some way from the docks, they began to leave the ranks. Then, having sold their picks and shovels, they returned home. Once they were seen back in their old haunts, says Galbraith:

> "The news that Paris had the mendicants and not the gold had an unsettling effect on investors and holders of the notes of the Banque Royale."

Soon it became necessary to ration the repayments. The boom was over. One day in July, says Galbraith, the crowd around the bank was so great that fifteen people were reputed to have been crushed to death. Whether that was true or not, the collapse of the whole house of cards could not be delayed much longer. After the end came, Law was smuggled out of the country by his patron, Philippe, Duc d' Orléans, and vanished into exile in Paris. There, Saint-Simon records, "he lived, in decent poverty. . . (and) died there. . . piously receiving the Sacraments of the Church." Charles Mackay (of *Popular Delusions* fame) writes that:

> ". . . the French are the most renowned for singing over their grievances. . . the streets resounded with songs. . . (one) in particular counselled the application of. . . (his) notes to the most ignoble use to which paper can be applied."

There now followed an interval of several months during which the English Chancellor, the Government and the financial authorities might have taken note of the collapse of the Banque Royale, and the widespread disaster which followed. But they neither took note, nor in any way heeded the warning. The South Sea Company went on from strength to strength, albeit largely on the strength of popular myth, and blue-blooded patronage. Bearing in mind the success the Bank of England was enjoying, it is easy to see why on 14th July 1711 the subscriptions had poured in; as, indeed, they continued to do whenever the public were called upon to subscribe. For example, in 1715 the Company's capital was raised to £10 million; and to £12 million two years later. By now, it represented more than half the capital of all the joint-stock companies put together, including the Bank of England and the United East India Company.

Many had found the South Sea Company prospectus both attractive and persuasive. So much so, that when Dean Swift (a shrewd man when it came to investment) read the offer document, he wrote to Stella, that he was "resolved to buy £500 South Sea stock, which will cost me £380." (Which fixes the price at £76 per cent at that early stage.)

John Blunt, secretary of the Hollow Sword Blade Company, now comes into the picture. Eventually he was to help to bring the South Sea Company down. As yet, he was still comparatively unknown, a dissenter who had made money, and started a bank. He was also a critic of what he saw as the luxury of the age. He recommended the purchase of South Sea stock, however, as an Englishman's patriotic duty.

The Treaty of Utrecht did not bring the hoped-for expansion of trade. There were troubles with Spain, which were soon to lead to war. The company was plainly over-capitalised, but it still had one thing: a long and impressive list of royal and noble subscribers. The Prince of Wales was one. He made a great deal of money by taking Walpole's advice and buying £20,000 of South Sea stock. One Thomas Guy received £234,000 for his shareholding, which enabled him to endow Guy's Hospital. It was true that the South Sea Company achieved very little. But, so far, there was nothing fraudulent in it. . . although the same could not be said for some of the other companies floated at the time. One was for "repairing and rebuilding parsonage and vicarage houses." Another, run by a clergyman, proposed to import "Spanish jackasses" to improve the British strain. There was a company offering a wheel for perpetual motion. Perhaps the most blatant of all was the one which promised to "carry on an undertaking of great advantage". But nobody knew what it was. The prospectus promised that every investor who deposited £2 per share would be entitled to £100 per annum. Within six hours £2,000 had been raised. Then the promoter vanished with the money.

The year 1720 saw the final rise and fall of South Sea shares. In January they stood at a premium of £28½. By March, they had climbed to £330. In April 1720, Sir John Blunt came up with a new scheme: to incorporate the funds of the Exchequer, the Bank of England, the East India Company and the South Sea Company. The Chancellor, John Aislabie, and the elder James Craggs, Joint Postmaster-General, examined the proposition. The Bank of England was opposed to it from the start. Sir Richard Steele was one of the many who disliked the whole idea. (Though there was but one who opposed it in the Commons, and he was treated like a pariah.)

The Prime Minister, Sir Robert Walpole, also condemned the scheme. He said it smacked of the the "pernicious practice of stockjobbing, by diverting the genius of the nation from trade and industry". He even published a pamphlet opposing the Bill. However, Sir Robert had already done very well out of the South Sea Company by selling his shares at the top of the market. He made enough to rebuild his home, and found a fine collection of pictures. But once before the Commons, the Bill was quickly passed. Five days later, the public was invited to subscribe £1 million at £300 for every £100 nominal. The issued was 100% oversubscribed, and the shares were soon standing at a premium of £40. Having announced a dividend of 10%, a second £1 million share issue then followed. This time the price was £400 per cent. £1.5 million had been raised in a matter of hours. The first to subscribe were the King and the Prince of Wales.

Among the foreign investors were several French noblemen, determined to recover what they had lost as a result of John Law's wild adventure! In May 1720, the word got around that John Law had fled. But not all who heard the news believed it. Nor were many people in England interested. South Sea shares now stood at £550. The following month, the Government pushed through the Bubble Act. This decreed that any company formed without a charter would henceforth be illegal. By now there were something like 100 "Bubble" companies; and more were being set up. June saw South Sea Company shares touching £800. In July, the shares reached their peak —£1,000 or 10 times the nominal value of the stock.

About that time, it was estimated that the advance in the price of all available UK shares (including the more fanciful "Bubble" stocks) was in the region of £500 million. That was almost five times as much as all the current cash held in the whole of Europe. On 24th August 1720, the Fourth Money Subscription for the South Sea Company was launched. Unbelievably, the whole issue was snapped up inside three hours. By now, according to contemporary accounts, a new stratum of the *noveau riche* had come into being. As Alan Jenkins reports:

> " 'City ladies buy South Sea jewels, hire South Sea maids, take new country South Sea houses,'; and this in turn bred a new race of estate agents, known as land jobbers. . . People might be wary of the small bubble companies (after the passage of the Bubble Act), but they still seemed infatuated with the big one: indeed there is evidence that many investors gambled in small bubbles so as to invest their profit in the big one. . "

But the end was not far off. Six days after the Fourth Subscription, Lord Bathurst wrote. . . "some of the Directors have endeavoured to run down the stocks after having sold their own out, in order to buy in cheap again. This has put people in a fright." Their "fright" would have been justified in any case, since, Jenkins tells us, at the top of each page of the subscription book there was a paragraph "awarding power of attorney to 'certain persons' so that subscribers had no claim if anything went wrong."

The crash came in September, when the shares fell to £175. Those who bought at the top had lost £825. By September 13th, Thomas Broderick, who was highly suspicious of the whole thing, was writing to Lord Middleton that he thought the Directors "had drawn out in good time." Thousands of families, he predicted, would be "reduced to beggary". Come December, the shares had slid down even further — down to £124. Mr Broderick was proved right. Countless small investors, who had mortgaged all they possessed to get hold of a few South Sea Company shares, were left with nothing. Nor were they alone. Many of the great and the good failed to sell in time — having ignored, or more likely never read, Joseph de la Vega's warning about the eel that "may escape sooner than you think." Sir David Hamilton, the Royal physician, was one. He lost £80,000 by holding on too long. John Gay, who could have picked up almost a quarter of a million pounds for his shareholdings, lost the lot. It was not until his *Beggar's Opera* became the "smash-hit" of the age that he recovered his fortune. Alexander Pope, who lost a good half of his investment, took a philosophical view of his loss: ". . . methinks God has punished the avaricious".

The Bubble had burst; with a vengeance!

On January 4th 1721, it was proposed that . . .*leave be given to bring in a Bill for restraining the Sub-Governor, Deputy-Governor, Directors, Treasurer or Cashier, and Accountants of the South Sea Company from going out of this kingdom for the space of one year. . . and for discovering the estates and effects, and preventing the transportation or alienating the same.* A week later a Committee of Secrecy was set up to investigate the Bubble. On January 23rd, Robert Knight, Cashier for the Company, fled in disguise to Calais, leaving behind a note admitting "indiscretions", but denying any guilt. Books were seized, arrests were ordered, including that of Sir John Blunt. The same evening, the Chancellor John Aislabie resigned.

The Committee emerged from behind locked doors to announce that the South Sea Company books had been "cooked", and fictitious stock had been distributed to members of the Government as an inducement to them to pass the South Sea Bill. Four individuals, including the Chancellor, were named. He was found guilty of the most "notorious, dangerous, and infamous corruption". Expelled from the House, he was committed to the Tower. Bonfires were lit throughout the City.

The Committee continued its sittings through March and April 1721. It was not until July that the South Sea Sufferers Bill received Royal Assent. The Bank of England and the East India Company each took over £9 million of South Sea stock: an early "lifeboat" operation. The Company continued to trade under its new directors. In 1748, the Port of London lost its slave traffic, and the South Sea Company ceased to trade. Nevertheless, it lingered on for more than a century, handling Government Securities. Charles Lamb wrote one of his memorable essays in memory of South Sea House, where he had been a clerk for a brief spell in the 1790s:

> This was once a house of trade. . . The throng of merchants were here — the quick pulse of gain — here some forms of business are still kept up, though the soul be long since fled. Here are still to be seen. . . imposing staircases; offices roomy as the state apartments in palaces —deserted, or thinly peopled with a few straggling clerks."

That whole affair, from first Bubble to last is one of the most extraordinary periods in modern English history. Yet even when feelings were at their keenest — and bitterest — that saving grace (or is it a national weakness?), the British sense of humour, came to the rescue of the culpable and wretched Sir John Blunt. The record shows that his "petition of innocence. . . moved the House (of Commons) to laughter." But the motion that he "should have but a shilling" was brushed aside; and the wretch was allowed to keep £1,000. Francis Hawes, Cashier of the Customs, did not fare so well. All he was allowed to keep of an estate valued at £40,031 was the sum of £31.

Why is it, you may wonder, that the salutary tale of the South Sea Bubble is dismissed so casually in most school books and almost every classroom, as merely an example of "what happens when speculation runs rife". Why are we so rarely told the truth: that it still provides one of the clearest warnings of what can happen when fate produces a combination of individual arrogance, professional incompetence, and corruption in high places? Perhaps it is yet another example of the kind of thing that we in our time would rather forget. It was, after all, an example of an early attempt at privatisation. In this case, it was a scheme to privatise the National Debt. It was promoted by top government figures and enjoyed the support of Royalty. It was launched by men with the highest motives. It commanded the support of the people. The pity was, that it was flawed from the start. The greater pity was that nobody of any importance could see that. Or, if they did, they did not say so. It forces us to ask whether such a thing could possibly happen in our enlightened times.

Of course not, you will say. But history tells us that the more things appear to change, the more they remain the same. Two *very* chancy undertakings were launched in Britain in the 1980s: Privatisation and Big Bang. Buy why Big Bang, first of all?

Why Big Bang?

The origins of Big Bang are not hard to find. They were in the first instance political, and motivated by that blend of envy, hostility and contempt felt by the Left towards any élite, professional body it cannot understand. But Big Bang could not have taken on its present form had it not been for the unpredictable attitude of the Thatcherite Conservative administration, and a failure of nerve on the part of the Stock Exchange itself. But that has been water under the bridge since October 27th 1986, when the traditional ways of dealing in City markets — both good and bad — were completely overturned in the course of one day.

Though they may be well known to a few, the main stages on the road to Big Bang are still worth recalling. In a sense, Shirley Williams was responsible for turning the attention of Sir Gordon Borrie and his Office of Fair Trading to the Stock Exchange and its ageing Rule Book. In 1976, when Mrs Williams (still a member of the Labour Party) held office as Secretary of State for Prices and Consumer Affairs, she extended the scope of the Restrictive Practices Act to cover "services" as well as manufacturers.

From earliest times, the Labour Party and the Trades Unions had nursed a grudge against the City in general, and the Stock Exchange in particular. On one hand, they referred to it contemptuously as a "gentlemen's club". On the other, they condemned it as a "casino". From the moment Shirley Williams included the service industries in the OFT's target area, the age-old vendetta against "privilege" and "élitism" quickly developed into a concentrated and skilfully orchestrated attack on the "capitalists" in the City.

There was nothing surprising about Labour's manoeuvres, holding the views it did. Nor was there anything surprising about the steps taken by the Office of Fair Trading. Both rated "competition" as the essential ingredient in the "fair trading" they were seeking to promote. However, the City in general and the Stock Exchange in particular saw other qualities as more important. Fairness, in the City's view, was not to be achieved by unbridled competition. That was for the High Street and for back-alley markets. What mattered in the City was the creation and maintenance of a community in which stability and probity were valued more; in which the best protection for the investor (or indeed for each other) lay in the observance of practices based on a generally accepted code of conduct, which had painstakingly — and, at times, painfully — developed over the centuries.

When a City man said, "My Word is My Bond", he was not striking a moral attitude. He was merely stating the premise upon which all the City's customs, conventions and day-to-day procedures are based. If standards were to be maintained, the responsibility rested on the community itself. Hence its necessary restriction to a certain kind of individual, who subscribed to a clearly definable and mutually acceptable set of beliefs. In short, the City was one of the few surviving examples of the mediaeval closed society. True, the Middle Ages had been over for several centuries before the members of the Stock Exchange began to match, however imperfectly, their own concept of a fair and honest market. At least, they could claim that while the Lord Mayor and the Common Council had become largely symbols of a great past, the Stock Exchange, the Banks and the other markets were serving the needs of their time. It is true that quite a few City men since the 1960s had begun to wonder whether it was true any longer. But at least, London was still one of the three major financial centres of the world; with Japanese and American banks, brokerage houses and other financial interests setting up shop within, or adjacent to the Square Mile.

It was not, as I have said, the attitude of the Left that was so surprising. It was rather that of the Thatcher administration, and of the Stock Exchange Members, when they came under fire from the OFT. Writing in *The Guardian*, shortly before Big Bang, Hugh Stephenson, a member of the Wilson Committee on financial institutions (1977-80) took up the question of the puzzling attitude on Throgmorton Street:

> "The Stock Exchange, badly advised from 1976 onwards, took the view right
> up to the last moment that *any* change in its rules or conventions would
> tacitly weaken its multi-million pound defence of its Rule book before the

> Restrictive Practices Court. . . By trying in vain for ten years to hold the
> old dyke, it ensured that the head of pressure would be uncontrollable."

By the time Cecil Parkinson was serving, for a brief spell, as Secretary
of State for Trade, the Stock Exchange was already locked in conflict with
the Office of Fair Trading, which had the law on its side. Indeed, Sir Gordon
Borrie was preparing to use it to haul the Stock Exchange before the
Restrictive Practices Court and require it to justify its Rule book. Not that
the OFT thought it could!

There were several things that the OFT and Sir Gordon disliked about
the Exchange's rules and practices. One was the fixed commissions which
brokers charged their clients. Prophets of the Consumerist Creed have always
hated fixed charges. Some time earlier, as you may well remember, the OFT
had gone after the High Street Banks to stop what it considered an "unfair"
trade practice. It was, in fact, the arrangement whereby the main clearing
banks would accept, or cash, each other's cheques without charging the
customer. It was an arrangement which suited the banks *and* their customers.
After all, if you wanted to cash a cheque in a County town, and it happened
to be market-day, you simply had to look around until you found the bank
which had the shortest queue. But this was anathema to the OFT. It was
a form of cartel; an evil thing which should not be tolerated. As a result,
the banks had to drop the concession which, if it restricted anything, cut
down on non-productive paperwork. If the OFT seriously considered that
such conformity really restricted competition, then — to be consistent —
it should have done something about banks' opening at precisely the same
time, on the same days, for the same hours! That, unlike the previous
arrangement, did quite definitely restrict consumer choice. In any case,
it is doubtful whether many "consumers" of bank services would thank
the OFT for its intervention. However, we are not involved here with
commonsense, but with political ideology.

The OFT also objected to the way the Stock Exchange scrutinised potential
new members, excluding those it regarded as unsuitable or as "outsiders".
The Exchange's reasoning was quite straightforward. Since experience had
shown that wealth, connections, and influential friends were not necessarily
a guarantee of probity, the Exchange, like any other *private concern,* reserved
the right to choose its members, and choose them with care. As with any
traditional Englishman's club, the members knew the damage that a
"wrong 'un" could do in a very short time. So — better be safe than sorry!
As for foreigners, they might be splendid fellows on their own patch. Indeed,
members might be delighted to do business with them. But, however long
they lived in the country, however "integrated" into English society they
might become, they would still never "belong". Furthermore, if they were
honest with you, they'd admit that they knew they never would. Their
children, possibly. But not the first generation.

Interestingly enough, the more independent life of the banker — especially
in the merchant banks — has made it easier for the stranger to be accepted

there; as some of the best-known names in banking show. But the City has long demanded that a new member should be naturally "clubable". Rarely the characteristic of a stranger!

This must sound arrogant and divisive. But, as an American, living in Britain since the 1960s, I know I am right — unpopular as it may be to say so! I can also give you an absolute guarantee that the rules and regulations that have been changed under the banner of Big Bang will do nothing whatsoever to remove the underlying sub-stratum of prejudice that has built up over centuries. Who has ever put in a kindly word for Merrill Lynch, the world's biggest stockbrokers? It was not because of a wealth of fellow feeling that they were dubbed "The Thundering Herd". There is something very pragmatic about the beliefs and behaviour of the reserved, conservative City man ("conservative" with a small "c"). His reactions may be compared to those of Queen Victoria, when she heard of the Government's intention to hold competitive examinations for admission to her Civil Service. She took some persuading, because — as she said — what happens if you pick a brilliant young man, who passes all the examinations, but turns out to be deficient in his *character?*

In the City, a man or a woman's character is as important as ever. Perhaps, as the complexity and the pressures of the market mount, it may become even more so. For it is at moments of stress that training and character show themselves. Even though every 'phone call may be monitored and recorded, there will be times when a man's or a woman's word *must* be their bond. When the pressure is on, markets cannot operate in any other way. Certainly, legislation and supervisory bodies are no substitute for individual calibre and personal integrity. That, after all, is why overturning a system based on well-tried ways has left gaps which no neat, new set of rules is going to fill.

To those (and there are many) who charge that brokers and jobbers are merely trying to protect their own position and incomes, an honest answer would be that in many cases it *is* a consideration. Unless they prosper, they will be a poor bet for their clients. Besides, in the past fifteen years or so, there have been several bad shake-outs; cutting staff, persuading partners to retire, or soldiering on until they have been forced to quit the market altogether. That is certainly one of the reasons why the bulk of the business in equities has been conducted through 25 brokers or less; with most of the shares being handled by one or two jobbers. That is why over 80% of Gilts business has been done through three brokers and a couple of jobbers. But this, one has to recognise, was noted and brought up as another of the City's "restrictive practices". The brokers and jobbers who gave up because they could no longer make a living would scarcely be impressed by that line of official reasoning.

For the record, it was as long ago as 1697, that the Government first brought in an Act to "restrain the number and ill practices of brokers, etc". Under the Act, brokers were required to keep proper books, to take no more than one-half per cent commission, and to act as agents, dealing solely for clients. They were required to swear that they would "truly and faithfully execute and perform the office and employment of a broker between party and party." Brokers would never be permitted to play "jobber", and deal on their own behalf. It is true that the Act lapsed in less than a dozen years, but a principle had been established: namely that the separation of the roles of jobber and broker was to be observed as the best practical means of avoiding conflicts of interest prejudicial to the client. At any rate, it was the best that anyone could devise in this patently imperfect world.

Single capacity, unique to the UK Stock Exchange, had been practised throughout most of the 19th century. Then "high technology" intervened. The introduction of the telephone made it possible for brokers to eliminate the jobber on many occasions; and double commissions might be earned provided buyers and sellers could be brought directly into contact. Jobbers too could use the telephone to make contact with provincial brokers, cutting out the London broker. By the time the Royal Commission on the Stock Exchange completed its enquiry in 1878, an informal commission scale had been agreed. But by now there was concern over the practices of some foreign banks in Britain, and particularly the German banks, True, they were putting in large orders, but they were also demanding substantial discounts on the commissions due.

In 1908, a new rulebook was introduced, re-establishing single capacity. But the arguments about commission rates continued. They were finally settled by balloting the members on March 12th, 1912. Fixed commissions won the day; but by a majority of only 119 votes. 1,670 members voted for, and 1,551 against. Thereafter brokers would be judged by their skill and by the range of services offered. Price competition is not always so "healthy" as it sounds. Some professional men are better at one thing than another. Therefore the client should be seeking the right firm, with the right expertise, rather than one offering the market's "best bargain". Yet it is quite amazing that so many people still talk as though price competition was all that mattered. Britain's recent, unhappy experience in cotton and allied textile exports shows that British weavers and finishers may beat the French or Germans by 20% on price, but poor design, unreliable delivery and inadequate sales services left Britain unable to stand up to its EEC competitors.

The casual way in which single capacity became a casualty within a few weeks of the Parkinson/Goodison compromise passed almost unnoticed. The way both parties acted — or failed to act — was probably a fair measure of the confusion that prevailed in the crucial months that followed the deal.

Almost equally disturbing to many professionals was the feeling that the whole sensitive business of reform was being tackled piecemeal and clumsily. "Like putting a watch together again in boxing gloves", was one comment. Scandals in the Lloyds insurance market had already led to a searching investigation and precise recommendations. Since investor protection was, is and will continue to be the very heart of the matter, one might have expected that the lessons learned from the Lloyds experience would have been taken in at once by those still groping in the dark, in the hope of stumbling over an ideal solution. By now, remember, they were not concerned with the stock market alone. There were the almost totally unregulated markets to be considered; not least of all, the Eurobond market. Yet, at the very moment that Government was insisting that the roles of insurance-broker and underwriter be kept separate, to avoid injurious conflicts of interest, single capacity for jobbers and brokers was allowed to fly out of the window, as though no longer necessary.

Whether this was a correct conclusion is open to argument. What is *not* so easily shaken off is the feeling that the thought process which led to this conclusion was muddled, illogical and confused. It began with acceptance of the OFT's demand that fixed commissions would have to go. Then it transpired that without fixed commissions, jobbers and (many) brokers felt they would be unable to continue. Assuming that they were right, the next step would appear to have been argued in a truly Alice-in-Wonderland fashion. Indeed it is tempting to reconstruct the inner dialogue which must have gone on:

A: Negotiated commissions have been prescribed. That is that! We have agreed.

B: True! But we are now told that single capacity cannot survive with *negotiated* commissions.

A: Correct! But unless we go for negotiated commissions we cannot hold to our agreement.

B: So?

A: So. . . we would have the OFT on our backs again.

B: (Somewhat sanctimoniously) Am I to understand that avoiding trouble takes precedence over eliminating conflicts of interest, detrimental to the investor? (Craftily) I thought THAT was why you were seeking to increase the competition.

A: (Bridling) We are introducing greater competition because IT IS A GOOD THING.

B: Who told you that?

A: You know *perfectly well*.

B: And you believe them?

A: Not *necessarily*. But that is where the power lies. In any case. . . there are more ways than one of skinning a cat.

B: You DO have a formula to replace single capacity?

A: We're working on it!

B: And you're sure there IS a better way?

A: There MUST be! Otherwise we would be in an IMPOSSIBLE situation. Which, by definition, is not possible.

B: Why?

A: Because we are doing the RIGHT THING.

It is the brand of chop-logic employed one wet afternoon in East Berlin by a large Russian lady in uniform. A group of Swedish academics were attempting to board the Aeroflot jet to Hanoi. Their baggage had already been placed aboard, and they were told to wait until the passengers were called. When the call came, this fearsome-looking individual barred their way at the top of the steps. *"Niet"*, she said abruptly. "You are not permitted to take this flight."

' "Why not?", they asked.

"Because another group with even higher priority will travel in your place." Knowing that it would be useless to argue, the group leader gave a most aimiable smile and — pointing through the porthole — said, "Very well, Comrade. But may we have our baggage, please."

The Uniformed Figure bridled. "You ACCUSE me that I have your baggage?" (This dialogue was going on in the most unbelievable American English.)

"No, no, Comrade. . . it's just that it has already been put aboard."

"Nonsense," came the reply. "It is impossible! Your baggage will have been placed ONLY upon the plane in which you travel. You agree? Yes? No?"

"Affirmative," said the group leader, trying very hard to smile once more. (He dreaded what was coming.) Dry-mouthed, he said, "That is why they took our bags and put them on the plane, Comrade." At this, the large Russian lady became extremely angry. "You are telling me Nonsense again!" she cried. "If you were travelling on this flight, then your baggage would, indeed, be on it. But you are NOT travelling on this flight. Therefore your baggage CANNOT BE ON THE AIRCRAFT. Stand aside, please!"

This kind of new-speak, or dim-think, is something we will meet time and again as the saga of Big Bang unfolds. Discounting either deliberate perversity or simple stupidity, it is difficult to see how the same administration, dealing with the same financial markets, could be so inconsistent. The truth, I suspect, is that by the time Mr Parkinson had decided to further Labour's cause, and the Stock Exchange had decided to let him, there was a period of disbelief and confusion as each side tried to sort out precisely where it stood. It is an experience the City has been through many times in the past; when old, familiar principles have been thrown aside, because, for the moment, it has seemed expedient.

One is bound to return to the fundamental fact that much of the pressure exerted by the OFT was for what? For the sake of *ostensibly* getting rid of minimum commissions for the sake of the consumer. I stress the word *ostensibly,* because I believe that before long we shall find that the number of broker-jobber-conglomerates willing to handle small investor business will be few indeed. Some will deliberately make high charges to keep the unwanted client at arm's length. The institutional investors will have the muscle to *negotiate* commissions and other charges. But the small investor — about whom the OFT, and the Thatcher Government have been shouting for the past three years — will be forced to take or leave it!

So far as fees go, shortly before Big Bang some banks and stockbrokers were offering a lower grade of service, to make up for the lower minimum charge. An outline tariff, published a few days before the "Off", demonstrated how difficult it will be for the newcomer to the market to decide where the best value lies — even opting for the simple Dealing-only rate. For example:

Dealing-only rate

Broker A	1% with minimum £12 and maximum £100
Broker B	1.4% up to £7,000;
	0.4% up to £15,000;
	0.3% up to £100,000;
	over that, by negotiation; minimum £20
Broker C	Plans discount-service, possibly by end 1986

Brokers A and B offer revised rates for their top "Advisory" service. But Broker C states: "Sticking to existing commission rates." Fair enough! Another Group, formed from seven regional brokers, could theoretically find itself in something of a predicament. In the "bad" old days, they could have set a common rate at the start, and stuck to it. That, today, would be against the rules. No fixed commissions! So they are able to say no more than:

"Looking at common rates for all firms but most are likely to stick with current scale in short term." So far as a Dealing-only rate goes, the answer for all eight is: "None".

But does this not constitute "price-fixing"? A second Group, comprising eight regional brokers, states:

"Rates to be harmonised, with some reduction for larger private clients. Looking at annual management fee."

But shouldn't it be "fees", plural? As for the Dealing-only rate, it's a simple "No". At least that is one thing they are agreed upon already. But the position of such loose groupings could be tricky. They may end up with the kind of absurdities that a landlord has to face, when he needs a hefty cellar-man, but decides to play safe by advertising for:

"Cellar-person, Scrum-half preferred."

One of the last things anyone would wish to see is a price war within the City. Cut-throat competition would tempt those with the longest purse to behave like the High Street grocer, who goes in for round after round of price-cutting until he's driven the "competition" into liquidation. Then he can make the most of the monopoly position he, and his long purse, have created, and jack the price up again. That is why, when you come to think about it, competition should be treated as a two-edged weapon, to be handled with care. In the wrong — or careless — hands it can produce the very result everyone was trying to avoid. Therefore, however highly competition may be valued, it must be contained within reasonable limits. But after the Crash of '87 the individual investor was soon made to feel an unwanted pest.

The Conservative Enigma

When Cecil Parkinson took up the ammunition prepared during the period of Labour rule, he did not hesitate. He carried on the attack made possible by Shirley Williams in 1976. Shortly afterwards, as we have seen, the Stock Exchange was to amaze onlookers by throwing up its hands and surrendering. Cecil Parkinson, who plainly knew as little about the workings of the Square Mile as most of his Cabinet colleagues, managed to persuade the Chairman, Sir Nicholas Goodison, and the rest of the Stock Exchange Council to give in without a fight, on the offer of moderate terms.

The explanation, repeated many times since, was that London's dealing system was antiquated; that American and Japanese institutions could not be relied on to continue doing so much of their business (and more than half of London's) in a market from which, as foreigners, they were excluded. Commissions in London too were higher than in the more competitive international markets. Worse still, London commission rates were (theoretically) not negotiable. Failure to respond to the challenge, ran the argument, would be tantamount to inviting the Americans and the Japanese to carve up the expanding world market between them. Once that happened, London would be left behind on the shore, like a stranded whale.

The Stock Exchange Chairman, Sir Nicholas Goodison has said that the threat hanging over the market was not forcing the pace of reform, but inhibiting it. So he welcomed the breaking of the log-jam. Although he did not try to minimise the risk, he did believe that London would capture a larger share of international business once its markets were opened up. On the day the Stock Exchange voted to accept the Parkinson/Goodison compromise, Sir Nicholas was interviewed on BBC Radio Four's programme, *The Financial World Tonight*. Welcoming the changes that were coming, he stated that he did not wish to see banks holding large blocks of shares as they did in Germany. Nor would he welcome the creation of large American-style conglomerates which would do virtually every kind of business. In that respect, he must have been a disappointed man long before Big Bang on Monday, 27th October 1986.

In the early stages of the new regime, we saw the fruits of too hasty a move into a computerised wonderland. Breakdowns were to be expected; but not faulty planning. "Visibility" was supposed to make up for the loss of single capacity. In the first weeks, the Topic computers (which hold the file of share prices) kept breaking down. The explanation (or, as many saw it, the excuse) was simple: too many people were trying to access the system at the same moment. "Hard cheese!" was the response of one seasoned operator, "but at least I've won my bet!" At 12.55 on the second Friday after Big Bang, Epic managed to fail for the first time. Epic is the series of super-mini-computers which holds permanent files of market prices. That afternoon, a link between the Exchange and its technical HQ failed. This broke the link between three of the eight Topic computers and the Exchange's own SEAQ system. At once 2,500 Topic users lost access to competing quotes. So SEAQ had to be suspended for a third time, in fairness to the market as a whole. It took 20 minutes to restore normal service this time.

In all, the electronic system was out of service for around an hour; but the final suspension came shortly after three-thirty. This thoroughly incensed those traders who were taking the opportunity (available after 3.30 on the last Friday of the old account) to deal without penalty for the new. Some of the gilts trade done with the new group, James Capel Gilts, was being put down (said the firm's finance director) to the account of James Capel and Co. Not because of computer failure, but merely because the wrong number had been put on one of the firm's pitches. When the market finally closed, it left 50,000 uncleared trade reports — almost as many as in the first week. Later, uncleared bargains became a serious problem.

Unforgiveable in the eyes of some traders was the revelation that neither the Topic nor the Epic system had been provided with a "hot-standby computer". So there was nothing to take over instantly if — or rather when — the main system went down. This, they argued, could not be blamed on "the fortunes of war". It was just "bad staff work". "Wasn't it Voltaire," said one analyst with a chuckle, "who observed that in England it was considered rather sound to hang the odd admiral. . . from time to time. . . *pour encourager les autres*, as he put it?"

A Kleinwort Grieveson director, who had told the press that he blamed bad organisation and poor personal liaison for the problems, thought that to have to close the market to launch British Gas would be bad public relations. But some of his fellow members remained apprehensive at the thought of having to use the still unfamiliar (and so far unreliable) system to handle the massive British Gas flotation in a few weeks time. By Grey Friday, something like 7 million people had indicated a desire to buy British Gas shares. That was one million more than NM Rothschild, the bank handling the issue, had originally indicated. This would be the equivalent of floating more than a score of medium-sized companies on the Exchange all at the same time. Somehow the market stood the test.

Away from the market, we could already detect signs of unrest within some of the freshly formed alliances. Older, senior staff were being "allowed to retire". The accent (like the money) was on youth. But for how long? The more realistic of Big Bang's Golden Lads and Platinum Girls were already asking that question among themselves. Not a few of the mega-money establishments, which had originally bought a token stake in one of the more prestigious London houses, were assumed (correctly enough at the time) to be planning a 100% take-over. Some had decided to give up the idea. One or two were still undecided, and were hanging fire. They might stay, they might sell out. But for the moment, they were not saying. Why should they? Not when they were prepared to put in big money for a year or two — a multi-million dollar toe in the water!

Behind closed doors of more than one of the mutant hybrids, personal relations were deteriorating fast, with some extremely unwelcome moves being made. For instance, the "outside" element had settled in fast and were effectively in control. Now they had begun setting up rival factions within the firm, specifically to compete with the UK jobbers or brokers they had grabbed when the starting-gun was fired and the first waggons crossed the line. Like any successful prospector in the roaring 'forties, they knew it was a gamble. But if they ultimately decided to take a hand in the game, they did not want to find that no one around the table was prepared to deal them in.

Most of the big-money players will succeed in establishing a permanent penetration of the City's defences. Some will succeed spectacularly. A few are bound to fail; or decide the game's not worth it. Although they are most unlikely to wait around for long. Given a couple of misdeals, a run of poor cards, and they'll be up, off and away. Moreover when they do pull out, they will not have the slightest qualms about dismantling the structure which cost them so much time and money to build up. There can be no mistake about it. The top prospectors, and their lesser pan-handlers on their staff, are all proven survivors. They have years of experience of corporate in-fighting behind them. Not that they had to fight their way into London. "Frankly", one hardened newcomer testified, "There's never been a Gold Rush like it. The nuggets practically gave themselves up!"

Nor, if and when they leave, will there be any UK cousins to worry about; no old family retainers to be remembered in their will. Not that there will be much to leave. In all probability, they will strip down the "old firm" until there's little left, apart from the once familiar name, reduced to a line on the writing paper. It figures. That's why it is a pity that those who were so keen on reform seem to have learned nothing from The Tale of Little Red Riding Hood. Invite a wolf into an English nursery if you will. But don't expect it to turn into a Long Haired Sheepdog overnight!

Make no mistake; those bright, alert young men and women with their crisp transatlantic accents may be most courteous. They will call you "Sir" or "Ma'am" with machine-like regularity every fifth or sixth sentence. But if cutting losses means cutting a few throats — so be it! No hard feelings!

These are well known as the barracudas of the securities industry, well schooled in the martial arts. It's all part of the job. They could justifiably share the motto of one of the US Marine Corps Regiments in Vietnam. They put up a sign close to one of the sniper-ridden highways near Danang. It read:

"Though We Walk Through the Valley of the Shadow of Death, WE are the Meanest Guys in this Valley!"

Even before the stock market crashed in '87, the bail-outs had begun.

Softly, Softly

In the provinces, there was a higher (and some would say healthier) level of scepticism towards Big Bang. In Edinburgh, some of the leading establishments in Charlotte Square made no bones about it. "We have relied on our favourite London brokers for their contacts and research. But are they going to let us have it when they've got the Americans and the Japs breathing down their necks? That is. . . if they haven't already taken over?" Many English provincial brokers confessed that they could not understand why London had brain-washed itself into believing it could hope to win this larger slice of international business by opening membership to its American and Japanese rivals. Surely Britain would be better off hanging on to what it already had; exploiting the much vaunted advantages that London was supposed to enjoy — 200 years of know-how, its location on the Greenwich Meridian, an unrivalled reputation for skill and integrity. . . etc! Far from increasing Britain's share in the world market, said the cannier of the provincial brokers, throwing wide the door to all comers would merely clear the way for giants like Salomon Brothers or Nomura Securities. Once inside, they would take a lion's share of the domestic market.

The further you were from London, the easier it seemed to be for people to see the wood. "All they're doing down in London," said one insurance man on Edinburgh's George Street, "is to count the rings and admire the trees! Meanwhile, the foreigners are working out how much they should cut, and how much they'll get for it."

One Yorkshire financial middle-man — who was by no means opposed to change — summed up the feelings of many of the older hands in the City when he said, "Cecil Parkinson and Nicholas Goodison thought they were just opening the back-door a few inches. In point of fact, they were breaching the dyke."

With blessed hindsight, quite a few of those who were "Don't Knows" at the start, have come round to wondering whether it wasn't a bad mistake to give in to Cecil Parkinson. Instead, they claim, the Stock Exchange Council should have said, "Right, we have a good case, and sound reasons for doing things the way we do; so we'll fight it out!" That way, the City would be

putting its case not merely to the Court, but — far more important — to
the Public at large. Their ignorance of what the City does and tries to do
was (and still is) profound. Even at the time, they were saying in some
quarters of the City that it was no bomb Parkinson was brandishing. . .
merely a "Thunderflash", the kind of "banger" used to enliven the final
stages of the day's manoeuvres. The odds were, therefore, that calling his
bluff would have been too much for any Conservative Cabinet, once it began
to count the political cost. Some extreme optimists even thought that a few
politicians might learn something to the City's advantage.

But the way in which events began slipping inexorably out of control,
and the painful and muddled handling of the key Financial Services Bill,
suggest that there was no great desire to learn in the Lower House. But
all credit must go to the House of Lords for its diligence in handling the
Financial Services Bill, and for its many amendments.

It is true that Wall Street went through the painful and costly process
of deregulation when fixed commissions were abolished on May Day, 1975.
But, as Hugh Stephenson, a member of the Wilson Committee which reported
on the City in 1980, wrote shortly before Big Bang:

> "When fixed commissions were abolished in New York. . . it happened
> in the context of an industry that had experience of over four decades of
> statutory regulations, since President Roosevelt invited Joseph Kennedy to
> turn gamekeeper and set up the Securities and Exchange Commission in
> 1934. The Americans had long practice of regulating the direct conflicts
> of interest, for example, when the same firm is dealing for itself and for
> its clients."

But on October 27th, all the City of London's traditional demarcation
lines were swept aside:

> "(In September) the Stock Exchange itself was forced into a shot-gun
> marriage with an upstart trade organisation, the International Securities
> Regulatory Organisation, which did not even exist a year ago, in order to
> keep billions of dollars worth of institutional business in London from going
> walkabout. . . There needs to be a statutory authority, clearly accountable
> to Parliament. . . Instead the system of regulation we are getting is going
> to be a dog's breakfast."

But what is that "dog's breakfast" going to cost in the end? And who
is going to pay for it? Before the end of 1987 people were to see it was too
late to do anything but pay up, and look cheerful?

The Walls of Jericho

The formation of conglomerates comprising banks, brokers, market-makers
and other types of fund manager have given a whole new dimension to

conflicts of interest. Moreover they can arise every step of the way. There can be a conflict of interest, for example, when a broker's analyst uncovers some price-sensitive piece of information. To whom does he owe his first duty? To the client, for whom the broker has acted for years as agent and advisor? Or should the analyst trip down the corridor to the market-makers' suite? The school-solution is that both should be told simultaneously. But since the market-makers are closer to the action — and in effect it is their finger on the trigger — they, not the client, will generally come off best. That was scarcely what the OFT can have had in mind when it turned the market upside down!

One major conglomerate, BZW, recognised this particular problem from the start. So the research team from de Zoete and Bevan took on the task of talking to clients; and the smaller research team, from the former jobbers Wedd Durlacher, were left to service the market-makers. So long as other teams did likewise, you might say, all would be well. But how long will this particular Chinese Wall prove effective? Time and again, share prices have often moved significantly before a particular rights issue or bid approach has been announced. Could this be put down to intelligent anticipation? Or was it a series of controlled leaks? Or chance remarks overheard in a wine bar? This sort of thing has always gone on, and is bound to continue. Neither computer screen displays, nor a mass of rules backed by the force of law, are going to change the fundamental nature of the market place; or the way the game is played. One side will always be trying to find out what the other side would rather it didn't.

From the investors' point of view, it is not only the rogue against whom they need protection. It is safe to say that although the villains have lifted millions off them over the years, investors have lost more money through their ignorance and ineptitude than through all the trickery and deception that the industry was capable of.

In fact, the first-time investors, whose numbers rose from an estimated 2 million before the British Telecom issue to 7 million by Big Bang, are different from those at any time in the past — except perhaps during the Railway Mania, or the ten years that the South Sea Bubble was being inflated. Many of those who entered the market from the British Telecom sale onwards have been encouraged to do so by the Government's campaign for wider share ownership. They were rarely individuals with the necessary thousand pounds-worth or so of "cool money", that is to say money they could afford to gamble with, and — above all — could afford to lose! They were, therefore, extremely vulnerable. That was why some City men were concerned when they discovered that new investors had never heard of "cool money". Some of them had taken their bank or building society accounts the small amounts of cash they had put away against a rainy day.

These are not the sort of clients who would normally have turned to a broker; nor are they the kind of client that a broker will go out of his way to attract. But there is no reason to think that the share shops and banks, and other institutions with shares for sale will be over-squeamish. Some of the newcomers on the salesman's side of the counter are genuinely doing their best to advise less sophisticated clients. But good intentions are not enough. The best advice that can be given to many of the new would-be investors is to persuade them to go home and have another "think". Indeed, one Investment Panel, organised by the Birmingham Stock Exchange, has made no bones about it. When a member of the audience gets up — as someone always does — to say, "My Aunt has left me a thousand pounds; what should I ask my broker?", the advice given without a moment's hesitation has been, "Ask him the way to the Post Office." I repeatedly tell my audiences that the Stock Exchange is far too dangerous a place for investors!

One of the complaints levied against the stockbroking community as a whole has been that they have tended to make the small investors unwelcome. As a result small investors have just not tried to buy shares on the Stock Exchange. But, in view of the kind of would-be investor coming forward since the wider share ownership drive, those stand-offish brokers would appear to have been performing a public service.

Already though, some first-time investors have taken the attitude, "What's the point of paying more than you must, when you know that the bank or broker you go to will probably be buying and selling shares on their own account as well as for the big institutions." One solution will be for the individual investor to seek out one of the brokers who intends to remain an independent agent. He, or she, may not necessarily belong to a large firm. In the Gilts market, for instance, one leading broker, Capel-Cure Myers decided not to join the ranks of the market makers. Instead C-CM, by adopting the agency broking solution, believes it can continue to be guided by the traditional principles of impartial advice, and "best execution" of the client's instructions. For the large institutions, the lower commissions they will be able to negotiate, and their long experience in the market means that they can deal with the market-makers direct. We have to see whether this is a competitive strategy. Those who attempted to do so after Big Bang in America failed.

Consider the amount of money that has been absorbed by British Telecom and British Gas, and will be absorbed in future by further privatisation issues. . . a minimum of £15 billions a year for the next two years. This could prove a very risky ploy, leading to a dangerous "crowding out." In front of the TSB launch, there was a huge net outflow from the building societies for the first time in 16 years. Subsequently there was a steady outflow from the Unit Trust industry, with redemptions exceeding sales. This trend is going to compound, and the end result will be a counter-productive, and self-destructive process in the course of which Unit Trusts, and other large holders of shares, are going to become illiquid. They will then be forced to dump a large quantity of shares on to an equally illiquid market. From the standpoint of market sentiment it will be a self-feeding process. What most newcomers fail to recognise is that eventually the privatisation issues will fall in the deflationary climate they have helped to create.

There is an extremely crude American expression applied to the stock market. It goes: "When the cops raid the whorehouse, they take all the whores."

It is bad enough that such a danger should exist, without the vast majority of the population — who would never normally wish to own a share — being set clamouring to join what they imagine as the favoured few. How far from the truth that really is! Donald Cobbett, who first joined the Stock Exchange in the 1930s, during the Great Slump, warns in his recent memoirs, entitled *Before the Big Bang* that:

> ". . . the strong will grow stronger, and the weak markedly more debilitated. The institutions. . . now have the ball wholly in their court. Of the future, the danger. . . visualised for the mass of investors, is of a two-tier, perhaps even a three-tier, market. An adequate market perhaps in 200/300 of the top equities; but an extremely questionable, perhaps wholly one-way, ultimately non-existent, market in several thousand capital issues for the rest of us. . . the Government through the agency of its lackeys, talks blandly about the advantages of choice! I ask. . . what choice for the small individual other than to invest at second hand via the vast collecting agencies for the public's savings?"

Now, we are told, all that belongs to the past. Banks, insurance companies, building societies. . . just about everyone is going to be selling shares. On Grey Friday there was news that badly shook many of the new investors. Teams from the Department of Trade and Industry moved in and closed two London "share shops"; and the department pressed a petition for the compulsory winding up of City Investment Centres, a company which ran the Finchley Road and New Bond Street shops. (The petition was presented under Section 440 of the 1985 Companies Act, which enables DTI to apply for a winding up order where it appears to be "in the public interest.") The DTI's action followed a four month investigation into complaints about late payment or late delivery of share certificates. This has been fairly frequent in the case of some firms conducting over-the-counter transactions; firms, it may be said, which continue to operate.

The question is, how long will the DTI be able to devote four weeks, let alone four months, to investigating clients' complaints now that Big Bang is behind us?

Much political capital has been made about the flood of new investors: the pioneers of *People's Capitalism*. A great deal of money has been spent launching British Telecom, TSB and British Gas. Not surprisingly, the attendance at *The Money '86 Show* at London's Olympia was extremely high. On the Saturday alone, no fewer than 6,000 people, of all ages, paid for admission. That is the same as the number of people now living within the London's Square Mile, generally supposed to be peopled by caretakers with wooden legs and lean, grey cats. Around 4,500 of them live in the 2,000 or so flats and maisonettes in the City Corporation's Barbican complex. It is still minute compared with the 130,000 or so who lived within the City's boundaries before the Great Fire of London, in 1666; or the 40,000 who inhabited London in Roman times. But it is a vast improvement on the miserable 4,200 or so — which included nurses, caretakers and the like — counted as residents in the 1971 census. The City is now fashionable, and set fair to become even more so. I moved in there myself sometime ago.

I wondered how many of the 6,000 Money Show attenders that Saturday were there because they had acquired their mortgage and still found their salary rising faster than inflation. How far was it a reaction to the Government's ceaseless litany, extolling the virtues of a mortgage-paying, share-gambling democracy. . . which is, incidentally, borrowed up to the hilt.

There were all the usual offerings to be found at such a Show. With Big Bang still reverberating in the background, British and American stockbroking firms were drumming away in strength. Among the banks, Nat West was displaying a touch-sensitive computer screen, currently under test. If the system passed the test, the bank's customers would then execute share transactions from some of Nat West's High Street branches. Never before in the course of market history had there been such an array of high-tech devices designed to attract and seduce the infant investor!

At the Money Show there were a large number of investors whom I have long called in my regular LBC broadcasts "the financially unwashed". They keep presenting proof of their identity by repeating the same mistakes over and over again. They can be distinguished by the great air of authority with which they will quote back to you the last thing said by the last person they met on their way to the John: usually someone with vested interest and a persuasive line of talk. But this time, at Money '86, "the great unwashed" — heaven protect them — were outnumbered by a new breed I had never met before. The breed could broadly be described as "the financially unwashable". They were Dame Nature's "no-hopers". Recently infected by the People's Capitalism virus, they were longing to pour their small savings down the first Black Hole they came across marked "Investment Opportunity".

Their inherent ineptitude and potential for self-destruction was a shock to everyone — even to the glib young sales-persons with their Porsches and expensive French perfume. For this vast herd of "financially unwashable", even taking the advice of the "hot-shots" would be safer. But the only advice the "unwashables" were prepared to take was likely to come from the seat of their pants. But who were the pawns in this army of new investors? Would they multiplying as fast as we were told?

Only a week after Big Bang, Dewe Rogerson (the PR firm advising TSB) were able to tell the press that the survey they had conducted for their client showed that even before the massive sale of British Gas shares there were already something like 7 million individual investors. *One in six Britons now a shareholder,* was *The Daily Telegraph's* headline. With the total now standing at 7 million, it also meant that three times as many people held shares then as in 1983. Surely this was proof — if proof were needed — of the success of Margaret Thatcher's dedication to the cause of *People's Capitalism.* Dewe Rogerson's deputy chairman was quoted (in the *Telegraph*) as saying:

"There is a new investor generation rapidly emerging. Over the next decade the face of financial Britain is set to change fundamentally."

The survey, said the report:

"(showed that) shareholders are becoming younger and more evenly spread by social class and, on the basis that 46 p.c. of the population want to do something better with their money and savings, Dewe Rogerson estimates that £40 billion is looking for a new home."

Specifically, the survey showed that the proportion of the top social class (AB) had declined from 56% to 35%. Class C1 accounted for 30%, C2 for 34%. There was, said the paper "a surprising 11 p.c. in the bottom DE bracket." Why that should have been "surprising" is hard to see. In the first place, the prime target for the *People's Capitalism* musketeers had to be the Cs, Ds and Es, since it is in those mainly uninvested sections of the population the *People* (according to the Thatcherite Gospel) are to be found.

On closer examination, the figures thrown up by the survey were by no means so significant as they seemed at first glance. To begin with, the estimated 7 million was based on a sample of no more than 933 respondents. This, some critics felt, was too small, pointing out that "the total included those in employee share schemes", although "the overall total is close to the Government estimates." Moreover one of the days chosen for the interviews was the 27th October, Big Bang day, when the British Gas campaign was also in full swing. Furthermore, as the *Telegraph* pointed out, some 60% of the total had "only one share, principally BT". So that meant that no more than 40% actually held shares in two or more companies.

At once "Maggie's Miracle" begins to shrink. It positively shrivels up once that Old White Magic (simple arithmetic) is applied. The results of the survey were hardly world-shaking in view of the high-pressure, high-cost marketing spree and the political shenanigans.

Clive Wolman *(Financial Times)* picked on several interesting points in the survey. One was that individual investors in June 1986 "accounted for only 18.6% of all transactions by value, compared with 28.4% in early 1983." Another pointed to the fact that different surveys have come up with different results. And the reason:

". . . many people do not automatically think of themselves as shareholders. They often need their memories jogged or to be reminded about company share schemes. . . The responses to any survey thus depend on how the questions are phrased."

A better description of the habits, and habitat, of the "financially unwashable" would be difficult to find. Seen from the broker's side of the contract note, there is no great love lost for that kind of client who spends perhaps twenty minutes on the telephone, and then decides to "think about it tomorrow." That was why Hoare Govett and de Zoete's set up their VDU-screen services a couple of years before Big Bang.

Ever since I've been involved in the London stock market, which dates back to the 1950s, stockbrokers have been complaining that even the most trouble-free small client business is totally unprofitable. It's a fair complaint. Most stockbrokers have geared their entire strategy to wooing the big institutional investor, which makes far better sense. Several thousand poundsworth of commission can be earned by writing just one contract note. Hundreds, if not thousands of contract notes are needed to earn the same level of commission from private investor deals.

Undoubtedly, Margaret Thatcher deserves the credit for having successfully encouraged the biggest explosion of private client business in British history. That is to say, excluding the South Sea Bubble and the Railway Mania. So far, so good. Though it must be very disappointing for Downing Street to discover (according to Roland Gribbon's *Telegraph* piece) that the provisional evidence of the TSB commissioned survey suggested "the explosion in private share ownership is not influencing political opinion, one of the Government's hopes in its State asset sales." But what happens now? Who will be prepared to handle this huge volume of largely unprofitable private investor business? There is certainly no reason to suppose it will become more profitable in the future. Not when you consider the rising cost of securities trading.

To sum up this whole "negotiated commissions" issue, I would say the small man or woman has gained nothing at all. Indeed, they often find themselves much worse off, since by the end of '87 we found the broker-jobber-conglomerates keen to handle small investor business becoming few indeed. Unabashed, some were making their charges high enough to keep the unwanted client at arm's length. "Negotiated commissions" are not the same as "acceptable commissions". Or even "reasonable commissions". Nor is there anything that anyone can do, under the new rules, to compel a broker to accept a client he does not wish to deal with. Not unless the client is willing to say, "To hell with the price!", and make a bull-headed dash for "quality"!

So, it seems, we are back where we started. Institutional investors still have the muscle to *negotiate* commissions and other costs. But the small investor — about whom the OFT, and the Thatcher Government have been shouting for the past three years — is being forced to take it or leave it! That is something that the reforming zealots should have thought about, before they rushed widely into battle like so many financial *Mujaheddin*.

It is still too early in the day to say precisely where the markets are likely to end up. But we do know that the Gilts market — which until Big Bang was served by just two jobbers — started off with no less than 27 primary market-makers. Everyone of them will be enjoying access to the Bank, as well as to the new Inter-Dealer Broker network. One task of the IDB's today is to enable the primary market-makers to deal anonymously with one another, without disclosing their book position. The market-makers' profits, like those of the jobbers, will arise both from the "turn" on each transaction and their success in anticipating price changes and adjusting their holdings appropriately. It will not be an easy row to hoe. The general expectation was that by no means all those who chose to become market-makers will stay the course. That has proved to be a correct assumption.

In the equity market, the same uncertainty prevailed. If commissions were to be cut, revenues would fall right across the board, unless the volume of trade increased sufficiently to make up the shortfall. There is a further dimension which must be considered. Volumes rise during a bull market, and fall during a bear market. Take the contrast between April 1986, when volumes rose above 40,000 bargains a day, and 1974, as we approached the nadir of that bear market. During December 1974, we were seeing bargains of between 4,000 and 5,000 a day. If London continued to experience the fall in aggregate commissions which occurred after October 1987, as did the American market after de-regulation, we would have the formula for a decline in the brokerage industry of a severity we have not seen before.

The May Day Massacre

It was not like the St Valentine's Day massacre. That was all over in a matter of minutes. The May Day massacre, which took place on Wall Street, was a gradual process, although the strains appeared almost at once.

Fixed minimum commissions had been agreed by two dozen brokers under the button-wood tree when share dealings began in New York in 1792. Following the passage of 183 years, market pressure and government edicts combined to force the replacement of fixed commissions by competitive brokerage rates on May Day 1975. Just as the German and other foreign banks had successfully put pressure on the London brokers in the early 1900s, so the large American institutions had been squeezing discounts out of the brokers by divers means. One of the most effective (as always) proved to be the simple threat to take their business elsewhere. For some time the Anti-Trust authorities had been asking why brokers of all people should enjoy the right to choose their fellows. Why should they fix the price that their clients would have to pay for their services?

It is one of the facts of modern political life that once it is accepted that the authorities have a duty to proceed against any trust or cartel merely because it exists, there can be no justification for concerted decision-making. Were the authorities to ask whether or not the trust or cartel was a benign one, the outcome could be very different. But that is not the way such bodies work. Besides, it might complicate an otherwise clear-cut issue. "To be or NOT to be", as W. Shakespeare Esquire put it.

For institutions, de-regulation was a gift. Between 1975 and 1980, commission rates on the disposal of 10,000 shares or more fell by 70%. That was allowing for inflation. The cartel rate was 0.74%. With competition, the rate was to fall to 0.16%. As in Britain before Big Bang, brokers had charged a fixed commission, seeking to outdo their rivals with the research and other services provided. Once competition became the order of the day, the Discount Brokers moved in, offering a no-frills service, which saved a private client betweent 33% and 60% compared with the pre-May Day commission rates. Generally, though, for the *same* service the private client tended to pay more.

Big Bang in the United States was followed by a long and strong bull market. The increase in business which developed helped to ease the problems which would normally be associated with so large a fall in commission turnover. Nevertheless, one third of the stockbrokers vanished.

Will London be able to survive Big Bang without a serious fall in total revenues, leading to the collapse of firms, and the departure of a sizeable proportion of the highly paid operators recruited by the new City groupings? Some have already gone. The United States was far better prepared than Britain on the eve of deregulation. American brokerage firms were far more highly capitalised than their British equivalent. In fact it is well known that UK firms have been under-capitalised for their task. It might appear that the firms which took over London brokers have compensated for their under-capitalisation. But only time will tell.

It would be unwise to harbour the illusion that those institutions which have bought minority stakes in various stockbrokers are going to support those firms if they run into real difficulties. If, as seems likely, a bear market coincides with the failures resulting from too many heavily capitalised groups chasing too little business, some private investors are likely to be caught. If they are, they will have far less protection than their counterpart in the United States, where Congress set up the Securities Investor Protection Corporation in 1970. Its object was to safeguard investors against the possible bankruptcy of a firm. Stockbrokers' accounts are required to be insured for $2,000,000. Many firms supplement this with additional protection up to $25,000,000 through independent insurers. Here in Britain, the Stock Exchange has had its own compensation fund, which has decided how much of the clients' loss shall be covered. But the fund has never faced the heavy risk it faces today.

It was to avoid a repetition of the abuses of the 1930s that the SEC, the Securities and Exchange Commission, was established in the United States. It was the domestic scandals in the London markets in 1981 which decided the DTI to ask the country's leading expert on Company Law, Professor Jim Gower, to review the whole area of investor protection. Although Professor Gower was known to prefer a statutory body like the SEC, this was not what the Government and the City wanted. They preferred to improve the system of self-regulation. To this end they devised the present two-tier structure, with the SIB, the Securities and Investments Board on top, and the Self Regulatory Organisations, the SROs, below.

The SIB, under Sir Kenneth Berrill, will not have anything like the sheer muscle of the SEC in the States, even with the considerable powers which the Department of Trade and Industry will delegate to it. Nor were the SROs to be fully operational until late 1987. From a strictly legal point of view the new regime was launched without any of the new and complex protective measures set out in the hard-fought and much-amended Financial Services Bill. In any case, lawyers will always maintain that no new Act can be regarded as "fireproof" until it has been tested in court.

If things go badly wrong, it is always on the cards that Government and City alike could be driven to adopt the SEC-type of statutory control; the kind Professor Jim Gower would have preferred in the first instance. At the moment, however, the players in the new Square Mile game are concentrating on surviving — or at least until 1988 has shewn its hand.

When I wrote *The Downwave,* I was anticipating the normal type of investor loss associated with a severe stock market decline in keeping with the cyclical bear market, which appears to have started in April 1986. What I did not envisage at that time was the dislocation that could be associated with Big Bang, the privatisation schemes that have been launched, and the inadequacies of investor protection. Therefore the financial holocaust I originally envisaged is now likely to be far more severe than I imagined. What we saw in the United States in 1929, which we describe as the Great Crash. . . the greatest bear market in history, is likely to turn out to have been a Teddy Bears' Picnic compared with what London could well be exposed to as we move on through to the 1990s.

The crash I now expect is likely to take a different path from that which I originally anticipated. Compared to 1929, the disaster may emerge more slowly, but will last longer, with little prospect of a swift recovery.

In 1954, I bought a share called Oil Recovery. In 1956, I sold that share at $45. By 1978, twenty years later, the share had fallen from $45 to $2. . . where it stands today. This is the kind of crunch I'm expecting.

Ever since the Chancellor's autumn statement in November '86, there has been a new political dimension to be considered. This still calls for a degree of guesswork — I prefer to be honest about it. It could help to look back 13 years to that last winter of our discontent; which, alas, brought nothing approaching a glorious summer.

The Moment of Truth

In 1974, the young men and women at today's dealing desks and VDUs were still concerned with the reasons why Caesar divided Gaul into Three Parts — if he ever did! Or why the fictional Square Root of Minus-1 still earns its keep in the age of the pocket calculator.

Unless unduly precocious, they will not have taken much notice of an event which occured during the Christmas "hols" in 1974. It was New Year's Eve, in fact, when there was a late night announcement. The Bank of England had provisionally agreed terms for bailing out Burmah Oil, which had run into a liquidity crisis, after a year which had seen a really vicious bear market.

Prices began soaring. The secondary banking crisis of the previous year, which had worked its way into the property market, brought a disastrous upheaval. Lloyds Bank reported that its Lugano Branch had suffered huge losses as a result of mishandling of its foreign exchange business. Commercial Union — that bulwark of the insurance world — faced a solvency crisis. The list of disasters and near disasters seemed endless.

Burmah Oil's troubles not only put the stopper on a thoroughly forgettable year; it sent the stock market sliding over the edge. On the third trading day of 1975, January 6th, the FT 30 Share Index came to rest on the bottom, at 146 exactly.

In February 1975, Edward Heath made the mistake of asking the nation what THEY thought about the militant miners. He received a very dusty answer. Labour took office once more. But the troubles that year were not all financial; nor was Edward Heath the only politician to suffer the slings and arrows of an outraged electorate. The Labour Government were to have no easy ride. Their majority was too small.

Mr Dennis Healey stands out as a Labour Chancellor that any moderate, middle of the road Conservative would have supported. Indeed, many of them did! Among those who remember that period, he is still spoken of as "the last Tory Chancellor the country had". But, as was clear at the start of 1987, that would not prevent a large number of people in the City from reacting nervously as the General Election began to loom in sight; especially if the Thatcher Government looked like falling.

In view of recent developments in the City, like Big Bang and the vast multi-billion sums committed as a result of the drive towards *People's Capitalism*, the dislocation could have been horrendous. Even if it did not reach such levels, the degree of volatility in all markets was likely to exceed anything known in stock market experience. The Indices had already began reflecting the direction of each Poll, and exaggerating its findings as Indices always will. Each Labour lead brought a small fall; each Conservative recovery a corresponding rise, mainly because of the perception of what a Labour Government MIGHT do.

Some leading members of the TUC had long ago realised that this would happen; especially abroad. They also realised that there was nothing Labour, or the Trade Unions, could do in advance to change their stereotype. Perception is stronger than any promise — unreality more persuasive than reality! Since no one is going to wait for the die to be cast, the nervousness, the selling, the final stage of blind panic — if such a thing occurs — could be seen well before polling day.

With hindsight, Mr Nigel Lawson's 1986 autumn statement indicated a confidence that surprised many people. He appeared to be willing to spend so much. But the indirect taxation we enjoy today thrives on higher prices and larger volumes. Improvident spending, and dangerously high levels of borrowing, are the VAT man's friend. Mr Lawson made that clear in his Budget of March 1987.

Taking the number of stockbrokers who went bankrupt in the period 1972 to 1975, we could well see three times that number going belly-up in the remainder of the 1980s. Even the wave of panic selling after 1987's Black Monday failed to generate sufficient volumes to support all the market-makers, or make up for the increasing cost of each transaction, after so many millions had been poured into steel, glass, concrete and computerised gadgetry; to say nothing of the small army of highly paid young men and women engaged to cope with a tidal wave of highly profitable business which never arrived.

1987 will long be remembered for the general state of unreadiness which prevailed in the City of London, to which the mountain of uncleared transactions bore witness. Concern over investor-protection gave way to fears that the cost of the regulatory system, coming on top of the rising cost of maintaining a barely adequate Stock Exchange, would price the small investors out of the market. It will also be remembered as the year of the pathetic BP share issue failure; which nevertheless failed to deter the more determined privatisation addicts, who clamoured until the doors finally closed to be allowed to purchase their slice of an already established loss.

With the Stock Exchange Chairman, Sir Nicholas (Big Bang) Goodison and the Governor of the Bank of England, Mr Robin Leigh-Pemberton confirmed in their respective offices, 1988 began as 1930 had done — with the same effusion of facile "explanations" as to why the October Crash had occurred.

Even December's disastrous trade figures failed to shake the cofidence of the City's soothsayers, as they continued their chant, in praise of the UK economy, the Chancellor of the Exchequer and the recovery which would soon be on the way. Ominously, it took until the end of January 1988 before BZW became the first major "player" to openly acknowledge the arrival of the 1980s bear market.

Chapter Six

SHAMS, SCAMS, SWINDLES AND FRAUDS. . . "BIG BANG" STYLE

Beware of false prophets, which come to you in sheep's clothing, but inwardly are ravening wolves. Ye shall know them by their fruits.
                                                        Matthew 7:15-16

If Matthew, an apostle of Christ, had been around around to help the London Stock Exchange prepare for the "Big Bang", there's no doubt that the outcome would not have been as calamitous as it was. Before he joined the disciples, Matthew was one of the shrewdest money managers around at the time. His original training was as a professional tax collector for those wheeler-dealer Romans.

Matthew and Jesus Christ were as natural a team as Hoare & Govett. Jesus Christ was certainly on a par with any of the foreign exchange dealers of today. He was quick to spot the machinations of the priests, who had devised a scheme for making a double profit from the exchange of currency. When he discovered what was going on at the Temple, he called it "a den of thieves" and slung the money changers into the street. Matthew also observed, "Every good tree bringeth forth good fruit; but a corrupt tree bringeth evil fruit."

Matthew 7: 15-17 was written in a vastly different atmosphere than that which prevailed following London's "Big Bang". It is nevertheless applicable to the capital markets we have today.

Alfred North Whitehead, the philospher and mathematician, spent a lifetime pursuing the evanescent discipline of logical thought. His claim was, "Two thirds of the people who can make money are mediocre; and at least half of them are morally at a low level." His comment on the morality and competence of those capable of amassing wealth must be considered the product of extremely astute personal observation.

In *The Downwave* I discussed the anatomy of a speculative orgy, and the changes in public morality that occur at the various stages of the Long Term economic cycle. At the terminal stage of the Long Term upward cycle, and at the late stages of a speculative boom, cheating and swindling become so common-place that thievery and malpractice are perceived as the norm. Business becomes brisk. The volume of transactions becomes enormous. The paper mountain makes the individual feel that detection is well-nigh impossible. The unscrupulous flourish. There seems to be a negative correlation between business ethics and the level of the various stock market indices during a boom.

Charles P. Kindleberger, in his classic work *Manias, Panics and Crashes*, says, "Commercial and financial crises are intimately bound up with transactions that overstep the confines of law and morality, shadowy though these confines be." The tendency to swindle, and be swindled, seems to run parallel to the extent and duration of the speculative boom. The numbers of swindlers and those being swindled would appear to rise in direct proportion to the number seduced by the speculative mania. The reasons are multifarious. Obviously, the number of swindles will increase in step with the number of sheep available for slaughter. There is also a tendency during a speculative boom for those with a modicum of ability, and an inclination towards thievery, to rise to positions within the securities industry where their inherent traits can be exercised.

Each boom-phase tends to develop from the ashes of a previous boom that has collapsed. The inexperienced and unknowledgeable usually suffer the most during such a collapse. At the early stages of a boom, the active participants are therefore likely to be the most astute professional investors, who are able to quantify and accept risk. At the early stage of a boom, most small investors, caught in a prior collapse, vow never again to become involved in speculative markets.

It was J.K. Galbraith who remarked, "Financial genius is a short memory in a rising trend." As a new boom emerges from the debris of the previous collapse, an increasing number of investors are attracted by the glitter of rising prices. The greater the amplitude and duration of a boom, the larger the number that become mesmerised by it. The average level of expertise and experience, therefore, falls as the average price levels rise.

Ultimately, "The Greater Fool Theory" becomes the driving force. People purchase investments for no other reason than the hope that a greater fool than them will appear, willing to pay even more than they did for the speculative 'counters'. As the speculative boom becomes a mania, all and sundry begin speculating, gambling with their savings, with borrowed money. . . and, sometimes, embezzled money. The thought that the price level of the vehicle of speculative pursuit could ever fall is unthinkable. . . inconceivable!

When the speculative boom enters its final stages, the rational profit potential that tempted sophisticated investors in the early stages completely evaporates. As the boom progresses, an increasing number of investors are attracted merely because of the steady rise in prices, nothing more. The greater and more protracted the price rise, the more people are willing to take action completely uninhibited by thought. The level of intellectual achievement shared by the average investor declines in inverse ratio to the price of the boom vehicle.

The Greater Fool Theory introduces a steady stream of speculators willing to pay progressively higher prices for the same intrinsic worth. But ultimately the Greatest Fool of All makes his entrance, willing to pay so high a price that he'll never find anyone to sell to. So once that last buyer, the Fool of Fools appears, the professionals — who have been impatiently awaiting his arrival — know there is only one way prices can go now. . . and that's DOWN! A long, long way down. At the peak of a speculative boom the financially unwashed, and the financially unwashable, become a dumping ground for over-valued, over-priced parcels of garbage shares that professional dealers always try to unload before the smell attracts too much attention.

At the incipient stages of a crisis, a divergence begins to appear. An increasing number of traditional areas of investment begin to show signs of weakness, as a result of professional liquidation. Marginal ventures begin to merge, in an attempt to show greater promise that the more conventional investment. New financial products are devised. Imitations of earlier ventures that have proved profitable appear in fancy packaging, especially for the new breed of financially unwashed and unwashable. Such investment vehicles have long lost their lustre for the more astute investor.

Greed, and the desire for a quick profit, lead the newcomers further and further away from normal market criteria and established investment channels. Impecunious market operators appear in increasing numbers, promising the unskilled and unschooled all manner of fantastic gains. Frauds and swindles proliferate. What has been described as a "mania" and a "bubble" is the ultimate result. According to economist Hyman Minsky the word "mania" emphasises the type of irrationality that occurs during the final stages of a boom. The word "bubble" foreshadows "bursting" which inevitably occurs.

The financially unwashed, and the financially unwashable, entered the market place of the 1980s firmly convinced that share prices would rise in perpetuity. They held with the conviction that should share prices fall, the fall would only be temporary, and that prices would soon rise again to even higher levels. This attitude, reflected in the lemming-like behaviour of the average small investor on the eve of the British Gas flotation, has been precursor to every single capital market crash in history — from Tulipomania to the bursting of the Hunt brothers' Silver Bubble.

In certain circles, they call it share-pushing. In Canada, it attracts the attention of the Royal Canadian Mounted Police. In America, you go to a federal prison for it. Under the Thatcher administration, it is called advertising and promotion; and you pay £200 million to achieve your object!

The series of privatisation commercials (that would have put any bucket shop to shame) saw a mad stampede to purchase these issues. So seductive have been the advertising and promotion, that people have been ready to draw heavily on their savings accounts. National Savings were especially hard-hit before the British Gas flotation.

People have given their savings, persuading themselves into believing they were investing. In all reality, they had been doing nothing more than speculating with their hard earned cash. In most cases, the new breed of investor has little or no idea of the intrinsic worth of what he is buying, or the many factors that govern future potential performance. One issue after another has been over-subscribed. People have simply been buying because other people have been buying, whether the privatisation was British Gas or the Sahara Harbour Board. It wouldn't have made a difference. They have been prepared to pay several multiples of the companies' value in the expectation of a quick profit.

It was a costly business for the taxpayer, according to some critics. Within an hour and a half of the start of dealings on Monday 8th December 1986, the number of British Gas shares traded broke through the 520.8 million level — the record established for a whole day's equity trading on November 14th. By the end of the session, over 800 million British Gas shares had changed hands. Most small investors were unable to sell their shares until they received their allotment letters more than a week later. This fact alone, said some observers, created what amounted *de facto* to a false market in the shares. They questioned whether any corporation in the private sector would have been allowed to hold back a section of shareholders in this way. Technically speaking, it was NOT a false market, since there was nothing to stop the private investor from selling. . . except the near impossibility of finding someone prepared to buy the shares that the investor thought (or hoped) were his. Tony Blair, a Labour Party Treasury spokesman, estimated that the premium at the start of dealing meant that foreign interests should have earned more than £75 million which:

> ". . . will be made on the first day of trading by foreign interests, many of whom will take this sum immediately as profit. This is roughly equivalent to the amount given by Britain to Live Aid."

Overall, he reckoned that underpricing BG shares would have cost the taxpayer £600 million — equivalent to £30 from each household in the UK:

> "It is not encouraging a long-term bet on British industry, but a one way bet against the Exchequer."

The Labour spokesman also released a letter he had received from the Financial Secretary to the Treasury, Norman Lamont. This claimed that "the price of the shares was set in the light of market conditions and took account of the interests of the taxpayer."

Despite many warnings to deal through Stock Exchange member firms — and thus enjoy some cover — the delay before they could get to the official stock market with their British Gas shares tempted quite a few people to sell through well advertised, over-the-counter dealers. Most came to no harm. But in one case, almost 1,000 investors came to grief. Since the Financial Services Act was still not in force, they had to bear their own losses. But, even if they had received their letters of allotment in time to sell through the Stock Exchange on December 8th, many no doubt would still have been lured to the over-the-counter dealers by the promise of low charges. Even before the British Airways offer closed in February 1987, one enterprising dealer was making a price on the *grey* market.

The archetypal newcomers seemed to think that all they were required to do was to drop the coin into the slot, and wait for the candy bar to fall into their hands. The element of fantasy ballooned in direct proportion to the size and advertising budget of each successive issue — British Gas being the biggest, and therefore the grandest of them all. The Gas flotation, as you may recall, introduced the mythical Sid. Three days before the issue, the elusive Sid dissolved into misty vapour on the mountainside. Alas, the odds are that the high bonus of many an eager newcomer will have the same unsatisfactory ending.

As though there were not enough traps for the unwary already, January 26th 1987 was nominated for the launch of the so-called Third Market: the forum for the shares of comparatively new, unquoted companies. Other companies were expected to come from the former over-the-counter market, and the ranks of the mineral exploration companies, whose shares were previously traded under Rule 535(3). By 1988, the Stock Exchange predicted some 60 companies would have joined. Accountants Touche Ross expected to see as many as 200 companies on the Third Market by then. Whether this will ultimately prove a blessing, or a pitfall for the inexperienced, remains to be seen. On the basis of recent experience, I fancy it is more likely to be the latter.

Innocents Abound and Abroad

It is not in industry alone that there is cause for concern; and a huge gap between the perception and the reality. For example, I was alarmed at the contrast between the type of investor at the 1986 Money Show and his or her counterpart a year earlier. At the 1985 Money show, the numbers had been nothing like so large. But the level of interest shown was far higher; the enquiries were more intelligent and to the point — often, actually, deflected by thought! During the series of lectures I gave at the 1985 Money Show, there had been a degree of reason, and some knowledge behind most of the questions they asked me at the end of each session. There was nothing like that at the 1986 Money Show. Then, I suspect, a high proportion of those who attended my lectures did so merely to hear me tell them what they felt they wanted me to tell them; to be convinced of the things of which they wanted to be convinced.

I suspect they saw me as a kind of medium, a Spirit Guide to the financial afterworld; there to provide a link between their very earthy desires and the magic land of Rich Ever After, on the Other Side. I am sure that the number of television appearances I made during 1986 had far more to do with the level of attendance than the quality of the information they were seeking. In terms of telling them what they wanted to hear, I'm afraid they were to be disappointed. No sooner had they taken their seats, than I was challenging their most cherished preconceptions. . . crushing their dreams of the Great Wealth that was there for the taking. Little wonder that I encountered their vehement indignation! Especially when I spoke disparagingly of the nonsense that had been dinned into them in their homes by the media; or the brain-washing they had been subjected to by those with vested interests in the Securities Industry, who saw them as pigeons to be plucked — or as a bottomless well of juicy commissions.

During 1986, the methods used to promote People's Capitalism were the epitome of share-pushing. Shops were opened on the High Street, selling shares like cans of peas. There are now areas within major department stores where you can select shares along with other "trivial pursuits". The sales staff in some of them claim you can complete the entire transaction and walk away clutching your contract note inside ten minutes. Potential investors could be seen poring over the chalked up lists in the High Street shops and Department stores, selecting. . . 100 of those! Say, 200 of those! And, I think, 150 of *that* lot. . . there! Like choosing a selection of sweet biscuits.

Whereas in the past the majority of the investing public made contact mainly with agents pure and simple, some of the dealers they encounter will be out to sell shares which they own. Writing in the *Daily Mail* on October 25th 1986, two days before Big Bang, Michael Walters warned that:

> "Banks, and even some building societies, may soon display share prices on a screen in their office. . . Members of the Stock Exchange, respectable names, may start to telephone you at home to push their wares. . . The person who telephones you with a deal — any deal — always has an angle, he wants your money."

If it was difficult to take everything a salesman said for granted in the past, it is likely to be an even more dicey proposition in future. Is it reasonable to suppose that any firm — whether a big name or a back-alley dealer — is going to send its pushiest salesman after you merely because they want to do you a good turn? Or is it because they feel they simply MUST warn you not to buy those *terrible* shares they bought for themselves in a fit of absent-mindedness? Michael Walters summed up the position post-Big Bang without pulling any punches:

> "Life out there in the share jungle is going to grow more dangerous than ever for the unwary. On Monday, two hundred years of Stock Exchange history is going to be blown sky-high. . . The bright young men are polishing their Porsches. . . and half the senior stockbroking partners have retired quietly to the country to count their cash. . . What's in it for you?"

It must be borne in mind that the euphoria over the new generation of shareholders, like that over the growing army of mortgagee-occupiers, was not without its uses. It tended to cover up the decline in the real economy in general, and manufacturing in particular. One of the saddest spectacles during December 1986 was that of the state-owned Rover Group's so called £100 million "Development Plan". It was announced with a flourish by Rover's Chairman, Graham Day: the man called back from Canada, at the behest of the Prime Minister herself. On his appointment, this brusque, no-nonsense tycoon was lauded by the media as the man who would SAVE Rover from a fate worse than that of the BL Group, the name discarded in the hope that the public — who'd been paying — would soon forget the Group's earlier losses.

The dynamic saviour's development plan turned out to be no more than a plan for a massive shopping centre development at Rover's redundant Bathgate truck plant centre in Scotland. Said Graham Day:

> "We were faced with the option of simply doing nothing and waiting for
> a developer to come along with a project or coming up with our own idea.
> The site is costing us money and is not producing revenue."

It did not occur to Mr Day that he had another, even more obvious option: to sell the site for what he could get and concentrate on improving the core business.

There was not long to wait before there was more news from what the *FT*'s Midlands correspondent called "Austin Rover, the UK volume car company." It was disclosed on New Years Day, 1987 that Austin Rover was seeking another £400 million to cover losses as well as funding the Rover Group corporate plan, submitted to Government just before Christmas. Observers believed that as Mrs Thatcher's choice, Chairman Graham Day was in a strong negotiating position. Some Ministers might object to more money being poured down the same hole, but they would know perfectly well that the refusal of indirect State aid for the West Midlands' components companies would be tantamount to throwing away several marginal Conservative seats.

Rumblings were to be heard from some very unexpected quarters as 1986 came to its close. Small British companies — supposedly the darlings of the Thatcher administration — were effectively being denied access to EEC loans because the Government had withdrawn currency exchange risk cover in the past 18 months. Without that cover, the loans available from the Community were not attractive to small firms.

The *Director* magazine is the organ of one of the most alert and active right-wing lobby bodies, the Institute of Directors. As such, it belongs in a very different camp from the *Guardian, Observer* or *Independent*. Yet the editorial in its January 1987 number took a remarkably jaundiced view of the designation of 1986 as "Industry Year":

> "It doesn't seem to have achieved all that much, except to give journalists
> an opportunity to interivew a selection of the great and the good on the

perennial topic of our national decline. . . I haven't met many business men who have been totally enthused by Industry Year. Their most common comment. . . is that, like Japan, 'every year should be industry year'."

From an independent source, Monks, remuneration consultants, came evidence of further cause for concern. Despite all the speeches made about the importance of engineers and engineering, it transpired that engineering executives were the lowest paid. Finance and planning executives could command an annual salary of £30,000; administration and secretarial executives, £27,500; but technical executives, £25,000. In metals and mechanical engineering, chief executives could command no more than £40,250. In construction and building materials it went as low as £37,600.

Finance, it appeared, is a readily transferable skill, commanding a premium over all other functions but general management.

A report was published three days later, by the Electricity Consumers' Council, pointing out that 2.5 million families would lose the extra supplementary payments to help with heating when the new Social Security Act came into force. The author of the report, Professor Jonathon Bradshaw, of the Social Policy Research Unit at York University, said:

> "The biggest losers (would) be tenants on estates with heating systems designated by the DHSS as exceptionally expensive to run. Around 80,000 householders are involved and they will lose up to £8.80 a week."

The Act was due to come into force in April 1987, but was postponed for a year because of "administrative difficulties". Would it be too cynical to say, "For *administrative difficulties* read *electoral reasons.*"?

You will have noticed by now that very little of all this fits in with the advice (or the promises) that Nanny Thatcher — and the "older boys" — have been giving the "little ones" over the past seven and a half years. Nevertheless, there have been some revealing moments: for example when Lord Whitelaw told a Conservative Women's Conference that he kept hearing people say they did not like the way Conservative policy was being presented. That usually meant, he told them, they didn't like the policies. He then passed quickly on to the next question. More recently, there was Energy Secretary Peter Walker's New Year plea to Government to ensure that Britain did not increasingly become two nations — "one employed and one unemployed, a prosperous South and a poor North".

Was this anything more than a routinely pious plea?, asked some Conservatives. After all, who could claim that it had not happened already? A *Mori* poll, conducted for the *Economist* magazine, and published in the press on 2nd January 1987, pointed out that nearly half the electorate disliked the idea of a hung Parliament. (Which meant that *more* than half were probably in favour.) The most apt comment on that poll came from another Conservative. She said simply, "It depends who's going to get hung!" But what do the electorate really believe? And how far is their belief based on anything more than habit or a sudden gut reaction? The minority vote which returned Margaret Thatcher for a third term, must give some indication of the nation's feelings.

Face to Face with the Greater Fool

During the course of one of my lectures at the 1986 Money Show, I decided to encourage a little audience participation. At the beginning of my lectures, I show a video that gives details of my background, experience and past achievements. At the end of the video, on this occasion, I explained to my audience that since they knew quite a bit about me, I thought I might learn a little bit about them. And since *they* were going to ask me questions at the end, I thought I might begin by asking *them* a few questions at the start. I first asked how many of them had read my book, *The Downwave,* and listened to my broadcasts on LBC. Considering the size of the audience, the number who appeared relatively — and regularly — well-informed were alarmingly few. (These occasions really do nothing for the *Ego.)*

I then asked how many thought we were now in a bear market. . . and how many were *certain* we were now in a bull market. After counting hands, I stepped down from the platform and walked over to one man who had put his hand up for the Bulls. "Why do you believe we're still in a bull market?" He eyed me somewhat suspiciously. "Put it another way," I said, "where's the evidence?"

"Well," he replied — somewhat defensively, I thought, "Anyone can see that the economy is doing well. Corporate profits are doing well. The stock market is still going up!" He had a really self-satisfied look on his face. I ignored that. Instead I challenged him straight out, "C'mon, you must know that a bear market starts well before corporate profits begin to turn down, and when there isn't a cloud in the economic sky. Besides, in April 1986 the FT Share Index reached 1,425. Yet in the summer of '86, it went below 1,200. At the time this Money Show opened, it was only 60 points or so above the summer lows. So. . . where's the bull market?

The man looked at me. I think he wished me dead. I moved in for the kill! "1,425 in April. . . and what now?" I forget the precise figure, but it was well down. I said as much. One or two people around him nodded. They could see I was right, but they still resented my putting them on the spot. "Put it another way. . ." I continued. "What WOULD convince you the Bears had come to call?" The man just looked away. "Right!" I thought. So I switched the approach. "OK. . . *you* tell me how far the market's got to fall before you'll see the red light and start selling." *That* hit home. I pressed him further. "Would it have to fall, say. . . 10%, or 15% or 20%? Just tell me. . . how much?" (Dammit, I thought. He must have some idea!) He looked up at me, in a kind of defiant way, "I'd say. . . 30%". The guy next to him nodded in agreement.

I wanted to be quite clear about this: so I repeated the figure. "If the FT 30 fell 30% you'd think of selling. Is that right?"

"Sure that's right," the man replied grudgingly. Those sitting around him seemed to agree too. . . to judge by their expression. So I turned and went back on to the platform. "Ladies and Gentlemen." I said to the audience at large. "You realise the FT 30 Share Index is a Blue Chip Index. . . like the Dow Jones Industrial Average." Again, general nods and grunts all round. (Though I knew that the expression "Blue Chip" was way above the heads of some of them.) "However. . . ," I said, letting my eye roam over the assembled multitude. "Not *everyone* has a portfolio stuffed entirely with Blue Chip. . . top quality shares. Most of us have quite a few second-line issues too. Right? They many be fine. . . when the market's fine. But if the FT 30 Share Index falls by 30%, I guess you can expect those other shares to fall by as much as 50%."

The odd tense cough. A little foot-shuffling. Silence again. This was the time to strike. "It seems our friend. . . down there. . . is actually prepared to see half the value of his shareholding cut right away before he's willing to admit. . . even to himself. . . that the Bears have replaced the Bulls in the market's Great Menagerie. Would you call that a sound investment strategy?" I looked around the hall. . . at the front rows, left and right. At those at the back. . . at the furthest, darkest corners for the last time. "Right then. . . " The silence by now was so intense that you could almost feel it. "Right, then. . . " I said. "That's your choice. It's your privilege." What I didn't say was that I had suddenly realised the Greatest Fool of All Fools was sitting right there. . . in the front row. . . with others of his fraternity in the adjacent seats.

The Insider Stealers

When *The Downwave* was published in 1983, many of the components required for a genuine speculative mania were already at hand. . . just waiting to be put together. I'd seen speculative manias before. . . and the Bubbles they produced. By '83, I reckoned, the Bubble was big enough to produce a shattering detonation once it burst. Now, three years later. . . four years later, I realise we'd really seen nothing in 1983. Nothing, that is, to compare with the unparallelled, misguided waves of speculative fervour of '86. It was more intense than anything I had seen in my 30 years as an investment analyst.

I also realised that until the autumn of 1986 one vital ingredient had been missing: an ingredient which has, without exception, deflated most speculative Bubbles. I mean the presence of the swindler and fraudster. In November 1986, that arch-demon made his appearance in the guise of the Insider Dealer — the *Insider Stealer* as he's come to be called.

The first example of financial fraud was fairly innocuous, involving the multiple application for shares in the Trustee Savings Bank. Accountants Peat Marwick, who were employed to weed out the multiple applications, investigated 5,000 forms for more than 1,000 applicants. Twenty people were eventually referred to the fraud squad for making illegal applications. The names reported by the TSB were linked to more than 1,000 application forms in September 1986.

On the other side of the Atlantic, as the Trustee Savings Bank fraud was being flaunted in the media, allegations were levied against Dennis Levine, Managing Director of Drexel, Burnham Lambert Inc.. Levine was charged with acting on inside information obtained in conspiracy with others. Following an investigation, two prominent US investment bankers were identified by the SEC as supplying Levine with confidential material.

The Trustee Savings Bank fraudsters were not considered to be of any great significance. Multiple applications for new issues that were likely to be oversubscribed have been a City tradition. But as a result of the massive privatisations and flotations, and the numbers involved, multiple applications could no longer be tolerated. The City and members of the investing public assumed that the charges made against those who were submitting applications for TSB shares, were intended as a warning to others.

At the time the news became public, the activities of Dennis Levine were considered a "one-off" affair rather than the thin edge of the type of mass fraud that has served to prick the speculative bubbles of the past. It is sufficient to say that public concern was not aroused by either the Dennis Levine affair or the Trustee Savings Bank scapegoats, albeit an amber light was flashing.

A development that did arouse the Department of Trade and Industry concerned irregularities in the High Street. The sudden closure of City Investment Share Shops, deemed by the DTI to be in the public interest, began to arouse public concern in early November 1986, following reports that many investors who had purchased and paid for shares from the convenient High Street shops, never had sight of any share certificates. In a large number of cases, the share shops had received the money for the shares, but the registrars of the companies had not received the share transfer forms within the time scale normally expected.

Nat West informed the DTI that they had received a number of inquiries from other anxious customers who had bought Britoil shares through the share shops but never received certificates. Nor was there any evidence, said the registrars concerned, that the shares had ever been purchased. It seems that a similar situation came to light at Lloyds Bank, the registrars for British Telecom. In an inordinate number of cases, the Lloyds Bank registrars' department could find no evidence that the individuals inquiring about their share certificates had ever purchased the shares.

In the case in point, the Department of Trade and Industry also became concerned because creditors of companies related to the share shops had filed petitions for winding-up.

City Investment Centres was not a member of the Stock Exchange. So investors who dealt with them were not covered by the Stock Exchange Compensation Fund, or any other fund for that matter! The Financial Services Act, which is intended to introduce an industry-wide investor compensation scheme for investors, was not yet in effect at the time the share shops were closed. Investors who had given their money to the share shops would appear to be in the same position as those who lost their money when MacDonald Wheeler, the money management group, failed in September 1986. For many years I have warned investors of the dangers of dealing with other than a recognised member of the Stock Exchange. But avarice habitually lays caution to rest. The licensed dealers in securities, who are not members of the Stock Exchange, offer dealings without commissions; and will frequently offer to pay slightly above the odds for shares they think people might want to sell. The temptation appears irresistible to the greedy, inexperienced investor who has yet to learn there is no such thing as a free lunch. When it comes to securities dealings, the cheapest "lunch" can turn out — literally — to be ruinously expensive in the end. And excruciatingly difficult to swallow.

The City, which is synonymous with the nationwide securities industry, is full of special types, nearly all of whom are arrogant. Some of them are very rich; and some of them, according to the rules the average citizen obeys, are very crooked. Behind the gleaming smiles, the pin-striped suits, the school ties and the red carnation lies very often an inner contempt for the average investor. He or she is seen as a willing receptable for the remnants of a new, shaky issue; or some tired share that the City's firms or its principles would like to unload.

The rules that govern the securities industry are written by the City and endorsed by its members. The rules which were drafted in anticipation of Big Bang would allow the City and its members to be even more larcenous than ever before should they choose to be. The City still acts as though it is immune to the Common Law, even though dishonesty is well documented. Its sorry record stretches back a very, very long way.

In the 1720s, when the stock market swindle known as the South Sea Bubble was exposed in England, it rocked the Crown. But this fraud was only froth compared to the vast number of scams, frauds and swindles on the contemporary scene, which the City has failed to prevent.

The Witch Hunt Gains Momentum

The pursuit of some fully accredited witches began in the autumn of 1986, following the failure of the Macdonald Wheeler Group and the closure of the share shops.

The first "witch" to be discovered was Geoffrey Collier, a 35 year-old performer in the securities industry, who was rocketed from a junior post with stockbrokers Grieveson Grant to become head of Morgan Grenfell's newly created securities business. This was built on the Big Bang urge to integrate Morgan Grenfell's acquisition of stockbrokers Pember & Boyle and stock jobbers Pinchin Denny.

Collier, whose annual earnings were reported by the media at various levels between £100,000 and £300,000, was accused of buying 50,000 shares of AE, a Midlands-based engineering firm which was then engaged in fighting a takeover bid by Turner & Newall.

It is believed that Collier effected the purchase as a result of inside information to which his position at Morgan Grenfell gave him access.

The share purchase was made through a Cayman Island company which Collier controlled. This company was also believed to have been used for the purchase of two residences in America. As an employee of Morgan Grenfell, Collier was under a general instruction that any share orders he made, both in his job and privately, should be placed through Morgan Grenfell's own securities subsidiary, of which he was joint Chief Executive. The purchase of the 50,000 AE shares was placed with Michael Cassell, the head of Vickers da Costa's stockbroking office in Los Angeles.

A reconstruction of events is believed to run as follows: Sometime during 2nd November 1986, Collier was contacted by the Corporate Finance Divison of Morgan Grenfell for the purpose of receiving a briefing on the bid that Robert Maxwell's Hollis Group intended to make for AE. Morgan Grenfell's task was to advise Maxwell on the terms of the bid which was to be announced when the stock market opened the following Monday. At 8 o'clock in the morning on 3rd November, which would have been midnight 2nd November in Los Angeles, it is thought that Michael Cassell of Vickers da Costa received the telephone order to buy 50,000 AE shares. Cassell relayed the instruction back to the Scrimgeour Vickers office in London. The order for the 50,000 share of AE was then split between Scrimgeour's own market-makers and the Chase Securities market-makers. By approximately 8.15 on 3rd November, 45 minutes before dealings were to begin on the London Stock Exchange, the Cayman Island Company, of which Collier was in charge, was in possession of its 50,000 shares of AE at 236 pence.

At 9 am on the morning of the 3rd November, as dealings began on the London Stock Exchange, an announcement was flashed on to the TOPIC screens in the City. Robert Maxwell's Hollis Group was making an agreed cash offer for AE, worth 260 pence a share. Within seconds, the price of AE stock jumped by 31 pence to 267 pence. What happened following that eventful moment, remains a mystery. It probably will always be a mystery. According to various press reports, Chase Securities and Scrimgeour were deeply concerned over the 50,000 AE share transaction and decided to move into action. I find this somewhat difficult to grasp. Deals of this nature are going on all of the time. I really cannot see why this particular transaction should have aroused such suspicion. It was not that large, nor was the profit;

not compared to certain other transactions of a similar nature over the years.

But, as the story goes, Chase Securities and Scrimgeour, jointly and simultaneously, found the purchase of the AE shares too timely and too obviously well informed. The order that came from Los Angeles was quickly traced back to Collier, who used to work for Vickers da Costa as head of its North American operations. Cassell had been a subordinate. Scrimgeour Vickers called in lawyers on both sides of the Atlantic to trace through the stages of the deal. Solicitors Linklaters and Paines were retained in London. Collier resigned his position at Morgan Grenfell and prepared to face criminal prosecution.

The entire affair has the aroma of a chosen scapegoat for reasons best known to the wardens of the City game reserve. After all, Geoffrey Collier was a shrewd operator. He had been around the City for quite some time, and was fully aware of the methods that could be used effectively to escape detection. Collier complained vociferously that he was being fingered for activities which are endemic in the City. One newspaper reported that Collier alleged that several Fund Managers dealt on the basis of inside information.

There is little doubt among those acquainted with the regular antics within the Square Mile, that there are a large number of "inside" deals and "inside dealers". Of this, there can be no question. Stock Exchange officials have complained for years that their investigations of "gangs" of insider traders habitually run up against a battery of offshore companies, nominee names and secret bank accounts, held in countries where financial privacy and secrecy are the rule. For the shrewd operator the risk of detection is minimal. Prosecution is even less likely, as the small number of prosecutions for insider trading bears out.

Files have been submitted to the DTI for many years. They have decided there was insufficient evidence for a successful prosecution. Since it was made a criminal offence in 1980, several hundred cases of alleged insider deals were pursued in six years. Of 108 cases meriting investigation, thirty-five involved a full scale probe. A mere five cases, involving seven individuals, were investigated by DTI inspectors. Of the seven, four were found guilty, two were acquitted and one case was still outstanding in November 1986. "Everybody knows it is happening, and we even have a fair idea who is doing it," was the statement of one senior City figure in a discussion with *The Sunday Times,* "But proving insider trading is notoriously difficult. The SEC only got Levine because the Bank Leu in the Bahamas co-operated."

It was the Stock Exchange's *ad hoc* committee of investigation that sent the Collier documents to the DTI. Following the Collier affair, Vickers da Costa, the stockbroking firm owned by Citicorp, discovered further transactions executed by Collier. Jeremy Paulson-Ellis, Chairman of Vickers da Costa and non-executive Director of Scrimgeour Vickers, received a menacing telephone call at his office, threatening him and his family. After that, when Paulson-Ellis went out in London at night it was with a bodyguard.

Police in Kent, where he lives, were also alerted. We used to think in London we had nothing in common with the Chicago-style bootlegging days of the 1920s, where blood flowed freely in the streets, or with the wars of the Mafia lawlords in New York in the 1930s and '40s. But this is the level of morality that prevails in the City of London in the post-Big Bang days of the 1980s.

Supporters of Big Bang, and what it entails, insist that the Geoffrey Collier incident was initially unconnected with Big Bang. The builders of the Chinese Walls claim that this kind of thing could have happened at any time. What else would you expect them to say? The fact is that it didn't.

One spin-off of Big Bang and computerisation has thrown up a new and more efficient form of insider trading. Every Friday afternoon, the wheeler-dealers rally around the video screen to plan the following week's deals. It's a comparatively simple process. First they look for the fastest rising shares on the week, and then on the day. After that they pick up Crawfords Directory to see which banks advise those companies whose shares have become fast movers. Next comes a quick glance at the Bankers' Almanac to see who is employed in departments of those companies advising possible takeover candidates. After that, a few discreet telephone calls and a luncheon invitation for those who are notoriously loose-lipped about takeover activity. Without the new computerised dealing systems, none of these wondrous feats would be possible.

In America They Do It Bigger. . . A Lot Bigger!

An influential ingredient in the witch-hunting that nearly always occurs during a long-term market decline is the element of envy. There are those who would like to cover their own tracks by providing scapegoats as a focus of attention when pickings are slim. There are also a large number who never did all that well when pickings were rich. They gain great pleasure from informing, where they can, on those who did exceptionally well. Such is the concept of morality of the City of London and Wall Street.

It was an informant who brought about the disgrace of Geoffrey Collier, who did reasonably well, although on the purchase of the AE shares all he came out with was a profit of £15,000. It was also an informant at Bank Leu in the Bahamas who brought about the downfall of Dennis Levine. He had amassed a fortune of $12 million! But there could have been no better target for envy in the securities industry than Ivan Boesky. He amassed a fortune of $200 million, the greater part of which is now believed to have come from insider dealing.

The Ivan F. Boesky scandal broke soon after the Geoffrey Collier affair. Ivan F. Boesky, Wall Street's leading arbitrageur, was permanently barred from the securities industry and agreed to disgorge $50 million in profits from dealings and $50 million in penalties, in the largest ever "insider dealing settlement with America's Securities and Exchange Commission".

The SEC discovered a link between Ivan F. Boesky and Dennis Levine, who merits further attention. The SEC claimed that Levine provided Boesky with "inside" information about ending deals with several companies between February 1985 and February 1986. During one of the most prodigious waves of merger mania in Wall Street history, Boesky allegedly made a profit of $4 million from the Inter-North/Houston Natural Gas deal. A smaller deal, which only netted him a profit of $975,000 was the FMC Corporation reconstruction deal. Other deals which brought in similar amounts were those involving American Natural Resources Company, Boise Cascade Corp, General Foods Corp and Union Carbide.

It was the claim of the SEC that Dennis Levine began to cultivate a relationship with Ivan Boesky which ultimately led to the unlawful exchange of inside information. In April 1986, it was agreed that Boesky would pay the sum of $2.4 million to Dennis Levine at some future date. This would be Levine's share of the illicit profits that Boesky would make through the inside information Levine promised to produce. Levine was to get 5% of the profits which accrued to Boesky and Co, for any share purchase recommended by Levine. Their agreement also provided that Boesky would pay Dennis Levine 1% of the aggregate profits resulting from Boesky's share dealings, where Levine's information influenced a decision either to hold or liquidate an existing position. Dennis Levine was arrested and brought into custody on 12th May 1986. As of that date Ivan F. Boesky ceased to pay Levine any part of the $2.4 million dollars that was agreed. Dennis Levine then grassed on Boesky.

On Dennis Levine's arrest, most of the Wall Street establishment dismissed him as a loner who had simply gone wrong. Later, Levine's position with Wall Street's establishment appeared to have much more sinister undertones. Wall Street watchers feared that Levine's activities — conducted from such a great height at Drexel Lambert — could be Wall Street's "own Watergate". Levine began talking in order to mitigate the possibility of a long prison sentence for himself. As a result, investment bankers at three different firms, and a prominent takeover lawyer, were charged with the regular swapping of inside information and using it to reap enormous trading profits. But Ivan F. Boesky was the biggest fish netted at that stage of the game.

It's still early days. Investigations of the type that began in the autumn of 1986 can take years! Many of Boesky's friends and Wall Street partners have been extremely nervous as to what could happen next, as government investigations of Boesky and his contacts continue. It was reported that for three months prior to his indictment, Boesky had a tape-recorder permanently attached to his person, recording many incriminating conversations during that period.

In the 1985 Economic Report of President Reagan, the White House effectively endorsed the ethos of Ivan F. Boesky and that of the corporate raider, rejecting any further government regulation in the area of takeover activity, much to the delight of Boesky and others like him.

For many corporate raiders, that was the green light, unleashing dozens more multi-billion dollar takeover deals and mergers. The light has now turned red. Boesky has until 1st April 1988 to unwind his affairs. It was the intention of the Securities and Exchange Commission to minimise the risk of default that an immediate ban on his activities would have produced.

In just a few short months, the financial community had been hit with the illegal activities of Dennis Levine; the failure of the Macdonald Wheeler money managing operation; the closure of the share shops by the DTI; the reference of more than 20 people to the Fraud Squad for illegal multiple applications in the TSB flotation; the warning by the London Stock Exchange to its members covering the legal implications of dealing in shares paid for from monies believed to have come from drug trafficking. Then we saw the insider dealings of Geoffrey Collier and those associated; threats of violence made to Jeremy Paulson-Ellis, the head of Vickers da Costa who reported Collier's activites. Finally, there was the huge Guinness scandal.

If ever there was a cesspool of iniquity, it was certainly to be located in the international capital markets after London's much heralded Big Bang. For a brief period, Big Bang was an audience grabber. But, to employ an American expression, it turned out in the final analysis to be no more than "an off-Broadway production."

By December 1986, it was pretty clear that despite the excited chatter in London, it was New York where the True Life Scandals, with a sensationally dazzling cast list, would be "coming in from the Sticks". The Wall Street High Drama Season had certainly got off to a great start with the sensational, modern Morality, "The Fall of Boesky". It had the critics tut-tutting on the edge of their seats, and the brokers in the audience nervously biting off their finger-ends. Highly inventive black comedy scripts, and Crime-fi scenarios began to pile up in the SEC's front office. But no one was *quite* sure when the Extradition Award Winners would be announced; or which seedy little side-show would suddenly win the title of "Scam of Scams, 1986". There was understandable anxiety among the production teams responsible. Would they be able to cash their Bail Bonds? Or would they have to "do a Boesky" — and start singing — in order to dispose of their Jail Rights!

The Beginning of the End of the Beginning

Since *The Downwave* was published, we have seen a number of components which have invariably been the precursor to a collapse in share prices of dramatic proportions. The number in place by the first quarter of 1987 was overwhelming, The bubble may not have burst but it had developed a menacing slow leak! The Government certainly had a great deal to answer for with regard to its privatisation plans and its liberal attitude towards deregulation. On the one hand, private investors far and wide had been invited to take their savings out of the building societies, banks, and other china pigs so they could become share owners. On the other, the effort that had been made to provide adequate protection for share holders in Britain might have appeared strenuous, but the actual level of protection from scams, frauds, swindles and deception, was virtually non-existent.

It is certainly through ignorance that self-regulation was chosen in preference to statutory regulation following Big Bang. The avenues of self-regulation have been well documented for decades. One must certainly ask the question "Does Government control the City or does the City control the Government?" Professor Carrol Quigley, author of *Tragedy and Hope* would testify to the latter.

The US Securities and Exchange Act of 1934 should have served as a model for the legislative programme that accompanied Big Bang. Within this act is a "suitability" clause. The regulations require the acting stockbroker, when recommending investments, to consider whether they are *suitable* in view of the financial status and needs of the investor. The rules are explicit. Penalties are incurred if they are violated. No such rules have been adopted to protect British investors. Surely, this *suitability* provision is vital for the inexperienced investor.

Thousands upon thousands of investors have been duped by acting on the basis of stock brokerage house estimates of prospective earnings. Stockbrokers are permitted to forecast whatever earnings please them for a company, using these forecasts to deal in shares in which they will be making a market. In many cases in the past, when half-yearly or annual earnings were reported, they showed no relationship to the forecasts. This was casually dismissed by the City as merely representing earnings that were "not as good as expected." In the meantime, the original forecasts may have caused severe loss to the investor. It would be reasonable to expect brokerage houses to be restrained from announcing prospective earnings, and to refrain from publishing reports without adequate proof, assuming responsibility for the misinformation. In the various recommendations made in the Finance Bill, this subject appears never to have been touched upon. Of course, the earnings numbers game is sacrosanct. It's one of the stockbroker's best marketing tools!

Big Bang has now permitted dual capacity. As a result a stockbroker can act as both an agent and a market-maker. As an agent, there is more than sufficient documentation to reveal how stockbrokers can do a disservice to their investors. As "stock jobbers", which is the other function they will be able to fulfil, an even greater number of abuses can be added to the existing ones. For example, the average investor will never know if the market-maker is taking a short position in the shares he is buying; or whether the market-maker is in a strong position to know which way the price of the shares may be heading. There is ample evidence that those making markets have at times deliberately spread rumours about the issues they handle for the purpose of rigging the market. Some market-makers have been known to give "inside information" to their friends, and take orders directly from them. Given current technology, a wholly computerised dealing system could be devised to mitigate many of the possible abuses. No thought whatever has been given to introducing such a system.

Dual capacity presents one of the most serious potential threats to the private investor yet devised. Stockbrokers, or other market-makers, are allowed to take a position in any shares they plan to purchase or sell to members of the public. They may then induce members of the public to buy or sell shares in whatever manner suits the previously established personal position of the broker. This could mean a deliberate attempt to depress prices to an unrealistic level, or push them higher to an equally unrealistic level. In this way they can create a false market. In 1968, the American Stock Exchange ordered stockbrokers to cut back on their own house accounts because of the frenzied speculation they induced. The individual brokers persisted in disobeying these instructions, and proceeded to create the illusion of major buying and selling and even more speculation.

I woke one morning in November 1986, picked up a copy of my *Financial Times,* to read that yet another licensed dealer in securities had failed. This time it was the Hamilton Hogg Group, which occupied a one-room office in London Wall in the City. A winding-up order was made by the Department of Industry in the public interest. Mr Peter Lawless, the sole director, admitted that Hamilton Hogg had creditors totalling £138,000, while it could indicate specific assets of only £14,200. The company had not held a dealing license for five months following June 1985. Nor had clients' ledgers been posted since that time. There was no record of the securities held by the company; and the company had failed to deliver the proceeds of sale and documents of title to its clients. Mr Lawless said the company's difficulties had arisen principally because of "the adverse state of the licensed dealers market in the wake of Big Bang".

For London, the closing weeks of 1986 saw publicists in the City, Whitehall and Westminster pulling out the stops, in a bid to elevate London — at least in their own eyes — from third place in the International Market Stakes, after New York and Tokyo. If their antics were unconvincing to the averagely sophisticated, they served to keep the new-style investors' minds off the inadequacy of the safeguards built into the Financial Services Act, as well as the sheer cost of maintaining any sort of protective cover.

After the DTI inspectors had called on Guinness, one of the best known of the Blue Chip companies, a deal with Boesky was uncovered. Revelation followed revelation. Worse, in the eyes of the British public, the finger of suspicion was seen to point at the very heart of the Establishment. In Threadneedle Street, the Bank of England's forecast of a 20 dollars a barrel oil price by 1988 was believed to have been leaked ahead of the publication of the Quarterly Bulletin, and a firm of gilt-edged market makers were also believed to have taken advantage of that information. Frankly, the Bank's estimates should have come as no surprise to anyone who read the economic forecasts from the leading brokers and commodity houses. True, there was one of those near-hysterical reactions when the Bulletin hit the market but that could have been expected by anyone who followed the market.

The forecast itself was no major revelation. It was the fact that the Bank of England endorsed the forecast made elsewhere that produced the market reaction that others may have taken advantage of. However, if the game is to be played by nursery rules, then Nannie's word is Law in the Land of the Bib and Feeding Bowl.

Now, in case you didn't know it, Insider Dealing encompasses far more than simply buying shares in a company before it's taken over. According to the new Financial Services Act, Insider Dealing involves taking an unfair advantage over the general investing public, by buying (or selling) a given company's securities while in possession of *unpublished information of a price sensitive nature*. The mind boggles! No one can be certain whether information is "price-sensitive" until the price has become sensitive. Besides, it's a fact that every investor is on the lookout for that stockbroker, or investment adviser, who's able to pass on information not generally available to the investing public. . . and which *is* price sensitive.

The whole concept of Insider Dealing (and the relevant legislation) is totally bizarre. It becomes even more arcane when you think about it. I remember, back in the early 1970s, a very large firm of stockbrokers was in the process of preparing a report on Shell, the oil company. The report was months in preparation, and it was generally felt in the City that the report would be a positive one. The report was, indeed, positive. It projected profits per share for five years to improve, and many other goodies! But, upon release of the report, the share price fell, and continued to fall for the two years that followed. By the strict letter of the Law, anyone who had purchased the shares of Shell prior to the publication of this report, would have been guilty of insider dealing. Of course, that insider dealing would have meant a loss for them. The question is — would this have been a crime? Or is necessary to *make* money out of the information first? In essence, it is clear that one investor should not be at an advantage over another investor. Presumably, it would indicate a strong probability of guilt to have anything above an average IQ in the City! Thus reducing the safe level of skill, expertise, and achievement to the lowest common denominator.

It comes to something when the atmosphere of crime and punishment invades certain extremely reputable City firms. Shortly after Big Bang — and well before news of the Guinness affair broke — a capable and well-respected economist in his thirties was heard to complain:

> ". . . we really don't know where we are these days. Let's say we do an especially good piece of research — visit the company, and manage to catch some of the more obvious straws in the wind, which. . . quite properly. . . we pass on to our clients. What's more, suppose the client makes a killing before the rest of the world has woken up to the obvious!

"In the old days, we'd have earned a bonus, the firm would have made a packet on commissions. . . and we'd be left with a contented client. But now — if we get it spectacularly right, the client could well receive a visit from the dreaded DTI inspectors, and we could be hauled up before the senior partners and be told — in effect — to prove our innocence!"

In other words, no investor (or his advisor) should ever be allowed to out-smart another. Or — in accordance with the current, non-competitive code — all the players should have an equal chance of coming last! But, as George Orwell taught us, some will always be more equal than others.

Carried to its logical conclusion, the present attitude to insider dealing could lead to an extremely undesirable state of affairs, with the general level of professional skill in decline, and the career conscious seeking safety in routine mediocrity. Why should they risk having to justify their actions to an in-house "compliance officer?" Were auditors and company secretaries to be pressured into acting as spies and informers — as some establishment figures would like — it is impossible to calculate the harm it could do to London as a major international market. For one thing, it could drive many clients into the arms of New York or Tokyo. For another, the combination of excessive legislation and over-zealous bureaucrats could well provoke a backlash. Not that the protest would be vocal. That is not the way with the more determined and enterprising members of the financial community. But they could be driven to operating on the very fringe of legality, stepping smartly across the line from time to time, provided the rewards appeared commensurate with the risk!

Not that the risk need be all that great, since it is unlikely that the investigators' success in the period immediately after Big Bang can be maintained for very long. Their initial triumphs were in some degree due to the energetic wielding of "new brooms". Moreover, some of those caught taking the inside curve had been lulled in the past into a sense of false security, because a wide range of sharp, if not actually *illegal,* practices had become commonplace within some of the most reputable houses over the years. Deplorable as it may seem to an outsider, the kind of men and women who succeed in the market place frequently have a touch of the buccaneer about them. They are not the kind that's easily frightened off. Nor are they over-impressed by shocked expressions on the faces of the righteous.

In any case, the more truthful small investor knows perfectly well (although he may not be prepared to admit it) that those who boast of what their broker tells them, or admit to subscribing to a tip-sheet, expect a little "extra" for the time and money involved. The same applies to the even larger army of indirect savers, who approach the market through an Investment Trust or Unit Trust, an Insurance Company or a Pension Fund. It is rare, indeed, to hear them complain that the management they rely on seems to "know too much" On the contrary. Too often they behave like the spoiled brat who eyes the cherries in the bowl and cries, "Don't count, Mummy. Just give me more."

As I said in one of my LBC broadcasts, I personally feel this entire insider dealing witch-hunt to be an ugly farce. The damage done to individual investors is probably minimal. Meantime, the inequities that are really costing investors a great deal of money hardly get a mention. The practice of "churning" — or encouraging investors to buy and sell shares with greater frequency than is either necessary of prudent — gets a bare five lines in the Financial Services Act. There is still nothing to prevent investors losing their savings as a result of firms like Macdonald Wheeler and Norton Warburg suddenly failing. Inexperience, ineptitude, irresponsibility, self-delusion and stupidity do not even get a mention in the Act.

One major problem with relying too heavily on the use of the law as a "frightener" is that ordinary people ultimately start to rebel. The hitherto law-abiding citizen cuts corners, takes chances and finally says, "To hell with the Law!" Beating "them" is seen as a challenge. When questions are asked, the ranks close. Memories fail. The never easy task of building up a case and securing a conviction becomes all but impossible. The police know that perfectly well as they patrol some of Britain's "problem" areas. Not even Dixon of Dock Green would be safe there after dark.

By the end of the worst week in 1986 for revelations, the City (and Britons at large) turned to the more pleasant task of preparing food, drink, and favours for the week-long, neo-Pagan Festival that has gradually replaced the simple commemoration of the birth of the Christ-child. What more could the year bring forth? It had been a bad shock to find the poisoned finger of suspicion pointing to the nation's official watch-dog, the Department of Trade and Industry, which shares with the Bank of England the task of keeping the City on the straight and narrow. It would be "the end". . . if the authorities uncovered evidence of insider dealing among its own civil servants! It would mean that it was not only in the Temple of the City that the less than honest money-handlers were in operation. Though, to be fair, neither Christ, nor Matthew, Mark, Luke nor John had ever suggested that there were no thieves elsewhere. Their point had been that the Temple in Jerusalem was the one place where the players *could* have been expected to shake the aces out of their sleeve before dealing.

At last the Bacchanalian ritual of the 1986 round of office parties emptied registry and dealing room alike. Secretaries and senior partners joined the boisterous Yuppies (and Already-Uppies) in holly-decked boardrooms, reception areas, canteens, bars and restaurants throughout the Square Mile. For an hour or two, the overheated computers and all but forsaken trading floor were forgotten. When the topic of insider knowledge accidentally arose, the thought was quickly brushed aside.

There was much laughter, as there always is at these highly liquid gatherings. Then one middle-aged market-maker ("I still think of myself as a jobber!") observed, somewhat lugubriously, that it was strange to think that the "Old" Exchange had to be opened, just over a century ago. . . in January 1885. . . because the members had outgrown their old home! Now, with Big Bang behind them, most firms had already vanished to their computerised cells "upstairs", deserting the familiar trading floor in a matter of weeks. There was even talk of selling off some of the unwanted space. So much for the "New" City!

By now it was as dark in the streets outside as in the dimly lit bars. Gradually the laughter died away — as the convoy of home-bound traffic rattled past. Then someone at the end of the bar said something. . . half in jest. . . about the wave of suicides that might take place during the Christmas holidays. "Guilt's a terrible thing", said his partner, echoing Ben Johnson.

I was not all that sure that our friend was joking. For, according to one City inebriate I know, those Boesky tapes were more far reaching — and incriminating — than had, by then, been recognised. Certainly, there were quite a few "City gents" who would not be very keen to return from the festivities, to face the uncertainties of the New Year. However, I did feel on Xmas Eve as though the last core sample of UK's untapped corruption potential for 1987 had been taken. But events a couple of days after Boxing Day showed how wrong that was, as a whole string of unpleasant surprises came tumbling out of the Guinness/Morgan Grenfell stocking.

I was reminded of a passage in that poem by one Minnie Louise Haskins — *God I Know.* It had been quoted, I am told, by King George VI in his Broadcast to the Empire on Christmas Day, 1939. It seemed to me to be highly appropriate. . . almost half-a-century later:

". . . I said to the Man who stood at the gate of the year: "Give me a light that I may tread safely into the unknown."

On the Precipice of the Forbidden Unknown

Unreliable as much of the information that comes our way turns out to be, it is the best we can hope for. So we must make what we can of it. Merely to throw up our hands, and complain that "It isn't fair", won't get us very far. After all, when we come to an indecipherable signpost, and a choice of three ways, we should not give up and spin a coin. We should try to make some sense of the clues we have to hand. First, we must have a rough idea of the direction in which we should be heading. That can help. Then, on the basis of past experience, it is fairly safe to assume that if there is a single finger-post, it is likely to be pointing down the lane which the locals at least regard as the most important. Therefore, if we take *that* route, we are likely to come across something, or someone, which will help us towards our destination. . . and so on. A dash of logic and an ounce of commonsense!

There is no need to labour the point, but we can work out quite a lot for ourselves, provided we make the effort. So it is with markets, despite the shortage of reliable information. We should not, therefore, immediately spurn the help of the first "Insider" who happens to come along. A recent

Business Week/Harris Poll, showed that 55% of American investors would not *hesitate* to take full advantage of any "inside information" they managed to get hold of. It is difficult to imagine that the true figure would be any lower in the UK. But respondents might be more reluctant to give us as truthful an answer.

Strange, you may think, that people can be that squeamish so close to the edge. One reason, of course, is that so few of them are prepared to recognise the existence of an edge; let alone accept that we are getting closer to it every day of every week.

I thought we were on the edge in 1983, while I was finishing off *The Downwave*. In the US edition, I opened the chapter I called GLOBAL BANKRUPTCY. . . THE COUP DE GRACE by pointing out that the developing countries were "in the stranglehold of an insuperable debt burden"; and that world trade, which was contracting, was "under threat from escalating protectionism." Domestic industry, agriculture and domestic households alike were "locked in a spiral of borrowing which (was) becoming even more menacing as inflation (turned) to disinflation and disinflation to deflation." The lenders, the banks, were:

> ". . . (staring) hopelessly at a black hole which swallows up more and more debt on the hopeless premise of staving off domino default. With the passage of time, the secondary depression of the 1980s will bring excruciatingly high unemployment, massive bankruptcies. . . a collapse in capital markets, a sustained decline in property values and a great deal of hardship for many people. Throughout the process international tensions will heighten. Countries will scramble to protect shrinking markets. Deficits for the developing countries will balloon while the temptation to default becomes increasingly more attractive. The *coup de grace* will be global bankruptcy as the *nadir* of the depression approaches."

Little wonder that when a few of us "take up a newspaper and read it" we certainly do see (as Ibsen put it) ghosts "creeping between the lines." When I wrote the passage quoted above, I added:

> "There is a Chinese philosophy that states life is a circle, We're still in the circle."

A circle is the closest we get to infinity and perpetuity. Must we not, therefore, learn to read the signs? Obviously, we cannot afford to ignore, or disbelieve, everything that comes from the Government, the leading brokers, the business schools. But, knowing what we now know about the art of misinformation, we must exercise a reasonable degree of caution. We must also "learn the language", so to speak. But extreme caution is essential here.

There used to be two schools of thought over the issue of language proficiency for Colonial Service cadets and junior subalterns serving in "foreign parts". The conventional view was that the neophyte should be encouraged to become proficient in the local dialect during his first tour of duty. Apart from anything else, it would keep him busy — when he wasn't playing games or trudging 20 miles a day through the bush, drawing maps or shooting small birds. Hopefully, as well as giving him some skill in "speaking the lingo", it should keep him out of trouble. "Trouble" in that context meant going to bed with local women or — even more dangerous — with the bored wives of senior officers.

The alternative view was that it was better to go slowly. Plenty of sport, yes! Bags of long, tiring marches carrying a heavy gun — excellent! But so far as women went, it was up to one of the seniors to detail a slightly more senior cadet (perhaps a chap on his second tour) to show a young friend "the ropes".

As for learning the "lingo", that should be allowed to come naturally. And it would, so long as the chap mixed a bit. . . within reason, of course! The logic behind this argument was that the local chiefs and politicos were "a dashed cunning bunch. And not above the odd bit of trickery." One favourite trick was to let slip some apparently indiscreet word or two in the newcomer's presence. Just as though they hadn't seen him standing there. Naturally, since they were speaking in their own tongue, the young man would probably be convinced that what they were saying *must be* true! That was why it was far better from him not to know too much about the language until he'd learned enough about the locals themselves to be able to *sense* when they were having him on.

An outstanding example of a well-played misinformation game was played in November 1986, at the time of the dismissal of Sheikh Yamani, Saudi Arabia's almost universally popular Oil Minister. Yamani was far from being the "fair-haired boy" of King Fahd. Many felt that King Fahd would have liked to see Yamani taking a firmer line over production quotas during the OPEC meeting that was concluded two weeks before Yamani's dismissal. Immediately after his dismissal, the oil price plunged since it was believed that in Yamani's absence King Fahd would take a stronger line on production quotas, which would ultimately lead to the type of free-for-all price war that occurred during the previous summer.

What followed was a second version, to the effect that Yamani had *actually* been fired for offering a 50 cent price discount on a netback basis without telling the King. The King, it was said, would in fact be going for higher prices rather than higher production levels. In the market, the price per barrel reacted accordingly. It moved up. The history of OPEC is riddled with this type of disinformation and misinformation, designed to influence price levels, through the medium of forecast feed-back.

Then Charles T. Maxwell, Senior Energy Strategist of Cyprus J. Lawrence came on the scene. Maxwell is probably one of the five most influential energy correspondents in the world. His track record is excellent, and his assessment of situations such as we are in now is accepted internationally. Maxwell claimed that the first explanation had been the correct one; the second version had been issued in an attempt at deliberate disinformation. King Fahd, said Maxwell, was the one who favoured netbacks. Yamani was not. Moreover the King wanted Saudi Arabia to abandon its recent role of swing producer, which Yamani had been supporting. Maxwell explained that there was a further conflict between them, dating back to the spring of 1985. The King and the Princes, Sultan and Salaman, had decided it would be wise to pursue market share — even though it meant driving down prices. This, they hoped, would drive out the non-OPEC producers, who were handicapped by having to meet higher break-even prices. Free from non-OPEC competition, Saudi Arabia would then be able to pick the right moment to go for a higher price, in an attempted replay of the early 1970s.

Meanwhile the congenitally gullible were rising to the disinformation bait. On the assumption that the worst was over for the oil market, the Taiwanese have been behind the purchase of oil wells from hard-hit owners in Louisiana and Oklahoma. Much of Taiwan's $13 billion trade surplus with the United States has been invested in what they saw as depressed US assets, available at bargain prices. They expect that rising oil prices will restore the value of the wells they have been buying. But what gives them that idea?

It would not be unreasonable to assume that the Taiwanese were deliberately allowed access to a "confidential" CIA report. According to this report, to which I have also had access, OPEC is still capable of creating economic turmoil throughout the Western World. Supposedly the Grand Design outlined by the CIA would have a devastating impact on the finances of every single American, as well as threatening the security of the United States itself. This, naturally, was music to the ears of anyone involved in Far Eastern Trade.

The scenario was as simple as it was seductive. The Saudi bloc deliberately engineered the oil glut, bringing the price down from $44 p.b. to under $15 p.b.. According to the CIA, the reason was to stop American "counter-measures" from being launched in an attempt to reduce US dependence on Middle East Oil. The next possible move — say the highly imaginative compilers of the report — is that the Saudi bloc, having achieved stage one of its objective, is poised to initiate another price hike. This time, the game will be played in a "softly, softly" manner, to avoid waking the dog. The CIA believes the Saudi bloc has the muscle to do it, and claims that neither President Reagan nor Washington is prepared to meet such a strategy.

To return from the realms of fantasy and misinformation to the real world, falling oil prices had led the US President to cut back drastically on the topping-up rate of the Strategic Petroleum Reserve. Oil companies and consumer industries followed. Mr Reagan cut the development programme, and slashed subsidies for oil conservation schemes, such as home insulation. Plans to rescue the coal industry were also abandoned.

A leading Fleet Street journalist once estimated that 10% of what he wrote was fact; and 90% fiction. It was up to the reader to decide which was which. Much the same might be said of this "confidential" CIA Report, which the whole world appears to have read. And it is highly likely that the Taiwanese *entrepreneurs* got the facts mixed up with the fiction.

Some will remember an earlier "confidential" CIA report about Mexico, circulated a few years ago, and are entitled to their suspicions. The report in question concerned the tremendous oil reserve South of the Border, and the extent to which Mexico would experience nothing short of re-birth, as the oil came steadily on stream. This CIA report transformed America's poor neighbour into an Eldorado of the oil world. Ultimately — thanks to its massive reserves and low production cuts — impoverished Mexico could well end up more powerful than even Saudi Arabia. That was the message.

Those of little faith will stress that about this time Mexico was heavily in debt to the United States. What's more, some US bankers and politicians were getting very worried; and several large Mexican debt issues were looking for a home in European markets. Then, just as the Taiwanese would be buying oil wells, so the Europeans started buying copious amounts of Mexican debt. Was it all that surprising that, as European holdings of Mexican debt began to rise and rise. . . the United States was steadily getting rid or its Mexican paper? Well, say the fair minded, the Europeans had to buy it from *someone!* I personally would be most unwilling to do any deal on the strength of the CIA's "confidential" say so!

If the Taiwanese believed the CIA oil report (always assuming they ever saw it), it must have brought considerable comfort to several extremely anxious south-western senators. They had been desperately seeking help for the US oil industry, where drilling was at a 46 year low. Therefore, if all it took to sell some of their dormant wells to foreigners was a report from the CIA, then it was a cheap way of bailing out those banks which had been holding on to a hitherto unsaleable asset.

I have to say that my view is coloured by the CIA's experience and record in the international disinformation business. On that basis, it would seem sensible to interpret their prediction of higher oil prices as a reasonably firm indication that prices would — after an initial surge — resume their downward path for some time to come.

It is also pretty certain that the Saudis were playing their own dis-information game; and that the return of the Iranians to centre stage should not be dismissed too lightly. Remember that the Iranian Majlis was advised, shortly after the Second World War (and by a former American executive from Saudi Arabia) to step up the pressure on the oil majors. It was Prime Minister Dr Mohammed Mossadeq who was responsible for the first post-war oil crisis, after the Majlis had approved the Nationalisation Law on May Day, 1951. Later it was the Shah who would force the oil majors to increase production to give him the bigger income he needed; and it was the Iranian — not the Saudi — Oil Minister, who was in the Chair at the end of 1973 when the big price hike took place.

After Yamani's dismissal towards the end of 1986, the Saudis called for another OPEC meeting to consider a proposal to raise the price per barrel to $18. The Iranians insisted that production would need to be cut to achieve the Saudi objective. Alan Abelson, writing for Barron's, noted that the new management of OPEC was coming more and more under the direction of Ayatollah Khomeini — "that level-headed old charmer". In Abelson's view:

"Yamani's absence and Kohmeini's increased presence means there will be politics, rather than business as usual at the cartel. . . In other words, if you like tag team wrestling, you'll just love future OPEC meetings."

However, before getting too involved in what The White House or The Pentagon may be up to, it would be wise to recognise that the range of major issues which Britain is still able to decide, must depend — if are prepared to be realistic — on what is happening in the main international arena, in which the United States, West Germany and Japan have in the past few years earned top billing. For Britain in the Fall of 1986, the future was perceived by many to hang on one main issue — whether or not interest rates could be prevented from rising sharply, as the United States deficit-financing crisis entered what the *International Currency Review* for September, published in New York, called:

". . . a dangerous and traumatic phase which could lead to the worst of all possible worlds: much higher interest rates, raging inflation in the United States, the headlong further depreciation of slump conditions to non-dollar economies, and ultimately to a breakdown of the prevailing free-wheeling environment of unfettered capital movements."

How, it may be asked, had we reached this pass? It is a question which can be answered only if we are prepared to go back to the base line established at Bretton Woods, when the International Monetary Fund (IMF) was set up.

The Crumbling Alliance

Forewarned is forearmed! The international events, as they are likely to unfold, will probably bear no relationship to the popular perception — as portrayed by the media — of how the world works and will probably continue to work. Britain as a nation may be an island geographically, but it is certainly not insulated from the world of international politics and economics. In the period ahead, there is a wide range of truly monumental issues upon which Britain will have to decide. It still has an important place in the OECD community of leading industrialised nations; a community which the United States, West Germany and Japan have tended in the past few years to dominate.

It was 1944, the year of the Russian offensive in the Ukraine, the American landing in the Philippines, the imprisonment of Marshal Pétain, the abdication of King Victor Emmanuel, the execution of Foreign Secretary Count Ciano, the Soviet capture of Budapest, the end of despot Horthy's 24 year rule, the declaration of Vietnamese Independence under "Uncle" Ho Chi Minh, the invasion of Europe on one side of the world and that of the Marshall and Admiralty Islands on the other, the failure of the July Plot against Hitler, the V1 and V2 assault on Britain, and the re-election of President Roosevelt for a Fourth Term.

Literature and the Arts that year threw up Camus's *Caligua,* George Macaulary Trevelyan's *English Social History,* Picasso's *Seated Woman in Blue,* Bliss's *Miracle of the Gorbals* and Prokofiev's *Symphony No 5 in B flat.* Elsewhere, the Butler Education Act introduced secondary schooling for all British children, the Fleming Committee reported on Public Schools in England, the British Medical Council decided to investigate hearing aids. That year, the Dumbarton Oaks Conference at Washington led to the establishment of the United Nations Organisation, and finance ministers of 44 countries met under the UN umbrella at the summer resort of Bretton Woods, New Hampshire — to create a system for greater international co-operation and stabilisation of world trade.

From Bretton Woods emerged the International Monetary Fund (IMF), the International Bank for Reconstruction and Development and the General Agreement on Tariffs and Trade (GATT). These events, as Douglas Jay describes them in his book *Sterling:*

> ". . . were largely the product of Keynes's reflections and of Anglo-American talks on the best way to avoid in future the vicious spiral of retaliatory trade restrictions forced by deflation in the early 1930's. . . Since the deficit of one country necessarily implied the surplus of another, the downward spiral could be avoided if, by means of a central mechanism and reserve, the creditor at some point in effect lent to the debtor. But mounting American pressure, based more on a simple nineteenth century faith in fixed exchange rates rather than on serious economics, grafted on to the scheme the new exchange as a sort of a modern refinement of the old gold standard."

The new regime of fixed, but periodically moveable exchange rates broke down in 1971-72. In the end, the exchange rate obligation had proved too much for even the United States to bear. In August 1971, President Richard Nixon suspended the convertibility of the dollar. In December, the new arrangement was formalised under the Smithsonian Agreement, which established new parities for the Group of Ten developed countries. The immediate effect was the devaluation of the dollar, and a rise in the gold price from $35 to $38 dollars an ounce. Sterling, which had risen to $2.53 between August and December, stood at $2.55 on December 20th. By 1958 the Bretton Woods initiative was universally proclaimed a huge success. International trade was booming; but ingenious administrators had begun to devise a range of non-tariff barriers. They looked "respectable" enough, but effectively cut down the flow of imports preserving the country's competitive edge.

The United States had its own recipe. It observed "voluntary" restraint on the import of foreign textiles, and the export of US portfolio capital and direct investment. There was an interest equalisation tax. Duty-free import allowances for tourists were reduced. Government agencies were allowed to buy foreign products *only* if they were priced 60% below the US substitutes. Sanitary rules were strictly enforced; and rules on quality and labelling were designed to discriminate against foreign imports.

Europe's way was to introduce "temporary" surcharges on imports, using value added taxes and turnover taxes to raise funds for subsidising exporters. Cheap export credits were also used to evade GATT rules. Nor were the less developed countries without blemish. They had complex tariff systems, producer cartels and buffer stocks; all devices to take the edge off free trade.

At least it could be said that the Bretton Woods plan had held up for more than a quarter of a century. In spring 1983, when *The Downwave* was published, the United States and Europe were at loggerheads. Japan emerged as the prime target for criticism. But, wisely, Tokyo continued to accept the rebuff, and went on building up its export markets, as well as setting out to start manufacturing inside target market areas. The 40 year-old Bretton Woods agreement had become a shambles, and a full-fledged trade war was threatening. It was clear that the trade barriers which fuelled the Great Depression were in place. As a matter of fact, as early as 1977, Japan's Prime Minister Takeo Fukuda had warned that protectionism could take us all back to the 1930s, when:

". . . major countries, one after another, abandoned the open economic system of free trade, switching to the closed system of protectionism. I am not suggesting that we are once again on the road to World War. Yet, I feel deep anxiety about the social and political consequences. . . if we slide once again into protectionism or a break up of the world economy into trade *blocs.*"

Naturally, every statesman of any standing agreed. Lip-service is cheap, and in plentiful supply. Objectively, national governments could see that the global international structure was interrelated and interdependent as never before. Again, every leading figure (from the industrialised and developing worlds alike) would use each and every opportunity to pay homage to the ideal of international free trade. Without a doubt, some must have been sincere. But so is the pauper, when he gets up, with tears in his eyes, to address the Neighbourhood Voluntary Aid Committee. "How wonderful," he cries brokenly, eyeing the well-dressed assembly."How wonderful. . . if we were *all* in a position. . . honourably to discharge our debts. . .!"

At the 7-nation summit meeting at Versailles in 1982, and again at Williamsburg, Virginia in 1983, the obligatory piety was displayed. Steps *would* be taken to restore some of the disciplinary elements of the Bretton Woods system. In the event, the Versailles 7-nation summit ended in acrimony; the Williamsburg summit produced a crop of fine sentiments. But that was that.

One "grand occasion" managed to rise above the routine platitudes — the so-called Group of Five (G5) Meeting in 1985. The professed aim was to bring down the US dollar, with the ultimate objective of reducing the huge US deficit. A more urgent requirement was to reduce the growing pressure on the Reagan administration from the protectionist lobby.

On the face of it, the G5 initiative worked; the dollar fell hard against both the Japanese yen and the West German deutschemark, as well as sterling. It looked as though intervention had proved effective. But, as the months passed, it was noted with dismay that the weaker dollar had not done anything to stem the flow of imports from Japan or West Germany. Pundits began to admit what they had tended to keep to themselves: that intervention *can* be successful so long as the intervenors are moving in the same direction as the market, which was the case in 1985. Another factor which had been present in 1985 was the willingness of the Japanese and the West Germans to go along with the rest of the Group of Five. By 1986, they were beginning to dig in their heels. Why should THEIR currencies (and economies) bear the brunt?

By beginning of January 1987, central banks were forced once again to try to turn the tide. President Ronald Reagan had come up with his first ever million-million dollar budget, supposedly designed to slash the US deficit by 50%. The budget also included a promise of "privatisation". On examination this proved to be mainly "privatisation" of debt — in other words, "securitisation" under a more fashionable name. More double-talk!

The EEC monetary committee (to say nothing of central bank and government officials) must have known all along that forcing *down* the dollar meant forcing *up* the yen and the deutschemark. But the strikes in France, which hit the franc, threw the EMS, the European Monetary System into turmoil. It was no longer safe to assume that the authorities could put off the inevitable realignment of the EMS currencies until — conveniently — after the West German elections on January 25th. The Baker-Miyazawa agreement to stabilise the yen's value was also severely under strain. Not because the yen or the DM were — as popularly supposed — the victims of the dreaded malaise called "currency instability"; but rather because governments (for their own purposes) were attempting to ignore what the international currency market was trying to tell them: that if traders moved out of dollars they would not go for the weaker, or potentially weaker currencies. Here we had a prime example of self-deception on a grand scale, on the part of those who profess to know better than anyone else — including the market.

When it comes to trade deficits, it is clear that by definition there must be an overall global balance. After all, if we take those dormant American oil-wells, the US states concerned may be contributing to the US overall deficit. But if the Taiwanese spend some of their surplus buying American oil-wells, it is in some degree redressing the balance. *But not necessarily on the same account!* While Western Europe's politicians were asking the

United States to cut down on its imports, and export more, they were threatening their own exporters, since a weaker US dollar can lead as much as tariffs to a reduction in American orderbooks. Moreover, if US business cuts its orders, for whatever reason, the rest of the world will feel it. Before long they will be reducing their imports.

"Ah," the export-orientated politicians (and the Business School theorists) tell UK manufacturers. "If you reduce your exports to the United States, you will be able to sell more to your partners in the EEC, and the Commonwealth. . . to say nothing of the Middle East and Japan." The reply they — or you — get from directors of the high-quality, wool textile mills in Hawick or Selkirk in the Scottish borders, will be a very frosty one:

"Thank you, (they'll say). We don't export to countries, or areas of the Commonwealth. We serve individual customers. We *already* export to Japan and the Gulf, thank you! We have *some* customers in Europe. But the cloth we supply our Texan millionaires is designed to their taste. . . as it is for Tokyo or Riyadh. So we can't just pick up the 'phone and tell some Frenchman, 'Look. . . because of the brilliant plan to reduce the American trade deficit, we have several thousand yards of fine quality, light-weight cloth specially designed for the Houston oil-man. . . how about taking that too? T'would be great on a wet and windy winter's day in the Rue de Rivoli!'

"So if we lose customers in the USA, because the politicians at Westminster cannot accept the pattern of world trade as it really is, both *we* and *they* will be the loser."

The last time the question was raised with one such mill owner in the Scottish borders earlier in 1986, he looked puzzled:

"I dinna get it. . . we fight hard to get the order, we air-freight the cloth to Dallas, or wherever, and we get the money quick as we can. So what's all this worry about the American deficit? Either the daft, silly ******s down in London want us to do business, or they don't! To tell the truth, our accountant was saying only last week that if we'd give up the struggle and just closed the mill, we could accept the offer some Japanese high-tech wizards made us a few weeks back. After that we could certainly afford to go straight off to the United States and do our wee thing there."

In that brief anecdote from real life, you have an illustration of the difference between the facile rhetoric of the political and academic worlds — with their shifting values, and ever changing theories — and the hard, practical, irrevocable decisions which have to be taken, and kept to, in the real world.

The function of Government is to remain in power. The purpose of the investor is to make a profit. If Government predicts a rosy economic future, in the hope that a bit of forecast feedback can thereby be generated, no great harm is done if it's wrong. Government will simply switch to another ploy. Considerable harm can come to the investor if he accepts the Government's prediction as accurate and invests all his savings in those areas which will bring a reasonable return only if the Government's forecast is correct. An interesting equation now exists. For the first time ever, the UK authorities have an equal interest in the future of the stock market as does the investor because of the many privatisation issues. Considerable political capital will be lost if they show large losses (it could easily have cost the Tories the 1987 General Election). Should the price of the various shares attached to the privatisation issues fall below that of the issue price, a future Labour Government is committed to renationalise these companies at the issue price. It will be interesting to see how both sides handle that problem.

Authorities have many weapons in their armoury, enabling them to produce credible forecasts — even if they are dishonest ones. They know a large part of the electorate wish to see a high proportion of the GDP devoted to "investment". Governments are happy to oblige by predicting an "estimate" of investment, and then making economic forecasts and projections which based on no more than a desirable estimate. Obviously, the outcome can be whatever numbers are required to produce the desired effect, while retaining credibility.

False GNP predictions are among the favourite psychological weapons in the war waged by governments to induce an economic atmosphere which, hopefully, will reverberate the desired repercussions. The chaos of dishonest forecasting begins at the government offices. It then filters down through the press lobby. The optimistic forecasts then pass to the stockbrokers who — asked by the media to comment — perpetuate the myth.

Think about it! Think about it when you next read in your newspaper about the prospects for the economy. Where are the forecasts coming from? There are many brilliant *independent* forecasters in the universities and business schools all over the country. There are also a large number of independent forecasting bodies capable of anticipating the future course of the UK economy, employed inside the UK and outside. But where do the forecasts *you* read come from? Hardly without exception, these forecasts are either being produced by the Government or vested interest associations involved with the Government at local or national level — our friends the stockbrokers. Where are all the university professors and other independent forecasters? Why is it that you rarely discover what they have to say or write? This should indeed make you curious!

An extremely pernicious device used by forecasters for the purpose of achieving their desires is to present "targets" as forecasts. Suppose the Chancellor of the Exchequer decides on a "target" of 8-11% growth for Sterling M3 in the next fiscal year. He is implying that monetary growth will not exceed 11%. We all know how often we've seen monetary growth remain close to pre-set target levels. The same holds true for the Public Sector Borrowing Requirement, along with numerous other "targets", treated by Government as forecasts.

Establishing actual targets (or aims) which are physically achievable is of no use to a government which employs economic forecasting to achieve a political objective. Targets are often intended to produce a specific feedback, based on what is desirable rather than actually achievable. The electorate must be led to believe that authorities have foreknowledge of a beneficial outcome for the economy, rather than merely targeting an item that is actually anticipated, and could conceivably occur.

While nearly all forecasters and planners have an unconscious bias towards the ageeable rather than the disagreeable — which explains the plethora of excessively optimistic predictions — using targets for the purpose of producing pessimistic forecasts can be useful too. Opinions often differ as to the way people can be encouraged (or induced) to embark on a particular plan. Sometimes, the electorate needs that little bit of "negativism" to get them moving. During the mid-stages of an electoral cycle, the authorities often regard low GNP targets, dressed up as forecasts, as a springboard from which to exceed the seemingly dismal future. On other occasions, the electorate will react best to an unrealistically high GNP prediction, refusing to be downcast when the predicted goal is not reached.

Experience has taught executives in the jungle of intra-corporate jealousies that to exceed their own sales forecast does not lower their prestige. On the contrary! The corporate executives, or minister, will not be denounced for their faulty forecasting if targets are exceeded. Instead they will bask in the glory of having beaten — due to exceptional effort and skill on their part — an allegedly reasonable and realistic forecast. All of you are thoroughly familiar with the euphoria that can be produced by results that are "better than expected", even though those results might be dismal. Expectation is all! You are equally familiar with the shouts and cheers that accompany events that turn out to be not *quite* so bad as predicted — even though the outcome is atrocious. They can hoist the share price too!

The principle outlined becomes even more critical at the time of an election. A *secretly commissioned* public opinion poll — as opposed to a widely disseminated one — may reveal that both the Conservative Party and the Labour Party are neck-and-neck in the run-up to the General Election. If the incumbent party commissioned this special survey, and were to publish the information, it could be regarded as inexpedient and potentially damaging. On the other hand, to deceive the public could be considered praise-worthy if the party won the election as a result of the deception. The choice the authorities would face would be whether or not more political capital would be gained by telling the voters — according to reliable information gathered —if the party faced certain victory or defeat. On the other hand, it might also induce voters to climb on to the apparently successful bandwagon. Most marginal voters will usually turn to the winning side if they are spoiled for choice. If defeat is predicted, it will lower the spirits of existing supporters, but encourage them also to step up their efforts to prevent the prediction's being fulfilled. Political leaders in Britain have tended to believe that desirable repercussions and political objectives are best served by predictions erring on the side of the optimistic. In between predictions, the electorate are treated like mushrooms. . . kept in the dark and fed with manure!

If it is true that the British people as a group have been found to respond only to optimistic predictions, the honest forecaster in Britain is at a distinct disadvantage. The pound has been declining for 127 years. The standing of Britain, as a major power, has been declining during the corresponding period. Britain has now been overtaken in the production league by virtually every other industrialised nation. Health standards are poor compared to those of other countries. Exports are uncompetitive. Inflation in Britain is higher than that of most other OECD countries. These conditions may not be conductive to national pride, but they happen to be inescapable facts of life. The ongoing development of these conditions has been widely forecast and widely anticipated for many years. The forecasts were usually ignored, muted, dismissed, hidden or derided since they were not optimistic. In 1973, the Hudson Institute produced *Britain in the 1980s*, one of the most accurate future portrayals ever produced, which forecast with uncanny precision a picture of what Britain has experienced during the decade. When the book was first published, it was torn to shreds by most reviewers, who treated the work with ridicule, derision and hatred.

In 1981, James Bellini's *Rule Britannia* was published. In his book Bellini predicts the collapse of the manufacturing industry, and a return to medieval social relationships involving a harsh new feudal lifestyle. The book followed a TV series of the same name. In a spiteful attempt to suppress the work of Bellini, the BBC became subject to litigation which was directed toward a minor aspect of the TV series. Bellini's work is claimed to have subsequently become subject to censorship. Bellini, who hosted the *Money Programme* for three years, and was the presenter of a number of economic documentaries, is believed to have resigned from the BBC as a result of the censorship imposed. In late 1983, John Eatwell presented a programme for the BBC outlining his forecasts for Britain during the 1980s and 1990s. The slot chosen for showing the programme was during the early afternoon on New Year's Day 1984 — just the time when most people wish nothing less than to watch a programme on economic forecasting. John Eatwell's book *Whatever Happened to Britain?* painted an extremely dismal picture of the economic scene. We've never read a review of the book. When was the last time *you* saw John Eatwell on TV?

Are you aware of the large number of studies of the British economy, and its prospects, that are never reviewed, never discussed, never read? Along with authors of exceptional talent who are never heard from. In 1984, Keith Smith's book *The British Economic Crisis* was published, its revealing insights available to all. Have you even heard of it? In 1982, *The Wasting of the British Economy* by Sydney Pollard was produced. This is another book that you'll very rarely find or hear of. *Britain's Economic Future* by Christopher Hawkins was publised in 1983. How many reviews of this book have you read? Have you even seen a copy? It should be at your local library. Is it? In 1983 we also had *The Economic Consequences of Mrs Thatcher* by Lord Kaldor, who produced a detailed but dramatically scathing attack on the non-policies of the Conservative Government. This appears to be another study of British life which is unpalatable for the masses and therefore relegated to obscurity. *On Britain* by Rolf Dahrndorf was published in 1983. This further study of Britain suffering an inexorable, irreversible decline met only limited success, despite Dahrndorf's popularity on TV and his demonstrable brilliance as Director of the London School of Economics. In 1984 *Mrs Thatcher's Economic Experiment* by William Keegan was published. In 1985, *Britain Without Oil* by the same author was published. Neither book gives you a particularly attractive picture of Britain's future, nor has either reached the best-seller list just yet. William Keegan, Economics Editor of *The Observer* since 1977 and Associate Editor of the paper since 1983, is yet to achieve the TV status of his associates in the stockbrokerage community.

The tools of the forecaster's trade still leave a great deal to be desired. Economists, using the tools of their trade, express the future in terms of GNP, sales, hours of work, imports, exports, public expenditure, industrial output, new housing starts, unemployment, etc. In spite of the numerous elaborate models that have been produced, in the final analysis the forecasts that are produced represent little more than the result of placing a ruler along the tangents of an existing trend and projecting that trend into the future on a time frame. There are two things wrong with that approach that will certainly cause problems. The first is, there is yet to be devised an economic law that tells the forecaster which tangents he should choose. For example, if you placed a ruler along the tangents of the *Financial Times* 30 Share Index that developed after August 1986, you would find the trend was up. If you project that trend upward, you'd get higher share prices in the future. On the other hand, if you chose as your tangents the descending peaks and troughs that developed after April, you'd get a downtrend. If you extended that downtrend, the future for share prices would be lower. But, if you want a more optimistic picture, all you have to do is select as your tangents the ascending peaks and troughs that have developed since 1975. Then you'd have an uptrend again. Economists have the same problem when dealing with economic aggregates.

The second problem with the straight-line projection approach is that trends will often experience terminal junctures. The straight-line projection approach is unable to deal with terminal junctures. If you are limited to using the straight-line projection approach, terminal junctures don't exist. All that exists is a search for revised tangents, which is not a satisfactory method for anticipating the future, or for developing an investment strategy.

Even if we are to reach beyond the simplistic basis of straight-line projection forecasting, there are still many factors that are likely to render an economic forecast totally useless. It is a dangerous delusion to infer that because certain phenomena are depicted in economic language, their quantitative and qualitative dimensions are necessarily determined by economic causes. If we consider the egalitarian nature of the British Welfare State, Hitler's confiscation of Jewish shops, the land laws of Kenya, the effect of apartheid in South Africa and the horrific potential of AIDS — all these may be considered as appropriate subjects for economic evaluation. Though all but one is now a part of economic history, they were clearly not brought about by causal factors which are within the economists' professional orbit of evaluation.

Exposing the fallacies and foibles in forecasting by economists is intended to help you establish that the economic future is as elusive to economists as it is to other mortals; since, in so many cases, the outcome can often be determined by the intrusion of prodigious non-economic events. This can have devastating effects. A pragmatic and objective approach to the subject of economic forecasting should also help to restore the economic discipline required of the investor. As an investor committing your savings, it is vital to have an undistorted understanding of the past and the present. It is equally important to try to recognise the consequences flowing from an interplay of given accurate factors. These are within the realms of useful economics, and can help the laymen understand and anticipate trends that *may* shape the future.

An overindulgence in prediction — as opposed to forecasting and the anticipation of likely events — will deflect those interested in the subject of economics from using the economic information in its most meaningful form. Currently, people are being bombarded with all manner of economic forecasts, predictions and *gurus*. Lord Bauer made an extremely interesting observation in this respect: *A great upsurge in forecasting is usually evidence of an unhealthy state of mind, especially of a readiness to welcome panaceas. A society which worships predictors and oracles loses its critical outlook. In an age which worships soothsayers, the emergent credulity threatens to drown rational appraisals that take account of present life with all its sordid and disagreeable revelations.*

But. . . !

> The prophets prophesy falsely, and the priests bear rule by their means; and my people love to have it so.
>
> JEREMIAH

It is probable that the 1980s will go down in history as the decade when British businessmen went into Government, and Government went into business — to their actual disadvantage. Once governments begin to intervene in trade, they are liable to wind up doing a great deal of harm. The lesson learned from sending looms to France in the early 1800s, and advanced cotton textile machinery to countries like India a century later, appear to have been forgotten. In November 1986, for example, the British Overseas Trade Board announced the publication of a *comprehensive market report* on current and future investment and export opportunities for British firms in Brazil's textile machinery sector. According to the BOTB announcement:

"The Brazilians envisage a doubling of their capacity in their textile industry by the end of the century. . . In June 1987 the BTMA (British Textile Manufacturers Association) are planning to send a BOTB-supported mission to Brazil. . . (and) also hope to arrange an inward mission of Brazilian textile machinery manufacturers."

I would now put the question, what is the sense of *increasing* the pressure on UK textile manufacturers, unless it has been decided centrally that textiles (like Sterling M3) may safely be ignored, and textile machinery (like the Exchange Rate) is what matters? There can be arguments for, as well as against, centralised state planning. There is little to be said for haphazard, uncoordinated *state interference.* If textile firms and machinery manufacturers decide to fight it out on a beggar-the-other basis, so be it. Provided neither party asks for (or receives) special help from Government. But with the Multi-fibre agreement, and constant diatribes condemning East European and Far Eastern countries for competing *unfairly*, it is clear that Westminster sees itself in control. Fact or fiction?

You must judge. What we have seen is a confluence of feigned agreements, disinformation, misinformation, confusion, duplicity and heavily disguised vested interest, leading the world into a malaise of incalculable dimensions.

Debts, Debts, and More Debts

Following the global bankruptcy of the 1930s, a *new deal* was inaugurated. Controls over government spending were tightened, so were banking regulations. New regulatory bodies were set up to ensure that a calamity of like proportions could never happen again. Nor would the seeds of debt be so easily sown. For ten years or so, it seemed to work. Shortly after World War II and the implementation of the Bretton Woods plan, the seeds of the process that had brought the international banking collapse of the 1930s, were being scattered across the credit-thirsty fields once again. But this time, it was on a larger scale.

First, the war-torn economies had to be rebuilt. They borrowed for the purpose. Debt was piled on debt. War recovery debt was horrendous. Debt spread from the developed world into the Third World. Credit-worthy consumers were persuaded to borrow well beyond their capacity to earn. When the consumer sector was saturated in loans, corporate borrowing was the next to be encouraged. When both consumers and corporations had reached the limit of their debt servicing capacities, further borrowing was encouraged to *remain afloat* until the next economic recovery. There was a great boom in commodities shortly before the 1973 oil crisis. Third World producers appeared eminently credit-worthy. There was a mad scramble among the geobankers — and particular in the USA and Britain — to go on lending to the developing countries, so they could expand their steel plants, build electric power dams and spend on all forms of capital project.

Then the commodity boom faded. World growth slowed. Many of the new Third World schemes turned out to be white elephants, and the borrowers were left with huge debts to service. An aggressive band of less developed countries (LDCs) began demanding a larger share of the proceeds of world trade. They included the OPEC states, and others which fancied that they too had the West at their mercy. Western reformers and pro-Third World lobbies encouraged them to ask for more. To their surprise, it just didn't work out. The OPEC bloc failed to land the industrialised countries in trouble for the simple reason that they kept buying Western and Japanese goods and launching vast, costly development schemes. So the huge and growing mountain of petrodollars exacted from the West flowed temporarily into the coffers of the Oil States, and then straight back to the West again in exchange for its goods and services. The burden of the increase in the world price of oil hit those least able to pay — the LDCs.

The external debt position of the LDCs worsened rapidly. By the end of 1979, their medium-term debt had reached three times their 1973 level, and equivalent to a quarter of their total output. A memorandum at the Office of the Comptroller of the Currency in Washington, dated May 17, 1977, had already spelled out the danger:

> "Large outstanding international loans to developing countries and financially weak developed countries are a matter of great current concern. Such loans usually finance basic economic development in emerging nations and, more recently, cover national balance of payments deficits. In either case the prospect that the country involved will be able to generate the sizeable balance-of-payments necessary to pay loan interest and principal, in this author's opinion, is dim, even over the very long term."

In 1980, United States interest rates soared over 20% at one time. The debt of the LDCs by now was a monstrous albatross. Over the next two years, their liquid reserves had been drained away. They borrowed now to survive. That too was why the bankers continued lending — to avoid collapsing themselves. According to the IMF, by 1983 the total debt of the LDCs had doubled again to more than $600 billion.

The first shock-wave was felt in late 1981. The epicentre was in Eastern Europe, rather than one of the LDCs. No less than $80 billion was owing in Bulgaria, Czechoslovakia, East Germany, Hungary, Poland, Romania and the US. $80 billion that will never be repaid! In June 1983, the rescheduling of Poland's debt was taken up again. Poland, it must be remembered, has its own strong, ethnic lobby in cities like Pittsburgh and Chicago. It was from America's Poles that the first money was sent to re-build Old Warsaw after 1945.

The next shock-wave came from Mexico — the land that was to become Eldorado! On August 20, 1982, more than 100 bankers were told bluntly that Mexico could not repay its debts. (Mexico's medium term debt was as great as that of all the Comecon debtors put together.) In a matter of

2 days, a rescue package of $1.85 billion was put together by a group of central bankers, acting through the Bank of International Settlement (BIS). The geobankers and the IMF together raised a further $8.6 billion. At the meeting of Third World Debtors in Lima, Peru, at the beginning of November 1986, Mexico was waiting for the IMF to give the green light for the latest loan package. Promised the previous summer, it was worth SDR 1.4 bn (£1.18bn). A few days later the Citibank led committee of leading creditor banks confirmed that it had raised 90% of its $6 billion loan package. In anticipation of the IMF move, the World Bank had already announced that it was prepared to release $30m of the £500m "trade development loan".

Since the 1970s Brazil, Argentina, Zambia and others have all made their contribution to what Secretary of State George Schultz first called the "debt bomb". The bomb is still ticking away. But will it ever stop ticking and just go off? Citibank's Chairman, Walter Wriston, said at the end of 1982 that the possibility of that happening was *about as close to zero as anything that human beings can predict.* That statement reminds me of the one made by Professor Irving Fisher of Yale University. He was a man of many talents: one of the founders of econometrics, and the inventor of index numbers. He was an advocate for eugenics and stock market speculation. He was a practical man too. In his early life he had invented a card index file, and sold it to Remington Rand. With the proceeds, and his skill as a speculator, he made a sizeable fortune. In 1929 he said that the stock market and the American economy had reached a permanently high plateau. Many believed him. In the aftermath of the 1929 crash he lost between eight and ten million dollars — according to his son, Irving Norton Fisher's biography, entitled *My Father-Irving Fisher.*

Fritz Leutwiler, president of the Swiss National Bank (and of the BIS) was another who saw "the danger of a chain reaction", as banks called in loans in an "every man for himself mentality". Chairman of the US Federal Reserve, Paul Volcker sounded a clear note of warning on November 16, 1982. He spoke of "a threat without precedent in the post-war world". If the worst happened, no country would escape the consequences.

In 1980, I wrote an article for the *Crown Quarterly* entitled "Global Bankruptcy". One banker told the Crown Agents that what I had written was pure lunacy. Beckman "lunacy" has since been adopted as the banking orthodoxy of the 1980s. In 1986, debt rescheduling and rollovers are still the order of the day. To most people's surprise, the disasters since 1982 have mainly been due to domestic rather than international failures. When Penn Square went bust in 1982, the $2bn loan portfolio it had sold around the market place was leaking bad debts like an old fashioned ball point leaking red ink. . . into a white shirt pocket. Then Continental Illinois fell flat on its face.

The World of Rock and Roll Banking and Grocery Store Finance

Throughout 1987, the reverberations of the fall of Ivan Boesky continued to ricochet from one side of the globe to the other. In addition to the investigation into Guinness, the Fraud Squad in London has probed a subsidiary of Exco International, Britain's largest money broking house. On the other side of the Atlantic, the Securities and Exchange Commission were still digging into a compost heap of corporate takeovers, junk bond financing deals and suspected insider trading. Members of the US Congress were threatening drastic action, exciting an almighty howl from Washington against the so-called "parasites" who prey on strong healthy companies. With each new investigation and indictment, it grew louder. It was clear that as the roar grew louder, there would be more investigations and indictments against the wheeler-dealers. The high-interest, low-quality junk bonds that had been used to finance the mergers and takeovers — which had already fallen in value quite sharply — would *continue* to fall in value. Ultimately, any bond issue that lacked a rating better than A+ would become suspect and perform accordingly. Obviously, the more exposure these scandals receive, the more frightened and disillusioned investors will become.

Ivan Boesky can never for one instant have dreamt he would have such an effect on the present and future of the world's stock markets. His influence is likely to stretch even beyond the world's stock markets. Returning once again to the Wall Street scene, some disturbing behind-closed-doors developments were causing grave concern in many quarters, especially the Federal Reserve. During several heated discussions, Federal Reserve Board Chairman Paul Volcker repeatedly warned that junk bonds were dangerously volatile and could set off a Wall Street explosion. Very few investors were aware that the US Savings and Loan industry held a massive $6 billion-worth of junk bonds that had been used for financing the mega-mergers and takeovers for the past couple of years. The fall in value of a large number of these bonds caused severe loss to many of the Savings and Loan institutions holding them. It was clear that if these bonds continued to fall in value, there could be a spate of failures among the savings and loan groups, with the attendant implications for the commercial banking sector.

In December 1986, Paul Volcker was extremely worried about the position of several large commercial banks that had helped finance the corporate takeovers and mergers that we'd seen. The crack-down on insider trading abuses could land the money centre banks with some massive bad loans, given the size of the deals that were financed. The picture was an extremely grave one, coming at a time when the US banking system was already resting on a bed of quicksand. If just one of the big banks went under, it could pull down the entire system within months.

In 1986, the deflationary forces raging through the global banking system produced 120 bank failures in the US. That was already above the 1985 level of bank failures, with three more months' figures still to come. A conservative estimate of the full years' number of bank failures in the US for 1986 was expected to be in the area of 140 plus, a post-1930s Depression record. Confidence remained shaken during 1987.

There was no disputing the immensity of the problem, although it appeared that the US media had been instructed to keep it all under wraps. When the Continental Illinois Bank was rescued by the Fed in 1984, it was only the fourth time in US history that a commercial bank had had to be saved and kept open by the infusion of massive FDIC funds. Only four commercial banks were subject to a similar type of rescue in 1986. US Treasury officials were believed to be discussing the possible dangers under the strictest security.

According to reports towards the end of 1986, the biggest worry of all concerned the failure of a major bank, and the possible implications due to the fragility of both the system and the US economy. US Treasury officials kept referring to the problem as the potential "credit implosion", an apt description for an economic hydrogen bomb that could produce devastating fall-out. The failure of a major mega-bank would certainly lead to a chain reaction, causing the failures of inter-connected mega-banks and smaller banks. As a result, the supply of credit to the corporate sector of America would suddenly evaporate; the banks that remained would be able neither to purchase the debt issue of major corporations, nor to issue further short term debt issues. The bill market would come to a standstill. Companies would be unable to finance their operations, and any plans they might have for expansion. Loans would be called in as desperate bankers tried to stave off the day of reckoning. Debt defaults and corporate bankruptcies would balloon as loans were called while financing proved impossible. The US economy would be brought to its knees; and, no doubt, the phenomena would be exported to Europe and other parts of the globe, as a result of the multinational links in the banking system.

"The problem with the major banks", explained one US Treasury official, "is that they *are* the system". In the US there are something like 15,000 independent banking institutions. All 15,000 are inextricably linked together through a network involving cheque clearing, wire transfers, data processing, loan sharing, share dealing, international banking and investment advice. Each day, over $1 trillion worth of transactions are processed through the interlocking network of these banks. The continual maintenance of efficiency and stability along this conveyor belt of credit is not only essential to the smooth operation of the banking system, but also to the nation's economy as a whole:

> "A sudden failure of one institution, particularly of substantial size, can interrupt a long chain of payments and dramatically and unexpectedly affect other, unrelated institutions, some of which may not even have a business relationship with the institution in difficulty and have themselves been well managed and sound."

This was the warning given by Paul Volcker to a special Congressional committee early in 1986.

By the start of 1987, $400 billion of Latin American debt, as well as domestic energy debt, agricultural debt, property debt, and junk bond debt were all in the process of going sour. It was more than likely that the passage of time would take its toll on at least one of the big money centre banks, if not two or three — so deeply involved as they were in the ballooning bad debt situation. Three years earlier, President Reagan had been advised that if such a set of circumstances ever did develop — as could have been the case even at that time — the consequences would cause financial chaos unparalleled since the Depression of the 1930s.

The Grand Design

Several inter-agency reports have found their way into the underground press in America, which make extremely interesting reading:

> "It must be recognised that traditional methods of handling bank failures are probably unworkable in the case of a banking crisis."

appeared one supposedly guarded inter-agency memo:

> "The traditional methodologies would result in disruption of service and would fuel the public perception of financial disaster."

The document offers firm evidence that a mega-banking crisis is being considered in Washington DC as a distinct possibility, and further declares that if one of the major banks were "in jeopardy" the existing system that is in place would be unable to function — *due to a dearth of eligible bidders, the necessity of raising a lot of money under the darkest of financial scenarios, and/or a lack of time in which to consummate a transaction.*

A blueprint for what will be effectively the nationalisation of the US banking system was drafted at top security meetings among the highest ranking officials of the US Treasury, the Federal Reserve and the Federal Deposit Insurance Corporation. The nationalisation programme would be spearheaded by the Federal Reserve during a major crisis since — by law — the Federal Reserve may make unlimited loans to the financial system at its discretion. Another inter-agency report issued by the Fed states:

> "The Federal Reserve System has adequate powers and considerable capacity to provide liquidity to the banking and financial system of the United States when that system is under stress."

The Federal Reserve is the bankers' banker, assuming the role of the lender of last resort. The function of the Federal Reserve is to provide liquidity in an attempt to prevent the failure of a bank if the problem is one of temporary illiquidity. If a bank actually does fail, the Federal Deposit Insurance Corporation steps in. The function of the Federal Deposit Insurance Corporation is to make certain that depositors are protected and to attempt to negotiate the sale of the defunct bank to a healthy one after liabilities have been met.

The first step in the grand design was underway by December 1986. Contingency plans which had been kept at each of the Federal Reserve banks for the emergency measures needed up until then, were under review. In total, the Federal Reserve banks held unissued currency of about $19 billion. A small part of this $19 billion was strategically placed outside the vaults of the individual Federal Reserve banks in various places of safekeeping for the immediate use of any depositary institution which might need funds during non-business hours. At the Federal Reserve bank in Culpepper, Virginia, the largest portion of the fund, $2.6 billion, was held in the vaults of the bank for use in the event of a national emergency. It was generally believed that these provisions should be adequate. The economic advisors to the Federal Reserve expressed the opinion that the amount of physical currency required to meet a series of "runs" on distressed banks, would come out to a sum lower than the total of any bank's estimated losses. It was envisaged that the major portion of any sum needed to avert a bank closure due to a "run" would be redeposited in other banks, and remain within the banking system. A part of the contingency plan proposed by the Federal Reserve would be to transfer currency directly from a bank that may be taking in deposits to one which may be experiencing a "run".

Given the increasing difficulties encountered by the FDIC in negotiating sales of defunct banks in recent years, there had been an amendment to the existing contingency plans. In the event of a large failure, traditional methods of handling bank failure might no longer be workable. As a result, a further plan was formulated. This, in essence, provided that the Federal Deposit Insurance Corporation — acting as a receiver — was now able to execute the temporary operation of a newly chartered bank that assumes the assets and liabilities of whatever bank may fail.

Part of the grand design to avert a banking crisis involved the declaration that the 10 largest banks in the US are now considered sacrosanct. It has been decided by the authorities that the Federal Government would intercede — with taxpayers' money if necessary — to maintain the liquidity and solvency of the 10 largest banks as first priority. In the event of bank failures outside the "Big Ten", the FDIC would choose an institution to form a bank holding company. The FDIC would then purchase the holding company's stock, and provide capital to the newly nationalised bank. Additional aid would be provided, as and when required.

During 1987, the Federal Deposit Insurance Corporation intended to ask the US Congress for a bill to give them more authority and more money in order that threatened institutions could be saved before they went under. Before such a bill became law, there were likely to be many minefields to cross. Furthermore, there were certainly a number of flaws in the grand design.

There was firstly no guarantee that the amount lost when a "run" occurred on a bank or series of banks, would be fully offset by deposit-taking institutions not experiencing "runs". Nor could it be usefully ascertained that the $19.6 billion reserve would prove adequate in the event of a banking crisis. The system was in unknown and unquantifiable territory; if, for no other reason, than that the prodigious off-balance sheet risks could absorb the $19.6 billion in its entirety.

Over the past several years hundreds of smaller banks have been allowed to fail. Most of the uninsured depositors have lost all or most of their savings. If suddenly, all creditors of the big banks were paid-off, following the heavy losses experienced by those who had invested with banks that had already failed, there could be a backlash shaking the entire *political* system, as well as the *banking* system.

A further political threat arises from the plight of the farmers. The farming community in the US has been among the hardest hit by bank foreclosures on debts which they could not repay. The farmers certainly won't stand for the US Government's blithely absorbing the land debts through non-farm bank customers in the cities. That would certainly aggravate their poverty. The 1986 elections showed the farming community to have much more clout at the polls than the politicians had recently believed.

Another impediment to the Federal Reserve's grand design was Senator Proximire, appointed new chairman of the US Senate Banking Committee. Proximire — no friend of the profligate bankers — is considered to be one of the meanest, most tight-fisted, penny-pinching politicians in America. It was fairly certain that Senator Proximire would not entertain a plan allowing bad bank managements to be let off the hook.

However the US banks are rationalised, and whatever the grand design, the bail-out of any major bank or banks is going to require the infusion of hundreds of billions of dollars. The $19.6 billion reserve won't even scratch the surface in the event of a serious calamity. There should be no doubt that the US Government does not have hundreds of billions of dollars immediately available for the purpose of bailing out the banks. While the Federal Reserve is *permitted* to lend unlimited amounts, the Federal Reserve is strictly limited. The US constitution does not permit any government agency in Washington to "print money."

Not withstanding the intentions of well-meaning regulators, the grandstand play over Insider Trading at the end of 1986 spread a thick smokescreen over the far more crucial, underlying problems that investors face. The cost to the investor of insider trading is infinitesimal compared to the potential losses from other causes.

In *The Downwave,* I predicted the sharp fall in the price of gold, the slump in commodity prices, in oil, and the escalation of the LDC problem. I also predicted bank failures taking place in the United States — and in Britain. Above all I forecast the change-over from inflation to deflation; from a near hysterical clinging to the belief that markets could only go up, to a sober realisation that the writing was on the wall. The message read: *This way to reality!*. Slowly, by Christmas 1986, the fact that deflation was a way of life in the United States had begun to be acknowledged. Investigative press coverage of *America's Deflation Belt* and the like, showed that the subject was being broached. Although many remained to be convinced. Deflation was by then quite a problem. The fact that the benign — if misleading — term "disinflation" was in everyday use, showed the customary unwillingness to use the hard word. It has always been the case that words like "liquidate", "take-out" and "eliminate" will be employed in preference to short, hard words like "kill"; even among — or *especially* among — professional killers. Similarly the word "disinflation" is used to take the edge off the word — if only for the speaker!

But deflation is not merely the slowing down of inflation. It is an actual collapse in price levels. It has been more destructive of wealth than inflation. It is certainly more difficult to control. It is unfortunate that so few in positions of control and trust have never actually met it. An article in *Business Week* summed up the position as succinctly as any:

> "(After) four decades of almost uninterrupted wage and price increases, the idea that a broad range of prices and incomes could see a decline seems as outmoded as paper collars and running boards."

A "running-board", it may be necessary to explain, was the ledge each side of the car (below where the door sills now are), linking the front and rear "mud-guards" over the wheels. You stepped on to the "running-board" to climb aboard. If it's necessary to explain *that* for the younger readership, you can see how difficult it is for them to imagine what deflation can do to an economy, and to an individual's way of life.

Therein, perhaps, lies the greatest danger: unfamiliarity — as well as familiarity — can breed contempt!

The Misinformers. . .

"It is true", said Lincoln, in his last public address, "that you may fool all the people some of the time; you can even fool some of the people all the time. . . " It would appear that, based on this assertion, great wealth has been built by members of the Securities Industry. Without listening any further, modern politicians added their own rider to Lincoln's familiar declaration. It runs: "There is a further truth, that we hold to be self-evident. . . that most people — fortunately — don't even realise they *can* be fooled. Even fewer seem to realise that they *are* being fooled. Least of all do they recognise their role as willing pawns in the great Deception Game."

Acting on that convenient assumption, politicians — and vested interest lackeys, who do their bidding for them — waste no more time on what Lincoln, or any other dead statesman may have said. They buckle down to, and get on with what they regard as their mission in life: the winning of office, the gaining of popularity, and the acquisition of wealth and power.

To that end, they unhesitatingly seduce members of the public into believing that things are far better than they really are. They are helped by the fact that it is not very difficult to convince people of the things people would like to believe in the first place: to wit that things *are* a great deal better than they could possibly be. The worse conditions become, the more desperately politicians and vested interests strive to prove that they are "actually better". The more anxious the times, moreover, the more eager the public become for reassurance. Little wonder that politicians place so much confidence in the two most common aids to political success — disinformation and misinformation, supported by half-dressed truths and plain, naked fiction. Today the disinformers and misinformers are in evidence on a greater scale than ever before, and in a much more skilful and organised manner. George Orwell's Newspeak and Double-think are now a stark reality.

Since the premiership of Harold Wilson, No 10 Downing Street has tended to build up its own exclusive policy and "information" teams. It tends to lead to confusion if No 10 and the Treasury, say, hand out two conflicting versions of the same story. But that occurs very rarely. Usually it will be when No 10 has failed to brief the Treasury Press Office on the official "line" to take; or when someone has forgotten to tell the Treasury, or some other department, to keep quiet. . . and say nothing.

Unfortunately, officials and others at Westminster (and in Washington) are extremely adept at the misinformation and disinformation game. It is easier to practise in Britain as — unlike his American counterpart — the UK citizen has no Right to Know. Indeed, some Governments appear to act on the assumption that it would be better if the electorate knew nothing! It is preferred they be like mushrooms: kept in the dark and fed with rubbish. The need of the politician to get his views across (whenever possible without debate) and the national craving for the "inside story" find expression in the Parliamentary Lobby system. The Lobby Correspondents, fed on scraps, are required to guarantee that they will be of good behaviour. They will accurately report what they are given to report. But they will leak nothing they are not *required* to leak.

Visiting correspondents — especially those from the United States — are constantly amazed at the way in which seasoned political journalists will subscribe to what one Washington columnist called "a grown-up version" of the English prep-school code of ethics: "Fear God, Obey the King and Make Sure the Other Side Don't Get Hold of the Ball." The truth is that journalists are quite like ordinary people in many respects. They love a secret. But they feel they cannot fully enjoy it until they have found someone they can share it with — "in the strictest confidence, old man!"

It would be easy to treat the whole Lobby system with contempt. But it would be a mistake to pretend it is not still effective. Indeed, it may well become more so. In October 1986, the Government instructed five key civil servants not to answer questions put by the House of Commons Select Committee investigating the Westland helicopter affair. On December 18th,

1986, Terence Higgins, chairman of both the Treasury and Liaison committees, attacked the Government's hasty decision. It could have "far-reaching" and damaging consequences for the entire committee system. The significant fact about the whole affair was that in an unguarded moment the Government had revealed its true feelings about Parliament's Right to Know. The manner in which Sir Robert Armstrong, the Cabinet Secretary, gave evidence at the MI6 book case before an Australian court was also most revealing. "He didn't just appear contemptuous of the Court and its proceedings," said one Australian journalist, who was present for most of the trial, "He seemed to me to be contemptuous of the whole bloody lot of us." It must be disturbing for the Mandarins of SW1 to discover that the world is less impressed than they are by their own kind.

For the ordinary member of the public, who does not have the time, (or inclination) to go through every official statement with a fine tooth comb, I am bound to repeat that *any* official statement must be regarded with suspicion. How often have I advised subscribers to *Investors Bulletin* never to believe anything from "reliable" sources unless it's categorically denied? But these days, experience dictates that official denials and "leaks" must also be regarded with suspicion.

Not that the journalists are entirely without blame. They like to write. They like even more to be read. Maybe they disappoint us because we *expect* them to be more reliable today then, say, in Alexander Pope's day. We know what *he* thought about them!

"All, all but truth, drops dead-born from the press."

Despite their shortcomings, Press Lobby offerings probably do less harm than most other forms of disinformation. For one thing, they can be recognised as a rule by their stilted language. For another, half-a-dozen papers will carry the same story. . . virtually word for word; despite the suggestion that "our reporter" was the only one to enjoy the Great Man's confidence! Those whose suspicions are not alerted by the indentical phrases all the way from *Newsnight* to the *Daily Mirror,* deserve what they get. The kind of story that *can* catch almost anyone out is one which has the claw marks of a genuine news story. Television is extremely good at this. It is far more difficult to judge their worth than to assess the value of the naked propaganda put out by a host of highly skilled lobby groups, many of which make no bones about their aim — to put pressure on Government. Their statements, surveys and statistical reports are accurate so far as they go. They are too wise to be caught passing inaccurate statistics. They know they can rely on the media to select the "juicier" passages. Most treacherous of all are those lobby groups which make out that they are "independent" or "anti-government", but in reality exist to further Government's aims. Where they exert any pressure at all, it is pressure on the public at large.

But nothing these days is more blatant than the fudging of official statistics. An excellent example is tinkering with the unemployed figures, by changing the basis on which the count is made. To say nothing of the use of "job creation" schemes to cosmeticise the figures. It can rarely be more than that, since the creation of real jobs is just about the last thing a "job creation" scheme can hope to do.

The emasculation of the leading cyclical indicators, by removing *hard* numbers relating to bankruptcies and substituting CBI "expectations" was a subtle example of the same technique, intended to reduce the "bad news" potential of these pointers to the future performance of the real economy. Another recipe for "statistical fudge" was to change the mode of presenting the Money Supply numbers. That was done in November 1986, following a broad hint dropped by the Governor of the Bank of England. He intimated that the Sterling M3 broad money aggregate might be discarded, since the "distortions" in M3 meant it was no longer a "reliable" indicator of monetary growth. Just more rubbish to pile on the mushrooms!

It might be said that since November 1986 the Bank's own figures have become less reliable as an indicator. The change from mid-month to calendar month reporting made it more difficult for a while for outsiders to measure and assess the significance of the Bank's monetary statistics. The Bank did say that the biggest problem would arise in attempting to assess the significance of seasonal adjustments applied to calendar month data. These adjustments, warned the Bank, would be less reliable and more liable to revision. Outsiders would find it more difficult to interpret Sterling M3 figures because the Bank would no longer publish seasonally adjusted data for the Public Sector Borrowing Requirement; nor would the public have details of the banks' external and foreign currency transactions and non-deposit liabilities. These sets of data are all key components of broad money.

This may seem too technical for people to worry about. However, they *should* worry — to the extent that an important source of information has been taken away from the financial institutions. It is information which the authorities have hitherto claimed they need to know. The simple fact is that the monthly PSBR figures published by the Treasury in cash terms provide no more than a very rough guide to the underlying trend of government borrowing. This is due to the timing of tax payments and the large seasonal fluctuations in departmental spending.

The October 1986 figures shewed no more than a modest rise in the broad measure of money, Sterling M3. But on an annual basis, growth came out at between 18.25% and 18.5%. That was well above the target range. To say that the M3 figure is no longer significant is one thing; to say, in effect, "Ignore the September figure. . . because we know how *that one* came about" is quite absurd. Money supply, like any other government figures, are supposed to show what has happened. If something occurs in real life and "spoils the curve" — hard luck! No doubt if the Plague had descended on London again last year, some bureaucrat somewhere would still be tut-tutting over the grave "distortion" it had caused to the mortality figures.

It is obvious that the inflation of Sterling M3 caused by the heavily oversubscribed TSB issue in September '86 broke the pattern. But it was an established fact. It happened. To have dismissed it as merely a "distortion", unwound during the October was absurd. Since privatisation issues are likely to continue to have a similar effect, it will seem more than a little disingenuous to make that particular excuse each time.

The fact of the matter is that since the arrival of the Thatcher administration, Sterling M3 has grown by no less than 190%. This is the largest growth in British Money Supply in over two thousand years! It happened, moreover, at a time when the virtues of "sound money" and "tight money" were being extolled by the Tory Establishment. Lies, deception, rock-and-roll banking and grocery store economics reached unparalleled dimensions in the Britain of the 1980s. So did the girth of the speculative Bubble.

It would be too flattering to both of Thatcher's Chancellors to suggest that everything that has happened since 1979 was the result of their radical policies. The last lingering impression that this might have been so was dispelled most skilfully by Gordon Pepper of Greenwell, when he addressed the Forex Association in London, on December 2nd, 1986. I confess that I had been an admirer of Gordon Pepper's, and of his outspoken, and incisive style back in the days when he wrote Greenwell's *Monetary Report*. It was Pepper who explained better than anyone the influence of the 3Ms (M1, M2 and Sterling M3). He did so at a time when most people thought of the Ms as motorways — or small, round, coloured sugar-coated candies with chocolate centres. On this occasion, Pepper was speaking about the Government's so-called Medium Term Strategy. It had been introduced in 1980 as the then Chancellor's perceived solution to all that ailed Britain.

Over time, the original Medium Term Strategy has been eroded out of recognition. When it was no longer possible to keep some of the early changes from the public, the Prime Minister herself attracted the attention of the crowd with her now famous shriek, "The Lady's Not for Turning." Not that I, personally, could ever see Margaret Thatcher making a U-turn. To do that, you must first know the direction in which you are going. Neither "the Lady" herself, nor her two Chancellors were ever quite sure about that. Obviously, they knew where they *would like* to be going. But that is by no means the same thing. Not, said Gordon Pepper, that there were deliberate, abrupt changes:

". . . policy has not been chopped and changed but. . . there has been a continued drift, the possibility of which was clearly envisaged in 1980, both from broad to narrow and towards greater emphasis on the exchange rate, especially in the latter when data for the money supply is suffering from distortion."

It was not long, however, before escape clauses began to be inserted into the Medium Term Strategy. In 1980, Pepper went on, the position was set out quite clearly:

". . . (No) single measure of money supply can be expected to fully encapsulate monetary conditions. In assessing monetary conditions, the authorities have to regard a range of indicators. The way in which money supply is defined for target purposes may need to be adjusted from time to time."

The message was there in plain language for all who cared to read it. If the Chancellor didn't like the way £M3 (or any other measure) was running out of control, it could be dismissed as "unrepresentative". He would then be free to replace it with a truly "representative" measure. That is one which was growing at an acceptable rate. This was the first statement of what we might call *Lawson's Law*.

Lawson's Law. . . Margaret Must Win

In 1980, £M3 ballooned throughout the year. In 1981, the authorities decided that the growth in £M3 had been "misleading". The Chancellor said as much:

"Taken on its own, £M3 has not been a good indicator. . . in the past year."

Would the Chancellor have been so disparaging had Sterling M3 numbers remained within the confines implied under the Medium Term Financial Strategy? In any event, targets were re-established for the three main measures of monetary growth for 1982 — M1, M3 and PSL2. The broad measure, M3 and PSL2, were given priority. M1 took second place. During 1982, however, broad money was on the rampage once again. In 1983, the Chancellor decided to reverse the emphasis. We were told to keep our eyes glued to the narrow measure of money supply; the *real* measure. Perversely, M1 was also way above target. Thereupon it had to be admitted that M1 was not the appropriate measure after all. So M0 (M Zero) made its entrance. M0 — notes and coins — was the one to watch, for a *true* picture of the way the money aggregates were performing. Watching M0, it was possible to see that the Thatcher administration, which had come to office on the back of a "tight money/sound money" policy, was one of the most profligate in British history.

Chancellor Lawson had to change again in 1984, because of the unsatisfactory performance of the money aggregates whether the emphasis was placed on M3 alone, or M3 and PSL2 together, or when narrow money (M1) was substituted for broad money as the primary indicator. That didn't leave very much to go on with. Especially when even the substitution of M0 for M1 presented the same picture of run-away growth. For 1985, we were told, both broad and narrow money should be given equal importance. But the schizophrenic authorities were to change their minds once again during the course of the year. In his Mansion House speech for '85, the Chancellor announced that he was:

". . . no longer seeking to control the recorded growth of £M3 by systematic overfunding. . . "

That is to say he would stop selling more Government paper than was strictly necessary to plug the gap. The trouble, explained the Chancellor, was that the target for M3 "was clearly set too low." No one was particularly surprised after that, when Lawson began to place the emphasis on narrow money once more, in early 1986. In his Lombard Association speech, M3 was downgraded and M0 elevated afresh. In the 1986 Mansion House speech, Chancellor Lawson claimed:

> "neither broad money nor credit was a trigger for this week's rise in interest rates."

But he did say that the manner in which the "more reliable" M Zero had moved higher could not be ignored. Credibility was beginning to wear thin, If, nevertheless, we persist in wanting to understand the reasoning behind this apparent shilly-shally, Gordon Pepper's analysis is helpful:

> "The detailed elaboration of the process of (policy) evolution has been given in a number of speeches by the Chancellor. The most important of these were in the 1983 Mansion House speech; the 1984 Mais Lecture; the 1985 Mansion House speech and the 1986 Lombard Association speech.
> "Mr Lawson's first Mansion House speech in 1983. . . described in detail the way in which policy had evolved under his predecessor, Sir Geoffrey Howe. (Lawson) then 'kite flew' . . . the evolution to come. At the time. . . with the benefit of hindsight it becomes clear; the decision not to overfund persistently and, if need be, to downgrade £M3, had already been taken."

The Government's efforts at managing the money supply may have been unsuccessful, but their success in handling the media has been superb. Scarcely a mention was made in the press of the Government's monetary policy debacle. For the great mass of the public, who know only one exchange rate — the pound in terms of the dollar — it is difficult to grasp the extent of sterling's decline against the world's other major currencies. One thing which kept the pound's "effective" rate so high was the weighting given to the dollar within the "basket" of currencies. The dollar may have fallen, but its weighting in the basket has not changed.

Between the second half of 1985 and the start of 1987, the pound was substantially devalued against the DM. But that did not reduce the propensity of the British to import rather than buy the domestic alternative. Nor did the weakness of sterling make UK exports that more attractive. Had the UK been a member of the EMS, it might have drawn the public's attention to the weak state of sterling. No doubt some superficially appealing explanation would have been devised — if the two Chancellors had really set their minds to it.

In his address to the Forex Association, Gordon Pepper reminded them that the growth in the importance of the exchange rate had also been reported in much the same way as the switch to and fro between broad and narrow money:

> "As early as 1982, the Government explained how the exchange rate became crucially important when the monetary aggregates were known to be distorted. A fall, or a rise, in sterling is often the result of an easing, or a tightening, of monetary pressure in the UK relative to abroad. So the exchange rate can indicate a change in monetary pressure but its movements must be interpreted very carefully; they may arise from non-monetary causes."

At the close of 1986 it was extremely difficult to tell whether sterling's persistent weakness and currency level was the result of monetary or non-monetary factors. There was a good gain in the exchange rate, early in December, when it was revealed that the Conservative Party had a 6% lead over Labour in a public opinion poll. The previous week the pound had slumped when another poll placed Labour in the lead. The pound swung back and forth, too, with the fluctuations in the oil price. They were comparatively large movements, in view of the small — almost miniscule — movements in the price of crude. Time and again the Chancellor stressed that the exchange rate was not serving as a reliable indicator when influenced by non-monetary factors. Therefore, he argued, no one should think there was a simple formula relating to monetary conditions.

If the Chancellor is to be taken seriously (other than as a Party politician facing an election), he was saying, in effect, that the slump in the mini-pound had nothing whatsoever to do with the Government's monetary policy. As I wrote in *Investors Bulletin* on December 13, 1986:

> "If you believe that, then you'll also believe that hyper-inflation in Germany during the 1920s had nothing to do with the fact that the authorities were printing money as fast as the presses would roll until a point was reached when the money that was being printed was literally not worth the paper that it was being printed on.
>
> "In spite of the fact that while the mini-pound has fallen from $2.56 to $1.03, while the rate of inflation has fallen . . .to under 5%, the Chancellor is trying to convince the electorate that the reason the pound must be defended is because of the inflationary consequences if it's not defended."

The truth, as anyone with half an eye can see, is that by the end of 1986 the speculative balloon, which was being flown through an easy money environment, had divorced the City from the poverty and penury to be found in many areas outside the South-East. The real economy, it was claimed, was being artificially buoyed up by the financial economy. That, in turn, was being sustained by the consequences of the previous fiat monetary policy, and a continuing headlong monetary expansion. I came to the conclusion, in the same issue of the *Bulletin* that:

"It is this factor above all — profligate monetary policy — which really underlies the international lack of confidence in the mini-pound, and which is the underlying cause of Britain's high interest rate structure. If the UK's real productive economy, labour market and balance-of-payments (excluding invisibles) were functioning in a satisfactory manner, and were not under such pressure and subject to such uncertainties, the currency would be far less vulnerable to fluctuations and non-monetary influences such as the oil price or the political situation. As things stand, the pound is so inherently vulnerable that any perceived negative which might ordinarily have no effect on the exchange rate is immediately translated into lower quotations."

Accepting that the aim of the Medium Term Strategy was to restore the *financial system* to a period of health over the medium term, it plainly failed. Not that the City objected, bearing in mind the manner in which revenue had been directed towards the financial services industry. Privatisation was a boon to those who thrive on commissions, since the higher volume of business served to soften the blow which might have been felt from lower commissions. But, at the close of 1986, there was neither joy nor cause for joy beyond the City, and the property-rich Southern counties.

Here we saw another propaganda trick being played. It starts as a rule with the construction of a crude politico-economic model which is (as we say of a computer) "user-friendly". After a while it tends to change its meaning; which is where the trouble starts. Take for example the concept of "Third World". At first, it merely meant the non-aligned bloc within the UN General Assembly: the bloc which tried to remain aloof from both the "East" (the Russians) and "West" (the Americans and us). The idea attracted considerable attention after the Bandoeng Conference of Afro-Asian States in April 1955. From time to time, Pandit Nehru's India, and President Tito's Yugoslavia were seen as nations seeking to tread the narrow path of non-alignment as members of the Third World.

In time, however, the term "Third World" acquired heavily economic overtones. It began to be used as a synonym for the "developing world"; itself a euphemism for the "under-developed world". In recent years talks between the industrialised West (or the OECD countries) and the Third World (or Less Developed Countries) were dubbed the "North/South Dialogue". The assumption was that the Northern Hemisphere had the resources, as well as the know-how; and the Southern Hemisphere lacked just about everything except huge, hungry and politically unstable populations. No one — or, at least, no one with any sense — bothered to point out that the "West" included Japan; or that Australia, for all intents and purposes part of the "West" — and therefore the "North" — was to be found in the Southern Hemisphere!

Over the past couple of years, the growing gap between London and the South East and the rest of the country — in terms of house prices, jobs, investment under the Business Expansion Scheme and the general level of expectations — has been called the North/South Gap. By the end of 1986, when the difference between the South and the rest of the country became too marked to ignore, the Government and some sections of the press began to poo-pooh the idea that any such divide existed. Why. . . they exclaimed. . . there were some very rich people in the so-called dying towns! They lived in fine houses, took two holdiays, sent their children to elitist boarding schools and bought expensive foreign cars. Whereas in the South there were some horrifying areas of impoverished and undernourished families, harassed and angry ethnic minorities, crimes-of-poverty, bed-and-breakfast families, overcrowded hostels, and 17-year-old down-and-outs (of both sexes), sleeping "rough" under the alleyways off the Embankment and in the new "cardboard cities" which sprang up wherever a supply of empty boxes was readily available.

Such sophistry did at least show one thing: how desperately the Government and its media supporters were seeking to hide the truth — if only from themselves.

At least things might have been worse, as a paper by economist Giles Keating entitled *Fooling All the People* pointed out. Had the *original* MTFS been followed through, the outcome for inflation and unemployment would have been even more dire. This was partly because public expectations about government policy are a key influence on the economy itself; and in early years of the MTFS, the continuing expectation was that it would have to be abandoned. Market forces, therefore, acted against the policy, leading to its modification.

At the beginning of December 1986, an all-party committee of MPs accused the Chancellor of operating an "obscure" monetary policy, and failing to set a coherent framework for fiscal policy. The Treasury and Civil Service Commons Committee — which had a Conservative majority — insisted that the Chancellor had made a "substantial change" in the Government's economic policies which should be explained. You see? It was not just Beckman who was belly-aching about the state of the nation! Or the stories that were being fabricated.

Leading analysts too were to come out with lacklustre forecasts for 1987. But the way these forecasts were presented by the media would suggest unreserved optimism. One particular point was the manner in which the media chose to isolate the subject of unemployment, as if it had been highlighted by the forecasters. But it was not highlighted at all. According to the Mori Poll, the principle political issue at the next General Election would be unemployment. If one had studied the various, differing media presentations with the forecasts that had been made, it would have appeared that the forecasts were principally concerned with forecasting unemployment for 1987. But, again, they had not been. Every year the *Financial Times* usually prints a table of the forecasts of Britain's leading forecasters. For the first time in memory, in 1987 — as we approached the General Election — that table was omitted. Ironically, this happened with the *Wall Street Journal*. That too usually prints a similar table. In 1987, it was omitted.

Many of the forecasts that *were* published pointed to an intolerable level of domestic debt in UK, and the twin shadows of protectionism and sovereign debt abroad. In a more reasonable world, they might have been expected to take the shine off shares. But, in a media-dominated world, where forecasts appear to be twisted and distorted to suit the desires of the incumbent Party, fourteen of the world's sixteen largest stock markets were hitting, or all-but-hitting, fresh All Time Highs.

Some saw the lack of any correlation between stock market performance and the real economy as the most nagging worry at the start of 1987. Others looked towards sterling. Many were puzzled. Which way *was* the pound heading? The explanation was quite simple. There was a massive divergence between the actual forecasts and the manner in which they were presented. This may be considered as the media's contribution to the cause of misinformation and disinformation.

Returning once again to the plight of the mini-pound, which the media chose to bell at the beginning of 1987, the Bank of England's Index (Base Average 1975=100) is the most generally quoted — apart from the £/$ rate. However, 1975, when the Index was last "fudged", belongs to another age. More revealing in many ways is the relative strength of the main currencies as shown on the Percentage Changes on the Morgan Guaranty scale. This shows how currencies have moved from their 1980-82 level. Despite the supposed weakness of the dollar, it had still added 0.4% on January 9th. In many parts of the world its non-European trading partners still regard the $ US as a strong currency. On the same date, other leading currencies stood as follows:

Yen	+54.5%	Lira	−16.6%
D. Mark	+21.6%	F. France	−13.0%
S. Franc	+21.5%	C. Dollar	−12.1%
D. Guilder	+14.3%	Sterling	−24.8%

While considering domestic attitudes to the Mini-Pound, we must always remember that media presentation is one of the major factors influencing the currency. One of the reasons the dollar was relatively stable against the pound during 1986 was due to presentation. It is an inescapable fact that the American economy, and the dollar, are far more *visible* than any other economy or currency in the world. The dollar's strength occurred in the period beginning in 1981, when the global economy was moving into recession. What could be seen at the time — though it was not appreciated before — was the underlying weakness of other economies compared with that of the United States. The US also moved into recession during 1981. But while the American recession was a comparatively shallow one, it was quite severe in mainland Europe, biting deepest of all in Britain. We may expect that when the world moves into recession once again, the same underlying weakenesses will reappear. It will then be seen that the American economy, and the dollar are far more resilient than the currencies and economies of Britain and Europe.

Canadian-born Dr Paul Chertkow made his name in this field as Chief Economist of currency consultants International Treasury Management. He joined Hoare Govett, around Big Bang, as their Currency Economics Director, and continued to produce his revealing monthly review of developments across the exchanges. With 151 national currencies, the task of reviewing the market — let alone forecasting trends — is far from easy. As Chertkow put it:

> "All that can be expected is that a carefully prepared forecast will provide a better indication of a currency's future value than a simple extrapolation of past values or than a single flip of a coin."

He also said, on a number of other occasions, that the claim by governments to turn the tide by intervention should not be taken too seriously. He had this to say for the future of sterling, after the Election:

> "(Once) the election is over, the foreign exchange market will focus its attention once again on economic fundamentals. Factors which now appear favourable (like the increase in government expenditure) because they should enhance the Conservatives' electoral prospects will then appear negative because they bode ill for inflation and the balance of payments.
> "To forestall another currency crisis, we believe that the next government, whatever its political complexion, will decide to participate in the exchange rate mechanism of the EMS, possibly with the same 12% bands as Italy."

The same "12% bands at Italy?" If Chertkow is right. . . how far, indeed, have the Mighty Fallen!

All the ambiguities and deceptions I have been describing influence business conditions and capital markets, domestically and internationally. They have been used as part of the propaganda campaign to expand the speculative bubble; and used by the most potent insiders of all — the Government.

There is a tendency to believe that insiders must always do better than anyone else, simply because of the information that is exclusively theirs. Add this to the immense power — and influence — wielded by Governments and we should expect them to be bang on the button every time. This, however, is an illusion. In his book published in 1987, George Soros — president of the highly successful Quantum Fund — devoted some 350 pages to the task of exploring what really goes on inside the financial markets. He included in his book, called *The Alchemy of Finance,* what amounted to a detailed investment diary covering a year in which the Fund appreciated by 123%.

On Sunday, November 2nd, 1985 he wrote:

> "I got my timing wrong. My dollar sales looked good until the Japanese Central Bank surprised me and the rest of the market by raising short-term interest rates. I took this as a new phase in the Group of Five Plan in which

exchange rates are influenced not only by direct intervention but also by adjusting interest rates."

A week later he wrote:

"My views on currencies are being tested. After a sharp rise in the yen, there was a sharp reversal last Thursday. . . I refused to be panicked."

Saturday, November 23rd, 1985:

"The markets continue to pre-empt me. . . The Japanese bond futures market collapsed (from 102 to 92) when the Japanese Government raised short-term interest rates. . . (This) is bound to be temporary: the Group of Five wants to stimulate worldwide economic activity, not to dampen it. . . We may be on the verge of a great stock market boom."

We remain indebted to Mr Soros, "the most successful pure investment manager in history", as Barton M. Biggs of Morgan Stanley once called him. Not many in his position would be so frank. Nevertheless, you may be thinking, an Insider among Insiders like Soros is rather like the hero of a high-grade TV Soap. He is bound to triumph in the end! To take first things first, George Soros confesses in the Epilogue to his book that as a young man:

"I fancied myself as some kind of god or an economic reformer like Keynes. . . My sense of reality was strong enough to make me realise that these expectations were excessive and I kept them hidden as a guilty secret."

When it came to the Big One — the stock market collapse on October 19th, 1987, George Soros admits he got it wrong. On 14th October the *Financial Times* published an article in which Soros argued that a bust was coming — in the Japanese market. He was right in so far as the Nikkei Stock Average peaked that very day at 26,646. But though Tokyo experienced a shake out, Wall Street and London were the markets to feel the full impact of the blow.

Later, Soros told the *Financial Times* (January 23, 1988) he had misjudged the political situation:

"If it hadn't been for the intervention the market would have crashed. But it is clear that the Japanese Government is on the line to prevent a crash, and I give them credit that once they have made a decision on policy they can take the steps to prevent a crash."

"Aha," you say, "end of story!" Not so, because it still leaves open two key questions — both of which will need a lot more time to answer: how was it Japan got away unharmed, but why did the markets collapse anyway?

It is worth bearing in mind that by the time the magic 100 days were up, the 2,443 "blue-chip" stocks in the 24 countries covered by the FT-Actuaries

World Index, shewed falls of around 19% — 10% on the crash, and a 9% drift-down thereafter.

The UK, on the FT-Actuaries World Index was down 28%, France 30%, and Japan — despite its relative invulnerability — down 16%. Tantalisingly for those who were ready to blame the United States for the whole shebang, Wall Street, which fell 20% on Black Monday, managed to recover some 8%, leaving New York considerably stronger than many by the 100th day.

As well as slashing share prices, the October collapse saw trading volumes fall right away, thereby reducing the commission revenues of the broking and market-making insiders. Even before Big Bang, it was clear that there would be too many dealers in every area of the new City. Even before the stock market collapse a number of City houses had closed down certain of their activities. After the crash, planned redundancies were replaced by swift, and often brutal, firings. At one American bank the first time staff knew they were for the axe was when they were instructed to hand in their security cards.

So far as the upper echelons of the City went, when they were not murmuring words of comfort, they appeared genuinely puzzled. But even they were less puzzled than that other breed of insider, the American (and UK) Business School fanciers. Their whole market theory rested on the assumption that markets behaved rationally and efficiently. For some, it was the only justification for the market's existence. Yet here they were, on October 19th and the days that followed, as disorderly as a bar-room filled with drunks and madmen. It was as though the City had been taken over by a whole army of lunatics, familiar to readers of my *Investors Bulletin*. They are the guys that so often take the controls of the market elevator. Only this time they had quit their glass and metal boxes and were rampaging through the dealing rooms, creating mayhem as they went.

Perhaps the most disturbed among the insiders were the concerned Governments and the market authorities. They gave the impression that the market collapse not only puzzled them, but left them angry and thoroughly disgusted. When Government insiders disapprove, they like to "take steps". It was the disapproval of the City, as we have seen, which led to the imposition of the reforms leading to Big Bang — for which, as 1988 dawned — the City was still not ready. Disapproval in Washington produced the idea of imposing trading limits on equity trading. At one time, the idea of the United States under Ronald Reagan interfering with price movements in a free market would have seemed as outlandish as anything the Soviet bloc might have dreamed up. Impose limits on equity trading through the exchange and back alley trading will follow — with the most insider of insiders scooping the pool. It would mean that the investor hit by a major fall could be locked in, perhaps for days, before prices had edged down to their soft landing. Fear of being locked in, coming on top of apparently ever increasing dealing charges, may well in the end make the new breed of investors feel that they are once again regarded as rank outsiders. The Stock Exchange Chairman,

Sir Nicholas Goodison, voiced his fears in January 1988 that the new investors could well retreat from the market to which it had taken so much effort — and so many privatisation issues — to attract them.

In many ways, it would be comforting to think that the Real Insider at government level possessed some special knowledge and ability denied to lesser mortals. Yet, after the dismal record of the Group of Five (of which more later), and after countless attempts at solution by summit — whatever the problem — we are eventually driven to the realisation that if Governments were more open with us, we would merely realise a little sooner how impotent they are.

How refreshing it was to know that when Japan's Prime Minister Noburu Takeshita is asked by journalists what is the right level for the dollar, he invariably replies, "Only God knows."

This book is about successful planning. If you are to be successful in your planning, and are able to anticipate the events likely to occur, it is quintessential that your judgement is based on information as opposed to disinformation and misinformation from political and other sources with vested interests. Not that vested interests are really necessary. It is a known fact that engineers can often prove a disaster running their own engineering company, because they are constantly seeking to "improve" their products. In a similar way, statisticians can become over-obsessed with their craft. They get out their rulers and extrapolate to such an extent that they deceive the user as much as they deceive themselves. As one business casualty of a severe miscalculation (which saw him expelled from the Board Room) claimed:

> "Looking back, I realise that instead of trusting to, and using what I heard around the place. . . which is all a man trying to anticipate changes in fashion can do. . . I made the mistake of hiring experts. Then, instead of telling them what I wanted from them, I more or less put myself in their hands. You could say that the road to my particular hell was paved with first class market researchers and statisticians."

You could say that my life and my work have been devoted to helping people anticipate the future, and arrange their financial affairs with a reasonable degree of success. I have always recommended acting on the assumption that the future will unfold in accordance with the unalterable principles that have governed economic activity through the ages. The laws of the market place suit our purposes. . . our preconceptions, or our desires! If we are to succeed in planning for the future, and anticipating the events that are likely to occur, it is again quintessential that our judgement should be based on information; rather than the disinformation and misinformation gleaned from political sources, or those with vested interests. It should be obvious that information from suspect or tainted sources will not serve you well. Ironically, this often includes those who have the greatest vested interest.

Chapter Seven

INTO THE UPWAVE

At any rate they seem to have been strangely forgetful of the catastrophe.
Plato, Laws iii

History is sometimes kind, and sometimes not so kind to those ahead of their time. Man discovered fire to warm his dwelling, and assist in the preparation of his food. Not too long afterwards that same man was burned at the stake with the fire he had discovered by those who considered him a witch or heretic. Man invented the wheel which would help transport him and his goods from place to place with greater efficiency than ever before. In due course, members of his species discovered they could use that same wheel to build a rack with which to tear their fellow men limb from limb if ever the dictates of the masses were denied.

The Vikings were the first Europeans to reach North America; but never received recognition for their explorational accomplishment. It was only after the Crusades, when Europeans had acquired a taste for spices and other products from the Far East, that Europe was ready for the accidental discovery of North America. Columbus set forth to find the "New World" and received full recognition for its discovery, even though Christopher Columbus never planned to arrive at the destination of his discovery.

History was kind to Christopher Columbus. It was equally kind to Winston Churchill. Had Churchill not been adamant about the German threat in his speeches during the 1930s, he probably would never have become Prime Minister in World War II. The premiership was his reward for the many warnings he had given the British people. But history was not so kind to Roger Babson, who predicted the impending stock market collapse of 1929. For years Roger Babson had warned his investment clients of the instability of the financial system and the inevitable holocaust. Yet, during the period of his incessant warnings, people continued to accumulate profits in the stock market, and Babson was denigrated and ridiculed for his pains. J.K. Galbraith issued similar warnings just before the "Great Crash" while shares were still rising. Among the letters he received was one threatening his life, if he didn't stop saying "nasty things" about the stock market. Although countless people are aware of J.K. Galbraith, it is not in connection with his forecast of a "Great Crash". Roger Babson was probably the first to anticipate the problems ahead, but very few people had ever heard of him.

In the early 1970s, I first began publishing my findings and studies in long wave economic theory. I predicted the longest and most glorious bull market in British history to coincide with a fall in the rate of inflation. In my publication *Investors Bulletin,* based on my use of the Elliott Wave Theory, my target for the beginning of the bull market was 146 for the Financial Times 30 Share Index. I made that forecast in October of 1974. In January of 1975 Britain embarked upon the longest and most glorious bull market the country had ever seen. In the following years, inflation plummeted from an inter-year high of 28% to an inter-year low of 3.5% during 1975. Very few people remember that forecast because it was made at a time when the City of London was imbued with pessimism, and the stock market was falling rapidly. By October 1974 the Financial Times 30 Share Index had lost over 65% of its value; and many City pundits held the view that the bear market would continue well into 1975 and beyond. It was generally perceived that buying shares was the most foolish thing anyone could do. Indeed the catch-phrase in January 1975 was, "We are now witnessing the end of the capitalist system as we know it".

During the bull market of the 1970s, I became extremely enthusiastic about oil shares. I was the first super-bull of British oil shares, predicting that oil shares would outperform most other groups. Inspired by the potential profitability of those companies which were suppliers to the North Sea, I developed Britain's only North Sea Service Group Index which was a regular feature of my weekly publication. I was also enthusiastic about the Engineering Sector and the Construction Sector. In fact, I was a buyer of most groups of shares with the exception of finance, insurance, property and banking. At the time, I believed that Britain would prosper on its ability to "make things", rather than by manipulating the efforts of others.

In early 1975 I advised subscribers to my *Investors Bulletin* to "buy with both hands". I continued to issue this advice periodically throughout the early years of the big bull market. As astonishing as it may now seem to many (based on my recent analyses), I earned the reputation of being a perennial bull during the late 1970s. "No matter what happens Beckman believes shares will always go up", was the comment made by one of my contemporaries. By then my bearishness in the late 1960s, and my advice to buy gold when it was trading at $35.00 an ounce, had been forgotten.

My studies of long-term cycle theory never suggested that any trend would continue in perpetuity. My clients had profited handsomely during the early stages of the bull market that began in 1975. By the early 1980s, the profits had been piling up nicely. But I knew the bull market must end. My job wouldn't be finished until I secured the profits that had been made, and invested them in an area with equal profit potential, but less risk, than the overvalued bull market. In January 1979, on my daily LBC broadcast, I forecast a recession in Britain, beginning during the fourth quarter of the year. On cue, that recession began in the fourth quarter. By 1982, it turned out to be the worst recession experienced since the Depression of the 1930s. The first major downward spiral that was likely to continue for 10 to 15 years. . . possibly more, had begun. I quickly reduced my position in equities just before the recession. The only investments I kept were the oil shares. In early 1981, I became nervous about the prospects for oil shares, and disposed of them also.

In 1981 I also began to see the beginning of two new bull markets: one for the US dollar and one for the US bond market. Rather than enter an equity market that I felt offered limited potential, I shifted my emphasis to US dollar fixed interest investment. I went on to forecast the biggest bull market in bonds since the 1920s. That is precisely what took place while the US dollar soared.

Most of the reasoning behind my strategy was outlined in *The Downwave.* In 1983 when it was published, I predicted an eventual collapse in the UK equity market, which would be as severe as the Wall Street Crash of '29. I also forecast a fall in residential house prices that would continue for 10 to 15 years. Among the other forecasts in the book were an 80% fall in the price of oil along with a banking crisis; sharp falls in farmland prices; a secular downtrend in most commodities; rising unemployment, and the decimation of UK manufacturing industry. Finally, I predicted a depression.

I saw growing protectionism as one of the world's major threats, with countries adopting a "begger-thy-neighbour" policy, in a desperate effort to protect their markets, as we moved further into the 1980s. I also anticipated vast cultural and social changes, with the music of the time becoming progressively more peacful and tranquil. I foresaw changes in moral values, with a shift toward Victorian standards; and I anxiously awaited the reappearance of man's love for his fellow man; bringing an end to the uncaring orgy where women were treated as instruments of pleasure, and men were used as stepping stones to nothing more than acquisition.

To many, who could see no further than the financial implications of my work, it meant a darker world. Since the publication of *The Downwave,* I have been labelled a Cassandra, a Prophet of Doom. Yet what I envisaged was a far brighter world; a world where people might plan their future, and enjoy a stability of human relationships that has not been seen for many decades. The fact is that an extremely large number of the forecasts made five years ago have come to pass, giving further validity to the long term infrastructure of global economic activity implied by the long wave theory of economic life on this planet. Today the bright new world of my vision now has a far greater chance of emerging, because of the manner in which the components are falling into place, than was the case when I wrote *The Downwave.* Of course, in the early part of 1987, as I complete this manuscript, stock markets around the world are booming; property prices in the South-East of England are rising by leaps and bounds, and we've yet to see any evidence of depression. To those who believe that a falling stock market and the prospects of a depression are the worst of all possible scenarios, the rise in property prices in the South-East, and the soaring stock market, have been advanced to refute the message outlined by the long waves of economic behaviour.

Those who ignore this message do so at their peril. True, there will be another long and satisfying period of sustainable expansion in most countries, when man will again rise to new heights of achievement. But the long term period of contraction must first have spent its force. The message of Black Monday, in October 1987, has still to get across.

Why Britons are Getting Poorer When They Think They're Getting Richer

If you are the type of person who is determined to take a rosy view of Britain's future, and believe only what is palatable to you, despite all the evidence to the contrary, then there is probably little point in reading any further. The power of Government to persuade is formidable. They employ a vast army of propagandists to tell you all the things you would like to believe to begin with, while patting themselves on the back for making all of the half-truths and naked fictions possible. On the other hand, if you have an open mind and realise that if I *could* tell you tales of a prosperous future for Britain I would — read on!

As I pointed out early on, we all have our ups and downs. Economic activity is no different. No economic development moves in a straight line. There are several trends of economic activity operating simultaneously all the time. There is the very long-term trend of economic activity which I have used as the basis for my long-term projections. This long-term pattern involves a period of expansion lasting 30 to 40 years. Next comes a period of transition lasting about 10 years. This phase is followed by a period of contraction lasting from 15 to 20 years. The short-term and medium-term behaviour of the economic aggregates, along with their relationships, vary in accordance with the nature of the overriding trend.

The last long period of expansion began in the late 1940s and continued until the early 1970s. Within that long-term expansionary trend were several recessions, which tended to be relatively brief and shallow. The transition phase of the early 1970s involved a recession that was longer and deeper than any of those that had punctuated the previous long period of expansion. The even deeper recession which began during the fourth quarter of 1979 in the UK served as the terminal juncture of the transitional phase.

For all intents and purposes, the long-term trend of economic expansion began in the 1940s and ended in 1972. The classical transitional period spanned the years 1972 — 1979, described by Alvin Toffler as an "eco-spasm". Between 1972 and 1979, the forces of inflation and deflation fought for supremacy. In 1979, the forces of deflation emerged triumphant, launching the long period of contraction which will lead ultimately to a global depression. During this depression, some countries will be hit harder than others. Britain will be among the hardest hit.

Let us pause for a moment to look once again at the idealised economic Long Wave model (p34). From that it will be seen that just as each long period of expansion is punctuated by brief and shallow recessions, the long period of contraction is punctuated by equally brief periods of recovery and expansion. These recovery movements, within the overriding period of contraction, are notably sluggish and lopsided. They are completely different from the type of recovery usually experienced following a recessionary phase within a structure of long-term expansion.

The recession that began in Britain during the fourth quarter of 1979, and continued through the second quarter of 1982, was deep and savage. It brought more economic dislocation (and higher unemployment) than any recession since the 1930s. Both the recession that began in 1979, and the minor recovery that began in 1982 in the UK, were classic in every respect within the category of long term economic cycle theory. The recession was prolonged and degenerative, greater than that of any normative recession that occurs during a period of expansion. The recovery that began in 1982, and many claim to have continued through 1987, had been characterised by the persistence of high unemployment in the UK, as elsewhere; stagnation in basic industries, with continuing deindustrialisation had been culminating in falling prices, and inflation and slow rates of growth of both input and output. The apparent recovery beginning in 1982 was certainly not the same kind of recovery experienced during the genuinely expansionary period of the 1940s-1970s.

Since no two cycles are identical, we must expect to find differences between the behaviour of the economic components now and those of 60 years ago. What must be recognised, however, is that while the similarities are *major,* the differences are *relatively minor.* This in no way invalidates the overall prospects for the future. Among the differences between the experiences of the 1920s and those of the 1980s in the UK, are a relatively stronger pattern in final output prices and buoyant incomes in certain areas of the private sector. During the 1920s, as we are seeing now, public attitudes toward economic conditions were relatively calm until the Wall Street Crash of 1929, which heralded in the Great Depression. During the early part of 1987, a stock market crash, either in London or on Wall Street, was the furthest thing from the minds of most investors. They believed that share prices would rise in perpetuity. These differences represent little more than a lag in the time sequence, before the FT 30 reached its all time high of 1926.2 on 16th July. By 9th November it had fallen almost 700 points to 1232, a loss of over 30%. Let's take a closer look at how we got to where we are.

As most of you are aware, inflation was rampant during the 1970s . It was considered an intolerable way of life for Britain, which suffered more than most countries due to the inherent weakness of its long term economic infrastructure. It was because of this inherent weakness that Britain was — and is — more prone to depression than most countries. Globally, during the 1970s, long-term credit markets were contracting quite severely for Britain. One Swiss bank placed British Government Securities on the "highly speculative" list. In 1976, the Labour Government under James Callaghan was forced to go cap-in-hand for a loan to the IMF.

Ultimately, the explosive rise in consumer prices proved too much for the stock market. Between 1972 and 1975, the British equity market (as measured by the *Financial Times* 30 Share Index) lost 73% of its value, rivalling the Great Crash in its intensity. For decades it was believed that the stock market would always be able to keep up with inflation. But the inflationary fires of the 1970s were too much for the equity market to handle. There was a stampede out of all forms of paper assets to buy "things", beginning with gold and gold related assets. The rush to buy what were defined as "real assets", as opposed to dubious financial assets, spread from gold to other precious metals, then to diamonds, gem stones, works of art, coins, stamps and a whole range of alternatives that many people had never before considered as investments. I heard of one man who collected old toy electric trains as a hobby. He was offered 2,000 times what he had originally paid for his electric train set, most of which was bought as "junk". A lady of my acquaintance collected dolls as a hobby, although she had never placed any value on her collection. When she was offered £20,000 for 20 dolls she found the temptation irresistible. The buyer explained that he wanted her dolls for "investment purposes".

During the 1970s almost anything was regarded as a "tangible asset" with a higher future potential value. Articles which previously would have been reserved for the refuse collector, acquired the status of "art nouveau". Contemporary art, incorporating discarded automobile tyres and chromium-plated Coca Cola bottles, fetched thousands at the auction houses. The desire to own "things" — any kind of "things" rather than paper financial assets, reached panic proportions in Britain during the 1970s.

It wasn't long before members of the public discovered that the acceleration in the money supply and profligate government spending were the primary reason they were suffering from ever rising prices. This tendency began to be associated with Socialist policy and Keynesian economics. As the 1970s progressed, inflation seemed to be a permanent way of life. Many fingers began pointing at the Labour Party and the Socialist movement in Britain. Suddenly, it was clear: a new political platform was in the making. Prior to the General Election of 1979, the Conservative Party preached a policy of "sound" money and "free" markets. It declared inflation to be Public Enemy No. 1. It had to be defeated. The British electorate bought the story. In 1979 Labour was defeated, and Mrs Thatcher came to office promising a bright new future, based on an alternative economic strategy. For the first time in living memory, Britain had a Prime Minister with a mandate to pursue a tight money policy. Keynesian economics, with all its deficit financing, was out. Milton Friedman's with "gradualism" and "monetarism" was in.

As I further pointed out in *The Downwave,* the terminal juncture of the long period of expansion occurs in proximity to a peak in wholesale prices, followed by a peak in retail prices, involving a peak in the rate of inflation. Following these secular peaks, the economy becomes progressively more prone to depression — a situation which can be aggravated by any monetary contraction. For the first time since the depression of the 1930s, Britain had a Government committed to the pursuit of a tight money policy. The transition spanning the period from expansion to contraction was complete in 1979 with the appointment of Mrs Thatcher as Prime Minister. The British economy had reached a point where the same engine that was preventing deep recession was the same engine that was fuelling inflation. That engine was fiat money. In 1979, Mrs Thatcher promised to shut the engine down. The consequences were inevitable. It was time for the long wave of contraction to begin. During the fourth quarter of 1979, the most menacing sequence of the long term economic cycle got underway, coincident with the end of the transitional phase. It was characteristic of the long-term economic cycle.

The recession in 1972 that followed the peak in the growth of the wholesale price level, was exceptionally severe. The recession that began in Britain during the fourth quarter of 1979, under the aegis of Mrs Thatcher, was far worse. Suddenly the manner in which decades of fiat money policy, and rampant social spending, had covered up the deteriorating infrastructure of the British economy was revealed as the recession bit far deeper in the UK than in any other country. It remained only for the global forces of deflation to gather momentum during the early 1980s.

"It breaks my heart to see what is happening in our country today", said Harold Macmillan in the House of Lords in November 1984. The passage of each day meant that 1,000 more people had joined the dole queues, while 1,500 a day were being added to the numbers on supplementary benefit. During the recession of the 1980s, 30 companies a day were going to the wall. Credit problems were acute. At the nadir of the recession, corporate and personal bankruptcies alike were higher than ever in the Great Depression. British manufacturing industry suffered its worst slump in 60 years. The electorate experienced the sharpest fall in living standards since World War II.

However you measured it, the decline in the real economy between 1979 and 1982 was inescapable. The production of wealth in Britain fell by 4%. Output of manufacturing industry declined by 19%. Investment in manufacturing industry fell by an alarming 36%. Competitiveness with other nations fell by 20%. In Norway, Austria and Japan unemployment was still under 3% in 1982. In Britain it was the highest of any industrialised nation at 13%. The total had risen in the UK over those three years by 2 million.

Within manufacturing industry, the output of textiles and clothing was cut by nearly 35% during 1979 and 1982. Steel production was slashed by 50% *in each of these years.* Less steel was being produced in Britain during 1982 than in the 1950s. Automobile output was down by 25% over the period

1979-1982, falling to its lowest level since 1957. The production of commercial vehicles fell to below the 1950 level.

In 1982 alone there were 12,000 company liquidations in England and Wales — more than two and a half times as many in 1979, *and the highest level ever recorded.* By 1982, personal bankruptcies were 60% higher than in 1979. Many firms, that for decades had been household names in Britain, were forced to close down or merge with others. The following is a list of some of the companies that came to grief in the recession of 1979-1982.

Airlines:	Laker Airways, British Cargo Airlines
Carpets:	Homfray Carpets, BMK, Forfar Carpets
Clothing makers:	Janet Reger (underwear), Morland (sheepskin wear), Libro (leisure wear), Lovable (bras), Alligator (rainwear), Nelbarden (swimwear)
Engineering:	Alfred Herbert (machine tools), Stone Platt (textile machinery), Aurora Holdings (Britain's last full-range special steel manufacturer), Carron's Iron Works, Wilson Watson Engineering, Fairbairn Lawson (foundry), Mallins
Financial Institutions:	Warburg (investment advisers), Hedderwick Stirling Grumbar (stockbrokers)
Football Clubs:	Wolverhampton Wanderers, Hull City (rugby league), Blackpool (rugby league)
Furniture:	Austins, Liden, Jaycee, Harrison Lebus, Orthopaedic Bedding Co., New Age Kitchens
Household goods:	Aeonics (duvets), Royal Stafford China, Viners (cutlery), Ronson (lighters, etc)
Shoes:	Norvic, Mr Henry
Shops:	Jacksons of Piccadilly, Swan and Edgar, Bourne's, Timothy Whites, Dicky Dirts, Crocodile, Supasave, John Michael, Biba
Toymakers:	Airfix, Lesney, Berwick Timpo, Dunbee Combex Marx, Triang
Vehicle Makers:	De Lorean (sports cars), Foden (trucks), Hesketh (motorcycles), Bamfords (agricultural machinery), Caravans International, Westerley Marine (boats)
Others:	Oxley Printers, Fakenham Press, Alan Pond (garages), Lockwoods (canned foods), Atcost (farm buildings)

One of the most remarkable aspects of the 1979-1982 recession, ostensibly triggered by a tight money policy, is that monetary policy was not actually all that tight. Moreover, inflation remained a serious problem, although not quite so serious as previously. In 1980 inflation had peaked at 28%. In April 1983, it was down to 5%. In spite of the recession, Britain was still showing the highest price rises for any major country, apart from Italy, Spain and France. Between 1979 and 1982, British prices rose by 50% compared to an average of 40% for the other industrialised countries. In the meantime, the price of goods supplied by the nationalised industry was hiked by 86% between 1979 and 1983 compared with 51% overall. The average rate of inflation for the period 1979-1983 was 13%. The engine that was fuelling inflation may have been slowed down, but it wasn't turned off. If it had been turned off, the consequences would have been unthinkable.

Britons will still have to pay the price for the excess reintroduced into the monetary system since 1982. The price will be even heavier than the price paid during the last recession, since the economic infrastructure has deteriorated that much further.

There you have a brief synopsis of the effects of the 1979-1982 recession on Britain. What I have described is not merely the prognosticative design of a pessimistic forecaster. It is the reality of that recession. Having seen the extent to which a mild slow down in the growth of the monetary aggregates was exacerbating the trends of a highly depressed and depression-prone economy, the authorities turned expansive. In 1982 they created conditions that were conducive to what the electorate might perceive as an "economic recovery" during the General Election of 1983. But perception and reality are two different things. During the long term expansionary phase, it is possible for the authorities to mitigate the duration and depth of a recession; generating economic improvement through an expansion of the money supply. This is not impossible during the contractionary phase of the long-term economic cycle. During the downwave, monetary expansion produces nothing more than a cosmetic effect, covering up the deterioration in economic activity and adding further excess to the system.

Although the authorities continued throughout 1982 to preach an anti-inflation-tight-money policy, the initially cherished economic policies of the Medium Term Financial Strategy were abandoned. Having invested many years of misleading propaganda (to promote the fictions that the Government's brand of monetarism embraced) the recessionary forces that were ravishing the economy proved politically too overwhelming in the year before a General Election. During 1982, the floodgates that were holding back the fiat money, opened wide. The idea that the economy would adjust benignly to a regular moderate flow of money rather than a steadily increasing flow, was forgotton. The approach of depression was hotly denied. A normal, sluggish, degenerating, secular expansion, which is characteristic of all expansions in the contractionary phase, got underway. It was aided and abetted by a generally expansive policy worldwide. But, just as Britain suffered more than any other nation during the recessionary period of 1979-1982, the secular expansion that began in 1982 was weaker than in most other countries.

In the years following 1982, there was a mild improvement in economic activity. But the price paid was indeed high. The price that is *yet* to be paid will be higher still. Since 1982, the monetary aggregates have exploded, exceeding all of the Government's previously established targets. Public spending has again been rampant. During 1986, the Government claimed that the Public Sector Borrowing Requirement for 1987-1988 was on target at a projected 1¾ % of GNP. But this was a statistical deception, distorted by the proceeds from privatisation sales. Adjusted for the sale of natural assets, the total Public Sector Borrowing Requirement for 1987-1988 would be in the area of £15 billion or approximately 4% of Gross National Product. The likely proceeds of asset sales are unreliable, representing neither a permanent flow of revenue nor a permanent reduction in expenditure. Therefore, the Government's fiscal stance and future implications can be ascertained only by treating asset sales as an item completely independent of Government financing requirements.

If a company were to sell a subsidiary, the profit from that transaction would be presented as the difference between the cost of acquisition and the proceeds of sale. If the company sold its subsidiary and treated the entire proceeds of sale as profit, and included this profit in the balance sheet, the directors would probably be guilty of a criminal offence. Yet, the manner in which the UK authorities have been treating the proceeds of privatisation, representing it as a reduction in the Public Sector Borrowing Requirement, is precisely the same as if a company were to treat the proceeds of the sale of a subsidiary as profit. Privatisation leaves the Government with a smaller asset position and smaller contingent liability position. The ratio between net assets and contingent liabilities can only remain the same.

Since it is most likely that private ownership of state assets will prove more profitable than when they were state owned, there is little fiscal gain for the Government by selling state assets rather than funding through the traditional debt market of Government Securities. In either case, funding current spending represents borrowing from the future, which is primarily responsible for Britain's current problems. The legacy that the British electorate are now due to inherit, as we move into a further phase of the contractionary period, is more of a threat than a blessing.

The White Paper on Government spending released early in January 1987 reveals for the first time what lies in store for the years 1989-1990. After allowing for inflation, the spending total is planned at £142.1 billion, representing a rise of 1.5%. The document also gives details of tax reliefs which count in the national accounts as "reduced Government spending". The most notorious of these "reliefs" is mortgage interest relief which is expected to cost the Exchequer £4.5 billion during the financial year 1986-1987. A married man's personal allowance comes to £13.1 billion; investment income of occupational pensions totals £4.6 billion. Employees' and employers' pension contributions come to £3.5 billion, and corporation tax relief is estimated somewhere in the area of £5.5 billion. Revenue forfeited through the absence of any capital gains tax on the sale of an owner occupied main residence was calculated at £3 billion.

Those who measure Government spending can come up with as many variations as a six-year-old with a Lego kit. Included in the Government's funny money numbers are asset sales running at £5 billion a year, along with the interest the Government has to pay on its debt. This is a frightening £17 billion for 1986-1987. There is a further sum of £6.5 billion, representing allowances for items such as non-governmental borrowing of public corporations being privatised!

The spending plans for the financial year 1987-1988 are £4.7 billion higher than for the previous year. The priorities are indeed interesting. Spending on housing, which fell by 6% between 1979 and 1986, was expected to rise by 1988. However, after the General Election spending on housing was expected to resume its downward trend. Since 1979, spending on social security advanced by 39.5% in real terms, due to the sharp rise in the level of unemployment. Social Security spending should remain stable over the next few years, unless there is another unexpected rise in the level of unemployment or public pressure on the Health Service!.

Between 1979 and 1987 Government spending increased by almost 14% in real terms, with defence up by 28% and spending on law and order up by 50%. The largest percentage increase of all was on matters related to job creation. This advanced by 90%, but had yet to bear any visible benefit.

When the Medium Term Financial Strategy was introduced in 1980, the Government claimed it was going to reduce public expenditure by 4% during 1983-1984. This was never achieved. Spending continued to rise, while the authorities mouthed their tight money policy. Spending continued to rise until it reached the same proportion of GNP as the Government inherited in 1979.

Spending plans for 1987-1988 were based on the assumption that unemployment would average 3.05 million the following year. If unemployment remains at 3.05 million, inflation must move higher — given the manner in which the British economy is currently structured. If inflation moves lower, unemployment and the spending attached to it, will of necessity move higher.

Along with claims of economic improvement in Britain, there have been claims of an improvement in the prospects for employment. Both claims are equally fictitious. Supporting claims that employment prospects were improving was the fall in unemployment between August and December 1986. A closer examination of the way the unemployment figures are calculated arouses considerable suspicion. If you take the measure of the labour force in December on the basis of previous calculations, and subtract the number of people in work, the result gives you the number out of work. It will be found that the numbers in August 1986 and December 1986 are identical. *In other words, there had been no real fall in the level of unemployment at all, as measured by the number of people who are actually out of work.* There had been a fall in the official rate of unemployment because many people had been pushed off benefits, or had refused benefits and were therefore no longer "counted" as unemployed, even though they were clearly out of work. It is estimated that the Government's new and more detailed "availability-for-work" test reduced the number of claimants at the beginning of 1987 by 4%, while an additional 2% were refused benefits. The number of people who were actually working in Britain had yet to rise. As a proportion of the population of working age, this number had fallen substantially. There are now fewer people than ever *in regular full-time employment* in Britain. The trend established after 1986 could be intractable.

Yet, in the five years or so since the trough of the recession in 1982, every official statistic emerging from Whitehall suggested a booming Britain. Real incomes during the third quarter of 1986 were ahead on the previous 12 months by a staggering 5%. Non-North Sea profits from industry were said easily to have overcome the depressing effect of lower crude prices on the income of oil companies. Retail stores reported record sales, suggesting a Klondike-like boom in the High Streets throughout 1986. This picture was repeatedly painted by the media over and over again. But there is a much darker picture beneath the glossy veneer that few seemed prepared to discuss.

1986 was a year of unrepeatable events. Figures show real income grew strongly. The growth in real incomes was the result of a combination of polarised earnings bouyancy and regional lags. There was also a redistribution of the tax burden that people thought were tax cuts, encouraging further spending. There was also a fall in the rate of inflation, producing a 5% growth in real incomes between the third quarter of 1985 and the third quarter of 1986. This was matched by an increase in consumer spending. There was no change at all in the savings ratio, standing at 10.6% of income in the third quarter of 1986 compared to 10.5% in the third quarter of 1985.

Those who like to convince you that the British economy has been improving continue to point to consumer trends, which offered the sole source of economic improvement. Many attempted to promote the concept of a "consumer-led boom", just as they tried to promote the concept of a country that was booming because of strength in the service industries. In both cases, this focus was highly misleading.

It is not possible for an industrialised trading nation to build an economy based on service industries. The very idea is absolutely ludicrous. For service industries to survive, there must be a viable industry to serve. At the same time, it is endemic during every period of economic deterioration for the service industries to lag other industries. When a recession begins, the slowdown in aggregate demand can be seen first in the level of commodity prices. The evidence of recession then spreads to heavily capitalised areas of manufacturing industry. During the sequence, secondary companies that rely on the larger companies feel the effect of recession. Through the continual progression, service industries are near the bottom of the list to experience the forces of recession. According to the work of A.C. Pigou, the consumer is the very last to feel the effects of recession. In Britain, the recessionary forces have been building momentum for over eight years. It is a simple fact that these recessionary forces may not have filtered through to the service industry level or to the consumer living in areas of service industry employment. The forces of recession have certainly hit the consumer in the industrial areas. He's out of a job! On the dole, many have defaulted on mortgages and are homeless. In sum, the prosperity that Britons believed they were enjoying, as we entered the latter part of the 1980s, was based on nothing more than false optimism generated by an easy credit-boosted, consumer spending spree; and supplemented by dubious claims for falling unemployment.

What Britons were told was an "economic recovery", fuelled by higher earnings and lower inflation, was nothing of the sort. This can be seen readily in the consumer credit statistics for 1986. The rise in outstanding consumer credit during that year reached 14%. It rose more than three times the rise in prices, and double the rise in earnings. In the past, the bursting of the easy credit bubble has always had dire consequences for the balance of payments, the exchange rate, mortgage rates and the rate of inflation. It is clear that the rise in consumer credit has been influencing Britain's trade figures for quite some time, through the attendant strong rise in imports.

In the past 7 years, the amount of credit extended to personal consumers had grown three times faster than incomes. Since the authorities abandoned consumer credit restraint, money owed on credit cards and hire purchase agreements has advanced at the rate of 20% per annum. At that rate, the debt burden doubles just about every 3½ years, while the ability to repay is cut by half. (Remember — the Rule of 72).

In 1980, the estimate of money owed represented slightly more than 7% of income. During 1986, credit outstanding was estimated at £31 billion. This was equivalent to 12% of income. Since 1980, the amount of credit outstanding had risen by 180%, compared with an increase in incomes of just over 60%. While the growth in incomes is likely to remain static — or fall — the growth in credit has been continuing to accelerate. If current trends persist, the level of outstanding debt by 1990 will reach more than 25% of incomes. The British consumer, in other words, will be in a similar position to that of LDC borrowers.

Not surprisingly, the suppliers of credit fully support loading the consumer with as much debt as possible, regardless of the consumer's ability to repay. On an actuarial basis, if a credit supplier can borrow money at 10% and lend at 25%, the profit margin allows for a large number of defaulters before a serious bad debt situation arises. Credit suppliers argue that the possibility of default is not a problem — any more than the level of consumer debt. They claim that people have become more sophisticated since using plastic instead of cash. They insist that most people pay off what they owe on their credit cards before the debt even accrues interest, suggesting that the level of debt is transient and misleading. The most pernicious aspect of the entire affair is that this argument is supported by the Office of Fair Trading and the Government alike, both of which have encouraged consumer debt.

The facts behind the rhetoric are that people have been using their credit cards to purchase basic items such as food, and that approximately 1% of card holders are now in default, finding difficulty in repaying the credit card company. Barclaycard alone accounts for 8,700,000 cardholders. Access accounts for 9,000,000. The default level at the start of 1987 meant that 176,000 people were having problems with these two credit suppliers alone. Given the plethora of other credit cards, it is likely that the defaulters numbered something in excess of 350,000.

It should also be recognised that figures for consumer credit include other sources of credit apart from credit cards. Actually, credit cards account for only approximately one quarter of outstanding debt. The remainder is mainly accounted for by traditional hire purchase agreements. Credit suppliers certainly cannot use the same argument for people who purchase goods on hire purchase as they do for those using their credit cards. But the consumer credit figures do not include mortgage debt. If this is added to consumer credit debt in addition to bank loans, total personal-sector debt in 1986 came to approximately £207 billion, representing about 80% of personal disposable income. In 1980, the figure had been £72 billion, or no more than 45% of personal disposal income. In just a few years, individuals will no longer have any personal disposable income at all if the proportion of debt goes on rising at the same rate as in 1986-7.

Overall, outstanding consumer credit grew from approximately 7.2% of personal disposable income in 1981 to 11.9% during 1986. Banks and building societies lend up to three times income for house purchases. This means that individual outstanding debts amount to something like 300 per cent of income. Add credit card debt, hire purchase debt and bank loans, and the debt burden rises close to 500% of incomes — if not more.

Now, let's look at a few basic economic facts. When an individual buys a TV set or a car on credit, he is effecting his purchase with income which has yet to be earned. That income, in turn, has to be earned on the basis of goods and services that are yet to be produced. As a result, the items he purchases on credit are not offset by an equivalent supply of goods and service, which would have been the case had he paid cash. The effect is an artificial level of demand and a growing economic imbalance. For as more and more goods are purchased through credit, less and less goods are being produced in terms of what would be normal in an evenly balanced economy.

At the same time, purchasing goods and service on credit is welcomed by just about everyone. The employee gains instant gratification, and is allowed to enjoy *now* the fruits of his future labour. Businessmen are pleased to offer credit, because they are able to sell goods and services which otherwise might not be saleable. Bankers love the whole idea, since profit margins on consumer credit are far greater than on business loans. (That is because the consumer is not interest rate sensitive, while the businessman must be to remain solvent.) Politicians are simply wild about consumer credit! It helps them generate an illusion of the prosperity they habitually promise voters.

But there is a darker side to the credit cycle, which has ominous implications. When an economy is hooked on credit, it becomes an insatiable "debt-junkie". It takes more and more credit just to keep the engines of economic activity turning over at the same steady rate. Any sudden reversion to simple cash transactions brings an immediate drop in economic activity, which could topple the economy into a depression.

When the consumer assumes more and more debt obligations, he finds his ability to repay those debts diminishes. That is because an increasing portion of his income is being used to repay the debt, while he is forfeiting an increasingly larger part of his future income. At the same time, businesses are lulled into a false sense of complacency. They expand their inventories and facilities to meet demand levels that are the result of a growth in credit. But at some stage they must reach a point of diminishing returns. Obviously, as the borrower commits an ever increasing amount of his income to repaying debt, his ability to purchase goods must be diminished — even if these goods are also to be purchased on credit.

So long as credit levels keep expanding, borrowers mortgage an increasingly larger amount of their future income. Suppliers of goods and services enjoy conditions that increasingly become divorced from any level of activity justified by prevailing economic conditions. As the credit cycle approaches its nadir, the economy still appears to be buoyant and booming, encouraging the spread of euphoria. But, slowly and steadily, severe deterioration takes place in the economic underpinnings. A grotesque imbalance develops. It is extremely difficult to pinpoint the precise level at which credit expansion reaches the point of unsustainability — the stage which precedes the inevitable credit crisis and depression.

It is the way in which a depression relates directly to the problems of the consumer that distinguishes a recession from a depression. A recession usually occurs when business people find themselves with excessive inventories, and cut back on their orders from manufacturing industry, which in turn must reduce output. So long as the overriding trend in consumer demand is upward, the recession becomes self-correcting. So it will not take long before the balance between sales volume and inventory is restored. That was the experience of the forty years of expansion from the 1930s to the early 1970s. Throughout that period, there was a steady expansion of consumer demand, with consumer credit remaining containable.

A depression occurs under totally different circumstances. First, the consumer finds himself with excessive debt relative to current and future income. This leads to the same conditions that occur during a recession; but with a difference. The economic contraction takes far longer to complete, because of the sharp cutback in consumers' purchases necessitated by debt servicing. Self-feeding debt liquidation is the only cure. In the meantime, the consequent fall in demand means that industries' inventories and plant capacity increasingly become excessive, leading to a snowballing of the problem. It takes years for equilibrium to be restored.

Since consumer debt at the levels experienced in 1986 is a relatively new phenomenon in Britain, I am going to take a leaf out of the book of the Great Depression in America. Consumer credit there has been a way of life for quite some years. The decade of the 1920s was known as the "Roaring Twenties" in the United States. Toward the latter part of the 1920s, severe cracks were beginning to show in the international economic infrastructure. But the orderly growth of the 1920s was gradually transformed into an unsustainable boom, as the decade moved swiftly to its terminal juncture.

The boom market, accompanied by a steadily rising stock, led to widespread euphoria. The urge to borrow money for all sorts of things became uncontainable. As usual, the bankers were eager and willing.

A great deal has been said about the stock market boom and the manner in which shares purchased on "margin" powered the speculative binge, culminating in the collapse. But far more significant to the economy as a whole was the accelerating surge in consumer debt. Between 1928-1929, total instalment debt leaped from $2.32 billion to $3.52 billion — a two year gain of some 52%, while disposable income grew only by 8%.

Given that type of consumer debt structure, it took no more than a mild recession to tip the economy into the abyss. An economic contraction in 1930 meant a decline in personal incomes. The surge in consumer debt was promptly reversed. The decline in incomes and rapid rise in unemployment led to a wave of consumer sobriety. Many began to cut back on their purchases, fearing to make new debt-financed transactions. They had witnessed the increasing problems of their neighbours. In the meantime, the repayment of outstanding debt had to continue. Total debt began to shrink, and the process of a self-feeding debt liquidation got underway. The US economy went into an irreversible contraction, culminating in depression.

Involuntary debt liquidation swelled as a number of individuals, with no means of meeting their debt obligations, were forced to file for personal bankruptcy. As an increasing number of individuals and companies were forced into bankruptcy, their creditors suffered heavy losses. They too had to file for bankruptcy. In the 1930s, the mushrooming defaults and contractions in consumer credit, and the subsequent collapse in consumer demand, sent a serious shock-wave throughout the entire US economy. Business inventories swelled beyond recognition; accounts receivable and bad debts ballooned. Bankruptcies begot bankruptcies at an ever increasing rate. The entire affair was brought to a resounding climax in 1933 when the US President, Franklin D. Roosevelt, was forced to close all of the banks in America.

There have been many claims by several pseudo-economists, which have been supported by the Government, to the effect that the British economy was experiencing a consumer-led boom during the mid-1980s. This so-called consumer-led boom was portrayed as the addendum to a boom which was being led by the service industries of Britain. The notion is pure nonsense. For reasons which I have gone into at great length, a boom led by the service industries is pure fantasy. Such a boom is not possible, since there can be no sustainable growth in service industries, if manufacturing industry is in attrition. Quite simply, service industries will have nothing whatever to serve if manufacturing industry continues to decline. An equally fanciful illusion, which has no substance, is that Britain is now able to make economic progress on the back of a consumer-led boom. This is also impossible when such a boom is fuelled by the continual expansion of credit. What Britain actually experienced during the long-term phase of the early to mid-1980s was an abnormal growth in consumer credit expansion, producing artificial and unsustainable growth in consumer demand. That is what politicians were calling an "economic recovery". Just as the abnormal consumer credit expansion produced demand for goods and services incompatible with the underlying economic infrastructure, so credit contraction will cause demand to fall suddenly and sharply to well below normal levels, bringing about a severe depression in a surprisingly short time, once the consumer credit bubble bursts. The ultimate conclusion, again forecast in *The Downwave* remains firmly in place. There has been a delay due to the explosive rise in consumer credit during 1984-1986. Unfortunately, the British people will face far more suffering, in far greater numbers, once the depressionary forces begin to emerge than would have been the case, had the consumer credit bubble not been allowed to reach such alarming proportions.

Encouraging people to "live on tick", in an economy that cannot afford to support them, has been having an extremely serious affect on home owners. For the years 1982-1986, the number of mortgage defaulters doubled each year and every year. As Britain bathed in the glory of its politicised "economic recovery" during early 1987, repossession of homes was increasing at a rapid rate in the West Midlands and South Yorkshire. In these areas, house prices fell in real terms. People were forced to give up their homes as, lumbered with debt burdens, they searched for a new home. It was precisely as I had predicted in *The Downwave*.

By the end of 1986, the official number of homeless people in Britain was estimated to be 100,000, which was double the level of 1978. In Scotland, Wales and Northern Ireland, the homeless figures were not known. The figure also excluded unmarried homeless people and childless couples. During 1986 more than 200,000 households applied to the local authorities in England for housing under the Homeless Persons Act. One in ten homeless families found themselves in that situation through mortgage default.

As a result of increased social spending pressures in 1986, and the need to cut expenditure, the authorities introduced legislation. Anyone who became unemployed would have only half the interest on their mortgage paid on supplementary benefit for the first four months. Prior to the new legislation, the interest was paid in full, but not the capital. At the time of the introduction of this new legislation, mortgage repossessions were averaging 1,800 a year in the North-East alone. According to *Shelter*, the housing charity, repossessions in the period ahead could treble as a result of this legislation.

During the depression of the 1930s, the Chancellor of the Exchequer faced the need to cut spending due to the pressure on revenues from declining business activity and rising unemployment. The Chancellor decided to cut the dole. This exacerbated the forces of deflation and depression, and caused a public outcry. According to popular belief there are now "safety nets" and Government "mechanisms" which would prevent that sort of thing from happening again. As the current trends in housing demonstrate, the more things seem to change the more they stay the same.

Purchasing Power Parities and International
comparisons of price levels and real per capita GDP
in OECD countries

GDP per capita (US$)

	1985		1986	
	*Real**	*Nominal†*	*Real**	*Nominal†*
US	16,494	16,494	17,200	17,200
Canada	14,959	13,636	15,700	14,100
Japan	11,666	10,997	12,200	16,200
Austria	10,610	8,743	11,200	12,500
Finland	11,421	11,024	11,900	14,400
Norway	14,098	13,960	15,100	16,500
Sweden	12,586	12,006	13,200	15,800
Belgium	10,718	8,022	11,300	11,300
Denmark	12,322	11,312	13,000	15,800
France	11,333	9,251	11,800	12,800
West Germany	12,158	10,243	12,900	14,700
Greece	5,914	3,294	6,100	3,900
Ireland	7,062	5,123	7,300	7,000
Italy	9,445	6,278	9,900	8,800
Luxembourg	13,636	9,745	14,300	13,900
Netherlands	11,332	8,628	11,800	11,900
Portugal	5,212	2,032	5,500	2,800
Spain	7,629	4,255	8,000	5,900
UK	10,882	7,943	11,400	9,600

* Converted at PPPs. † Converted at exchange rates.

Figure 16

Recently the OECD (Organization for Economic Cooperation and Development) completed a study intended to compare living standards between 19 nations. Standards were highest in the US, Canada and Norway. Living standards were the lowest in Portugal, Greece and Ireland. Britain was well down the league table, ranking number 12 in terms of living standards. In Europe, the standard of living was higher in most major countries including France, West Germany, the Netherlands, Finland, Norway, Sweden, Denmark and Luxembourg.

Britain is a depression-prone economy. The evidence is clear for all who are prepared to look beyond the political rhetoric. It is not a question of a depression developing at some date in the future. Britain's depression is under way clearly. But the perception of a depression among most individuals is far, far different from the actual reality. Many people still harbour the view that a depression descends like a swarm of locusts, sudden and all devouring. It doesn't happen that way. A depression will begin in the most vulnerable areas and then spread slowly to encompass an increasingly wider range of society over time.

Our position in the context of the long-term *schema* and our performance over the last five years point to the inevitability of a depression within the next few years. Thereafter, a long and glorious period of economic expansion involving a shorter working week, more leisure and a standard of living currently beyond human comprehension, is also inevitable. But only after we have experienced the long period of economic contraction, endemic to the long waves of economic life on this planet.

The global expansion I envisage is likely to begin during the early 1990s. Unfortunately, Britain may not be in a position to enjoy the fruits of the next long-term period of expansion to the same extent as other nations. The position of this country within the framework of the long-term global economic cycle may make this impossible. For purposes of forward planning, this aspect of the long waves of economic behaviour calls for extremely careful consideration. Certain elements of the political cycle, which in turn are a function of the economic cycle, place the British electorate in a somewhat invidious position, involving a major socio-political shock.

The end of every period of expansion produces cries among the electorate of more. . . more. . . more. . . more. . . more, more, more, more! Needless to say, it is the Government which the electorate feels should provide that more, more, more, more. At the terminal juncture of a period of expansion, the political party which promises the most (and asks the electorate to produce the least) will be the party to gain favour with the electorate. This tendency is more prevalent in some nations than others. It depends very much on the attitudes that have been encouraged amongst the electorate during the long-term history of several expansions.

Eventually a point is reached in the long-term political cycle where no political party of any persuasion, or ideology, is able to satisfy an electorate weaned on a socialistic, "government-will-provide-all" philosophy. Decades of political promises lead to heightened expectations among the electorate, who become totally unprepared to accept the slightest sacrifice or inconvenience. At the first sign of economic difficulty, the Government is blamed. Then it is ousted for failing to provide the unprovidable. Complete political disarray follows. It involves changes in political ideologies which often lead to a coalition government — while there remains hope for the electorate. Unfortunately, in many instances, economies that are overly mature find themselves moving toward a state of dictatorship and the enslavement of the electorate.

I doubt if there is an individual in Britain today who would remotely consider himself a slave of the state. Yet, in terms of their aggregate behaviour, Britons conform to the type of slavery that ultimately has encompassed slave-states. The electorate continues to clamour for additional tyrannical government security, just like any slave would do. The true libertarians, who acknowlege government as a parasite, are steadily dwindling in number. How did we arrive at this point in Britain? The answer can be found in the political development of the country over the past century or so, while providing a window for the future.

Britain. . . An Inflession Prone Economy

The United States declared its independence in 1776 — not all that long after the start of the Industrial Revolution. Britain had been a wealthy country during the 18th century, and it would not have been unreasonable to expect Britain to reap equal, if not greater, rewards from the major new technologies of the Industrial Revolution than the United States, which was still a developing country. Indeed, for a century it worked out like that. But gradually, Britain fell back, and the United States and Germany moved out in front. Britain — which had held the mantle of world leader during the 18th century — then entered a period of long-term decline.

In the past 200 years, Britain has, indeed, fallen a long way as the decline in the pound sterling shows. Many economists accept that broadly speaking the true strength of a nation is reflected in the value of its currency. At the time of the American Civil War (1861-65), the pound stood at $16.48. By March 1986, it had fallen to $1.03.

This at once prompts the question why the United States grew and grew until it assumed the mantle of world leader, while Britain continued its long-term decline. It used to be believed that the decline began in 1914. Now many economic historians would argue that it began as early as the 1870s. Some attribute the decline to the end of Britain's creative phase; others on the way Britain turned from Europe to the markets of the Empire, leaving rivals to compete for — and capture — Europe's market citadel. That is merely *what* happened. The more important question is *why*.

Throughout history we have seen the rise and fall of great nations. For a while, they have led the world in innovation, technology, production and living standards. Then, through the passage of time, these truly great nations have yielded up their crown, entering a prolonged period of decline. Some one-time world leaders — like Greece or China — are now among the Lesser Developed Countries. One of the more recent cases is that of Spain! — once among the most powerful. The country we are most concerned with is, of course, Britain. Sad as it may sound! So, let us look more closely at the reason why this is happening; and the inexorable precedents that history has provided.

Most economists accept the principles involved in short-term business cycle periodicity and the logic of the business cycle. Economic activity does not ebb and flow in a random fashion. There is evidence to demonstrate a stochastic behaviour pattern of unquantifiable duration. This notion is quite simplistic. The concept of the business cycle becomes a bit more esoteric when dealing with the cycles-within-cycles as demonstrated by the chart of the 20th century business cycle. What can be seen is the interaction between the short-term business cycle of Juglar along with the medium-term business cycle of Kitchin and the Long Wave fabric of Kondratieff. It was Professor Schumpeter at Harvard University who developed the theory of the three cycle *schema* and the effect of coordinated terminal junctures on the interaction of the independent cycles. In view of the remarkable manner in which the Long Wave cycle once again has conformed to the experience of the latter half of the 20th century, an increasing number of economists are beginning to conduct extensive investigations into the Long Wave phenomenon which I first introduced to readers of *Investors Bulletin* in late 1974.

THE 20th CENTURY BUSINESS CYCLE
AND CRISIS POINTS
(Calculated Path)

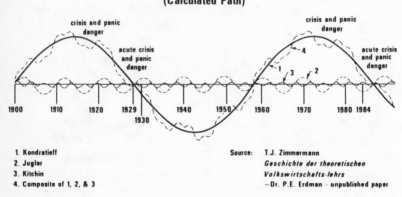

1. Kondratieff
2. Juglar
3. Kitchin
4. Composite of 1, 2, & 3

Source: T.J. Zimmermann
Geschichte der theoretischen
Volkswirtschafts-lehrs
—Dr. P.E. Erdman - unpublished paper

Figure 17: The 20th Century Business Cycle and Crisis Points (Calculated Path)

What very few have recognised is the existence of an even longer cycle than the 50-60 year Long Wave cycle. This explains why the extent and duration of depressions varies from country to country, yet occurs with the same frequency. This longer-term cycle also gives an indication of the type of depression we're likely to see in Britain along with the manner in which the UK is likely to participate in the next long-term period of expansion. . . the Upwave.

First, let's review the principles involved. During the course of every long-term period of expansion, there are recessions which tend to purge the system of the cumulative excess that occurs during the period of prosperity. As the long-term expansion progresses, governments turn increasingly to expansive monetary policies in order to lessen the effects and duration of the recessionary phases. As a result, the excesses that develop in the system are never fully purged and form a cumulative residue. This cumulative residue means that each recession requires a greater level of monetary growth to blunt its forces. Each time fiat monetary policy is introduced as a means to blunt the forces of recession, the residue gets larger. Eventually a point is reached where the excesses in the system become insatiable. The long-term period of expansion ends and a long-term period of contraction begins. During the course of the long-term period of expansion, recession becomes longer and deeper with the maturity of the cycle. During the period of contraction there is a steep depression and panic, as can be seen in the chart of the 20th century business cycle.

A similar phenomenon occurs over an even longer period. This period involves a cycle of world supremacy that lasts about 150-200 years. It comprises three Long Wave cycles and three major depressions, all of which vary in intensity, relative to the level of world dominance and the maturity of the economy involved.

Most Long Wave cycle studies begin with the latter part of the 18th century. Of course, Long Wave economic activity had been taking place long before that period. The problem lies in attempting to correlate the data prior to that period where records are somewhat more obscure. Yet we do have trends in interest rates going back to 2,500 BC that conform to the same Long Wave economic cycle as that which as utilised by Schumpeter, Kondratieff, Jay Forrester and other economists who have studied long-wave economic phenomena. A periodicity conforming to Long Wave economic activity can also be found in the price series of a host of the items such as gold, copper, wheat and various raw materials. There is overwhelming evidence to suggest that the Long Wave cycle was present, not only during our industrial society, but also during our agrarian society.

By piecing together the nature of economic activity peculiar to various countries in the period when these countries were the world's dominant power, some extremely exciting correlations emerge.

In general, what can be seen is that following a nation's first major long-term expansion during its period of world dominance, the initial depression which acts to purge the system is the most severe. Subsequent depressions are less severe. But the economy becomes more inflation prone. There are also significant socio-political factors which rise to the surface as a nation loses its global dominance. Britain is probably one of the best examples of this at present. But let's look at a few examples which are offered by other nations. In that way we can get a better picture of where Britain has been, and where it may be heading.

The chart on Page 31 shows the development of four complete Long Wave cycles of economic activity spanning the period from 1700-2000. The last fifteen years are projected in accordance with the nature of the activity of the previous 200 years.

We can construct a relatively reliable model showing shifts in world dominance since global leadership was inherited by the West about 400 years ago. Unfortunately, reliable economic data is not available for much of that 400 year expanse. Where historical data was available it has been used. For much of the material I have been forced to rely on descriptive historical accounts to ascertain the nature of economic conditions. In this respect, the historical accounts of Fernand Braudel have been of exceptional value.

In spite of the lack of statistical data for periods during the 16th and 17th centuries, the evidence to support the Long Wave cycle thesis, and that of the overriding thesis of cyclical global dominance, is even more overwhelming than that revealed in the four cycles corroborated by the statistical evidence of Josef Schumpeter.

During the early part of the 16th century, Spain was rapidly becoming a global leader. In 1582 Philip II made a momentous decision. Two years earlier, at the height of Spain's political domination of Europe, Philip II had conquered Portugal. That done, Philip and his Government elected to take up residence in Lisbon. Philip felt that looking over the ocean was an ideal vantage point from which Spain could rule the world. In 1583, with Philip's support, and the presence of government, the Iberian fleet drove the French out of the Azores, hanging all the prisoners from the yard-arm. The occupation of Lisbon in the 1580s left Spain in a position from where the entire Spanish Empire, and its economy, could be expanded and controlled. No longer was the might of Spain imprisoned in Madrid, the landlocked heart of Castile. Spain was now the possessor of what was deemed to be "The Invincible Armada". At the time time, Spain was the world's leader in the grand fashion.

The Spanish economy then embarked upon the most explosive growth phase of its history. . . and also a series of depressions, having taken the mantle of world leader from Portugal. The first major depression occurred in Spain during the 1630s. The economic carnage that began in the 1630s continued until the 1640s. The growth phase that emerged following the depression of the 1630s, was again dynamic. But it never had the same impetus as the earlier growth phase. Another depression hit Spain in the 1680s, approximately fifty years after the initial depression. A third depression engulfed Spain in the 1730s, just about 100 years after Spain had experienced its first depression as a world leader.

The depression in Spain that spanned 1680-1689 appeared to be even greater than the depression of the 1630s. During the latter stages of the expansion that followed the depression of the 1630s, Spain suffered from chronic inflation. It remained intractable during the early stages of the 1680s depression. Although the deflationary depression of the 1630s reduced price levels in Spain by 9%, the excess accumulated during the previous period of expansion was never totally eliminated. The expansion that began after the depression of the 1630s lacked a solid foundation, in case more drastic measures were required to purge the economic system. As usual, the designs of government were to blunt the effects of recession and depression, through the use of the monetary aggregates. At frequent intervals during the last half of the 17th century, Spain suffered the evils of inflation, calling for corrective deflationary action. Sharp declines in the prices of commodities ensued, and the inevitable commercial crisis erupted. The War of the Spanish Succession developed during the final stages of Spain's time as world leader. It culminated in the long period of decline from which the nation has never recovered. According to *Forecasting International Inc,* the economic condition of Spain by the 21st century will be similar to that of Poland today. But it was certainly not the War of the Spanish Succession which brought about the demise of the Spanish Empire. The seeds had been sown long before that war, as successive governments sought to spare the people the inconveniences associated with depression through the profligate creation of fiat money.

Following the War of the Spanish Succession, France became the new world power, and embarked upon the inevitable road to its rise and fall. Having inherited the crown from Spain in the early part of the 18th century, the French economy expanded. However, as we know, the ultimate fate of every expansion is to end with over-expansion and inflation. By the 1720s the inflationary fires began to burn in France. A depression ensued during the 1730s. The depression of the 1730s plagued France for approximately ten years. But it was not unduly severe as depressions go. As was the case for Spain following the first period of expansion whilst global leader, the French effort to purge the system of its excesses was not particularly thorough. The economic consequences were therefore preordained. Since the inflationary pressures prior to the depression were never adequately eliminated, the expansion that followed was never so vibrant as in the first expansionist phase as global leader. In addition, there were still some excesses in the system, which ultimately would have to be corrected before equilibrium could be restored.

The first depression which France experienced as world leader ended during the 1740s. The subsequent period of expansion continued until the late 1770s, when the daunting spectre of depression began to reappear. The French depression of 1780-1790 provides a classic illustration of the kind of Herculean efforts that governments exert to prevent, or cushion, the effects of depression. Throughout the ages, governments have turned continually to the same solution to ward off economic collapse; shewing that they have learned nothing. The results are always the same, regardless of which country we study or which century we monitor. To blunt the forces of deflation, the French embarked on a policy of uncontrolled money creation during the latter part of the 18th century. The result was hyper-inflation, which led to the near total annihilation of the wealth of the middle classes. While the forces of depression may have been postponed for a while, they were certainly not averted. The French economy was to be subjected in the end to an excruciating whipsaw effect, which the economic and political institutions of the French Empire were unable to withstand. There you have the background to the French Revolution; a totally new form of French government, and the rise of the dictator, Napoleon. Napoleon's first order of the day was to ban the printing of fiat money, and stop hyper-inflation dead in its tracks.

Hyper-inflation, and a subsequent depression, hit the French people during the second period of contraction while France held the role of world leader.

This was the epitome of the type of chaos generated when the authorities try to fight off the inevitable consequences of depression. Ultimately the penalties are far greater than ever envisaged. They are more far reaching, and of a greater magnitude, than they would have been had the deflationary forces been allowed to run their course. During a depression large numbers of people are thrown out of work and suffer destitution and penury. This is true. As much as 25% of the workforce may be affected, which is painful for society as a whole. But there are far worse things than 25% unemployment. . . far, far worse. During a normal depression, as I mentioned in *The Downwave,* 25% of the work force may be without a job, but that still leaves 75% of the work force *with* a job. The wealth of the middle-classes may be dented during a typical depression. But it is certainly not completely destroyed, as can be the case with hyper-inflation. While a depression produces human suffering of seemingly impossible dimensions, the pain inflicted is far less than that wrought by the type of inflation that first destroys the currency of a nation, along with the wealth of all classes, leaving the people to face a depression immediately after they have emerged from the hyper-inflation. Under these conditions — as history has demonstrated in the case of France and others — the existing political and social structures have no hope of survival. Governments which continually pump money into the economy in order to spare the population the inconvenience of economic contraction, are merely setting the stage for the destruction of the very social and economic fabric they are trying to preserve. Thereafter, some violent upheaval or revolution is virtually guaranteed.

The accelerating money infusion helped to postpone the depression in France that was overdue from the late 1780s until the 1790s and early 1800s. This in no way invalidates the long-term cycle *schema*, which in any case is not a cycle of fixed periodicity. The processes at work which would produce the depression were firmly in place during a period well within the hypothetical time frame of the Long Wave cycle. It was political intervention that delayed the arrival of that depression, which further confirms the inexorability of the long wave of economic behaviour.

A country that experiences its third depression, having assumed the role of world leader, is usually about to be reduced to the status of a second-rate power. France suffered a further depression during the 1830s. But already it had surrendered its title to England in 1815, following the Battle of Waterloo.

The Colonial Experience

History can have a telescopic and distorting effect, making some isolated events — like a war — appear to go on for ages. Yet long-term social and industrial developments appear to be over in virtually no time at all. It is further accentuated by the tendency on the part of historians and their publishers to accentuate the isolated event, rather than explore — and explain

— the circumstances and the condition of the environment at the time. That is certainly the case with the history of the United States.

For example, few people today realise (unless it is pointed out to them) that there were was something like one and three-quarter centuries between the establishment of the first successful English Colony at Jamestown, and the end of the War of Independence, signalled by the surrender of Cornwallis and his forces to General George Washington. There is also a tendency to treat individual participants (unless they happen to be *very famous),* as cardboard figures — mostly of one kind. The inhabitants of the early American Colonies tend to get lumped together as "Puritans", friends and families of the "Pilgrim Fathers", who landed at Plymouth Rock, Massachusetts, on a day in 1620. Their arrival is usually portrayed as the moment of Victory; the way it used to be portrayed in the school-room pictures of our childhood. The truth was somewhat closer to the old joke:

> "When the Pilgrim Fathers landed, they fell upon their knees — and then upon the aboriginees."

As William Bradford described it in *The History of Plymouth Plantation,* their arrival was not so much the Moment of Triumph, as the first glimpse of the Valley of Travail:

> "Being thus passed the vast ocean, and a sea of troubles before in their preparation. . . what could they see but a hideous and desolate wilderness, full of wild beasts and wild men? And what multitudes there might be of them they knew not. . . For summer being done, all things stand upon them with a weatherbeaten face. . .".

What is also rarely remembered is the arrival the previous year in Jamestown, Virginia of a Dutch ship bearing the first cargo of African slaves. From the very earliest time, the contrast between Puritan Massachusetts and Planter Virginia was too deep to ignore.

The New Englanders of Massachusetts and Connecticut saw themselves as God's agents; entrusted with the task of making a home for God's "chosen" and converting — or disposing of — "those miserable Salvages"(sic). The author of the religious compendium, *Magnalia Christi Americana* (1702), one Cotton Mather (son of Increase Mather), explained the presence of these "Salvages". They had been decoyed there by the Devil:

> ". . .in the hopes that the Gospel of the Lord Jesus Christ would never come here to destroy or disturb (the Devil's) Absolute Empire over them."

Everything, it seemed, that was not ordained by God must be contrived by the Devil. Indeed, when Cotton Mather lost the texts of some lectures, he decided that, "Spectres, or Agents in the invisible world were the robbers."

William Penn, who founded Pennsylvania, handed out some very down-to-earth advice to would-be emigrants in 1685. Although there was a strong moral undertone in his advice:

"Be moderate in expectation, Count on Labour before a Crop, and Cost before Gain."

A very different attitude prevailed among the planters of Virginia. There was a wealthy, English-born planter and diarist, William Byrd of Westover. Many called him "the American Samuel Pepys". In his *History of the Dividing Line* — the story of the early Virginia settlements — he observed that the settlers:

". . .extended themselves as far as James-Town, where like true Englishmen, they built a Church that cost no more than Fifty Pounds and a Tavern that cost Five Hundred."

From early on the seeds were sown of the cruel conflict which would tear the new nation apart within a century of independence. Meanwhile, both types of community made haste to establish schools and colleges. The foundation that later became Harvard University was instituted in 1636, with a printing press set up nearby some three years later. By 1755, William and Mary College had been established in Williamsburg, Virginia. So had Yale, at New Haven, Connecticut, Princeton, at New Jersey and Columbia, in New York. Nor were trade and banking neglected because of principles. The Quaker city of Philadelphia was well to the fore in commerce; and the first issue of paper money in Pennsylvania came in 1733, following the example set by the Massachusetts Bay Colony more than 40 years earlier. Massachusetts had sent an expedition of irregulars to seize Quebec. In this they failed. Nevertheless the expedition had cost a great deal of money. But as J.K. Galbraith puts it, in his book, *Money*, there was:

". . .no enthusiasm for levying taxes to pay the defeated heroes. So notes were issued to the soldiers promising eventual payment in hard coin. . . presently the notes were also made legal tender for taxes. For the next twenty years the notes circulated side by side with gold and silver of equivalent nomination. Notes and metal being interchangeable, there was, *pro tanto*, no depreciation."

Soon other colonists realised that notes were a useful, general-purpose alternative to taxation. Since the promised redemption was postponed time and again, prices specified in terms of the notes went on rising. Eventually the notes were redeemed at a few shillings in the pound, taken from the gold sent to pay for Queen Anne's War. Rhode Island and South Carolina took the message and followed suit. This alarmed Massachusetts, which had taken the first step towards credit-by-printing-press. In 1740, a Massachusetts commentator complained that Rhode Island was buying from Massachusetts Bay:

". . .all Sorts of British and Foreign Goods with this Paper Manufacture which costs nothing, which enables them to rival us in trade."

It was also noticed that rising prices, as Galbraith tells us, "stimulate the spirits of entrepreneurs and encourage economic activity just as falling prices depress both." It was for this reason that Pennsylvania had issued its first paper money. When prices recovered, it stopped. The performance was repeated once more in 1729. Thereafter, New York, New Jersey, Delaware and Maryland all followed suit. Needless to say, the Mother Country was not amused. In 1751 the English Parliament forbade the issue of any further paper money in New England. The ban was extended to other Colonies in 1764. Even in the Colonies themselves, opinions were divided over the issue of paper money. So much so that Davis Rich Dewey's *Financial History of the United States* (1903) reports:

". . .a substantial element of the population, particularly in the larger cities in the East. . . stood aloof from the revolt against England. . . because of the fear that independence would bring excessive issues of paper money with all its consequent derangement to business affairs."

One important lesson may be drawn from the history of money, and the American Colonial experience, observes Galbraith:

"Having recent experience of inflation, people cherish stable prices, and having long experience of stable prices, they become indifferent to the risk of inflation. And, on the whole, older communities are less inclined to monetary experiment than newer ones."

After Independence, paper money was no longer an experiment in the former American Colonies. Realistically, there was no alternative. The Revolution had been paid for with paper money. When prices rose at an ever increasing rate, it was necessary to ensure that no one started to cast aspersions on the paper in circulation. In 1776, Congress passed the necessary resolution that:

"Any person who shall hereafter be so lost to all virtue and regard for his country, as to refuse to receive said bills in payment. . . shall be deemed, published and treated as an enemy in this country and precluded from all trade or intercourse with the inhabitants of these Colonies."

Alas! Prices still went on rising. Shoes in Virginia cost $5,000 a pair in the local currency, and a full outfit of clothing cost upwards of a million. Creditors, the records show, sheltered from their debtors like hunted things for fear that they might pay off their debts in worthless paper.

England: Ploughshares Into Lathes

While the American Colonies were gaining their independence, England was about to be caught up in the French Wars; first against Revolutionary France, then against Napoleon. Although no one could have realised it at the time, England was shortly to become world leader. During the reign of George III, the population grew from seven-and-a-half to fourteen million. Fortunately, England had already embarked on a massive programme of agricultural reform. It was so successful that it was possible to feed the rapidly growing population throughout the Revolutionary and Napoleonic Wars. During those years, English agriculture boomed; partly because of increased demand, but even more because of the huge technological achievements of men like Coke of Norfolk, who had spent half-a-million pounds on his estate; and Arthur Young, who successfully campaigned for the enclosure of the wastelands, and put an end to the traditional open-field system, with its inefficient strip-cultivation. The reforming landlords of the 18th century may have been acting in their own best interests. But the result was to breed better stock, supported by vastly higher crop-yields, which thus were available when the nation needed them.

Just as in the Second World War, Britain's moorlands and chalk lands were brought under the plough. Landless labourers, and cottars displaced by the enclosures, provided abundant cheap labour. Farmers made money hand-over-fist. When the war ended, and the price of corn fell, farmers and landowners alike demanded protection. In 1815 a Corn Law was passed, to prohibit the import of corn until the domestic market price reached 80 shillings a quarter. It meant that the poor could ill afford their loaf. Farmers found it increasingly difficult to sell their other, more costly, products. Nor did the import ban bring the price stability. Prices fell, rents fell, the number of unemployed grew rapidly, and bankruptcies increased.

Inevitably there were those who did well out of the conditions which others found so crushing. On one of his *Rural Rides*, six years or so after the Battle of Waterloo, William Cobbett found evidence of the suffering and injustices to which the displaced, disinherited poor were subjected. He wrote:

> "There is one farmer, in the North of Hampshire, who has nearly eight thousand acres of land. . . He occupies what was formerly 40 farms! Is it any wonder that *paupers increase*?"

In the census of 1831, there were nearly a million families engaged in agriculture. 686,000 families of labourers worked for a wage. At the same time, 145,000 families of owners or farmers *"hired no workers whatsoever!"* When the starving field workers in the South of England rioted in the cause of a wage of 2/6d. . . half-a-crown a day, three were hanged, and 420 transported to a penal colony in Australia.

To make matters worse, a new class of landed gentry were replacing those "known to every farmer and labourer from their childhood" . . .the old style country gentleman. They, said Cobbett, had regularly taken part in those familiar country pursuits "where all artificial distinctions are lost". The *new* gentry as a rule cared little for "country-delights". They were distant and haughty in their behaviour:

> ". . .looking to the soil only for its rents, viewing it as a mere object of speculation. . . and relying for influence. . . upon the dread of their power. The war and paper-system has brought in *nabobs* (of the East India Company), negro-drivers, generals, contractors, pensioners, sinecurists,

commissioners, loan-jobbers, lottery-dealers, bankers, stock-jobbers. . . You can see but few good houses not in possession of one or the other of these. These, with the parsons, are now the magistrates."

Historian David Thomson warns us to remember that hostility to the red-faced *nabobs* and stock-holders of the national debt was well established by the early 1820s, but he reminds us that:

"There were some 2200 offences for which the death penalty could be imposed; although it was not often exacted because judges had consciences and juries might refuse to convict. . . capital offences ranged from highway robbery and murder to such curious crimes as injuring Westminster Bridge or impersonating out-pensioners of Chelsea Hospital."

In 1815 — the year of Waterloo — game laws made it illegal to buy or sell game. It was a boon to professional poachers! It was also illegal for anyone other than the squire or his eldest son to kill game. Under a law passed in 1816, any cottager who went out with nets by night risked transportation for seven years. Until 1827, spring-guns and mantraps might be employed to protect pheasant preserves.

Although the streets of London might not be paved with gold, the health and cleanliness of Londoners were improving. The death rate continued to decline. Foreign visitors commented on the well-dressed, sturdy appearance of the working people.

The Corn Laws, supported by landowners and farmers, were opposed by the cotton-goods manufacturers. They too wanted to see prices stable, but as low as possible. This would keep their wages bill within bounds. At the same time, they wanted to see corn imports rise. Then agricultural producers abroad would be able to afford the cloth and cotton goods spun from the raw cotton imported from America. Already, the mills of Lancashire were using steam-driven machinery. In the woollen industry, machinery was in the process of driving out the hand-worker, although power weaving would not become universal for another generation. With the same object in mind as woollen manufacturers, others campaigned for Free Trade. When you dominate the world market, it makes sense to keep all doors open!

Iron, coal and engineering were next in importance after textiles. The growing demand for machinery of all kinds increased the demand for iron and coal. In 1815, England's annual output of iron was little more than 250,000 tons. Twenty years later it had quadrupled. By 1848, annual output had doubled in 13 years to 2 million tons. Coal production also expanded rapidly. Between 1815 and 1835, it grew from 16 to 30 million tons per annum. By 1848, it had reached 50 million. By then, England was producing half the pig-iron used in the world. So far as technology went, Joseph Bramah, Henry Maudslay and others had laid the foundations for an engineering industry by the early 1820s. In a few years, machine tools would be made by other machines. The great railway age would dawn.

England in the 1820s enjoyed two major advantages. She had less than half the mouths that France had to feed; and a few more than Prussia's. But her industrial techniques, her commercial strength and her naval power were unequalled anywhere in Europe, which was still predominantly agricultural. Russia, Britain's most serious rival in the Levant and Asia Minor, was kept at a safe distance from the West European market by the Hapsburgs, the Turkish Empire and Prussia. In the West, Italy still comprised half a dozen states; Germany more than a score.

With France safely out of the picture following Napoleon's defeat, and Amsterdam no longer the financial centre it had once been, the City of London was the undisputed economic capital of the world. Indeed, it was not until the last quarter of the 19th century that London had anything to fear from foreigners on either the political or the economic front.

Richard Cobden, the leading advocate of Free Trade, described England's commerce in the most glowing terms. He saw it as:

". . . the grand panacea, which like a beneficent medical discovery will serve to innoculate with the healthy and saving for civilisation all the nations of the world. Not a bale of merchandise leaves our shores, but it bears the seeds of intelligence and fruitful thought to the members of some less enlightened community. . . while our steamboats, that now visit every port of Europe, and our miraculous railroads, that are the talk of all nations, are the advertisements and vouchers for the value of our enlightened institutions."

Britain's traffic on the high seas grew 4 times in bulk between 1847 and 1880. Excluding coastal and Anglo-Irish trade, 14.3 million tons of shipping entered and were cleared from British ports. In 1880, it had grown to 58.7 million tons. Half the world's ocean-going tonnage was British in 1851 — the year of the Great Exhibition. It was to grow even faster once the Suez Canal had been opened, 18 years later. In 1879, some 1.7 million tons out of a total of 2.3 million tons passing down the new waterway, was British.

Cobden's rhetoric on the glories of trade was excelled only by that of *The Times*, which reported the opening of the Great Exhibition in Hyde Park, on May Day 1851:

"In a building that could easily have accommodated twice as many, twenty-five thousand persons, so it is computed, were arranged in order around the throne of our SOVEREIGN. . . some were most reminded of that day when all ages and climes shall be gathered round the throne of their MAKER. . .".

It is strange to think that apart from the main London Railway termini, the Crystal Palace was the only truly functional building of distinction erected in the 19th century.

There is little wonder that the beginning of the 19th century saw a shift in the economic order of the entire world — from China to the Americas. Or that it was England, lying at the heart of that world, which took the lead against all comers.

With leadership came expansion. Following the expansion came over-expansion and, in the end, depression. Britain's first depression while holding the role of world leader began in the 1830s. Unlike those of Spain and France during the parallel period of history, the depression in England was extremely sharp and severe. Prior to the depression, the expansion had been relatively orderly. It had never reached the levels of over-expansion characteristic of the initial expansionary phase in France and Spain. This placed Britain in an ideal position to enjoy the economic recovery that followed the depression of the 1820s-1840s. Especially since that deep depression appears to have eliminated fully the non-productive, inflationary excesses of the British economic system at that time.

The depression during the first quarter of the 19th century was truly devastating for England. It was the product of an earlier over-expansion of the cotton mills. The period has often been described by historians as England's period of "creative destruction". Various historical accounts place the timing of that depression from 1825-1847. There were some intermittent upturns and brief improvements in economic activity during the twenty-two year period of economic decline. The overall ramifications were quite prolonged. But from that disastrous depression emerged England's golden period. Few, if any, countries had ever experienced the long-term growth, and increase in living standards, that took place in England in the 1840s and lasted until the 1880s when Britain experienced its second depression as world leader.

England's depression in the 1870s and '80s involved an interesting development in the Government's use of fiat money. For the first time a government could be seen actively using the monetary aggregates for the purpose of keeping technically defunct companies and institutions afloat. It was a pattern that would be pursued further in the following decades, leading ultimately to the economic demise of the country.

In Britain fiat money policy bore little resemblance to the sharp vertical drop in the level of the monetary aggregates during Spain's second depression. It was also completely different from the socially destructive, undisciplined monetary policy in France that led to hyper-inflation. In effect, the British Depression of the 1870s to the 1880s, although quite severe, was strictly controlled and "fine-tuned" compared to the previous depression of the 1830s, or the second depression in Spain and France. The nadir of the depression, which came during the period 1874-1879, involved a fall of 9.2% in the production of consumer goods and services. As I have demonstrated previously, consumer panics are usually the most difficult to control. For a time, it seemed as if the panic of 1874-1879 was being held in check. But Britain received a second dose of depression following a brief phase of pseudo-recovery in the early 1880s. During the early part of the second phase of depression, few recognised (or wanted to recognise) what was taking place. People are usually content to accept the *status quo*, believing the things they want to believe. Much as today, the newspapers and forecasters, during the second half of the 1880s, painted a very rosy picture of England. Most refused to recognise the periods of decline until recognition was unavoidable. If forced to accept that economic activity was less than inspiring, the forecasters would promise that they would turn better at any time. With each miniscule recovery within the confines of the secular decline, the incantations and promises of hope would immediately revive.

But the long depression, and the manner in which the authorities used the monetary aggregates to support non-productive, loss-making enterprises, sapped England of its ingenuity and pre-eminence as a world power. Just before the beginning of the 20th century, Britain entered her third 50-year period of global supremacy. She was ill-prepared for the military threats of Germany, and bereft of the qualities that previously helped her maintain a dominant role in world markets. If Britain had allowed her lame-duck industries to reflect the decision of the market place, sufficient capital would have been freed to allow Britain to participate fully in the expansionary period of the early 20th century. Instead, the lack of massive liquidations and the support of non-productive enterprise left Britain unable to carry out the modernisation required for the first expansion of the 20th century. The British industrial base was outdated, resulting in higher priced, and less efficient, products. This finally left Britain with a sharply declining currency, and the loss of its economic market supremacy.

The Chanceller of the Exchequer during the 1870s-1880s depression seemed to have a "Medium Term Financial Strategy" which involved a "soft landing" approach to depression. Although that depression may have been sharp in a statistical sense, it did not complete the one useful function of any economic contraction — namely to reduce fiscal excesses, and so provide a launch pad for the recovery that must follow. One of the most devastating aspects of the depression of the 1870s-1880s in England was the shattering of the high expectations that had prevailed prior to that period of economic woe. Following months of insufferable predictions of economic recovery, and a new period of economic growth, individuals, businesses and the Government finally got down to accepting the realities of life. They also found themselves making sharp downward revisions in future expectations as Britain's basic industries wallowed in stagnation and export markets vanished — or were never recaptured in the first place. Meanwhile, Britain had to grapple with the worldwide trade protectionism, so characteristic of the late 19th century.

Running concurrent with the loss of trade in Britain, in the late 19th century, were heavy social responsibilities which the authorities had decided to accept as an addendum to support for lame-duck industries. As a result, the population took an ever increasing slice of the nation's contracting economic pie. If a nation consumes and fritters away the profits of the past and present, rather than reinvest in order to stay one step ahead of the competition, then obviously the competitor takes over. By the time Britain sank into its third depression as world leader, the competition was ready, willing and able to take over. The depression of the 1930s fell on an England whose economic infrastructure had been damaged beyond repair. The US promptly assumed its role as world leader during the expansion following the 1930s depression. In the subsequent years, there was very little change in British fiscal and monetary policy. In fact, the excesses that brought Britain's decline about became even more aggravated and exaggerated.

Now let's see what we've learned from the correlations and precedents involved in the shifting pattern of global supremacy cycle over the past 500 years. One thing we've seen is that the world supremacy cycle for an individual country lasts from 150-200 years. Timing of such great magnitude is relatively unimportant. Far more so is the position of a nation within the framework of the long-term cycle *schema*. A country will usually experience three complete Long Wave economic cycles during its reign as world leader. There will be three periods of major expansion, and three periods of contraction. There will also be three panic phases during the 150-200 year time frame.

The Global Supremacy Cycle. . . The Mirage

During the first Long Wave cycle in a country's role of supremo, the public is relatively unaware of the power of monetary policy. Monetary profligacy is deemed a politically acceptable course. It allows the authorities to induce progressively larger changes in output and spending, relative to prices. Prior to the first period of expansion as world leader, a transfer of sovereignty occurs between the existing but deteriorating world power and its successor. By the middle-to-end of the first expansionary phase, the transfer is complete. The falling star is replaced by the rising comet. But the new star of the global economic showcase is rather like an inexperienced lover who must learn the penalties for premature ejaculation. He becomes over-excited and over-indulgent, adopting an almost licentious approach to his new role. The result is a severe depression, It is usually the most devastating the country will ever see. But because that recession is *so* severe, the purge of the entire system which follows halts the construction of an economic base on which long-term sustainable growth can build during the second fifty years of global supremacy.

During the second period of expansion within the 150-200 year global supremacy time frame, the new world leader consolidates his position as the world's most formidable economic force through the expansion of trade and accumulation of wealth. In addition, there will be a widening of the sphere of political influence and power. The second period of expansion within the longer term cycle is usually viewed as the "golden era" for the world leader. During this time, the citizenry experienced new heights of achievement. The expansionary phase of the second Long Wave cycle is exceptionally dynamic and involves far greater participation amongst the population. This particular phase of expansion engenders tremendous enthusiasm. The prospects of a depression recurring are seen as a nightmare — so long as the memory of the previous depression lingers on.

During the second phase of expansion in the Long Wave supremacy cycle, monetary growth is better understood. It is no longer considered to be an instrument that can safely be used without restraint. Money growth is largely seen as a precursor to higher inflation (relative to economic growth) during this phase of the world leader's development. Society becomes very conscious of monetary forces. It adjusts its expectations in a rational manner, after the experience of the severe depression that ended the growth phase of the first Long Wave cycle in the 150-200 years of global domination.

The pain and hardship experienced during the first depression of the three Long Wave cycle *schema*, leads to the provision of safety nets, bureaucracy and company bail-outs as the second wave of expansion matures. The key factor that changes the pattern of the Long Wave from cycle to cycle is the degree of governmental intervention, involving large deficits and social welfare nets. But in so intervening, the imbedded inflationary pressures which otherwise would have been self-liquidating, had the system not been tampered with, remain a festering core, impeding economic achievement during the third period of expansion in the global supremacy cycle. Although psychologically devastating, the depression of the second long-wave economic cycle experienced by the global leader is nowhere near as savage in concrete terms as the first. But the price that must be paid by a nation for this small comfort is a very high one. . . the loss of global supremacy and reduction to the status of a second rate. . . and finally. . . a third-rate power.

During the third and final period of growth in a nation's supremacy cycle, the financial capital, which spurred the second phase of growth, is not forthcoming. The national deficit of significant proportions, which develops during the second Long Wave of the supremacy cycle, is never fully reduced. A combination of bureaucratic safety nets and military operations leads to a guns-and-butter surge of government spending. By now the authorities are reluctant to raise taxes for fear of the deflationary consequences. Tax increases, therefore, are insufficient to match government expenditure. This leads to a gaping deficit, a massive money pumping exercise to finance that deficit, and an unavoidable surge in inflation.

Because of the bureaucracy and the built-in safety nets, a thorough liquidation of the debt excesses and inflationary excesses is never achieved. Companies that should have been liquidated are patched up. Debts that should have been repaid are disguised by rescheduling. The result is a deflationary process that is less rapid, and less thorough, in cleansing of imbedded inflationary pressures, than was the case during the depression which followed the expansion of the first Long Wave cycle in the global sequence. Venture capital for new innovative processes is now less abundant than after the first depression. The economy is riddled with a plethora of antiquated companies that continue to be suckled on scarce financial resources, because society, in its altruistic way, shrinks from outright liquidation. Because a firm foundation following the second depression is never established, the seeds for strong growth during the third wave of expansion are absent. The resistance to deep-going change, limiting the growth of the third long wave of the global supremacy cycle, is the cause of many of the negative features of that phase of expansion. In this way, it contributes to the loss of global supremacy.

In every case over the past 500 years, the old world power has been dethroned during the third Long Wave of expansion, when some newly emerging power has taken its place. By the time the third wave cycle has moved on to the depressionary phase, the old world leader has become a second-rate power. Thereafter, the ex-world leader will continue to decline. By this stage depressions tend, relatively speaking, to be less severe. This is because the encrusted bureaucratic institutions and the social safety nets cushion the impact of the forces of depression. The shock will be reduced, but the cost will be high. When a nation loses its claim to world leadership, as Britain has done, its deeply-imbedded, depression-prone inflationary economic infra-structure makes it impossible for it to experience anything but stagnation. Fairy-tale economics, and political bedtime stories will be used to ease the situation to some extent. But only insofar as it momentarily eases the pain, and tranquillises the victim.

The depressions experienced by ex-world leaders are influenced mainly by the economic blunders of those nominally in charge, but who — in reality — have lost control. Once a country has moved from world leadership to the second rank, it is already on its way to the third rank. At such a stage in the inevitable decline, the social consequences are probably more debilitating than the purely economic.

At first sight it may seem that economic decline could be defined as the reverse of economic growth. This would not be a logically circular argument, since statistical economic growth can be defined with reasonable precision. Theoretically, a nation could grow in perpetuity. But decline cannot go on forever. Beyond a certain point, the contracting society would simply perish and disintegrate. However, history tells us that nations neither grow in perpetuity, nor perish. Nations rise until they achieve global supremacy, then falter and decline. Thereafter they muddle along in a state of limbo for several centuries before they rise and fall again.

Spain relinquished its title as world leader in the 17th century. Then it went into a steep decline lasting for approximately 60 years. At the beginning of the 18th century, it seemed as if the attrition in the Spanish economy had ceased. But, since most other nations were experiencing growth at a much more rapid rate, the Spanish nation never recovered to any degree its former pre-eminence. Indeed, it continued progressively to lose more ground. In the final phase of their economic history, the Spanish experienced a decline in relation to other countries although continuing to grow in absolute statistical terms. This is much the same position that Britain has been in for quite some time. The truth is that societies reach a point in their cycle of maturity where they become third-rate. Decline essentially becomes relative decline.

One of the most masterly of the many obituaries written on the British Empire and the Commonwealth that have appeared in modern times, is that of the historian Correlli Barnett. Barnett describes the subject as "not the decline and fall of the British Empire", but "the decay and collapse of British power. . ." It is an entirely different, far more important and hitherto neglected approach, which would appear far more appropriate in current conditions.

The resurrection of the British Empire could take place through industrial reconstruction *only if it occurred in tandem with a revival of British power.* Since this is not even a remote possibility, it must be accepted that Britain will continue in relative decline for many decades to come.

In the days of its supremacy, British imperialism penetrated almost every corner of the globe. It was respected in hundreds of territories, large and small. But those areas of the British Empire which counted as tangible sources of power during Britain's reign as global leader were essentially three in number — Canada, Australasia and British Southern Africa — now the South African Republic and Zimbabwe. The Malay Peninsula might also be included. It alone was most highly valued as the world's largest single source of rubber and tin. When Britain lost vast tracts of its Empire, it ceased to be a global leader; not because of the symbolic independence of hundreds of millions of Africans and Asians, but through Britain's irreversible loss of influence and power in those areas.

There are four basic phases in the continuous cycle of the rise and fall of an Empire.

Before a nation can come near to being a global leader, the philosophical basis for such leadership must be firmly established, along with a territorial imperative. During the pre-supremacy stage of any world power, territorial acquisitions multiply at an accelerating rate. There are wars and conquests, and considerable internal strife culminating in civil wars. The pre-supremacy phase of the cycle could be described as the Age of the Warrior, when an efficient and strong military complex is developed — the first step towards global leadership. With territorial expansion comes the establishment of an ever widening industrial base, supported by an extended trade base. The final component qualifying the nation to become a world leader is advanced technological and agricultural systems. Obviously, no nation can possibly be a world leader if it has to beg for food, or import what it needs from others.

Before the mantle of world leader can be assumed, internal conflicts (which impede a unified social and economic development) must be resolved. The civil wars, characteristic of the early stage of the pre-supremacy cycle, have been resolved in the past through an internal struggle ending with industrialists imposing their will on less progressive agricultural interests. As we move into a post-industrial society, a similar struggle is likely to occur with post-industrialists striving to overcome the intransigence of those attempting to preserve less progressive labour intensive industry.

In the second phase, deeply imbedded inflationary pressures, profligate monetary policy, heavy government obligations and huge deficits weaken the economic underpinning of the world leader about to surrender his role. The successor is ready to emerge from the formative years of the pre-supremacy cycle and enter the first Long Wave as world leader. An inherent characteristic of that first wave is the evolution of free trade and capitalist tendencies. The capitalist approach will tend later to take on more socialistic overtones as the no-longer-new world leader matures and ages. But, in order to provide the philosophical background needed for the initial thrust to global dominance, an increasingly capitalistic approach must prevail at the early stages of leadership. This implies well-defined individual rights, and a background that encourages entrepreneurial endeavour. It is the spirit of unfettered free trade, and support of individual capitalist initiative, which lead to the exploitation of new innovative processes — the envy of the world during the first Long Wave of global dominance. As a result, the wealth of the nation, and its productive capacity are boosted quite significantly. Above all, it is the individualistic and capitalist tendencies that spark the required energy and wealth to propel the newcomer to the pinacle of world leadership. But, as we know, all booms reach for extremes. During its initial phase as world leader, the nation succumbs to a speculative bubble. Ultimately it bursts, bringing on a savage depression of the kind which occurred in England following the South Sea Bubble, and the aftermath of "Tulipomania" in Holland. It happened too in the United States after the speculative binge of the 1920s. The terminal juncture of a nation's first Long Wave cycle as world leader is characterised by a deep depression.

The third phase occurs during the second 50-65 years as global leader. This is its Golden Age: the second Long Wave economic cycle within the global supremacy cycle when the nation experiences its most rapid rate of economic growth. During this phase, its power and wealth are unmatched by other nations. At the same time, the leader-nation becomes complacent. Having experienced the comfort associated with the building of a vast empire, its leaders assume the trend to be permanent — likely to continue indefinitely. Attention then turns to social reform and other progressive issues. The capitalist and the individualist are no longer allowed to flourish as they were in the first Long Wave economic cycle. The political mood is to feed on previous decades of wealth accumulation. More of the nation's resources are directed towards relatively non-productive areas. During the second long-wave economic cycle since the assumption of world leadership, there are the usual periods of economic weakness as the cycle progresses. Memories of the deep depression during the first Long Wave cycle run deep. The world's leader therefore builds bureaucracies and safety nets to mitigate the impact of recession and depression. This traditional reaction ultimately leads to debasement of the nation's currency, and its demise as world leader.

Having passed through the pre-supremacy period, its initial phase as world leader and finally its Golden Age, the nation reaches the third economic Long Wave. It is during this third 60-year cycle that the nation loses its position as global supremo. The introduction of non-productive social programmes, bureaucracies and social safety nets attacks the nation's capital and industrial base. This means it cannot keep up with current technological changes — the harbingers of growth during periods of global expansion. Capitalists and entrepreneurs become lambs on the sacrificial altar of socially conspicuous consumption. They now lack the incentive to take the types of risk that spurred economic activity during the earlier stages of the world leader's development. The internal pressures on Government to aid the ailing sections of the economy, and to promote social welfare, rob the nation of the resources needed for research, development, and the promotion of innovative technology. The ageing world leader is dethroned. A new, vibrant and economically more efficient nation takes over as world power and world leader. Once a nation has lost its hold on global leadership, the inexorable decline ensues.

A nation's rise to world leadership and its subsequent decline to the status of second rate power, spans approximately 250 years — give or take a few decades. The plight of a nation during the period following its loss of title as global leader is bleak. Socialism becomes extremely intense. High taxes, wealth confiscation, the loss of personal freedoms and poor economic performance accelerate the decline towards the second rank. In many previous cases, the process of socialisation has weakened nations to such a degree that they have become backward and poverty stricken. One need not look very far for examples. No doubt the most extreme case is that of the Soviet Union. By strict control of human behaviour since the fall of the Tsar and the October revolution, the Russian economy has largely avoided the ups and downs of economic activity, and avoided the consequential impact of global depression. In order to achieve this, increasingly repressive actions have been undertaken by the authorities. The standard of living in Russia is relatively low compared to that of most western, industrialised nations. While the Soviet Union appears to have achieved relative economic stability, avoiding the wild swings seen in the West, it would be safe to say that the Soviet Union is in a *permanent* state of depression.

The disintegraton of the British Empire accelerated sharply in the quarter-century following World War II, as Britain lost the basis needed to compete among the leading world powers of the 20th and 21st century. But Britain lost even more than that. She lost her very means of survival as an independent power in the world of today, when she lost the means of independent economic existence. . . essential for an independent *political* existence. There should be no doubt whatever about Britain's current role in global society. While the rhetoric tends to blind people from the reality of this country's position, it is an undeniable fact that Britain lacks many of the vital natural resources needed for modern industry, and for maintaining the living standards to which British people are accustomed. Among the UK's international competitors today are two countries with vastly greater productive resources — West Germany and Japan. In any case, most countries trade less with Britain than they used to. Relatively speaking, British capital counts for less internationally than ever before. In other words, Britain is now a country passing painfully through the post-supremacy phase. Since publication of *The Downwave,* I have modified my thoughts on the extent of the depression which I envisage in this country. The policies of the Conservative Government since 1983, when my book was published, appear to have delayed the onset of recession, and possible depression. The depression I envisage for Britain may not be so severe as I originally thought it would be, but the price that is being paid is heavy indeed — the loss of economic and social freedoms, and the choice between becoming a slave state or a pauper state. Possibly both!

The pre-requisites of the Long Wave economic cycle will certainly be fulfilled. On a global basis, economic contraction will continue, with a depression encompassing the panic stage as I envisaged. The self-feeding process of debt liquidation will be completed, and a new Long Wave economic cycle of sustained expansion and economic growth for many countries will emerge.

Since my book was published, and despite the free-market economy rhetoric of the administration, an increasingly socialistic infrastructure has been maintained in Britain. This may reduce the severity for this country of the global economic contraction which is gaining momentum. But it will also limit Britain's ability to participate in the next period of expansion. Unfortunately, as I write these words, Britain is moving steadily in an inflation-prone manner which is unlike that of most other developed nations. It is very similar to the direction taken by Germany in the years that led up to the nightmare hyper-inflation of the early 1920s. We may certainly expect a long and glorious "Upwave" as we move into the 21st century. Unfortunately, as it appears today, one country — Britain — is unlikely to participate.

Britain on the Winding Road to Serfdom

Real economic achievement and security are achieved only through the assumption of risk. In consequence, economic security is a by-product of risk assumption in the market place. This is why a national environment that encourages and promotes individual talents, individual freedoms, productivity and creativity is so vital to collective human security. But the British, as a people, seem to have forgotten these basic principles. Instead of attempting to achieve personal security, they have elected successive governments to carry out this function, thereby abdicating personal responsibility. In their quest for security, Britons have allowed themselves to slip into the bondage of dependence. The bondage of dependence leads in the end to slavery in one form or another.

Britons look toward governments, labour unions, and bureaucracies to provide for them — rather than having faith in their individual ability. In Britain, nearly two thirds of the nation are actually dependent on government for their income and survival. Britons rely, for their survival, on a National Health Service, which is breaking down at an accelerating pace. Britons rely on a welfare system to support them if they are out of work — or can't find the work of their choice. Britons rely on government to produce a political version of a "free market": a contradiction in terms! Britons now look to government to produce shares to trade in their socialist substitute for a free market. Britons have been seduced into a collective form of pseudo-security under the direct control of government. This is slavery.

Slaves are totally dependent and irresponsible. They may look after property, and even believe they own it. But the master controls that property. The slave is responsible to the master. But the master is responsible only to himself. Free men own and control their property. They are responsible to themselves, not to a master. When, however, men are the subordinates of other men, and this represents the basis for society, we have a society of secular humanism. In truth, the philosophy of secular humanism is the philosophy of slavery. It is a condition where man, and his efforts, are the product of a controlled environment. The logical result is hopeless determinism. At the same time, man has no responsibility for his actions, because the results of those actions are determined by the masters of his environment. Secular humanism is the close companion of Marxism and its doctrine of "dialectic materialism". According to the Marxist doctrine, man does not control his existence. He is the product of his economic environment. Whoever controls the economic environment, therefore, controls man. In other words, man is a slave to his environment and to whomsoever controls that environment. This is in stark contrast to the aggressive, confident, hopeful, free-enterprise philosophy that led to Britain's assuming the mantle of one of the world's greatest-ever powers.

You may feel that by using words such as "bondage" and "slavery" I am over-reacting to the problem, and thereby encouraging *you* to over-react. This is not so. The major developments that have taken place since *The Downwave* was published have given me cause for deep concern. In order to assess more accurately the magnitude of the problems facing those living in this country today, it would not be inappropriate to examine the foundations of modern political philosophy; and do so in the context of the type of global economic activity I envisage for the remainder of this decade.

I strongly believe we are heading for a massive deflation and global depression. Unemployment will soar. There will be bankruptcies and failures of alarming dimensions in all industries. World trade will come almost to a stop. Property values will fall sharply. Stock markets, along with commodity markets, will crash. Poverty, penury and destitution will spread, and all that has ever been associated with the depression of the 1930s will reappear in most of the industrialised countries. The predictions that I made in *The Downwave* now have, in my opinion, an even greater chance of being fulfilled than at the time they were made.

So far as Britain was concerned, when I made those predictions back in 1982 they were made on the assumption that the British Government was an example of benign government. According to the pattern of the next five years, I changed my mind. I had the impression that this benign government was turning malignant. In electoral terms, the Conservative Government of Mrs Thatcher gained office by default. Media presentation had convinced the electorate that socialism was failing. The rhetoric of the Conservative Party was deemed to be a new approach; one which would compensate for the failure of the socialist Labour Party. But many people began to see that "Thatcherism" had not been a resounding success either. There was considerable unrest among the electorate as the early months of 1987 brought us closer to the General Election. There was the possibility that traditional political polarisation in Britain might have been superseded already by an authoritarian type of regime in keeping with the more extreme type of socialism normally associated with a nation in its post-supremacy cycle. It is ironic that both capitalism and communism share the same idealistic objective — the minimisation or elimination of external government. Capitalism sees the function of government as limited to maintaining peace, ensuring justice, and enforcing law and order. The final stage of communism is reached when state government has been subjugated to obscurity — when the State, as they used to say, has "withered away".

The rights of the individual form the basis of the capitalist philosophy. Property rights are inviolate since an attack upon the property of an individual is essentially an attack on the individual. "Human rights" under capitalism means the right to choose your own way of living and of earning a living. These rights are also deemed to be inviolate but exclude the right to expropriate (or interfere with) the rights of others. In order to function, the capitalist system requires a free market of goods and services and unrestricted, open competition to actuate the normal functions of supply and demand.

Under a capitalist system, self-reliance and entrepreneurship are encouraged. State dependence is discouraged. The function of government is to alleviate whatever might hamper the creation of wealth, encouraging whatever would enhance the wealth-creation process. In a truly capitalist economy, state welfare is limited by the amount of tax collected. Recipients of state benefits would be deprived of the franchise whilst dependent on the state.

The essence of moderate socialism is expressed in its attempt to provide a life of ease and comfort for every citizen "from the cradle to the grave", whether he contributes to the wealth of the nation or not. In a socialist economy, the ability of the government to provide welfare services is not limited by the amount of taxes that are collected. The only limitation on the amount spent on welfare is the ability of the administration to create debt.

It should be noted that under a capitalist system "property rights" are not confined to the ownership of property, but include the control of that property. Property which is owned by an individual, but controlled by the state, is not full ownership. A state which, for example, obliges a property owner to seek planning permission, or requires a farmer to sell his milk through a marketing board, is not a truly capitalist state. It is a 20th century socialist hybrid.

The form of utopian socialism envisaged by Karl Marx involved the total elimination of private enterprise — with all individuals working for the state. There are, of course, many variations on that theme. Prophets of a moderate persuasion believe that only basic industries should come under state ownership. Those of a more extreme view feel that *all* economic activity should be subject to central planning.

Regardless of the commitment to the basic ideal, both capitalists and socialists acknowledge the necessity of investing in the future to generate the income needed to support government services, regardless of how extensive (or how limited) those services may be.

The major ideological difference between socialists and capitalists on investment and wealth creation is the *source* of the investment decision. The socialist believes that controlling the national income, and investing it, achieves a higher degree of efficiency than if individuals are left solely in charge of the wealth-creating and income-producing process.

In practical terms, there is very little difference politically between socialism and capitalism in the UK. Both systems ultimately defer to the demands of the electorate, and are essentially democratic by nature. It is when there is an erosion of the democratic rights of the individual, and his free choice of an elected government, that we must fear that a point of departure from both socialism and capitalism may have been reached.

In early 1987, a Private Member's Bill which sought to incorporate the European Convention of Human Rights into British law was defeated. This is a menacing sign for the future rights of the British citizen, and the current intentions of the British authorities.

Both communists and extreme socialists share the same economic ideologies. Both believe in central planning. Both systems would run the national economy in just about the same way. The basic difference between socialism and communism is a political one. Socialists will bow to democratic rule, allowing their party to be voted out of power if this is the will of the electorate. Communists will not permit the ruling power to be voted out of office. Essentially, the communist system in Britain would be a one-party system. Whether or not we still have anything more than a one-party system in Britain is highly debatable.

Capitalists and socialists will use every legitimate method available to persuade the voter that their system is the superior one. The communist will also attempt to persuade the citizen that his system is the best. But the means of persuasion may not be so legitimate. Should persuasion fail, the communist will not be bound by public approval. He will always maintain office, and the dictate of government. He will probably not resort to force until all forms of persuasion have failed. In Britain, persuasion has so far been successful so the use of force does not arise. Although this may be a debatable point, considering the methods of Customs and Excise and Inland Revenue in Britain. . . along with the greater powers recently given to the police.

However, the essence of communism is beyond doubt the complete subservience of the individual to the requirements of the state. In other words, communists and their political allies each strive for the 20th century version of human bondage and enslavement, both physical and pyschological.

When a country adopts fascism, it has reached the depths of economic and political degradation on the winding road to serfdom. A fascist dictatorship is the end of the line for a country in its post-supremacy phase of global involvement. There is really no political difference between the fascist and communist systems. Both operate with the same ferocity and forceful rule. The difference between the fascist and communist state lies in the individual ideological interpretation of economic central planning.

The fascist is far more devious than the communist. The communist insists on state ownership and control of all property. The fascist will allow property to be owned by the individual — providing that property is used in a manner directed by the central planning board. Failure to comply would mean the ultimate confiscation of the property. But those who live in a fascist state may not be aware of this until they actually fail to comply. It therefore stands to reason that a fascist government would encourage private ownership of property, particularly if it served to increase the amount of wealth the government could control.

Among the basic characteristics of the fascist system is its tendency to maintain control through various forms of deception. In George Orwell's *1984,* an important function in the maintenance of continued suppression is "war hysteria", and the conduct of "continuous warfare" without victory and with "no danger of conquest". This latter function is particularly important to what Orwell defines as "all of the Inner Party" which "Big Brother" presides over and where the "true war enthusiasm" is to be found. Orwell's people of 1984 under the facist dictatorship of "Big Brother" had to be prodded into frenzies of "fear and hatred" on an intermittent basis. This is an integral function of control.

But the most important function of all, overriding every other goal and objective in Orwell's world of 1984, is the preservation of permanent power by the "Inner Party", and "Big Brother". As O'Brien, the anti-hero of Orwell's novel puts it:

"The Party seeks power entirely for its own sake. . . we are interested solely in power. Power is not a means; it is an end. One does not establish a dictatorship in order to safeguard a revolution: one makes a revolution to establish the dictatorship."

According to the Orwellian nightmare, the use of power is predicated upon two assumptions: the first is the "mutability of the past" and the second is the "infinite malleability and susceptibility" of human nature. Many in the 1940s considered Orwell's work as predicting a communist dictatorship into which the socialist fabric of Britain might be heading. Orwell's dialogue was intended to be nothing of the sort. What Orwell portrayed was Britain — not under communism — but under a fascist dictatorship subjected to the tried and tested methods of the demagogues who preside over such a system.

To a certain degree the fascist state tries at first to exude the atmosphere of pseudo-freedom. In this respect, the fascist state is more insidious, and far more pernicious, than the communist state. Right from the beginning, the communist state makes it clear that no form of individual freedom will be tolerated. The fascist philosophy and method are designed to allow people to *think* there is still a resemblance to capitalism in their society. The regime also appears to be encouraging freedom, while in reality it is cunningly implementing an autocratic and totalitarian planned economy.

The Western world has been taught to fear communism, considered to be the greatest threat of all to freedom and the capitalist system. I have no doubt whatever that many fascists have assisted in the perpetuation of the idea of communism as the enemy of our society. By diverting attention to the communist menace, the far greater threat of fascism remains undetected.

The communist is a socialist who finds that persuasion has failed and turns to force. The fascist is a communist who finds that force has failed and turns to force and deception — both on a grand scale. Many of these converts are quite sincere in their impulsive, self-righteous attempt to impose their regime on others. They are essentially well-meaning, strange as that may seem. There is probably some twisted character trait that tells a national leader that the imposition of his will and belief on others — at whatever cost — will be for their own good. I've always been very suspicious of the individual who feels driven to impose his will upon several million people. That type of over-sized ego must have its roots in some disturbing character deficiencies.

The shift that occurs in the post-supremacy cycle of a nation, from capitalism, to socialism, communism, and finally, to fascism, may at times be dramatic. Usually it occurs gradually. Regardless of whichever is the case, it is the unrelenting change from democratic principles to those incorporating force and deception that transforms a capitalist society into a fascist nightmare.

In Britain today, with genuine and created grievances among the various sections of our unemployed and polarised society, undertones of violence are never very far beneath the surface. They could easily erupt to produce an uncontrollable wave of riot and disorder if the nation were faced with an economic crisis, which proved far worse than anything I envisaged in *The Downwave.* Should the authorities continue to encourage a profligate monetary policy, which has been the pattern since the beginning of the Thatcher administration, a resurgence of chronic inflation could ensue. This could create even more chaos and distress than the last bout of inflation. There has been an alarming weakening of Britain's economic infrastructure over the past 15 years. Such a crisis could produce even greater polarisation amongst the electorate. Such an atmosphere would be tailor-made for the demagogue. It would allow him, or her, to seize power by persuading the public that a strong benevolent "Father". . . or "Mother". . . should take a firm hold of the nation, and rule it with an iron hand.

It is vitally important that we do not delude ourselves into believing that an authoritarian regime will be kept within bounds simply because the regime claims to have the welfare of the electorate at heart; and that it is seeking power merely to safeguard the public interest. An authoritarian party will seem like any other party, present or past. It can adopt a political platform to match the promises of the opposition, guaranteeing economic and political stability. The dangers of allowing any authoritarian party to form a government lie in the basic ideologies which will "provide a life of comfort for every citizen from the cradle to the grave, whether he works or not". There is an even greater danger in the use of whatever means are necessary, whether force, deception, or otherwise — to achieve that objective. The fact is that the objective is not achievable. The force and deception that bring so much human misery during the attempt to achieve the unachievable are at the core of the problem. Fascism is basically a planned type of economy in which individual effort is demanded by the state, and directed towards the aggrandisement of the state. Hitler's National Socialist German Worker's Party seemed tolerable and constructive in the early stages. But history has shown that even if a party is initially well-intentioned, it must become increasingly suppressive in order to maintain power. Because the system of central planning doesn't work, hasn't worked, and never will work. It is a misguided political ideology shared by misguided and impractical academics.

Under a fascist administration, the state gradually changes. It begins as one that has received its power, authority and right to tax the individual from the individual. Eventually it will be transformed into an authority where the state has become all-powerful; and the individual, stripped of all rights, is relegated to the role of state supplicant, chattel and slave. The ultimate state of degradation would be control by a Hitler-type regime. In which case, it could be many decades, or even centuries, before the once-free state known as the United Kingdom, is returned to its rightful owners.

Britain is now on that winding road to serfdom. As history demonstrates, there are degrees of serfdom. Many individuals currently enjoy their role as servants of the state, oblivious to the implications. Regardless of the state of the nation as we enter the next phase of global depression, no worse investment for the future could possibly be made than to elect a government which could prove difficult (if not impossible) to remove from office — other than by force or by open revolt.

Power. . . The Face and the Mask

You can't beat the game if you don't know the rules. In fact, it's pretty damn foolish even to become involved if you don't know the rules. The first rule you must consider is "The Golden Rule". That's a simple one; and one which makes an ideal point of departure for all investors. "The Golden Rule" says: "Those who control all of the 'gold' make all of the rules". And you know who controls all of the 'gold' . . . the Government!

George Orwell's concept of "newspeak" is being demonstrated with a vengeance by the British authorities. Nigel Lawson, Chancellor of the Exchequer, told a group of Liverpool businessmen that "only charlatans know the future". In "newspeak" that means all economists are "charlatans" with the exception of a Government economist. He tells the truth! Therefore, you should ignore totally any economist who disagrees with him, or any other Government spokesman out of tune with the party line. Nigel Lawson periodically studies the forecasts of the bunch of civil servants employed as "charlatans" by the Treasury to provide him with the predictions of the future upon which he will prepare the annual Budget. This is the kind of duplicity that has become characteristic of the statements made to the media by the Government.

One must always give credit where credit is due. The Government's manipulation of the media, and its repeated dogma, have been enormously successful. The entire nation has been mesmerised by what it perceives as "Thatcherism", and a "new way". Experienced economists actually believe her Government has made progress toward improving the state of the British economy. They believed that the "tight money" policy that Mrs Thatcher had adopted would produce longer term benefits. They believed that "Thatcherism" was dedicated to making people more independent and self-reliant. They believed in the Government's commitment to curbing inflation. So persuasive was the rhetoric, and so effective the suppression of views that might contradict the rhetoric, that it was accepted as truth. Yet, when asked to quantify the achievements of the Government, those who hold such an unyielding faith in "Thatcherism" are suddenly at a loss for words. On the other hand, the small number who condemned the methods and achievements of the Thatcher regime were able and willing to produce a plethora of statistics demonstrating the inexorable deterioration of the British economy since the start of the Thatcher Regime. Much of the contraction in the British economy was caused by the global recession, and so had little to do with the Government. However, the fact that most people were unaware of the depth of the domestic and global problems was entirely the result of the propaganda into which the Government put such effort.

The reader may come to the conclusion that I am anti-Government, and may be an anarchist, or a subscriber to some way-out left-wing philosophy. I can assure you this is not the case. I must be apolitical and totally objective in every respect if I am to unearth those factors which are important in the decision-making process. It has never been my intention to foster or denigrate political objectives. First and foremost, my role is to provide information. I am no evangelist.

To understand the political environment sufficiently to be able to deal with it, you must have some grasp of the true nature of two hierarchies. Nations are rather like a shop-keeper with two sets of books. They keep one set of institutions and organisations for their overt dealings. Each also has its established rules and conventions. There is no mystery about these overt hierarchies in the West. Theoretically, at any rate, they are ultimately answerable to the people. There is in Britain a body of elected representatives who sit in the Lower House of Parliament (the Commons) and act as the Legislature. They make laws. There is an Upper House of Parliament (the Lords) which forms part of the Legislature, with somewhat limited but still important powers.

The political party with the most members in the Commons (but not necessarily an overall majority) acts as the Executive. The Executive is also represented in the Upper House. When Parliament passes a Bill, it becomes law — again theoretically — once it has received the Royal Assent. So the supreme authority in Britain is "the Queen in Parliament". It is an answer which will earn the requisite number of marks in an examination. But it tells only part of the story. Much the same could be said of the second hierarchy — the Military. The Military exist as a legal entity because Parliament has voted that they should. Theoretically, the Armed Services could be voted out of existence.

The third hierarchy — the Economic, lurks in the shadows. Theoretically, the Chancellor presents his Budget annually to a committee of the whole House of Commons; a Finance Act is passed; and by the time MPs go on their summer holidays, the necessary funds will have been voted by Parliament for the various Departments of State; and the Inland Revenue, in particular, will have been told how much to collect in taxes. Where there is a gap between income and expenditure, it has to be made up: by borrowing or by the sale of State assets. QED.

The great difference between Britain and the United States is that the two Houses of Congress (Senate and the House of Representatives) have a legislative function. The Executive Power resides in the Office of President; but Sovereignty is vested in the United States Constitution.

In both countries, the judges and the courts carry out the judicial function, thereby affording the citizen the protection of law. Lastly, both countries tell the world, "We are not as other inferior regimes. *We* live by the Rule of Law." Unfortunately that tells you about only *one* set of books — the one we are proud to show off. The other set is not open to anyone, because it tells how things really happen.

The first of the hierarchies, the Government, is not in fact so dependent on the individual citizen and the national consensus as might appear. In Britain there is only a comparatively small number of Commons seats which normally change hands at an election. The candidates chosen for the majority of seats, which in varying degrees will be considered as "safe" seats, are virtually hand-picked for the green leather benches of the Commons. The candidates themselves often know perfectly well which of their number is likely to be elected. So, in reality it is the various political parties' constituency organisations which are the real power in the land when it comes to sending their man (or woman) to Parliament. Thus we may say, even from this simple example, that the results of an election do not necessarily represent the will of the people. Add a further dimension — that the winning candidate in Britain has to gain just one vote more than any of his or her opponents. This is called the "first past the post" system. Theoretically it means that the Party which wins the most seats — however narrowly — derives greater strength in the House than the mere counting of heads (proportional representation) would give them. It also avoids the kind of horse-trading that goes on after the votes have been counted under proportional representation. This, it is argued, can land the electorate with alliances in the House which will follow policies contrary to those the voters thought they were going to get. But with the present UK system, a candidate who has attracted more anti-votes than pro-votes can still get elected for the constituency. The Conservative Government was elected on that "ticket" in 1983, and in 1987.

Again theoretically, Britain has civil servants, powerful men and women who hang up their political bias (and some say their consciences) with their hats and coats. They are the highly skilled non-political servants of the public. They will continue to run their departments irrespective of who gets elected. In point of fact some civil servants, being virtually appointees of the Prime Minister, are as powerful as any Minister. The Westland affair, the Australian MI6 case, and many other instances involving "leaks" on defence and security matters have displayed to the public a side of civil service life which has alarmed them.

There was the controversy over the alleged plot by MI6 "activists" to discredit the Wilson Labour administration; and the difficulty the Commons had in trying to get an answer out of the Prime Minister on the subject. There is the role of some of the leading members of Mrs Thatcher's Downing Street entourage. . . or Mr Harold Wilson's for that matter! The performance of the Cabinet Secretary at the Australian spy-book trial was none too edifying to strict constitutionalists. But these days they must be counted among the few surviving romantics. "Revelations" of so many kinds have made even "cynics" uneasy. It is arguable whether it is not perhaps doing a disservice to the public at large to make them uneasy about things they are never going to change. Even members of Parliamentary Select Committees feel frustrated when Government instructs civil servants on the kind of questions they may, or may not answer. Tell some backbenchers today that there is always Question Time, when they can challenge leading Ministers, and they will give a sad, hollow little laugh.

The Military establishment derives its power and political importance from the fact that it is the only legal body entitled to deploy physical force to the limit. How long will it be, though, before the gap between the police and the military is closed by the introduction of para-military forces — the logical development after the introduction of CS gas, baton-rounds and snipers' rifles. Today it is not only questions of national defence that worry the ordinary citizens as they watch the escalation of civil disobedience and its gradual drift towards violence. The Stonehenge incidents of 1986 were a nuisance to the authorities, and angered the local farming community who saw their crops and their fields — and so their livelihood — damaged. But what will happen if the masses of young unemployed, who have been told to "get on their bike", and "move on", and "keep moving", begin to drift together across the face of the countryside. . . pausing (as the Stonehenge travellers did) to collect their social security money before making camp a little further on — as did the wanderers in 1987!

Some think it was premature to go so far as to abolish the Riot Act. It has already become clear that one day it could be needed: not just in Northern Ireland, but on the mainland. Every child's text book tells — if only in a few lines — of the Luddites, the Tolpuddle Martyrs, the Chartist Rioters, "Orator" Hunt and the Massacre of Peterloo. How will the next generation's text books handle the first of the Notting Hill Riots, shortly after the Second World War? Already it seems so long ago, that many have forgotton it happened — if they ever knew!

That the Military are powerful in political terms is undeniable. They wield considerable clout when extracting money from Parliament — which means the taxpayer. It should not be underestimated. But there is a more worrying aspect. We may seek to comfort ourselves with tales of what happened in East Germany and Hungary in the 'fifties; and how badly the Russians did in Czechoslovakia in the '60s. There was the Solidarity struggle in Poland; and more recently the role played by Soviet forces in Afghanistan. But older readers will recall the role played by the military in Algeria: how tanks and armed men stood ready on the Paris streets as de Gaulle gathered up the reins of power — and above all — how close France came to open revolt when de Gaulle turned his back on the French 'colons'. Then there were students' demonstrations in Japan and in Europe. True it was almost a generation ago. So were the troubles at the Sorbonne, the near riot at the London School of Economics, the Trenton riots, the black mobs on the streets of Washington, the shooting of students on the campus. . . to say nothing of the anti-Vietnam War demonstrations. The Bader-Meinhof gang, the militant Japanese students, the "Weathermen" (mainly well-brought up young women), who robbed a military armoury and accidentally blew themselves to pieces in New York.

Just over a decade ago in Britain we had the 1976 Notting Hill carnival riot. The London "Bobby" was forced to take up a defensive weapon to protect himself from the missiles. . . a dustbin lid! Commissioner Sir Kenneth Newman of Scotland Yard has called it a "rather unedifying spectacle". In Lewisham, the following year, the police arrived on the scene of a clash between Left-Wing demonstrators and the Right-Wing National Front, carrying riot shields for the first time in public. Three years later, the Bristol riots led to looting of the shops, and the donning of reinforced helmets by the police. The very next year, police were petrol-bombed in Brixton. Outside the South-East, Liverpool endured the Toxteth riots, where the missiles the mob used were building materials, piled by the road, for use in the "re-gentrification" of what had once been an upper-class re-gentrification residential area.

The miners' strike brought trouble nationwide. There was fierce hand-to-hand fighting, and the police charged the crowds on horseback. On numerous occasions, roadblocks were set up on the motorway. Potential trouble-makers. . . as the police saw it. . . were turned back. Handsworth added a new and frightening dimension to race violence. The disturbances at Wapping, and the October night riot at Broadwater farm brought a further escalation of hatred and bloodshed. The night scenes on television were reminiscent of the troubles in Belfast and Londonderry. Shortly afterwards police began training at their specially built "Riot-City". In 1986, Territorial support groups were formed to provide a reserve of 1,500 police officers, in highly trained teams. At the beginning of 1987, the Army loaned the Metropolitan police their first armoured vehicles. . . known as "pigs".

So far, in so few years! But how much further will it go by 1990? Shall we see a renewed role for the military in aid of the civil power? Not as today in Northern Ireland — but here on the mainland? No one in their senses would any longer say, "It couldn't happen here." You may well ask, "*What* couldn't happen?" The answer is, we just don't know.

The third hierarchy, the Economic, or "Plutocracy", is made up today of governments that have gone into business; as well as businesses which — you might say — have gone into government. The power wielded by the top 200 multi-national corporations is awesome indeed. The turnover of that top 200 would shame many a sovereign state. But these are "grey eminences". They shun the limelight. They have too many enemies. Too much is at stake. The prey they stalk is the unwary politician to whom power is a way of life, a goal overshadowing all other goals. The collectivist whose sole ambition is to wield power over others is a prime target for ultimate manipulation by the pragmatic, grey, faceless men who control the limbs. . . and smiles. . . of these multi-national robots. True, the men ostensibly in charge control these monsters from the Boardroom. But it is far harder to pinpoint the exact seat of power. Over the years the multi-national corporations and multi-national bankers have been at pains to cultivate the belief that the proprietary base is widely scattered, and that the "management" is actually in the driving seat. They like to encourage the myth that they are the victims of government. In reality they come close to controlling governments.

In *Tragedy & Hope*, Professor Carrol Quigley, of the Foreign Service School, Georgetown University (formerly of Princeton and Harvard) wrote a book which has become the Bible of conspiracy theorists, who may study their subject in some American universities. He highlighted the influence of international bankers going back to the Hapsburgs. Their influence — on the whole — has been benign. Professor Quigley hopes this pattern will continue, despite the forces currently working against them in the never-ending power game of politics and economics.

Governments have been aided in promoting this important aspect of disinformation (by journalists, sociologists and historians) by labelling anyone challenging this plutocracy as some form of extremist, anarchist or radical. Of course, the reasons for such accusations are purely self-interest. Top academics teach at top institutions and top institutions have boards of trustees which resemble a miniature *Who's Who of Finance and Industry*. The trustees decide in most cases who gets promoted to positions of authority; who receives tenure of employment; who is recommended for early retirement. . . and who is dismissed and relegated to obscurity. Part of the disinformation process involves the argument that decisions of this nature are likely to have been determined by the plutocratic trustees who have insisted they be well attuned to the economic interests, and prejudices, of their masters.

"When authority presents itself in the guise of organisation it develops charms fascinating enough to convert communities of free people into totalitarian States."

It was this quotation that F.A. Hayek chose for the introduction of the 13th chapter of *The Road to Serfdom*. The quotation came from *The Times*. The extent to which propaganda and disinformation play a part in shaping and modelling attitudes under the direct control of the authorities must never be forgotton. We can see with utter clarity how the power of the press, behind which lies the power of government, has over the years fomented an entirely new climate of thought and sentiment among great numbers of the population. Perhaps only the senior generation has been aware — and less affected.

In the process of Britain's decline and loss of Empire, the role of the international media should not be underestimated. Tightly-knit press control has been instrumental in shaping public opinion; convincing people that one of the most socialistically motivated leaders in British history — Margaret Thatcher — is actually a Conservative advocate of free markets. In much the same way, a media influence has been instrumental in shaping public opinion in the countries that used to comprise the Commonwealth. What some people may have assumed to be "grass roots" sentiment toward Britain, shared by her neighbours and protectorates, is likely to be as much the product of a propagandist press as any of the opinions encountered in this country on domestic issues. Those in the British Empire did not suddenly wake up one morning and decide that Britain was no longer suited to be their Mother Country. Nor did they demand independence out of the blue. The process was far more subtle and protracted. Attitudes were influenced almost imperceptibly by the organs of mass communication. In precisely the same way, the British electorate did not merely come to the sudden conclusion that this country should shed its Imperial heritage. People here became acclimatised to the idea by a process of slow, gradual conditioning that took place over decades, with the media acting as the principal tutors and suppliers of the necessary disinformation.

There should be no doubt whatever that the media have become an instrument of power politics. Democracy is intended to provide government by the people, for the people. The media have been used to support government *by* government, *for* government thereby depriving the individual of his democratic right to choose the government. "There is no other choice" has been the pernicious catch-phrase of the Conservative Government. In the election, the media referred to the Labour Party as "the loony Left", denigrated the Labour Party leader, and emblazoned on the front page and the screen, the unpopular policies that would be adopted if a Labour Party were to assume office. The media — as the army, navy and police force used to be — are now such a factor in the conquest and control of the masses that we may unite with Spengler in his claim that "printing and gunpowder belong together".

The media want you to buy what they have to sell. In order to get you to buy what they have to sell, they have to tell you what you want to hear. In the same way, a politician gets your vote by telling you what he *thinks* you want to hear. What most people want to hear is that they deserve more of everything; and that it is government's duty and responsibility to make certain they get it! What the media will not do is call upon the many rational, intelligent, economic experts in Britain who understand the fiscal realities, who realise what is bankrupting the nation, and who can offer a credible alternative to the pusillanimous, congenitally optimistic piffle that comes from political sources. True prophets have never been overly popular. Mainly because people do not take kindly to those who predict that they are about to be chastised for their irresponsible, profligate ways. That makes it extremely easy for the government and its media pawns to take over. In addition to the regular media "experts", Whitehall maintains a sort of standing army — on call at a moment's notice — to wipe out the blasphemous prophets whose voices may inadvertently be heard.

Whenever any of the truly great economic commentators of our time. . . men like Harold Lever, Frederick Hayek, Lord Bower, Christopher Story and Richard Eastwell. . . begin to make the slightest penetration of the mental recesses of the British electorate, the socialist media (who now pretend to be a conservative media), simply open their magazines, newspapers, TV networks and radio stations to the propagandists. They are then given free access to British homes for as long as may be required to dent the credibility of those forecasters not in line with party dogma. These assurances are quite effective, since the true economic prophets have no comparable means of replying on a mass basis.

My own personal experience adds testimony to the persistent pattern. As a result of my work, I have earned a fairly high media profile. I'm beginning to feel such a profile may be counter-productive in my efforts to speak the truth. On radio and TV, I insist on live performances unless I am relatively certain that my work will be subject only to innocuous editing. There is a direct relationship between the amount of press comment I attract and the number of live appearances I have made on radio, TV and in lecture halls. Of course, I have no way of responding to those press comments. Many newspaper articles claim I have been predicting an apocalypse for ten years. Ten years ago, I was forecasting the longest and most glorious bull market in British stock market history. If the press commentators were to admit that, it would lend my current predicitions far too much credibility for their liking. "Beckman's been wrong on property", they say. "Beckman said property would crash and it's gone up instead". They forget to mention that my forecast on property was based on a 10-15 year time frame, not on a few weeks or a few months after the forecast. They also forget to mention that the only place where property prices have been rising has been the South of England. Elsewhere, property prices have been behaving exactly as I predicted they would. But any such admission would enhance the nature of the forecasts they wish to remain muted. "Beckman's been wrong on the stock market", they say. "He predicted a crash and shares have been going up over since". Once again they forget to mention that I was predicting the ultimate crash. . . the operative word being "ultimate". The timing is imprecise. The consequential risk is quite precise.

Throughout history, we've seen the same sequence of events repeating itself over and over again. Yet the majority of individuals remain oblivious to it all. As a period of long-term economic improvement approaches a terminal juncture, and over-optimism, over-speculation and mindlessness appear to prevail, the men of wisdom will come forth and warn of an approaching cataclysm. In response, government spokesmen, and those that governments manipulate, will assure the public that these "scaremongers and doom merchants" are probably a little bit funny in the head since. . . "IT" could never happen here, or "IT" could never happen again, or "IT" could never happen today. The next step is for the masses to disseminate the soothing assurances amongst themselves until the biased unrealities become perceived truths. At that stage, anyone who calls attention to the increasingly more obvious realities is labelled a "doomsayer", "doom and gloom merchant", "perennial pessimist", "doomer", "gloomer". . . ridiculed

276 Into The Upwave

or simply ignored. The final step comes when the cataclysmic event that was denied has come to pass.

This three-step sequence has been observed in nation after nation, with monotonous repetition. We saw this sequence unfold in the civilisations of ancient Greece. We saw the sequence unfold again in the civilisation of ancient Rome. We saw it happen in Spain. We saw it again in pre-Napoleonic France of the 1790s, and yet again in Russia prior to the Bolshevik Revolution in 1917. How can we fail to recognise what has been happening in Britain for the past 100 years? Yet, notwithstanding the lessons of history, Britons prefer to cling to folly, and accept the assurances of those responsible for all of their problems to start with.

You must accept, and expect, the chorus of propagandists to shriek with even greater fervour as the disastrous series of events we face unfold. They are unaware that the majority of the people neither seek the truth, nor want to hear the truth. As we travelled into the second half of the 1980s, people became accustomed to their false prosperity, and would prefer that it were not challenged. As the background becomes more foreboding, the majority of the people will find an even greater need for someone — anyone — to say all is well. That being the case, the originators and disseminators of disinformation and propaganda will gladly oblige, in exchange for support and the power support brings.

Unfortunately, reality cannot be diverted by ignoring it. Historical determinism will not go away with the ploy of casual dismissal. The time-bomb of human bondage and state control will not stop ticking away — merely because someone is trying to call the public's attention to it. . . while there is still time.

Chapter Eight

THE SUN RISES IN THE EAST

We have not the freedom to reach this or that but the freedom to do the
necessary or to do nothing. And a task that historic necessity has set will
be accomplished with the individual or against him.

Oswald Spengler.

Civilisations are born, develop, mature, stabilise and die. Visualise a long, sweeping, forward leaning letter "S". This growth curve was first developed in detail by Lowell J. Reid and Raymond Pearl of John Hopkins University in the 1920s. The civilisation starts with a long period of slow growth, similar to the first gentle curve in our "S". This period of growth gradually accelerates and turns into an exponential curve of growth, not unlike the long sweeping upward curve in our figuration. Eventually, the growth rate flattens and the civilisation dies and a new one takes its place.

That there are great cycles in civilisations is certainly not a new concept. In 1805 in London, William Playfair observed the phenomenon in *An Inquiry into the Permanent Causes of Decline and Fall of Powerful and Wealthy Nations.* Historian Arnold Toynbee also viewed civilisations in a cyclical perspective. Since the rise of human settlements (or of our written records of these), there have been, according to Arnold Toynbee, twenty-one different civilisations, of which Western society, as a cultural unit, is but one:

"Societies rose, existed as civilisations,, and then crumbled. The system was one of growth, breakdown and then dissolution".

Pearl's growth curve, the sweeping "S", is found again in Oswald Spengler's work. Spengler saw the life of a culture as paralleling the life of an individual. As he describes it in *The Decline of the West,* the life of an individual and the span of culture may both be compared to the seasons. Every culture has its spring, summer, fall and winter. The first curve of the "S" begins in the springtime. It will be found that corresponding events occur at precise points in the curve, relative to the development stages of each of the twenty-one civilisations categorised by Toynbee. The peak in architectural development is common to the same growth phase of every culture, whether it be the Ming Dynasty or the Roman Empire. The same holds true for mathematics, painting, music, fashion, religion, the physical sciences and politics. Each crops up in identical form, at identical phases in the development of each of the civilisations of the past few thousand years.

Spengler, like Pearl, was convinced that the future course of a culture can be accurately drawn once the early dates in its history have been established.

Spengler called the winter of the culture — the final stages of a civilisation — the age of "Caesar". In other words, the age of the dictator. During the course of cultural development, feudal rule of the elite passes into democracy, then into mobocracy and finally into "Caesarism" when the culture is ready for dissolution. The building of great cities is another aspect which determines the final stages of a civilisation. It is here that Spengler sees Caesarism developing, during the 20th century of Western civilisation.

Writing his great thesis during the course of World War I, Spengler felt quite certain that the Great War, which the world was experiencing, would be only the first of many. According to the painstaking, sociological correlations of Spengler, life in the second half of the 20th century would involve the awful age of ". . .contending States when dictators would arise". Spengler, who died in 1936, was equally certain that democracy would shortly give way under the ". . .march of the Caesars". The Caesars habitually destroyed democracy and money. Had Spengler lived just three years longer, he would, perhaps, have recognised in Hitler the first of the many Faustian Caesars under whom he foresaw "the world trembling, the money collapsing and the blood streaming".

Dr S.H. Lee, in his studies of Chinese history, adds considerable corroboration to the works of Spengler. The history of China goes back further than any other. Dr Lee finds two 800-year periods in China's history (and the beginning of a third) which show corresponding parallels along the lines indicated by Spengler. Their frequency, Lee says, "far exceeds the limits of probability".

Each period in Chinese history began with a short dynasty with great military strength, unifying the country after centuries of strife and disorganisation. During those centuries of deprivation, other civilisations held the dominant world role. Then came four to five hundred years of peace; a change of dynasty; wars — and especially civil wars between the North and the South. The wars culminated in the subjection of the dissidents, signalling the end of the culture.

Spengler found that in the springtime of a culture, architecture blooms. Not the architecture of the cities, but architecture similar to that of the cathedrals of our own Renaissance. Dr Lee too, in his study of Chinese history, mentions the undertaking of vast architectural projects in the early part of these great civilisations. Colossal palaces sprang up in the opening years of the first of the dynasties comprising Lee's 2,000 year study. The Great Wall was built under the Ch'in dynasty, the dynasty which probably gave its name to the nation! The early years of the second of the 800-year periods saw more palaces of great magnificence, and the Great Canal. The beginning of the third and most recent period brought the re-building of the Great Wall, new canals and dams, along with the city of Peking.

Without any doubt, the most important implication of these long term, historical correlations is the existence of a pattern of world dominance. That particular issue has a special poignancy at this most important terminal juncture of our Western civilisation, as we've known it. The works of Spengler, Lee, Toynbee, and others, all seem to reveal a dominant rhythm of about 500 to 600 years, representing the birth and maturity of a civilisation. More intriguing still, is the tendency for world dominance to shift from East to West and back again in accordance with this observable rhythm. If we accept the long-term historical patterns, the shift from West to East is due to take place some time during the 20th century.

In prehistoric times man passed through progressive growth stages, distinguished by the nature of the tools he used, and the materials from which he made them. That is why these stages are known as the Stone Age, the Bronze Age and the Iron Age. The Stone Age may be divided roughly into two parts. The first, the Old Stone Age, lasted about 100,000 years, ending somewhere between 8,000 and 10,000 years BC. During the Old Stone Age, man's principle "tool" was a rough stone, held in the hand to crush things, and other stones. Later, man attached a handle to the stone, making the first axe or spear. This marked the arrival of the New Stone Age, which lasted until about 4,000 years before the birth of Christ.

Old Stone Age man was a cave dweller and a hunter, who killed wild animals for his next meal. By the New Stone Age, with the help of more efficient tools — spears and axes — man left his cave and put up a wooden dwelling in the open. As he passed through the Bronze Age and the Iron Age, he learned three other arts, which greatly helped him to advance. The first was the art of cultivating plants — the dawn of agriculture. The second was the art of breeding and training wild animals, so that they became domesticated. Finally, he learned to make pottery, giving him a range of household utensils. As a result of these three arts, man became less of a nomad. Groups of men and women began to settle during the months when they were no longer seeking fresh pastures. So, crops could be planted and harvested. The food supply for man — and whatever he called a family — was assured. Man could now begin to plan his future.

As all these changes took place in prehistoric times, the population grew and men were no longer content to live in primitive huts. They began to build cities with well-defined boundaries, thus establishing a territorial imperative. In other words, circa 4000 BC, man was becoming civilised. For civilisation means only the art of living in cities. It is at the point when man began to live in cities, that history truly begins. From then on, we can study the rise and fall of the great civilisations of history.

The earliest civilisation (in the sense of city-dwelling) sprang up in Egypt and various parts of Asia — from China in the Far East, to Mesopotamia, the land of the Tigris and Euphrates. Great civilisations arose in Egypt and Mesopotamia, while the people in Europe continued to live in extremely primitive conditions. The Americas were completely unknown. The Egyptian civilisation is one of the oldest known to history. Up to the year 3500 BC there were two separate Kingdoms. Then they were united, and there began a long period of development under successive dynasties, or families or rulers, called Pharaohs. While Egypt flourished, another civilisation was developing in Mesopotamia, originally colonised by the Sumarians. Here we have the first recorded *decline* of a civilisation. Somewhere between 3500 and 2700 BC, the Sumarian empire was overthrown. About 500 years later, a people called Amorites arrived in Mesopotamia, and established a new civilisation. Under the great King Hummurabi, about 1800 BC, they launched a series of conquests. Subsequently, they built the City of Babylon on the Euphrates, which ultimately became the heart of the powerful Babylonian Empire.

In about 1100 BC, we have the second decline of a civilisation. Babylon was captured by invaders called Assyrians, whose military strength lay in their clever and strategic use of horses and chariots. Nineveh, on the Tigris, became the capital of the Assyrian Empire. As is characteristic of the spring-time of a civilisation, the Assyrians built beautiful palaces and magnificent temples, making Nineveh the finest city in Asia.

Another 500 years passed. In 612 BC, Nineveh was destroyed by new Assyrian invaders, the Chaldeans. The great King Nebuchadnezzar rebuilt Babylon, and it became even more magnificent than before. On the roof of his palace in Babylon, Nebuchadnezzar created the famous Hanging Gardens, which the Greeks held to be one of the Seven Wonders of the World.

Historians have called the century or so starting in 540 BC, "The Age of Tyrants". The Chaldeans enjoyed a very brief reign, and were finally invaded, and destroyed, by the Persian King Cyrus. In the 6th century BC, Cyrus led his armies from his territory which lay to the east of the Tigris. When he invaded Babylonia, the Chaldean armies proved to be no match for his skilled archers and swift-footed cavalry. The Persians then went on to conquer Syria, the rest of Asia Minor and Egypt.

From Asia Minor, in 520 BC, the Persians advanced on Europe, where they soon met the determined resistance of the Greeks. Here yet another civilisation emerges 500 years after the decline of the Assyrian civilisation. The course of global dominance was moving from East to West.

The ancient Greeks, who were city-dwellers and seafarers, founded the first European civilisation. The inhabitants of their two major cities, Athens and Sparta, were isolated from one another by the lie of the land. As a result, both cities grew into independent States, each with its own government and laws. Greeks from the various cities would come together for such festivals as the Olympic Games. Greek civilisation spread to the many colonies founded on the coasts of the Mediterranean and Black Sea; especially in Sicily and Southern Italy. It was from the Greek colony of Marseilles, that Pytheas sailed into the Atlantic, and explored the coasts of Britain. By establishing their colonies all over Europe, the Greeks increased their trade and manufactures, as they went on improving their skills at shipbuilding and waging war.

Like every young civilisation, the Greeks had to fight for their existence. The first major conflict was against the Persians (500-448 BC). The Athenians first defeated the Persians at Marathon. Then Xerxes overcame the Spartans at Thermopylae and captured Athens. But he was ultimately defeated at sea near Salamis, and on land at Plataea. The war, which was carried into Asia Minor, ended in triumph for the Greeks in 448 BC, just over a century since their first encounter with the might of Persia.

The period 460 to 430 BC was the Age of Pericles. It was also the *Caesarian* phase of Greek civilisation. Pericles was a great leader. He beautified the City of Athens and encouraged sculptors and architects like Pheidias and Ictinus. But the growing decadence in Greek culture began to show through in the work of playrights such as Aeschylus, Sophocles and Euripides. The Greek civilisation experienced its first major shock when the Athenians were defeated in the Peloponnesian War (431-404 BC). That civil war was symptomatic once again of the Caesarian age of a civilisation. It finally weakened all the Greek city-states, setting the stage for the decline of the Greek Empire itself. King Philip of Macedon reigned from 359 to 336 BC, and created a powerful army. His successor was the most powerful of all Greek leaders, Alexander the Great, champion of the Greek "Caesars". Alexander, who reigned from 336-323 BC, conquered Asia Minor, (including Syria), Egypt, Persia, part of Turkestan and India. After Alexander's death, the Greek Empire fell into the hands of its Generals who were constantly, and bitterly, at odds with one another. Disunity finally led to the collapse of the once great Greek Empire.

In the 500 years or so beginning about 670 BC, the glory of Greece and the power of the Ptolemys continued to decline. Rome came on to the world stage as their successor. In the 8th century BC, the Romans founded their City, and established a Republic. By 270 BC they had conquered the rest of Italy. In the three Punic Wars (264 BC-146 BC) they went on to crush the Carthaginians, destroying Carthage and adding North Africa and Spain to their domain. Turning eastwards, they conquered Greece, and established the Province of Asia (200-130 BC). Around 100 BC, the Romans completed the conquest of Cisalpine Gaul. In the meantime, starting from the Mediterranean coast and spreading over Southern Gaul, they established the Province of Transalpine Gaul. As Governor of this Province, Julius Caesar conquered the remainder of Gaul, from the Atlantic to the Rhine, and up to the North Coast (58-50 BC). Caesar twice invaded Britain. Once in 55 BC and once again the following year. On both occasions he failed to hold the country. Indeed, it was not until sixty years later (in 14 AD) that Britain was finally added to the Roman Empire — an Empire which by then was nearing its end.

Rome, which began as a simple city-state, had become the capital of one of the most prodigious empires the world has ever known. As the Empire grew, its cities in other lands became more splendid, more magnificent. But the citizens of Rome became more idle. As they did so, the Empire began to decline. In 166 AD plague struck, killing large numbers of the population. The long Roman peace suffered a violent disruption in 193 AD, when marauders raided its frontiers and outposts. The Sassanid Revolution against the Parthian Kings in AD 224 had brought to power a new dynasty, which saw itself as successor to the Achaemenids, creating at the same time a powerful and highly centralised state in Persia. Having expanded and taken over the Kushan Empire to the East, it began to pose a threat to Rome to the West. The Emperors Diocletian and Constantine both attempted to overhaul the administration, and divided the Roman Empire between East and West. But they failed to make it strong enough to keep out the people who lived beyond its frontiers. Nor could they make it flexible enough to absorb them. By now the seeds of Roman decay were too firmly rooted. Between 235 AD and 284 AD, Roman civilisation collapsed. It disintegrated in squalor during a prolonged period of civil wars, barbarian invasions and disputes over succession to the Imperial Office.

However, no civilisation dies overnight. Once an Empire begins to decline it can still take a century or two before the nadir of degeneration is reached. The Roman Empire began to decline in 60 BC, around 500 years after the Greek civilisation had started to run-down. While the Roman Empire was thus immersed in an irreversible process of disintegration, new Asian empires were beginning to develop once again. The crown of world dominance was now to pass from West to East once more.

Around 200 AD the centre of the civilised world lay in the Middle East. From the Caspian to the Hindu Kush, the serried array of the Iranian baronage stood guard against raiding horsemen from the steppes. The Iranians had sturdy mounts, heavy armour, and powerful bows, together with a readiness to take the field at a moment's notice to protect the peasants upon whose rents they lived. Thus they provided the heartlands of the Middle Eastern and Indian civilisations with an effective and inpenetrable line of defence. Unlike the situation on the increasingly vulnerable Roman frontiers, a raiding party that tried to penetrate the Middle Eastern boundaries had to pass through continuously protected territory, where the most technologically formidable warriors of the age would be lying in wait. Few raiding armies made the attempt. Even fewer repeated it.

Secure behind this barrier, both the Indian and revived Persian civilisations attained new levels of elegance, sophistication and religious virtuosity. The Gupta Empire in India was the first native State to establish itself since the fall of the Mauryas. The Gupta Empire based its power on the Ganges Valley. At its height it held sway over much of the sub-continent. India had entered upon a golden age, which remained "classical" for subsequent Indian generations. The expansion of Indian civilisation to South East Asia, and its impact on Chinese, Korean and Japanese styles of life, imbued the civilisation of more than half the human race with a common tint. Insofar as Asia has any community of cultural tradition uniting the Indian people with those of China, Japan, Korea, Mongolia, Tibet, Burma, Cambodia and Ceylon, it is due to the influence of ancient Indian civilisation. The achievements of Hellenism were certainly no greater.

In the meantime, the Roman Empire was being transformed into the Byzantine Empire by the Emperor Constantine, who ruled from 306 AD to 337. Constantine changed Roman Government in two important aspects: he established a new capital at Byzantium, which he renamed Constantinople, and he made Christianity the approved State religion. The new capital of Constantinople was well situated, both for trade and defence, since it was relatively easy to supply the city from distant coastlands of the Black Sea and the Aegean. The uninterrupted survival of Byzantine Imperial Government is believed to have saved Romans from becoming barbarians.

The Byzantine Empire, the Gupta Empire and the Sassanid Empire all flourished simultaneously. But about 450 AD, 500 years after the start of the decline of the Roman Empire, the Eastern centres of power began to self-destruct. In 316 AD, the Hsiung-nu overran Northern China, and divided it into several kingdoms. Between 375 AD and 410 AD several peoples crossed the Byzantine frontiers, and remained there — permanently. Throughout the 5th century the Hephthalites (often referred to as the "White Huns"), launched a number of campaigns against Bactria. This eventually forced a reorganisation of the Sassanid Empire, on a strictly military footing, under Khosrau I. The "White Huns" are often credited with the collapse of the Indian Empire of the Guptas. With hindsight we can see that the centre of world dominance was ready to shift from East to West again, as the Empire of Charlemagne, along with Britain, rose to prominence. In 527 AD, when Justinian became Emperor in Constantinople, the West was the most hopeful spot on the horizon.

From the second half of the 4th century AD, the Roman hold on Britain began to weaken. By now the island came under the relentless attack of the barbarians. Three different sets of invaders occupied the country: the Angles, the Saxons and the Jutes. From settlements in various parts of the country, the Anglo-Saxons moved on to conquer virtually the whole of Britain. From their landing beaches along Britain's coast line, the Anglo-Saxon invaders gradually spread across the country, as the war of conquest developed. The general effect of Anglo-Saxon occupation was to replace a mature civilisation, which it had destroyed, with one which was still in the early stages of development.

As more and more territory fell under Anglo-Saxon control, the position of the chief military leaders grew in importance. Several Anglo-Saxon tribes formed an alliance, for the sake of greater tactical strength. This made the chosen leader of the amalgamated tribes even more powerful. In time the military leader was made King, and enjoyed the loyalty of all the highest to the lowest in the land. Royalty emerged in Anglo-Saxon England around the middle of the 6th century with the King and the royal family supported by nobles and *thanes*. Few men were born noble. Those of lesser standing who had served the King well were often rewarded for their services with grants of land. They grew into a powerful body of landowners called *thegns* or *thanes*. It was the *thanes* who were to form a body of Advisers to the King known as the *Witan,* or Council of Wise Men.

Thus the King grew from being a military leader to sovereign ruler of an area of a whole territory. The country was divided up into kingdoms, each dominated by a different king. Soon the kings of the various domains began fighting with each other. It should come as no surprise that internal civil war ultimately led to the destruction of that particular civilisation.

While Western civilisation was developing in Britain, an outpost of Western civilisation advanced westwards under Charlemagne. Charles the Great (as Charlemagne was called) united the Franks on both sides of the Rhine; spread the Christian faith in Germany; and set up the Spanish March against the Moors. As King of the Lombards, Charles was also of great help to the Pope. In return, His Holiness crowned Charles Emperor on Christmas Day 800. Thus the Holy Roman Empire came into being, marking the end of the early medieval period. Grand as it sounded, Charlemagne's empire proved quite incapable of defending itself against the Viking and Magyar raids. As a consequence, military and political leadership passed into the hands of the rough-and-ready, local lords and men-at-arms. The whole civilisation began to decline. Between 960 and 1470 AD world domination moved Eastward again into the hands of Genghis Khan and Kublai Khan, until the mighty Ottoman Empire emerged.

Close ties between steppe nomads and the civilised world had been maintained for centuries before 1000 AD. Until the 16th century, this brought a series of infiltrations and conquests that took the Turkish and Mongol rulers to China, the Middle East, India and Eastern Europe. In AD 1000, Turkish-speaking tribes were already living in the middle reaches of the steppes, from the Attalia mountains as far west as Southern Russia. In eastern Iran, there had already been extensive penetration of Moslem towns by Turkish nomads. The Iranian barons, who for so many centuries had held the steppe nomads at bay, ceased to be effective after about 900 AD. About this time the culture of Islam moved into decline, along with those of Britain and Charlemagne's empire.

After about 900 AD Turkish mercenaries found themselves in a position to hold to ransom the Moslem heartlands of Iran, Iraq and Syria, completely dominating the political life of Islam. The Turkish newcomers next extended the frontiers of the Moslem world quite considerably. They launched their deep penetration of India with massive raids launched by Mahmud of Ghazni, in 1000 AD. By the 14th century the southern part of the sub-continent alone had escaped Moslem conquest. In the 13th century, the Turkish advance into India and Europe was halted by a sudden storm emanating from Mongolia. The founder of Mongol greatness had been Genghis Khan, who succeeded in welding together a vast military confederacy among the people of the steppes. Genghis Khan went on to carry out a series of successful raids in every direction — southward into China, westward against the Moslems of Iran and Iraq, and against the Christians of Russia too. On his death, Genghis Khan's empire was divided between his four sons. They replaced the massive raids of Genghis' time with a more stable form of political rule. According to Mongol custom, leadership was vested in Genghis's youngest son, and that son's heirs. These were the rulers of Mongolia and China, and the commanders of the vast Mongol army.

When Kublai Khan came to the throne, he held sway over more people than had ever before fallen under the authority of one man. Before he became Emperor, he did something which was almost unprecedented under the rule of the Khans. Instead of rewarding his conquered enemies with the customary fire, rape and slaughter, Kublai Khan offered them help, once they submitted to his rule. Kublai was probably responsible more than any of his predecessors for the development of the Eastern civilisation of that time. The astronomical instruments made at his request remained in Peking until 1900, when the Germans took them to Berlin. The great traveller from the West, Marco Polo, expatiated on the good government, hospitals, printed books and other signs of progress during Kublai Khan's rule in China. The Grand Canal was much improved. Competent Turks, Persians, Armenians, Byzantines, and even remote Venetians, like Marco Polo, were welcomed. What's more, some of them were appointed as governors, advisers and physicians. Although Kublai Khan placed few Chinese in high positions, the people as a whole liked the Khan, despite his nomad origin. They were prepared to overlook the practices of his predecessors, the pagan shamanists, who treated the human beings in their power much as they treated their animals. . . tending to them or slaughtering them as convenience might dictate.

In the sixty years between Kublai's death in 1294 and the end of the Mongol Empire in 1355, the nine descendants of Genghis Khan who succeeded to the throne are said to have been weak; not all that unlike the descendants of Julius Caesar. After the death of Kublai Khan, China faced one of the worst physical periods in all its history. Droughts, and often floods (and the accompanying famine they brought), were exceptionally frequent and severe in North China. According to the records of Yao, the year 1325 saw floods occurring every month from January through December. Almost every province suffered. Moreover, it was about the same time that the dreaded Black Death, the worst known plague in the history of mankind, broke out and spread westward. Such disasters almost inevitably bring political disruption, banditry, invasion and rebellion in their wake. No civilisation could survive such conditions. Given the problems of the period, it is remarkable that the Mongol dynasty lasted so long as it did. It would seem the overriding 510 year cycle is even more powerful than these events which man has long described as "Acts of God".

The Mongol dynasty left the legacy of a rich civilisation. Many leaders of the kith of Genghis Khan were great administrators as well as soldiers. Akbar is an example. On his mother's side, and possibly also on his father's, he was a descendant of Genghis Khan. Akbar ordered careful surveys of all property, and on the basis of those surveys introduced a mode of taxation that brought, and encouraged prosperity throughout his dominion. Having set up semi-feudal military systems, he established schools for Hindus, Moslems and Parsees alike.

In art too, the descendants of Genghis showed exceptional ability. There are few more famous buildings than the Taj Mahal, the magnificent tomb of the favourite wife of Shah Jahan, at Agra. Nor does the Taj Mahal stand alone. Among many other palaces and monuments is Agra's Pearl Mosque, which — with its pure white marble set off by delicate gold tracery — appeals to some even more than the Taj Mahal.

In 1513, the first Portuguese merchant visited the South China coast. By then the Ming regime, the final edifice of the Mongol influence, was already showing signs of the ills typical of a decaying dynasty, and the end of a civilisation. Inequitable taxation (together with Court and clique intrigues), provoked sporadic uprisings in the Chinese provinces. The raids from the steppes, and from the sea, were also becoming serious. The final collapse of the Ming dynasty — and the end of that civilisation — came in the traditional way. In 1644, acting in concert with a Ming General, a powerful and well disciplined barbarian war band from Manchuria entered Peking under the pretext of helping to suppress a domestic rebellion. Once they had the capital, the Manchus refused to co-operate with the Ming dynasty any longer. Their own leader, who successfully claimed the title of the Son of Heaven, founded a new dynasty, the Ch'ing. Another civilisation had fallen in the East, just as a new civilisation was approaching its period of dominance in the West. It was five centuries since the civilisation founded by the Turkish invaders had led to the reign of Genghis Khan. Then, after 1470, came Europe's great moment of unification, and its establishment of imperialistic domination over the world. Soon another great world power would appear in the West, the United States.

The new civilisation in Europe in many ways represented the rebirth of the Byzantium civilisation. It exhibited a pronounced tendency to militarism, which penetrated all ranks of society in a fashion unknown elsewhere among civilised peoples. This imparted a degree of formidability *vis-à-vis* their more polished neighbours, allowing the Europeans and Americans alike to borrow whatever they felt beneficial from the civilisations of these neighbours. Yet they could do so without in any way surrendering their sense of superiority, or their cultural individuality. The decline of the Eastern civilisation of that period took place between the 14th and 17th centuries. The flexibility and capacity for growth of the civilisation of the European countries meant they were ready to mount the throne of world dominance by about 1500. By that time, they had arrived at a level of culture, and a style of civilisation, that in most respects could bear comparison with any other in the world of their time.

The growth of Western civilisation over the past 500 years, which involved the Industrial Revolution and two great wars, needs little elaboration here.

What is important to recognise is the fact that our European civilisation *is* now more than 500 years old. According to Spengler, Western civilisation should now be in severe decline. And it is! The criteria which Spengler saw as evidence of a civilisation entering old age have been met. This means the maturing of Western civilisation into its final form — before its enfeeblement against the competition of rapidly rising civilisations, eager for growth, in the East.

Spengler is certainly not alone in his views. In *Time of Troubles* the great historian Arnold Toynbee comments:

> "If the analogy between our Western civilisation's modern history and other civilisation's *Times of Troubles* does extend to points of chronology, then a Western 'Times of Trouble', which appear to have begun in the 16th Century, may be expected to find its end some time in the Twentieth Century, and this prospect may well make us tremble."

According to many historians and futurologists, the beginning of the next major shift in global power from West to East should now be due. There is significant evidence to suggest that the massive changes in the structure of the world economy over the past decade may be more than simply an economic dislocation at the terminal juncture of a cycle. But who is ready to accept the mantle of world dominance as we move into the 21st century? It is tempting to think of China, with its 800 million people. It may look like a big, tough superpower. But it isn't. While China could clearly trigger dangerous situations around the world, it can still be argued that the US and her European Allies — or the Soviet bloc, for that matter — need not fear China even if it is the most highly populated country on this planet.

At one time China was the dominant civilisation in the world. . . orderly, rich and highly advanced. One of the frustrations that early Western travellers experienced was that the level of acumen in China was much more advanced than their own. The kite, geometry, the concept of earthquake-detection, geology, fireworks, gunpowder, printing, the collar harness, the magnetic compass, weights and measures, the spinning wheel, paper-making, cast iron, mechanical clocks, astronomical instruments, chopsticks and even the fishing reel. . . were all known to the Chinese long before they appeared in the West. As recently as the year 1800, China had a higher per capita income than Europe. Then time stood still for China. A deep freeze set in, as Western industrial civilisation reached its zenith; and the Western powers invaded (and opiumised) China treating it as their domain.

Even now, China has little influence economically in world affairs. Before China could again become powerful, it would have to eliminate two-thirds of its ever-growing peasantry. But China does not wish to employ human selfishness as the engine of society. Unfortunately, that human selfishness is one of the most impressive engines a country can use. This has been demonstrated time and again throughout history.

Although China's annual per capita income is growing, it was until recently no more than $200; one of the lowest in the world. If China is ever to become a powerful world force it must achieve impressive and recognisable economic growth. Yet China works only for the Chinese. But there is nothing in 20th century culture to say that a country should be judged primarily from the viewpoint of GNP. In the traditional sense, China meets the five guarantees for human survival: adequate food, clothing, education, shelter and medical care. The people are protected by their government from the Soviet Union and the United States. More important in many ways is the fact that the Chinese think of themselves as the centre of the world. . . top dragon. . . Number 1. And *ego* counts for a lot, even in China. The Chinese would appear very satisfied with their current status; and for that reason, it is most unlikely that China will share in the spoils of world domination by the East for quite some time.

The position of Russia and the Eastern bloc is more difficult to assess. In geography and culture, Russia bridges the gap between East and West. It seems likely that the current part played by Russia in the role of global superpower is going to turn out to be transitional; resting partly within the cycle of Western domination, and partly within the projected period of Eastern power. Both the United States and the Soviet Union have been losing considerable influence all over the world. Their dominance is seeping away like sand in an hour-glass. There is an almost mystical notion that Russia was destined to see the birth of a great new civilisation, but that it lost its way — selling its birthright for a conglomeration of Europeanisation. Most Europeans and Americans have trouble with the idea that Soviet civilisation would have been better somehow if Russia had stayed aloof from Western Europe. The thought seems quite plausible to many Russians.

There is little doubt that Russia would have suffered far less making the same industrial progress without the revolution. The bountiful Ukraine would have done especially well. Had it not been interrupted by war and revolution, its growth is likely to have been achieved in a far more meaningful way than has been the case. Had it not been for the revolution, Russia is likely to have been the recipient of steady economic participation from Europe and the US. The nation's growth rate could have been double what it is now, with much less anguish. Misinvestment and mismanagement — often the result of faulty training — have wrought economic ruin on Russia.

It is true that the Russians have achieved exceptionally impressive progress in certain areas. But their basic skills do not really lie in the field of either industrial civilisation or post-industrial civilisation. Industrialisation, modernisation, organisation and efficiency, seem to be qualities which Russian people tend to lack. They do not appear to have the first-rate managerial skills which will be needed in the post-industrial society of the 21st century.

When we consider the requirements of our post-industrial society, neither Russia nor China would seem to be in a position to assume the role of world leader. But China's neighbour, Japan, has one-eighth the population, twice the gross national product, and has been growing at more than treble the rate of China. Japan could staff any system, including that of a world empire. By the end of this century, I believe that Japan will very likely be the most successful industrial society in the next cycle of global leadership. . . the economic superpower of the world during the next upwave.

The Miracle of the Japanese Superstate

Starting well below where Brazil is today, Japan has outgrown Britain, West Germany, France, Italy and most other industrialised societies. Economic capability has been doubling every six or seven years. Japan will probably pass the United States in *per capita* income by the next decade; and, in terms of gross national product, by the turn of the century. The Japanese have an unsurpassed capacity for purposive communal action. With the Government providing high-quality direction, they have outperformed the most optimistic expectations. The original objective was just to catch up with the West. The oriental desire to "save face", and maintain prestige was the spur; not national security, or a higher standard of living. Their innate qualities, coupled with the fact that the Japanese have the world's most achievement-oriented culture, will be the driving force which will enable Japan to assume the role of world superpower after such forces have evaporated in the West with the decline of its culture.

In order to maintain economic momentum in the next decade, and develop a really high quality of life, it is estimated that Japan will spend half a trillion dollars, or even more. If it proceeds with its usual efficiency and purposiveness, Japan will emerge as the first humanised post-industrialised and ecologically-adjusted nation in the world. The Japanese have shown a unique talent for borrowing from foreign cultures, maintaining the quality of achievement, and remaining Japanese through the process. That is why Japan moreover, has benefited from the economic success of the West without repeating the economic failures which are the result of the decline of Western civilisation.

Herman Kahn, in *The Coming Boom,* pointed out that many of the so-called innovations with which the Japanese have been credited were learned from the Americans about 30 years ago. For example, "the so-called quality-control circles. . . were originally transmitted to them. . . by Edward Deering, an American expert in quality control."

In the 19th century, Britain's *per capita* income grew one to two per cent a year. In so doing, it was the wonder of the world. In an effort to spare the electorate pain wherever possible and, at the same time, avoid electoral disfavour, through profligate monetary policy, successive British governments have ensured that *per capita* income continues to grow at no more than one or two per cent per year. Whereas the British Empire was once the "window of the world", it is now the *economic calamity* of the world. The Japanese have not made the same mistake. Japan has been the only country since World War II willing to experience the necessary sharp, severe depressions which serve to correct expansion which runs beyond economically justifiable levels. There have been six such depressions, in which the Tokyo Government has refused to interfere. They caused considerable suffering among small industries and small under-capitalised businesses. With few exceptions, the Government has demonstrated a steadfast — almost ruthless — refusal to support lagging businesses and industries. After each recession, the Japanese economy has been able to resume growth, having established a firmer base from which to operate, thanks to the elimination of the excesses which weakened the expansionary phase. The national economic law has been allowed to take its course.

Personal savings are the lifeblood of industry. The Japanese propensity for saving is in no small way responsible for the economic achievements of the past few decades. The Japanese put aside about twenty yen for every hundred yen they earn. This compares with fourteen marks per hundred by the West Germans, and about five to seven cents in the dollar for Americans. Personal savings in Japan amount to 13% of GNP. In West Germany the figure is 9%. In America, it is not more than 4%. Personal savings in Japan are encouraged by tax incentives; and the average Japanese employee often receives a major part of his remuneration in the form of a mid-year bonus. This is another important factor in maintaining the high savings rate which works to the benefit of society and industry.

Japan has a population of 117 million people, all of whom are confined to an area about the size of Wales plus the whole of Ireland, North and South. Or, if you like, you can compare it to the State of Montana. Most of the population is concentrated in large and medium-sized cities. The fact that such large numbers can be moved to work and back again each day with relative expedience is a triumph of logistics; helped by the fact that Japan's transportation network remains extraordinarily efficient, and Japanese commuters are almost invariably patient and courteous. In spite of the overcrowding, Japan is generally considered a desirable country to live in. A study prepared in 1981 showed that on a scale of one to one hundred in terms of environmental living conditions, Sweden received a rating of 97 while Japan, Iceland and the Netherlands ran close behind with a rating of 96. Canada and Switzerland had a rating of 95. The United States, United Kingdom, France, Finland and New Zealand had a 94 rating. Australia, Austria, Belgium, Czechoslavakia, East Germany, West Germany and Ireland, were rated 93. Italy and Luxemburg, were rated 92. The Soviet Union, Poland, Bulgaria, Hungary and Spain had a 91 rating. Ethiopia and Guinea were rated 20, Somalia 19, Afghanistan 18, Angola 16, Mali 15 and Niger only 13.

While suicide is frowned upon in the West, the ritual of *Hari-Kari* is an ancient tradition in Japan. It is considered more a symbol of honour than dishonour, when an individual decides to take his own life for reasons of sacrifice, renunciation or apology. A Japanese student who fails a university entrance examination for the second or third time (having studied) night and day for a year or so between each attempt) may well choose to exit the world via *Hari-Kari*. As will lovers who have been denied parental permission to marry; mature men who have failed in business; young men who wish to expiate the debts and sins of their fathers; or young widows who are having trouble raising their children. One would, therefore, expect a relatively high suicide rate. But this is not the case. Japan's suicide rate is about 15 persons per hundred thousand of population. This is higher than the United States. There the rate is eleven persons per hundred thousand of population. But it is lower than in Hungary, Austria, West Germany, Denmark and Sweden.

Japan has approximately one policeman for every seven hundred and twenty-nine inhabitants. The United States has one for every five hundred and two. France has one for every three hundred and forty-seven. A Japanese policeman is given more training and more discretion than law enforcement officers in most countries. The effect of this can be seen in the relatively high rate of arrests compared with other countries. Japan's police force has a 51% arrest rate for all crimes, compared to twenty-five per cent in the United States and thirty-five per cent in Britain. In cases of robbery, the Japanese arrest rate is eighty-three per cent; versus thirty-eight per cent in the United States. The arrest rate for murder is ninety-eight per cent in Japan, compared to ninety one per cent in the United States. Tokyo, whose population is about 8.5 million, experienced eight murders in 1980. New York, with a similar population, had twelve times as many murders, and fourteen times as many rapes. The comparatively low crime rate in Japan has as much to do with a traditional respect for authority — and family pride and honour — as with the effectiveness of the country's well-trained, highly disciplined police force. Peer pressure is a strong deterrent to misbehaviour in a country where virtually every individual is a member of a group; and where there is relatively little alienation from society.

A survey, taken in the mid-1970s, asked Japanese men whom they would telephone first if there were an earthquake. A mere nine per cent said their wives. Thirty-seven per cent said their employers. The Japanese call this devotion to the company *Aisha Seishin*. Once again we can see why the future success of Japanese industry is beyond the capabilities of declining Western civilisation.

There has been an explosion in the number of passenger cars on Japanese roads. In 1960 the country had no more than 440,417 private automobiles. By 1970, the number had risen to 6,776,949. Five years later Japan had 14,882,193 passenger cars; and by 1980, 21,542,000. In 1960, when Tokyo had only sixty thousand automobiles on its streets (compared to several million now), traffic conditions were by no means as good as they are today. That is because streets and avenues have been widened at enormous cost;

freeways have been constructed; gardens have given way to garage space, and there are massive underground parking complexes.

Only Sweden, Denmark and the Netherlands have more bicycles *per capita* than Japan, which in February 1979 had about forty-seven million, or one bicycle for every 2.3 people. When oil prices skyrocketed for a second time in 1979, bicycle ownership increased even further, since the rise in oil prices made driving to work prohibitively expensive.

In 1977, Japan passed Sweden to become the country with the world's highest life expectancy. Life expectancy for Japanese men is 72.7 years, and for women 77.9 years. In the United States, life expectancy among men is 70.2 years, and women 77.8 years. According to the *Guinness Book of Records,* no-one in history has lived longer than Schigechiyo Izumi of Tokunoshima, Kagoshima Prefecture. He was born in 1865 and died on the 29th June 1979 at the age of 114.

Between 1970 and 1980, Japan's exports to the world increased seven times in current dollar terms. Her exports to the EEC alone increased ten times. By contrast, the exports of the remaining nine OECD countries in the industrialised West increased only five times. EEC imports from Japan continued to grow at nearly twice the speed of its imports from the world. At the same time, Japan's exports to the EEC grew faster than her world exports. Imports from the EEC grew slower than Japan's world imports. The result was that through the decade Japan had a larger than ever trade surplus in Europe, reversing the historic role of a deficit with Europe for the first time in one hundred years. In 1966, GNP overtook Italy. In 1967 it overtook the UK. In 1968 GNP in Japan was greater than France. By 1969 Japanese GNP exceeded that of Germany. In 1960 the volume of trade between the European Community and that of Asia was more than twice that of Japan. By 1970, for the first time in modern history, Japan had overtaken the nine countries of the European Community in exports and imports alike. That trend has continued throughout the 1970s and into the 1980s. Japan's trade with Asia is now one and a half times that of the entire European Community. Japan now has three to four times more invested in South Korea, Taiwan, Indonesia, the Philippines and Thailand than do all of the countries of the European Community. Japan has more than one-and-a-half times the level of investment in Hong Kong than the European Community and slightly more in Malaysia.

Anyone visiting Japan during the early 1960s, and again in more recent years, will certainly notice some startlingly visible signs of the replacement of Europe. At first it was by the United States. . . now even the United States influence has been replaced by domestic pressures. Over the whole country today, in the town and the village alike, practically everything that moves on powered wheels is of local manufacture. That goes for the cars, the trucks, the tractors, the motorcycles — even the bicycles — as well as neon lights, radios, stereos, TVs and videos, sewing machines, clocks and the watches. You could say that virtually all the paraphernalia of modern life, which used to be made in Europe or America, are now made in Japan. These consumer durables are another striking sign of the massive flow of exports, as well as the investments, that continue to pour into the country.

The achievements of the past three-and-a-half decades have given Japan one of the most affluent societies in the world. More than 98% of Japanese households own refrigerators, colour TV sets and washing machines. More than 85% own vacuum cleaners. More than 80% own cameras, kerosene room heaters and sewing machines. More than 62% own their own homes, which is as high a percentage as that in any European country. More than 60% of the people own their own automobiles.

The reasons for the Japanese "miracle", and for its continuation, are multifarious. At the core of Japan's success is a kind of coalition between management, labour and government. All work together in a harmonious consensus. This helps to increase productivity and to improve the operation of the industrial system. But probably it is Japan's current state of development as a culture — and the cultural differences between East and West at this time — that make this harmonious integration between government, labour and management possible. While many things that are currently benefitting Japan would also benefit the West, many just won't. That is because Western culture has long ceased to be a homogeneous society. Collusion amongst management, dissention among the labour ranks and conspiracy in government circles do not seem to be a creative, productive, or constructive option in Western society.

Herman Kahn in his book, *The Coming Boom* provides an outstanding example of the enormous difference between Japanese and Western commercial psychology. Let's suppose the Japanese Government decides to allocate a territory to two Japanese companies, dividing it half between East and West.

Then, says Kahn ". . .each company would kill itself to show that it could do more with its territory than the other company".

On the other hand, if two American companies were given the same divided jurisdiction, and knew it was safe to relax and do as little as possible, they would. The same would hold true of commercial psychology in Europe, probably to an even greater extent. Neither in the United States nor in Europe would the managers, or workers, feel the competitive sense of honour that compels the Japanese to try to excel each other. This aspect of the culture is another reason why the Japanese system is likely to race ahead in the years ahead.

The Japanese culture is special in many ways. Much of the industrial progress that has occurred in Japan can, as we have seen, be attributed to methods originally copied from the United States. But while the Japanese have an extraordinary ability to imitate, they are originators too. It should also be noted that only the Japanese and the South Koreans have been able to create the type of large corporate trading entity that plays such a vital role in the industrial development of both countries. Large corporations of this type are an extremely useful aid to rapid economic progress. The Taiwanese and Hong Kong Chinese have also attempted to create organisations of this kind. Frankly, they have failed. The difference between Japan and other countries that have tried to emulate the Japanese success pattern, would appear to be the ingrained capacity for loyalty inculcated in Japanese and South Korean children at a very early age. As adults, this loyalty is transmitted through the employer.

National character is, or course, extremely difficult to quantify. Many aspects of national character must be inherently subjective; subject to change, qualification and exception. Japanese national character is highly complex and subtle by Western standards. In Western terms, an interesting comparison can be made between Japanese culture now and that of Western culture during the Middle Ages. Imagine an idealised world of the Middle Ages transferred to the 20th century, complete with all the feudal virtues of loyalty, devotion, deference, humility, honour, obedience and absolute solidarity under one banner. If you can also visualise a crusading order (similar to the Templars) operating a factory, then you have an approximate idea of what the work ethic is like in Japanese industry. Often to go on strike in Japan means no more than wearing an arm-band on the job. The Japanese worker wouldn't think of slowing down production. He would as soon miss the daily company hymn song!

Number one on the Japanese industrial hit parade in the early 1970s was the following little ditty, sung each morning by management and labour in the factories of Matsushita Electric, one of Japan's most successful companies:

"For the building of a new Japan,
Let's put our strength and minds together,
Doing our best to promote production,
Sending our goods to the people of the world,
Endlessly and continuously,
Like water gushing from a fountain,
Grow industry, grow, grow, grow,
Harmony and sincerity,
Matsushita Electric."

Songs of that type are sung only by people with a high morale; like children at school, supporters at football matches or armies marching to victory. Fight team, fight! Lack of songs is a sign of low morale. Western music has indeed become less tuneful. The lyrics of the popular songs of the day are virtually undecipherable, merely the noise generated by grunting and writhing. When British Leyland and Chrysler both take on a vocal coach, there may be hope for the West. . . but not before. Not if one believes the long-term cycle of world dominance will continue.

In addition to songsters, Matsushita has a worker-control room. On Friday afternoon, workers beat dummies of their foremen with bamboo sticks. This is how they let off steam. Grievances, tensions and frustrations vanish before they head for home and family life for a peaceful weekend. Matsushita has a virtually unbroken record of growth at 30% per annum for nearly 40 consecutive years. In recent years though, it must be admitted, growth has been slowing a bit.

Japan on an Oil Slick. . . A Blessing in Disguise

The Japanese civilisation is now at the dawn of a new era. While Western culture is in the process of stagnation and decay, it is the purity of the Japanese culture that will enable the country to survive and flourish in a world where the West has lost its way. The emphasis is shifting from West to East.

Yet, it would be unwise to assume Japan is without its problems. The cyclical continuity of the long waves of economic life is a global phenomenon. It affects all countries in all parts of the world. During the early 1970s, the growth phase of the industrialised economies reached a terminal juncture. The deflationary effects of the downwave will affect Japan as well as the rest of the world.

In fact, nowhere in the world is the onset of the downwave likely to be more marked than in Japan. But, at the same time, no other economy in the world has survived the first decade of the downwave better than Japan's.

In relative terms, Japan has to import more raw materials than any other major country, so it was more vulnerable than most to the explosion in general commodity prices in 1973 and in oil prices in 1974. In that year, Japan's inflation rate was the highest of any major country. But, a decade later, in 1983, it was the lowest. The shock effect of the oil crisis was greater upon Japan than elsewhere — partly because its growth rate had been both higher and in various ways more dependent on cheap energy. Take ship-building. One of Japan's more sensational achievements in international trade in the 1970s, was her complete domination of the world ship-building market; and particularly the VLCC super-tanker market. With the oil shock of 1973/74, that market all but disappeared at a stroke. The oil market did not, of course, disappear. But in 1973, growth in the overall trade in oil was being projected at 7% per annum for the foreseeable future. It is estimated that three-fifths of the output of the world's tanker yards in 1973 was destined to meet the demands for new ships resulting from this growth in the oil trade — and the growth disappeared overnight. But it was even worse than that. The oil market actually began to shrink. So the demand for replacement of old tankers also dried up. This meant there was practically no demand for tanker building at all.

The same kind of thing happened in some other areas of the capital-goods industry on which Japan was particularly reliant. In 1973, Japan's automobile industry already dwarfed that of Germany or France. The long post-war boom in automobiles was already tiring by the early 1970s. The oil crisis finished it off. Naturally, this hurt Japan's auto manufacturers, but no more than any other country's. It was a different matter in the market for machine tools and plant used in the manufacture of the automobiles. Here again, output had built up on the basis of a growth in demand which suddenly vanished. No new capacity was needed, which meant virtually no new plant and machinery. Inevitably, the dislocation in Japan was greater than elsewhere *precisely because its earlier growth rate had been so much greater.* Between 1973 and 1975 industrial production swung from a growth rate of 15% to a *contraction* rate of 15%. During the years 1960 to 1973, prior to the first oil crisis, the annual growth in Japan's economy had been no less than 12.5%

Inevitably, the slowdown at the onset of the downwave was dramatic — the rate fell to 2.4% in the period 1973 to 1980. It was much more dramatic than the decline in the US and in Germany. There the respective declines were from 5.4% to 1.85% for the US and 5.2% to 1% for Germany. But the point about the latter period is how well Japan survived the much greater unheaval to its economy. In the internationally depressed years at the start of the 1980s — particularly 1980 to 1982 — Japan's growth rate was over 3%. The rest of the world was in recession. More significant still, Japan was not suffering from the high unemployment which has been the tragedy of the global economic scene in the 1980s. Nor has it run foul of the major constraints which threaten the US economy, in the form of the famous "twin deficits" — on Federal budget and on current balance of payments.

In the days of Japan's earlier post-war boom, in the 1950s and '60s, it tended to run small deficits (or surpluses) on its current trade account. A ballooning surplus in 1972 and 1973 was the sign of things to come. But it was cut short, and turned into a *big* deficit, by the soaring cost of imported oil. In the old days, Japan's exports had certainly made their mark in the market-places of the Western world — partly because Japan's exports tended to be concentrated in sectors where Japan had specialised. Ships have been mentioned as key exports; but there had also been cameras, watches, zips, transistor radios, ball bearings, motor cycles. However, after the oil shock of 1973/74, Japan embarked on a more broadly based export drive. In the Middle East and the developing countries, Japan found a hunting ground where it could compete on an equal footing with its American and European rivals. The oil crisis had made OPEC $70bn richer, and the oil importing countries that much poorer. Their recession was OPEC's boom. Remember, Japan, as a nation, was reacting to its particular sense of vulnerability to oil supplies, and the national response was impressive. It was rapidly felt by Japan's trading rivals in the West. The chosen ground for the battle was where the real money was — in contracting, steel and other building supplies, earth moving equipment, cranes and trucks. Also in the major consumer areas of automobiles, air conditioners, hi-fi equipment and the like.

Symbolic of the movement was the emergence of a totally new automobile manufacturer, Honda; which, as everyone knows, turned at that time to motor cars, having previously dominated the world motor-cycle market.

In was the Middle East boom which allowed Honda to make this remarkable transition. The first (small) Honda was launched in the Middle East and in other pockets of prosperity among the developing countries. It rapidly became a favourite throughout the Middle East, from Amman to Alexandria, from Teheran to Taiz. Then — but not before — it was launched in America or Europe. One way or another, in the second half of the 1970s, Japan set out to dominate the OPEC import boom. What's more, it succeeded. Japan secured a leading share in practically all OPEC markets. One way or another, other Japanese companies besides Honda used their success in these developing export markets as a springboard from which to launch an all-out attack on their European and American rivals on their home ground.

Protectionism Casts a Long Shadow

The world oil shortage of 1979 produced a similar story all over again. This time, the oil price soared from around $13 to $35. Japan, like most Western countries, plunged into deficit on current account payments. Indeed its deficit this time around was much deeper: three times deeper than in 1974! Although the percentage rise in the oil price was lower, the rise in absolute dollar terms was far greater. But, in due course, the deficit turned round as a further export drive got underway. This time the story that emerged was somewhat different from the last time. Deep structural changes had been taking place in the world economy. During 1982, Japan's renewed export drive faltered, and ran out of steam. At the time, one or two observers attributed this pause to the chickens finally coming home to roost — and assuming the dreaded role of protectionism. However, during 1983-1984 two events combined to set Japan's current account balance soaring again. One was a fall in oil prices; the other was the expansion of the US economy and the unheard-of explosion in the American current payments deficit. These two events helped to conceal the numbing impact of growing protectionism on Japan's penetration of the developed West's markets. Protectionism is an old bogey in Japan:

> "Japan has entered upon a commercial war against the great industrial nations of the world with the same energy, earnestness, determination and foresight which characterised the war. . ."

The quote is taken from an American trade journal of 1896 and the "war" referred to was Japan's victorious war with China in 1895. Forty years later, during the Depression, a Japanese Ministry of War pamphlet of 1934 told a similar tale: "countries suffering economic stagnation and anxiety concerning the international situation are jealous of the Empire's foreign trade expansion and her growing political power". It went on to assert that the nation had been able to rationalise its industries with new equipment because of a degree of co-operation among its workers which was notably lacking in Europe. Whereas Japanese labour was thrifty and hard-working, in the West "labour aimed at working as few hours as possible, doing the minimum of work for the highest possible wage". The quotations are drawn from Endumion Wilkinson's celebrated book *Misunderstanding*.

Of course these arguments have a remarkably familiar ring today. But the point is that it has all happened before — at least twice before. The 1890s were years of world depression. They were Downwave years. So, of course, were the 1930s. The voices of protectionism, not unnaturally, are raised in hard times. The collapse in world trade in the 1930s is widely attributable to protectionism. In the post-war period, protectionism has to date clearly had no fatal effect on world trade. The history of trade relations between Japan and the West has aroused strong passions at various times among interested parties, and accounts tend to vary according to where the interest lies. But there is broad agreement on the following facts and trends.

After the Second World War, Japan embarked on the international commercial scene with an economy which (for historical reasons) was largely closed to foreign trade. Just to give one illustration: as late as 1973, when its automobile output had reached around 4 million, Japan's automobile imports amounted to a mere 37,000 — which is less than one per cent. In the early days, high tariffs had formed the obvious barrier to exports to Japan — a price barrier. In 1955, Japan joined the General Agreement on Tariffs and Trade (GATT); and under the Kennedy and Tokyo rounds of tariff reduction agreements, the price barrier was progressively reduced to relatively insignificant proportions. As this happened, Japan's trade rivals focused their criticisms on so-called non-trade barriers — government regulations of one sort or another covering health, safety or environmental standards generally. In the specific case of automobiles, Japan's automobile-type-approval procedures came under increasingly bitter attack in the mid-1970s.

But as the decade of the 1970s wore on, it became increasingly clear to one and all that Japan was winning markets (and holding on to its own market). Increasingly it was winning on grounds of competition — in terms of quality as well as price. In 1980, for example, Japanese wages in the automobile industry were higher than those in Britain, France and Italy. But Japan's labour productivity was much higher. It was in fact the highest in the world. In due course, it was the markets of the West that, one by one, fell back on protectionist measures against Japan. In the early to mid-seventies these mainly took the form of "gentlemen's agreements" with Japan that she should observe voluntary export restraints. These "orderly marketing agreements", covered an increasingly broad spectrum of products. In addition to automobiles, they covered radios, tape recorders, TV tubes, ball bearings and steel, during the 1970s. By 1983, every major export market had quantitative restrictions on Japanese automobiles — ranging from around 1.8 million units in the US to a 3% market share in France, and just 2,200 units in Italy.

So the pendulum of protectionism had swung fully back against Japan.

On balance this appears to date to have done Japan no harm. The chances are that it will do less and less harm — short of all-out trade war — as Japan's strength in the market-places of the world moves further and further up the range of high technology. It is too late now for protectionism to pose a really serious threat to Japan. Unless it turns into a large-scale beggar-my-neighbour movement which would hurt Japan's partners as much (or even more) than Japan, eventually crippling world trade, leading to a domino default throughout the indebted LDC world.

By 1983, about a third of Japan's exports were in the high technology, very high value-added area. In 1960, over half her exports had been in labour-intensive products like textiles and leather, which are the typical surplus product of the newly industrialised countries (NICs). Today the proportion is insignificant. The list of the product areas in which Japan now claims world leadership (indeed dominance) takes in factory robots and video recorders. Hewlett-Packard, the US electronics group, is one of the largest consumers of semi-conductor memory chips. Early in 1984, it proclaimed to the world that the "best" US supplier of memory chips was "three times less reliable than the average Japanese vendor". This was not the first time Hewlett-Packard had criticised the quality of American memory chips. Yet despite major efforts by the industry to improve, "the average step-up" in US chip reliability had apparently been "half that achieved by Japanese" suppliers over the period. In 1980, Japan held 25% of the world memory chip market. In 1983, its share was 46%. The current generation of memory chips has the so-called 64K chip, which can record 64,000 bits of information. It was to be superseded by the 256K chip. According to Hewlett-Packard, three Japanese suppliers had already qualified their 256K chips with it, while no US maker was ready to meet the company's quality standards.

So the question is: are Japan's chip-makers vulnerable to protectionism? Will the European and American anti-Japanese campaigns succeed in the long run? As soon as that sort of question is asked, the answer is returned in the form of another question. What sense does it make to deny your electronics industry the best, the most reliable chips available? If the US electronics industry is denied Japanese chips, others in Britain, France, Germany, Holland, Sweden, Israel, Hong Kong, Taiwan, South Korea, Brazil — even Russia — will beat a path to Japan's door. During the 1980s, it has been perceived that Japan has emerged as a joint leader in high technology along with the US — as a kind of *Avis* to the the American *Hertz* in the field of hardware for the information industry. Japan has more robots in its factories than the rest of the world put together. This fact can be seen as a symbol of Japan's claim to a leading place in the post-industrial society. For the robot is precisely a symbol of the elevation of men over and above the menial role of manufacturing; a role which in the post-industrialised society would ultimately be performed exclusively by the machine in general, and the robot in particular. The culture and civilisation of Japan are a post-industrial culture and civilisation. Japan is the first country in the world to achieve that status.

The truth is, it is now probably too late for protectionism to have any special effect on Japan. In the early 1930s, when world trade went into a nosedive, Japan was the only industrialised nation which actually succeeded in increasing its exports. The various protectionist measures taken against Japan during the 1970s, in such areas as steel, ships and ball bearings, failed to halt the growth of Japan's exports of these products. The quantitative limits on Japan's automobile exports to the US, and many European countries, have had three interesting effects. In the long run, they all may prove counter-productive to the aims of the self-protectors. First, they have given Japanese motor cars an automatic scarcity value. As a result, they have been sold at higher prices than would otherwise have been the case. Enhancement of their profit margins has increased the resources the Japanese auto-makers can devote to the development of even more competitive models. Second, it has forced the Japanese producers to compete all the more aggressively for a share in the markets of the Pacific Basin which promise faster growth anyway. Third, by shielding them from cyclical fluctuations in demand, it has simplified planning, and reduced financial gearing, in such a way as to free financial and skilled manpower resources for deployment in other industrial areas with more promise of growth. This is particularly relevant in Japan where (by contrast to the pattern elsewhere) the big motor manufacturers typically form part of a larger industrial empire.

In short, there has been a contest for supremacy in world trade. Japan has won the contest. The means used to win the contest are past history. But the record should at least be set straight.

One charge of "foul" — that was still being levelled at Japan in the early 1980s — was deliberate under-valuation of the yen, by manipulation of one kind or another. A close study of the history of the Central Bank's market intervention over the yen shows not only that it had been unsuccessful in depressing the value of the currency, but that it had not been tried — except when outsiders deemed the yen to be "high" as in 1978.

Equally, the charge that interest rates had been artificially depressed in Japan, for the purpose of keeping the yen's value down, does not hold water. In the first place, interest rates and long term bond yields in Japan over more than two decades had swung just as widely as in any free-market economy. The one exception was in the States in the special circumstances post-1980. Secondly, the acid test of whether a country's interest rates are artificially high — or low — is the relative level of real bond yields, adjusted for inflation. On this measure, Japan's rates have been among the highest in the world. The charge of deliberate under-valuation of the yen would be particularly absurd when so many of Japan's most successful export lines are straight-jacketed by quantitative restrictions.

The Plaza Agreement. . . An Agreement to Disagree

A new phase in the seemingly endless poker game between national banks and the international foreign exchange market began with a shuffling of the pack at the game set up at the Plaza Hotel in New York in September 1985. One experienced spectator was Professor Martin Feldstein of Harvard, a former member of the Presidential Council of Economic Advisors. When he heard of the game, he asked:

> "Can you bring five people into a room and significantly lower the value of the dollar? You really can't."

But US Treasury Secretary James Baker believed you could; as did the finance ministers of France, West Germany, and Japan and the British Chancellor of the Exchequer. When the Group of Five met at the New York Plaza, they declared their intention — to see a reduction in the strength of the dollar. Over the next few weeks they were gazed at in wonder as the strength of the dollar oozed away. It is not known how far the statesmen themselves appreciated that in the market's view the dollar was already ripe to be sold. In one sense, it did not matter greatly, since one of the main purposes of the Plaza get-together had been to reduce internal American pressure for protectionism; pressure which — by the beginning of 1987 — was once more registering "Concern" on the international political barometer. As one observer put it:

> "There was poor President Reagan, still wearing his mantle of righteousness (slightly soiled by scandal) hopefully tapping the glass in the hope of diverting the world's attention away from Irangate, towards the errant Japanese; while his surrogate god-child, Margaret Hilda Thatcher, provided a shrill backing to cries of 'Look what they're doing!' from Mr James Baker and other members of the Administration's more vocal Group."

Back in September 1985, the representatives of the Group of Five managed to persuade the public, if not themselves, that forty years after Bretton Woods, with the foreign exchange system in a shaky condition, they had set things right. Their aims, as Britain's Chancellor described them, were to achieve further progress towards price stability; to reduce public expenditure and the burden of taxation; secure the effective working of the labour market, and resist protectionism. It was no less worthy an intention than those expressed on other similar occasions.

In January 1985, the United States had been resisting pressure for intervention against the dollar, as concern over the massive US deficit mounted. Then came the Bonn Summit in May, and in September '85, a reaffirmation of the declaration made at Bonn; notably the belief that:

> "Sustained growth in world trade, lower interest rates, open markets and continued financing in amounts and on terms appropriate to each individual

one are essential to enable developing countries to achieve sound growth and overcome their economic and financial difficulties."

After that, a pause for breath or for silent prayer! The dollar had to be brought down, as a means of helping to reduce that massive US deficit. It seemed to have escaped attention that the architects of the system, created in 1944 at Bretton Woods, had held that over- or under-valuation of a currency had to take into account voluntary long-term investment flows as well as current settlements, and the comparative cost of a restaurant meal or a suit of clothes, in different countries. The truth was that at that moment, the United States was the quarry, and the target for opprobrium and abuse. It may be noted that when equilibrium is lost — for whatever reason — it is the convention that "someone must be to blame". Once the "guilty party" has been identified, pressure will be applied. The ritual of "purification" by slander begins. October 1985 saw further intervention.

By January 1986, it had been decided that the appropriate treatment now was to cut interest rates, without — as was said at the time — "upsetting" exchange rates. To give him his due (which in recent years has tended to be denied him) Chairman of the Fed, Paul Volcker, was not all that keen on any interest rate plan. Indeed, he made clear that the *right measure* to take was inescapably the measure which was *right for that particular economy at that particular time.* Right or wrong as he might be in both diagnosis and treatment, he did not believe in prescribing a given remedy — quack or otherwise — merely because it was the current fad. Secretary Baker was more sympathetic to the interest rate treatment, which Japan was calling for. By January 20th, 1986, the dollar had fallen some 10% since the Plaza agreement. At the same time, as some of the headlines were putting it, A STABLE DOLLAR IS NOT ENOUGH. Not that anyone of standing had ever said it was. But no matter! That was the mood, and the mode.

It was decided around this time that it would be wise to prevent the dollar's falling too far. By now, it was beginning to dawn on all but the most hardened players that it is impossible to cure the "over-valuation" of one currency without causing an upward movement in others. Already the Japanese yen and the deutschemark had begun to look over-nourished. As the *International Herald Tribune* put it, on January 21st 1986:

" 'There is a desire for lower interest rates', said a high Treasury official, who declined to be identified."

That was the intellectual level on which the game was being played. Some G5 members began to think it might be preferable to return to the practice of holding secret meetings, as they used to in the 1970s. Not that they had achieved much success even then. But, at least, their failures attracted less publicity. One of their far-from-happy developments was the transformation of the Group of 10, as it was in 1972, into the Group of 20. It took until spring the following year, before it was clear to all concerned that such an unwieldy body was not going to achieve anything. Then came the autumn, the *Yom Kippur* War and the first oil price explosion. After a stressful period lasting more than a half-year, the Group of 5 met before the IMF Annual Meeting in 1974, at the behest of the then Secretary of State, Henry Kissinger. But they were not to call the shots. 1974 belonged to the OPEC producers.

In 1981, following the second oil price hike, the statesmen (said some observers cynically) "discovered" interest rates. But they still couldn't decide what to do about them! In July 1983, they discussed debt. . . somewhat in the abstract; and later — over a weekend — they drew up a blueprint for currencies and trade. After that dismal record of non-achievement, it is not surprising that their apparent success in September 1985 went to their — and their international fan club's — heads.

By April 1986, the dollar had fallen through the DM 2.20 floor; and the rate against sterling was $1.51 plus. Now Japan began to take centre stage. In Tokyo, in May 1986, the Group declared its intention once more. This time it was to:

> "promote better international economic co-operation, and better international coordination and lead to a greater stability of exchange rates."

Some would say this was not strictly true, since the declaration was little more than a pious hope. It was not a *programme*. The hope was that *without* better co-operation and coordination (which experience had shown to be a forlorn hope) exchange rates might somehow be manipulated to everyone's advantage. But how to do it? Answer came there none! It was all a bit of a fantasy. It must have been understood around the table that the dollar could not be allowed to fall too far — which at once raises the question "How far would have been *too* far?" But the players evaded that one by calling for a new pack.

To be realistic, it was clear that the dollar could become too weak. That would please neither the West German nor the Japanese Government, since the deutschemark and the yen would now become too strong. But how could these two currencies be *too* strong, if the overall objective was to secure an appreciable reduction in the US deficit by sapping the strength of the dollar, and so making it easier for the Americans to export to Europe and Japan, thereby reversing the flow of trade? The answer was twofold: the Japanese and the Germans had no great desire to reduce their exports, and the US administration was well aware that (beyond a certain point) too weak a dollar would lead to some very unpleasant side-effects. After a while it became clear that American discomfiture in itself did not guarantee a reduction in either the Japanese or West German trade surplus. However, the original statement looked far better from a political — and PR — point of view; especially with the US mid-term elections due in a few months time.

In the second half of 1986, there was little to indicate that the Group's major objectives were being attained. . . By September, (*Financial Times*, September 17) the press reported open, and public, disagreements between

Group members. Attempts, it was claimed, were being made to heal the rift. Or — some asked — were they merely trying to keep the noise down? By the end of the month, *The Times* was reporting a Nine Point Statement by the Group, which stressed their responsiblity to implement the decisions outlined in the Tokyo declaration. The Group, now numbering 7, agreed once again on close and continuous coordination of economic policy "in the period ahead". The impression at the time seemed to be that the Group had produced little beyond the usual "fudge" and "compromise."

Early in December 1986, it was expected that the Group of 10 — no less! — would meet soon to "tie up loose ends". Japan and the United States were said to be keen on another meeting. A glance at the day-to-day movement of their currencies, and the performance on their respective stock markets, will help to explain their enthusiasm. *The Times* reported (January 26th, 1987) that Treasury Secretary Baker and Japan's Finance Minister Kiichi Miyazawa had met for "tough talks". By the beginning of February, the United States was the one to press for a futher meeting. On February 8th, *The Sunday Times* predicted that there would be EARLY DOLLAR TALKS. On the exchanges, the yo-yo-ing continued regardless. On 10th, Secretary Baker was blamed for the dollar's sharp fall; and the dollar closed in London at DM 1.8100 and 152.40 yen, with $1.5175 to the pound.

Hopes of a G5 meeting grew as the February passed, with Germany and Japan pressing hard once again. At last it look place in Paris, with Canada and Italy in attendance. By now, the French were recommending "reference zones", as their recipe for stable currencies. But Paul Volcker made clear, as he had done countless times before, that there was no point in such remedies; designing "references zones" in the absence of economic policy coordination. . . would achieve nothing.

Once again, Treasury Secretary Baker appeared more keen to show his cards to the onlookers than get on with the game. By now the protectionists at home were taking over in Congress as well as the media. This was probably the most significant development since the Plaza meeting in September '85. No longer was the Administration attempting to contain protectionism; rather it appeared to be encouraging it, justifying its increasingly bitter feeling attacks on Japan and its trade policies.

Secretary Baker came out with the firm pledge that the United States would cut its deficit from 3.9% to 2.3% of GNP by 1988 — election year! Clearly, said observers, Secretary Baker must have been counting on a rise in GNP. The Japanese, for their part, promised to cut tax, to "provide steady expansion of domestic demand", as Satoshi Sumita put it. This came at a time when the Prime Minister was in fact planning to reduce income tax, and cut corporation tax, with the loss to be made up by the imposition of a politically controversial 5% Value Added Tax. Japan, like Sweden incidentally, has shown that a high marginal rate of income tax does not discourage economic growth. Will it be possible to say the same of a Value Added Tax? At the moment, a 5% rate looks extremely modest. But the experience of other countries shows that once VAT is in place, it takes very little to tempt the authorities to raise the rate.

The West Germans, for their part, promised to increase the tax cuts already planned for 1988. However, West Germany is a country where it is not so easy to make the population spend. It is like trying to think up a gift for the Man Who Has Everything. The German propensity to save is legendary. In any case, observed Martin Feldstein, neither countries' tax cuts would have much effect unless they were far larger than they are ever likely to be.

Nevertheless the Paris meeting won a good press. It tempted *The Guardian* to come out with one of its classic headlines:

"AT LAST THE RICHEST NATIONS HAVE AGREED TO BURY THEIR HATCHETS AND FIGHT OFF RECESSION."

The United States and Europe certainly seemed to agree where those hatchets should be buried. . . in every available Japanese enterprise; but in consumer-electronics generally, and telecommunications in particular. The National Telecommunications and Information Administration in Washington admitted that the deficit with Japan in their line of business had doubled over 4 years. Japan was exceptionally successful with radio transmission equipment, telephones with multiple lines and small business exchanges. The United States saw itself as under a withering attack from Japan. Nor was it any too happy over what it saw as the European threat. In one case in 1987 there was a contest to supply the French CGCT with a sizeable order. ITT had joined Philips in competition with Siemens of Germany. Pressure was put on Siemens which was threatened with obstruction to any attempt to win a contract with US regulated networks. Mark Fowler, a former head of the Federal Communications Commission expressed a view shared by many US business interests:

"I want to remind Europeans that we have one of the most open markets in the world. (There are). . . efforts by certain European companies to close their markets to American companies."

William Sullivan, an analyst with a White House policy committee spelled out the limits for European companies:

"There is land available to foreign companies here (in the United States), they can hire American engineers and they can set up distribution with no difficulty. Yet we find we are restricted overseas."

Many Americans blamed de-regulation for the influx of foreign competition; an idea dismissed completely by M. Michel Carpentier, head of the EEC's Directorate General for Telecommunications:

"It is a myth that US deregulation has led to an invasion by European telecommunications products with no equivalent opening of the major parts of the European market to the US."

The sharp hostility of the Americans to Europe (and America and Britain to the Japanese) is understandable in view of "pecking order" of the winners and the losers at the telecommunications game at the end of 1986:

Winners:
Japan, Sweden, West Germany, Canada, France, Taiwan and Hong Kong.
Losers:
United States, UK, Italy.

International Trade During the Remainder of the Downwave

A key feature marking the international economic scene since the start of the 1980s has been the 'twin deficits' of the US — the burgeoning deficits on current account and on Federal budget account. The former was being put at between $65 and $85bn for 1984, having been a positive balance as recently at 1981. The latter had swollen to $190bn in 1982/83 having been below $50bn in 1980/81. Many economists consider that there is a link between the two, namely that the big budget deficit is in part responsible for the big current account deficit. This they argue has happened in two ways. In the first place, the current level of budget deficit was so high — higher than total consumer savings — that as a result, borrowing needs of the Government forced up interest rates and held them at a much higher level than they would otherwise be. It is true that by almost any measure, US interest rates were high — higher in real terms than in any other major economy. This made the dollar a very attractive currency and pushed up its value. As a result, US goods became less competitive on world markets, whereas imports became much cheaper. Hence a mushrooming trade deficit in the US. Secondly, economists also argue that if the Government's borrowings, needed to cover the Federal deficit, exceed personal savings, then money has to come from somewhere else (namely abroad) to make up the gap. This flow in itself would tend to push up the dollar, and might also require high interest rates. So, the two arguments are like two sides to the same coin — though nobody is quite sure how it works.

Almost all economists agree that the present situation has become unstable, and cannot be left to work itself out. History argues the same way. The rate of economic growth in the run-up to the US Presidential Election certainly looked unsustainable. That growth rate, sucking in imports from abroad, was largely responsible for the growing current payments deficit. The best assumption for the mid-1980s was that the US current deficit would gradually shrink to break-even and maybe turn into surplus. The impact on world trade could be tremendous. But it didn't happen!

The outlook for commodity prices under these circumstances would not be propitious unless growth in Europe and Japan was able to compensate for the slow-down in the US economy. With a shrinking export market to the US, the combined effect on the export prospects of the LDCs —

and particularly those of South America which are especially dependent on trade with the US — would be menacing. These were the precise circumstances during which a worldwide depression. very similar at an international level to the depression of the 1930s, becomes a very high probability. There are even better reasons today — which have already been outlined — for believing that once again Japan would be the most vulnerable of all the industrialised economies to any envisaged collapse in world trade. Its imports are only a little over one tenth of its national income, against figures of around a third for the European Community, for example. Manufactures have accounted for only a quarter of Japan's imports, as against half for the USA and two-thirds for much of Europe. Many of Japan's imports have been luxury goods. The balance, raw materials, are necessities almost by definition. But, as we have seen, these are likely to be declining in price in the hard times ahead, especially oil, which accounts for around a half of Japan's raw material imports. The sharp and prolonged collapse in oil prices in 1986 served only to reinforce that view.

It seems to follow from much of this that — apart from the developing countries — the chief victim of a trade war in coming years will be Europe. That doesn't mean Japan will be without its problems, as we enter the final stages of the downwave. There will be many problems, which will be quite severe. But Japan's problems — unlike those of Europe and the United States — are likely only to be transient, having a cleansing effect and serving to build a firm base from which Japan will enter its "Golden Era" as we move into the upwave.

The Constraints Within. . . The Distress Without

Now comes the nightmare which must have haunted Paul Volcker, Chairman of the US Federal Reserve Bank. As the cyclical momentum of the post-1982 US economic upturn seemingly gathered pace, the monthly consumer price figures threatened to speed up and fan the flames of inflationary expectations among America's financial community. Interest rates, it seemed, could start to rise, as they have always tended to do in the late stages of any economic upturn. Inflationary fears would undermine the confidence of the international community in the stability of America's money, and the dollar would fall. This would further exacerbate inflationary fears. For people would see that the cost of imported goods must rise, and US corporations would feel free to raise their domestic prices. As a consequence, interest rates would spiral upward in line with inflationary expectations. The Fed would feel powerless to intervene by increasing liquidity. It would be left in no doubt that, at the slightest sign of throwing in the sponge in its long battle against inflation, the credit markets would go into a nosedive. The rise in interest rates would threaten to strangle the economic upturn. It would also threaten to escalate the budget deficit, and the cost of servicing the national debt. This would worry the US financial community still further. As interest rates rose again, and the US stock market plunged deeper, consumers would feel less rich and less confident. The economy would move into recession, led by a sharp drop in housing starts, house purchases and auto buying.

That was the nightmare. By the beginning of 1987, events had take a very different turn. It was clear all along that the richest country in the world could live with an extremely high level of risk. But for the debtor countries of South America, the situation was infinitely more perilous. In the months following Mexico's default in mid-1982, the debt burden of the LDCs became progressively worse, not better. As late as the beginning of 1984, it was still possible for some to hope that steady expansion in world trade, along with stable interest rates, pointed the way to a longer term improvement in the LDCs' condition. But, even then, the world's banks were growing increasingly reluctant — as they saw it — to pour good money after bad. As and when all hope had to be abandoned on this score, rising interest rates were likely to prove the final straw for the more heavily indebted LDCs, who would see no sense in playing the game of pretence any further, if only because it would bring them no more credit! Outright default would then be the order of the day for most of the countries of Latin America, as well as other countries in Africa, the Pacific, and elsewhere.

Suppose there were such a collapse? What would be its effect on the Japanese banking system? Thanks to their vigorous activity in sovereign lending in the late 1970s, the exposure of the Japanese banks to LDC debt is at least as great as that of any other major banking system.

Traditionally, Japanese industry has been more indebted — more highly geared — than industry in most Western countries. This is quite understandable in view of the much higher growth rate of Japanese companies and their resulting need for finance. The basic viability of so much of Japanese industry at the level of international comparison goes some way to compensate for this higher gearing. So does the general slow down in the Japanese economy in the past decade. This has reduced financial needs in relation to internally generated resources from profits. But in troubled times, when the problem is liquidity, the consideration of long-term viability has a habit of taking a back seat. In a scramble for money, what counts is money *now,* not money next year. Moreover, in recent years, Tokyo has had its fair share of sensational bankruptcies, just as New York, London, Frankfurt, or Lugano have. In short, the Japanese banking system could prove quite vulnerable in certain areas.

The urban property market in Japan also looks a tender spot. We have seen how the very nature of the property market makes it particularly vulnerable at times of liquidity crisis, whether it be in New York, Paris, Rome, Hong Kong, London, or the Upper Regions of Lower Slobovia. The London panic of 1973-1974 showed how troubles in the commercial property market almost triggered a total collapse in confidence and nearly brought Britain's whole financial industry to its knees. In 1982-1983 it was Hong

Kong's turn. A financial property crisis was saved from total debacle by the coincident rising tide of confidence in the US. In 1983, Singapore experienced its first serious trouble in the property field. A potential property collapse failed to snowball into a full-scale crisis since the economy was on the mend, and confidence among the financial community generally was on an improving trend. The trouble in each of these centres was that the urban property boom had been over-exaggerated. Land prices in the East were just that much higher than in New York, or Paris, or Amsterdam. Or most other places, for that matter. The reason? "Shortage of land", the estate agents will say. "They don't make it any more". . . Remember?

On the face of it, the land shortage argument seems to have some force — especially in Hong Kong and Singapore, both small islands. It may appear to have some force in the City of London too, with its much prized 'square mile' at the heart of the financial centre. The argument has also been applied to Tokyo's densely populated downtown area, where property prices are as high, or higher, than anywhere else in the world. But the argument is valid only when demand exceeds supply. There is, in fact, always plenty of land just outside the coveted areas. When trouble really strikes real estate, it takes the good and beautiful along with the bad and ugly. I suspect the Tokyo property market may find its first taste of real trouble before the 1990s.

Despite these two qualifications, a close examination reveals that Japan does not suffer from the series of constraints that confront the major economies of the West — like a minefield with a precipice beyond. America, as suggested, is well down a road of excessive monetary growth, involving understandably high levels of budget and trade deficits. Europe has a wholly intractable unemployment problem, and, in some cases, has had an even worse budget deficit. Just about the only bright spot in Europe is a reasonable balance/surplus on current payments — due, directly or indirectly, to the corresponding US deficit, which will probably disappear sooner or later. Wherever economic recovery appeared, it was based on consumer dissaving and on a stock market boom, apparently based on the acrobatics of prices on the New York, London and Tokyo Stock Exchanges — showing the reckless abandon of a wild party on board the Titanic. It is only fair to point out that until 1983, one ingredient had been missing in the very close parallel between the early 1980s and the late 1920s. That was wild speculation in shares. Then it started again with a vengeance.

Japan seemed to be blissfully free from most Western constraints around 1983-4. Unemployment might be understated in the official figures. But at around 2%, it was nothing like the problem it was in the West. The current payments accounts was in massive surplus — structurally, as we have seen. Inflation was the lowest in the world. Current economic growth posed no strains, and higher interest rates no threat. Not a cloud in the sky? Apart from the dark clouds that threaten the economic world as a whole? No! There *was* a problem. The Japanese eat too well! That is to say, they eat too healthily. Just as, by the start of 1987, they were saving too much. The Japanese, it seems, are living to a very ripe old age, and there could be a tough price to pay for this in the future!

In truth, in the 1940s Japan was very slow to fall into line with Western customs in funding public welfare — in particular pension liabilities. By 1982, it had caught up fully on health benefits, and total social security benefits had risen to 11% of GNP (from a mere 4% in 1970). This was in line with the 10-12% average of the six other foremost economies of the OECD. But its aging population poses a special pensions problem. In 1980, one in eight of the population was aged over 65. It is expected that by the year 2000 the figure will have risen to one in five. So, the overall pension burden on the economy is expected to rise from 4.3% in 1980 to 12% in 2000. (Incidentally, it is already over 10% in the US and Europe). The Tokyo Government's share of the burden is expected to rise by 3½% of GNP over the period. The Japanese authorities affect great concern over the current level of the budget deficit. But, I think Japan will be able to handle this Herculean task with the same determination and cultural integrity that has served the country so well, thus *permitting the natural economic forces to eliminate the excesses,* rather than inventing self-serving mechanisms, which has been the direct cause of the decline of the West.

With the commencement of the Downwave in the early 1970s, came deep structural changes in the world's economy which affected Japan as well as the West. During the period of secondary recovery from 1975 through 1980, the ability of the Japanese economy to recover from a period of global contraction provided clear evidence of the economy's tremendous resilience, indicating an inner strength which was not apparent in Western economies.

The three important changes that have occurred in the world's economy after the early 1970s can be summed up as follows:

1. For the first time since the Industrial Revolution in the West, the pace of advance in total output and per capita output in Western industrialised countries fell slightly below the average of the world output and world *per capita* as a whole.

2. The unfavourable differential between world output and the output of the West continued to widen after the early 1970s. That meant that the Western industrialised nations' share of total world output, although still accounting for two-thirds of that total, was declining.

3. There were extremely large differences between the rate of growth in Japan, and the non-Western industrialised nations. The rate of growth in South Korea, a newly industrialised nation, was the most striking. This development had gradually been changing both the share of total world production generated by the West, and their position and importance as a world power.

During the last 13 years of the Upwave, from 1960 to 1973, Japan achieved the highest rate of growth among all of the industrialised nations. More importantly, during the first nine years of the Downwave, circa 1973-1984,

Japan still maintained its position at the top of the growth tables:

Growth rates in real gross national product (% per annum).

	1960 to 1973	1973 to 1982
OECD	4.8	2.4
United States	4.2	2.4
Japan	10.5	3.4
European Community	4.7	1.9
Other OECD	5.4	2.1
France	5.7	2.6
Germany	4.8	1.9
Italy	5.2	2.5
United Kingdom	3.2	0.6

Figure 18

As previously mentioned, Japan is a country endowed with virtually no natural resources other than labour and human skills. This unalterable factor renders the Japanese achievement during the past three decades even more of a "miracle" than would otherwise be the case. Through the 1960s, Japan was able to build up a modern industrial society with first class manufacturing capacities of which the abundant use of imported natural resources, including crude oil and iron ore, was a necessity. At the beginning of the 1970s, Japan was hit by a double shock. The first was the warning from the so-called Club of Rome, whose members appealed to the world for the adoption of conservation measures because of the limited availability of many natural resources around the globe. The Club of Rome sent out grim warnings about the scarcity of raw materials on the one hand, and about the dangers to the environment on the other. "Small is beautiful" became a catch phrase. In respect of global economic development, intense dangers were outlined for the single model, and large scale approach, of the industrial economies upon which the Japanese "miracle" was based. The Club of Rome called for more attention to efficiency-minded and quality conscious strategies. . . the kiss of death for a rapidly expanding economy reliant upon the unlimited use of imported natural resources. Although the Club of Rome was to repudiate its position that the world was running out of resources — which the Hudson Institute challenged at the time, the Club's publication *Limits to Growth* (and the report prepared for President Jimmy Carter, *Global 2000*) still proved a considerable shock to the nerves at the time.

On the heels of the Club of Rome's declaration of 1970, came the massive oil price hikes by the exporting countries. The shock to Japan was greater than in most countries, in view of the Japanese industry's heavy reliance on imported crude. Growth in the Japanese economy slowed significantly. Because of the ingenuity and perseverance of the Japanese, however, the extent of economic deterioration was far less than elsewhere. Britain, a producer of oil, saw its growth rate slashed from 3.2% (the average for the period 1960 to 1973) to 0.6%. That was the average for the period 1973 to 1983.

To meet the difficulties of a world recession and an explosion in energy costs, the Japanese Government embarked on several policies. These measures proved quite effective. The Government instigated an emergency stockpile programme for crude oil. Then, in an effort to control inflation, it imposed direct controls over the price of some daily necessities. In a co-ordinated effort, the Japanese business sector also enacted a range of new measures. The most important was the streamlining of administrative systems and production lines, along with an intensified programme of research and development, to minimise wastage and maximise thermal efficiency. Within ten years, expenditure on research and development in Japan quadrupled. It rose from 1.2 trillion yen in 1970 to 4.7 trillion yen in 1980. By 1982 the sum was further increased to 6.5 trillion yen. As a percentage of GNP, research and development expenditure rose from 1.6% in 1970 to 2.0% by 1980. By 1982 it was 2.4%. Of the total increase in research and development expenditure, only one quarter was financed with public funds. The balance was financed by private financial resources, which is in sharp contrast to other major industrial powers, such as the USA, USSR, UK, West Germany, and France, where more than 40% of research and development expenditure has been financed through public funds.

The rapid response to the problems of the early 1970s and early 1980s was carried out with abundant human resources of excellent quality, both in the laboratorial professional sphere and at the blue-collar level. The results of the research and development programmes were vast improvements in the manufacturing processes, primarily in terms of energy efficiency, but also in terms of overall cost inputs. Japan demonstrated quite forcibly its ability to overcome the oil price shock, where others had failed dismally. It is interesting to note a wave of optimism among businessmen. The main force behind the change in perception was the United States, where it was claimed that the economy grew by 9.6% in the first quarter of 1983.

Unfortunately, it was clear even then that the optimism was likely to be misplaced. The deep structural changes that had developed in the world economy during the 1970s remained in place; the long-term, secular trend of the economy remained downward. However, economic activity never moves in a straight line. It fluctuates. While planners were becoming accustomed to the type of scenario where three or four years of economic growth are followed by one or two years of recession (which, in turn, are followed by three or four years of growth), that relationship was changing. For the period that remained until the early 1990s, planners anticipated having to become accustomed to a change in relationship between economic contraction and expansion. At the risk of over-simplifying the situation, they expected three to four years of economic contraction, followed by one or two years of economic improvement. After that would come three to four years of economic contraction. ... at least until the early 1990s. Essentially, they saw this reversal in relationship between contraction and expansion as one of the major dynamic forces that distinguished the Downwave from the Upwave.

During the second half of 1984, it appeared that growth in the world economy was likely to be slowing down again. Japan certainly did not look like being able to sail through the depression completely unscathed. However, in spite of the resilience demonstrated in the Japanese economy (first during the 1973 to 1975 recession, and again during the recession of 1979 to 1982), it seemed that the Japanese could suffer more than other nations from the approaching depression. But it will be poised for a more dynamic recovery than other countries during the early 1990s, when a truly long-term sustainable global recovery is expected to begin.

In the meantime, as we entered the concluding stages of the Downwave, in early March 1987, the GATT secretariat reported that 1986 had seen "one of the poorest performances in three decades" by the trade in manufactured goods. If we ignore the recession years of 1958, 1975 and 1982, the increase in the volume of trade in such goods — no more than 3% — was the lowest since the 1950s. The average annual growth of 3.5% during 1985 and '86 was likely to fall to 2.5% in 1987. GATT attributed this decline to two factors: slower economic growth in the industrialised countries, and lower demand from the primary producers, due to the fall-off in earnings from commodity exports. Exports of manufactures from the United States (among other countries) had only recently begun to respond to the depreciation in their currencies. West European and Japanese exports had been choked off by the appreciation of *their* currencies.

Although restrictions on automobiles, clothing and textiles, consumer electronics and steel had reduced the trade in such items, the GATT report stressed that they had not been the sole — or even the main — cause of the slow-down. The 7% increase (by volume) in the trade in mining products (including oil) was spearheaded by a 9% surge in the volume of the petroleum trade. This was stimulated by the fall from around $30 a barrel to a low of $10 for a while in 1986. Even the $18 a barrel agreed by OPEC was not necessarily going to hold.

It was West Germany which made the most mileage in 1986, overtaking the United States, although the value of its exports declined from DM 537bn in 1985 to DM 526bn in 1986. At the same time, the trade imbalances in the United States, West Germany and Japan increased. GATT's view was that the competitiveness of US producers improved markedly in 1986. This ran contrary to the theory that the decline in the dollar's nominal value did not reflect the *real situation*. GATT also appeared to side with Chairman Volcker, in so far as it argued that imbalances were not reduced in 1986 because the various exchange rate realignments had not been supported by changes in macroeconomic policies.

The question was raised once again when there was a concerted intervention stabilising the dollar. This took place on March 25, 1987, and was described by the *Financial Times* next day as:

> ". . .the first open demonstration of the Paris accord in action. Simultaneous buying in New York, Frankfurt, Tokyo and London . . .was sufficiently unusual to stop speculation in its tracks."

But would it hold? Or would its effects, like those of so many earlier central bank demonstrations, prove purely transitory? Two further questions had to be answered, opined the *FT* leaderwriter:

> "First, has the dollar yet declined far enough to encourage the massive adjustment which is needed? . . .And can the Paris agreement survive the long gap before the promises to co-ordinate policy begin to be fulfilled? . . .Progress in changing macro-policy in Japan and Germany remains almost imperceptible; and while the US Administration appears patiently understanding at the moment, Congress is less so."

It had been late in 1985 before the major powers fully acknowledged that the growing threat of protectionism could ultimately bring world trade to a standstill; and — having done so — that it could serve as the precursor to a 1930s type depression. The first Group of Five meeting was set up in response to that threat of a possible trade war; the objective being to bring nations to an agreement which would limit (or even avoid) the necessity for trade sanctions, or any other protectionist device such as competitive devaluation.

Paul Volcker, as Chairman of the Federal Reserve, again insisted that any attempt to achieve currency stability in a vacuum, by merely engaging in sterilised intervention, must fail. There had to be some distinct and visible changes in the economic policies of the leading industrialised nations. It was true that each of the meetings of the major powers brought a brief period of currency adjustment and relative stability. But each had proved short-lived. For in the absence of genuine changes in economic policy, the uncontrollable, global force of deflation emerged inevitably as the over-riding influence.

As we entered the second quarter of 1987, the fine utterances of another meeting were already borne away on the wind, soon to vanish echoing into empty space. During the course of a Parliamentary session in mid-March 1987, there was a furore in the Commons as Alan Clark, the UK Trade Minister, announced that Britain's deficit with Japan came to £3.7 billion for fiscal 1986. The UK Trade Minister blamed this massive deficit on the unwillingness of Japan to honour its agreement to open her markets to foreign competition. Mrs Thatcher, the Prime Minister, muttered darkly about the manner in which the new Financial Services Act could be employed to blunt the effectiveness of Japanese financial institutions operating in Britain — just one of a number of trade sanctions that could be imposed against Japan if need be. The UK Trade and Industry Department said that the lack of any positive Japanese response to the United Kingdom's requests for fairer trade meant that Britain would have to consider the full range of retaliatory options, including the erection of non-tariff barriers. As part of that "full-range" of options, the active co-operation of the United States was being sought. President Reagan had already announced punitive measures against Japanese electronics firms, on the grounds that they had failed to honour the Washington/Tokyo agreement on semi-conductor "dumping", concluded in September 1986.

By 30th March 1987, it appeared that an international trade war was in full gear — or about to move into full gear — as I had anticipated in *The Downwave*. The Paris accord — which was supposed to have brought currency stability and international co-operation once and for all — was in shambles. The dollar was in free fall against the yen. International bond markets shuddered. Equity markets plunged. On the 30th March, the *Financial Times* 30 Share Index in London staged its biggest ever one-day fall. It plummeted 38 points, slashing nearly £10 billion off the value of shares.

Thus the inexorable forces of the Downwave were massing.

The Global Order of the Twenty-First Century

The hiatus in international trade over the past few years had nothing whatever to do with the violation of agreements or unfair trade. Had global economic conditions been buoyant, there would have been no threats of protectionism, or trade war.

Rival nations had simply been clamouring to retain a share of the pie that's been continually shrinking in size. Some nations have been better equipped to compete than others — which is always the case whenever depression approaches. It should be clear to the most casual observer — as we enter the decade of 1990s — that we are enmeshed in a global trade recession, which is likely to be the precursor to a world depression. We may expect a series of "domino effect" financial crises, and eventually a backlash on US and European growth; as the US and her European counterparts are drawn downwards into the vortex of declining trade and debts that keep on growing and can never be repaid. The principle source of the crisis has been the decline in the power of the United States, which is in the process of relinquishing her role as the leading world power. The depression will run its course — just as it has so many times before — until a new world order emerges. We are also at that point in the global supremacy cycle where we will not only see a restructuring of global leadership, but the new leadership is likely to shift from West to East as Western nations and Western civilisations continue to decline.

As we draw closer and closer to the depression of the 1980s, it is likely that a high level of speculative activity — carrying with it the potential for a financial holocaust — is more likely in Japan than elsewhere. This is largely due to the over-expansion of recent years. Japan is also likely to experience a more severe financial dislocation than other countries, during the oncoming global depression. To even the most objective observer, the Japanese stock market has risen far further and fast than anything which could be termed "fair value" by the first quarter of 1987. The figures set out below make this clear.

Capitalisation of US and Japanese Stock Markets.

	New York	Tokyo
1976	856	179
1977	794	205
1978	937	327
1979	960	274
1980	1,240	357
1981	1,145	403
1982	1,308	410
1983	1,578	519
1984	1,593	617
1985	1,955	909
1986	2,203	1,746

Figure 19   SOURCE: *Morgan Stanley*

On Sunday 5th April 1987, *The Sunday Times* estimated that between 30th March and 3rd April:

> ". . .the Tokyo stock exchange's market value finally caught up with Wall Street for the first time, reflecting a remarkable surge in the Japanese Market during the past 15 months. . . Tokyo broke through to reach an estimated value of $2,661 billion, against $2,652 billion for American markets."

In those 15 months, Tokyo share prices had risen 184% from $909 billion to $2,588 billion, just before the final three-day spurt.

On top of the price levels attained, there was a 40% appreciation of the yen against the dollar. At the end of March 1987, when the "trade-war" panic stories broke, the dollar was to fall below 150 yen. Heavy intervention by central banks failed to have the "magic" effect that the politicians were banking on. The over-valuation of stocks and shares, and the increasing strength of the yen, were to drive the Japanese economy into recession during the first quarter of 1987. Increasingly effective competition from other Asian and Pacific Basin producers reinforced the recessionary pressures. Some Japanese corporations sought to offset the tightening squeeze on industrial profits by speculating in the stock market — in Japan and elsewhere. Given this cast-iron formula for financial chaos, the Bank of Japan was caught in a vice. On the one hand it was under pressure to go on providing the credit required to moderate the rise in the yen, and hold back — if only for a time — the forces of recession. Yet it was obvious that the relaxation in monetary policy must provide fuel for further speculation. Finally, when the Bank of Japan raised margin requirements in an attempt to curb speculation, shares on the Tokyo Exchange only moved higher.

The Japanese/American trade war threat showed just how brittle markets were. On March 30th, the news — and the rumours — gave the Dow Jones Industrial Average its third worst day ever. It shed 57.39 to 2,278.41; earning it the sobriquet of *Black Monday*. Yet, by Friday of the same week, after a quarter-point rise in US prime rates, Wall Street was roaring ahead once more with a 69.89 point rise to a new peak of 2390.34. That was a rise of 54.54 on the week. As the *Financial Times* pointed out, it was only six sessions earlier, on March 26th, that the market had reached its previous record of 2372.59, before going into "a two session tail spin that landed it 94 points lower at the close on Monday" The *FT* reported to Monte Gordon, of Drefus, as saying:

> "The market revealed its fears for one flashing moment at the beginning
> of the week and investors learned what they should be cautious about."

By *Black Monday*, London had still not been fully drawn into the Washington/Tokyo dispute. Nevertheless, Monday saw the FT 30 Share Index take its biggest-ever one-day fall. By 4 o'clock it had plummeted 42.4 points to 1,578.2. The more broadly based *Financial Times* Stock Exchange Index dropped 51.9 — its biggest fall ever. The *Datastream* 1,000 Share Index showed that, at 4 o'clock a total of £9,840.000 had been slashed from the value of shares in the worst ever one day market plunge. The previous record fall was on 24th September 1986, when £5,690,000 was wiped off the value of shares. The clouds were gathering.

Understandably, the herd began looking over their shoulders and asking, "Is that a Bear we see in the undergrowth?" But not the chartists. They were predicting an 8% rise, taking the Dow to the magic 2,500 level some time during the year. In any case, as we know how it goes from long experience, while the market is anxious, nothing terrible will happen. It's when the sun is shining and God's in his heaven. . . and the pundits have told you it was no more than a "technical correction". . . that disaster strikes.

By Friday, 3rd April, the sun had gone down for the London traders, who were rattled by the Government's threat to refuse licences for Japanese banks. Already, Sir Nicholas Goodison, Stock Exchange Council Chairman, had condemned any such action as counter-productive. Some considered that attempting to put pressure on the large Japanese security houses and banks would be tantamount to throwing away a fair slice of the benefits to be derived from Big Bang. Not surprisingly, the FT 30 fell 21.2 points, leaving the index 74.2 points lower on the week. The FT/SE 100 dropped 22.6, increasing its five day loss to 83.5 points. On Saturday, EEC finance ministers and central bank governors met for two days' talks in Knokke-le-zoute, in an attempt to achieve a common position ahead of the IMF meeting in Washington. But, after the weekend, it was Wall Street's Friday night recovery, and the pro-Conservative slant of the weekend Opinion Polls, which gave the London market a shot in the arm.

Elsewhere in the world, markets had been hitting the high spots. On Friday the 3rd, Canadian stocks reached another closing high, after a two day rally that wiped out their 67-point fall on *Black Monday*. Since Australian brokers are abed by the time London has really got going, Monday down-under had seen a record on the All Ordinaries of 1712.1. On the following Friday it was to be raised to a new high of 1721.5. That same Friday, foreigners took their profits on the German Exchanges, and foreign buyers invaded the Paris Bourse. Singapore and Hong Kong were preoccupied with their own problems.

In the next issue of *Investors Bulletin,* on 4th April '87, I wrote:

> "What should be clear from the action of last Monday is that sentiment is fleeting and a bear market can start like a bolt from the blue. . . The type of action that was witnessed is certainly not the type that comprises healthy corrective action in an ongoing bull market. What you have been watching is the way a stock market crash begins."

The last time the London market experienced a real collapse was 15 years ago, between 1972 and '75, when the FT 30 lost over 70% of its value, and the price of many individual shares fell more than 90%. By the time the average "new" investor found how fast. . . and how far. . . share prices can fall, it would be far too late for the majority to do anything but try to pick their way out of the financial debris — clutching what remains of their portfolios — and their shattered hopes.

A crash on the Japanese stock market would trigger off similar crashes across the markets of the world, as happened after Wall Street's "Great Crash" in 1929. It has to be remembered that by 1987, Japan had taken over the role of world banker — the part played by the United States in the 1920s, and OPEC during the 1970s. In 1985, Japanese banks had already overhauled US banks with loans of $650 billion against America's $600 billion. In the first quarter of 1987, Japanese banks accounted for almost 40% of foreign currency loans in London, and 5% of sterling loans. At that time just under one hundred Japanese banks, insurance companies and security houses were operating in London. According to *Business Week International,* Japanese investment in the US trebled between 1980 and the end of 1986, from just under $10 billion to just under $30 billion.

It meant that any interruption to the flow out of Japan to the rest of the world could interrupt global markets totally, with an unpredictable, but devastating effect.

During the early part of 1987, there had been indications that Tokyo authorities were getting concerned over the level of speculative activity in Japan, having seen for themselves how a move to curb speculation had actually *encouraged* speculation. If concern continued to build to a point where the Japanese authorities were more exercised by excessive speculation in the markets than by deflationary tendencies in the economy, a stock market crash would be bound to occur. But Wall Street and London were to get there first!

Luckily, the sooner speculative excesses are reduced, as markets crash and economies move into decline, the sooner a base will be built as a springboard for the type of long-term expansion witnessed following World War II. As we move into the next Upwave, several nations will be vying for position as world leader. The primary candidates are Australia, China, Japan and the Soviet Union. China is an exceptionally strong contender, sharing similar cultural attitudes as Japan, but with a much larger work force, commensurate with the larger land mass. China's ambitious attempt to modernise and reform its economy will do more than shape the future of the Chinese people. It could prove a dominant influence the world over. After a period of relative isolation, trade between China and the rest of the world is undergoing a renaissance of remarkable proportions.

China has a domestic market of 1.2 billion consumers, the largest in the world. It is also the largest developing country and one of the fastest growing. China's national income has been rising at an average 8.7% per annum since 1978. The "Open Door" policy means the "People's Republic" is now a major market for exporters, investors and banks. Since 1980 China has become one of the largest recipients of new foreign investment, and the leading developing country for trade volumes, bank borrowings and new capital-market issues.

The impressive growth performance of China essentially stems from three major factors. Most important has been an end to the disruption caused by the Cultural Revolution, permitting a renewed emphasis on economic growth and development. Of almost equal importance, is the manner in which the many reforms since the demise of the Cultural Revolution have served to encourage private and public investment alike. Finally, a healthy savings ratio of over 30% of GDP gives the Chinese economy an exceptionally strong underpinning, matched in very few other newly-industrialising countries.

Nevertheless, China suffers certain drawbacks which could impede its assuming the mantle of world leader. To begin with, we have never known a world leader that has not been both capitalist and oriented towards the entrepreneur. China, on the other hand, is a socialist country, and Chinese socialist principles are bound to limit the scope and speed of reform. There are four aspects of Chinese socialism which are not likely to change; indeed, they are regarded as sacrosanct. First, all economic, social and political facts must remain firmly under the control of the authorities. State ownership of the dominant share of industry is not likely to be diluted in any way. There will always be a limit to the degree of inequality, in terms of wealth and income, which the authorities will be prepared to tolerate. Above all, the No 1 priority for Peking will remain to secure the basic needs of the population. That will not change; not so long as the current style of government continues.

It would seem, therefore, that China has too many problems to resolve before it can realistically hope even to *approach* global supremacy. True, it has been hard at work correcting these defects. But Peking's efforts gave the impression of being defensive measures, rather than a genuinely offensive programme. As a result, China's extensive modernisation plans are likely to be strongly keyed towards defence, before their well-oiled *offensive* powers can be set in motion. The Chinese have a profound fear of the Soviet Union, which is why a great deal of their defensive thinking is directed towards that quarter. Furthermore, China lacks the industrial complex necessary for agricultural self-sufficiency, and the creation of a modern military complex.

In recent years, Peking has introduced a degree of free trade, with the aim of putting the economy on a firm course towards rapid industrialisation. But the sheer scale of China's population — around 1.8 billion, and still growing — means that the Government's ultimate objectives will take many years to achieve.

According to the theory advanced by Spengler in *Decline of the West*, global domination will rest in the East for the next 500 years or so. Sometime during that period, China is likely to inherit the mantle; but probably not for 150 years or so. In the meantime, China will remain a serious contender in the world economic growth league. Certainly, the new China will be seen as an excellent area for potential investment.

The publicity given to Mrs Thatcher's visit to Moscow, and the emergence of *glasnost* under the leadership of Mr Gorbachev, suggested that dramatic changes had been taking place in Kremlin circles during the 1980s. It appeared that — with the blessing of Britain and the United States — cultural exchanges between Russia and the West were about to transcend the mere swapping of a ballet company for an orchestra. During the first six months of 1987, there was a broadening of the types of exchange permitted. It was most striking. For example, doctors and scientists from both sides were able to meet — and evaluate — each others' developments. Most surprising of all, perhaps, was the sight of Soviet nuclear scientists stepping out of a jet on Californian soil. They had come to inspect a US missile site; the intention being that each side could thereafter discuss the means of verifying the extent of each other's nuclear arsenals. Ultimately, it was hoped, they could evaluate the reports, and satellite pictures, that landed on their desk.

There is growing evidence, too, that certain aspects of capitalist philosopy — as well as day-to-day market oriented procedures — are becoming accepted in the USSR, moderating the raw edge of communist practice. To some extent these changes could well help to rectify some of Russia's longstanding, internal problems; and put this other vast and determined Euro-Asian nation in a stronger position to bid for world leadership, as the global power centre moves Eastwards before the next major long-term expansion.

The Soviet Union has many attributes qualifying it to become world leader in terms of business and political influence. To begin with, Russia's sphere of influence is already world-wide. The USSR also has the backing of its people for a strong and efficient military regime, allowing ample spending on heavy engineering and electronics — the foundation of a modern armaments industry. Outside its borders, Russia has pursued a policy of quasi-colonisation. Afghanistan is a prime example. Little or no effort was made by the West to counteract Soviet moves, since the UK and Europe tended to regard Afghanistan as outside their sphere of influence, leaving it to the United States to make play for Afghan favours. Here we see the claw-marks of the New Russia, which is in a prime position — in the absence of any meaningful intervention — to build up a massive, trans-continental power base, the prerequisite for global hegemony.

Russia also exerts an indirect influence on several strategic areas around the world, through its strategically-placed surrogates like Cuba, Vietnam, and latterly Nicaragua. They are vital components in a long-term plan of the USSR to achieve control — by military or other means — of global key locations. The Russians have deliberately chosen to operate in a way which avoids direct contact with the Western military machine. By the tactical use of subversion, they have gradually undermined the ability and will of the Western Powers to counter the unrelenting Soviet drive.

Step by step, the Soviet Union is winning hearts and minds, and gaining ground, enabling Moscow to take further measures — direct and indirect. It has learned to use its policy of quasi-colonialism to surround, then isolate, a country or a sphere of influence. This is the first step towards restricting the development by others of new markets in the East, in countries close to their borders, and in the vicinity of their more distant strategic strong-points. The new markets, which the USSR ensnares in a web of subversion and propaganda, are all markets vital for the survival of Western capitalism. To survive — let alone to grow — the capitalist system must continue to develop new markets, which can be integrated into the *Western* sphere of influence; not by bribery and intimidation, but by the genuine pursuit of mutual advantage.

In the absence of new markets, to be cultivated to serve as a means of absorbing and fuelling expanding production, the capitalist economies of the West will simply stagnate and turn inwards; becoming progressively more protectionist and socialistic. . . which, of course, is precisely what has been happening over the last decade or so.

In addition to Russia's programme of colonisation and the control of strategic global locations, which can be used as a restrictive weapon toward business in the West, she has also been regularly introducing capitalist type incentives in her system. Thus the appearance of *glasnost* represents a wholly new attitude. These pseudo-capitalist objectives are directed towards both the agricultural and industrial sectors for the purpose of boosting production, reducing dependance on Western grain and technology.

As we complete the period of global contraction and move toward a period of long-term global expansion, the Soviet Union can be seen to be implementing a two-pronged strategy. It puts the nation in position where it could easily assume the mantle of political and economic leader, during a period predestined to see the Eastern hemisphere gain dominance over the West. The long term objective of the USSR, formulated to produce a territorial imperative which would restrict the West from gaining access to any further markets, is in perfect alignment with Marxist ideology. Marxists and Trotskyites, more than anyone, are aware that by preventing the West from gaining access to new markets, they can effectively capture the world leadership; as they sit by and push the Western industrialised nations into decadence, social unrest and anarchy. By utilising this two-pronged cold war, Russia has reduced the Western industrialised nations to the condition of a medieval monarchy under siege from all quarters. Russia's tactics have gradually deprived the West of an increasing number of the economic opportunities vital for its survival. Obviously, if the West finds its markets in the East shrinking — while markets in areas where the USSR have a powerful, *indirect* influence also contract — it will mean an expansion in the markets available to the Soviets alone. Therefore, as the second element of the two-pronged effort, Russia has been preparing for an economic upsurge; endeavouring to acquire economic status through the regular employment of capitalist techniques in agriculture and industry, as already mentioned.

What we are now witnessing in the Soviet Union is a modification from the approach of Marxist Socialism. But it is not a deviation. The measures being taken remain within the bounds of communist ideology, which insists on central government control of the masses, and of the means of production. Physical and intellectual slavery remains an integral part of the Soviet approach.

According to pure Marxist doctrine, which established the basis for the political philosophy of the USSR as early as the 1920s, capitalism was a self-defeating economic phenomenon. It could be assumed that markets would ultimately become saturated through the type of over-production engendered by the basic hypothesis of encouraging a free market. All that was necessary under the Marxist strategy, to put an end to capitalism once and for all, was to restrict as many markets as possible. This would bring about the slow strangulation of the capitalist system — without the need for military action. During the depression of the 1930s, it was widely believed that the last nails were being hammered into the capitalist coffin. But Marx had been wrong. Indeed, the Russians now recognise the major weakness in the Marxist strategy. What Marx failed to envisage was the cyclical revitalisation of capitalism through innovation, and the application of these innovations to existing markets; making these markets more efficient, once a base for further exploitation had been built. Contrary to the expectations of Karl Marx and his followers, the depression of the 1930s did not bring about the extinction of the capitalist philosophy. In fact, it served as a springboard as we've now seen. Nor was capitalism self-defeating. On the contrary! Given the continual encouragement of free markets, capitalism was self-regenerating. Nicolai Kondratieff, one of the innovators of Long Wave economic cycle theory, argued this point — much to the dismay of the Soviet authorities. Kondratieff was right, indeed, about the self-generating nature of capitalism; and many other facets of economic life on this planet. His reward for discovering a phenomenon to which the Soviets now appear to have acquiesced, was deportation to a prison camp, where he died in misery and penury.

There are many weaknesses in the Marxist approach, as the Russians have discovered; and these are currently being countermanded. To begin with, the traditional slow strangulation approach, inherent in the Marxist strategy, takes a considerable amount of time, an exceptional amount of long term economic and social deprivation, along with vast resources. But there is yet to be any convincing evidence to suggest that Marxist strategy will *ever* work. In the meantime, compared to the West, the USSR has been in a permanent depression since the concept of Marx's utopian socialism became a part of Soviet political and economic policy. Furthermore, the pure Marxist approach leaves Soviet policy continually affected by the actions — and subsequent economic conditions — of the West and its Allies. By employing capitalistic techniques where appropriate, and offering capitalistic incentives to agriculture, trade and industry, — and, to a degree, encouraging some form of free market flow — the Soviets are in a far better position to control their own destiny, and seize the mantle of global leader when it proves most opportune.

To many observers, the suggestion of a free market philosophy in the USSR may seem outlandish. But most so-called observers are not very good at observing, and are mostly wrong, most of the time. Too many of them have an in-built, anti-change mechanism that continually subjects their psyche to the acceptance of unchallenged stereo types. Take those of Russian soldiers breathing fire, and equipped with two horns and a long red rail with a spike on the end.

Recently, cinema audiences were exposed to the sight of vicious, seething Russians, sadistically torturing the saintly epic hero, Sylvester Stallone in

Rambo. The same viewers were horrified by a film made in 1984 (*Invasion, USA*), in which immoral, contemptible and unfeeling Russian soldiers watched a sweet, innocent little girl decorating a Christmas tree. Then they blew up the little girl, her family, the house and the Christmas tree. This is the type of stereotyped propaganda put out in the West, so that we shall remain on the alert for the Russian menace to strike. Our leaders encourage us to live by these contrived caricatures of other countries, lest we become too complacent. If we didn't accept these stereotypes, we might come to the conclusion that we are all variants of the same human species, and that the same variations exist in other countries the world over. This discovery might mean we could be less willing to support our leaders, and we might lose some of our nationalistic and patriotic fervour.

Like religion, political ideologies and a belief in Santa Claus, there is a place for nationalism and patriotism in every household. But neither nationalism nor patriotism should be allowed to destroy your judgement, or your powers of observation; not when it comes to anticipating the future, in order to plan your lives and those of your loved ones. People in the USSR are also nationalistic and patriotic; and their leaders are just as pragmatic as our leaders. They are equally intent on manipulating the world in which we both live to their own design — as our leaders are. The Soviet leadership is now showing very clear signs of adopting a far more practical approach to their role as a global power, in stark contrast to the dogmatic approach that was the keynote of the political and economic philosophies of Russia during the early 1900s. Many observers feel the Soviet authorities would never permit the type of reforms that would enable Russia to sequester the role of world leader from the United States on capitalistic ground. But these changes and reforms are surfacing throughout the Soviet Empire at an accelerating pace, as the Russians make their major play for global economic and political domination. In Soviet bloc nations such as Hungary and Poland, exceptionally advanced, undiluted capitalist ideas are being encouraged and adopted. Nations within the sphere of direct (and indirect) Soviet influence are now being encouraged to incorporate capitalist practices in their socialist systems; while there is seemingly a concurrent shift towards greater individual freedoms. Under the Soviet long-term Grand Design, it is likely that once the mantle of global leadership has been put on, these freedoms will be short-lived. For Russian philophers genuinely believe that personal freedom undermines authority and weakens central control. In the meantime, it is a means to an end; the end being to threaten world democracy and the free market, capitalist way of life that we know.

As I have demonstrated, we are now at a period in the long-term cycle of global supremacy where a transfer of world economic and political supremacy to another nation is due. According to Oswald Spengler's classic treatise *Decline of the West*, the nation that will become the new global leader will be an Eastern nation, geographically speaking. Territorially and strategically, the nation which seems most likely to achieve the status of new world leader is the USSR, with all the incumbent political implications their leadership would involve. The hungry fighter fights the hardest. The West has become fat, tired and decadent. It is no longer a match for a hungry fighter. The USSR is that hungry fighter.

The Russian people have lived in a congenital state of depression under Soviet rule for decades. The Soviets have unrelentingly and unyieldingly stifled free thought. Moscow has used the time to develop the infrastructure needed for Russia to rise like a Phoenix from the ashes of the Tsarist Empire, which went up in flames during the October revolution, to become an industrial and military colossus. Now, the Soviets are about to use the Gorbachev gambit. *Glasnost* has given the Russian people a glimpse of hope they have never had before. The Kremlin appear to be relaxing individual restraints in an effort to win friends and seduce their critics in the West. At the same time, Soviet leaders are attempting to bring trade, industry and agriculture up to Western standards, while still retaining the inherent communist ideologies characteristic of Marxist-Leninist philosophy.

In the past, when the mantle of world leader has been passed from one nation to another within the same hemisphere, the dislocation associated with an alien culture, forcing its ideologies on the *waning* culture, has never been a major concern. But we are now at that position in the long term cycle when global supremacy will pass from one hemisphere to another: from the Western Hemisphere to the East. To many, subjugation to a Soviet culture and political regime is an unthinkable consequence. But as un-thinkable as such a future may be, it must be fully recognised that under current circumstances, and with their current policies, the Kremlin are the leading contenders for the role of global leader; which would mean establishing Soviet ideology as the dominant economic and political force in world affairs.

Of all the Western nations, some believe that Australia is the only nation capable of countering the attempt of the Russians to become the next global leader. Strategically, Australia also has the requisite economic buffer — natural resource wealth, along with self-reliance in agriculture. But, severe constraints reduce the ability of Australia to become a global leader. As already outlined, the Soviets are in an exceptionally strong position to resolve their problems on their own. They are now demonstrating this capability. While Australia is in a position to offer substantial resistance to a Soviet threat, Canberra would have to enlist substantial aid from a number of her trading partners, who may not be in a position to supply the degree of support required. Statistically too, Australia is a strong contender. Ancilliary factors suggest that Australia would be a most unlikely heir-apparent to world leadership, which in turn makes the threat of Soviet domination that much more profound.

Are we doomed therefore, to suffer the dictates of Soviet domination as we move into the Upwave? Does the future have nothing to offer other than grey submission or life in a *gulag*? Maybe not! The one element that offers a ray of hope happens to be one of the economic scenarios that is feared by most, but offers the most serious deterrent to Soviet hegemony. The development which would completely counter the prospect of Soviet domination would be the onset of a global depression. As simple as it may sound, it is the problem of providing food for the people that will determine the future stability of any nation as a depression deepens. Widespread hunger, across many parts of the world, has been an inherent characteristic of every depression in history. As we move into a global depression once again, the same problem will emerge. What has often spelled the difference between national survival and national catastrophe is a country's ability to grow sufficient crops to feed itself; while maintaining a reasonably stable currency, and a sound balance of payment position, enabling the government to purchase the recovery food products on the world market, should crops fail and production prove inadequate.

During the early phases of a depression, there is invariably a glut of food products, as farmers attempt to offset the fall in price levels associated with acute deflation by increasing production. The glut is then intensified. What frequently follows, in an attempt to restore price levels, is the destruction of crops and animals in order to reduce the surplus. Eventually, the depression deepens and the deflationary forces intensify. Then an increasing number of farmers will be forced out of business. This will lead to inadequate food supplies, which will become a primary source of political instability. Countries attempting to maintain sound currencies, and able to avoid the temptation of trying to reflate their way out of a depression by adopting fiat money policies, should remain in a relatively good position — both to buy food and to maintain a democratic form of government. On the other hand, a country that permits the destruction of its currency through the excessive inflation of the monetary aggregates, or through restrictive currency controls, will face increasing instability. It will eventually have severe difficulties in financing any external purchases. Russia, Eastern Europe and the Third World will suffer the most, as the depressionary forces mount. The plight of Russia is likely to be the most disruptive.

During periods of global depression, the Russian people have invariably suffered greater (and more excruciating) dislocations from a lack of food supplies than any other major power. Even now, were it not for the availability of foreign purchases on credit, and the temporary viability for its commodity-based export industries such as oil and gold, the Soviets would be experiencing extreme difficulties. They would certainly not, in any way, be a serious contender for the mantle of global leader when the present sphere of influence shifts from West to East.

The evidence strongly points to a global depression, which is now building in momentum. As the depression spreads and intensifies, there will have to be further concessions in commodity price levels. Russian commodity exports will suffer accordingly, reducing the country to penurious levels of economic activity. Massive food shortages are then likely to develop as a result of the Soviets' inability to effect further credit purchases in any meaningful amounts.

When internal instability grows in Russia, in tandem with the deepening depression, the Soviet authorities will be faced with one of two choices. Either they can cut back on military spending and concentrate Russia's capital resources on agricultural development; or they must seek new sources of food, through the military exploitation of more fertile neighbours. In either case, a depression will debilitate the qualities which the Soviets now feel will enable them to seize the role of world leader.

The two countries which currently are best placed to withstand the ravages of a depression are the United States and Japan. Even under the worst conditions imaginable, neither the US nor Japan should experience any great difficulty in providing its citizens with the basic necessities of life. This will be so regardless of the degree to which international trade may be reduced. During the depression of the 1930s, the US became the receptacle of the world's wealth. This time around, during the deepening depression, it will share that role with Japan's financial institutions, as risk capital — including gold — is rapidly transferred to the financial systems of both nations, at the expense of the rest of the world.

Once the depression has spent its force, I believe Japan will emerge as the next global leader. As we move into the Upwave, Japan will display a strong sense of nationalism, along with the financial and industrial ingenuity which previously gave the US its role as global leader. Then Japan will readily be seen as the dominant economic and military force of eastern Asia whose influence will be global. Japan currently has the lowest level of national debt, the highest savings ratio and the most sophisticated government and industrial complex of any major nation. Obviously, Japan is heavily dependent on exports. During the early phase of depression, it is likely that Japan will suffer more than most nations and experience the type of depression that occurred in the US during the 1930s. Yet, as the nadir of the global depression approaches, economic activity in Japan will be the first to show signs of improvement. Subsequently, the economy should readily adapt to the newly emerging economic order of the next long term period of global expansion.

I hold the view that as we move into the Upwave, and the sun rises in the East, it will shine on Japan as the global leader of the 21st century. This assumption is based on the resolution of economic forces, undeflected by the profligate tendencies now being witnessed in the West.

In the meantime, with each bulge of the money supply, and each debasement of a currency among Western nations, the Soviet presence becomes more imposing. The shadow it casts on the democracies continues to lengthen.

Chapter Nine

BRITAIN. . . THE ALTERNATIVE SCENARIO

Lenin is said to have declared that the best way to destroy the capitalist system was to debauch the currency. By a continuing process of inflation, governments can confiscate, secretly and unobserved, an important part of the wealth of their citizens. By this method they not only confiscate, but they confiscate arbitrarily; and while the process impoverishes many, it actually enriches some.

J.M. Keynes *The Economic Consequences of Peace*

The history of the Great Depression has been told and retold. The facets of this amazing period appear to be unlimited. The structural progress of the world's economy during the 1920s and 1930s provides an ideal model for the 1970s and 1980s. Unfortunately, the only lesson from history that is apparent with any degree of consistency is that very few people learn much from history.

In October 1932, most of the world's stock markets were in ruins, after the decimation of the global economy during the previous three years. It was at that time that one of the greatest speculators in history decided to republish a 90 year old book on mass psychology entitled *Extraordinary Popular Delusions and the Madness of Crowds*. A well-worn copy of that book has always graced my office. In the foreword to this monumental work by Charles MacKay, Baruch made the following observation, "If in the lamentable era of the new economics culminating in 1929 we had all repeated, 'Two and two still make four', much of the evil might have been averted."

At the start of 1987, bull markets were still roaring away in New York, London, Tokyo and elsewhere. Merger mania and takeover activity were rife. Billions were being borrowed to finance the private and institutional mania. In the background, the world's financial system was in complete disarray and on the verge of collapse. That was not a prediction. That was a fact! We saw the signs among OPEC members; among commodity producers; and most markedly in the world's banking system, where the roots of a financial Armageddon had been planted. I was on record as forecasting a 1930s type deflationary depression. That's no longer a forecast. It's currently taking place. The second great deflationary depression of the 20th century began in Latin America during the late 1970s. Africa joined the depression crowd in 1982. More will join with the passage of time. The deflationary cycle, which I had forecast several years earlier, was following closely the pattern of the 1920s and 1930s. Back in the 1920s, commodity prices were exceptionally hard hit. They were the first markets to collapse. As I have stated on several occasions, raw materials represent the first stage in the manufacturing process. When there is a long-term terminal juncture in raw material prices leading to a deflationary secular downtrend, all other markets ultimately follow suit. The rate of growth in commodity prices peaked in the mid-1970s. In absolute terms, commodity prices have been falling for over seven years as I write. Very few investors have come to grips with the nature and behaviour of the deflationary cycle. Just like inflation, deflation begins gently and then builds in momentum encompassing an increasing number of markets and assets. Many investors have begun to associate deflation with *disinflation,* which is a misnomer. There is no such thing as disinflation. There is only deflation or inflation. Disinflation is supposed to suggest a falling rate of inflation. People have been programmed to believe that a falling rate of inflation is good for the economy. What has been defined as a falling rate of inflation is the composite result of laggard inflationary trends and lead deflationary trends working together at the same time. Just as a *bit of deflation* — under the disguise of disinflation — is now considered to be good for business and the economy. It was that *bit of inflation* that was also considered good for the economy during the 1940s and 1950s. In the end that inflation became deadly, and was denounced as Public Enemy Number One. Deflationary trends are basically the same. However, there is one major difference. Deflation is much more difficult to control than inflation, and generally unfolds at a much more rapid rate and causes much more devastation in its wake.

I say "generally", because beyond a certain point inflation is the more deadly force. But, because instances of runaway hyper-inflation are mercifully not that frequent, we are more afraid of deflation and depression. They are, we tell ourselves, "the devils we know". Believe me that experience — and history — shew there are worse demons!

When I predicted that recession and depression were on their way in *The Downwave,* I was forecasting what I saw to be a distinct possibility. Today I go further: I can see no possibility of our escaping that recession, which must lead us into a depression comparable with that of the 1930s. Many find that possibility too frightening to accept. Others — equally frightened — are using their position of power to devise every and any means to put off what they dread as the evil day. But as I shall show, by recalling what actually happened in Germany in the 1920s, how painful and destructive the alternative of hyper-inflation must be. At the same time, you will see how the very means employed to fight off the inescapable slide into depression can result only in making that alternative inflationary scenario inevitable and even more disastrous. *That headlong rush into the flames of hyper-inflation is what I see today as the alternative scenario for Britain.*

A recession is supposed to have a cleansing effect, alleviating uneconomic excesses and serving to correct pockets of disequilibrium that appear at the mature stages of economic development. Once the excesses are corrected, the economy has a strong base from which renewed growth can take place.

During the Upwave that began after World War II, the recession was cut short through the introduction of monetary stimuli before the natural economic forces had a chance to work. Each recovery phase since World War II began with a greater number of businesses employing human and physical resources for progressively uneconomic functions. Three men were employed to do the job of one. Double resources were employed to perform the task that half could have accomplished. The burden for the productive elements of the economy became increasingly acute as uneconomic functions tended to drain the world economy of its resources. This meant that even more stimulation was required to keep the productive elements efficient, and the unproductive sectors afloat, when both showed signs of faltering. Throughout the various phases of expansion and contraction between 1947 and 1973, each phase of expansion required more profligate spending than the one before — to produce an even lower level of growth. Each recession required more government support to prevent the system from sinking deeper into the morass. During each recovery phase, the problems for the unproductive countries, individuals and white-elephant industries increased in scope and number, rendering the situation more and more intractable. In the process, a large chunk of the steel industry was lost. A reasonable chunk of the British banking system was lost. De-industrialisation has taken place at an accelerating rate. Manufacturing firms have been contracting. The process continues.

The 1973-1975 recession occurred at a time when liquidation of the global debt would have caused the greatest implosion of money in the history of Western civilisation. The unbelievable debt mountain that governments, individuals and corporations had accumulated throughout the post-war period not only had to be serviced, but had to be supported at ever increasing cost; with interest rates rising to levels that hadn't been seen since the days of the Roman Empire. The cost of servicing that global debt acted as a drag on economic improvement. The lifeblood of business and of a nation is capital. *Capital was being used to service debt rather than generate profits.*

If the authorities had failed to stimulate the economy through the introduction of more monetary excesses on top of existing monetary excesses, (just to keep the game going) we would have had a 1930s-type depression and a series of self-feeding bankruptcies and concurrent debt liquidation — all totally out of control. As the secondary prosperity of 1975 began, there was certainly little scope for any government to move into surplus. This led to the most unstable of any secondary prosperity phase in the 200 year-old-record of the long wave economic pattern.

The longer governments continue to fight the deflationary forces that have been working through the system; the longer they refuse to permit the global economy to correct the excesses of thirty years of profligate spending and debt accumulation; the greater will be the monetary and fiscal stimulation needed to offset the cumulative effects of these deflationary forces. The greater too will be the tendency for price inflation to escalate during each period of pseudo-economic improvement. The result will lead to successively higher interest rates and successively higher inflation, until such time as unsustainable hyper-inflation is reached.

Now you may say, "Ah, Beckman, you've admitted it! The depression in the Downwave *can* be averted. Governments *can* continue to stimulate the economy, so we may not get a depression after all. We may get hyper-inflation, but isn't that a helluva lot better than hyper-depression? After all, we've learned to live with inflation. It wasn't *that* bad!"

It is my contention that the weight of evidence supporting my conclusion is overwhelming. The deflationary aspects of the Downwave are perfectly in place. The infrastructure of the Long Wave cycle of economic continuity has proceeded in precisely the same manner as it has done since the beginning of the Industrial Revolution. As we move towards the end of the 1980s the probability of a scenario similar to that experienced during the 1930s (and previous periods of cyclical depression) is exceptionally high. If I were asked to put a number on it, I would say there is a 90 per cent chance that we shall see an action replay of the 1930s depression.

When it comes to dealing with probabilities, the odds may be 100 to 1 in your favour. . . But there is always that damn *1*. What might conditions be like if that *1* comes up? What would the alternative to the Downwave be? There can be only one alternative. It would be hyper-inflation. In the unlikely event that financial markets are able to tolerate further expansion, governments may continue to debase and inflate their currencies, using Keynesian reflationary techniques to blunt the forces of deflation, and disguise the inevitable economic deterioration as economic improvement. All of this would be taking place on top of an existing debt mountain, and an economy stretched far beyond its means. The object would be to postpone the day of reckoning for as long as possible, accepting the consequences; and for a miracle to make all the badness go away before the situation degenerated into chaos. If companies headed for bankruptcies are big enough, government will bail them out. If unemployment gets higher and the government has to increase its so-called job creation schemes and transfer payments, they'll print the money that's required.

The structural differences between the US economy now, and the nature of the US economy during the early stages of previous Downwaves, are significant. The level of wages is far less flexible now than in the 1920s and '30s. During the 1920-1922 recession, wages fell sharply. In the depression of the 1930s, they fell even more. Cuts in salaries were commonplace. This is not true today. The only significant change in the salary structure has been slower growth. We can probably expect to see a much higher level of unemployment for any given degree of deflation, and therefore a heightened level of social tension. This should be particularly true in urban areas, where unemployment is highly concentrated and the threshold of social pain is already an extremely low one. Then we shall see what we have seen in the past. History is replete with examples of massive state interference once the political discomfort of deflation and unemployment begin to threaten the ruling party.

During the early stages of earlier Downwaves, there was little government intervention. That did not come until the more pronounced stages. One of the main explanations for the deep recession that follows the peak inflation is in the decline of government expenditure. Recently, both the UK and the US governments have — despite their talk of cuts — been increasing their expenditure on automatic stabilisers and the military.

Any deceleration of money and credit at this time would send the economy into a relapse, casting us headlong into a depression, with a massive debt liquidation and the subsequent collapse of the financial system. This scenario is certainly recognised by the authorities. Nor will the policy of state interference be thrown suddenly out of the window. Shortly after President Reagan took office he stated, "We will not fight inflation on the backs of the unemployed." The Secretary of the Treasury later stated that we could not have another depression because the Federal Reserve would never let money supply shrink to the extent it did in 1929-1933.

Another respect in which the current downwave differs from previous declines is that several years ago governments removed any external impediments that could blunt inflationary forces through a regression to floating exchange rates. The current system has created an engine for inflation, unprecedented in any other than the hyper-inflations of the past. Countries no longer lose significant reserves when they have a payments deficit. In a world of floating exchange rates, there is no run on the gold reserves. The country simply lets the exchange rate drop. At the early stages of previous Downwaves, the fall in the reserves tended to reduce the domestic money supply and act as an automatic governor, limiting the fuel for inflation. This self-activating mechanism is no longer available. Countries with massive deficits are free to increase their deficits still further. They expand their money supply when it should be contracting.

Economically, we are in uncharted waters. We have discontinued the disciplines originally designed for our protection. We have created a locomotive that could run away in either direction — into the deepest depression since the late 18th century and the dawn of the Industrial Revolution, or into a disaster rivalling the hyper-inflation which destroyed German society in the 1920s.

The Nightmare of Inflation. . . You May Have to Sell Your Ears!

Just before World War I, the German mark, the British shilling, the French franc and the Italian lira, were all worth about the same. The exchange rate was around four to five to the dollar. Ten years later, you could exchange one shilling, one franc or one lira for up to 1 trillion marks, provided you wanted marks. Most were unwilling to touch marks. The mark was worth one million-millionth of its pre-1914 value.

Before World War I, the industrialised world lived under a gold standard, enjoying price stability and stable exchange rates. Germany, as an industrial power, ranked high among the trading nations. The country's prosperity was protected by the monetary rules laid down by the Bank Law of 1875. The Central Bank, the Reichsbank, issued the currency. One-third of the currency was backed by gold reserves. The other two-thirds was backed by commercial paper of persons or businesses of proven solvency. The amount of bills taken by the bank was in proportion to the level of economic activity. The amount of currency in circulation was governed also by the level of economic activity.

The outbreak of war placed the German economy in a critical position. The blockade imposed by the Allies all but killed the international trade that Germany had depended on for its prosperity. When war fever reached its peak in July, 1914, a substantial exodus from Germany began. Certain sections of the German public began to panic, and turned to the Reichsbank to convert their money into gold (as they were entitled to do). Within a short time, the gold reserves were drained by 100 million marks. As a consequence, wartime legislation was passed abolishing convertibility of the currency into gold. In everyday language, Germany went "off the gold standard". The door to inflation was opened.

Since its international trade had come to a standstill, Germany was forced to borrow to finance the war. The Government approved credit of 5 billion marks. At the same time, three-month government Treasury bills were substituted for commerical paper to serve as a backing for bank notes. The Central Bank was authorised to take up, and discount, unlimited amounts of Treasury bills. Unlike commercial paper, these did not represent the underlying security of a solvent borrower. Treasury bills were merely government obligations, sold to the Central Bank by the Government, allowing it to create money at will. With currency issued on the strength of Treasury bills and loan-bank credits, the inflation began. In just two weeks, the amount of money in circulation rose by 2 billion marks.

Germany's total expenditure during World War I amounted to the then colossal sum of 164 billion marks. The war cost 147 billion marks. The country had a total income of 121 billion marks. The 43 billion marks gap was covered by Treasury bills. The unfunded indebtedness of the Reich was 50 billion marks. By the end of 1918, the amount of money in circulation had reached the sum of 35 billion marks, about five times the pre-war level. The profligate issue of currency brought a fall in the value of the mark. It fell by 50 per cent between 1914 and 1918. In 1919 the mark halved again. Prices inside Germany had roughly doubled.

On November 11, 1918, when Germany signed the armistice in the forest of Compiègne, the economy was gutted. A large portion of German industry had been destroyed during the war. There were some 6 million war casualties, and the mortality rate of the civilian population had risen considerably. Productivity had fallen and the reserves of food and raw materials were depleted. In addition, the conditions of the armistice called for the surrender of huge quantities of war materials. The Germans were also required to deliver 5,000 railway engines, 150,000 railway wagons and 5,000 trucks. The social and economic dislocation that accompanied the transition of a defeated nation from a military economy to a peacetime economy contributed to the overall chaos.

Germany needed money and needed it badly. Money was needed to buy food and raw materials from abroad. Demobilisation of the armed forces was a costly business. So was the unemployment caused by the return of the soldiers, and the redeployment of industry. War victims had to be cared for. Pensions had to be paid. The Government could have resorted to tight fiscal measures to finance a slow and painful recovery. Instead it decided upon what it saw as a quicker method: the bulk of government expenditure would continue to be covered by borrowing, deficit spending and printing currency. Between November, 1918 and July, 1919, the deficit grew by a further 50 per cent. The issue of currency marched in step. Internal prices advanced by 42 per cent.

In 1919, the mark began to fall rapidly. By February, 1920, prices advanced by 42 per cent, and the exchange rate against the dollar reached 100 marks, nearly twenty-five times its pre-war parity. The Cost of Living Index (published by the German Statistical Office) showed a rise of 847% over the pre-war level. By mid-1920, conditions had begun to stabilise. The mark began to hold its own in foreign exchange markets, following the deep devaluation. But business conditions were far from buoyant. Wartime price controls had continued long after the war ended; and even when controls were relaxed, firms were unable to boost prices to levels which would compensate for rising costs. During 1920, the net profit of 1,485 German companies averaged only 25% of pre-war earnings. (Adjusted for monetary depreciation, but not for inventory profits).

In 1920 the whole world was plunged into recession. It was to be the deepest recession since the depression of the 1890s. The timing could not have been worse for Germany, still desperately struggling to restore industry to its former glory. Most of the industrialised world remained on a gold standard, and acquiesced to the deflationary and restrictive disciplines that a gold standard imposed. Germany decided to move in the other direction, seeking to blunt the forces of global recession through more monetary and fiscal stimulation. Thus was the pattern set.

The recession took its toll on Germany's overseas markets. Between May and December 1920, exports fell by 40 per cent. Unemployment shot up from 1.9 per cent in March, 1920 to 6 per cent by July. From June, 1921 through November, 1921, the mark began to fall again, gathering momentum in the descent. During that period, the mark lost about three-quarters of its value against the dollar. The dollar rate rose to 270 marks. This was a precursor of worse to come. . . far worse.

Desperate times make politicians desperate. The year 1921 was a desperate one. The German war reparation payments were due for negotiation. At a conference in Paris, the Allies decided that Germany should pay the reparations in amounts of between 2 and 6 billion gold marks per year, spread over a period of forty-two years. Controls would be set up to safeguard the payments. It was at that time that the British criticised Germany for its fiscal policies, stating that the financial burden to be borne by the German people was ridiculously low, compared to that of the people of the victorious Allies.

The Allies' reparation demands were rejected by the German government. The Allies replied with trade sanctions against Germany, and occupied three major German cities — Düsseldorf, Duisburg and Ruhrort — in the Rhine-Ruhr area.

On May 5th, 1921, David Lloyd George handed the German Ambassador what was to become known as the "London Ultimatum." The total sum of reparation was decided at 132 billion gold marks. This was to be paid in regular installments of 2 billion gold marks. To this a sum equivalent to 26 per cent of Germany's exports would be added. A down payment of one billion gold marks was to be made before the end of August. In the case of non-acceptance by the German Government, the Ruhr would be occupied.

The German Government resigned, refusing to accept the ultimatum. A new government was quickly formed. The ultimatum was accepted. The down payment of one billion gold marks, due in August, was made as stipulated, although the German authorities had great difficulty in getting the foreign currency required. The problem was further aggravated when one of the international loans contracted by the Reichsbank — 270 million gold marks from a Dutch banking consortium — had to be repaid at short notice. Foreign currency, ordinarily earned by trade transactions, was not available. The only way the German authorities were able to buy the foreign currency needed to pay the Dutch was through the sale of paper marks on the foreign exchange market. The paper marks were duly issued through the creation and discount of Treasury bills!

This transaction triggered off a wave of speculation against the mark. The situation was made even worse on October 20th, when the Council of the League of Nations decided that Upper Silesia should be partitioned, and its richest industrial area given to Poland. The ensuing gloom and despondency in Germany reached panic dimensions. The decision of the League of Nations was the kind of psychological shock that led to a flight of capital out of marks, *and* out of Germany. On November 29th, 1921, the mark plunged once more. It fell to 300 to the dollar during November, 1921. On November 15th, a further 500 million gold marks were due under the London Ultimatum. The sum was paid, but under protest. Following the payment, the mark improved, since it was deemed that the speculation was overdone. For some three months the mark was stable against the dollar at around 200. In March, 1922 the mark resumed its downward path. It was 270 to the dollar in June. The currency in circulation rose by a further 50 per cent between February, 1922 and June, 1922. The Cost of Living Index rose from twenty-four to forty-one during the corresponding period. Between June, 1913 and June, 1922 prices had increased by forty-one times.

For reasons related to economy rather than the potential inflationary impetus, the mark continued to fall throughout 1922. In addition to the scarcity of money, it was widely noticed that the earnings stated by German industrial companies, although declining, were still too high — and considered totally unrealistic if inflation were taken into account. Although the authorities attempted to tighten money, inflation continued on its way. The rise in inflation meant that whatever increase there might be in domestic earnings was being lost through the depreciation of the currency. The dividends that were being paid by companies represented a depletion of capital rather than a distribution of earnings, once the growth in the rate of inflation was factored into the result.

Efforts to control inflation by sporadic tightening of money proved utterly futile. The amount gained in terms of controlling inflation was offset by the hardships and political pressures the measures caused. By mid-1922 the German authorities had completely abandoned any attempt to control inflation through tight monetary policies. They gave in to the demand for easy money — and higher inflation. The Reichsbank began to supply credit directly to industries — and in copious amounts. It deliberately encouraged the wider use of commercial paper, which it readily discounted; putting more currency into circulation as it discounted the paper. During the course of 1922, the value of commerical paper discounted by the Reichsbank rose from 1 billion to no less that 422.2 billion marks. Commercial paper joined Treasury bills in their role as engines for the creation of more and more paper money.

By June, 1922 the mark was in free-fall. Between June and December that year the mark fell from 300 to 8,000 to the dollar. German inflation had entered a new phase. It now became clear, even to the most casual observer, that the mark was galloping downhill towards the abyss. By then, German industrialists had enough experience in dealing with a falling currency and rising inflation. Anticipating a rise in costs, they ruthlessly raised prices in response to every fall in the exchange rate. Confidence in the mark totally disappeared. It was replaced by a widespread obsession with *beating* inflation by *using* it. Industrialists played the game by speculating on further falls, thus inducing further falls. Speculating on the fall in the currency became the best game in town, circa the autumn of 1922. Wild spending sprees emanated from the ill-gotten gains of a falling currency. If the mark was dying, the Germans thought they might as well have their fun before the funeral. But the terminal stage of the game was far less rewarding than many had expected.

Between June and December, 1922 the Cost of Living Index in Germany shot up from 41 to 685. The prices of goods and services increased by more than 1,500 per cent in those six months. The currency circulation exceeded 1 billion marks. So did the German deficit. But, it should be noted that until the early part of 1923, printing money to keep the economy moving had its beneficial side effects, as it was intended to do. During the summer of 1922 there was full employment in Germany. The rate of unemployment was under 1 per cent from April to September 1922, rising slowly to reach 2.8 per cent by the end of the year. German industries, especially those in the export trade, were booming during the period when other countries were suffering the ravages of the 1920-1922 recession. In the fall of 1922, the working week of British coal miners was reduced to a mere two days. German miners were working over-time. They had to, given the disastrous fall in real wages as inflation galloped ahead. Yet, the 1,500 per cent rise in the Cost of Living Index in 1922 was nothing compared to what followed in 1923.

As that fateful year began, a dramatic development heralded the commencement of a new and more terrifying phase of inflation than the world had ever seen. It would terminate in the complete and irreversible collapse of the mark. After twelve months of nervous fluctuation, the mark plunged again in 1923, gathering momentum, dragging social misery, penury and political turmoil in its wake. At last, the German currency went over the cliff edge of sanity. It had, as it were, clung on for months by its fingertips. It has been said that capital markets can do anything they like, any time they like, without reservation. The annihilation of the German mark proved that beyond any doubt.

The straw that broke the camel's back was a consignment of 125,000 telegraph poles, plus a quantity of coal, that were part of the London Ultimatum. They were to be delivered to the French late in 1922. Germany failed to make the delivery. French and Belgian troops marched into the Ruhr and occupied the region under the sanction that was part of the ultimatum. The result was a public uprising and civil war in Germany. There were arrests, bloodshed and loss of life. Once again the internal strife had to be financed. It was the *coup de grâce* for the mark.

At the beginning of January 1923, the mark was trading at 18,000 to the dollar. By September 1923, the mark was trading at 100 million to the dollar, and still falling! The official German Government's reaction to the occupation was "passive resistance." The Government ceased all reparation payments of any kind, and ordered a general stoppage of work for civil servants and railway workers. In addition, there was to be a complete cessation of any activities whatsoever which could conceivably benefit the occupying powers.

Germany's passive resistance to the occupation of the Ruhr prevented the occupying forces from restoring production, in any meaningful degree. But the price paid was a high one. Not only did Germany lose the wealth-generating resources of the Ruhr when she could least afford to, but the country also had to provide for the unemployed and refugees who had lost their livelihood because of the passive resistance. On top of that, there was the damage caused to the rest of the nation by general unemployment, disruption, dislocation and administrative difficulties. For example, the German railways depended on coal from the Ruhr to keep rolling. Without coal from the Ruhr, food and supplies could not be delivered to the other regions. Germany was obliged to buy coal from Britain to maintain essential services. This mean the purchase of additional foreign currency, to the further detriment of the mark.

The Germans had only one method for coping with the situation: the printing press. Notes in circulation increased from 1 billion marks at the end of 1922 to 92.8 trillion by November 15th, 1923. By the end of the year the sum was a staggering 496.5 trillion marks. On November 15th, 1923, Germany's floating debt stood at 189 trillion marks. Three per cent of Germany's expenditure was covered by taxes and other income. The other 97 per cent came from the printing press.

Inflation reached such proportions that some employees demanded to be paid their wages two and three times a day, so as to keep up with rising prices. Emergency notes were issued by towns and cities throughout Germany. These were known as *Notgeld*. They were issued in huge quantities. The total number of *Notgeld* issues is fantastic. It is recorded that 3,500 cities issued a total of almost 50,000 different notes between 1914 and 1922. Eventually, 30,000 people and over eighty private houses were employed keeping up with the increased demand for paper money. Many of the earlier German issues of notes were overprinted, some of them twice on the same note.

The year 1923 was one of galloping inflation: galloping to such a degree that madness gripped Germany's financial authorities, and economic disaster overwhelmed millions of people. Under these conditions, life became

Figure 20: 100 million Reichsbanknote

grotesque and unbearable. The inflation was so preposterous that the story has tended to be dismissed as an historical curiosity rather than the culmination of a chain of economic, social and political developments of permanent significance. As money was dying of the inflationary fever, so were reason and common sense among the people. Printing presses all over the nation disgorged mountains of pieces of paper called "money". This was rushed — by rail and road — to desperately waiting crowds, who hoped to get hold of it in time to buy the necessities of life before inflation made the money worthless. Yet, however quickly they grabbed at the packets of marks that were thrown down to them, however swiftly they ran to make their purchases, more often than not they discovered that they were too late. The prices of goods they badly needed had jumped far beyond their reach — even as they were on their way to the market. And little wonder!

In Berlin, the price of potatoes, eggs and butter was changed six times a day. Grocers refused to part with their goods in exchange for paper money. Barter increasingly replaced transactions involving paper marks. The year 1923 brought catastrophe to the German *bourgeoisie,* as well as hunger, disease, destitution and sometimes death to an even wider public. Once the gold and jewels had gone, people were forced to offer their furniture and personal belongings to obtain their daily crust. Many had nothing left to offer. There was widespread undernourishment and near starvation. The angry and desperate masses became unruly. There was rioting in the streets. Throughout Germany, hyper-inflation turned the place into a national madhouse, with the inmates dancing a St. Vitus's Dance of the billions. . . and all this took a mere eighteen months to happen, from the time that Germany first abandoned its "tight money" policy in 1922 in a vain attempt to bail-out its ailing industries, and hopefully keep consumption rolling.

In 1923 the value of the German mark was a national preoccupation. But who could comprehend a figure followed by a dozen ciphers? In October, 1923, the British Embassy in Berlin noted that the number of marks to the pound equalled the number of yards to the sun. Dr. Schacht, Germany's National Currency Commissioner, explained that at the end of the Great War one could, theoretically, have bought 500 million eggs for the same price as one egg five years later. As the mark reached its nadir, and became exchangeable for gold marks, the sum of paper marks needed to buy one gold mark was precisely equal to the quantity of square millimetres in a square kilometre. It is far from certain that such calculations helped anyone understand what was actually taking place at the time. But the figures may help *us* to focus on the horror of hyper-inflation.

While the jobless, the homeless, the relief lines and the soup kitchens may appear individually synonymous with depression, it is actually difficult to describe the extent of the problems associated with the German experience. This was a difficulty noted by Lloyd George, writing in 1932. He said that words such as "disaster," "ruin," and "catastrophe" had ceased to rouse genuine apprehension any more — so widespread was the use of these terms.

During the German hyper-inflation, the meaning of disaster itself was devalued along with the mark. Erna von Pustau told Pearl Buck:

"Inflation finished the process of moral decay which the war had started. It was a slow process over a decade or more; so slow that really it smelled of slow death. . . in-between there were times when the mark seemed to stop devaluing, and each time we people got a bit more hopeful. People would say 'The worst seems over now.' In such a time Mother sold her tenanted houses. It looked as though she had made a good business deal, for she got twice as much cash as she had paid. But the furniture she bought. . . had gone up five times in price and. . . the worst was not over. Soon inflation started again with new vigor, and swallowed up bit by bit the savings accounts of Mother and millions of others."

William Guttman and Patricia Meehan, in their book *The Great Inflation*, tell a heartbreaking story. Dorothy Henkel recalled how:

"A friend of mine was in charge of the office that had to deal with the giving of salaries, pensions and special grants to the police of the whole district around Frankfurt. This was at the time when the bank notes were showing as many as twelve noughts. She struggled with her task very bravely. One case which came her way was the widow of a policeman who had died leaving four children. She had been awarded three months of her late husband's salary. My friend worked out the sum with great care, checked it and double-checked it and sent the papers on as required to Wiesbaden. There, they were checked again, rubber-stamped and sent back to Frankfurt. By the time all this was done and the money was finally paid out to the widow, the amount she received would only have paid for three boxes of matches."

It may be difficult to fathom the extent to which extreme inflation can ravage society. Probably the best way to demonstrate what was actually happening is through the price history of the period itself. The following table makes the point far better than reams of descriptive literature ever could. During the three months from August 1923 through October 1923, prices were moving hour by hour, at a rate that often took a year and more to accomplish in normal times.

Item Quantity	Pre-War Price	Price in Summer 1923	Price in November 1923
1 kg rye bread	29 pfennig	1,200 marks (early summer)	428 billion marks
1 egg	8 pfennig	5,000 marks	80 billion marks
1 kg butter	2.70 marks	26,000 marks (June)	6 trillion marks
1 kg beef	1.75 marks	18,800 marks (June)	5.6 trillion marks

A pair of shoes that cost 12 marks in 1913 cost over a million marks in the summer of 1923. By November, 1923 the price was 32 trillion marks. The price of a newspaper in November, 1923 was 200 billion marks. The price of one match was 900 million marks. Life in the city was complicated even more by the introduction of the "multiplier" which had to be used to adjust the price mechanisms for the spiralling rate of inflation, as and when required. An extended mathematical knowledge was needed just to keep body and soul together. Each morning the newspapers would publish a list of prices for public services. One billion involves nine zeroes. The number of digits on a price tag became so unwieldy that these multipliers had to be used. Every trade and each class of goods within that trade had a different index or multiplier. A purchase of the most ordinary items in a shop required several minutes of calculations to determine the exact price. Once the price was calculated, it then took several more minutes to count up the bundles of notes (with denominations of thousands, millions and billions) needed to execute the purchase.

Service	Price in Marks
Tramway fare	50,000
Tramway monthly season ticket for one line	4 million
for all lines	12 million
Taxi-autos: multiply ordinary fare by	600,000
Horse cabs: multiply ordinary fare by	400,000
Bookshops: multiply ordinary price by	300,000
Public baths: multiply ordinary price by	115,000
Medical attendance: multiply ordinary price by	80,000

Prices were moving up so rapidly that salaries (even though they were disbursed two and three times a day) could no longer be readily adjusted by the use of index numbers or multipliers. Business had become virtually impossible. People spent their waking hours with dazzling numbers spinning around in their heads. The publication of the exchange rate twice daily set the human calculating machines in motion, in an effort to determine how much money they would receive in their wage packets — and how much they could buy with it before prices went up again. Price calculations were multiplied by multipliers, then divided by the divisors, until people shook with hysteria before going out of their minds.

The brother of William Guttman, co-author of *The Great Inflation,* worked at the University Psychiatric Clinic in Munich. How the borderline between madness and reality was blurred is illustrated in his story:

> "When a new patient was brought in, the doctors started their investigation with a simple test to find out whether the patient was an obvious mental case or whether, at least on the face of it, he was normal. They would ask him a few elementary questions such as, how old are you, how many children have you got, what is the height of the *Zugspitze?* And the answers could be, I'm 25 million years old, have 1,000 or 15,000 children, etc."

The chronic instability of living in a world where money was dying drove the nation to temporary insanity. It was a moral insanity more than anything else. There was a diminishing ability to distinguish the difference between right and wrong. There was a callous and almost paranoid disregard for the rights of one's fellow man, in a society where materialism had reached its most horrifying extreme. "An age of Bedlam of unprecedented dimensions," and "a kind of lunacy gripping the people," were two of the phrases used to describe the collective madness of the German inflation by its chroniclers.

Stefan Zweig, in his memoirs, *The World of Yesterday*, recalls his horror at witnessing the spectacle of Berlin in the grip of inflation. According to his account, palaces of vulgar and coarse amusement mushroomed in the centre of the city. Male prostitutes would parade along the *Kurfürstendamm*, to a witches' sabbath. He likened the dances of homosexuals of both sexes to orgies transcending those of decadent Rome. The average sixteen-year-old girl in Berlin would have been insulted by the suggestion that she might still be a virgin.

Hans Furstenberg describes in his memoirs the revulsion he felt seeing the demonstrations of nauseating perversity along the streets of the city centre; the flagrant display of nude shows and nightclub spectaculars that flaunted every conceivable form of human and animal sexual degradation.

In the dimly lit, and not so dimly lit areas of the city's parks, trying to avoid stumbling over fornicating bodies was like running an obstacle race. One morning a young student was found dead, his hands and legs bound to a tree while semen dripped from his anus like water from a leaky tap. It was later discovered that he had been raped by a band of fourteen male homosexuals.

Berlin was dancing on a smouldering fuse, attached to a load of explosives. It was leading a life of unprecedented apathy without the slightest thought to what the next day would bring — it might be worse than the day before! Prices could double again, or maybe jump by a thousandfold. Nobody really knew. The money you spent on a bottle of champagne in the evening might only buy a matchstick by morning. Anyone, regardless of his walk of life, could be pushed into penury within hours.

People who could afford it, for as long as they *could* afford to, used whatever means available to escape their possible fate — or the thought of it. Gambling became excessive and widespread. The number of illegal gambling dens spread like an epidemic, attracting customers in search of diversion, eager to be rid of money that literally was becoming "not worth the paper it was printed on." Drug taking became extraordinarily fashionable. With the demand for drugs, came a vast army of peddlers and pushers who supplied confirmed addicts, as well as those who were being trained to become addicts. Cocaine became a symbol of the age for a delinquent population, which — out of a sense of frustration, or the desire to discover a new and more lasting form of escape — plumbed the depths of human depravity.

Human values fell in proportion to the rise in the rate of inflation. Crime of every kind was rampant. The statistics of the time speak for themselves. The number of criminal convictions in Germany rose from 562,000 in 1913 to 826,000 in 1923. The largest gain in the number of convictions was in the area of theft, rising more than 300%, from 115,000 in 1913 to 365,000 by 1923.

Stealing proliferated on an unimaginable scale among the middle-classes. Apart from the comparatively excusable motives of desperation and poverty, a lack of inhibitions among the people made stealing anything whatsoever a normal and acceptable way of life. No copper pipe, or brass armature, or sheet of lead on a roof was safe. No car was safe without someone to prevent the "gas" being siphoned out of the tank. Nor were even the railway carriages safe from the passengers, who stripped them of their curtains and leather windowstraps. Young boys would wander the street, unscrewing metal doorknobs and the metal number plates from doors, wherever they could be found. It was easier to buy food with a piece of metal that could be melted down for scrap (or leather that could be used to repair a shoe) than with paper money.

Life for the majority of Germans during those years was a time of animal, sordid, grinding poverty. Overall standards of well-being declined. Mortality in general rose. Stomach disorders and scurvy grew alarmingly. Typhoid and skin diseases became frequent because of a lack of hygiene in the handling of food. There was an increase in pneumonia and rheumatic complaints. Many simply could not afford fuel or warm clothing as prices rose far out of the reach of an increasingly larger proportion of the population. Children suffered especially. Infant mortality rocketed along with rickets and tuberculosis cases. Most school children were severely underweight.

Food virtually disappeared from the shops. Farmers were simply unwilling to sell their produce for paper money. Supplies that did manage to get through had to evade the clutches of millions of hungry, desperate people on the way. There was a scarcity of potatoes because of the danger of transport. Goods had to be moved after sundown, disguised under canvas and tarpaulin. Any visible food transported in the daytime would have invited hijacking.

Between 1913 and 1923, the consumption of beef fell by 50 per cent. The consumption of horse meat remained relatively constant. Dog meat was the only meat that showed a rise in consumption levels. In Germany, in the third quarter of 1921, 1,090 dogs were slaughtered for human consumption. In the third quarter of 1922, 3,678 dogs were slaughtered for the same purpose. In the corresponding quarter of 1923, 6,430 dogs found their way to the dinner tables of the German people.

One landlady was particularly noted for her ability to keep her boarders regularly supplied with meat at the evening meal. She said she had a secret supplier in Münsterberg. Every Thursday she would travel to the city, where she was able to buy as much meat as she wanted and at an especially reasonable price. Münsterberg was the city where the mass-murderer Denke conducted his operations in 1923.

During the depression of the 1930s, hunger and poverty were to lead to the rediscovery of brotherly love. People knew they needed each other. They helped one another. That was not so during the Great Inflation of the 1920s. Callousness was unparalleled. People would humiliate each other without the slightest hesitation. There is the macabre and disgusting incident told by the daughter of a once wealthy landowner in Germany. The local parson demanded as payment for the father's funeral service one of the last remnants of the vanquished family's fortune. . . a few silver spoons.

Milk was another item in short supply due to hoarding. People couldn't obtain milk in the ordinary way unless they had a certificate to prove there was a baby in the family. A young mother tells of her experience when moving to Berlin: as a visitor to the city, the first thing she did was register with the local authorities so she could get milk for her baby. The woman in charge of disbursing the milk dismissed the young woman's request in a rude and abrupt manner: "We haven't any milk for you." "But, I have a small baby and I'm entitled to it," pleaded the young mother. "Why do you bring babies into the world?" was the reply. "Drown it!"

No doubt the next chapter in the story of the German hyperinflation is the worst of all. By November, 1923, Adolf Hitler believed his hour had struck. The German currency was worthless. The purchasing power of incomes and salaries was reduced to zero. The lifesavings of the middle-classes and the working-classes were totally wiped out. The faith of the German people in the economic structure of German society was obliterated.

"What good were the standards and practices of such a society," asks William L. Shirer in *The Rise and Fall of the Third Reich:*

> "A society which encouraged savings and investment and solemnly promised
> a safe return from them and then defaulted? Was this not a fraud upon the
> people?"

We live in a world where you have to pay back borrowed money. But in the case of Germany following World War I, paying back what they owed would have meant immediate hardship for the people. The politicians — who wished to spare the people any hardship (and to remain in power) — decided they didn't want to pay what they owed in goods and services. So they printed paper money, and built up a staggering debt. The inflation could have been halted by balancing the budget. But, politically, such a move would have been unfavourable — and therefore impossible. Adequate taxation could have mitigated the soaring inflation, and debasement of the currency. But the new government was afraid of losing office if it imposed adequate taxation. Above all, the politicians wanted to keep their jobs. Instead of drastically raising taxes for those who could afford to pay, the German Government actually reduced taxes in 1921.

Aided and abetted by foreign bankers, industrialists and landlords stood to gain enormously through foreknowledge of government policy. The German masses were financially and morally bankrupt. The government sat idly by while the market tumbled and inflation soared. The State was freed of its public debts and managed to wriggle out of paying full value for its war debts. The destruction of the currency enabled the bankers and industrialists to wipe out their indebtedness by repaying their obligations in worthless German paper money.

It took the German people many years to discover what had actually occurred. They never imagined how profitable their demise had been to the industrialists and bankers, the army and the State. All the people did know was that large bank accounts couldn't even buy a spindly bunch of carrots, a half pound of potatoes, a few ounces of sugar or a pound of flour. They knew the hunger that gnawed at them daily. The time was ripe for a man called Adolf Hitler; who wrote in *Mein Kampf:*

> "The Government calmly goes on printing scraps of paper because if it stopped that would be the end of the Government. Because, once the printing presses stopped. . . and that is a prerequisite for the stabilization of the mark. . . the swindle would at once be brought to light. . . Believe me, our misery will increase. The scoundrel will get by. The reason: because the State itself has become the biggest swindler and crook. A robbers' state!. . . if the horrified people notice that they can starve on billions, they must arrive at this conclusion: we will no longer submit to a State which is built on the swindling idea of the majority. We want a dictatorship."

We in Britain and the United States have been programmed to fear a depression, as if it were some form of bubonic plague. Inflation is perceived to be preferable. As I have shown you, there are far worse alternatives than the depression of the 1930s, or the depression that I envisage for the 1980s. Have politicians learned anything from the macabre events that surrounded the German inflation? Is this an isolated case out of the history books that can never happen again? Can we comfortably believe the Central Banks can solve our problems by printing more money, bailing out the banks and lame duck companies?

For those who think the fiat money route is the way to go, the Brazilian economy provides a perfect object lesson. Not too long ago Brazil was extolled as a country which had learned to live with inflation. Those who advocate an easy money policy pointed toward Brazil as an economy that seemed to survive an inflation rate of 127 per cent. Survival, of course, is qualitative. Brazil became a bankrupt nation that owed $105 billion. Earlier in 1983 there was rioting in the streets of São Paulo because the Brazilians refused to accept the austerity measures the Government wished to impose, in a bid to return the country to stability. Fearing a revolution the Government acquiesced to the demands of the people. The result was the near default on a $400 million bridging facility that was due in May, but not paid until mid-July. Many bankers feared that Brazil would ultimately default. How were the Brazilian people coping with inflation? One way was by selling human flesh.

CORNEA FOR SALE. . . PLEASE CALL WORKING DAYS

This ad appeared in a local newspaper in Rio de Janeiro, the city where the wealthy lavish millions of dollars on plastic surgery, while the poor and the destitute try to make ends meet by selling their kidneys, corneas and blood. You can get $35,000 for a nice fresh cornea. Kidneys are more abundant. They go at a much lower price. If you're a Brazilian, you'll only get about $15,000 for one of your kidneys. There have been times when the rate for blood hit rock bottom, with more donors than people who need a transfusion. Two bucks and a bowl of soup is about the most you're going to get for one pint of Brazilian blood that patients in the hospital pay $45 for. Another reason for the low price of blood is that disease and infection are widespread in Brazil. Special costly measures have to be taken for purification of the plasma. Now the spectre of AIDS has cast its ubiquitous shadow.

Extraction of a living person's cornea will cause blindness in one eye for life. People donating corneas usually do so by signing permission for extraction to take place after death. But, in the summer of 1981, the Brazilian Red Cross sponsored a national campaign to solicit cornea donations for transplants. Squeezed by 100 per cent inflation at the time, along with galloping unemployment, many poor people began to place their corneas and kidneys on sale, advertising their organs in local newspapers — for immediate delivery!

One Brazilian, who offered a cornea through the papers, had to support a wife and child on the money he earned working at Rio de Janeiro International Airport. He figured that if he could get his asking price for the cornea, it would give him enough to pay for his young son's education. He would also be able to secure his own future as one of the partially handicapped, entitled to claim government subsistence. He felt the loss of the sight in one eye was a reasonable price to pay for ensuring his son's education, along with his own personal survival. What he didn't know is what that education will cost when the time comes. It is always possible that his partial blindness may buy nothing more than a pencil when the day arrives to pay for his son's education.

Many offers to sell organs with the promise of immediate delivery appeared in the classified columns of the Brazilian newspapers under the "medicine and health" columns. These offers were merely an extension of the long-standing controversy over the still generally legal practice of the poor selling their blood during this period of intractable inflation. About 75 per cent of the blood used in Brazilian hospitals has been supplied through commercial blood banks, usually located in the impoverished outskirts of the major cities. Regular blood donors tend to be the unemployed, sick and undernourished. In 1980 a documentary film was made on the blood trade. An incident was recreated involving an unemployed labourer, living in Rio, who died of anaemia after selling his blood repeatedly in order to feed his family. In spite of the film, the commercial blood banks in Brazil continued to do a booming trade. Some estimated the traffic at 2,500 gallons of blood a day.

In the surburban slum of Madureira, a blood bank called the Natal Blood Bank faced the railroad station, which is used by thousands of commuters to go to work each day. Another commercial blood bank stood where thousands more poor and starving embark to earn their daily bread. It was not uncommon for a large number of these working-class commuters to sell their blood to raise the money to pay for the train fare. . . the equivalent of 10 cents!

As an American sitting in your comfy condo (or a Brit watching your favourite American "soap"), you may harbour the illusion that Americans could never stoop to those levels. "If Uncle Sam is going to print money, he knows how to make it work," you may say. Oh, yeah!

Darline Vanderpool, living in California, was willing to sell one of her kidneys just to get the price of a square meal. After seven days with nothing to eat but a can of tomato soup, and no prospect of any money for at least another week, Mrs. Vanderpool attempted to sell one of her kidneys through a classified ad in the newspaper. "There are so many people without kidneys, I thought, surely, *I* could sell one," she explained. Mrs. Vanderpool's efforts failed. The newspaper refused to accept the ad, since California state law bars the sale of human organs from live donors. As inflation rampaged in America, there were large numbers of people selling their organs through the American newspapers before the law was passed.

Right now, governments around the world are faced with the same choice the German Government faced in the 1920s. Sovereign debt soars. Most of it will never be repaid. The biggest debtor of all, the US Federal Government.

The notion that the Federal Reserve can make everyone better off by intervening in money markets, bailing out lame duck companies and printing money to foster financial economic recovery is the same notion the German people were led to harbour before the nightmare inflation. Central Bank intervention in money markets has proven itself to be the most persuasive, dangerous, destructive and mischievous of all intentions; primarily because the irreparable damage that it causes doesn't reveal itself for quite some time. The Federal Reserve intervenes by buying paper assets in the same way as the Reichsbank bought Treasury bills. These paper assets are mostly newly printed government securities. The Government buys these paper assets by simply printing pieces of paper that you keep in your pocket in the form of Federal Reserve notes. Sounds familiar?

The Downwave has come. The message is, it's time to pay the piper! The mountain of debt that has been accumulated through the Upwave must now be repaid. It can be done in one of two ways. Payment can be made in worthless paper currency, debased and expanded by government. Or, it can be repaid through the liquidation of assets that have been accumulated but never earned. Given the horrendous level of current debt exposure, and the amount of money that will be needed to fund that debt, the first method will produce the kind of nightmare inflation experienced by Germany during the 1920s. The second will produce a 1930s type depression.

Stockton and Jarrow

Mention the word "depression" in connection with the 1920s and '30s, and the man-in-the-street in Britain will at once think of unemployment. It started soon enough at the end of the Great War; with Churchill, as Secretary of State for War, having to slow down the rate of demobilisation in January, 1919. But the boom that year made it possible to release 4 million men within the next 12 months. This meant that large numbers of women were pushed out of their jobs to make room for the returning "heroes". The same thing was to happen in Germany. It made many women bitter. Some became militant in later years. One small girl, who saw her mother and "aunt" treated in this way, became notorious. Her name was Ulrike Meinhof.

In 1919, there had been two major advances in technology. An RAF bomber flew the Atlantic, and Sir Ernest Rutherford described the first "artificial transmutation of matter". He had "split" the Atom. But the public's attention was largely taken up with jobs and strikes. There had been Police strikes in 1918 and 1919; and a sudden week-long railway strike in September, 1920. In the 1921 slump, the unemployed rose to more than 2,170,000. Fortunately, the Unemployment Insurance Acts of 1920-22 introduced "uncovenanted payments" — better known as "the dole". By 1924, unemployment was down from its peak. But it was still firmly fixed at over a million. There had been mass unemployment in pre-war days from time to time. It lasted until the market recovered. Now a new kind of unemployment was turning once prosperous towns into "depressed areas". They called it "structural unemployment."

There were two events in the latter part of 1986 which should have reminded us that there is nothing new in our current concern over unemployment, and the polarisation it brings. They were the death of Lord Stockton, the former Prime Minister Harold Macmillan; and the 50th anniversary of the Jarrow March.

When he first entered Parliament, Harold Macmillan was something of a radical. From the first, he followed the principles he had set out in his book *The Middle Way,* in 1938:

> "The fixing of a minimum standard of life must not be regarded as merely humanitarian. It is closely related to the whole question of economic stability. There is a clear relationship between the purchasing power in the hands of the people and the demand for consumers' goods and the level of employment among workers engaged in producing those goods."

J.K. Galbraith went further in his book *The Affluent Society*, focussing on the problem of a community which — like the rich uncle — already "had everything":

> "To have failed to solve the problem of producing goods would have been to continue man in his oldest and most grievous misfortune. But to fail to see that we have solved it and to fail to proceed thence to the next task would be fully as tragic."

The next task, said Galbraith, should be investment in "men" rather than "things." Easier to say than to achieve! Although a Tory and married to a Duke's daughter, Macmillan did not insist that "free enterprise" or a "property owning democracy" was the next inevitable step. On the contrary, he was prepared to adopt "the Socialist remedy" where private enterprise was shewn to have:

> ". . .exhausted its social usefulness, or where the general welfare of the economy required that certain basic industries and services need now to be conducted in the light of broader social considerations than the profit motive will supply."

Echoing Gladstone on the Railways! The second evocative occasion during 1986 was the 50th anniversary of the Jarrow March, reviving memories of a time when the profit motive had ceased to be enough to keep a town alive. Ellen Wilkinson ("Red" Ellen) summed up Jarrow's plight in a memorable passage in a Left Book Club publication entitled *The Town that was Murdered* (Gollancz, 1939):

> "Charles Palmer started Jarrow as a shipbuilding centre without considering the needs of the workers. They crowded into a small colliery village which was hurriedly extended to receive them."

As an enterprise, Palmer's town was a great success. Here the British armour-plate industry was started. Floating batteries were constructed for the Crimea. Iron ships, screw colliers and liners were all laid down in Palmer's Yard. Jarrow in its day was a triumph of planning. It was thanks to Charles Palmer, who was one of the first entrepreneurs to see the advantage of making a plant an integrated whole. He offered employment to the thousands of labourers, or "hands", who came pouring in from the North of England and from Ireland. Between 1851 and 1921, Jarrow's population increased tenfold to 35,000. However, the majority of workers lived in shocking conditions. Augustus Hare found a clergyman friend of his living:

> ". . .amidst a teeming population of blackened, foul-mouthed, drunken rogues, . . . in rows of dismal houses, . . . where every vestige of vegetation is killed by noxious chemical vapours. . . the furnesses (sic) vomitting forth volumes of blackened smoke."

The workers, wrote "Red" Ellen:

". . .paid with their lives for the absence of any preparation for the growth
of such a town. And in 1933 another group of capitalists decided the fate
of Jarrow. . ."

They were to do so without reference to the workers, whose plight was
that much worse because they had been "far-sighted". A number had invested
their savings to help keep Palmer's going. Some had put up as much as
£300. That, in 1933, was more than the national average wage. It was no
consolation to those who were *not* taken on by one of the demolition gangs,
to find that marsh birds could again be heard calling, as they swooped down
on to the Slake; or that the sky was clear again for virtually the first time
in eighty years.

In 1935, Stanley Baldwin became Prime Minister, and "Red" Ellen took
her seat as member for Jarrow on the benches opposite. Ellen was a fighter.
She led a group of young men and women 15 miles, one stormy day, to
see (and hopefully to win the support of) Ramsay MacDonald, then visiting
his constituency. MacDonald's only response was to ask Ellen why she didn't
"go out and preach Socialism, which is the only remedy for all this?"

In despair, but with great courage, the Jarrow workers decided to march
to London and confront Parliament — just as they had confronted Ramsay
MacDonald. On the first Monday in October, 1936, three hundred marchers
set off on the 300 miles to London. But Jarrow's men and women were
far too proud to set off, as countless others had done, on a "Hunger March".
Their march was to be a Crusade, led by David Riley, a Jarrow Councillor,
who had first thought of the idea. Striding forth in his bowler hat, he stood
out from the rest in their "trilbys", cloth caps and scarves.

On November 1st, in the midst of a cloud-burst, the marching column
reached London. In retrospect the Crusade, which appeared to achieve
nothing at the time, acquired a symbolic importance. For many, Jarrow
became a milestone on Labour's line of march. Like the Tolpuddle Martyrs,
they were not begging for a job and a crust. They were demanding their
rights. The Crusade also shewed up an unexpected split between the higher
ranks of the clergy. They tended above all to be members of the establishment.
Dr. Gordon, Bishop of Jarrow was believed at first to have given the Crusade
his blessing: a fact which drove the Bishop of Durham into a fury. But later,
even the kindly Dr. Gordon was to turn his coat, declaring that he had not
given the *march* his support. He had merely prayed for God's blessing on
the men and women who *took part* in the march. This time it was the
Archdeacon of Northumberland's turn to become angry with Jarrow's Bishop.
The Archdeacon, more to the point, issued a restatement of the aims of
the march. It was published by *The Times*.

Later it turned out that the Jarrow Crusaders had been unlucky with their
timing. Had they moved off a few weeks earlier, political attitudes would
not have hardened while they were on the march. But the marchers were

approaching London when the Government decided to discourage all such demonstrations. On October 22nd, when the Jarrow marchers had been on the road for two-and-a-half weeks, more than a thousand Blackshirts had marched into Bethnal Green, headed by a drum and fife band, escorted by mounted police and constables on foot.

Up to that time, the authorities had been extremely patient. Some said *too* patient. As long ago as June '34, a mass meeting at Olympia had led to such brutal handling of the opposition that Parliament and the country were deeply shocked. As a result, the Incitement to Disaffection Act had been passed. But it was not until 1936 that the Public Order Act became law. This extended police powers, banned the wearing of political uniforms, and limited the holding of "provocative" processions.

Inevitably the Act was seen as a blow to personal freedom and political expression. But the Government had no choice. As Ronald Blythe wrote in his book, *The Age of Illusion*, the conduct of the Blackshirts' had brought:

> ". . .the strongest objections from borough councillors and priests, whose streets and parishes were submitted to disgusting scenes of violence and Jew-baiting. . . During this year, too, there took place the first British march against the Dictators, when scores of idealistic young men volunteered for the International Brigade in Spain. . ."

The past sixteen years had been far from peaceful — at home or abroad. When the first march of the unemployed took place in October 1920, memories of the October Revolution in Russia were still fresh in the minds of both sides. The demonstration had been broken up by the police with great violence; and establishment figures like the then Bishop of Durham found it necessary to warn the nation that England had ceased to be a consititutional monarchy, and was taking its first steps towards "the dictatorship of the proletariat". It is only surprising that for so many years the unemployed confined their activities to marches and demonstrations; are were not seduced, or provoked, into violent protest — or in the worst areas — to open revolt. Even the General Strike of 1926 had been a comparatively tame affair. Nevertheless, the marches and demonstrations represented a form of social protest which clerics like Durham regarded as a form of organised mob pressure. He warned:

> "If generally adopted. . . it may bring us before the winter is out into grave public confusion and danger. . ."

When "Red" Ellen and the Jarrow marchers reached Charing Cross, the big moment was at hand — the presentation of their petition to the Prime Minister in the House of Commons. "Red" Ellen spoke. Then Stanley Baldwin made a brief, factual reply to her question as to how many letters and resolutions he had received from individuals, public bodies and corporations. The Premier then passed the matter on to the President of the Board of Trade, Walter Runciman. At that point, writes Ronald Blythe:

> ". . .the amazed marchers listened while (Runciman) solemnly told the House that the unemployment position in Jarrow, while still far from satisfactory, had improved in recent months. . . When a Welsh member asked the Prime Minister whether it was in the public interest that a private company should be free to barter away the livelihood of the whole population of a district like this, Baldwin refused to answer."

Disappointed, the marchers returned to Jarrow. There they found the Unemployment Assistance Board were deducting between four and eleven shillings from their allowances, since they could not have been "available for work" while they were on the road.

The cruel irony of the situation was that Baldwin was one of the few front benchers who genuinely sympathised with the jobless. It was Baldwin who had looked around the Commons after the "Coupon Election", which followed close on the heels of the signing of the Armistice. There, on the benches, he had seen "a lot of hard-faced men who look as if they have done very well out of the war". His biographer wrote later how upset Baldwin had been by unemployment, which in the period 1920-38 remained at around 14.2 per cent. Unemployment had always meant waste in terms of manpower; even between 1884 and 1914, when the mean rate was around 6 per cent. The "structural unemployment" of the 1920s was not a kind which would go away with a revival of trade. Therefore the Government could not be blamed for the fact that it persisted in areas like Tyne and Tees and the Welsh valleys, when they — and the people — had become outmoded and redundant.

Government came under criticism, nevertheless, for its lack of positive regional policy. For in 1936 the authorities were still refusing to site the new factories, called for by the rearmament programme in depressed areas like Wales and the North. Instead, factory workers were brought into the South-East, where industry was already flourishing as never before. In Middlesex, unemployment was as low as 4.3%. In Glamorganshire, it was in the region of 33.4%. For a time it looked as though rearmament would cure unemployment at long last; especially as some of the factories in the depressed areas came alive once more. But even here, the looked-for improvement was short-lived. By 1938, the year of the Munich crisis, unemployment suddenly returned. Had it not been for the outbreak of war, historian David Thomson believed that depression might have set in once more. As in the 1980s, the level of unemployment in the 1930s, and the depth of poverty in the depressed areas, served only to widen the gap between the two nations. They made the people of the old industrial areas feel they were a different species. In his *Pelican History of England (No 9, England in the 20th Century)* David Thomson writes:

> "It continued to be the old industrial north and the great nineteenth-century industries of coal, iron, shipbuilding, and textiles that suffered most. The

south, especially the busy Home Counties of housing estates and streets of surburban villas, was the home of twentieth-century England. . . The 'condition of England question', as the nineteenth century called it, returned as the foremost social concern."

Even here appearances were deceptive. Certainly there was prosperity in the South. But it was patchy. What's more the unemployment and distress to be found there was mostly disregarded by politicians, voluntary workers, the churches and the media alike. Sermon after sermon was preached on the slums of Birmingham and Walsall. None were preached on the slums of Brighton or the Wessex towns. It was understandable, since the impact of mass unemployment fell mainly on the industrial "working-class". Unions may have felt largely impotent in the industrial towns, but they still had a voice which they did not hesitate to raise. After all, they could lose nothing by calling attention to plight of their members. But in the South, the unemployed office workers, like the educated middle-class, were more reticent. They might not "have much". But they *did* have their pride. Besides, no potential employer would be prepared to take on a book-keeper, salesman or manager who had shewn he was capable of "making a scene".

There was considerable reaction to books like George Orwell's provocative study, *The Road to Wigan Pier,* Walter Greenwood's novel, *Love on the Dole* and J.B. Priestley's semi-documentary, *English Journey.* They all served to widen the intellectual gap between North and South, and helped to push public opinion a little further to the Left. As one Sheffield councillor complained at the time:

> "All those plays they keep putting on at The Playhouse. . . Priestley and the like, what *they* do is simply to make the average Sheffielder think that "poor" is synonymous with "good", and that you call a man's reputation into question if you dare to refer to him as "prosperous".

Not only did the Depressed Areas move weeklies like *New Statesman and Nation* to sympathise with the people and their plight. Depressed Areas also made good copy — especially if based on the kind of "fact" which many seemed to think had been discovered for the very first time by *Mass Observation.* In the *Penguin Special, Britain (1939),* M.O's "study of everyday behaviour in Britain" took the form of a collection of essays on topics ranging from Armistice Day and Astrology to All-in Wrestling. The one thing they had in common was that they all pointed very firmly towards the Left. M.O. was an immensely powerful influence too on many who would have been horrified to be considered "Left". They would maintain that Mass Observation had opened their eyes, and they were merely reacting as any decent Christian should.

As the North/South gap took hold of the imagination, so did the idea that only the Left "cared", a view which a flood of Left Book Club publications, the *Left Review* and even *Picture Post* sought to reinforce. Unfortunately, it was the kind of over-simplification which invariably exacts its price. Over this issue, they made many middle-class, lower-middle class, and working-class readers in the South feel extremely uncomfortable. They sought refuge in trying to be "realistic" and "fair", but positively refused to have the wool pulled over their eyes by a load of Left-wing propaganda. After that they could dismiss all these disturbing reports as "like those atrocity stories" during the 1914-18 War. The more things appear to change, the more they stay the same!

In any case, the South — and especially the South Coast — had its own unemployment problem. A great deal of the work was seasonal, with a limited amount of longshore jobs or light industry. The unemployed comprised a mixture of catering and leisure trade workers, office and other white collar staff, and younger members of the educated middle-classes, unable to find a "suitable opening". The middle-class jobless were reasonably inconspicuous in their blazers and sports-jackets, grey flannel "bags" and "plus-fours". Although this was as much a uniform as the industrial worker's shiny black suit, neckerchief and flat cap. But middle-class "casualties" were reluctant to sign on the dole. They did their best to remain "independent". Like countless young ex-officers in the early 1920s, they sank their savings into various — usually unsuccessful — enterprises. Many sold eggs or brushes, insurance or encyclopaedias door-to-door. In the end, they were prepared to take "any job". This could mean collecting money for the deckchairs, or keeping an eye on the slot-machines at the end of the pier.

Class Attitudes

It is worth recalling the Hudson Institute's study of Britain in the 1980s. After exhaustive research into Britain's history, and contemporary condition, the Institute concluded that the primary problem in the United Kingdom, and the reason for its lack of progress, were a product of the indigenous class system. Their report sent a shock wave through the political and economic establishment of the day. Published in 1972, it was greeted with derision or simply ignored. Even if there was an *element* of truth in the Institute's conclusions, it was felt in many quarters to be "disloyal" to risk "talking the economy down" by even *referring* to the study.

To some readers, it will seem strange to bother with "class" at all these days. It is fashionable to say, "There is no longer a distinct 'working-class' in Britain, or the United States, today." Either, you will be told, we are becoming a "classless" society, or — except for down-and-outs and aristocrats — we already belong to the same, broad middle-class. However, it would be difficult to find a market researcher or public opinion pollster. . . or an investment advisor. . . to agree with that! Even if either assertion were true, what matters more than the class *we* claim to belong to is the class from which the previous generations came. Because each newcomer brings along some of the beliefs and predispositions that his (or her) forebears once cherished. Therefore, to attempt to understand our past (so that we may have more success in coping with it in the future) we must take account of class history, and family history too, for that matter. Often, too, when we look into the matter, we find that family and class issues are too closely intertwined for the one to be considered without the other.

There is another reason why we should not pay less attention to oral history than to the printed word. Books contain facts which can be accepted or rejected at will. The text will stand unchanged, whatever our reaction or our mood at the time. Whereas our story-teller will react, and respond to our mood. Our questions, or even our open disbelief, will awaken memories that have scarcely stirred for a dozen years. Yet it is customary to attach greater weight to written history, or statistics, than to oral testimony. The first may be regarded as "authoritative"; the latter tends to be dismissed as merely "anecdotal".

This is taking too simplistic a view. It is advisable, first of all, to be certain what we are reading. If it is a treatise or thesis intended to impress, then be impressed. Or not! But do not leave it around for the more vulnerable members of the household. If it is the plain setting down of a man or woman's recollections, aspirations and beliefs, then very different criteria should be applied. Take a book that was once pronounced "seminal", and treated with the reverence usually reserved for a new cult. I mean Richard Hoggart's analysis of "the assumptions, attitudes and morals of working class people in Northern England and the way in which (the media) are likely to influence them." Packaged under the title, *The Uses of Literacy,* it was first published in 1957:

In the very first sentence of the first chapter, he demolishes the idea that there were (in 1957):

> "no working classes in England now, that a 'bloodless revolution' has taken place which has so reduced social differences that already most of us inhabit an almost flat plain, the plain of the lower- to middle middle class."

It is striking the way he enables his readers to find their own place in the developing story of the late 19th, and early 20th century, by the simple process of identification with the members of his family:

> "My grandmother married a cousin and at that time their family was still rural, living in a village about a dozen miles from Leeds. . . Some time in the 'seventies she and her young husband were drawn to that expanding city, into the service of the steelworks. . . All over the North and Midlands the same thing was happening, the villages losing their young people. . ."

What was happening elsewhere about that time? In France, a major strike swept the textile and metal-working plants in Alsace in July 1870, with some 20,000 workers out in the vicinity of Mulhouse. In some towns, strikers kept the non-strikers out by force. Troops were called, and 70 arrests were made. Mining strikes around the same time were far more violent. The previous June, at St Etienne, 15,000 miners had struck. The troops killed 13 and wounded another nine in what was to be called "the massacre of La Ricamarie". At Aubin, later the same year, troops shot 30 to 40 strikers attempting to break into a metalworking plant. They killed 14 on the spot. After the Paris Commune in 1871, strikes grew in amplitude and frequency. Elsewhere in Europe, the deep political division between North and South in Italy complicated the situation. But the transition to modern forms of violence appeared in the North around the time of unification. Later, in Milan's *faggi di Maggio*, at least two police and 80 demonstrators were killed. In the South, food riots and tax rebellions continued until the turn of the century.

In the United States, where the frontier was still advancing westwards, the Civil War marked a watershed in violence. Before the War, the most prevalent types of crime had been horse theft and counterfeiting private banknotes. After the Civil War, there were train robberies started by the Reno Brothers of Indiana, and bank robberies by the James-Younger gang of Missouri. The era between the Civil War and World War I produced the family blood feud — notably the Southern mountain feud in Kentucky, West Virginia and Virginia. Between the 1860s and '70s, urban violence died away — except for Civil War draft riots.

By the 1870s, when Richard Hoggart's grandparents were settling down in "the vast new brick acres of Hunslet", the US labour movement had lived through a century of sporadic violence. Though there had been no organisation of labourers as such in the port cities of the colonial period, sailors, longshoremen and other members of the maritime industry rioted from time to time. Then, with the mushrooming of industry generally after the Civil War, the labour organisations mirrored industry's growth, throwing up such powerful bodies as the Knights of Labour, American Railway Union, American Federation of Labour, Western Federation of Miners and the Industrial Workers of the World. In 1877, a nationwide railway strike began along the Baltimore Ohio Railroad, and spread to the Far West. The strike came close to open insurrection, when riots "blistered" Baltimore, and left great stretches of Pittsburgh in smoking ruins.

The ten-year old "Molly Maguires" troubles came to a climax in the hard coal fields of Eastern Pennsylvania. The "Molly Maguires" were a secret band of Irish miners who literally fought their employers. A series of riots and mayhem culminated in the dynamiting of the *Los Angeles Times* building forty years later! Shortly afterwards, Colorado's "Thirty-Year's War" climaxed in 38 skirmishes in which 18 persons were killed.

The work ethic — indeed the "life" ethic — were both very different in the two English speaking nations. That was partly because the early colonists had taken a number of important beliefs and rights with them from Britain. For example, in 1780, at the time of the anti-Catholic riots, the French historian Elie Halevy pointed out that it was still valid to claim that:

"A government without a police force was powerless either to prevent these (current) outrages or repress them promptly. The right to riot or, as it was termed by the lawyers "'the right of resistance" was an integral part of the national traditions."

In J.W. Ward's collection of *Letters to Fry*, one passage, dated December 1811, makes clear the kind of "police" the French employed:

"They have an admirable police in Paris, but they pay for it dear enough. I had rather half-a-dozen people's throats should be cut in Ratcliffe Highway every three or four years than be subject to domiciliary visits, spies and all the rest of Fouché's conspiracies."

In Britain, there was always a fear that the new police, which Sir Robert Peel introduced in 1829, would end up as an instrument of state — or Party — as did Captain Ernst Roehm's *S.A.* or *Brownshirts*. Although there were some clashes between the police and strikers, there was nothing like the violence experienced in the United States. Philip Taft and Philip Rose, of Brown University and State University of New York, at Buffalo have claimed that the United States had the bloodiest and most violent labour history of any industrialised country. They were contributing to *The History of Violence in America*, a report prepared for the National Commission on the Causes and Prevention of Violence, set up in June 1968, while the nation was still mourning the assassination of Senator Robert Kennedy:

"The precipitating causes have been attempts by pickets and sympathisers to prevent a plant on strike from being reopened by strikebreakers, or attempts of company guards, police, or even by National Guardsmen to prevent such interference. . . No major labour in American history ever advocated violence as a policy, even though the labour organisations recognised that it might be a fact of industrial life."

One exacerbating factor was (as a Report to the Second Session of the 50th Congress shews), the use of special "police":

"In Pennsylvania, every railroad in 1865 and every colliery, iron furnace, or rolling mill in 1866 was granted by statute liberty to employ as many policemen as it saw fit. . . armed with such weapons as the corporation determined — usually revolvers, sometimes Winchester rifles or both — and they were commissioned by the governor."

The report related to labour conditions in the anthracite regions in 1887-88. In other States, "sheriffs and other local officials were authorised to appoint persons paid by the employer for strike and police duty." (Taft and Rose) Unbelievable as it may seem today, the coal and iron police continued to be commissioned until 1931, when the Pennsylvania mining companies were allowed to utilise police under their own control in labour disputes. Nor was it in the *heavy* industries alone that violence broke out. In New York, in 1909-10, the International Ladies' Garment Workers' Union was involved in two strikes. More than 750 pickets were arrested; nineteen ended up with jail terms in the workhouse. Wrote Taft and Rose:

> "The pickets, on the other hand, complained that they were victims of repeated assaults by the police and hired sluggers. . . The union charges were supported by a number of social workers. . . The settlement of the strike was followed by a cloak-makers' walkout, involving more than 50,000 workers. . . The employers engaged dozens of private guards, the union. . . (hired) its own strong-arm men. During one encounter a private detective engaged by one of the employers was killed. . . several union members were tried for the offense but were acquitted."

Because American society is far more open and transparent than British society, the public and the media tend to focus on the more sensational aspects of American life. But life in the first half of the 19th century Britain had been hard enough in the new industrial towns. It was fortunate for Hoggart's forebears that they did not leave their village until the 1870s. By this time urban life was improving fast. J.L. and Barbara Hammond are renowned for their study of life at the beginning of the last century — or as they called it (and their book), *The Bleak Age*. They quote Wordsworth, who had a strong practical streak, and observed that the invention of the steam engine had "saved the countryside". The "mills could now be built in the ugly towns instead of spoiling the streams and valleys."

One trouble was the speed at which the new towns grew. Take the census figures for 1801, 1831 and 1851.

000's	1801	1831	1851
Manchester and Salford	90	237	400
Bolton	18	42	61
Blackburn	12	27	65
Bradford	13	44	104
Halifax	12	22	34
Leeds	53	123	172
Oldham	22	51	72
Sheffield	46	92	135

The flood of Irish immigrants to Boston is part of American history. But the flood of Irish to the new towns of England is less well known. Few realise either that 150 years ago, as the Hammonds pointed out:

> "It was easier to reach Lancashire and Yorkshire from Ireland than from Norfolk or Dorset. . . The Labourers sent to Lancashire by the Poor Law authorities were taken to London, put on a boat of Pickford's at the Paddington Basin of the Grand Junction Canal, and carried to Manchester in four or five days at the cost of fourteen shillings. But an Irishman could cross to Liverpool for half a crown in fourteen hours. . ."

And the Hammonds added:

"The Fleming woollen weavers, the Huguenot silk weavers, the German tailors, brought to England. . . a special skill. "But (said Sir George Cornewall Lewis) the Irish emigration into Britain. . . (spread) themselves as a kind of substratum beneath a more civilised community."

In 1841, the Irish comprised one tenth of the population of Manchester and a seventh of the population of Liverpool. In the ten years following the potato famine of the 1840s, half a million Irish were to arrive in Britain. Add the Jews fleeing from Tsarist domination and other refugees from oppression; and, by 1900, the newcomers were flooding into the urban conurbations where they could find work.

Beginning in the late 1800s, there was more rapid mobility between classes, with increasingly higher living standards. Witness the progress in this of the Hoggart family:

"(Grandmother) was a first-generation townswoman. . . Meanwhile a second generation was growing up. . . from the time of the Third Reform Act, through the series of Education Acts, the various Housing Acts, the Factory Acts and Public Health Acts. The boys went to 'Board' (free primary) school and so into steelworks. . . or into the more genteel openings, as grocery assistants or salesmen. . . this was regarded as almost a step-up in class. . . The second generation had fewer children, and. . . were glad that 'the lad's chances in life' had improved, but began to worry whether he would get his scholarship. . ."

Richard Hoggart wrote that in the mid-1950s. Since then another generation — that of his children — has grown up, and gone on 'improving' their 'chances in life'. Suddenly the escalator has stopped. The *Social Trends* report published in January 1987 shewed the gap between rich and poor growing wider once again. Professor A.H. Halsey, Director of the Department of Social and Administrative Studies at Oxford University, suggested that the 30-year-old post-war period for Britain and other industrial countries ended in 1973-74 with the first oil crisis. Nevertheless, upward *social mobility* was not checked. More than 60% of younger people had been limited to the same jobs as their working-class parents. By 1983, the proportion had fallen to just over half. Now, said Professor Halsey, "this picture of continuing advancement has to be modified by considering unemployment."

Although Professor Halsey did not use the shorthand expression "the North/South divide", he did point to the changes within the regions, not dissimilar from those of the late 1930s. There had been a further shift away from the areas associated with 19th century industrial manufacturing. This in turn had produced rising unemployment in the inner city, with a move towards the suburbs, the New Towns and the South-East. On the face of it, there had been one striking improvement. Between 1982-4, redundancy had affected one employee in 65. By 1985 it had fallen to 1 in 90. Against that, in 1979 those out of work for more than a year represented 25% of the jobless. By July 1986, they accounted for 41% of all benefit claimants. In the process, Professor Halsey went on:

". . .a pattern has emerged of a more unequal society as between a majority in secure attachment to a still prosperous country and a minority in marginal economic and social conditions — the former moving into the suburban locations of the newer economy of a 'green and pleasant land', the latter tending to be trapped into the old provincial industrial cities and their displaced fragments of peripheral council housing estates."

The Census of Employment showed that between 1979 and 1986, 415,000 jobs had been lost in the North-West. Although job losses in some other areas, which included Yorkshire and Humberside, were smaller than originally thought, Yorkshire and Humberside still came second after the West Midlands which came next with 234,000. Even the fortunate South-East lost 131,000. Between May 1979 and November 1986, there was, in fact, a 224% increase in the unemployed in the South-East, including the area of the former Greater London Council. Within the GLC area, the increase was even higher, at 242%, with a total of 359,000 jobless — as then defined. This was 40,000 more than the count for the remainder of the South-East.

Even taking the self-employed into account, the job losses in the North-West remained double those elsewhere. As though underlining afresh the Hudson Institute's forecast for Britain in the '80s, job losses in engineering, metals and cars continued to climb. Between September 1981 and September '84, 429,000 jobs vanished. That was 160,000 more than previously estimated. Moreover a venture capital survey in 1986 shewed that as little as 5.1% of funds invested were going to the North, North-West, Yorkshire and Humberside. Whereas no less than 63.5% was finding its way into companies in Greater London and the South-East. David Trippier, Minister for Small Firms called it a disgrace, especially as barely 1% of the UK's multi-billion pound pension (and insurance) companies were prepared to back small, growing companies not quoted on the Stock Exchange. With most supporters of the Small Business movement admitting a failure rate of 1 in 3, it is understandable why those responsible for the savings of others did not rush to invest in what Mr Trippier glowingly described as "young companies which will grow to become the employers and wealth creators of the future."

Overall, in the period of the first two Thatcher administrations, at least 1,026,000 jobs vanished in engineering, metals and cars. This represented more than half the loss to manufacturing as a whole. The cutbacks in their turn brought a fall in the numbers employed in catering, distribution, hotels and repairs. But job growth in services, including the financial services sector, took up much of the slack. Between 1979 and '86, 559,000 new jobs were created in banking, finance and insurance.

At the beginning of 1987, the City, like just about everyone else, began to talk about "political risk", whether before the approaching General Election or afterwards. They increasingly hedged their bets, and qualified their forecasts. At the same time, highly vocal, key Ministers, like Lord Young (Secretary for Employment), began uttering more frequently than ever. The media also began carrying more information gleaned mysteriously from various "private" meetings. One which attracted considerable attention was a meeting at which Kenneth Clarke, Lord Young's deputy, was less than enthusiastic over the idea of putting more limitations on social security benefits. Lord Young's committee on employment policy (according to the *Independent* 9.2.87) maintained that the "existing array of schemes" for job creation, expanded in January '87, "were tackling the unemployment problem". Mr Clarke was on record as saying, in response to back-bench hardliners, "We are not proposing to change the rules of entitlement to benefit, nor that the refusal to take part in the scheme should, in itself disqualify anyone from benefit." However, claimed the *Independent*, "ways of reducing benefit are being studied."

Always a believer in the right *word*, at the right time, Mrs Thatcher was also said by the *Independent* to have:

> "agreed in principle to the Department of Employment being given a revised role as the Department of Enterprise after the general election in a wide review of possible Whitehall reforms."

The rumours — as so often — proved to be true the moment you looked into them more closely. Disposable incomes, according to the *Social Trends* report, rose by 229% between 1975 and '85. Allowing for inflation, this represented a real increase of 24%. But the income of the bottom two-fifths fell from 10% to 6% of the total. That of the top 20% rose from 44% to 49%, before taxes and benefits reduced the gap. Home ownership trebled from just over 4 million in 1951 to almost 14 million in 1985. But homelessness also escalated. According to the *Social Trends* report, homeless households in '85 totalled 109,000, against 97,000 the previous year. Some sources were claiming an even higher figure by the first weeks of 1987.

Writing in the *Lombard* column of the *Financial Times*, on January 29th,1987, Joe Rogaly summed up the position as he saw it. Most of us in the UK were better off beyond any doubt; real household disposable incomes rose by 11% per head between 1980 and 1985:

> ". . .the penetration of the washing machine exceeds 80%, as do the telephone and, naturally, the colour TV. Just on a third of households have a video recorder. . . Only the dishwasher is spurned. . ."

But the fact remained:

> ". . .too many people are travelling in the opposite direction, on the downwards escalator. . . We. . . know where most of the deprived people are: in the inner cities, and some of the council estates. But there are too many of us, and we are too drunk on the sweet nectar of acquisition to take much notice."

Handsworth and Brixton are parts of the inner city. Broadwater Farm was one of those "council estates". Professor C.H. Carstairs, then Professor of psychological medicine at Edinburgh, set out *his* "alternative scenario" in the Report on Violence called for by President Johnson as long ago as 1969, after the death of Robert Kennedy. The Professor ended with this warning:

"Unless the masses of our city poor can be persuaded that there is a future for them too. . . their morale is likely to crumble until vast human communities degenerate into the semblance of concentration camp inmates, if not even Zuckerman's pathologically belligerent apes."

The Choice before us. . . Policy or Politics

We have recalled how hyper-inflation destroyed the German middle-classes in the 1920s, plunging the country into mass unemployment and depression. We saw the price of that. We have seen the consequences of hyper-inflation elsewhere too. Nevertheless, most people would probably still opt for inflation. Because, as I've already said, they fear deflation and depression more. That is due partly to the widespread nature of the Great Depression of the 1920s and '30s, which was felt so intensely throughout Britain and the United States. It is also because the history of the *hungry years* has become a folk legend, whereas inflation — be it in Germany, Argentina, Brazil or elsewhere — concerned other people. It happened "over there", not "here at home". Therefore it is difficult to make people grasp that the consequences of inflation are far more horrifying than those of depression. Not to mention the fact that it is possible to recover from depression without immediately running into inflation again. But hyper-inflation is bound, sooner or later, to plunge the economy into deep depression. So, given a minimum of common sense, it should be clear which alternative is the more cataclysmic.

When I wrote *The Downwave* in 1983, it was my conclusion that the forces of deflation and depression were building. Fortunately, those forces have continued to build! I say, "fortunately", because experience shews that if governments had succeeded in deflecting the forces of deflation, we would possibly be facing the kind of scenario for disaster that overtook the Germans during the Weimar Republic. I believe that the forces of deflation are likely to go on building in the period ahead. There is one thing, however, I should make clear. Many people who read *The Downwave* believed that what I had outlined was a neat, tight programme for the next six months or so. That was not my message. So why did they choose to read it that way?

Unfortunately, many people with good sight, lack foresight. Theirs is not a problem of poor sight so much as faulty perception. This is particularly so when they are forced to recognise that they stand face to face with depression. We have seen many signs that all is not well today: signs which Joe Granville described so well in his book, *The Warning*, published in 1985. Taking up the point I made two years earlier in *The Downwave*,

Granville noted that during the Upwave, most crimes are against people, but:

> "As the downwave develops, there is a shift to crime against property — fraud, embezzlement, arson, etc. Current crime figures shewed that this was happening (in 1985). . .

I made clear in an earlier chapter that the world is NOT suddenly going to wake up one morning, pull back the curtains and exclaim, "Shit! We're in depression." It doesn't happen that way. A depression begins in the smokestack industries — as the Hudson Institute pointed out in 1972. It hits the highly capitalised industries first. Then it spreads to the secondary, supportive industries. Depression spreads on both an economic and a regional basis. Ultimately, debt and an all-enveloping depression become ostentatiously obvious. That, as a rule, is only after 5 years or so of gradual erosion as the forces of destruction work their way through the economy. That's how it happened in the 1930s. That is how it will always happen.

Now, as then, there will be pockets of prosperity within the global economy. These we shall watch, almost totally disregarding the pockets of weakness. That is to say — unless we are unfortunate enough to be personally involved. People have said often enough in the past that "These things can't happen today — we know too much. Communications are too good. Thanks to advancing information technology there are no secrets. Nothing can just 'creep up on us.'" Unfortunately, we are not inclined to accept evidence which tells us something we do not wish to hear. In 1941, Stalin ignored the warnings he was given that the Germans were about to invade Russia. He was behaving then in the same way that so many of us *always* will.

Today many people pin their hopes on regular Summit meetings, on regional groupings, on powerful national "tie-ups" like the Group of Five, which began its struggle with the twin problems of the US dollar and the US deficit back in the autumn of 1985. "With international co-operation of that kind," say the herd, "we're *bound* to get *somewhere*." Their aim, they tell themselves, should be to engineer prosperity for us. Beneath the billowing rhetoric lies a hard, unchanging bed of fact. It is a fact that deep differences continue to divide the nations, for all their smiles and protestations. Yet they are determined to cling so tightly together that we are driven to wonder whether they are trying to rise together, or making certain that when *they* sink, the rest sink too!

Essentially, we have what we always have had at times like this — a balloon which is being inflated in a darkened room. No one actually knows how much air the balloon will take, not even after October 1987. There are no printed specifications to tell us how far the economy will take the strain. We only know one thing: that eventually it will be stretched beyond capacity. Then the balloon will burst — the economy will collapse — perhaps next week, or in five years time. But, if we all keep blowing. . . because we don't know how to stop. . . the bursting of that balloon is what will blow us right off course. That's no prediction — it's a cast iron guarantee.

In the event, it may leave us with depression or hyper-inflation. It's bound to be one or the other. If we are lucky, it will be depression. The alternative scenario is unthinkable. Nevertheless, as we saw in the 1920s and '30s, there will always be those who are able to adapt their ideas in time, and go on calmly managing their affairs. . . while the vast majority merely moan, as they sink deeper and deeper into the morass. Those who *can* act, and push ahead are the ones — the *only* ones — to translate the inescapable into opportunity.

That — as we consider our strategy for the immediate future — should be our aim: to join the ranks of those who, like the Chinese centuries ago, learned to equate risk with opportunity. We should waste no time in seizing it.

Sadly, that is not what appears to have happened. Britain, in my view, has gone a good way down the high inflation route since I wrote *The Downave*. Then it looked as though the authorities were at least getting the measure of the global forces of deflation gathering at that time. The hope for the UK was that those forces would be strong enough to neutralise the inflationary side-effects of any monetary counter-moves the Government might be driven to make; driven by its rigid ideology and political needs. It is plain that Westminster and Whitehall have been studiously following the same hyper-inflationary route which was taken by Germany in the 1920s; exposing Britain, as they did so, to the alarming risk of inviting similar consequences. Or have the invitations already gone out?

What if the worst does happen? Suppose — for reasons we cannot even guess at — that the whole, or even part of Western Europe fails the test, landing us in political disorder and social chaos. What then? One thing is certain. Sooner or later *some* sort of saviour will emerge, and a sigh of relief will go up across the continent. But before settling down with our colouring books and crayons, we might recall the words of a former *national hero*, who successfully defeated the Communists, built a network of magnificent highways and rescued his fellow citizens from crippling unemployment:

> "That is the miracle of our age (cried Adolf Hitler), that you have found me, that you have found me among so many millions! And that I have found you, that is Germany's good fortune."

Chapter Ten

YOU AND THE GULAG ANGLO-PEDIGREE

A world of unseen dictatorship is conceivable, still using the forms of democratic government.
Kenneth Boulding, University of Michigan
(Quoted in *The Hidden Persuaders* by Vance Packard)

Already I can hear the screams of protest, trapped inside quite a few skulls: *Unseen dictatorship? Using forms of democratic government?* "That's pretty snide," they're saying. "Besides, that Vance Packard guy was a rabble rouser. In any case, do you have to go back all of 30 years?"

The answer to the mini-tirade is, "Yes. . . but we're going to have to go back far longer than 30 years to get things in perspective." We're going to have to go back to the beginnings of what we know as government because, from earliest times, we've known that the essence of government has been (and still is) coercion. One of the tools governments will often turn to these days is deception. It's not, let me hasten to say, because they are particularly mean. It's just that they have got into a hole they can't climb out of — not without losing face. To make matters worse, they cannot arrest you, starve you, beat you, torture you and (when all else fails) hang, draw and quarter you. The law doesn't allow it. But no law says they're not allowed to put you under a great deal of pressure.

That happens regularly when someone who ought to know better steps out of line and challenges either the establishment itself, or the thought-mode it has so successfully imposed on "thinking people". Take our old friend the "conspiracy theory". At its shrillest and most absurd, it sees fascism — nowadays classified as a form of political perversion — behind every Red under every bed. Some con-theorists have reached the point when they accuse the guy in the bed of having put them there.

Paranoia, it may well be! But the tale of intrigue, bungling and duplicity over the arms for Iran affair amounts to nothing less than conspiracy. It is one which puts the sexual antics of John F. and Robert Kennedy into the same category as a few mild pranks at the annual choir outing. Already not a few people are beginning to wonder whether after Irangate (to say nothing of the shenanigans involving the Vatican bank), apologies to Richard Nixon might not be in order.

That said, we are left with the basic facts. And now we've gotten hold of them, let's proceed.

I am not suggesting that all this means that we have to resent, or oppose government. We may have our reasons for so doing, but — in the main — we should be prepared (and probably are) to accept that we owe a duty to the state, or to government, in return for its role as adjudicator in disputes. Otherwise we would be left on our own to fight — perhaps literally — for our rights. The state also protects our property from our fellow man who, without the long shadow of the law, could well get wrong ideas! Finally, but by no means least, we hope the state will be willing (and able) to protect us from foreign threat. Be it an attempt to violate our territory, employ unfair trade practices, exert excessive economic pressure or threaten our health and way of life, by poisoning, or wilfully destroying our environment.

"So what!", the persistent heckler will cry. "Where's this 'world of unseen dictatorship' to be found?" One address, I can give you right away. It's No. 10 Downing Street, where you find the Prime Minister and the Cabinet (when they happen to turn up). That's according to the Constitution. You will also find what can only be described as a "private circus". It's rather like the nest of advisors which Prime Minister Harold Wilson introduced when *he* was in office. That, incidentally, is something you will *not* find in the Constitution. But they're there all right. At this point I hear a small, persistent voice asking:

> "How can you talk about an unseen dictatorship and such like? What about the sale of Council houses. . . which has transformed Mr and Mrs Featherbed into fine, outgoing, upstanding members of the mortgage-paying democracy? And what about the Grabbit family? They were smart enough to see when we offered them shares in the nationalised concerns (to almost all of which we had contributed a great deal from our taxes), that it was because some of us genuinely wanted them to become members of that other Tory fan club, the shareholding democracy. Even if they did take their tiny profit with indecent haste."

Since we have gone through all that in earlier chapters, there is no need to do more than nod politely and pass on. But what if they ask, "Do you *honestly* believe the rule of Thatcher is turning into a form of dictatorship?" They are entitled to an answer. And they'll get one in due course, because first, we have to look back quite a way so we can see where we are actually going, and how far we have changed direction. Looking back is important, because if you don't know where you've come from, you can't really tell where you're going, or whether you're actually moving at all. So — back to fundamentals, starting with what Mr Vance Packard actually said — and meant.

The "symbol manipulators", as Mr Packard called them in his book, focussed their attention on politics in the 1950s. Then, in a few short years, they turned to the currently acceptable art of image-bending. (Remember the 1987 UK General Election Campaign?):

"They were able to do this by drawing upon the insights of Pavlov and his conditioned reflexes, Freud and his father images, and Riesman and his concept of modern American voters as spectator consumers of politics."

Social scientist David Riesman pointed out in his book, *The Lonely Crowd*, that just as glamour in packaging and advertising of products substituted for price competition, so:

". . . glamour in politics, whether as *charisma* packaging — of the leader or the hyped-up treatment of events by mass-media, substitutes for the type of self-interest that governed the inner-directed."

But how precisely to do it? Adolph Hitler had carefully explored this territory some thirty years or so earlier, and had written down his thoughts, along with his plans in his book, *Mein Kampf*. He had a great deal to say one way and another about "persuasion" being a master at the art:

"The broad masses of the people can be moved only by the power of speech. All the great movements are popular movements, volcanic eruptions of human passions and emotional sentiments, stirred either by the cruel Goddess of Distress or by the firebrand of the word hurled among the masses."

At first, the American public were not actually *sold* their President like soap powder. They were merely sold *politics* as such. The experts also began testing and exploring the attitudes of potential voters, instead of taking them for granted. In 1952, one ad agency went so far as to examine the opinions — and personalities — of the "don't knows," with a view to discovering their "underlying emotional tone." The switch voter, the ad man discovered, often:

". . . switches for some snotty little reason such as not liking the candidate's wife."

Most disillusioning! In 1956, *Nations Business* published by the US Chamber of Commerce, stressed that when it came to a party's attempts at "merchandising its candidates and issues":

"Candidates need, in addition to rich voice and good diction, to be able to look 'sincerely' at the TV camera. . ."

After that, the politicians, and their policies, were ready to be distributed in their high-integrity, fancy packs. By now, you didn't so much decide to *buy* them, as *succumb* to the irresistible force the market radiated. Nevertheless, despite the method employed — which in some people's eyes degraded the whole process of free, democratic choice — the things you wanted from government, the reasons you accepted the coercion, were the same as they have been from time immemorial. Indeed, in recent years, anthropologists have discovered that the most primitive societies have frequently had a surprisingly advanced system of government, and pattern of everyday behaviour — confirming the view Macaulay expressed in his *History of England:*

> "In rude societies the progress of government resembles the progress of language and versification. Rude societies have language. . . but they have no scientific grammar. . . Rude societies have versification. . . but they have no metrical canons. . . As eloquence exists before syntax, and song before prosody, so government may exist in a high degree of excellence long before the limits of legislative, executive, and judicial power have been traced with precision."

During the centuries which followed the departure of the Romans, when it used to be thought "nothing happened", the Saxons and the Danes began to lay the foundations of English law and legal procedure. It was, Macaulay complained, a system dominated by the Church, but:

> "A society sunk in ignorance, and ruled by mere physical force, had great reason to rejoice when a class, of which the influence is intellectual and moral, rises to ascendancy. Such a class will doubtless abuse its power: but mental power, even when abused, is still a nobler and better power than that which consists merely in corporeal strength."

It was certainly "corporeal strength" that enabled William, Duke of Normandy to rule Britain for 21 years. In those days, the ruler *ruled*. Democracy was unheard of. Personal freedom for the native English was firmly squelched under foot. Under the system introduced by the Normans, taxes were mainly paid in kind — so much grain, so many horsemen, so many days' service. The Domesday Book provided a far more comprehensive record, and set of valuations, than any computerised record that Inland Revenue or any other Department of State has been able to create so far. Though we should not crow too soon!

The Normans ruled for less than 90 years, to be succeeded by Henry II — first of the Plantagenets. They completed the foundations of the English and Welsh legal system. After Henry II came Richard I, who was rather pre-occupied abroad, and left England to its own devices. He also left his English subjects at the mercy of the nobility of Norman-French stock. (The tale of Hollywood's folk-hero, the legendary Robin Hood, tells it all). Richard's successor John was driven from France; and the barons now had sufficient power to force John to sign *Magna Carta*, accepting that he could not impose taxes without consent. But, observed Macaulay, the English kings might be:

> ". . . interdicted from taxing; but they claimed the right of begging and borrowing. They therefore sometimes begged in a tone not to be distinguished from that of command, and sometimes borrowed with small thought of repaying."

Although the Kings who came later were by no stretch of the imagination absolute monarchs, it did not prevent individuals being arrested and tortured on no authority other than the royal command. The fall of the House of Stuart led to the Commonwealth and Protectorate. Under Oliver Cromwell, the ideal recruit was one of "grave character, fearing God and zealous for the public liberty". But it was the "public liberty", rather than individual freedom, the Civil Wars was all about. Still no sign of what we — let alone the Athenians — would call democracy.

The Restoration of the Monarchy, as we have seen earlier, brought licence to the few, but not freedom for the many. Indeed, it was not until the 18th century that we find a new emphasis on personal freedom which reached its peak — for the middle classes at any rate — in the mid-1800s. As historian Arthur Bryant points out, Liberalism:

> ". . . was the most dynamic force in Britain. It derived its strength from the urban and educated middle classes who enjoyed electoral supremacy between the first and second, from the manufacturers who wanted nothing to stand between them and their search for wealth, and from the still unenfranchised masses of the industrial towns. . . For fifty years British legislative annals mark the steady removal from the statute book of every law that offended against individualistic reasoning."

At last — free enterprise was given its head. All that remained was to give everyone the vote. That's how it looked. Although women under 30 had to wait for the vote until the 1920s; and it was not until 1950 that we had one-man, one-vote. Alas, reactions to social and political changes tend to be over-done. Macaulay, writing around the mid-century, was bowled over by the wonders about him. There were the marvels of the railways and industry, to say nothing of the new electrical devices. Somehow he managed not to notice the social and political agitation going on "below stairs". Like many today, Macaulay was so "hooked" by the high tech of his period that he exaggerated the therapeutic effect of what he regarded as instant communication:

> "We live in a highly civilised society, in which intelligence is so rapidly diffused by means of the press and of the post office, that any gross act of oppression committed in any part of our island is, in a few hours, discussed by millions."

The difficulty is that governments can change their policies in a flash, should they be so minded. But people cannot change their minds, or revise their judgements so easily. The general perception since Macaulay's day has been one of progress. Progress, we're told, is what we've had, are having and ought to have! Whether true or not, the Victorians claimed to have made Britain the leading industrial nation. At the same time, though more gradually, Britain edged forward, reform by reform, to become the nearest thing to a genuinely democratic country in the whole of Western Europe.

There are many in Britain today who still wear Macaulay's blinkers. They have not yet noticed that a state of armed insurrection, bordering on Civil War, has existed in these islands for almost two decades. For the past century, the torch of political violence in the British Isles has been carried mainly by the Irish revolutionary factions. All too often they have succeeded; unlike Guy Fawkes' gunpowder plot, or the Cato Street conspirators of 1820. (*Their* aim was to murder Lord Liverpool's Tory Cabinet and seize London). More important, the blinkered brigade do not seem to have realised that since the 1960s, successive governments in Britain have been gradually encroaching on the freedom of the individual, although the outward forms of democratic government have remained for all to see. And that's the heart of the matter; the reason for quoting that text by Kenneth Boulding of Michigan University.

What is this "unseen dictatorship" which is said to be developing in the environs of Whitehall and Downing Street? How has it arisen? So far as the present Government goes, a complete change in its fortunes — and its image — came as a result of its pursuit of the Falklands War in the second quarter of 1982. Sam Brittan, in his book, *The Role and Limits of Government*, published in 1983, detected a "decisive turnround in the Thatcher government's popularity" after the Falklands War:

"It cannot be entirely a co-incidence that there was a concurrent coarsening of government economic policy. . . and an ideological opposition to devaluation going way beyond anything justified by theory or experience and eventually flying in the face of what the foreign exchange market was in fact doing."

Significantly, documents leaked in Febuary 1983 shewed that:

"A healthy desire to free the individual citizen from the power of professionals such as doctors, teachers, and social workers, became mixed up with a desire to tell citizens how to use their independence."

About this time, it was noticeable that civil servants were frequently complaining — in private naturally — of the extent to which their advice was being disregarded. Strange to find members of the Administrative Class talking their way into solidarity with the unwanted and oppressed! Nevertheless, what possible explanation could anyone — including Sam Brittan — give for all this?:

"Peculiar features are bound to arise when the traditional party of authority tries to become the spokesman for individual freedom. It is all part of the tragic division between political and social liberalism, which has moved to the right."

That seemed at the time a fair and charitable interpretation of the party's and particularly the leader's split mind on so many issues. One Tory backbencher of long-standing remarked a little later:

"When I first entered the House, after the War, I felt very keenly the fact that I had not come from what was then the accepted Tory background. Now we are all so much more democratic. But it is not necessarily all that wonderful for the country. It is not that we Tories, with a middle-middle-class background, are actually cold and standoffish with the masses. It's just that *noblesse oblige* is something which does not come naturally."

A far less kindly critic of the Thatcher administration is Tam Dalyell, a Scottish aristocrat who happens to be a Labour Member of Parliament. In his book, *Misrule*, he describes how and why he came to clash with Mrs Thatcher over the sinking of the Argentine warship *Belgrano*; over the Westland affair, which led to the resignation of two Ministers; over the Libyan bombing; over the MI6 book trial in Sydney, Australia; over the 1984 Coal Strike, and the raid on the BBC's Queen Margaret Drive building in Glasgow, in February 1987. At the beginning, in 1979, he suggests:

"Mrs Thatcher behaved not very differently from her immediate predecessors. Harold Macmillan once tersely observed, when asked what had influenced his Government, his style and his policies, 'Events, dear boy, events!'' And in the same way, it was a single event which brought about the seachange that resulted in Mrs Thatcher's grip over government in Britain: the Falklands War."

With the Falklands War, the Lady *did* start turning — assuming there was an intended direction in the first place. She herself talked about the effect the war had on her to George Gale of the *Daily Express:*

"In a way the Falklands became my life, it became my bloodstream. . . "

And after the surrender was confirmed:

"I knew that whatever the problems and troubles I could have in the rest of my period in office they were as nothing then and now."

In their study of the Lady, Nicholas Wapshott of *The Times* and a colleague, writing in 1983 (an election year) observed that no one could have predicted Mrs Thatcher's post-Falklands popularity two years earlier:

". . . with Thatcher the most unpopular Prime Minister since polls began, and Britain severely disrupted by rioting in cities as the summer wore on. . . In no (election) campaign since Churchill's in 1945, had one person so dominated the political landscape. Most Conservatives hoped the comparison would stop there."

Older Conservatives would remember that it was largely Sir Winston's speech about the socialist "Gestapo", delivered in a cigar-laden growl, which helped more than anything to alienate the Forces' voter in 1945.

Winning the leadership of the Party, as Mrs Thatcher did, after a hard-fought battle to dislodge Ted Heath, she did not have an easy passage in her early days at No. 10. After she became Conservative Leader, some members of the parliamentary party had already been heard to grumble that so little had been gained by replacing Ted Heath with Mrs Thatcher. As Bernard Levin put it in *The Times*: what was the point of jumping out of the "igloo" into the "glacier"?

Certainly, Mrs Thatcher's manner was abrasive. Even if her abrasiveness was somewhat exaggerated by one of *The Daily Telegraph* leader writers who had already become a powerful influence on her and Sir Keith Joseph. Experts in foreign affairs were not all delighted with her carefully cultivated image as the *Iron Lady*. On social and economic matters, she was troubled by the so-called "wets". In many cases, their "wetness" was due more to their anger over the dismissal of Ted Heath than to the "leftist" nature of their views. All the same, she may have been discomfited, but she was in no danger. Tam Dalyell points out that even at her most unpopular, Mrs Thatcher was virtually invulnerable to any attempt to dislodge her from the Leadership. This was partly due to the then "new" method of choosing the Party Leader. In times gone-by, when the Conservative Party in some mysterious way "recognised" the consensus feeling when choosing (or cold shouldering) the Leader:

> ". . . the Marquis of Salisbury could assemble six grandees of the Conservative Party willing to go along, tap a Prime Minister on the shoulder and say, 'Your time is up'. . ."

But today, the appointment — or replacement — of the Leader requires an election. This involves the striking of bargains, and takes time. Besides, the contenders for the post, and their supporters, are suspicious, and keep their counsel. So it was clear that, provided Margaret Thatcher could "stick on ", the more hurdles she took in her stride made her appear even more firm in the saddle. Rivals were free to criticise her style as ungainly, or "not the thing"! But they could go no further. Potential plotters would have realised how difficult it would be to unseat her — unless she came a cropper of her own accord. But as one authentic knight of the shires and a lover of the chase put it:

> "She'll stay on all right. It's what she's doing to the National horse that doesn't bear thinking about. It will be a broken down old hack by the time *she's* finished riding it."

Dalyell identifies another factor on Mrs Thatcher's side: the comparatively recent admission of the "open question" at Prime Minister's Question Time. In the 1960s, the only questions which could be placed on the Order Paper for the PM to answer were those pertaining to the PM's actions or responsibilities. Then along came the open question, which could relate to almost anything. Dalyell blames his own party:

"The rot began. . . with Harold Wilson, who would insist on showing off in the Commons how much he knew about every facet of Government. . . In 1968-70, Harold Wilson (on his return to office) reverted to his bad habits of being the universal expert on Tuesday and Thursday at 3.15 for a quarter of an hour or more. . ."

The natural consequence was a temptation — which few members could resist — to "have a go" at political-points scoring. This gradually became accompanied by raucous "cheering and counter-cheering, snarling and counter-snarling (and farm-yard noises)":

"The result of this is that it is virtually impossible to hear what the Prime Minister says and latch on to those questions which are clearly inadequate. . ."

The hullaballoo may sound like an anti-bloodsports demonstration. But it gives Ministers an open field and an easy ride. Particularly since Neil Kinnock, as Leader of the Opposition, decided to treat Prime Minister's Questions as an opportunity for a regular passage of arms with Mrs Thatcher who (to be fair) has probably seen him off on most occasions.

Dalyell, like many other observers of the Whitehall and Westminster scene, advances a further reason for the security of tenure Mrs Thatcher enjoys. From the day of Bagehot onwards, it has become increasingly obvious that the power at the disposal of the Prime Minister has been steadily increasing. One of the reasons for this is the practice of recent Prime Ministers to hand-pick the most senior civil servants. This gives No. 10 tremendous power, as the late Lord Crowther-Hunt (a one-time minister under Wilson, and Rector of Exeter College, Oxford) pointed out on numerous occasions. Sitting, as he did, on two long and detailed enquiries into the working of Parliament and the Civil Service, he became convinced that a strong Prime Minister wielded more *personal* power than an American President. You could probably argue that a Prime Minister, who has appointed his, or her, top civil servants (the so-called "mandarins"), can sleep nights as peacefully as the incumbent in the White House, once he has managed to pack the Supreme Court with just the right men — with just the right ideas.

No Prime Minister can avoid making the occasional mistake — particularly in his, or her, judgment of people. It is more than a little ironic that Clive Ponting (arrested, tried and acquitted for leaking state documents to members of the Commons) is reputed to have owed his last post to Mrs Thatcher's personal intervention. According to the story, she thought he was not going to get the sort of job he deserved!

So far as the Whitehall "mandarins" go, there are just over 40 of them. They hold the key posts at the head of departments and divisions serving the government of the day. James M. Perry writing in *The Wall Street Journal* was greatly impressed by what he had seen of them:

"While other countries may have their own civil-service elites, the mandarins are uniquely British. . . aloof, secretive, privileged, highly educated. Some critics maintain they are Britain's real ruling class, responsible in no small measure for the nation's political and economic decline since World War II."

Sir Frank Cooper, a former Permanent Secretary at the Defence Ministry, claimed that the great value of the mandarins was that they provided continuity. "Politicians come and go. The permanent secretaries are there for life." What he did not say was that the style in permanent secretaries changes, albeit more slowly than that of their political Masters. Sir Robert Armstrong, the Cabinet Secretary, bore a double responsibility. He was head of the domestic civil service at the same time. His successor, Robin Butler, was Mrs Thatcher's Principal Private Secretary from 1982-85, having served as a private secretary to the Prime Minister's office with Edward Heath and Harold Wilson. As Cabinet Secretary, Mr Butler will be the most influential official adviser to the Prime Minister, with direct access to her. In his dual capacity, he will take over a 600-strong staff, and sit at the right-hand of the Prime Minister in Cabinet. When a Cabinet is so dominated by the Premier, as it is understood Mrs Thatcher's Cabinets have been — and when the Cabinet Secretary has such a considerable say in what the UK civil service gets up to — it does not require telepathy for the Premier's ideas to get across to the lower echelons of her administrative services. One moderately important civil servant said wryly of the current climate:

> "It must have been rather like it is now in the days of the Commonwealth, when Oliver Cromwell ran everything."

There are times, Tam Dalyell maintains, when even superbly polished and skilful Arch-Mandarins like Sir Robert Armstrong are handed an impossible task. Head boy at Eton and scholar of Christchurch, Oxford, Sir Robert Armstrong "epitomises the pinnacle of verbal skill in the English language". In 1986, when he appeared before the Parliamentary Committee enquiring into the Westland affair:

> "Sir Robert hedged with an elegance which would have left the authors of *Yes Minister* gasping for breath. It was the John the Baptist performance before Australia and the Peter Wright case."

But in sending him to Australia, in the Wright case, Dalyell maintains:

> "Mrs Thatcher bounced (him) into a task which he did not want, which was none of his business. . . and which he knew from an early stage was a certain loser."

In the Commons, on 3rd December 1986, Roy Jenkins attacked Mrs Thatcher for:

> "her extraordinary capacity to expose to danger. . . those who are closely associated with her. . . Private secretaries and press officers are treated like

junior officers, constantly called upon to go over the top in a desperate partisan assault not made more attractive by the fact that the Prime Minister's orders are to safeguard the political life of their colonel-in-chief, the Prime Minister."

That Mrs Thatcher is powerful and has little or nothing to fear from any rival, is beyond doubt. That her influence is firmly entrenched in Whitehall, and that she is loyally served by some of the finest minds in the country, may be taken as read. But why has she become the target for so much extremely bitter criticism?

As Roy Jenkins put it, at the end of the passage from Hansard which Dalyell quotes:

> "My advice to the substantial number of notable civil servants who worked with or for me is, 'Do not get too close to this Prime Minister. She is an upas-tree — the branches may be splendid, but the contact may be deadly."

Can it possibly be because she is a woman? A woman, it must be said, who believes firmly that she knows her mind, and has the courage to see that her ideas — right or wrong — are carried out? In her sympathetic biography of the Premier, Penny Junor leaves the reader with the firm impression that Mrs Thatcher from an early age has been "programmed" to succeed. Moreover, success appears to have been represented as the one test by which a life may be judged.

By the time Margaret, second daughter of Alf Roberts, of Grantham, was emerging from her teens, her biographer tells us she displayed:

> ". . . an intense, and some would say arrogant certainty that she was right; and was never shy about declaring herself."

She was immensely proud of her father, who saw to it that her "learning never stopped. The whole of life was a process of education, and a serious business." Since one or other of her parents had to stay behind to look after the grocery, they could not go on holiday as a family. Mother and the two girls would go off first to a boarding house, where they usually catered for themselves. Father would then take his holiday later, to coincide with Bowls Week. By most people's standards today, it was neither the most colourful nor humanising upbringing for any child. Nor was there much chance to leave the home, since Margaret wasn't allowed to play childish games, and had few friends out of school:

> "Her time was taken up with homework, work in the warehouse at the back of the shop, or church in one form or another."

Diligence, and the dedication of her parents, brought Margaret a County Minor Scholarship before she was 11. Although she generally came top of the class in exams, writes Penny Junor:

"This was not because of brilliance but rather through sheer hard work."

In due course, hard work and her parents' encouragement won her a place at University in 1943. She was then 18. There she frequently repeated, with great pride and assurance, the familiar sayings of her father. With a rare, but endearing touch of human vanity (Ms Junor tells us) Margaret would refer to "Daddy, the Mayor of Grantham", rather than mention the grocery shop connection. The young Margaret Roberts left no one in any doubt as to her belief in herself. She had, says her biographer:

". . . the certainty and confidence of a crusader who has glimpsed the holy grail."

Politics were an early ambition. What's more, she had scarcely graduated when she told friends she should never have chosen chemistry:

"I should have read law. That's what I need for politics. I shall just have to go and read law now."

Ms Junor's account of Margaret Thatcher's early life leaves us in no doubt whatsoever that when this "perfect little girl" became "a perfect lady," she still depended to a great extent on the approval and support of a father figure, whether her own father or an older, more experienced man belonging to the circles into which she now moved. At a crucial stage in her career, Airey Neave (who was killed by a car bomb at the House of Commons) was at that time the most important of her surrogate fathers.

Her early life was circumscribed by the moral — and practical — compulsion to work hard in order to "get on". Little wonder that today she hates holidays; has such an obsession to get on with the job; has a sharp and critical mind. But, as a senior civil servant who worked closely with her observed, it is by no means a creative one. On a number of occasions, at rallies and conferences, on television and at "walkabouts", Mrs Thatcher has displayed a certain theatrical gift; though not that of an actress playing a part. It has rather been that of the evangelist, who knows that when preaching the Word, the right emphasis, the right tones, the right costume, the right gesture. . . and the right pauses. . . will help to put across the message. Especially to those who are somewhat lacking in faith! The Prime Minister has strong beliefs; and is no less zealous in putting them across.

The day Mrs Thatcher heard about the loss of life aboard the *Sheffield* during the Falklands War, she was to address a Women's Conference at the Albert Hall. On hearing the news, she changed her speech, and changed her mind as to what she would wear. She went on to the platform dressed head-to-foot in black. At the conclusion of her speech (as those who were present still recall) she did not do as she usually did — extend her arms, inviting applause. Instead she bowed her head, allowing her arms to hang limply at her side. How well she had judged the occasion. After a deep silence, the audience came alive. They cheered, they roared. Then they roared and cheered again.

Even Mrs Thatcher's instinctive "feel" for the right word and gesture can let her down at times. In Whitehall on an important occasion for the Windsors, the Royal Family appeared in discreet, but scarcely sombre clothes. Mrs Thatcher, on the other hand, chose to dress all in black, from head to foot. She embarrassingly over-dressed, considering the comparatively minor role she had to play that day. To those who remembered the advertisements posted up in the tube after the Second World War, the Prime Minister of the United Kingdom looked like the "Black Widow" in one of the famous "Keep Death Off the Road" posters.

Given her third successive victory at the polls, Mrs Thatcher's political opponents were not alone in asking themselves whether a third term, with her in charge, would be good for the party or the country. Apart from anything else, Mrs Thatcher would be bound to maintain an even tighter (and more personal) grip on the nation.

T.E. Utley, one of the main "thinkers" in the Conservative Party, wrote a piece in *The Times,* on Monday, June 22nd 1987, which will be well worth reading again in four or five years time. Students should make a note to look it up:

> "On the very night of victory, while the champagne was still flowing, she was exhorting us all not to slack. She does not simply have in mind the task of getting on at the double with her libertarian programmes. . . Much more significantly she directs our minds to the need to do even better electorally next time."

If, in the event, Mrs Thatcher sees that her policies have failed to produce results, she will not be the first Prime Minister to have set out so hopefully, to end so sadly. Many of those who experienced disappointment and disillusion managed to rise above it. But anything short of complete success will be painful to Mrs Thatcher.

Failure to be elected for a *fourth* term could be interpreted as "failure". For even on the night of victory, wrote T.E. Utley:

> "Prime Minister and some of her more enthusiastic colleagues (were) faintly entertaining the illusion of political immortality. It is an illusion to which all victorious politicians are prone, and some vanquished politicians. . . are tempted to the view that there is no life after political death."

Elections for those conditioned to "winning" — whether in the examination room or at the hustings, are there to be won! Each fresh hurdle is further proof of success. Many worship success. Some crave it. For them, there can be no *moral* justification for failure, partial or complete.

For most of the electorate, it is different. What matters more than elections is how well the country is governed in the years between; and whether people, regardless of social or economic level, get what they expect — or what they imagine the winning Party promised them. Will there be lower taxes? Or will the much vaunted reduction in income tax be no more than a transfer by sleight-of-hand? That is to say, will the reduced revenue from income tax be compensated by higher National Insurance contributions, and huge swathes of VAT harvested in a High Street where credit appears unlimited? Will funds be available for a full range of health and social services? Or will the man-in-the-street be forced to "go private" to secure the right treatment within a reasonable time? How much further will the doctrine of privatisation be carried?

Ostensibly, the Thatcher Government is keen on privatisation as a means of returning power to the people — the financial counterpart, if you like, of the sale of council houses and the encouragement of home ownership. The sale of council houses grew originally out of a desire to reduce the increasing burden on local authority rates and central government funds. Maintaining council properties was, in many areas, less onerous than maintaining the often extremely costly administrative structure. Privatisation released an instant inflow of capital, which helped to balance the books. Similarly, the sale of the nationalised industries entails a further load-shedding. But, given the far greater control to be exerted over the professional, industrial, commercial and financial life of the nation, the third Thatcher Government is achieving the dream of every government, to enjoy the fruits of power without the burden of responsibility.

Will the public outcry over the arbitrary and pig-headed behaviour of some of the operatives of firms entrusted with the task of "wheel-clamping" act as a warning? Or will the system be allowed to continue; with contractors tendering for all the difficult, dirty and disagreeable tasks which central government and the local authorities alike would prefer to be shot of. Given the go-ahead, contractors could tender for a wide range of franchises — running prisons and homes for the aged; organising "cost-effective" care for the mentally sick and the terminally incurable; providing temporary shelter for the permanently homeless, and supervising work camps for the young school-leavers, conscripted into training-schemes. Some of these franchises would be so worth having that further privatisation could add significantly to the number, and range of vested interests.

In moving from the present centralised system, to one in which the right to carry out essential services can be bid for by private contractors, the government is abdicating the responsibilities assumed in the last century. They were not seen at the time as "burdens". They were an essential part of a programme of rationalisation and reform, designed to clean up the corrupt and inefficient existing system. That many local (and central) government services are costly and inefficient, cannot be denied. But the aim of any rational government should be to *make* them cost effective, not to evade responsibility by restricting (or abolishing) services, or handing them over to private contractors. Understandably such firms, must give first priority to increasing their profits, and maintaining the price of their shares.

Government propaganda has described the process of privatisation in rainbow colours. But to any thinking person it must be seen for what it is — the failure of Government from the word "go".

If no one else, one might expect the traditionalists in the modern Conservative Party to remember Disraeli's words:

> "Permissive legislation is the character of a free people. . . you must trust to persuasion and example as the two great elements if you wish to effect any considerable changes in the manners of the people."

Sam Brittan makes a similar point in his book of essays, where he stressed the importance of maintaining a proper balance between the basic freedoms. But he sees the dilemma:

> "There is a crucial connection between personal and political freedom, on the one hand, and economic freedom on the other, as *The Road to Serfdom* (by Hayek) clearly established. In the decades since it appeared there has not been a single example of a fully collectivist economy retaining basic freedoms. Yet the only societies which seem able to protect a market economy from erosion by interest-groups are certain Pacific Basin countries in which either political freedom or democracy, or both, are absent."

We could be in danger of self-deception were we to take that passage too literally. A book is only a book. In this case it is one which Hayek himself confessed took about ten years to write, to think about and write again! It was not a blueprint for DIY democracy. It was a reflection — half hypothesis, half prayer. Brittan spells out the *impasse* confronting the politician seeking a practical solution:

> "If, as I believe, this authoritarian cure is worse than the disease, what reforms are possible in liberal democracy itself?"

The answer to that might well be — first catch your *genuine* liberal democrat! Particularly since Brittan goes on to admit that:

> "Hayek does not analyse the question of how legislatures should tackle entrenched interest-group powers without undermining liberal principles by the methods used."

It could well be that this is one of the many instances in which we should give up any idea of finding a "solution" and deal with each bucketful — good or bad — as it comes up. That's how we have had to react to governments all down the ages, unless we were political commentators or potential martyrs. After the Second World War, they used to say, "If you must lie down in the road, make sure the oncoming tank is British." That may not be such sound advice any longer. Not in Thatcher's Kingdom!

I use the term "kingdom" advisedly, because there is a touch of the regal about Mrs Thatcher from time to time. We cannot ignore the fact that this country has never known so powerful a woman, apart from two great Queens — Elizabeth I and Victoria. This must have occurred to Mrs Thatcher more than once. It could explain a great deal.

They say "to know is to understand, and to understand is to forgive." Some feel that Margaret Thatcher has a great deal for which to be forgiven. On the other hand many women maintain that her male critics are mistaken; Mrs Thatcher is behaving like any other woman running her own "household". Whether right or wrong, the problem remains. The United Kingdom is not a "household". But Mrs Thatcher has no political rival of sufficient stature to point this out. More significantly there does not seem to be anyone left in her Cabinet (and very few on the backbenches or within the Party at large) to whom she would listen. After eight years in office, she managed to purge her "court" — for that is what her inner circle resembles — of the last of the turbulent "wets". What she had in mind was made plain in the highly controversial Queen's Speech in the summer of '87. Within 24 hours, Conservatives joined in the outcry over the proposed poll tax.

A poll tax, as countless generations of British schoolchildren have been taught, was one of the things those "continentals" used to impose on their hapless people. Old attitudes, engrained in the classroom, die hard. So do prejudice and mistrust. That is why the reaction to Mrs Thatcher's announcement that she intended using part of the Parliamentary recess to visit the derelict "inner cities", was to ask: "Why now, in 1987. . . and not in 1986, '85, '84 or '83? And what does she intend to do when she gets there?" Sooner or later, we shall be told that such criticisms shew there is a "conspiracy" against her and her senior colleagues. Who then will be held responsible? The extremists, the militants, the Reds and anyone else who happens to be out of favour at the time. Which brings us back to that Joker in the political pack, the "conspiracy theory".

Conspiracy or Coincidence?

That, as Hamlet said over an entirely different issue, is the question! To begin with, conspiracy is a term to be used with care. But it rarely is. Sometimes the so called "conspiracy" is no more sinister than any very big, very dirty business. For example, it was hailed as the break-up of a major conspiracy when, in June 1987, Gaetano Badalkamenti, the ex-Sicilian Mafia boss was sentenced to 45 years imprisonment, along with Sal Catalano, who controlled the New York end of the so-called "Pizza Connection" drug network.

The term has been employed to describe Insider Dealing — presumably because of the complex network of covert operations involved. Historically, the British have long been sensitive to the "international conspiracy", particularly when aimed against the Empire. At the turn of the century,

Tsarist Russia was said to be plotting to gain control of the Khyber Pass; despatching undercover "agents" to the bazaars of North India, seeking to stir up disaffection among the peoples of the North-West Frontier, and subverting the local tribesmen.

Some international associations, which seemed quite proper when first founded, have acquired sinister overtones with the passage of time. For centuries, wrote Gary Allen, in his book, *None dare call it Conspiracy:*

> ". . .there has been big money to be made by international bankers in the financing of governments and kings. . . (and) the ultimate advantage the creditor has. . . is that if the rule gets out of line the banker can finance his enemy or rival."

The House of Rothschild, he pointed out, was particularly active and successful during the last century, when every war in Europe ended with the establishment of a "balance of power". For the banking house founded by Meyer Rothschild in Frankfurt, there was business to be done in London, Paris, Vienna and Naples. Meyer was fortunate in having sons who could take it on. Nor were the Rothschilds alone in the international banking business. The J.P. Morgans and Rockefellers and others also played their part. The Left have always attacked the "international bankers cartel", as they saw it.

In the 1880s, Cecil Rhodes had a personal income of at least a million pounds sterling. When he died in 1888 he left a fortune to found, in 1891, a private society (some called it a "secret society") with the purpose of furthering Rhodes's ideas for the extension of British rule throughout the world. Under the title of *The Round Table*, it was run by Lord Alfred Milner, who worked behind the scenes to influence the British Government's handling of foreign affairs and its conduct of the First World War. After the war, came the creation in England of the Royal Institute of International Affairs, and in New York the Council on Foreign Relations (CFR). The CFR became an extremely influential body, frequently described as "the invisible government" or "the Rockefeller foreign office". Members of the group have not been politicians or bankers alone. Men from the great corporations, along with some of the labour leaders, have also played their part.

On an international level there is the Bilderberg Group, so called because it first met in Oostebeek, Holland in May 1954 at Hotel de Bilderberg. This too has a membership of top people in virtually every calling. When they meet, they do so in great secrecy. No word of their deliberations leaks out — despite the fact that participants have included editors of the media from across the world. Is this maintaining a closed forum in which men of standing can speak freely? Or is it a "conspiracy"? There is also the Trilateral Commission, which draws together North America, Western Europe and Japan. The idea is that the "best brains in the world" should meet privately:

> ". . . to collect, and synthesise the knowledge that would enable a new generation to rebuild the conceptual framework of foreign and domestic policies."

Who you might ask, could object to that? Or treat it as sinister? The answer is, Barry Goldwater for one, in his book, *With No Apologies:*

> "In my view, the Trilateral Commission represents a skilled, coordinated effort to seize control and consolidate the four centres of power — political, monetary, intellectual, and ecclesiastical."

Against this, it can be argued that the very stature and "job description" of those participating has been such that they have no need to attempt to "seize control". They already exert considerable power within the "establishment". Obviously, there are several ways of looking at these private international fora. One may say, "If they have nothing to hide, why don't they come out into the open?" That tends to be the American view, since every United States citizen has a Right to Know. On the other hand, it can be argued that there are some matters which — if they are to be discussed at all — must be discussed in private. Hence the rule that nothing said at any meeting of the Royal Institute of International Affairs may be attributed to the speaker unless specific permission has been given. Although the gist of what was said, the conclusions reached and the sense of the meeting, may well be reported.

In the case of my own Offshore Conference, in Monte Carlo, in June 1987, the press were not invited. That was no oversight. Had they been present, there would have been far less to report. Many of the things speakers were able to say were said, because it *was* a closed conference. But that is not to say there was anything secret or sinister about the proceedings, or that it was any form of conspiracy. You will discover that for yourself, if you continue to read on.

In Britain we have never been so keen on "open diplomacy" as in the United States. And for the reason given by one cynic:

> "With secret diplomacy, you don't have to tell so many lies in public."

There can be no doubt that there are secret gatherings of conspirators, every hour of the day, every day of the week. The former White House aide, Lt-Col Oliver North, of the US Marines, gave the Congressional enquiry into the Iran-Contra scandal the answer: the first essential for covert operations is to *remain* covert. This applies to all conspiracies worthy of the name. Where it is decided that certain conspiracies should be denounced, it is customary to describe the menace in highly coloured language, coining some such apt phrase as the Yellow Peril — the threat from the Far East early this century. It is necessary for the witch-hunters to stir the emotions, and divert attention from other threats nearer home. As another cynic put it:

> "If God ran Harrods, he'd organise the most tremendous thunderstorm every time the shop looked empty."

The popular version of "conspiracy theory" is that plots are hatched by megapowers (or their agents), by multinationals, international bankers, the military or other covert interests, each seeking to gain control of an industry, a political party or national government. In the United States, the John Birch Society, with its 25,000-strong membership, is convinced that there is an international, monolithic, godless, Zionist-Communist conspiracy — a Grand Design or Masterplan to unite all nations into a mongrelised one-world government. Others see countless conspiracies to seize power in one area or another. Sometimes they plan to do so by main force. At another time, they will attain power by means of a gradual and insidious takeover. Robert Welch, chieftain of the John Birch Society, once went so far as to accuse the Beatles of being:

> "Part of a systematic plan geared to making a generation of American youth mentally ill and emotionally unstable by timing musical rhythms to the actual physical pulse beat of the teenager, thus anaesthetising the control centre of the brain, demoralising and destroying him."

So far as the media and the general public are concerned, the fact that a group of rich, powerful or otherwise influential people meet in private to discuss some matter is sufficient to justify a cry of "conspiracy". They ignore the realities of everyday life. Interested parties — oilmen or bankers — may well meet to discuss a common plan. But it is possible they have agreed to meet only because they wish to limit, or even dissolve that agreement. But it is safe to say they will rarely come out of their corner unless they can see an advantage in so doing. Some will attend because they know that if they are *not* there when the cake is cut, they will be left with no more than a handful of crumbs. In every organisation, within any community, some will be better at cake-stealing than others. The principle which applies to all cake-cutting exercises — from take-over negotiations to the reading of a will — is "To Each According to his Greed." In any case, genuine conspirators are most unlikely to meet in major International Hotels, with fleets of black Mercedes saloons — blinds drawn — ferrying the great and the good, and the internationally famous, from the heavily guarded airport to their high-security destination. Behaviour of that sort would be a gift to the media. Especially to television, which could then report, "Our correspondent was not allowed to film the arrival of these world figures." It would not even be necessary to name them! In terms of selling newspapers, or attracting viewers, it would be a far better bet than attempting to put across in 90 seconds what the European Agriculture Ministers said about pig meat.

Conspiracy theory was raised at Monte Carlo at the *Investors Bulletin* Offshore Conference, when we presented both sides of the picture. Larry Abrahams, author of the *Insider* report — a world expert on conspiracy theory — tended to endorse the Gary Allen view of the game. Bringing it down to an everyday level, Mr Abrahams claimed that the oil glut which caused so much concern in February 1986 was "as phoney as the crisis of shortage was in 1974."

Whether you "buy" *his* conspiracy theory or Plato's Conspiracy Theory, or Cicero's Conspiracy Theory, or Machiavelli's Conspiracy Theory, Larry Abrahams believes he's "in pretty good company". So will many of the public, who are devoted fans of the related areas of conspiracy and self-deception. They show this by their eagerness to consume all the junk-fare the media has to offer. In this sense, many of the public are casualties of our time; the new-disabled, whose energy and enterprise have been drained away over the years by a despairingly passive life-style. They crave something to lift their minds, and spirits, out of the slough of despond.

Create, or recognise, the public's craving for candy-floss conspiracies, and someone will be ready to cater for it. There's big money in conspiracy as a branch of show business — especially for the conspiracy pedlars. Some will go out on the road to promote and further their own political or religious aims. It may be in some cases to spread "the truth", as they see it — a service to humanity. It may be for no better reason than to promote — or raise funds for — their cult or movement. Some conspiracy pedlars (among them some of the most successful) are plain, old-fashioned paranoid schizophrenics.

The other conspiracy expert at the Monte Carlo conference was Bob Eringer, author of a lengthy study of this dangerous fraternity. It was entitled *The Conspiracy Pedlars — A Review of the Conspiracy Media in the United States* (1981). He was *not* a supporter of Gary Allen or the John Birch Society:

> "I have a problem with the word conspiracy because the word paranoia is often close to conspiracy. I look at it as sort of "influence peddling". I think the power elite do try the best they can to control things. People always do. But I don't think they are very successful."

Clearly, one must keep a sense of perspective. That means — among other things — it would be unwise to assume that a conspiracy ceases to be a danger merely because the parties fail to agree. Or because they turn out to have been double-crossing one another! That *can* be even more dangerous. At such times it's the innocent who are likely to be caught in the cross-fire. Again, it would be wrong to over-estimate the effectiveness of the pressure exerted by vested interests. Self-deception can be an equally potent force. One well sign-posted route to self-deception was pointed out half-a-century ago in J.M. Keynes's *General Theory*. (It is no less valid for having been so widely quoted):

> "Practical men, who believe themselves to be quite exempt from any intellectual influences, are usually the slaves of some defunct economist. . . . It is ideas, not vested interests, which are dangerous for good or evil."

When it comes to what Bob Eringer called "influence peddling," Vilfredo Pareto (in his *General Sociology*) believed that men and women cannot be controlled by changing their reasoning. It is necessary to go deeper, playing

on their instincts and emotions. The psychologically effective approach to
the public — whether as voters, shoppers or volunteers for some dangerous
mission — is something we take for granted. But when are we going to
ask about the psychological make-up of our leaders? Or those who might
try to manipulate them?

It is important to recognise the power of an institution or a leader. But
it is also advisable to examine the source of that power. A dedicated, energetic
and effective politician, motivated by high ideals and aided by a healthy
life style, is one thing. An equally dedicated, energetic and effective
politician, who is a life-long manic-depressive, is quite another. Such
individuals may appear to be powered by the same deep, inner convictions.
In reality, they may be driven by their inner maladjustment, and guided
by the advice of the last person under whose influence they fell.

In this connection, we must also consider an even more disturbing angle.
If the conspiracy is sufficiently well-planned (and the secret sufficiently
well kept) the intended victims themselves may unknowingly become pawns
in the game. History has shown that even the most powerful ruler may become
the victim of a malign influence. That is the warning implicit in the strange
tale of the monk Rasputin and Alexandra, Tsarina of All The Russias. There
are times too when those who secretly support a cause, or its leader, find
they have underestimated the strength of the man, or movement, they imagine
they are manipulating for their own ends. In Germany, a number of
landowners and the leaders of heavy industry poured millions into the coffers
of the emerging Nazi Party. They saw it as a tool with which to smash the
German Communist Party. That achieved, they believed that they could drop
the Party — *and* its leader. They were wrong. Just as wrong as the ultra-
conservatives who, on 30th January 1933, applauded the bestowal of the
Chancellorship by President Hindenburg on Adolf Hitler. History, they told
themselves, had made *them* the nation's leaders. So they could afford to
play Herr Hitler's "game" a little longer. . . just until it no longer served
their purpose!

One of the incidents from our own time, which Tam Dalyell recalled in
his book *Misrule,* was the receipt by the deputy leader of the Labour Party
in 1974, of photocopies of documents purporting to show "proof" that he
had opened what would have been an *illegal* Swiss bank account. It was
sent to him by a reputable journalist who wanted to get his reactions. After
two weeks it was established that the documents were forgeries. There was
no doubt about it. Someone had been "having a go" at Ted Short, when
the Labour Party was about to face its second General Election within a year.

The simple, honest citizen, brought up in a Christian household, with
a high opinion of the system, might have anticipated that the resurrection
of ancient tales of anti-Wilson operations by MI6 would have irritated the
establishment — especially when they attracted the attention of a determined
campaigner like Tam Dalyell. When it was clear that the stories would not
lie down, the reasonable citizen might expect the authorities to settle the

matter once and for all. Not so! Tam Dalyell wrote to the Chairman of the Security Commission, a distinguished High Court judge, Lord Griffiths of Govilon, requesting an enquiry under the 1921 Act. He received a courteous but disappointing answer:

"If. . . the Commission were of the opinion that the powers provided by the Tribunals of Enquiry (Evidence) Act 1921 were necessary for their investigation, they would so inform the Prime Minister to seek the authority of Parliament for such powers to be granted."

On 26 March 1987, Mr Dalyell asked the Prime Minister "if she will now refer to the Security Commission allegations of security services operations against Ministers of the Crown in the 1970s; and if she will make a statement." Mrs Thatcher's reply was brief and to the point. She said: "No".

One of the facts of political life is that while the authorities are apt to see plots and plotters in every corner, they greatly dislike anyone's pointing to conspirators under *their* bed. As Gary Allen indicated in his book, *None Dare,* those who do — at any time, in any country — will be asking for trouble. At the very least, steps will be taken to discredit them. They'll be dubbed "paranoid", or scatty conspiracy-theorists. One distinguished academic who took the lid off the conspiratorial network in the United States was the late Professor Carroll Quigley, of the Foreign Service School, Georgetown University. His book *Tragedy and Hope* did not make him very popular. Yet, Gary Allen reminds us, Franklin D. Roosevelt once went so far as to admit:

"In politics, nothing happens by accident. If it happens, you can bet it was planned that way."

Allen does not see conspirators as criminals, but as *insiders,* who "from the very highest levels manipulate government policy." The reason they do this boils down to a desire for power. It is a desire that can be kept under control a short time by success, and success alone. But even that wears off; and temporary gratification serves only to intensify the craving. How right we are to treat power as a drug! It is quintessential to remember that men and women can be "hooked" on power just like any other junkies. That means they will be willing to do anything — or anyone — for a fix.

The average individual finds it hard to fathom the perverted lust for power of men and women of their kind. The ordinary citizen, writes Gary Allen:

". . . wants only to enjoy success in his job, to be able to afford a reasonably high standard of living. . . to give his children a sound education. His ambition stops there. He has no desire to exercise power over others. But we must realise that there *have* been Hitlers and Lenins and Stalins and Caesars and Alexander the Greats throughout history."

We know Hitler's life story — that of a high-school drop-out with boundless ambition; a man the Junkers thought would help them to destroy the German Communist Party, and break its hold on the workers. That was why the big industrialists gave Hitler money; while the military, whose tradition was to stand aloof from politics, stood back until it was too late. In the end Hitler destroyed all who colluded with him, or came too close.

At the height of the First World War, another dreamer and revolutionary was locked in a sealed train with a consignment of gold and despatched to Russia. The reason was that the Berlin High Command saw Vladimir Ilich Lenin as *their* man. He would sweep aside the revolutionary government of the moderate Kerensky, take control of Russia, and end the War. This (the High Command reasoned) would relieve the pressure on Germany's Eastern Front. The inhuman terror, destruction, enslavement and death that Lenin and Hitler brought *should* have been predictable. History has always shown that those who hunger for power have not the strength to deny their appetite.

There is another danger. That is to assume that the power-hungry must come from the same narrow background. We see them as born and raised in poverty, or confined in their early years in a cramped and joyless environment. We see them as bent and twisted into believing that the pursuit of excellence or godliness. . . or both. . . are the sole channel of advancement and self-expression. But, postulates Gary Allen:

> "Is it not theoretically possible that a billionaire could be sitting, not in a garret (like Hitler and Lenin in their youth) but in a penthouse in Manhattan, London or Paris and dream the same dream as Lenin and Hitler? These men would. . . command immense social prestige and be able to pool astonishing amounts of money to carry out their purposes."

Allen goes further. He asks why should we assume there are no men or women alive *today* with a sufficiently perverted lust for power to emulate the destroyers of the past?:

> "And if these men happen to be billionaires is it not possible that they would use men like Hitler and Lenin as pawns to seize power for them?"

Or institutions like the key UN Agencies, NATO, the European Commission — or even the Mother of Parliaments?

There is all the difference in the world between a government's being deflected from its course by outside alien influences, and modifying its policies to remain true to its principles. Take privatisation and home and share-ownership. How do they stand the test of being measured against the underlying principle of modern Conservatism, that in the end the market view will — and, indeed, must — prevail?

The long-term promotion of the virtues of home-ownership will be consistent with basic Conservative beliefs only so long as it makes sense, in market terms, to buy — rather than rent — one's living space. The moment the market dictates otherwise, the government is faced with the choice between an unpopular U-turn and a betrayal of Conservative principle.

Much the same difficulty could arise over the drive to persuade all social and economic classes to become investors in British equities. What happens when the market no longer goes on rising? What advice will Government give if the market suffers a major fall?

Ostensibly, privatisation has been seen as a means of returning power to the people, as well as providing a fresh incentive for management and workforce alike. By mid-summer 1987, the effects of privatising British Telecom were the subject of public protest and concern. This surprised no one who had always been told — and, indeed, believed — that the only thing worse than a public monopoly was a private monopoly.

Given the Thatcher administration's determination to remain in control of the key industries, albeit from a distance, privatisation certainly enabled them to realise the dream of every government. . . achieving the maximum of power with the minimum of responsibility.

Wealth. . . transfer or confiscation?

The first thing you will notice when we take a closer look at some of the things government proposes to spend those taxes on, is that they're going to support what I, for one, do *not* regard as the legitimate functions of government. In fact, you'll find that some of the expenditure is on downright *illegitimate* activities. The first example is the confiscation of the property of one British citizen, who's earned the right to it, with a view to passing on a slice of it to someone else who definitely has not! In *my* book, this is legalised theft. Under that broad heading I'd also put confiscating the property of non-farm workers to hand out subsidies to farmers. The amount that has been paid out in subsidies through the Common Market's Common Agricultural Policy is horrendous.

Another form of legalised theft comes in the shape of hand-outs to "lame duck" corporate financing programmes. In that case the Government is again confiscating our property to give it to a management project which otherwise would fail. Suppose the manager of some multi-national corporation — a giant employing thousands of people — comes to my door and says, "Let me have a few thousand pounds for a bail-out, so I can keep my company going. . . even though it's losing money." I know what I'd do! I'd tell him to go play in the traffic. He knows that I would, too. If he's really smart, he won't come anywhere near *me*. Instead, he'll take himself off to Whitehall. . . or Westminster. . . to urge someone in the Government to use its agents to collect the money he wants: and, through its agents, to collect it from ME.

The agents are, of course, the Inland Revenue. Backed by the legislature, the Tax Inspectors are quite accustomed to taking whatever steps are necessary

to confiscate the property of certain individuals to give it to others to whom
— naturally — it would never otherwise belong. Now, in order to achieve
its quite illegitimate aims, government, and its servants — the so called "civil"
servants — must become as intrusive, obtrusive (and frequently abusive)
as possible. And they're good at it. As a result of the widespread powers
vested in government, for the purpose of achieving what are deemed to be
"higher objectives", government is going to bear down on the citizen to
the point where personal liberty is no more than a tertiary matter. As for
what those "higher objectives" of government actually are. . . I'll tell you!
They're what they call the fair (or fairer) distribution of wealth; care for
the poor, sick, elderly, disabled; and the general welfare of the non-poor,
non-sick, non-elderly and non-disabled. Quite a few types of people wait
for government to spread it around. . . and remember whose it is! Ultimately
the process must end in the kind of totalitarianism we are taught to abhor.
And *that,* when you analyse it, is nothing more or less than an alternative
form of servitude.

This malign tendency is a natural by-product of a nation in decline. When
an increasing number of people join the ranks of the needy, fewer and fewer
people are left to create wealth. This weakens the nation. It reduces its power
to resist pressures from vested interests, who offer their support. But at
a price. . . though it may not be mentioned at the time. Over the past few
decades, Britain has been moving steadily in the direction of a totalitarian
state, although it has maintained the outward signs of a highly developed
— and very high-minded — democracy. The move has not been rapid. On
the contrary, it's proceeded at a steady, deliberate pace, and on the whole
has remained hidden from public view. The authoritarian practices of the
Inland Revenue and the Customs and Excise (who look after VAT, remember)
have developed step-by-step — one small step at a time. A century ago,
there were no computers, credit cards, mailing lists, driving licences, census
records and the plethora of devices that Government now uses to track the
movements, and behaviour, of its citizens.

In the 1880s taxation was low — especially income tax. At the same time,
Britain set an example to the rest of the world as a smoothly functioning
democracy. Banking among private citizens was in its infancy. It was also
well outside the reach of government. A century ago, the citizen in Britain
did not have to bare his soul to the Tax Inspector, and spend hours of his
life filling in forms about himself and his finances. The Briton of today
is forced by law to reveal all to the servants of the state. By *all,* I mean *all.*

The ostensible justification for the continued attack on private property
rights, economic freedom and financial privacy can be traced to the desire
(I've already spoken of) to provide welfare and "do good". Not that these
are necessarily unreasonable objectives. . . within reason. Most people feel
that government *should* care for the poor, aid the disadvantaged and under-
privileged, provide assistance for the elderly, support failing businesses. . .
and thereby prevent unemployment. . . and generally give to the deserving

element in society. At the same time it must be recognised that government itself has no resources of any kind. Believe me, the Prime Minister, the Cabinet, Members of the House of Lords and Judiciary do not spend a penny of their own money. That's because, in the first place, the last place and all along the line, they don't have any money to spend. Neither is there a Tooth Fairy, Easter Bunny, or Santa Claus hanging around just in case someone asks them to come up with some.

Once it is recognised that none of the *authorities* possesses a penny, we have to accept that the only way the authorities can take a penny from the individual (who's earned it) to give to another individual (who hasn't) is through compulsory collection, backed by intimidation, threats and coercive action. The *galli-galli* man's "Now-you-see-it, Now-you-don't" approach is also employed with considerable skill. Income tax, we were told was being lowered. (Rejoice! Rejoice!) But that leaves Corporation Tax, VAT, Capital Gains Tax, and Inheritance Tax. Given a continued consumer boom, the "take" must increase. Then, to help it on its way, there are tax concessions to be reduced or removed.

If, by any chance, you feel that I'm being a little too liberal with such terms as intimidation, threats, coercion and paranoia, I suggest you wait until April 5th comes around next time, and then tell your Tax Inspector you're not going to pay because you don't feel like it. Try it! But only if you're keen to learn at first hand what it's like to be intimidated, threatened and coerced. And be careful! Get too ugly about it, and you'll end up behind bars. What's more they'll still squeeze every penny out of you. Down to the very last penny you never knew you had.

The truth is that under current legislation, governments are permitted to carry out acts which — perpetrated by a private individual — would undoubtedly be considered criminal. Like telling some sweet old lady you'll pull her arms out if she doesn't produce the cash! Do that, and you can expect to be arrested. Regardless, I may say, of the nobility of your cause. Yet I find it difficult to see any meaningful difference between that sort of conduct and some of the practices of the Inland Revenue.

Every year it demands so much money. If I pay late, I am fined. If I refuse to pay I'm gaoled. I'm definitely under duress, and in the end I get robbed. Robbery is theft. But since it's the Inland Revenue, I have no say, I cannot even stipulate how the government spends my money. Sometimes the ood character tries to do just that — on conscientious grounds. But in the end he, or she, gets locked up. Literally. You can read such cases in the paper. Mind you, I *know* it's useless to complain, because the law says the Inland Revenue may do what they're doing. In other words, I can't complain about their form of theft because it's been *legalised!*

By now it may be clear that you *don't* have to ask me when does Summer Camp become a "Gulag"? I know. But do you? Do most people in Britain today? The crux of the matter is that in any society — free or not free — quite a few objectionable things turn out to be legal. But that doesn't make them legitimate or *right*. The pre-war persecution of the Jews by the Nazis was legal. Laws had been passed saying they could. But it was horrendous. So is apartheid in South Africa. The snag is, apartheid is just as legal as the Nazis' anti-Jewish laws. But both are still examples of statutory injustice.

This brings us to the important grey area on the borderline of morality. It draws our attention to the distinction between what is *legal* and what, though legal, still offends against the rules of *natural justice*. Without attempting a definition, it is fair to say that for practical purposes *natural justice* is to law as *authority* is to *the exercise of power.*

Everyone ought to have a fair chance. That's one of the principles of natural justice. Generally we agree. People are innocent until proved guilty. That's another principle of natural justice which has been absorbed into the concept of the Rule of Law. Nor is there any reason to suppose that an "educated" person will judge more wisely, or fairly, than a badly educated one. We believe that every man or woman should be equal — which also means equally *accountable* — before the law. (But that doesn't necessarily mean that they are entitled to a slice of what I, and I alone, have earned!)

When we read in the newspapers that some government department has behaved in an arbitrary manner, we are outraged. But suppose — as in the case of Customs and Excise and Inland Revenue — they have been given wide discretionary powers? Then we probably can't fault them on the *legality* of their actions. We are thrown back on what is fair, decent and reasonable. We often condemn malpractices in a firm or a department because they diminish the rights of others. Maybe we *are* that high-minded. But that's not always why we get het up. In their work on *The Criminal, the Judge and the Public,* Franz Alexander (psychoanalyst) and Hugo Staub (lawyer) recognise that:

> "Acts of injustice become more and more the centre of interest of the popular masses. Every individual member of a given class perceives as his own the wrong which falls on another of the same social stratum. . . as if the individual says: 'This might happen to any one of us' ."

The psychological impact of injustice applies at *all levels of society.* It is just that the higher-status or better-off members have more options than those at the bottom of the pile. So they are less easily driven to frustration and self-destructive outbursts.

Back in the 1930s when banks were keeling over at a rate of knots, you might have decided that the sensible thing would be to buy gold and stuff it in your mattress. But that powerful elite anticipated this, and because your holding gold would have interfered with *their* plans, they just said you couldn't. To make certain, they passed a law to that effect. Was *this* fair?

In the 1940s, if you became nervous about the future of the pound, you might have contemplated moving into another currency and keeping what savings you had abroad. But Exchange Control laws said, No! Violation of those laws carried severe penalties. How about *that* for natural justice?

Then, way back in 1917, to finance the cost of World War I a massive 5% War Loan issue was floated. It could be redeemed, said the coupon, any time after 1929. The depression of the 1930s resulted in so sharp a fall in British Government revenues that the interest on this issue absorbed some 40% of all the money collected in. Certainly, the Government could not afford to redeem the bond, and escape that way. So — hey presto! The Government presented the public with the solution. They would generously be "allowed" to convert their 5% War Loan into a new issue bearing interest at only 3½%. Highway robbery, or an Act of State? For the individual it amounts to the same thing. Just about 24 hours before devaluation in 1949, the late Sir Stafford Cripps said, "No devaluation." He was lying. But that black lie was for the good of the nation! Like one of Colonel North's patriotic falsehoods.

No private firm would be allowed to behave so dishonourably. Or crookedly. Nevertheless, when Chrysler couldn't repay its debt, the US Government lent its guarantee to the debt. . . the debt that Chrysler couldn't pay.

Say you're planning retirement, aiming for a particular class of security; or intend to develop your business along certain lines — both being compatible with existing legislation. What happens if later your plans clash with new plans government has just thought up? You know well enough! A law will be passed in an overt manner through *de facto* legislation, or retroactively if need be. This is the way of government. Central planning by government means the superseding of an individual's plans by the powerful elite. As a country's fortunes decline, and the incompetent increase in number (leaving the wealth producers in a dwindling minority) laws will generally be passed giving the authorities powers to confiscate even more of the wealth created by the productive few. The country then finds itself in an irreversible spiral, as penal taxation drives out the wealth creators in increasing numbers, until only the non-productive element remain.

This pattern is superbly illustrated in Ayn Rand's inspired (and inspiring) novel, *When Atlas Shrugged*. The tale is about the Twentieth Century Motor Company, which decided to change its policies to benefit the workers, and reduce the number of strikes and confrontations with the union. In true socialist fashion, the company adopts the slogan, "From Each According To His Ability, To Each According To His Need." All the workers are expected to put in a full day's work and achieve maximum productivity. Instead, the guy with seven kids and one arm is seen to be likely to get paid three times as much as the single guy in robust health with no dependents. It was a great and noble idea. But it leads to disaster for all — including the needy.

What happens on the way is that those with any ability leave the company so soon as the new policy is announced. They are off to find employment where they will be paid in accordance with the volume and quality of the work they produce. Obviously the needy stay on. Where else could they be sure of being paid more and more for their ability to do less and less? Finally, the company is left with none but those incapable of achieving enough output to produce the profits required to cover their patently unearned salaries. Inevitably, the company takes a dive. What Ayn Rand wrote represents for me a microcosm of the way Britain has been heading for decades. A factory is not a natural resource — like a mine, a tree, a river or an oil well — that can be pillaged, plundered and exploited. Neither is a nation; and certainly not a people. But back to our immediate prospects.

In the circumstances prevailing immediately after the June 1987 election, we were bound to note the growing polarisation in the country, and ask what the social and political implications were likely to be. Were we likely to see more Brixtons, Toxteths, Tottenhams, and Wappings? Could there be a repeat of the country-wide miners' strike? The potential for violence was assuredly in place. As Alexander and Staub put it:

> "Before every great social revolution one usually observes an increasing number of miscarriages of justice which, while in no way being the cause, yet play the role of precipitating moments of these social changes — there always exists a *chronic* feeling of injustice because the individual always feels the restrictions imposed upon him by society. . . ."

In view of the outcome of the June '87 election, the new administration could well be in office for close to the full five-year term. It might be well, therefore, to recall the words of Polybius in the 2nd century BC:

> "Those who know how to win are much more numerous than those who know how to make proper use of their victories."

Any government can run into trouble, with the professions, the trade unions or the more hair-trigger minorities. Some governments seem from the start to invite trouble. Political circles, a few days after the election, were expecting (or warning) Mrs Thatcher's fourth Trade Union Act to be on the statute book by mid-summer 1988. What response, though, could be expected from the militants, who had already hinted at extra-Parliamentary action? One thing was clear. They would inevitably lose face if they failed to come up with an excuse — which the public would accept as a *reason* — for the action promised.

History records that the miners won the first round of the battle with Ted Heath in the '70s. Mrs Thatcher won hands-down in the '80s. Is it conceivable that either side will be content to leave it at that, rather than go for a once-for-all-time knock out? It did not take long in '87 for the newly appointed Energy Secretary, Cecil Parkinson, to announce plans to privatise the electricity industry by 1990, creating two giant private monopolies, neither of which would compete with the other. At Barnsley on June 20th, nine days after the election, Arthur Scargill told miners they might have to come out on strike against the new code of conduct the Coal Board had introduced; a code by which the Board gave itself the right to judge, and discipline miners

394 Into The Upwave

whose personal conduct — in their view — fell below the standard expected
of its employees.

In some ways, the prospects on the mainland are acquiring that grey,
hopeless look which characterised those uneasy years in Northern Ireland
almost 20 years ago, before the Six Counties went up in flames. Some felt
that the new administration would do well to recall the advice given to British
businessmen in 1961 by Nikita S. (We'll bury you) Kruschev:

> "When you are skinning your customers, you should leave some skin on
> to grow so that you can skin them again."

All in all, the individual Briton might be well advised to start considering
what he — or she — should do before the first signs go up, reading the
unambiguous message:

> "Keep Right for the *Gulag*"

Life in the Gulag

Let's return for a moment to first principles. By its very nature, the collapse
of a civilisation gains momentum along the way. The decline of the British
Empire can best be illustrated by a graph which accelerates exponentially.
More evidence of collapse can be seen in the fifty years from 1917-67 than
in the previous century. More signs of the disintegration of Britain as a nation
can be seen in the past 20 years than in the previous half century; and more
in the past 10 years than in the previous 2 decades.

The causes of the decline in a civilisation are more difficult to perceive
than the collapse itself. In a very literal sense, it's moral standards which
constitute the foundations of a civilisation. Is not morality what ultimately
distinguishes *homo sapiens* from the beasts of the wild? When the foundations
of a structure are destroyed, the structure itself must fall. We now live in
a society where many of yesterday's most cherished values and beliefs have
been dismissed as outmoded and useless; while some of the worst vices
of the past are now accepted — encouraged even! Licentiousness, promiscuity,
perversion, legalised thievery and a debt-burdened society are accepted as
the norm. Little wonder that the foundations of our civilisation are crumbling!

At the heart of our disintegrating society lies the abandonment of a belief
— once sacrosanct — in the inalienable rights of the individual. In its place,
we have put the inalienable right of the mob to rule. Down the ages, we
have been taught to distinguish Might from Right. Now, in effect, we say,
"Forget the old distinction. . . Might *makes* Right." We go further. "Right"
is whatever the most powerful group in the community says it is. The
dominant group may be many different things, and described in many ways.
We may talk of "the electorate", "the populace", "the people", or "the power-
elite". It is irrelevant whose influence extends over the group, or why. Where

it does, it does! Might becomes Right. We have no time for the old questions. We have moved on. We should be ready to recognise that our society no longer respects the rights of the individual. They might conflict with the rights of the all-powerful mob, which alone may rule.

Back in the days when we were widely seen as barbarians, the rule of the most powerful was the rule of the universe. . . as well as the rule of the animal kingdom. Laws and government are supposed to have changed all that. They did for many centuries. But now?

It is true that democratic principles have not entirely been abandoned. They are much talked of and praised. The word "democracy" is increasingly bandied about. The principles of democracy, however, are broader and finer than merely one man-one vote. But they have been twisted and perverted to support the new doctrine. The argument runs thus:

> "In a democracy the majority has its way.
> This gives power to the majority.
> In our society, the mob has the power.
> We are a democracy. Therefore. . .
> The mob is entitled to rule."

Faulty logic, lacking moral foundation. Yet this is what we continue to accept. Not that democracy has ever been perfect — depending as it does on the selection of representatives who, once elected, are virtually free to act as they please. Viewing the matter in practical terms, we have the verdict of history. It tells us that the majority have been mostly wrong, most of the time, about most things. But that is no justification for giving up; for granting a licence to one group to commit aggressive acts against another, merely because it has the power. Nor can we justify that one group seeking to do so, quoting the very "democratic principles" which have been so readily betrayed. When laws are ignored, and acts of violence by a favoured group are licensed by the State, we are heading fast down the road towards the Gulag.

Ambition, greed and envy are traits common to all men and women, at all levels of society, from the Norman baron to the chief executive of a multi-national mega-billion corporation; from the *villein* in the fields, to the latrine marines who scrub out the toilets in the headquarters of Meglamania Inc. When the State encourages such traits, it is colluding with the power-corrupted. Our whole system is debased beyond recovery. It happens, too, when politicians and union leaders are guaranteed a long and prosperous career — provided they can appeal strongly enough to the greed and envy of the voters. It also happens when the power-elite learn the way to manipulate the delicate mechanism of "majority rule" to serve their own ends. They can do it so skilfully that the clock goes on ticking — but it shows only the time they *want* it to show! At that point, friends, we have arrived. Our smiling guide comes out to meet us. Welcome to the Gulag.

Inside, it's just like the world we left. Here too, individual responsibility has yielded to mob-rule. Here too *desire* has become "need". But the *need-*

needs of the favoured few have been satisfied, the inalienable right of each individual to life, love and the pursuit of happiness is left on the threshold. Here the traditional rights of the individual must be exchanged for the inalienable right to credit, to own one's home, to eat more than required, and — if necessary — to murder the other creatures with whom we share this planet. There is, above all, the right to dip into the wage-packet of the creators and producers. . . provided one remains a fully paid-up non-producer! There is free education, medical care, and a chance to play the stock market. In other words, the inmates are entitled to all the goodies reserved for the young, the old, the infantile, the just born and the unborn in the society which began to emerge in the 1980s.

You will notice that the non-productives continue to overtake the productives. That is because the latter still hold out, refusing to abdicate personal initiative to the State. As we have already seen in this chapter, over-sized television sets — like money — do not grow on trees. And the State has no money! But that doesn't seem to worry too many of the Gulag dwellers. That is because one of the first things dinned into every inmate is that whatever is done in the Gulag is done "for the common good".

In her best selling novel, *The Fountainhead,* Ayn Rand had a great deal to say about the "common good of the collective":

"The 'common good of a collective' — a race, a class, a state — was the claim and justification of every tyranny ever established over men. Every major horror of history was committed in the name of an altruistic motive. Has any act of selfishness ever equalled the carnage perpetrated by the disciples of altruism? Does the fault lie in men's hypocrisy or in the nature of the principle? The most dreadful butchers were the most sincere. They believed in the perfect society reached through the guillotine and the firing squad. Nobody questioned their right to murder since they were murdering for an altruistic purpose. It was accepted that man must be sacrificed for other men. Actors change, but the course of tragedy remains the same. A humanitarian who starts with declarations of love for mankind ends with a sea of blood. It goes on and will go on so long as men believe that an action is good if it is unselfish. That permits the altruist to act and forces his victims to bear it."

Let's not say it too loudly, but the so-called democracy of the Gulag — for all the free speech, universal suffrage and the stream of fascinating opinion polls — is little more than a legalised mechanism for the sequestration of the wealth created by the few for the benefit of the more numerous non-deservers, by means of theft, force and fraud.

One good thing which can be said about the Gulag we love and know, is that the gates are still wide open. Maybe now is the time for those unappreciative, malcontents and ingrates — who still hanker after independence — to start packing up a few valuables, ready to make a move before the Head Keeper decides that the gates have been open long enough.

Chapter Eleven

ORWELL'S GUIDE TO THE GULAG
ANGLO-PEDIGREE

The Party seeks power entirely for its own sake. . . we are interested solely in power. . . Power is not a means: it is the end.

"O'Brien" (in *1984*)

Whoever you are, wherever you live in Britain, whatever your ancestry, however you spend your time and money, there is one thing of which you can be absolutely certain: you are an expert, inveterate player of an extremely risky "game".

You may never have remotely thought of entering a casino. It's more than likely that you are blissfully and totally unaware that you should never draw to an inside straight while playing poker, and you should always take the odds behind the line when rolling dice. If you're like a large number of sophisticated, thinking people who read books, you'll probably find Trivial Pursuit, Monopoly and Scrabble, paralysingly boring. You may visit the Cote D'Azur for sun, fun and food, unaware of the location or existence of the casino nightlife. And, you may even believe that Pacman is the job title of a shipping clerk. Nonetheless, you are involved in a game . . . a very ruthless, tough competitive game with exceptionally high stakes. The risks are your personal freedom and whatever material wealth you may have amassed up until now. The most pernicious part of it all is, you must play the game. You have no choice. Not to play the game is not to live in Britain . . . or not to live at all.

It should be perfectly clear that you're going to stand very little chance of winning any game unless you know the rules. In fact, it's pretty damn foolish to become involved in a game if you don't know the rules. Unless you can master the rules, there's little chance you'll even finish the game. The name of the game that I'm referring to is "Power Über Alles". The game involves the sequestration, confiscation and control of wealth along with the God-given — as opposed to Government-given — inalienable freedoms of the individual. The participants in the game are Government on the one side and the British electorate on the other. It's a war game in so much as the victors take all, while the losers are left vanquished.

The first rule you must become familiar with when considering the merits of the game and your chances of winning is "The Golden Rule". According to "The Golden Rule" of this game, those who control all of the "gold" make all of the rules. Now, you know who controls all of the "gold" in Britain. It's "Big Mother". Or, more precisely, the grey eminence who pulls the strings of power that serve to formulate the policies of your elected leaders, who are deemed responsible for the success or failure of whatever policies have been instigated.

In general, the rules of the game give Government the right to legislate and control the supply and distribution of money. In so doing, through taxation and other means, the Government is then able to confiscate the personal wealth of the opposing force, who are also stripped of their individual rights and freedoms in the process. In this case, YOU are the opposing force. You lose the game when the Government, through its power, is able to drive all the malcontents into the Gulag where the ultimate penalty is incarceration or death.

The weapons which are at the disposal of the electorate are wealth, the ballot box and the ability to take up arms. The strategies of the forces opposing the electorate are multifarious and devious. But, as the objectives become clear, and it is seen that Government is in the process of seizing what is rightly the personal property of the electorate, the battle rages as the electorate fight in every possible way to protect their freedom and possessions. Having exhausted all available legal (or illegal) means of lightening the tax burden, or whatever other means are being used to sequester their wealth, some may seek to remove their wealth from harm's way and surrender early in the game, departing for distant shores. Others may seek an advantage by using their vote for the purpose of neutralising the effects of the existing administration in favour of a more amenable one. They can, therefore, threaten an existing government with extinction, which can happen when a ruling party loses at the polls. Defeat, as we have seen from the recent plight of the Labour Party in Britain, can be so demoralising that a major party may be unable to provide an effective opposition for several administrations. As the game continues, and more bitterness develops between the opposing sides, individual governments and party members may be driven physically into exile. In a total defeat, the Government and its members may be literally obliterated. This will leave the electorate with an extremely formidable opponent in the form of a one-party system. I see this now taking place in Britain.

Given the power of the Government and the limited powers of the individual, you may feel you have little chance of being on the winning side of this game. That may be the case, but not necessarily. A lot depends on the "state of play". In their book, *Blood in the Streets,* Sir William Rees-Mogg and James Dale Davidson claim that communism was introduced into Russia by the megapolitical powers when it appeared that the Soviets were about to threaten the economic designs of the Western oligarchies. The same covert forces that broke up the old Tsarist empire, by implanting the germs of Marxism and Leninism, were successfully deployed to undermine the USSR.

The authors claim that communism no longer poses a threat to the mega-political powers, who are now moving at an accelerating pace in their efforts towards the construction of a one-world-government society. . . their government and their world. . . utilising totalitarian fascist techniques. That puts Moscow on the losing side of the game that's being played on the other side of the world. If the authors of *Blood in the Streets* are right, it puts a fresh complexion on the new mood in the Kremlin — especially if Moscow shares the view expressed by the authors in their remarkable treatise. At the same time, a new problem is posed for the electorate of Western governments such as Britain and the United States.

Apocalypse 2000, by Peter Jay and Michael Stewart, introduces a further variation on a theme. The sub-title of *Apocalypse 2000* is *The Economic Breakdown and Suicide of Democracy 1989 − 2000*. Like George Orwell's *1984* and *The Collapse of Democracy* by Robert Moss, the book is written in a "factional" style. . . fiction based on fact. The fact element which is the common denominator of all the works is the economic consequences of a totalitarian regime. The fictional element is that it hasn't happened in the Western industrialised countries. . . just yet. In their book, Peter Jay and Michael Stewart explain in great detail how the destruction of democracy could easily occur unless drastic policy changes are implemented by Western governments. By looking back in history from the vantage point of the early years of the 21st century, the authors depict a total disaster where monetary systems have collapsed, free trade is but a memory, while social and economic devastation is everywhere and rioting in the streets is the common-place, everyday way of life. The authors see a world that is not fit to live in — a world far more horribly plausible than the doomed planets we read about in science fiction novels — where the only escape from desolation and despair in the 21st century is the mental anaesthetic offered by drugs.

According to the historical dialogue, things began to go terribly awry for the West during the 1980s. . . in other words, just about now. In Europe, it is envisaged that a neo-Hitler figure emerges who imposes on the EEC his vision of a third economic and military super-power, capable of total global domination. While this neo-Hitler is using national pride as his principal political platform, seducing the European masses, a new President is elected in the United States. The new President is portrayed as a man of reason and statesmanship, who opposes the fascist regime that is gaining momentum in Europe. As a result, the US President is quickly deposed and replaced by a megalomaniacal right-wing extremist, who is also a religious fanatic. He gains control of both Houses of Congress, and becomes a supporter of the totalitarian alliance.

Coinciding with the lunatic leader in the White House, and the fascist leader in Europe, is a clash between Western consumerism and traditionalism in the Far East, along with a total upheaval in the Soviet Union. The final result is apocalyptic, involving a complete global economic break-down and disappearance of democracy. But the authors offer a ray of hope. It all need not end that way. In the game of "Power Über Alles", the electorate does have a chance, if it acts decisively and quickly enough.

One of the worst things that can happen to a society is to adopt a one-party system and embrace a government that's hard to get rid of. This appears to have happened in Britain with the election of the Thatcher administration for a third term of office. The odds in favour of the electorate winning the game of "Power Über Alles" are rapidly diminishing.

The Fourth Estate. . . The Black Knight

In the game of chess, one of the most treacherous pieces of all is the Knight. Unable to move as many squares as the Queen, the Rook or the Bishop, the Knight makes up for this disability by the unique manner in which it becomes an essential ingredient of many deceptive and devastating combinations in the end game. The Knights consequently pose an even greater threat than many of the other pieces, whose movements are far easier to anticipate. A grand-master chess player will jealously guard his Knight to a greater extent than pieces which have a greater value. He will use the Knight to its full potential for his opening gambit, through control of the centre of the board, finally launching him as the ultimate weapon in the end game. Control of the Knight throughout the game is quintessential. In the game of "Power Über Alles", the Fourth Estate adequately fulfils the function of the Black Knight, whose shadowy, semi-visible movements can dictate the terms, as well as the outcome, of the end game.

Before Edmund Burke, it was generally recognised that there were Three Estates in the Realm. . . the Lords, the Commons and the Clergy. It was Edmund Burke who drew our attention to a Fourth Estate. . . what we now refer to as "the media". A generation later, Lord Macaulay confirmed the status of the Fourth Estate. In his work, *Hallam's Constitutional History*, Macaulay said the gallery in which the reporters sat had become ". . . a Fourth Estate of the realm". To Thomas Carlyle, this was not merely a figure of speech, or a witty saying. To Carlyle, the Fourth Estate was decidedly becoming a force in its own right:

> "The stupendous Fourth Estate, whose wide world-embracing influences what eye can take in?"

Control of the Fourth Estate — the media — is a quintessential element for success in the game of "Power Über Alles". I know of no other governing party in Britain's history which has been so determined (and equally successful) in controlling the media as Mrs Thatcher's Conservative Government of the 1980s.

Without a doubt, one of the major factors that distinguish a dictatorship from a democracy is the extent to which government controls the media, and the various other mechanisms through which propaganda is disseminated, for the purposes of placing the Government in the most favourable light — as opposed to the reporting of facts as they occur. In Britain, the techniques employed by the Government in managing the news have become progressively more sophisticated, involving a combination of profound administrative secrecy with obedient and compliant political reporting. If Britain were a democracy, such a tendency would be considered unique. I no longer consider the British political system to be in any way consistent with the democratic principles upon which it was founded. Neither do I consider the methods employed to manipulate the media in any way unique.

For quite some time, British governments have sought to manage the news: focusing on whatever would be in the interest of the incumbent party. While suppressing anything which would not be in the best interest of political objectives, they are continually polishing the image of the party leader. James Margach, the former political correspondent on *The Sunday Times*, reported on the media activities of twelve Prime Ministers from David Lloyd-George to James Callaghan:

> "With obsessional ruthlessness and even ferocity they almost all sought to dominate the press, radio and television as the vital preconditions to their domination of Parliament, parties and public opinion. They desired to enrol and exploit the media as an arm of government. Two objectives possessed them. First to establish and fortify their personal power and second to reinforce the conspiracy of secrecy, to preserve the sanctity of government behind the walls of Whitehall's forbidden city".

Attempts to change the opinions of others through the manipulation of truth is probably as old as language itself. Through language comes the power to manipulate, or persuade people without necessarily resorting to physical force. Direct violence, or the threat of violence, may produce submission to the will of another individual or group. But thoughts are primarily created and modified through language — as spoken on TV or radio, and as appearing in the press and magazines. In the area of "brainwashing", words may be supplemented by unpleasant physical treatment. When attempting to persuade people to purchase shares in privatisation issues, the verbiage is supplemented by pleasing pictures and music. In both cases, the essential techniques of persuasion are verbal and symbolic, with the results aimed at the psychological. In general, and with very few exceptions, psychological transformations require psychological techniques. It is the deployment of psychological influences through the mass media, rather than external compliance brought about by force alone, that gives George Orwell's "thought police" such a prominent role in controlling the behaviour of the populace in his novel *1984*.

In an age of conflicting ideologies, entire nations are being subjected to group persuasion through new means of faster and more reaching communication, new techniques and the pull of mass movements led by demagogues. Malleability of the thought processes which dictate behaviour patterns is an important consideration for all who wish to exercise control over others. Some authorities hold the view that we are all virtually at the mercy of the mass media and the techniques used for group stimulation. It has also been suggested that "brainwashing" and similar techniques available to the modern mind-manipulator through the mass media are not only irresistible, but can lead to real and permanent changes in political outlook and ideologies. If these beliefs are well-founded — and I believe they are — the outlook for Britain is not very pleasant to contemplate. According to the other Fleet Street authors of *Sources Close to the Prime Minister*, Mrs Thatcher has won and held her lead at successive general elections primarily through the use of advisers versed in the most modern American media techniques. Such techniques have "reached new levels under Mrs Thatcher". In a scathing condemnation of the manner in which the mass media are now manipulated in Britain, Michael Cockerell, Peter Henessey and David Walker assert:

> "Facts are the raw material of democracy. Without them voters cannot make reasoned choices between parties or policies or politicians. Without them voters cannot call their governments into account. The British people live in one of the most stable and sophisticated parliamentary democracies in the world — yet in a vital sense that democracy is a sham because the British people are governed by a system which does all it can to deny them facts. A half-informed nation cannot take proper decisions about taxing and spending: decision making becomes the preserve of private government. Yet, Parliament, the people and the press not only tolerate this British obsession with secrecy, they allow it to act as a formal and intimidating apparatus within which governments may practise an anti-democratic technique to their heart's content."

Through the press lobby, and in turn through the mass media, Mrs Thatcher has continually and unrelentingly declared herself an enemy of big government, a partisan of the individual against the state, opposed to superfluous and inefficient bureaucracy. Ever since taking office in 1979, through three successive administrations, she clearly has been a dedicated supporter of the very secrecy which shelters the bureaucracy she has so scorned. She also has pursued policies diametrically opposed to the political platform presented to — and endorsed by — the media.

In Orwell's *1984*, it is the Ministry of Information, which having secured control of the Fourth Estate, proliferates "newspeak" and "double-think". It is my profound contention that by a similar brand of "newspeak" and "double-think", the British electorate have been irreconcilably seduced by the Thatcher administration. The mass seduction began in 1979, gently and subtly at first. By 1987, this mass seduction reached its most blatant, and was plain for all to see, early in October 1987, at the Conservative Party Conference in Blackpool.

Writing in the *Financial Times*, political editor Peter Ridell and his reporting team summed up the conference in terms which left little doubt as to the purpose of the *soirée*. The ironic remark by the Conservative Minister whom Ridell chose to quote, had in fact hit the nail smack on the head:

> "We've got a one-party state and it isn't going to change quickly."

This statement alone should have struck terror into the heart of every Briton. Without exception, history demonstrates — with bloodshed and lost lives — that power corrupts. . . absolute power corrupts absolutely. Yet, in the same manner that those condemned under the Third Reich cheered their orators — who were also their executioners — those attending the Blackpool Conservative Party Conference, ranted and waved their blue-dyed-red-flags in a standing ovation for the demagogy that was being slowly but certainly imposed upon them:

> " . . . the press benches in front of the platform were cleared of humble scribblers in order to make way for the photographers."

All available arts were employed in the build-up to the Leader's speech. And no wonder! In the old days, no Conservative Leader would attend the Party Conference. That was considered as a gathering of the privileged rank-and-file members. It was a form of recognition for those who worked tirelessly in the wards, collecting annual subscriptions, running coffee mornings, organising Jumble Sales and Bring-and-Buys, and — when the challenge came — attending campaign meetings and canvassing "on the door-step". A few Ministers would be invited to contribute to the debates, but few MPs would care to attend unless their Constituency Chairman said he would be *delighted* to see them "during the week".

As late as the 1960s, when Harold Macmillan intimated that he would not be leader for ever. . . even he was mortal! . . the old rituals had been observed. By the time he made his appearance at the rally, the appeal for party funds had already been made, bags had been packed and hotel bills paid. Now — at last — the Leader would speak. SuperMac was a master of such occasions, relying on his patrician mien and histrionic skills. For Edward Heath and the present Leader, an almost constant presence in the hall, smiling or frowning at the various speakers, popping up on "the box" from time to time, has made the task much more difficult. In Mrs Thatcher's case — what should she wear?

If the Leader's speech is to be the high spot (and not a let-down), merely making an appearance will not be enough. The chosen one, who all week has appeared in a range of familiar roles, cannot suddenly switch from stern but fair headmistress to Conservative Goddess — which is what the party faithful are entitled to expect. Therefore, she must undergo a complete transformation.

The necessary build-up today calls for more than a fanfare followed by mock Churchillian rhetoric. There must be music and lights, to reinforce the impact of the microphones and hidden auto-cue devices. At Blackpool in 1987, the atmosphere, reported the *FT:*

" . . . was heightened by the triumphal organ strain of the party's general election theme."

But when the Chosen One herself appeared on the platform:

" . . . this incongruously gave way to the tune of *I do like to be beside the sea-side* presumably as a gesture towards the populist nature of her regime."

Those at the Conference came away convinced that the third Thatcherite election victory was only "a staging post on a much longer journey." As for what may be expected along that way, two passages in the speech were worthy of note. First, a word on the state of the deeply divided nation:

"Recovery has come faster in some parts of the country than others. But now it's taking root in most depressed urban landscapes."

These words, as dwellers on Teeside, in Gateshead, Wolverhampton and the West Midlands will have noted, were uttered *after* the Leader had visited their part of the country. They were rhetorically formulated for the edification of those with little knowledge of that area of the country, just as the various economic projections of the Chancellor of the Exchequer are designed for those who know little of economics, and are unable to distinguish between the statistical economy and the "real" economy, where people have to live, work and eat.

At the Conservative Party Conference, which seemingly saw that no alternative party was at the pinnacle of its power, Chancellor of the Exchequer Nigel Lawson predicted that the British economy was set to grow at a world-beating four per cent — thanks to the discipline, tax reform and encouragement of individual initiative that the government had provided. This represented the first public confirmation by Mr Lawson of the revision upwards of the 3% growth forecast projected in the March Budget. Mr Lawson said that Britain would enjoy its best economic performance for 14 years. This was totally to disregard the OECD forecast made two weeks earlier, which stated that Britain was likely to suffer its worst decline in output growth for over a decade. At Blackpool, in keeping with the generally unfettered euphoric tone of the Conference — totally undeflected by reason — Mr Lawson said "the British economy has been transformed."

Now, in case you may have forgotten, it was early in 1984 that the same Chancellor of the Exchequer, Nigel Lawson, told a group of Liverpool journalists that "only charlatans know the future". In the true tradition of Orwellian "newspeak" and "double-think", the electorate have been told that all economists are charlatans, but some economists are more charlatan than others — implying that the economists employed by the Government

·are less charlatanistic than others. Indeed, they may actually know something about the future that non-Government sources don't know! In turn, you are being asked to ignore the predictions or forecasts of those "charlatans" which may conflict with those of the Chancellor — or of any other individual or group of individuals out of tune with the "party line".

The type of duplicity and misinformation I've outlined is characteristic of the statements made by this government to a media that have been more than happy to propagate and disseminate the propaganda offered as the truth; and to do so unthinkingly and unquestioningly. Throughout the reign of Mrs Thatcher, it has seemed that anyone who disagreed with the manner in which the government had presented itself, would be placed by the media into the category of imbeciles, heretics, madmen or left-wing extremists. Those who may have condemned the methods and accomplishments claimed by the Thatcher regime, and were able to produce the plethora of statistics that demonstrate the inexorable decline of the British economy under "Thatcherism", are either ignored, or chosen as targets for denigration and character assassination by the Fourth Estate.

"Let's get em!", was the shriek from the chorus line of Fleet Street hacks during Mrs Thatcher's bid for a third reign of power in the summer of '87. It is difficult to establish how far the syndicate of the Fourth Estate was politically motivated as opposed to the extent to which they were merely behaving in the time-honoured, venomous way the British press tends to behave on any "occasion" they are all forced to share. Regardless of the reason, one thing was clear at the time — there was a recognisable common denominator when it came to identifying the target. Any infidel with the slightest notoriety, who might possibly cast doubt on the sanctity of Mrs Thatcher's rule, was an automatic candidate for denigration or character assassination. Those who dared question the economic forecasts, and feasibility of the party political platform were eliminated as a source of editorial copy during the election campaign. Never before had I seen such unanimous support for any political party by the syndicate of the Fourth Estate as I witnessed during the run-up to the General Election of 1987.

Fleet Street is acutely aware that simple minds like simple things — such as catch-words and catch-phrases. The chosen catch-phrase for the Labour Party was "the Loony Left". It was a phrase designed for an unthinking electorate to commit to their psyche whenever reminded of the Labour Party.

In order to give the impression of objectivity and balanced reporting (which is vital if the Fourth Estate is to achieve the credibility it needs to maintain power), severe criticisms of the government are published from time to time. But, be sure, these criticisms will appear only after the source has been duly neutered through months of careful preparation. The catch-phrase, "Loony Left" proved exceptionally useful when applied to the Lambeth Council Leader Linda Bellos, who made the front page of the *Evening Standard* during the Conservative Party Conference with her castigation of the third administration under Mrs Thatcher:

"There is a streak of Nazism in the Tory party. I predict that so long as
we are ruled by Thatcherism, gas chambers will be here within seven to
ten years for lesbians, gay men, blacks and socialists. What we have seen
in the last eight years is a complete erosion of civil liberties, including the
social security proposals, the right of accused people to remain silent and
the poll tax.

"All these things together create a climate in which fascism is becoming
a reality. I am not just talking about people calling me a nigger in the street,
but black people are becoming more and more the victims of fire bomb
attacks.

"I am not personally accusing Mrs Thatcher of being a fascist. I am saying
that what is happening under Thatcherism is leading to fascism."

As a result of similar statements prior to that in the *Evening Standard*,
Ms Bellos had been stripped of her credibility through the various innuendos
and implications about her in the mass media for sometime. Ms Bellos had
been awarded the title of "Queen of the Loony Left" by Fleet Street. Had
this not been the case, and might Linda Bellos have retained any credibility,
it is most unlikely that her comments would ever have appeared in print.
Yet Linda Bellos is not a mad woman. She is an articulate, intelligent,
thinking human being with feelings and beliefs. There are obviously a large
number of individuals who share these feelings and beliefs, otherwise she
would not have been elected Leader of the Lambeth Council.

One must always give credit where credit is due. The Government's
manipulation of the media under the Thatcher regime has been enormously
successful. Since the transformation of the Conservative Party under Mrs
Thatcher, the entire British nation was mesmerised by "Thatcherism", which
was perceived to be a "new way". Experienced economists — whose
mutterings appear in print — led you to believe that even they had been
seduced by the persuasive rhetoric of the Thatcher administration, and that
the Conservative Party had actually made progress toward improving the
current and future prospects for the British economy. It was reported that
Mrs Thatcher had accepted that monetary.growth and consumer credit would
increase at a more explosive rate than at any time in history. Yet, the rhetoric
of the Thatcher administration remained unquestioned.

Many have been totally convinced that "Thatcherism" is dedicated to
making people more independent and self-reliant. There is certainly no
shortage of evidence to demonstrate that more people became reliant on
the state under the Thatcher regime than at any time since the 1930s. State
benefits and transfer payments reached an all time peak. Yet, so persuasive
was the rhetoric, so convincing the media's presentation of the Thatcher
dogma, that preconceptions that were subtly induced continued to hold.

Many still believe that a cornerstone of Mrs Thatcher's policy is the control
of inflation. Monetary policy has proved to be contrary to any which would
curb inflation. As we continue along the path of the "agonising '80s" we
find inflation in Britain creeping up again. We also find a vast polarisation
in regional inflation. While the nationwide average was stated in the autumn

of 1987 to be in the area of 4%, inflation in London was growing at the rate of 9.6%. Whatever self-congratulation the government had given itself in the past on bringing down the rate of inflation proved a fallacy. Inflation had fallen globally, due to global factors, which had nothing whatever to do with the policy of the Thatcher administration. The fact that most people are unaware of the depth of the domestic and global problems that exist is wholly the result of the propaganda effort instigated by this government, and promulgated through the Fourth Estate. So persuasive has been the suppression of views that might contradict the party rhetoric, that "Thatcherism" has been accepted as truth.

When the Conservative Government made its first bid for power during 1979, with a political platform promising greater freedom for individuals, lower taxation and the enhancement of personal initiative, I was wholly and unreservedly enthusiastic. I became suspicious of the methods and objectives of the Thatcher regime after the new Government's first budget. While this budget involved the same type of fiscal cosmetics as those of previous governments, the objectives seemed diametrically opposed to those which the pre-election platform of the Conservative Party had promised.

During the fourth quarter of 1979, signs of a recession began to appear. My concern deepened when I began to see the manner in which disinformation was being passed off as economic analysis during the early 1980s, when economic conditions in Britain were steadily deteriorating. Suddenly, there were substitutions in the economic indicators used by the Central Statistical Office. Indicators of economic activity were replaced by indicators reflecting nothing more than the opinion of the CBI. Such opinion, formulated by businessmen, echoed that of the politically inspired mass media, which supported the Thatcher regime in unison.

Base dates of economic indicators were changed under the Thatcher regime, with the explanation that these changes more accurately reflected economic activity. What actually took place was a break with the continuity of the past in an effort to present the British economy in a better light than would otherwise be the case. Since the present Government took office, there have been 22 changes in the way unemployment statistics are calculated. Once again, the people have been told that such changes are needed to give a more accurate picture of economic conditions. Ironically, every change has meant a lower number than would otherwise have been the case had the original figures been maintained.

My continued investigations into the various attempts to misinform the public satisfied me beyond all reasonable doubt that the distribution of disinformation and propaganda, taking place with increasing momentum, was on a scale never before attempted by any British Government. During 1983, I desperately wanted to alert people to the manner in which news and information were being suppressed and distorted, when it did not suit the objectives of the political elite, or the grey eminence who controls the political elite. The article was entitled *The Paper Curtain*. It was eventually published in *Penthouse Magazine*, which at the time was trying to improve its image as something other than a girlie mag. *Penthouse* was the only magazine willing to publish my article, which was rejected by everyone else who saw it.

Since then, we've seen the Fourth Estate coming under the domination of a decreasing number of interests — all with the sanction of the British government. During early 1987, Rupert Murdoch successfully by-passed the rules of the takeover panel in his efforts to acquire the *Today* newspaper. Others whose monopolistic endeavours were of far less magnitude had failed. Rupert Murdoch is a known admirer and staunch supporter of Mrs Thatcher's policies.

Actually, the Fourth Estate and the government have a common interest and motivation. Both are out to win the favour of the electorate, and so maintain supremacy over them. If people like what a particular TV programme has to say, they will cast their vote by watching that programme whenever it appears. On the other hand, if too many people do not like what they see (or hear) on a particular programme, they will vote the producers out of a job by switching channels.

Obviously, it is in the interests of the Fourth Estate to tell people what it perceives to be popular at the time, whether it be true or not. It has always been a popular political line in every age — throughout every area of the world — to tell the people the politicians serve more of everything. To tell them that they have *an inalienable right to more* of everything; that is the government's duty, and obligation, to make certain the people *receive* more of everything. In this respect, the government says it and the media swear to it. . .

In Aldous Huxley's *Brave New World*, the people are provided with "somas". The purpose of the "soma" was to divert attention from reality. In both Aldous Huxley's *Brave New World* and George Orwell's *1984*, the ultimate weapon in controlling the minds of the masses is to keep the minds of the masses occupied — and away from any kind of serious thinking — through constant transmissions over the varied means of communications available. The idea is to keep them laughing, crying, excited, hating the enemy — anything at all. Total mind control was achieved in Orwell's vision of the future by keeping the minds of the masses programmed, and occupied, at all costs. In our contemporary, real society, that means not only guilt- and envy- orientated news stories, but also situation comedies whose level of intellectual achievement never exceeds that of an eight year old child; an unending flow of trivia and minutiae dressed up as a crisis; degradation, denigration and sensationalism; sex, violence, football, darts, snooker, boxing — anything that can induce vicarious involvement, distracting the people's minds from the humdrum nature of their existence in the Gulag.

What the Fourth Estate will avoid like poison — and the authorities will censure — is the presence of any of the many rational, intelligent, economic experts in Britain or elsewhere who may have a clear understanding of the fiscal distortions which are bankrupting the country. Prophets have never been popular, primarily because most individuals do not take kindly to predictions that suggest they may be about to experience retribution for their apathy and licentious endeavours. It makes the task of mind-control that much easier, both for the government and its pawns in the Fourth Estate. As Humbert Wolfe said:

> "You cannot hope to bribe or twist (thank God) the British journalist.
> Considering what the chap will do unbribed, there's no occasion to."

In addition to the "experts" kept by individual members of the media on their "approved list", Whitehall maintains a sort of standing army of "experts" whose function is to be on call at all times to deny anything the blasphemous prophets might have to say. I had first hand experience of that "standing army" when I appeared on Capital Radio and forecast a fall in house prices. My broadcast was followed by a sharp letter from the Secretary General of the Building Societies Association who decried everything I had to say. A panel of "experts" was quickly assembled for a broadcast the following evening. These "experts", supposedly "objective," consisted of a solicitor who earned a good deal of his income from conveyancing, an estate agent who derived his entire income from the sale of houses, and a spokesman from a building society which thrived on granting mortgages. Their "objective" opinion was that there could *not be* a fall in house prices. They spent half an hour refuting what I had said in three minutes. But I was not given any opportunity to counter what they had said, nor was I invited to appear on Capital Radio ever again.

From time to time, an economist or commentator with a meaningful message manages to slip through the media's defensive screen. Whenever any of the leading economic minds of our time — men like Frederick A. Hayek, Milton Friedman, Ralf Dahrendorf, John Eatwell, Sidney Pollard, William Keegan, Andrew Gamble, Keith Smith, James Bellini, Andrew Glyn, John Harrison, Christopher Story — have begun to make the slightest penetration of the minds of the average citizen, the Fourth Estate throw open their magazines, television and radio stations to Whitehall's standing army of powerful, ignorant and morally corrupt economic puppets, who are given free access to British homes. They quickly assure the public that the forecasts of these economic "alarmists" are nonsense. The assurances given by the government's followers prove quite effective, since the true prophets have no corresponding means of responding *en masse*.

As it stands, the news and information circulated in Britain — and published about Britain for the rest of the world to see — is determined by the editorial policy of a frighteningly tiny handful of individuals. If these vested interests want you to see something in print, it appears in print. The same applies to your radio and TV. If *they* decide their interests would not be best served if you were told of the true state of the economy, or the impending failure of a building society, the likely failure of a bank, the dire straits of a company such as Rolls Royce, the problems Britain may be having with transfer payments, the artificial nature of invisible exports, etc. . . . *ad infinitum*. . . *ad nauseam*. . . either that information will be relegated to obscurity or left to the small group of independent journalists working on newspapers such as *The Guardian* and *The Observer* — or in what has been described as the "underground press".

Before you are permitted to read or hear an alternative view, it is likely that efforts will have been made to detract from the credibility of the sources and of the papers or programmes where that alternative view may appear. The propaganda machine has been moderately successful in spreading the word that *The Guardian* represents the "left-wing" press. While you may *read* whatever appears in *The Guardian*, as a supporter of Mrs Thatcher, you are expected to dismiss what you read, in view of the reputation of its origin. The same holds for individual media and news journalists like James Bellini or William Keegan. It has become popularly accepted that journalists who disagree with the policies of the Thatcherite administration, as portrayed in the popular press, must be anarchists or left-wing extremists. . . carriers of social disease. Such is the extent to which public opinion and thought has been manipulated.

When Might is Right. . . or Left!

History may be imperfect, but it is at least a matter of record — provided no one burns the history books. What is yet to become history can prove to be no more than conjecture. I have examined the methods by which the present regime in Britain has mobilised the syndicate of the Fourth Estate to gain greater control of the thoughts and desires of the electorate as it plays the "Power Über Alles" game. Where this road ultimately takes us is not yet a matter of history. Therefore it must be considered as no more than conjecture. In order to recognise the awesome possibilities, it would be useful to recall the ways in which the syndicate of the Fourth Estate has been used to further the objectives of powerful interest in the past, as well as to consider the dire hardship emerging from the callousness of those whom we elect to serve our best interests.

In the United States, in 1914, it was beyond any question of conjecture that J.P. Morgan, one of the world's most prominent bankers, was a leading member of a group of the most influential pro-war propagandists of modern times. Together with the Rockefellers and other leading bankers, J. Pierpont Morgan was responsible for floating millions of dollars worth of war loans. They wanted the USA to guarantee these loans by entering the war, which had broken out in August between Britain, France and Russia — the main Western Allies — and the so-called Central Powers.

J.P. Morgan knew it would be necessary to win over liberal opinion — traditionally *anti*-war. So in addition to his open advocacy of war, Morgan launched his intellectual counter-attack by means of a magazine called *The New Republic*. Not to mince words, Coley, who ran it for Morgan, was an archetypal fascist.

Tribute must be paid in all honesty to the success of J.P. Morgan's ploy. Having disguised the magazine as an unmistakeable liberal publication, Coley — in true fascist style — launched a successful reaction, gaining public support for certain aspects of medieval aristocracy. This he achieved by simply presenting them in liberal guise. His method was similar to that used by the Thatcherite Conservatives to present their left-wing policies under the banner of right-wing ideology. But more of that later.

The working press of the USA, which was largely liberal at the time, became vehemently bellicose in the period leading up to America's entry into the Great War in 1917. Without a doubt, a great deal of the pro-war propaganda appearing in the popular press stemmed from the inventions of Coley in *The New Republic*. When the United States Government seemed to be dragging its feet, unwilling to send its "boys" to join the conflict "over there", J.P. Morgan decided on a fresh ploy to speed the decision he wanted. Direct action!

It was Congressman Callaway (Texas) who shewed the direct link between J.P. Morgan's efforts and Washington's decision to join battle on the side of the Allies:

> "In March 1915, the J.P. Morgan interests, the steel, shipbuilding and powder interests, and their subsidiary organisations, got together 12 men high up in the newspaper world and employed them to select the most influential number of them to control generally the policy of the daily press in the United States."

The 12 men selected 179 newspapers. They then began a process of elimination, retaining only those absolutely necessary for controlling the general policy of the daily press coast to coast. They found they needed to purchase control of no more than 25 of the most important titles:

> " . . . an agreement was reached; the policy of these papers was bought, to be paid for by the month; an editor was furnished for each paper to properly supervise and edit information regarding the question of preparedness, militarism, financial policies, and other things of a national and international nature vital to the interests of the purchasers."

When the Serbian nationalists assassinated the Austrian Archduke, Austria was forced to assert itself. The Austro-Hungarian Empire was in dire straits. It feared that any failure to show strength following the assassination might encourage other acts of rebellion, leading to the break-up of the Empire. Russia, with ambitions to carve out an Empire of its own in the Balkans, mobilised in support of Serbia. From that moment, the die was cast. Since each side had its allies, major war was inevitable.

This put Germany in an exceptionally vulnerable position, surrounded as it was by the Franco-Russian alliance. Should the Austro-Hungarian Empire be defeated and dissolved, Germany would have lost its only ally. Rather than wait and risk being attacked at some later date, the military in Berlin argued it would be advisable for Germany to support the Austro-Hungarian Emperor against the Russians. The moment Moscow began to mobilise, Berlin — the weaker party — knew the time had come to exploit its only advantage by launching a surprise attack on Russia.

The moment Germany fell on Russia, France declared war on Germany. It may be argued that the French saw Berlin's action as more an excuse than a reason for retaliation; particularly as France's defeat in the Franco-Prussian War of 1871 had rankled ever since. The official reason given for England's entry into the war was Germany's violation of "Little Belgium's" neutrality, as its armies swept through the country in its aim of reaching Paris in six weeks. This, so far as it went, was true enough. Unfortunately the Kaiser and the High Command would not believe that England would go to war for the sake of a piece of paper. But, in any case, there were many in England who welcomed the excuse to "put the Kaiser in his place".

The hostility towards Imperial Germany was intense. It had grown increasingly so from the turn of the century as England and Germany became serious trade rivals, rivals in the colonial world, rivals on the High Seas. The attitude of the English press had been hostile to Germany for some years. The popular papers of the Left had run campaigns warning of the German menace. Some said the Germans were eager to stir up trouble in Ireland. Spy fever was rampant in the towns of England, and in the suburbs. A popular thriller of the day by Erskine Childers told how the Germans were preparing for *Der Tag*.

Germany was generally accepted at the time as the aggressor, because she had struck the first blow. Not surprisingly, this view was reaffirmed after Germany's defeat in 1918. The Germans — regarded as a nation of musicians, poets, engineers, soldiers, intellectuals and pork-butchers — had become the hated *Bosche*, the *Hun*, who (said the press) crucified their victims, tossed babies into the air and caught them on the point of their bayonets. Were they not guilty of every atrocity known to civilised man? And a few they had thought up for themselves! It meant that their women and children were a legitimate target — to be blockaded and starved into submission.

We may leave aside the terrible price that was paid years later for the excesses and hatred encouraged by those newspaper headlines as they screamed their message — "Hang the Kaiser" and "Make the Bosch Pay". The plain fact is that Germany was not the sole aggressor it was made out to be on the eve of the Great War. In retrospect, Germany can be seen as a frightened nation, surrounded by enemies — real or potential — who for their part were delighted to go to war. Not that anyone seriously imagined that having "given the Kaiser a bloody nose", it would not be "all over by Christmas". The situation was far better understood in the United States, where Russians, Germans, Englishmen, Irishmen, Italians and Poles lived — if not as neighbours — at least in adjoining neighbourhoods. The war and the rights and wrongs of the belligerents were seen in a different light by the immigrant Jews in Britain and the USA, for whom Russia was not a well-loved ally, but the country which had driven them, their parents and their grand-parents to seek refuge in the main English speaking countries in what they perceived as "The West".

Ironically, it was not the Allies but Berlin which acted after 1914 as the protector of the Palestinian Jews, putting pressure on the Turks not to conscript the settlers into the *Jaish*, from which few — Jew or Arab — were likely to return.

Gradually, in the United States, the jingoistic press managed to teach the American people what J.P. Morgan and his friends wanted them taught: German U-boats were sinking American ships without warning on the High Seas, in violation of the rules of war and international war. The prime case was the sinking of the *Lusitania*. We now know that the *Lusitania* was not the peaceful merchant vessel she was made out to be. She was a ship of war, an English auxiliary cruiser carrying tons of munitions. Moreover, she was armed and travelling through a war zone. In May 1915, she was sent to the bottom.

It need have come as no surprise to anyone had the facts been known. In this case the Fourth Estate was not alone responsible for the instant flow of lies and misinformation. The man in the White House, the former academic Woodrow Wilson, is generally regarded as one of the more highly principled of American Presidents. But war is war. It's even harder when you're still trying to "sell" the idea of war to the people and their legislators. So President Wilson lied about the incident in every possible way — from the nature of the ship to the nature of its cargo. He lied about the location of the allegedly unprovoked attack. He lied about the attack itself and the extent to which it was unexpected.

Something of the sort was bound to happen. At the beginning of the war, England and Germany had declared a blockade of each other's coasts. As they did so, they warned neutral vessels to refrain from carrying arms or other war material through the pre-defined war zones. The United States submitted to the British blockade.

But the highly bellicose American newspapers urged Washington to defy the *German* blockade. At the same time, there were always a few credulous travellers prepared to take the risk and travel on an arms carrier.

Some American citizens were lost when *Lusitania* went down. Although Americans had been warned in countless newspaper advertisements *not* to travel in what was strictly speaking a legitimate war target, they insisted on doing so. They knew what they were doing, and chose to take the risk. But *that* did not prevent the President's declaring that Germany had no right to sink British ships — not if American citizens chose to travel in them!

Nor did the lies stop there! When further armed carriers were sunk, the press put out more false information about the sinking of British ships and the casualties aboard American ships.

On May 4th 1916, in response to repeated threats from pro-war Congressmen, President Wilson requested Germany to lift her blockade. By not doing so, it was clear that Germany would sooner or later be starved into submission. On December 12th in the same year, Germany made a bid for peace on roughly equal terms with the Allies. But the Allies rejected the offer, refusing even to treat it as a basis for negotiation. Time — and Germany's capacity to feed her people — were running out.

On February 1st 1917, Germany resumed submarine warfare in an effort to starve England into submission before she was forced to give in. The re-activation of Germany's U-boats played right into the hands of J.P. Morgan. Coley was instructed to spearhead a high-powered, propaganda campaign in all the newspapers Morgan controlled. He did as instructed. The front cover of *The New Republic* launched J.P. Morgan's call to arms:

"Without delay diplomatic relations must be broken. The navy should be mobilised. Steps should be taken to arm all merchant ships. The terms and conditions of our entrance into the war should be announced."

Two weeks later Coley wrote:

"Americans would instantly respond to a deliberate defiance of Germany's threats. They would rejoice at being members of a nation which rose after long and just patience to answer so deliberate an enemy of western civilisation. The time to strike is now."

The rabble-rousing campaign, conducted by the jingoist press bought by J.P. Morgan, paid off. The White House asked for a declaration of war. Congress acquiesced. That meant an even larger fortune for Morgan. Most of the attacks launched on him at this time identified his motives for wanting America in the war with the war loans he had made to the Allies. His true motives went deeper than that. Very few people at the time managed to grasp the enormous power of the banks to create money out of nothing. Let alone the power of a Central bank to do so many times over! Even fewer people were aware of the colossal profits which accrue to bankers in times of war. Profits made no other way can ever accrue on a comparable scale. The purchase of those 25 leading newspapers was a small price to pay for the immense fortune which the House of Morgan would make once America had entered the war!

Washington's decision to join the Allies saw an end to the traditional notions of civil liberties, respect for the Constitution, democracy and freedom. They vanished. . . every one. . . in a mounting wave of war hysteria. This, after all, was a conflict the Fourth Estate had portrayed as:

"The War to Make the World Safe for Democracy"

To reinforce the war effort, the totalitarians moved in. They suppressed whatever elements of genuine democracy had so far escaped the authorities' control. They moved in fast. A Conscription Act was passed, containing a provision forbidding anyone to volunteer! Sedition Laws were enacted. These made it a criminal offence to criticise the United States Government. President Wilson — that saintly man — is known to have urged Congress to go along with a law allowing him *personally* to censor the press; claiming that this would be "absolutely necessary to public safety". Shenanigans of that kind were repeated often enough. But the case of J.P. Morgan 'Warmonger' is in itself sufficient to show the crucial part played by the Fourth Estate for any government — or faction — that is resolved to control the thoughts, and sap the resolution of a population without *appearing* to have thrown aside the basic principles of democracy.

As one ancient cracker-barrel philosopher put it, as he spat on the red-hot stove:

> "The democratic spirit is the Corn. The *forms* of democracy. . from the Supreme Court to the local hustings is no more than the Husk."

Whether the Government controls the media or the media controls the Government, is a moot point. At the moment, in contemporary Britain, a common interest makes each dependent on the other. The authorities will bestow favours on the media, while the media moguls extend their power. The media moguls will then act in support of incumbent government, manipulating the minds of their readers in whatever manner the authorities see fit.

If the authorities aspire to overt direct control of the media, they can have that whenever they want. The media moguls are aware of this. So is the government. In Robert Moss's *The Collapse of Democracy,* he describes a Britain where:

> "For the sake of the economy, the Government has reduced the number of newspapers to two dailies and one Sunday: The British Times, the Morning Star, and the one People's Mirror."

In his factional scenario of a future Britain, Robert Moss envisages the complete control of all forms of information input, including the importation of foreign newspapers:

> "It is difficult to gauge the mood of the times from these organs although their editors are mostly people who were prominent in Fleet Street or the provincial press before the General Strike. Television is, if anything, worse. The news documentary has disappeared completely — which is ironic in view of the fact that it was through this particular medium that the leaders of the present Government were able to present their version of events during the political storms of the 1970s.
>
> "Sport, old horror films, the Bolshoi ballet and historical sagas — many of them re-runs of serials popular in the 1970s — are now the order of the night. There are also the late night blue-movies on BBC2 which (rumour has it) were introduced to divert those insomniacs who might otherwise be thinking about politics."

In Britain, virtually everything we understand about the world in which we live, the nature of the British economy, the direction our government is taking us in, is the result of what appears in a network of newspapers, records, books, films, radio and TV owned by a mere twelve companies. These companies include household names such as EMI and Rank, along with huge combines such as British Electric Traction. Ninety-five per cent of the circulation of daily newspapers in Britain is now controlled by just five companies.

The way the world is portrayed through the mass communications network, determines what political parties and issues we support; the manner in which we may vote in a referendum and our feelings towards other members of the society. It determines how we spend our money, how much we borrow, where we live, with whom we wish to associate, and whom we feel we should discriminate against. It helps to define what our goals and objectives should be, how we should invest, how we should save and to whom we should owe allegiance. The concentration of ownership in the field of mass communications gives an immense power over our lives to those who use the media for propaganda purposes.

The press is probably the most striking example of all. In 1948, Lord Beaverbrook, then owner of the *Daily Express*, blatantly admitted to the Royal Commission on the Press:

> "My purpose originally was to set up a propaganda paper and I have never deviated from that purpose all through the years."

It is a matter of recorded history that other media moguls reported their political views in precisely the same way, inducing support for their political designs through the influence they held over their readership. Lord Rothermere, in the '30s, is known to have used his newspapers, including the *Daily Mail*, to provide support for the Nazis in Germany and Oswald Mosley's Blackshirts in Britain. His headlines proclaimed "HURRAH FOR THE BLACKSHIRTS". Readers were then given instructions as to how they might go about joining the British Union of Fascists.

The institutions of mass communications are extremely hierarchical. Even though controlled by relatively few, there are extremely close links between even this small number, who between them share a range of "official" and "acceptable" sources in Britain. It is for this reason that most of the news progressed through mass communication channels is presented in much the same way — as though there were no other way, and only one side to any story. As a result, people in Britain are exposed to a highly biased treatment of the way they are expected to see their country and the world in which we all live.

The background of a large number of journalists, and the circles in which they move, mean they share a common culture with some of the most powerful groups and interests in our society. The influence and aims of those in direct control can therefore be transmitted downwards through the tiers of the hierarchy without difficulty. Furthermore, "official" sources of information — the Treasury, the Bank of England, the Ministry of Labour and the Ministry of Defence — gain routine access to the media for the purpose of airing the views that will further the interests of Government. In a direct sense, the civil servants who act as spokesmen for the various government departments, can affect the livelihood of the journalists.

Obviously, "sources" close to the Prime Minister enjoy a monopoly over the news. Theirs is certainly the information that journalists wish to have access to as quickly as possible — preferably in advance of their competitors in other areas of the media. From time to time, Government spokesmen might leak the contents of a Cabinet discussion to those journalists who have proved the most supportive in the past. Press briefings are given to the favoured few, and the more powerful the interests at stake, the more closely guarded (and controlled) will be the "official" version.

In Britain, the Ministry of Defence has more press and information personnel than any other Government department, including the Central Office of Information. Senior news journalists in this area tend to have inordinately close military backgrounds themselves. Not long ago, Britons were presented with a series of shock-horror programmes dealing with the devastation a nuclear war could cause if there ever were a nuclear attack. Without any doubt, the prospects of a nuclear war as portrayed in these films was sufficient justification for living in dreaded fear of a nuclear war, above all other fatalities this planet could ever engender.

These films were hugely expensive to produce. I wonder how many people ever considered the question who financed and promoted these films. Was it the defence industry warning us out of the goodness of their hearts? I doubt it! It would certainly be in the interests of the defence industry to terrify the electorate, who in turn would be willing to support a government which favoured a massive defence budget. At the same time, public support of a massive defence budget can serve the purpose of easing the politically unacceptable burden of unemployment — at least to some degree. The defence industry wins. The Government wins. Even a few of the unemployed win. The price paid is that you are scared out of your wits.

The truth of the matter is that nuclear war is about as probable as the ancient belief in a massive cataract at the end of the Atlantic ocean. No country in the world would launch a nuclear war, given the prospect of turning themselves into a cinder, or inheriting a cinder if they win. Nuclear power is a deterrent. It always has been a deterrent. It will remain a deterrent. Yet through the power of mass communications serving their political vested interests, we have been brainwashed into believing that nuclear war is a realistic threat. So many of us have been ready and willing to support any cause which seems capable of eliminating the possibility of a nuclear war, and its likely effects; even though that cause may be supportive of policies and ideologies completely alien to us.

In order to see the world as those who control the Fourth Estate want you to see it, you must be prepared to turn somersaults with your values and ideals, expunging, or at least downgrading, any opinion contrary to the "official" line. The object of mass communications is precisely what it sounds like — communicating ideas to the masses, who will accept the ideas in the greatest number. The more widely accepted an idea, the more widely it is *likely* to be accepted, even by those considered as dissenters. This will be so whether the idea be true, false or completely inane. By adopting buzz words and catch-phrases, with the aim of presenting a view of the world which will appeal to the lowest common denominator of intellectual achievement, virtually any opinion can be injected into the psyche of even the most cynical. As Gustav LeBon tells us in his study of mass behaviour entitled *The Crowd*, when confronted with mass opinions the most astute individuals will succumb unwittingly to the belief of the crowd. In the area of mass communications, might makes right, even when right is left!

Let's look a bit more closely at the manner in which your views have been twisted and distorted beyond intelligent recognition in our contemporary British society. It is a widely shared view that one of the major problems for British industry has been the work force which habitually goes on strike. Never was this presentation made with more ferocity than at the time of the British Leyland strike and the miners' strike, when British workers were awarded the sole responsibility for the United Kingdom's poor economic performance as portrayed by the media. In January 1979, when Mrs Thatcher was preparing for her role as Prime Minister, the *Daily Telegraph* reported:

> "The public in every opinion poll shows that it believes the trade union situation to be more responsible than any other factor for the nation's problems."

Obviously, placing the blame on the trades unions for the nation's ills had been effective; and a government capable of harnessing the trade unions would be a popular government, since greater prosperity for the nation would be implied. If it were discovered that factors outside the realm of government control were responsible for the nation's ills, a platform geared to curbing the labour cartel would be ineffective. In fact, if the Government were forced to admit it had control over very little other than the way people think, feel and behave, most political platforms would fail to carry conviction or influence the electorate.

A closer look at the problems of British Leyland, which are shared by an exceptionally large number of companies in Britain, provides a shining example of the manner in which the truth has been disguised and distorted with the full knowledge of the government. The Ryder Report on Leyland, commissioned by the government, revealed that between 1968 and 1972 the company distributed 95 % of its profits in dividends. In those years, British Leyland made a profit of £74 million. Of that £74 million, £70 million was paid out to shareholders and £4 million was retained for re-investment. The reason was that such an approach was the most tax efficient in the context of government legislation at the time. The problems facing British Leyland's future were easy to see. BL, like many other companies, had more obsolete and decadent equipment than its competitors. In February 1975, the *Daily Express* reported that a Toyota worker in Japan was working with the equivalent of £11,780-worth of machinery while a British Leyland worker in Britain had but £1,000-worth. As a result, cars in Britain cost more per unit to produce, while the means of production were extremely unreliable. In 1975, figures produced at management level showed that British Leyland were losing far more money through ineffective machinery, and factors such as managerial ineptitude, than through strikes. Leyland had become a hotch-potch of different parts, which had been absorbed into it, with the result that different sections were actually manufacturing products in competition with each other. Management and the organisational structure of the company, like that of many other British companies, were utterly chaotic.

The facts and figures relating to British manufacturing industry and the level of investment fail to support the more common explanation — that the problems of industry are caused by strike-prone workers. There are a number of reasons why investment by Britain's manufacturers has been so low. The most obvious one is the vast amount of capital that has been exported to countries where taxation is lower and profits are higher. Another reason is that within the British economy, those in a position to invest will concentrate on the areas where the highest returns can be obtained. They have not been in manufacturing for quite some time. For speculative reasons, billions of pounds have been directed away from production into areas such as the buying up of commercial and industrial property, land, and most recently, domestic property and shares.

By effecting trade union legislation, and using the British worker as the scapegoat, the Government has given the appearance of improving the state of British industry. This is a far better ploy than attempting to attack the true source of the problem, which is lack of investment. It's easy for the Government to legislate against workers. It's not so easy for Government to seduce a reluctant investor — at least for the time being.

The key problem underlying Britain's economic decline over the decades has without question been a failure to invest in industry. The decline of investment has spanned the entire range of the manufacturing sector. Between 1960 and 1972, Britain re-invested 16%-18% of its gross national product each year. By comparison, Japan was investing 30%-35%, almost twice the rate. In 1978, the Government announced a grant of £100 million to the computer industry. At the same time, the Japanese Government and industrial interests were moving ahead with a plan to inject £350 million in their computer industry. The relative fall in investment has had a disastrous spin-off, aside from the nation's being deprived of its very backbone. Which is, and always will be, manufacturing industry. As a result of Britain's inability to compete in world markets, there is a serious prospect of protracted unemployment, at excruciatingly high levels, for decades to come. But the Fourth Estate has provided an answer for that also — aided and abetted by the government's propaganda machine. You have been taught to believe that your fellow countrymen who are out of a job are "scroungers" who don't want to work, who just want to live off the state. So effective has the brainwashing been in this respect, that in the run-up to Mrs Thatcher's second bid for power in 1983, the normally politically sensitive element of unemployment was not a major political issue. In part, it has been eclipsed, like so much else, by the post-Falklands euphoria — nevertheless the major stance adopted on the Labour Party's political platform was the excruciatingly high level of unemployment. By fighting the campaign on that issue, they lost the election.

The Fourth Estate in Britain has adopted a policy of one-dimensional news reporting that pursues a single explanation at the obliteration and expense of all others. Just as the coverage of industry by the Fourth Estate is organised around limited, simplistic, carefully orchestrated versions of the truth suitable for the common mind, so is news on the economy treated as a whole. Through a vast and continuing campaign, British people have been programmed to believe that inflation is now the product of high wage demands, linking this explanation to a political policy of voluntary wage restraint. Here again we are reminded that media coverage is directed more towards the likely response of working people, and the manner in which they can be manipulated into supporting government policies, than at analysing the "normal operations" of the economy and their ability to generate crises outside the realm of government control.

I have demonstrated in a variety of ways over the years in my editorial efforts — as have Hayek, Friedman, Von Mises and many others — that the cause of inflation has nothing whatever to do with rising wages. If there is a link, it's the *manner in which high wages are financed* that is the cause of higher inflation. Rising wage levels is an effect. . . not a cause. In the public sector, wages must be paid for out of the earnings of a firm. So long as the earnings of a firm increase, there are no inflationary consequences. When the Government pays for high public sector wage settlements, or bails out bankrupt companies with money that it prints, *then* you get inflation.

When inflation was screaming upwards in Britain during the mid-1970s, high wage claims were being offered as a contributory factor in rising inflation, as well as the effect of the oil price rises. While most agreed that the hike in oil prices had some effect, it did not adequately explain why inflation in Britain was so much higher than elsewhere, any more than it explains the continuing battle Britain has had with inflation long after the oil crisis. There has been only one source of inflation in Britain. That source is the Government! Not that the Government would ever admit to this, since the promotion of inflation through the creation of fiat money is one of the most effective methods the authorities have of taxing people without their knowledge or consent, sequestering the nation's wealth in the process. Lenin was the master who taught most governments which seek control of the electorate a great deal:

> "By a continuing process of inflation, governments can confiscate, secretly and unobserved, an important part of the wealth of their citizens. By this method they not only confiscate, but they confiscate arbitrarily.
>
> "As the inflation proceeds and the real value of the currency fluctuates wildly from month to month, all permanent relations between debtors and creditors, which form the ultimate foundation of capitalism, become so utterly disordered as to be almost meaningless; and the process of wealth-getting degenerates into a gamble.
>
> "There is no subtler, no surer means of overturning the existing basis of society than to debauch the currency. The process engages all of the hidden forces of economic law on the side of destruction and does it in a manner which not one man in a million is able to diagnose. . ."

There have been three main positions on the basic cause of the rampant inflation that attacked Britain in the mid-1970s and the reason that Britain's has been, and remains, an inflation-prone economy. Only one of the three directly attributes the cause to rising wage levels. Yet the results of the study carried out by the Glasgow University Media Group show that news statements claiming that wages were the main cause of inflation outnumbered the others by eight to one. In the period under study, there were 17 occasions when the view was expressed on the news that high wages and a policy of wage restraint, whether it be voluntary or otherwise, was not the best way to come to grips with the economic problems facing Britain. There were 287 occasions when the view that these were exactly what was needed was put across. If you are convinced that high wages are the cause of inflation, it would not be surprising — in view of the extremely limited exposure you have had to any other view.

Without a doubt, the biggest con trick of all has been the manner in which the electorate has been manipulated into believing that Mrs Thatcher offers an alternative to the political policies that have fostered the near total disintegration of British industry over the past few decades — a tribute to the tireless efforts of the Fourth Estate. What we have actually seen over the past few decades, which has escaped the attention of the electorate, is a narrowing of the polarities between parties. Conservative governments have ceased to pursue policies consistent with Conservative ideology, while Labour Party policies no longer reflect the original precepts upon which the Labour Party was founded. Expansionary monetary policy had in the past been associated with the Labour Party. Yet no government in British history ever pursued a monetary policy so expansive as that of the Chancellor of the Exchequer, "The Demon Barber" who nearly turned the British pound into confetti during his period of office under the Conservative administration of Ted Heath. The expansionary monetary policy associated with the Labour Party was actually reversed under the stewardship of Chancellor Healey, who pursued a far more contractionary policy than that of his Conservative predecessor. This is not to say the Conservative Party has turned expansionist and the Labour Party has become contractionist. What I am saying is that correlations of the past (which may be responsible for current preconceptions) no longer apply. In our current political environment, there is far less polarity than ever before. Policies which were previously associated with rival administrations have become completely interchangeable. Political polarity now exists in rhetoric only — the rhetoric which the Fourth Estate publish as fact. It is "policy" that determines whether or not a particular government is going to have a beneficial influence on the future — not rhetoric.

Most individuals in Britain have had their minds turned into mush and are content to believe we still live in a political environment that ceased to exist quite some time ago. In days of old, when there was a change in political party there was also a change in policy, which is the reason that people voted for a change in political parties. When the British electorate decided to oust the Labour Government in 1979, it was assumed (not unreasonably) that a change in government would bring about a change in policy, as had occurred in the past when Labour was replaced by the Conservatives. The British electorate saw nothing of the sort. All that *has* been seen is a shift in style and presentation which have been comparable to the changes in style associated with previous changes of government. There has been no discernible shift in policy whatever — merely an extension of government devoted to central planning, dressed up to look like the policy of previous Tory governments through a devious and unrelenting process of rhetoric and media control.

It would seem that many have forgotten precisely what a Conservative government is supposed to stand for. One aspect of Conservative Party policy in the past has been that of *less* government. No one with the slightest acquaintance of political affairs in Britain could possibly claim there has been *less* government under the Thatcher administration. Since 1979, the Thatcherites have interfered with business, taxation, personal liberties and the rights and freedoms of others, and done so more than any Labour Party that has ever held office. Hardly a day goes by that we are not reminded in some way of the presence of this leader, Mrs Thatcher.

Those who have been deceived by style and rhetoric believe this administration "favours the rich" at the expense of the middle and lower classes, but is committed to a policy of cutting taxes for all. The facts reveal this media-induced preconception to be pure nonsense. The current administration has been collecting a greater portion of the national income in tax than any other government in British history.

Stuffing pound notes in your shirt pocket, while lifting your wallet out of your back pocket, is an old confidence trick. The Government, through the media, has focused on income tax and lowering thresholds in order to support its rhetoric. At the same time an entire range of taxation has been introduced, from *de facto* tax increases through the wider powers given the Revenue and Customs and Excise, to more open tax increases involving fiscal drag and the widening of VAT coverage, along with pension restrictions and increased National Insurance contributions for the self-employed.

Since the advent of the Thatcher administration in 1979, continually rising taxation has become an in-built part of the system. The implementation of VAT makes certain this is so, because of the effect of inflation on incomes and prices. Inflation in Britain may have come down, but it has not been eliminated. During 1987 it was the highest of all Western industrialised nations. As prices rise — no matter how fast or slow — the level of VAT payments must also rise as a proportion of national output. When wages rise to keep up with inflation, so too will income tax payments, as the element of "fiscal drag" places taxpayers in progressively higher tax bands, while their net take home pay buys less. Generally, what has been perceived as a tax cut is really no more than a redistribution of the increasing tax burden, thrust upon an unsuspecting electorate, duped by the media, under the control of the Thatcher administration.

The apparent benefits of moving tax thresholds and cutting the standard rate of income tax have been more than offset by the extensive and more far-reaching methods that have been instigated. While the near total elimination of tax avoidance schemes, and tax efficient investments, have made the so-called "rich" increasingly vulnerable — rather than enhancing their tax position. Administering taxation has become so sophisticated and comprehensive under the Thatcher administration that many individuals are not even aware that they are paying far more tax than they ever paid when tax thresholds were lower, and tax rates much higher, than they are now. This holds particularly true for the wealthy.

As I mentioned, Conservative governments in the past have been associated with a "tight money" policy and stringent control of public spending. The administration certainly fills the bill as far as the rhetoric is concerned. But look at the administration's record, and we see a totally different picture. Year after year, budget after budget, the government has failed to adhere to its pre-established targets. So dismal has been the administration's performance, that Chancellor Nigel Lawson abandoned the traditional measures of monetary growth in favour of others which would make it look as though money supply was not ballooning at all. The Chancellor has claimed more than once that although the broadly defined monetary aggregates have been hopelessy distorted by technical changes in the financial system, "the replacement" MO was behaving well. During 1986-1987, MO was expanding at 4%. The rate rose to 5¼% at the time of the General Election of 1987, which left it still within the 2%-6% target range established for the "replacement" indicator of monetary growth. In sharp contrast was the growth in the traditional measure of the money supply, Sterling M3. In the year to April 1987, the growth rate was 20.5%.

The Thatcher administration has completely ignored every single one of the cherished economy and monetary policy guidelines which formulated the rhetoric by which it regained office. Having invested several years of misleading propaganda, promoting the fictions it embraces, we found during 1987 an even worse monetary shambles than that of the most profligate administrations. Sterling M3 had expanded by 190% since Mrs Thatcher came to power. In cash that works out at a monetary expansion of £190 billion mini-pounds, "printed" by a government advocating a "tight money" policy. Fiscal restraint had been completely abandoned. Wages and real earnings had been allowed to soar. Sterling experienced recurrent bouts of weakness on foreign exchange markets in the context of a rapidly deteriorating balance of payments position.

In another brilliantly staged public relations exercise, the British Chancellor of the Exchequer, aided by a gullible and sympathetic financial press, managed to dupe the financial markets and the domestic electorate alike into believing that the British economy was poised for continued growth. Nothing could be further from the truth. The appalling consequences of "Thatcherism" were, by the end of 1987, only too apparent in the real Britain, as opposed to the aberrant statistical creation of the Government's propagandists. Unemployment in Britain stayed at its highest level since the depression of the 1930s, with a catastrophic decline in British industry.

Matching the duplicity that has characterised the Thatcher regime, is the schizophrenic stance on defence. On the one hand, the government proclaims our defences to be inadequate. On the other, they have benignly allowed those industries capable of providing the basis for Britain's defence to shrink and weaken, until they ended up in a state of decadence and stagnation.

Mrs Thatcher's government will go down as the first in history to preside over the transformation of Britain's net trade balance in manufactured goods from comfortable surplus to careering deficit. The cost in economic and social terms cannot be hidden by any amount of Fourth Estate propaganda or political rhetoric. On the heels of the honeymoon after the 1987 General Election came the October stock market crash, bringing with it the prospect of a mammoth crisis of unprecedented dimensions. The ground for this had been prepared by an unbridled and licentious pre-election injection of liquidity into the system, causing personal and commercial debt to soar. The "official" propagandist view of the British economy bears absolutely no resemblance to the underlying reality. In the first few months following the General Election of 1987, Britons were enjoying the transient benefits of a pre-election, forced-fed consumption boom, which must eventually end in a cataclysmic policy reversal and a Gulag-type siege economy, for which very few are prepared. For *that* we may thank the disarming effect of the rhetoric and other techniques employed by the Fourth Estate.

The Orwellian Nightmare

It is my opinion, with the election of the "Thatcherites" for the third term of office, blatantly brandishing slogans such as "There is no alternative"

and defiantly admitting, "This is now a one party system", that the country
has lost its way. You are now rapidly witnessing the collapse of democracy
and the democratic way of life in Britain as we have known it. Those gifted
with any degree of political awareness must surely recognise that Mrs
Thatcher is not and never was a Tory — at best a misguided closet liberal,
perhaps a socialist — at worst the unwitting arm of totalitarianism.

Britons should actually be more sensitive, more acutely aware of the threat
of totalitarianism and the contributory role of a controlled press, in the light
of the folk memories of the 1930s and 1940s, when Mussolini, Hitler and
Goebbels dominated the international scene. The lessons of the Spanish
Civil War should have served to strengthen their hold on the imagination.
For many, Koestler's *Darkness at Noon* will remain a seminal influence.
But for a far greater number, it remains George Orwell's chillingly prophetic
novel, *1984*, appearing in 1948, that gave Britons a stark reminder of what
they had experienced with their ration cards, "points" and clothing coupons.
Two years before the appearance of the Orwellian treatise, Winston Churchill
made his Fulton speech, warning of the dangers that rest on the other side
of the Iron Curtain. There, another form of dictatorship was blooming.
Although seemingly in opposition to the fascist dictatorship of Adolf Hitler,
it was a force with which the Moscow ally had suddenly divided Europe
in an Orwellian mode. The time may be different. . . the place may be
different, but is not Solzhenitsyn's *Gulag Archipelago* a microcosmic
extension of the Orwellian nightmare?

People the world over, even to the present younger generation, who have
managed to acquire some rewarding comprehension in spite of the educational
system, have been fascinated by the awesome accuracy of Orwell's nightmare
vision. Many believe that *1984* has easily been the most influential factional
scenario for the future since World War II. They perceive it to be worthy
in every respect to be compared with the prophetic works of Jules Verne
and H.G. Wells, but far more penetrating in its appreciation of the world
in which we now live, and the direction in which we may be heading.

It was in Britain that the social and political drift of the 1940s provided
Orwell with his inspiration — the same Britain that inspired Frederick
Hayek's *The Road to Serfdom*. We've come a long way down the road since
Hayek first published his masterpiece in 1944. Over the next 40 years, the
Fourth Estate continued to maintain and imply that communism represented
the greatest threat to democracy. Hayek knew better. He was one of the few
to recognise the socialist roots of fascism. In the introduction to *The Road
to Serfdom*, Hayek writes:

> "(I)t is now necessary to state the unpalatable truth that it is Germany whose
> fate we are now in some danger of repeating. The danger is not immediate,
> it is true, and conditions in this country are still so remote from those
> witnessed in recent years in Germany as to make it difficult to believe we
> are moving in the same direction. Yet, although the road be long, it is one
> which it becomes more difficult to turn back as one advances. If in the long

run we are the makers of our own fate, in the short run we are the captives of the ideas we have created. Only if we recognise the danger in time can we hope to avert it."

In the 1940s, it was not the Germany of Hitler, or the Germany of World War II, and their resemblance to Britain that concerned Hayek in a physiological sense. It was the current ideas in Britain which he saw as displaying more than a superficial similarity to those of Germany before the war. These "ideas" were the seed corn of fascism. How does Hayek feel about his prophetic vision more than forty years ago? The answer to that question lies in the preface written in 1976 for the edition published the same year:

"The reader will probably ask whether this means that I am still prepared to defend all the main conclusions of this book; and the answer to this is, on the whole, affirmative.

"I have long resented being more widely known by what I regard as a pamphlet for the time than by my strictly scientific work. After re-examining what I wrote then in the light of some thirty years further study of the problems then raised I no longer feel so. Though the book may contain much that when I wrote it I could not have convincingly demonstrated, it was a genuine effort to find the truth which I believe has produced insights which will help even those who disagree with me to avoid grave dangers."

Hayek was firm in his view that should the correct policy changes be implemented, our society could be diverted from the totalitarian direction in which it appeared to be heading. Orwell's world was a world where those policy changes had not been implemented. In one area, there is a perfect dovetail between Hayek and Orwell. The legacy of Orwell's *1984* and Hayek's *The Road to Serfdom* can be traced through the development of a bureaucratic theory of a totalitarian society, and the definition of the functions required to eliminate political dissent. Both are a prerequisite for maintaining peace and control in the Gulag.

It was Hayek's contention that the feeling of oppression in totalitarian countries was far less acute than most people in a liberal society envisage, because of the success of totalitarian governments in arranging for people to think as they *want* them to think. Thought control is the major device. Hayek tells us that the most effective way of arranging for people to serve the single system of ends towards which the totalitarian plan is directed, is to convince them to believe in those ends. To render a totalitarian system complete in its functions, it is not sufficient that the electorate simply be forced to work for the same ends. Far more essential is that people should come to regard them as their own ends, through the use of propaganda and thought control. In so doing, the totalitarian regime avoids the risk associated with control through the barrel of a gun, which breeds anarchy and revolution.

In the totalitarian society of the Gulag, people must be made to accept not only the values of the leader but also the views about facts that support the underlying central plan. New values are made acceptable by introducing them under the names of old values, such as giving the totalitarians the label of "Tories". In order to achieve the level of thought control required for the continued maintenance of a peaceful and tranquil Gulag, no field of knowledge can afford to be left uncontrolled. The suppression of truth and freedom of thought must be the primary objective.

At the epicentre of Orwell's approach to the future is the political reality of the rhetorical trap, designed to seduce the electorate into a state of mindlessness, which must end in complete despair and desolation, which is where the Gulag mentality of transient, tranquil apathy ultimately leads.

If you genuinely wish to test and validate my concept and fears of the society in which we now live, it would be well to look deeply and carefully into the message of Orwell's *1984*. You may then be able to identify with a greater accuracy and understanding both the road which we in Britain are travelling, and its final destination. Later you may be able to recognise — and expose — the *hubris* of men like Orwell's character O'Brien. . . men and women who would like us to believe that *their* political "world" is capable of eclipsing the real world, and that reality consists of no more than human consumption.

You have been programmed to believe that you are now living in a stable, democratic society where repression is something which you hear about on TV, or in the news, as taking place far from the boundaries of this gentle island. As a result, Britons have been encouraged to adopt a superior tone about the prospects of "Big Brother". Of course, it would be ludicrous to suggest that we are *now* living in a country that bears much resemblance to Airstrip One — the nightmarish, all embracing, totalitarian Gulag state of *1984*. But strip away the paper-thin facade of a media-created environment, and a frightening pattern appears.

Paramount to the creation and fulfilment of the totalitarian dream is the aggrandisement of a leader who serves as the focal point of the Gulag. In the Orwellian Gulag we have "Big Brother". In the Britain of the 1980s we have "Big Mother". Margaret Thatcher is the only Prime Minister of this century to have given her name to both a style and a doctrine in the fashion of "Big Brother". No leader in Britain that I can think of has ever indulged in such an ostentatious omnipresence — never far from the news, TV screens, magazines, periodicals or whatever other organ can be used through which she can peer out at you — in the true tradition of Orwell's "Big Brother".

The total elimination of any form of political dissent is the ultimate objective for those presiding over Orwell's Gulag. By and large Britain in the 1980s, with the aid of the Fourth Estate, has dealt with political dissent in much the same manner as those in charge of the Orwellian Gulag. The Thatcherite Government of the 1980s has added an awesomely effective element to the time-old struggle between individual will, initiative, motivation and conscience on the one hand, and established authority on the other. That new element has been the manipulation of the general culture, while the "masses" have remained relatively passive. That is to say, content, complacent and generally apathetic — this being the transient phase of the Gulag. If you want proof, just look around! Ask any "Yuppie" how he's feeling these days, as he moves uncertainly in the twilight zone of the Gulag.

One of Orwell's fantasies that has turned out to be devastatingly accurate, has been his identification of technology as a tool that would be employed by the state to impose its political will. No doubt readers of Orwell's novel may still shudder at the suggestion of telescreens controlled by "Big Brother". Yet it is now a fact that British security forces have equipment at their disposal, far more sophisticated and far more intrusive than Orwell's telescreens over which "Big Brother" maintained surveillance.

In Britain, extensive secrecy masks from public view the incomprehensible activities of the 'security services' — from the Special Branch to MI5, SIS, and the Government Communication Headquarters in Cheltenham. In America, the same devices for surveillance are available. The Freedom of Information Act has allowed an occasional light to be shed, which prompted Senator Frank Church in 1975 to make reference to the technology available to the security services, warning that:

" . . .at any time it could be turned on the American people. . . the capacity
is there to make tyranny total".

In Britain there is no Freedom of Information Act. As far back as 1976, in *The Technology of Political Control*, it was suggested that Britain was moving towards a new state model, increasingly authoritarian and contemptuous of human rights. The roots of this new state were said to lie in traditional paternalism, authoritarianism and the government of the day. With the current problems of unemployment, impending recession and the possibility of civil disobedience — perhaps involving riots similar to those of 1981 — it is most unlikely that the paternalistic, authoritarian heroine of the Falklands confrontation would flinch from using all the resources of the state available for maintaining *individual* control.

In *The Downwave*, I explained how the final stages of rapid economic expansion and inflation are usually associated with a relaxation of values, a fall in moral standards, promiscuity and a high divorce rate. In fashion, as moral decadence becomes rife, men become more flamboyant in their dress. For women, what was previously a hemline becomes a crotch line, while necklines become nipple lines. When that long period of expansion ends, and a long period of economic contraction begins, there is a return to traditional moral codes and conservative standards of dress. At first, I was bemused by the stance adopted by Mrs Thatcher, who was urging a return to Victorian values. I am now beginning to wonder whether there may not be something a bit sinister and devious about this aspect of the Thatcherite facade.

Not only is thought control quintessential to the proper supervision of the Gulag, but "feeling control" also. In Orwell's Gulag society, carnal desire for another individual is castigated as a "thought crime". To come up with what may be interpreted as a subversive erection, or vaginal secretion, would constitute grounds for arrest and questioning — not for the old-fashioned moral reasons, mind you, but because carnality in the Gulag would diminish the all-seeking, all pervasive power of the state in the game of "Power Über Alles".

In the Orwellian Gulag, and — to judge by the way things are going — in the pseudo-Victorian Gulag of the Thatcherites, before long, the "sexual act successfully performed" could be deemed "an act of treason and rebellion" by some extreme zealot. When Orwell's downtrodden hero, Winston, plunges his unconscionable member into the vessel of the unholy spirit, and "successfully performs" the sexual act with Julia, they are both committing one of the most serious crimes against the state:

> "The aim of the Party was not merely to prevent men and women forming loyalties which it might not be able to control. Its real undeclared purpose was to remove all pleasure from the sexual act. Not love so much as eroticism was the enemy inside marriage as well as outside it. . . . The only recognised purpose of marriage was to beget children for the service of the Party. Sexual intercourse was to be looked on as a slightly disgusting minor operation, like having an enema. . . The sexual act, successfully performed was rebellion. Desire was thought crime."

A further facet of the moral dictates of the Inner Party is developed by Julia:

> "They want you to be bursting with energy all the time. All this marching up and down and cheering and waving flags is sex gone."

By contrast, the nether world of the proles in the Orwellian Gulag is glimpsed out of a corner of the eye, comprising a meaningless cycle of birth, copulation and death while a wanton, corrupted sexual hedonism is condoned — even encouraged — by the Party-controlled pornography industry.

In Britain today, while Mrs Thatcher preaches Victorian virtues, prostitution is legal. Some of the pillars of our community have been openly linked with prostitutes. A progressively more liberal attitude has been adopted toward perversion and homosexuality. The educational authority of one borough council was accused of virtually encouraging homosexuality among the young. Pornography is a major industry in Britain. In London's Soho, it is scarcely possible to find a cinema that features anything but hard core pornography. One of the major features of cable television has been late night films featuring sex, violence and bad language, normally categorised as "light blue" films.

It is not for me to pass a moral judgement on any of these activities. It is a reflection of Party policy that all this goes on while the leader of the Party preaches "Victorian virtues".

I referred to the sexual act "successfully performed" as "one of the most" serious crimes of all against the State. But, truly, the *most* serious crime in the Orwellian Gulag is thought crime. When Winston goes further and seeks to maintain his own private thoughts and "feelings", in a desperate effort to stay "human", he is committing a far more serious offence than performing the sexual act with Julia. He is deliberately flouting the instructions circulated by the Ministry of Information. Poor Winston does his best to reassure Julia. "They can't get inside you," he tells her:

> "If you can feel that staying human is worthwhile, even when it can't have any result whatever, you've beaten them."

In the novel, Winston and Julia arrange to meet O'Brien, whom they mistakenly believe to be a kindred spirit. They think he will assist them in serving the "Brotherhood" — the imaginary opposition. O'Brien pretends to go along with Winston's and Julia's plans and draws them into the illusion of a conspiracy. The task, O'Brien tells Winston, is:

> ". . .to extend the areas of sanity by a little."

At the same moment, back at the Ministry, the extension of reason is outlawed as the ultimate act of treason for anyone in the Gulag.

Predictably, O'Brien betrays Winston, employing a brand of deception similar to the kind of "dirty tricks" employed in British politics today. It emerges that Winston's terminal crime was to have been:

> ". . .capable of ordinary human feeling."

According to O'Brien, "Big Brother" is not in the least interested in the overt act:

> "The thought is all we care about."

Winston is seen as a "flaw in the pattern". However, O'Brien leaves Winston in no doubt as to what they will do to him. Having squeezed him empty, O'Brien promises, they will:

> ". . .fill you with ourselves."

Now stand back! Give some thought to the manner in which *your* thought process is directed, and *your* opinions are formed. What is your principal source of input? Where do you get the information on which you base your judgement of a political party or recent event?

You know the answer as well as I do. It's summed up rather neatly in that TV commercial for the *Financial Times*. You know the one I mean? Where the one man without a copy finally breaks down and confesses:

> "No *FT.* No comment!"

I'm willing to bet that your primary intelligence sources are the media. . . the Fourth Estate. Whoever controls the Fourth Estate controls, to a considerable degree, the way you think and feel about things in general — but especially the things you care most about! That in turn will influence the way you plan. . . or fail to plan. . . your life. Just recall for a moment how people reacted when Orson Welles broadcast that famous radio play and frightened literally thousands of radio listeners into believing the Martians had landed.

"That was an extreme case!", I can here you saying. But what about the steady drip, drip, drip — year in, year out — as well-meaning friends and family continue to feed you tales of what "they always say" about this, and that and the other? Remember the old tale they used to tell in East Anglia about the shipload of monkeys washed up on the beach? It was during the Napoleonic Wars. Convinced that they were part of Boney's army, the villagers hanged every one of the monkeys on the nearest line of trees, saying:

> "We'll do the same too for the next lot of Frenchies as dares to shew their ugly faces in these parts."

When the authorities are over-zealous, their very zeal can backfire. At the end of World War II, Menachem Begin (of the illegal *Irgun Zwai Leumi*) was being hunted as a "wanted" man. Posters bearing his picture were affixed to virtually every notice board and hoarding in Palestine. Although Begin was checked and screened on more than one occasion, he was never recognised. And for a good reason. Palestine police posters tended to make every wanted man look so villainous that he could hardly *be* recognised.

Like most successful villains, O'Brien in *1984* has "a certain charm of manner". Perhaps, suggests Orwell, O'Brien's political orthodoxy, "was not perfect". Like quite a few politicians today! That is an impression which must always be given in order to win — and retain — the trust and confidence of those who are to be put down. Without winning over the victim, the act of subjugation may be far more difficult. Moreover, if the victim does not trust his leader, there is always the danger of anarchy. Anarchy and resistance can spread. As I said earlier, at their first meeting Winston and Julia mistakenly identify O'Brien as a fellow conspirator, one who will help them in their cause. But, as the final confrontation draws closer, the nightmarish nature of O'Brien's true character shews through.

For the average reader, the way Winston is betrayed reveals O'Brien as the epitome of bureaucratic efficiency. Efficiency to the very highest standard has always been the ambition. . . and the temptation. . . of almost every civil servant or politician. If betrayal in Orwell's Gulag can be shewn to be a certain way of achieving the political objective, then betrayal becomes the recognised way to an efficient operation. In Orwell's Gulag, to ask, "Is betrayal a *good* thing?" would be absurd and irrelevant. We should enquire, "Is it efficient? Does it work?"

But surely, you may ask, are there no longer any moral considerations?

The truth, which I am bound to tell you, is that "morality" is not absolute. Whether an act is or is not moral depends on whether or not it is accepted by the "right people". In our increasingly bureaucratic society — as in Orwell's 40 years ago — the "right people" will probably tell you that the need to achieve is so great that the efficiency of the *means* is what counts. Therefore it is the "means" that justify the end, rather than the other way round. In Thatcherite Britain, efficiency and enterprise are the passwords which will get you safely past the remaining social or moral barriers that any old-fashioned moralist may try to put in your path.

The Orwellian Gulag relies on two main sources for its *Theory of Bureaucratic Suppression of Political Dissent*, which is recognised as endemic to any system of "mass organised lying". The first is the 22 page manuscript entitled *The Theory and Practice of Oligarchal Collectivism*, and the other is the transcript of O'Brien's lengthy interrogation of Winston. Taken together, these two documents constitute a bureaucratic theory of a totalitarian society; defining the necessary bureaucratic functions to which the Fourth Estate makes a major contribution. Orwell puts two of these functions into their proper context:

> "The day-to-day falsification of the past, carried out by the Ministry of Truth,*
> is as necessary to the stability of the regime as the work of repression and
> espionage carried out by the Ministry of Love."

The priorities are quite clearly defined in this passage, which merely reiterates that old cliché, "The pen is mightier than the sword". The true objective becomes concretised when O'Brien tells Winston, "We are not interested in overt acts". In other words, dead letter boxes, meetings in 'safe' houses, a bit of pair-bonding and notes under the hotel door are not really major issues in the Gulag. Prevention is always better than cure. The principal objective of the bureaucracy in a Gulag is to anticipate or remove any danger of overt acts through thought control. This is achieved by the skilful dissemination, disinformation, misinformation and propaganda, directed towards stirring the emotions and diverting any thoughts, tendencies or inclinations which might later emerge as a subversive overt act against the state.

You may now see the Official Secrets Act in a different light: at best a placebo, at worst a method for exerting pressure on the less sophisticated who may be inclined to talk too much. You may also have a greater understanding of why it is always more profitable for the leaders of a Gulag to subvert a publisher, TV personality or public relations officer than to encourage an MOD Colonel or FO cypher clerk to defect. The greatest threat to the totalitarian regime are people who think. If the thought process can be neutered, absolute power becomes assured.

Another important function used to ensure effective and continuous calm in the Gulag is to switch from the nurturing of national pride to raising

*A conscious or unconscious pun? *Pravda* is the Russian for *Truth*.

the nationalistic hackles and provoking a display of "healthy" jingoism. Remember. . . true jingoism always starts with a declaration of one's peaceful aims. As the original popular song put it:

> "We don't want to fight,
> But, by jingo! if we do
> We've got the Ships,
> We've got the Men,
> We've got the Money, too!"

The grand design in the Orwellian Gulag was the perpetuation of "war hysteria" generated by media-hype jingoism. Through the various channels for propaganda there was the "conduct of continuous warfare" without ever a victory, and with "no danger of conquest". The latter function was particularly important for "all of the Inner Party" where the "true war enthusiasm" was to be found. This "Inner Party", over which "Big Brother" presided, has its equivalent in the governments over which Mrs Thatcher has presided.

It was endemic to the Orwellian bureaucratic process that the inhabitants of the Gulag should be periodically prodded into sporadic frenzies of "fear and hatred"; just as Pavlov's dog was jabbed with positive and alternating impulses in the interests of producing a conditioned response. As was demonstrated by Pavlov's experiments. the use of alternating stimuli is perfect for turning a brain to mush and pulp, whether it be animal or otherwise. As I have stressed, thought control and mindlessness is a prerequisite of the Gulag. In the Orwellian Gulag of Airstrip One, the outputs of TV screens, controlled news and periodic circulars were the source of the alternating stimuli.

In Orwell's Airstrip One Gulag, the population has its emotional energy continually directed towards an external enemy, in the form of Eastasia and Eurasia. Constant and continuous warfare enables the bureaucracy to inflict restrictions on the inhabitants "in the national interest". They might not otherwise be tolerated. Similarly, through the justification of various "wars", a large number of the undemocratic practices of the British bureaucracy go unchallenged. Practices that would be wholly alien to a democratic society in peacetime are not only being secretly maintained, but reinforced. Their common target is said to be the "enemy within". It is possible to pinpoint three separate "limited wars" in which the British State has involved the electorate's co-operation in the acceptance of undemocratic acts. There is ideological war, "the war against crime" which is a regular feature on TV news programmes and in the news headlines, usually exaggerated well beyond their significance. There is the undeclared war in Northern Ireland, which has continued for years without any sane justification. There is also the "Cold War", which has provided the security forces with much of their experience. It has, moreover, provided the *raison d'être* for secrecy and personal surveillance, whether fighting suspected Marxist dissidents in the Colonies, or unmasking the perceived communist menace within its ranks.

When a level of "fear and hatred" is needed beyond that which these "limited wars" are capable of providing, more overt measures must be taken. Need we in Britain look any further than the invasion of the Falkland Islands to see how "true war enthusiasm" restored the waning popularity of the 4-year-old Thatcher administration? Many forget that just before that war, the Conservative Government led by Mrs Thatcher was one of the most unpopular in British history.

From invasion to cease-fire, was there ever an element of true "victory"? For Britain, there was certainly no danger of "conquest". The anglophile Argentinian author, Jorge Luis Borges, dismissed the affair as "a fight between two bald men over a comb".

When it was announced that the British militia had been despatched to the Falklands — and would arrive in *two to three weeks* — even the most patriotic observer must have seen that it was really the kind of stuff that lampoons are made of. Let's face facts. . . the *real* facts. Britain is no longer a first-rate military power, and hasn't been for quite some time. Argentine doesn't even rate the military status of a few kids dressed up in Star Wars outfits, engaged in intergalactic conflict on the green lawns of Hyde Park. When the British reacted to the Argentine takeover of the Falklands, it was like an overjoyed bull who had just bumped into a 97-pound weakling.

Judging from the number of troops, and the amount of equipment, sent to the Falkland Islands, it would not have been unreasonable to think Britain was about to declare war on the Kremlin and its forces. In the time honoured fashion, the first casualty of war was the truth. Characterised by a blind patriotism, a contempt for readers' intelligence and unquestioning belief in the infallibility of Mrs Thatcher — as would be expected of an organ in the Gulag — *The Sun* newspaper ran the jingoist slogan, "The Paper That Supports Our Boys", exploiting the wanton and unnecessary loss of human life to its full potential. *The Sun* habitually ran bloodthirsty headlines such as "GOTCHA", commemorating the sinking of the *Belgrano*. One grotesquely inaccurate story followed another throughout the Falklands campaign. *The Sun* announced the recapture of the Island of South Georgia before it had actually happened. But this was nothing unusual. A number of the newspapers followed a similar line.

In bureaucratic terms, the war had the desired effect. The media jingoism provided just the amount of frenzy, fear and hatred required to reverse the fortunes of the Conservative Party. It left Mrs Thatcher a national heroine and provided her with a landslide victory at the General Election which followed soon afterwards. In totalitarian terms, the end justified the means. Humanitarian terms are not an aspect for consideration in the bureaucratic Gulag.

A further prerequisite to the efficient functioning of a totalitarian bureaucracy is the preservation of permanent power by the Inner Party and the high political elite. . . "Big Brother". . . Or, in the current context, "Big Mother". The possibility of losing power to an alternative government is not even contemplated. There *must* be no alternative government! Does that sound familiar?

In Orwell's novel, O'Brien puts the matter quite succinctly, "The Party seeks power entirely for its own sake. . . we are interested solely in power." O'Brien then adds:

> "Power is not a means: it is an end. One does not establish a dictatorship
> in order to safeguard a revolution: one makes the revolution in order to
> establish the dictatorship."

The methods used to achieve "power for the sake of power", leading to the ultimate control and sequestration of all people and their wealth, are based on two assertions. The first, according to Orwell, is the "mutability of the past". The second, and probably the more important, is the "infinite malleability" of human nature. As H.L. Mencken pointed out, "through the application of enough pressure, we can be taught to cheerfully embrace polygamy, astrology or cannibalism". In this Britain of the 1980s, the people were taught to "cheerfully embrace": Left as Right, pornography, homosexuality, theft, deceit, hypocrisy, duplicity, gambling and unrestrained borrowing in the interests of consumption and instant gratification, portrayed as representing the only real world. There is little doubt that "Thatcherism" has provided all of that. The electorate were probably programmed to treat these misgivings as blessings, in total disregard of the consequences of such vices, which should have been learned from the past. But British politicians have been inordinately successful in exploiting man's "infinite malleability", and have been no less triumphant in their "mutability of the past".

Disinformation and repression have been properties of all bureaucracies in varying degrees. Assumptions based on "mutability" and "malleability" are what effectively distinguish authoritarian governments from the type of totalitarian government to which we may soon be subjected. The increasing power that accrues to a bureaucracy is not seized by that main force. It is handed over. . . voluntarily. The origins of the ultimate collectivist nightmare lie in the desire of individuals to abdicate and reduce personal responsibility for the benefit of the state. All bureaucracies appear to be well-meaning in their initial stages — as do their leaders; seemingly intent on saving us as a society. But it is by their collectivist methods that we are destroyed as individuals, to be thereafter confined to a mental or physical Gulag. . . or both.

Chapter Twelve

SURVIVING THE
GULAG ANGLO-PEDIGREE

The Chinese coolie lives in a palm-thatched hovel on a bowl of rice.
When he has risen to a higher occupation — hawking peanuts, for example,
from a barrow — he still lives on rice and still lives in a hovel. When he
has risen farther — to the selling, say, of possibly stolen bicycle parts, he
keeps his hovel and his rice.

C. Northcote Parkinson

It was the year 1995 — Friday noon — the week before Xmas. It didn't look as though it would be a white Christmas. The mist, slush, and type of damp cold that gnaws through to your bones, promised nothing better than the traditionally British grey Christmas. No matter! Only a handful of people still celebrated the Christian Festival. By the 1990s, most of the churches had been torn down to be replaced by tinselled supermarkets. The local pub had given way to the travel agency.

The scene takes place outside the railings of the Ministry of National Allegiance, which used to be called Buckingham Palace — renamed after the Royal Family went into exile. Two drably dressed individuals, down on their luck (like most people on the street that day) — catch sight of a solitary tourist. Could there be a remnant of that once universal Yuletide spirit hidden away in that foreign breast?

Without a moment's hesitation, the bolder of the two sidles up to the obviously American stranger with the customary, "Psst! Ya got any dollars, guv?"

A good question! A few months earlier, the official exchange rate had been frozen at £100 to the US dollar, just before the re-imposition of exchange controls, which occurred shortly after the Rt.Hon. Margaret Thatcher — now approaching her seventies — had been elected for her sixth, interminable term in office. (That is, if one includes the 8-month interregnum following the so-called Nuclear Nightmare, when vast areas of Kent and East Sussex had to be cleared, after the new Dungeness Reactor was sabotaged.) Within two hours of the news, Parliament had been suspended and the country had been placed under the quasi-military rule of Her Majesty's Emergency Commissioners, with Rt. Hon. Margaret Thatcher designated as First Commissioner. It was with relief that the nation heard the last Royal

Proclamation from the Palace which told a frightened and bewildered people of the Abdication. It was generally understood that the *quid pro quo* would be the return to Parliamentary Government after a General Election.

It was the last time that any genuine opposition candidates were to stand against the ruling party. From 1979 onwards, Margaret Thatcher had invariably been elected by a minority of the votes cast. By 1992, the state of the nation was too serious for the question of leadership to be left to chance. It had already been decided that a new computerised system would come into use by the following year. Unfortunately it was not ready, so the old-style system would have to be used. This meant that anti-Government names could be — and would be — placed on the ballot paper. There were scuffles at many polling stations, when those flaunting Opposition colours were turned away, or arrested on the grounds of "causing an affray" or for "obstruction." Later that night, angry scenes took place during the count. In some areas it was alleged that sealed boxes from anti-Government wards had been intercepted on the way and "interfered with". In most constituencies, party tellers had their notes and marked-up electoral rolls taken from them. This, it was charged by the Opposition, would enable the Ruling Party to make a note of the identity of anti-Government voters for intimidation purposes. Whether true or not, the next round of local elections was conducted on the basis of a greatly reduced Electoral Roll.

At the following General Election, the Act requiring Personal Registration at the voting station, on the day before the poll, had been introduced. Would-be voters were required to fill in a form stating their name, address, occupation, National Identity Number — and produce their medical and Poll Tax certificates. Only when satisfied that they had full details of the applicant, would the Polling Officers (seconded from the National Investigation Bureau) feed the data into the computer. Next day, many thousands of known anti-Government supporters, discovered that they had been omitted from the authorised print-out, due to "computer error". There were skirmishes in the poorer districts, and some arrests. Invariably the homes of those detained were thoroughly "turned-over".

Generally speaking, most opponents of the Government took the easy way out. Just as the Party's Political Psychology Centre had predicted, they gave up. So effective was the "treatment" that *de facto* One Party Rule was established with the minimum of coercion, and very little physical force. When the Thatcherites "went to the country" for the sixth time, they were virtually unopposed. The Government still claimed to support the concept of "Democracy". But it was something of a sham. The voter was faced with a simple choice: between voting "Yes" or voting "No" to the Leader's nominee. There were no alternatives, and to fail to register a vote was an offence. Some, it was said, stubbornly pressed the NO key set in the panel before them. How many did this — or what happened to them — was never disclosed. So far as the Government was concerned, it required only one "Yes" vote in each constituency to win a landslide victory.

This time, there were no angry protests, but there were rumblings of discontent. The Leader instructed her Minister-without-Portfolio responsible for the Re-Election Operation (as it was now openly described) to speak to the people on a national TV and radio hook-up. He was brief and to the point:

"The Ruling Party will at all times safeguard the right of every loyal and decent citizen to vote in a secret ballot."

When the victorious Party returned to Westminster, senior Ministers (who were mostly in the Lords) were able to assure the diplomats and foreign press that unlike Cromwell the New Conservatives had never once been forced to prolong the life of Parliament.

After the successful return to power of the Thatcherite Government in October 1992, the black market rate for dollars in Britain had risen fast. By the end of 1995, it was close to £1,000 to the dollar. Woe betide any UK resident — or UK citizen — found in possession of gold or foreign currency! The penalty for possession was instant arrest and detention for an indefinite period in:

. . . "such establishment(s) as may be prescribed by the Minister of Defalcation, and his officials, under the Act."

You may wonder at the temerity of those two drably dressed individuals, approaching a complete stranger from America in that way. For one thing, it was possible they were already under citizen surveillance. For another, the "American" in question could well turn out to be an *agent provocateur*. Frequently, these were wired for sound, and constantly monitored by one of the ever vigilant COTs — the Ministry's Camera Observation Teams.

It is most unlikely that we shall ever know precisely what happened to those two dubious individuals that raw December day. Had action been taken, the record would instantly have become classified. Had no action been taken, there would be no record, no confirmatory print-out. Defalcation Officials — like their colleagues in other Ministries — had long ago learned from experience that any "document" (or, more precisely, any data-base entry) bearing their name (or departmental number) could prove embarrassing at some time in the future. The rule in all Government Departments was that which dictated:

"Nothing that a Ministry does just *happens*. Therefore *someone* must be *held* responsible. In the event of failure to find the individual(s) responsible, the section, group or departmental head shall be so deemed."

Moreover, by the date in question, all UK prisons and "prescribed establishments" (including the Catterick, Ventnor, Tobermory and Lerwick re-education camps) had become disturbingly overcrowded. It was partly due to the soaring crime rate and the unshakeable belief of lay-magistrates in the efficacy of the custodial sentence. It was also due, though never officially admitted, to the level of disaffection among prison officers, which led indirectly to the resignation of two Home Secretaries in quick succession. Not for attempting to cover-up the inefficiency and corruption within the Prison Service, but for using Parliamentary Question Time to "leak" highly sensitive information which was being kept from the public.

The same information had been given to the elite of journalism, the Lobby Correspondents. Naturally they did not betray the Government's trust — by word, deed or innuendo. When the act of betrayal *did* take place, the full fury of public opinion — as interpreted by the media — was unleashed on the hapless Ministerial miscreants. The next Home Secretary made a never-to-be-forgotten appeal to the whole House that they should never again attempt to misuse Parliamentary procedure. That was well enough in days gone past, he said:

> "But what — in this Second Age of Enlightenment — have we to do with the meaningless, empty rituals of a bygone age like the so-called Speech from the Throne? Or the antics of Black Rod — played by some superannuated General or Air Marshal, who appears at the door of the Commons to have it slammed in his face. . . looking for all the world like an old actor playing Malvolio in the provinces.
> "As for Question Time. . . that daily opportunity for smears, slurs and innuendo. . . either you trust us. . . and the Right Honourable Lady we are proud, and privileged, to serve. . . or you do not! In which case I can only hold you to be utterly, and forever, beneath contempt."

The cheers and waving of Order Papers greeting this loyal and spirited declaration of faith was duly reported, and soon forgotten. The Overcrowded Prisons Problem was solved with great skill, and the threatening scandal was silenced once and for all. In a brief statement by a junior Minister on the day before the House rose for the Easter recess, the Government announced its intention to replace imprisonment in most cases with "new, humane and technogically advanced methods of dealing with offenders". As a result of the scant coverage given this piece of news, no one knew precisely what these "technologically advanced" methods were; although it was assumed they would be carried out by the white-coated "medics" at those Ministry of Defalcation establishments which normally handled such matters.

After a while even this somewhat frightening alternative to prison no longer appeared to be an effective deterrent. Secretly — and for understandable reasons — many offenders *wanted* to be caught. Such was the wretchedness of their conditions, that mental re-programming looked like a soft option. So the black market in dollars continued to flourish. There was the much quoted story of the Old Age Pensioner who lived for almost a year on a $10 bill smuggled into the country by a grandchild from Los Angeles. The child in question was admitted shortly before the curtain came down on the Kith and Kin (Visitor to Britain) Scheme. Already it took almost 6 months for anyone living in the "free-world" to obtain a visa for a 2 week visit. Very few visas were granted. It was all but impossible for the ordinary British citizen to obtain an exit permit.

At that time, the rate of decline in the currency was quite unprecedented. When the old lady first acquired the $10 bill, the black market rate stood at £100 to the US dollar. By the end of that same year, it had soared to £900.

The internal deterioration in the economy took more time, but it was no less painful. It reached a pitch at which it became clear to almost everyone that there was no need for a Stock Exchange any longer. The Prime Minister's declaration of a State of Emergency had come at the height of the Great Depression towards the end of the 1980s. This led to the nationalisation of banks, insurance companies, and all but the smallest manufacturing firms. It also brought about the decline, and eventual closure, of the Stock Exchange. Having remained empty for some time, the multi-storey tower on Throgmorton Street became the Headquarters of the new mobile police unit, the Volunteer Peace Brigade. By law, all members of the community were bound to "volunteer" to serve in this new mobile police unit for at least 4 hours per week. Their duties were not onerous. They were merely expected to report on the activities of their neighbours during their spell of duty.

Before the general decline heralded by the world-wide stock market collapse of October 1987, the odds on Britain's ever seeing a wave of nationalisation again were virtually *nil*. To suggest *re-nationalisation* of the recently privatised state-owned industries would have been dismissed with scorn. Indeed, in the summer of 1987, a large number of people had decided to vote for the Thatcherite Conservatives precisely because they had bought shares in the privatised companies. True, many of them had sold them at the first opportunity, in order to cash in on a quick profit. Nevertheless, they voted for Mrs Thatcher because they feared that a Labour Government might re-nationalise the former state-owned concerns, and take away the shares they had been talked into buying. There was an isolated incident in October 1987, when the failure of the BP share issue led to the introduction — on the advice of the Bank of England — of a so-called "safety-net" scheme.

The privatised shares had been sold in advance to some 250,000 investors at the fixed issue price of 330 pence, payable in 3 instalments. Before the offer closed, the price of the BP shares already on the market fell to below the privatisation issue price. The underwriters were badly caught out, and so were the buyers who were already irrevocably committed. Eventually, and against his will, the Chancellor was pressured into agreeing to a scheme whereby the Bank of England would buy back the privatised shares (for which 120 pence would have been paid) for 70 pence. The general public, egged on by the media, hailed this humiliating capitulation as a "triumph" for the Chancellor. What had escaped the notice of all but a few was that the Government had managed to raise all the funds it required, and now stood to gain even more by buying back some of the BP shares (with tax-payers' money) at a discount of 50 pence per share — the discount coming out of the pocket of the misguided buyers and the angry underwriters. Labour's Shadow Chancellor was one of the few in Parliament to recognise the true nature of the Government's sleight-of-hand: de-nationalisation and re-nationalisation at the same time.

By 1990, when the *Financial Times* 30 Share Index touched 200, most people were more than happy to sell their shares to *anyone*, at whatever price they offered. Between 1987 and 1900, ICI had fallen from £17.00 to 70 pence a share; and other companies — also household names — suffered a similar fate. The willing buyer had virtually become an extinct species.

True to the style of October '87, the Government announced their willingness to offer a few pence above the current market price for the top shares listed on "Footsie", the *Financial Times*/Stock Exchange 100 Share Index. The response from individual investors was instantaneous. Mindful of the long delays before the cash was paid out, the Government went one step further. It stressed that while investors were still *entitled* to sell through the usual channels — building societies, High Street banks and agency brokers — they were *advised* to go straight to Her Majesty's Share Shops. These had been set up in the many one-time Job Centres, which had lain idle since the supply of jobs had all but dried up. Never having dreamed for one moment that their savings could evaporate so swiftly, thousands of ordinary folk queued up outside the official Share Shops, fearful that the authorities might change their mind! The scene, reported one overseas columnist:

". . .was reminiscent of the good old days, when the British would queue up all night outside Oxford Street stores in the hope of snatching a bargain. The night might be long and cold, but what was that to shoppers who still shewed what their grandparents would call 'the Dunkirk Spirit'."

At any other time, the prices offered in the official Share Shops would have been regarded as derisory. But people were happy to take whatever the Government offered. Some investors were less fortunate. Those who held low quality shares had been beaten to the exit by the Institutions in the first few days after the collapse. By the time they had made up their minds and dug out their share certificates, they were left with a bundle of worthless paper, bearing the names of the hundreds of companies — still remaining on the Stock Exchange — which no one wanted to know about.

From the Government's point of view the share repurchase operation was a real *coup*. They had used the taxpayers' money to buy off a large number of individual investors, while reacquiring all the former state-owned companies they had sold to the public, at around 1/10th of the initial offer price. Furthermore, they had acquired a major stake in the remainder of the top 100 companies. And all for a song!

The summit of the Government's achievement was reached when the Stock Exchange — still theoretically a private company — decided on voluntary liquidation. The Cabinet, tongue in cheek, agreed. After months of hard bargaining, LIFFE, the active and aggressive London International Financial

Futures Exchange, was permitted to create a special division (in one corner of the Royal Exchange) to handle the few remaining responsibilities of the defunct Exchange. The Bank of England completed the process by taking over (and stripping) the two remaining Gilts marketmakers. Several UK merchant banks decided to merge; and one by one the foreign banks and finance houses departed. Only three decided to retain a token presence in London.

A long and honourable chapter in the history of the City closed the day that the first contingent of the Volunteer Peace Brigade established its new HQ in the Stock Exchange Tower. At one blow, the Right Wing Thatcherites — who still called themselves "conservative" — had succeeded in "nationalising" the City to a degree to which no Labour administration, from Attlee to Callaghan, had even dared to attempt. What's more, they had managed to persuade their followers that everything they had done had been in the best interests of enterprise.

The triumph of Westminster over the City, and of Thatcherism over traditional democracy, was attributed by some political commentators to the successful change in style, following a succession of shake-ups inside Conservative Central Office, after the departure of Saatchi and Saatchi. As the Party's official historian put it:

"By the end of the 1980s, it was no longer necessary to *sell* Thatcherism. Rather, it was time for the Leader to reveal her true strength. At the last Conservative Party Conference — to be known in future as the Leader's *Annual Briefing and Rally* — Margaret Thatcher said, 'I have entered on a performance which is without precedent, and will have no imitator.'"

Even those who recognised the deliberate misquotation from Jean-Jacques Rousseau's 200 year-old work, *Emile, ou De l'Education*, were impressed. A former broker, now one of the Leader's sharpest critics, replied with a quotation from the same work:

"A man says what he knows, a woman says what will please."

Not surprisingly, attacks on the Leader became conspicuous by their absence once the old attitude to Parliament changed. With the departure of the Royal Family, the whole concept of the role of Parliament had to be re-thought. Sovereignty resided no longer in "the King (or Queen) in Parliament". It was perceived to reside in the people, as represented by their Leader. Carefully, and without upsetting the more conservative members of the Conservative Party, the Leader finally "agreed" to the plea submitted by the Archbishop of Canterbury and the Master of the Rolls that henceforth the two Houses of Parliament should shed their ancient forms, to be replaced by the Congress of Benevolence. A mass meeting of members of both "Houses", and religious leaders from all sects and religions, assembled in the Wembley Exhibition Centre to hear the formal Ceremony of

Transformation. In his address, the Archbishop used the memorable form of words which, approved beforehand by the Leader's secretariat, has gone down in history:

> "After so many centuries, we have at last — in the Congress of Benevolence — the true Mother of Parliaments, fashioned in the image of Margaret Hilda Thatcher, the One True Leader of One Nation."

Political reform will usually command far more attention than any other kind of change. Not surprisingly, therefore, the close-down of the Stock Exchange computers for the last time brought little in the way of public reaction, despite the attempts by the media to make it an "occasion worthy of the event". Most members of the public remembered that the Stock Exchange had cost them dearly. Few blamed the Government for its "share-owning democracy", since Downing Street convinced them without too much difficulty that it was all the fault of the Americans. The man in the street was left to regret ever having had anything to do with stocks and shares. On the whole they praised the Government for having introduced its Share Shop scheme. Nevertheless, there were thousands who *did* grieve: the thousands employed in the City in the 1980s, during the so-called "Age of the Yuppie". They saw more than merely their livelihood pass away when the Stock Exchange and the other City markets collapsed, and the "Yuppies" were transformed in a matter of weeks into "Py-uppies" — the *previously* young and upwardly mobile!

A few of the Whizz-Kids, especially those who had come up from the back-streets, managed to keep their wits about them, taking unskilled or semi-skilled jobs. Some became drivers of milk-waggons, taxis and delivery vans. These were menial jobs. But a job, however menial, was a job in the 1990s. Besides, a job gave them plenty of scope for improvising the odd deal on the side — especially if they had transport. Having managed to look after their BMW or Range Rover, it was child's play "fixing" the petrol gauge and the speedo so as to bump up the van's official mileage, and have the odd gallon over at the end of the day. Besides, anyone who could sell Options or Gilt Futures, could make a small fortune peddling those everyday items — like auto-spares or building materials — which became increasingly scarce.

Less fortunate were those top City personnel, who had enjoyed an income of close on £1m per annum. They realised that they would have to learn to live on the meagre pittance provided by the Ministry of Equal Welfare — always assuming they managed to pass the Means Test.

Unemployment had by this time reached a dangerous level. It was made more so by the strictness of the authorities. The level of unemployment, which had shocked people in the 1980s, was growing worse and worse. Between 1987 and 1990, the number receiving State subsidy swelled by 1,000%. One trouble was that payments from the Ministry of Equal Welfare were so structured as to constitute an incentive to the recipient *not* to look for work — a state of affairs which, in some degree, had prevailed for nearly 20 years. Suppose the head of the family took a job (other than that provided by the Ministry of Work). Then State benefits would be cut by £1 for every £1 earned. Since the only employment available in the Gulag society of 1990 was neither lucrative nor remotely self-satisfying, most recipients of State benefits felt they might just as well *not* take a job. Little wonder that by the early 1990s there was virtually no job market to speak of. That, in fact, was the reason why a Ministry of Work was created.

The decision was taken when it became clear at last that unemployment would continue to grow, even if the Government was willing to go in for printing money and debasing the system on a massive scale. The creation of the Ministry of Work was intended to remove those receiving a free hand-out from the register of the Ministry of Equal Welfare, and put them to work. Thereafter it would serve as the employer of last resort. It did this by offering the unemployed a place on one of their "meaningful public-spirited work" programmes. Some were offered a place on a "programme" assisting in hospital or similar institutions; others helped to refurbish burned-out and abandoned dwellings in the inner cities. On the whole most stockbrokers, ex-jobbers, market-makers, managers and investment counsellors were grateful to the Ministry of Work, to which they owed their survival.

In the early days, however, many of those who had been able to sit back and draw Ministry of Equal Welfare benefits for some time — without interference — were in no mood for change. They resorted to every known dodge and strategem to hold out as long as possible, in order to avoid being drafted into one of the Ministry of Work's unattractive "programmes". Some held out, clinging like drowning matelots to the belief that sooner or later their expertise would be demanded once again — a delusion entertained by a surprising number of people in the Gulag of the 1990s. They failed to grasp that even if such esoteric skills as theirs were ever called for again, they would be the last ones the authorities would turn to.

The hard fact was that there was no room in the Gulag for "exceptions". The rules were strict, universal and rigidly applied. Whatever the small print might say, just about anyone was likely to be deemed "able to work" — including the elderly, the blind, the deaf and the semi-crippled. Those who refused to sign on as "ready and willing" would immediately forfeit all right to draw their Ministry of Equal Welfare benefits. How they managed to survive thereafter was entirely up to them. Moreover, in the harsh environment of the Gulag Anglo-Pedigree there were no second chances!

At the grass-roots level, there was certainly no shortage of work for those who did "sign-on" for a Ministry of Work programme. Probably the most prodigious task was the restoration of burned-out housing that left vast areas of London, Manchester, Bristol and Birmingham a scarred, smouldering expanse of rubble. The fair-haired, blue-eyed, ivory-skinned English Rose had been smoke-damaged.

The fires that raged through the inner cities — one fire every 67 seconds in the UK as a whole — were horrifying. They were a constant reminder of the extent of the break-down in law and order, as well as in the country's way of life and institutions. Many of these fires were due to the high level of violence, to the riots which had become an everyday occurrence, to individual vandalism, or to the carelessness of wandering bands of meths drinkers and hard-drug addicts. But that was not all. Many fires were attributable to the increasing number of "insurance fires" started by disillusioned landlords.

In the late 1980s and the early 1990s an Englishman's home ceased to be considered as his castle. This concept was capitalised during the 1970s and 1980s, when government officials latched on to the idea that by encouraging home ownership they could not only appeal to the individual's pride and self-esteem — for which they would receive ingratiation, the Government was also being offered the opportunity of immobilising huge tracts of the population, which implied tremendous electoral advantages. If nothing else, it prevented Opposition voters from moving in to spoil a safe seat.

The plan worked for quite a while, but it finally backfired as a result of the collapse in house prices that ran in tandem with the collapse of the stock market. House prices in Britain as a whole had been teetering on a knife edge since the middle of the 1980s. There was a collapse in house prices in Aberdeen, along with a severe slump in house prices in the Irish Republic. Elsewhere, with the exception of Southern England, house prices were sluggish in "real" terms, lagging beyind the rate of inflation, even though inflation had come down — before it started rampaging upward again.

Pushing the residential property market down the first slope of the abyss was the collapse on the International Stock Exchange (as it was then called), and its subsequent closure. This hit London and the South-East of England very hard. There was a sudden explosion of properties for sale in the stockbroker belt as the "upwardly mobile" quickly became *downwardly* mobile; and had to make a rapid adjustment of their life-style and expenditure. Aggravating the general situation was the Government's seemingly well-meaning, mad dash for a larger market in rented accommodation. The Government's desire for a bigger market in rented accommodation was a potential revenue raising exercise — a precursor to property tax and an unearned income tax. Although few of its supporters realised what the Government's intention really was, even fewer recognised how desperate for revenue the Government had become, due to the massive transfer payments that were being made in spite of the increasingly draconian social welfare legislation.

When the property laws were modified for the purpose of encouraging private landlords to let their property, there was an initial explosion in rents for those already in such accommodation. Although the Government raked in vast revenues during the first year or so, there was an explosive rise in homelessness, leading to a real threat of anarchy and revolution. Given the fact that the prisons and camps were full to overflowing with the prison staff "bolshie" and the police undermanned and restless, the Government did the only thing it could do. It reintroduced rent control. Said the new Urban Environment Minister in a statement to the Commons, the day after his appointment:

> "I regret very much that the former holder of my present office decided that she could no longer bear the heavy burden of office. (Cries of "Oh!") As this House will be aware, the appalling position in which the average private tenant (Cries of "There are no others!"). . . the average tenant finds himself, or herself, could not be tolerated. (Cries of "Shame!") That is why the Rt Honourable Lady regrets that she cannot be present in the House today to announce that Her Majesty's Government proposes to re-introduce Rent Control. . . because it is the most efficient way of ensuring an orderly. . . and I may say. . . free market."

The reintroduction of rent control nailed the lid on the coffin of the residential property in Britain.

Within a year of the introduction of rent control, Britain's inner cities began to burn. Too many people had too many incentives to throw a match. Some private landlords of abandoned buildings that brought in no rent at all, and literally could not be given away — began starting insurance fires. The ABC of Property Investment in the 1990s was the same as it always has been:

> "The market value of any property retained for income is relative to the net income the property produces."

When income is higher than prevailing financing costs, there is a positive rate of return for the landlord. If it is perceived that capital appreciation is sufficient to compensate for income levels which are below financing costs, once again there is a positive return for the landlord. However, if rental income is below financing costs and there is perceived attrition in capital value, the negative rate of return is compounded, and you can't even get rid of a multiple dwelling unit by giving it away. The buyer is not only stuck with maintenance costs, but also delinquent taxes in most cases. That was the state of the residential property market in the early 1990s.

But what of property outside the market, in the vast, de-populated areas created by the introduction of the National Re-housing plan? This had been brought in to cope with the acute shortage of housing in the late 1980s. The need for more dwellings was so acute that the authorities dismissed the bad experiences they had had with the multi-storey blocks of the 1960s, and returned to the strictly controlled building standards which prevailed during the construction of the Barbican, as far back as the 1940s. The pressure for accommodation was now so great that, instead of copying the Barbican's 41 storey towers, the authorities gave permission for towers of 50 to 60 storeys.

The re-housing plan was carried out in most major cities, and soon absorbed those displaced from the insanitary sprawl of ground level dwellings, where the main services were frequently on the point of collapse. In the worst areas, leaking sewers had polluted the water supply, and the collapsing main drains left the place a quagmire after rain. Driven in part by a sense of social responsibility, but mainly by the risk of a series of epidemics, the authorities moved faster than they had ever done before.

There was another reason for the fact that for the first time in a generation there was a housing surplus. That was, unhappily, the spread of AIDS. In the AIDS epidemic of 1993, 10% of the population were said to have been wiped out. The official figure was never published. By 1995, one in five of the population had become a victim of the dreaded disease. Active cases were hospitalised. Those who were too far gone for treatment were placed in some of the old mental hospitals, and kept under supervision until the end. Suspects and high risk individuals were "quietly persuaded" to go voluntarily to one of the Care Camps. Most were no more than detention camps. In this way, the demand for accommodation in the community was further reduced.

Luckily, by the time the AIDS epidemic struck, machinery to control the movement of population was already in place. The need had been recognised with the introduction of the Poll Tax. This led to the National Registration Act, which required everyone to carry an identity card. Random card checks were at first forbidden, until it became clear that without the utmost vigilance, every anti-social individual would be free to move about the country to escape registration and the Poll Tax. The original Identity Card bore no more than a photograph and the individual's name and Poll Tax number. After a few months they were replaced by a more sophisticated variety. This bore the holder's fingerprints, together with every conceivable piece of information about the holder, including blood group. Some of the information could be accessed only by one of the electronic read-out devices held in every official establishment, from the police to the Ministry of Humane Welfare.

Failure to produce an identity card when so requested by any official — or any other citizen with good reason — was an offence. No one without an identity card would get very far. He — or she — would get no benefits of any kind from the Ministry of Humane Welfare, let alone emergency treatment at any Casualty Department. A card was necessary in order to access one's bank account, buy a stamp, obtain a driving license, enter a municipal car park, purchase tyres, spare parts, oil or petrol. Inter-City bus or train tickets also required one's identity to be established; and without an identity card, it would be impossible to stay overnight at any hotel or — legally speaking — at any private dwelling. Nor could rationed foods be obtained without a card; and it was a punishable offence to *share* a food ration. The most important number-coded information related to the health of the holder; above all whether he or she was an AIDS victim, potentially at risk, or a known carrier of any one of the 284 contagious or infectious diseases prevalent throughout the UK. The problem of communicable diseases was linked directly to the severe drop in health standards, and the appalling hygienic conditions under which most ordinary people were forced to live.

Harsh as the registration and identify cards regulations may sound, they were neither imposed as a punishment nor intended to limit a citizen's legitimate rights. On health grounds alone, they were seen by most people as desirable; and they were defended by the broad mass of the clergy, on the grounds that:

"We must not let our natural desire for liberty rob others of theirs."

Britain's health code was both supported and welcomed by the International Health Authority, which not only supported the 9-innoculation protection standard for all visitors to Britain, but recommended that the returning visitor should undergo 12 weeks' quarantine before being certified FFI (Free from Infection).

When the UK Government tightened up the rules after the typhus scare, an order was passed through the Congress of Benevolence providing for the instant arrest of any person failing to produce a valid identity card. The authorities confirmed that in an emergency, a Citizen's Arrest might be justified. But the public were warned not to attempt any such action unless wearing the approved protective clothing. The Department of Health and Order deployed a number of legal arguments, of which The Lord Chief Justice was highly critical. The controversy raged for almost a week, until the Home Secretary pointed out on television that anyone who failed to carry his card was in effect depriving himself of the many services and benefits to which he — or she — was entitled. Surely, the Home Secretary concluded, such persons *should* be detained, otherwise the State would be denying them the care and protection they so plainly needed.

The many rules introduced during the early 1990s tended to increase, rather than check, the level of lawlessness. Many desperate and inadequate men and women began trying to avoid having to make the choice between regulation and a spell in one of the Care Camps. Some took the desperate step of joining the growing band of addicts and other "anti-socials" who had taken refuge in the depopulated areas. Countless small fires were lit night after night, regardless of the risk that the authorities would launch a snatch raid. Some of the fires were lit — as man has always lit a fire — for comfort, and to keep the cadaver-fed rats away. Others were lit to heat a billy can. But many of the fires were set off by drunks or drug addicts — many of them youngsters spaced out of their heads — who were merely trying to melt their heroin and roll their "crack" in the empty houses. All too often disaster overtook them. Unable to move, they, or their companions, would be burned to death. Others would stand back and deliberately set fires because, they said afterwards, they had "enjoyed watching the blaze."

There were also bands of "building strippers" wandering aimlessly up and down the country. Those from the North might end up as far South as Dorset or Hampshire. Those from Kent or Essex frequently turned up in the Pennines, as though somewhere — over the next hill, perhaps — they would find what they were looking for. In the meantime they would live off what they could find. It was useless sticking to the countryside; the farmers would come out with dogs and guns. It wasn't strictly legal, but if they blew one of the itinerants away, they would simply say the man (or woman) was an obvious AIDS victim, who had threatened to bite them. So, naturally, they'd shot them in self-defence. The plea was generally accepted.

Back in the ruins of the inner cities, they tended to feel safe. Sober citizens — and the police-militia — were normally too afraid of "catching something" to leave the main roads. There were large, hungry rats. Rats had fleas, which carried the bubonic plague. Nervous travellers forced to enter the dead-lands were forever examining their crotch and armpits for the first signs of swelling. There were typhus ticks on the low scrub; and the stagnant pools and runnels were an ideal breeding ground for mosquitoes. The Sunday papers had warned on more than one occasion that a mosquito bite could give you AIDS.

The "strippers" spent as little time in the dead-lands as they could. Anything portable had long ago been carried off. So now they must waste no time setting fire to crumbling flats and offices, taking care not to get trapped on an upper floor. In this way they could remove any copper tubing, lead plumbing and light fixtures, electric wiring, structural timber, or whatever else could be sold to pay for a bed and a meal — no questions asked! Once they had taken whatever was lying around, they'd prepare to make off, covering their tracks.

Usually, they would finish stripping the premises before they set light to it, so as to cover their tracks and ensure a swift get-away. Others, more desperate or impatient, would fire the building first, waiting until later to emerge from their hiding place to search the smouldering ruins for chunks of melted-down metal. Unfortunately, not all of the buildings were vacant before being set alight. Not that this greatly concerned the "strippers", who knew they would be able to supplement whatever they got for the fitments, by looking for the charred remains of their victims, in order to extract any gold and silver fillings they might have in their teeth. Rather in the way that some of the leading UK crematoria used to until the practice was outlawed in 1987. It was not unknown for the more hardened "strippers" to lop off their victim's skull, and carry it away with them to investigate in safety later.

The usual crimes of violence, from a casual mugging to calculated rape, continued unabated, which tended to distract attention to what was going on in the dead-land. Sometimes a wounded man, or woman, would be seen lying beside the road. But as they would often adopt this strategem in order to pounce on the unwary passer-by who came forward to help, the accepted rule was:

"Let bleeding 'strippers' lie"

After a time, however, it became apparent that not all the fires were started by vandals, "strippers", rioters or run-aways. A number appeared to be started by ordinary, law-abiding people who had set light to their own homes. When questioned, they said, "It was to better ourselves." On the face of it, burning down your home would seem a bizarre way of achieving such an objective. But, with social conditions what they were at the turn of the decade (to say nothing of the real destitution that prevailed) burning down their hovel was a small price for slum dwellers to pay when it was the only way open to them of escaping from the heinous conditions under which they lived.

This quite extraordinary state of affairs was due to a misguided piece of legislation introduced by the Minister for Humane Administration. It was based on an idea borrowed by Mrs Thatcher from President Reagan, before he faded quietly away to be replaced by a hard-money President. Like many of the over-legislative edicts of the Gulag, the original bureaucratic plan looked attractive on paper. In practice, it proved to be a strong incentive for arson — as well as providing a devastating insight into the workings of the bureaucratic mind.

For some time, many of those in receipt of State benefits had failed to be selected for a tower-block. Consequently, they continued to live in old, deteriorating properties, barely fit for human habitation, — forever at risk from marauding "strippers". Naturally, these vulnerable and unhappy people were anxious to move as soon as possible to the better accommodation they knew the Ministry for Humane Habitation could give them. Unfortunately, the rule was that those in receipt of a State subsidy were not entitled to claim moving expenses until they had occupied the dwelling for at least two years. There was, as the Ministry for Humane Habitation's circulars made clear, one exception. Any person *burned-out* of his (or her) dwelling would automatically qualify for a grant of between £1,000 and £10,000 (indexed to the rate of inflation) to cover the cost of new clothing, new furniture and re-location. The Bill passed through Parliament unopposed. It is true that under a One Party government, there *could* be no opposition. But it was also a measure which the highly unpopular Ministry of Fiscal Control felt would be warmly welcomed by a grateful electorate — as, indeed, it was. But not in the way the authorities had imagined!

The ink was scarcely dry on the Act, when frustrated slum-dwellers decided to take advantage of the new legislation by setting off a chain of fires, which ran through whole streets in the run-down areas of every major city in Britain. This new brand of arsonists — quiet, sober, respectable family men and women — genuinely believed they would now be entitled to claim the lump sum moving grant, as well as a better place to live.

Looking back from the vantage point of the mid-1990s, it is clear beyond doubt that the root of the United Kingdom's troubles was government expenditure. We have seen how unemployment soared, making ever-increasing demands on the nation's purse-strings. Higher unemployment called for higher taxation. Higher taxation led in turn to even more unemployment, with surviving firms ever more hard hit. In the first place, the only jobs they had to offer were low-paid jobs. Low-paid jobs became harder and harder to fill, since they compared so unfavourably with the generous welfare payments available. To recruit labour, therefore, firms were driven to paying their workers more than they could realistically afford. Furthermore, the overall demand/supply position of the labour market was moving against them. It was one thing to calculate the potential labour supply. To tap the *available* supply was quite another! The hard fact was that AIDS sufferers and drug addicts (both of whom drew Ministry of Equal Welfare benefit) represented one-in-five of the potential work-force.

On top of that, there were the "uncounted", hiding-out among the ruins of the inner cities, or travelling the countryside as "strippers". It was such a waste, especially as the "strippers" were often men and women with skills and a trade: electricians, machinists, seamstresses or carpenters; fitters, plumbers and mechanics! They were often young and fit, too proud, too eligible for registration and employment, but too proud and angry to settle for an unskilled job on the shop floor. In earlier times, one might have called them "outlaws". Not that they were Ned Kellys or Billy-the-Kids. They were more like the Englishmen who took to the countryside when the Normans stole their land; or the Highlanders hunted down and butchered after Culloden.

The dwindling labour force — and the growing costs of welfare — imposed a further still strain on government resources; and governments have only one way in the end of coping. So a company which had managed to overcome its recruitment problems — by paying over the odds for labour — could still be put out of business by the sheer weight of taxation. This, in turn, would increase the burden for the fortunate survivors.

In the Budget of March, 1995, the swelling tax burden was matched by higher taxes. VAT rose to 60% in the Budget of March 1995. Zero rating had already been abolished. When VAT was made payable on commercial transactions of any kind, every business and sole-trader was required to register for VAT. Excise duties were also raised. Those on cigars and cigarettes went up by 25 pence. That meant the duty on a packet of cigarettes (selling at £16.25) totalled £15.92. The duty on wines and spirits was increased by £2.00. The duty payable on a bottle of Scotch (selling at £120.00) rose to £115.00. Beer drinkers were dealt with less harshly. A £6 pint was still available in one of the few remaining pubs — licensed to sell spirits between 1pm and 2pm. The increased duty on that traditional pint now amounted to £5.60.

Having completed his "belt tightening" operation in the areas of indirect taxation, the Chancellor announced that the Standard Rate of Income Tax would be reduced to 20 pence in the pound. Since numeracy had never been a strong point in the British Gulag, the Chancellor's announcement was received at face value — and with approval, as few were able to appreciate the implications of combining a lower rate of tax on generally falling incomes, with a higher "take" from generally *rising* prices. It is safe to say that almost nobody managed to grasp the significance of the new tax on pensions, or the massive increase in National Insurance imposed on employers and employees alike.

Contributions were to be increased on a graduated scale. For the lower paid, there would be an increase of no more than 3% on the rise in salary above the indexed salary increase. However, the increase in National Insurance contributions on the index level of a wage increase would rise by 10% for each 1% above the level of the prevailing average for the preceding five years. For the higher paid, the 3% increase imposed on the non-indexed level of wages increase was to rise by a multiple of 1.4675 for each £2,500 of income. For those earning more than £10,000 per annum, indexation would be reduced to 75% of the rate of increase in the average rate of inflation over the subsequent 12 month period. National Insurance contributions would rise by 20% for each 1% rise above the prevailing average rate of inflation for the previous ten years.

These increases would not apply to civil servants. Nor would they apply to those employed by any government establishment, or any industry considered to be making a "strategic" contribution to the welfare of the nation. The good old "fiscal drag" trick never fails! While all were deemed equal in the Gulag, it was necessary that some should be treated "more equally" than others.

There were further subtleties in the March 1995 Budget. Income derived from rents from commercial property would be subject to a surcharge of 10% for the coming year, and for the previous three years retroactively. Income from residential property would be subject to a surcharge of 15% for the coming year and the previous 5 years retroactively. All profits from the sale of books, periodicals and other publications were to incur a "once only windfall profits tax" of 35% per annum, payable on the coming year and the previous three years. Government publications, and those registered at the Post Office as newspapers, would be exempt from the "once only windfall profits tax".

Finally, the Government took control of whatever foreign assets the citizen might hold. Several years earlier, following the American precedent, British citizens and residents had been taxed on all income received from any part of the world. This was followed by a wealth tax, applied to all assets held anywhere in the world. A large number of these assets had already come into Government hands when the authorities compulsorily acquired all foreign assets known at that time to be privately held. They offered in exchange the first issue of a new undated Exchequer 2½% loan stock. It was dubbed the Peace Loan. In the March Budget of 1995, a further tranche of the Peace

Loan was issued with the purpose of mopping up the remaining overseas assets in private hands, which a combined Inland Revenue and People Bank task-force had uncovered. To save time, and expense, an amnesty was offered — and a deadline given. Thereafter, said the authorities, all "illegal" holdings would be confiscated. Of course, if the errant individual cared to accept the Government's generous offer. . .!

Most errant individuals did. But to ensure that everyone got the message, the authorities reduced the coupon on the new Peace Loan to 1¾ %. The public accepted the offer. They had no alternative. But they did so with an extremely ill grace. "This is a wretched state of affairs," wrote one Party supporter. "We are, after all, the backbone of this country."

Far more wretched was the state of the majority of the nation! In less than 20 years, a radical Government of the Right had fashioned the Legislature and the Judiciary into an instrument of oppression, as skilfully as any Left Stalinist regime. Step by step, again in a strictly legal manner, the Government had managed to strip the majority of the British people of their wealth. In the process, the greater part of the wealth and the power of the country was placed in the hands of a powerful *clique* of place-holders and time-servers. By 1995, the ordinary man and woman had lost something more precious than freedom. They had lost hope, and with it their self-respect.

There were some outside the elitist circles who believed they could still manage to hold on to *something* — provided they signalled (and went on signalling) their unquestioning obedience. They were the Quislings of the 1990s. Some submitted out of fear. Many were able to mask their cowardice from themselves — like the collaborators of Vichy — through their ability to pretend whatever it was necessary to pretend. Probably the majority of the compromisers told themselves (and everyone else) "it could be worse." Thus they were able to grit their teeth and watch their less compromising neighbours suffer whatever came their way. But there were many who simply broke under the pressure of urban living, as conditions, even in the desirable tower-block localities, became intolerable. As one (subsequently banned) writer said, on his last appearance on television:

> "We have seen our wealth dissipated, our standards degraded; and now we have joined the Grey Generation; the age of the anxious and the fearful. Despite the ball-crushing, womb-withering boredom, they know they will never dare to set foot outside their grey tower. *That* would mean walking down those streets which have been ruled by the mugger and the rapist ever since the collapse of law and order in the 1980s. Pass down the main street with its deserted stores and corner shops, and you come to the once prim avenues of homes that cost some citizen a life-time's mortgage to acquire. The narrow, brick-edged beds of privet and laurel sprawl over the broken tiled path. But they cannot hide over-flowing garbage bins, and broken soil pipes, which give the area its distinctive odour.
>
> Empty garages and church halls house the vagrants, who long ago turned out the less offensive squatters. All in all, the suburbs have become part of the decaying inner-city, which even an Irish tinker would refuse to touch for fear of contamination."

Little wonder, with the towns so insanitary and disease ridden, that hundreds, if not thousands, of disgusted families drifted away to join the wanderers — the drab, grey columns of the rootless, who trailed through the counties, deep in misery and despair. They moved around in family groups, as the Stonehenge people once did in the 1980s. Now there were no demonstrations or mass pickets, since few would care to risk attracting the attention of the authorities. From the autumn of 1994, the wanderers became a familiar sight from Hadrian's Wall to Fishguard, and from Glencoe to the former middle-class "resort" of Bournemouth. They had chosen the open road as the only remaining alternative to entering a Care Camp. They were penalised by receiving the lowest level of welfare support of any group. But they were content, so long as they were left alone.

At first, the local people — the "settled" — protested loudly. In one county, when the bench refused to pay heed to their complaints, they marched up to the house of the Lord Lieutenant. He told them, in no uncertain terms, to get off his land or take the consequences. They left. They then tried lobbying their MPs, claiming that the wanderers were scum, and should be removed — with force if necessary. Failing to get satisfaction at Westminster, the farmers declared they would "get rid of the vermin" once and for all. They were as good as their word. Organising a full scale attack, and armed with shot-guns and baseball bats, twenty "locals" fell on one of the wanderers' camps near the Bulford tank training ground. A dog was killed, and a child and its mother had their skulls fractured. Otherwise, the casualties amounted to no more than severe cuts and bruises. Three hand-carts, which the farmers removed, were later burned at one of the tank crossings, forcing a long line of motorists to sit and watch.

Normally, you saw only the wanderers' women and children on the road. The men did their best to keep out of the way of the authorities. In any case, they were busy foraging for food. They would walk into the nearest town in the hope of finding the odd menial job for a few small coins. Some took the opportunity to "suss out" the lie of the land. They were by no means all angels.

The women on the whole looked clean and cheerful; the children well-cared for. The women worked hard, pulling the heavy hand-cart that every family somehow managed to acquire, or build for itself. On this would be piled the frame bed, the remains of a battered tent, their clothes and a few personal possessions. These usually included an iron stew pot and an enamel tea-kettle. There would also be a bundle of kindling sticks, so the children could set fire immediately they halted for the night, while the women prepared a meal for when the men returned. In some areas, where the "settled" were openly hostile, the men would return to the encampment after dark.

Very occasionally, you would see an old man or woman riding past in the family cart. But the "grans" and "gramps" among the wandering folk rarely survived a second winter.

As the country folk learned to accept the wanderers, conditions in the towns grew markedly worse. Poverty, inequality, injustice and punitive, one-sided legislation dulled the senses and mocked at ambition and initiative. Robbery, murder, rape and arson became as much a part of the everyday scene as the filth, and the rats, and the human excrement that bubbled up from the broken drains beneath roadways.

How could people continue to tolerate such conditions without a hint of protest or threat of insurrection? In 1995, shortly after that harsh Budget, a turning point was reached. Illegal publications of the kind circulated in the dead-lands began to appear on the city streets. One night in November 1995, literally thousands of leaflets were posted up on church doors, shop windows, and official notice boards across the land. Others were thrust through letter-boxes apparently at random. Though printed on small hand-presses, and somewhat crudely laid out, the message was always the same:

> "All Mankind must Die, at *some* time. But the cruellest Death of all is the Living Death of the Gulag Anglo-Pedigree."

Personal Planning in a Siege Economy

What you have just read is an excursion into faction. . . a fictional scenario based on fact. Life in the Gulag as I have described, is not in any way intended as an absolute prediction. The scenario is based on a straight-line projection of existing trends. We all could end up in the Gulag as it has been described, if existing trends are perpetuated without deviation and without the type of policy changes needed to mitigate their effect on the future socio-economic infrastructure of Britain.

What I envisage for Britain is a modification of the original thesis that was set out in *The Downwave*. At that time, my projections were based on the assumption that the global deflationary forces that were common to the particular phase of the economic cycle that prevailed at the time, would not be deflected by a fiat money policy that had been characteristic of British Governments in the past. As it happened, since publication of *The Downwave*, the British authorities have pursued a fiat money policy with fervour. The cherished economic and monetary policy guidelines of the Thatcher administration have turned out to be nothing more than rhetoric. Having invested several years of misleading propaganda in promoting the fictions which the original policy guidelines embraced, it clearly can be seen that the floodgates of fiat money have been opened far wider under the Thatcher administration than anyone had ever believed possible. Since Mrs Thatcher came to power, Sterling M3 has expanded by £110 billion, the equivalent of 190%. At no time during the Thatcher administrations was there any semblance of fiscal restraint. Wages and real earnings soared against the background of an artifically buoyant currency and a rapidly deteriorating balance of payments.

If you are the kind of person who wishes to take a rosy view of Britain's economic and financial prospects, in the face of the massive evidence to the contrary, it is pointless for you to give any further consideration to the proposals I am about to make. If I could write favourably about the British Government's economic and financial management stewardship, I would, of course, do so. But, regrettably, the record dictates otherwise. During the period from the 1920s to the 1940s, the Western industrialised nations experienced one of the worst depressions in history, followed by the beginning of one of the greatest and most protracted expansions in world history. I firmly believe that experience is about to be repeated. By the early 1990s I expect to see an Upwave emerging which will be of similar dimensions and duration to that spanning the 1940s through to the mid-1970s. But, as was the case following World War II, not all countries will benefit equally from the glorious expansion I envisage. Some countries will experience only a modicum of improvement in living standards. Others will experience little improvement at all, suffering protracted polarisation in the social structure similar to countries like Greece and those in the Near Eastern Soviet European bloc following World War II. Unfortunately, based on unchanged policies, it would appear that Britain will fall into the latter category during the next period of expansion as a result of the efforts being made to provide a "soft-landing" during the current period of contraction. It would therefore be in the interests of every individual in Britain to begin making preparations and building personal safety nets, the better to survive the Gulag mentality of a siege economy.

As Britain moves down the path leading to the Gulag, society will grow progressively more discontented. At the same time, polarisation of the community will mean that an inordinate percentage of the community will move below the poverty line, while progressively smaller numbers in the community are able to acquire conspicuously larger amounts of wealth. The natural spin-offs will be envy, resentment and an explosion in crime rates — particularly in crimes against property such as theft and kidnapping. Individuals who display their wealth by driving large, flashy cars, wearing expensive jewellery, living in expensive areas and generally enjoying a life style of conspicuous consumption will be running an exceptionally high risk in the Gulag society. Crime has been increasing rapidly for several years in Britain. The momentum of the increase declined in the years 1984-1987. But, as we move into a global recession, we must expect an acceleration in the crime rate to record level. For the thieves, the rewards are highest where they can be quantified. Those, as I say, who engage in an open display of their wealth and live in expensive areas will be the primary targets for the criminal.

Thieves are becoming increasingly more sophisticated all of the time. While technology in crime prevention and detection has been advancing, so have methods for *anti*-prevention and detection among professional criminals. Expensive alarm systems are rarely an effective deterrent. Professional criminals and their trainees are coming up with new innovations all of the time. It is now a common practice for thieves to scour the obituary columns and society pages, keeping a diary of those wealthy individuals who may be attending a funeral, a wedding or are, perhaps, away on a long vacation in some sunny, far distant land. These diaries provide the professional criminal with a ready time-table for his carefully planned attacks. In the underworld, thieves allegedly rent mailing-lists of high income investors, those carrying heavy insurance, yacht owners etc. and then attempt to determine when these individuals will be away from home.

Although the wealthy usually love to display the fruits of their labours, the direction in which society is heading makes it mandatory for the rich to adopt a low profile, unrewarding as this may seem. Conspicuous consumption at a time of growing polarisation, destitution, poverty and deprivation will only incite greed and envy, adding more inducements for those who may be criminally inclined. Most wealthy individuals are collectors of one kind or another, gaining great pleasure from displaying their collection. Owning works of art, jewels, coin collections and stamp collections, antiques and other items of beauty is really not much fun unless you can share their beauty with others. Unfortunately, in the Gulag society, the desire to display items of wealth has its price. The items you may wish to have on display become as readily available to the professional criminal as they are to you.

As an addendum to maintaining a low profile in our potentially crime ridden society, you must also try to make your home as unattractive as possible to the potential thief — both outside and inside. If possible, you will want bright lights, plenty of open space, along with fences and walls which make it slow and difficult to break in. According to police records, the professional thief will spend an average of less than three minutes committing his act. Anything that will appear to impede the speedy execution of a burglary will be an excellent deterrent. In my London apartment, I arranged to have revolving galvanised fencing material on the top of an existing iron-work gate. By no means was this combination impenetrable. It merely took a considerable amount of time to negotiate in the event of an attempted home-breaking. I also installed dummy TV cameras to give the intruder the impression that he was being photographed as he attempted to climb over my fence. There was ample evidence all around the perimeter of my apartment to indicate I had a comprehensive alarm system. In fact, the appearance suggested an alarm system far more comprehensive than was actually in situ. In addition, whenever the apartment was vacant, I would make certain music was always playing on a double cassette-player which would run continuously. The cost of this installation was a mere fraction of my insurance premiums. In addition, I incorporated a relatively inexpensive timing device to switch on the lights whether or not I was at home. All these items are extremely helpful when it comes to encouraging the potential thief to look elsewhere for a property offering greater ease of access. Conspicuous consumption must be avoided in the Gulag. Conspicuous protection is highly desirable.

Inside your home, there should be a variation on the protection visible from outside. Simply storing your valuables in places where a thief would be less likely to look, is probably the greatest deterrent of all. The conventional safe or storage vault is of limited value. It is too obvious. The majority of safes or vaults are quite light and can often be rolled away on castors to a waiting vehicle, and then lifted aboard with the aid of a hoist. Futhermore, the conventional safe is often constructed of sheet steel, with a cement filling between the layers of steel to provide weight and substance. Such safes are readily "peeled" by the professional safe-breaker.

Hidden compartments in your home are likely to be far more useful for protecting your valuables than safes. Your local police station will often have a crime prevention officer. His service can be indispensable. I asked the crime prevention officer to visit my home. After a half-hour inspection he chose a hollow light fitting as the ideal place to hide valuables. That was ten years ago. To date — although I've been the victim of several burglaries — no thief has ever discovered the hollow light fitting. One of the easiest secret compartments to construct is one behind the skirting board, or base boards, which are found along the walls next to the floor in practically every house and apartment. They cover the opening between the floor and the base of the wall. Choose a section of the baseboard that ends at a door, or a corner of the room. It then becomes a matter of simply hollowing out a cavity in the wall behind the baseboard, large enough to hold your valuables. These baseboards are so ordinary and commonplace that a thief will rarely give them a second look.

Secret compartments built into furniture make ideal hiding places. The removable arm of a settee which is hollow underneath is cheap and easy to construct. It also offers immediate access. Mouldings on furniture are similar in application to the baseboards along walls. It is a simple matter to remove the moulding from a table or a desk, using the hollow space behind to store valuables. The moulding can be held in place with magnets for ready access.

One piece of furniture that readily lends itself to concealed compartments is the bookcase. The lower shelf of most bookcases is several inches above the floor. The unused space is invariably masked by quite a thick moulding, easily removed. Access can be gained by either refixing the moulding with magnets or by removing the shelf that rests on top of the moulding — assuming there is a thin plywood covering beneath the shelf.

Wall panelling is a decorative item that also can be used for secret compartments. If an entire wall, or a room is panelled, it becomes a simple matter to make one or more of the panels removable, so you can use the large area of dead-space between wall studs to store your valuables.

If you happen to be a lover of indoor plants, these too can prove vital hiding places for valuables. If you happen to have a profusion of indoor plants against a wall, or in a conservatory, you can select one pot out of the many plants and build a false bottom into the pot. The possibility of detection will be minimal.

Without a doubt, one of the oldest techniques in history for hiding valuables is simply to bury them in the ground. So long as you are extremely careful to draw an accurate map, and leave the ground exactly as you found it, it is difficult to fault this time-honoured hiding place. In general, once you become aware that any seemingly structural space or object in a dwelling contains hidden space, and can therefore be utilised as safe storage, your own ideas for secret compartments will probably proliferate. A few words of warning, however! You must not try to show people how clever you are by revealing your hiding place. Reveal your hiding place to no one — otherwise people will talk and it will cease to serve its intended purpose. At the same time, you must allow for your accidental death. So tell your family of your hiding places, so they will have ready acccess to your valuables if need be. At the same time, members of your family who are aware of your hiding places, must be impressed with the necessity of keeping their existence a complete secret. If you happen to have a safe deposit box — which can be opened on your death — merely keep a typed list of these hiding places inside, and detail the contents available to your heirs.

Mitigating the Effects of Arbitrary and Confiscatory Taxation

The standard dictionary definition of "theft" involves "the taking away of another's property without his consent and with the intention to deprive him of that property." There is no qualification in that definition which makes it any different when it is Government that is doing the taking. Taxation is based on the assumption that it is the responsibility of Government to provide services for the people, and the further assumption that most people would be unwilling to finance services for others. Therefore, the only means available to Government for the provision of these services is the compulsory extraction of monies from the people — by threat or by force.

The Inland Revenue is able to maintain the myth of "voluntary tax compliance" primarily because a large slice of income tax paid is withheld at source! The taxes not withheld at source, are paid because of the fear that has been instilled in people over the consequences if taxes are *not* paid, or unpaid through false declarations. Voluntary tax compliance is about as genuine as your willingness to hand over your money to a robber with a gun to your head. If you don't *voluntarily* comply with the demands of the thief (or the Inland Revenue) you'll soon find that you are forcibly deprived of enjoyment of your property one way or another.

Both in Europe and in the United States, confiscatory taxation is becoming an increasing burden for the average citizen. In Britain, when one considers the vast array of taxes, indirect and direct — despite the Government's attempt to create the illusion that taxes are being lowered —it can be readily seen that anyone paying the highest rate of tax will be paying over 90% of some part of his income in tax. You must recognise that more taxes are on the way, and that for the foreseeable future, taxes will be *increased* not *lowered*. The latest invention here in Britain is the revival of the tax that caused so much trouble in the Middle Ages — the "Poll Tax".

As economic activity declines, and unemployment resumes its exponential rise in Britain, the demands for government services will escalate, as government revenues decline. The manner in which the Government will rise to this challenge will be the same way that governments have *always* met the challenge when public expenditure exceeds revenue. The Government will raise taxes, while giving those empowered to collect these taxes, even greater authority of execution. We have seen this taking place in Britain to an increasing extent over the past few years. While taxes have continued to absorb an increasing percentage of UK GNP, it has been generally perceived that the Government's finances and economic activity have been improving. It takes little imagination to determine the type of tax regime the authorities are going to come up with when it becomes ostentatiously obvious that economic activity is deteriorating, and government revenues are in steep decline.

As taxes reach unbearable levels, an increasing number of Britons will be tempted either not to pay, or actively to cheat on their taxes. This will lead to the emergence of an entire nation of lawbreakers — people who lie about their income and their assets in order to survive. Obviously, the best way to shed the tax burden is not to pay. But there is the right way to go about it, and the wrong way. Put it another way, there are safe legal methods and dangerous illegal ones.

I would now like to make it quite clear that in no way do I advocate illegal tax evasion. Nor do I encourage the use of the more devious and questionable methods that might be employed for the purpose. In fact, I would strongly advise against the use of any such methods, if only because your chance of escaping detection is becoming progressively more limited all the time. Moreover, your chances of finding yourself in prison are becoming greater all the time. This especially holds true for those who by choice, or by necessity, maintain a high profile. Inland Revenue and Customs and Excise make a special effort to use those in the public eye as visible "scapegoats", to serve as a deterrent to lesser mortals who may consider cheating on their taxes. I would state in no uncertain terms, the amount to be gained by cheating on your taxes is in no way commensurate with the risks you will be taking — that is, unless you're some kind of weirdo, who values money and possessions more than freedom. Even in those circumstances, the odds are stacked against you, and you might well end up losing both.

We live in a computerised world. Cross referencing of computer information among government agencies, done with the speed of light, is a reality of the Gulag society. There is the example of one individual who claimed he was not liable for UK tax during a particular period, claiming instead that he was non-resident at the time. The Inland Revenue were able to produce a parking ticket which had been placed on that individual's vehicle during the period he claimed to be out of the country. There is another example — where the cumulative total paid into a credit card account was in excess of the actual income declared by one individual on his tax return.

The average Briton will probably have his name on at least 40 or 50 files, which can be cross-referenced by the Inland Revenue and Customs and Excise. The following represent but a small sample of some of the data government has access to:

Motor Vehicle Licenses and Registrations
Welfare Payments
Unemployment Benefits
VAT Returns
Income Tax Return
NHS Medical Records
NI Contributions
School Records
Birth, Marriage and Death Certificates
Military Records
Police Records
Court Records
Property Deeds
Land Registry Records
Passports and Visas
Census Returns

While governments have direct access to the aforementioned, governments will also have access to a wide range of commercial records, through a variety of means. There is a large market for lists of various categories of individuals. Just as a commercial organisation can purchase lists, say, of those with an income over £50,000 per annum, so too can Inland Revenue. Through the use of high speed computers, government departments are capable of storing prodigious amounts of data. Not only is the government able to maintain vast quantities of data on individuals, but the type of purchases and the physical whereabouts of an individual can be monitored by "tapping-in" on electronic transaction reports — particularly those of banks, retail outlets, employers and insurance companies. All of this can be assembled in one grand Data Bank to which Government has access.

It is more than likely that most of the information governments are able to assemble is supplied by the individual. In many cases, there is no choice. Unless you complete the census form, you commit a criminal offence. Unless you complete the necessary form for inclusion on the electoral register, you will not only be unable to vote, but will also be considered a "suspicious person". If you apply for a mortgage, or any other form of credit, you must provide a great deal of information, or you won't get your money. If you want the contents of your home insured, you must make a full declaration of the contents — especially of your more valuable items — or the insurance company is at liberty to refuse to honour your full claim, that is according to the law! Insurance is an area where you can reveal an enormous amount of personal and financial information. . . without realising it.

The following provides a further example of records kept on the average Briton, to which the Government can gain access if so desired!

Insurance Company Records
Employment Agency Records
Private Medical and Dental Records
Credit Bureau Records
Shareholder Lists
Unitholder Lists
Records of Banks and Financial Institutions
Records of Stockbrokerage firms and Investment Funds
Records of Automobile Dealers, Mail Order Firms and Retailers
Building Society Records, and those for other miscellaneous Lenders
Records of Clubs and Organisations
Credit Card Transactions
GIRO Records
Church Records
Genealogical Bureau Records

It is most unlikely that you will be able successfully to mitigate your tax burden by attempting to cheat and lie. The odds on your being found out, if you *are* a tax evader, are extremely high. Even though you may regard the taxation of your hard-earned money as unfair, you will probably still be plagued with guilt feelings if you try to cheat — knowing that you are a law-breaker, and that the agents of the Inland Revenue or Customs and Excise (or both) may be even now secretly on your trail. Even more important! Can you live with the legal consequences if they catch you out? At best, you'll be facing interest charges, penalties, and fines. At worst, you could go down for a long jail sentence.

Many turn to the exportation of their wealth as a means of hiding their funds from the prying eyes of the authorities. If you have an undeclared foreign account harbouring untaxed earnings, there can be many problems. A major problem is the recent Exchange of Information Act, whereby the UK authorities can now investigate the accounts of foreign banks. There is also the problem of bringing those untaxed earnings back to the UK, even if your secret account remains undetected. Should you decide to repatriate some of the funds you have abroad, you'll have a tough time spending it. If you have been able to bring in some of the funds you have concealed abroad, you will still have to spend the money very quickly and unobtrusively, and maintain those funds in cash. You certainly won't be able suddenly to start living like a Lord, nor, more importantly, will you be able to invest those funds.

Tax evasion of any kind is manifestly not the route to take to mitigate your tax burden in our current and evolving society. However, there are a certain number of things you *can* do to cushion the tax bite, and reduce your exposure to onerous taxation. What I am about to recommend falls into three basic categories:

1. Maintaining a Bargaining Position.
2. Sheltering Your Assets.
3. Maintaining Maximum Tax Efficiency.

The Pursuit of Tax Efficiency

There are no free lunches, and there are very few routes down which to escape from the tax authorities — unless such a route proves to be ultimately to the advantage of government. One escape route that has been permitted, which governments believe will be to their ultimate advantage, is that of pensions. The tax-exempt pension is probably the most efficient form of tax avoidance that exists — provided it is handled properly. If handled improperly, the potential losses could offset the tax efficiency element.

If it is in any way possible for you to establish, or participate in, a pension scheme at your place of work, you should make every effort to do so; availing yourself of the maximum contributions you're allowed to make. The provision of a reasonable pension scheme is an ideal way of supplementing the State pension, and is highly tax efficient. Subject to the formal approval by the Superannuation Retirement Funds Office of the Inland Revenue, an occupational pension scheme will have some or all of the following features:

The employee's contribution may be deducted from income tax. An occupational pension scheme is not treated as a taxable benefit in the hands of employees.

The fund pays neither income tax on investment income, nor capital gains tax on realised capital gains.

The pension payable can be up to ⅔ annual salary after 10 years' service.

There can be a commutation of up to 1½ times the annual salary payable in one lump sum after a minimum of 2 years service with a company.

The fund may increase the level of payments after retirement to make some allowance for inflation.

An existing pension scheme may be "contracted-in" or contracted out of the State scheme. Where the scheme was contracted out, the employer undertook to make up the benefits the State would otherwise have provided. The new schemes available from July 1988 will be far more varied and flexible than in the past.

Occupational pensions schemes can be contributory or non-contributory. Non-contributory pension schemes are more costly for the employer and are likely to provide fewer benefits than contributory pension schemes. In general, I would advise taking advantage of a contributory pension scheme if possible. Individuals who would not ordinarily expect to obtain the maximum benefits under an occupational pension scheme — especially those nearing retirement age — should pay the most they can, "topping up" with additional contributions.

The most tax efficient schemes of all for directors of limited companies have been self-administered schemes, provided the individual directors are able to control the actual investments. Under no circumstances would I recommend any of the "off-the-shelf" schemes marketed by insurance companies or intermediaries. The individual should contact his own accountant in order to have a Trust Deed prepared specifically for him.

Before giving their approval to such a scheme, the Superannuation Funds Office have required that one of the trustees of the fund to be a pensioner trustee. The Superannuation Funds Office will wish to review the progress of any fund on a regular basis, particularly with regard to its investment policy, and to transactions between the trustees and the company. The SFO wants to be satisfied that the fund is being operated in the best interests of the individual pensioner.

One of the major benefits of a self-administered scheme is the ability of the pensioner to create, and structure, the plan in the way that best suits his or her objectives. It is for this reason that individuals should never become involved in schemes where the investments cannot be determined by the recipient of the scheme. The record of companies managing the pension schemes they market leaves a great deal to be desired — particularly during inclement market conditions. It is essential that any pension scheme be actuarially consistent with producing the maximum pension allowable at the time the pension is required. Pension fund managers immersed in the "performance" cult are often unable to determine the difference between what is *perceived* to be capable of producing a given pension, and what is *actually* capable. I feel it is mandatory for all investors who pursue tax efficiency through a self-administered pension scheme to be in a position to select the investments themselves; and have access to a fund manager who will construct a portfolio that will fall into line with *actuarial* criteria, rather than speculative criteria. The type of investments the scheme undertakes must ensure that the level of benefits promised to the recipients of the scheme *can* be met.

Members of a pension scheme can also be the trustees, which is one of the primary benefits of a self-administered pension scheme. As trustee, the member controls the investments. Self-administered pension schemes are extremely flexible. Although the principal aim is to secure pension benefits for members, such schemes can also assist in ensuring the success of the main business. For example, up to 50% of the pension fund may be lent, on commercial terms to the employer. The pension scheme may also invest in property, which in turn may be leased to the company at a commercial rent. The benefits for a company director controlling his own self-administered pension scheme can be arranged to suit individual needs. It is also possible to vary the level and timing of contributions.

A self-administered pension scheme should still be advantageous for high-rate tax payers, and anyone able to contribute £10,000 or more per annum. It is really quite foolish not to take advantage of any such valuable tax concession. The funds contributed are deductible from income, and therefore show an immediate return equivalent to the marginal tax rate for the particular level of income. The interest and dividends which accumulate in the plan are tax free, hence effectively far larger than if they'd been earned outside the plan. Capital gains are also tax free, amplifying the benefits of capital gains. The best possible investments for a self-administered pension scheme are those with a low level of capital risk, and a high current yield. Zero coupon bonds and Stripped Treasury bonds related to the time the pension will be payable are exceptionally attractive, since the beneficiary of the scheme is able to achieve a constant rate of compound interest through these instruments. This, too, is something which has not been available through any other form of investment.

There remain a number of cases of those who are self-employed, or in non-pensionable employment — where there will be no company pension scheme, or where a self-administered pension scheme would not be appropriate. For those, the greatest tax efficiency will be through a personal pension: the type available through the various Life Offices in Britain. As with a retirement annuity, the aim will be to invest a sum of money that will grow tax free until retirement. Then the funds accumulated will buy the best annuity available at the time.

There are two major drawbacks to the new personal pensions. The first relates to the maximum amount that can be put in one of these schemes. It can be less than what is allowed for a self-administered pension scheme, or contributory company pension scheme. The second drawback is the extent to which the purchased annuity will be able to provide the pension required, because it is the level of interest rates which dictates the pension payable. In such an unstable environment as we have in Britain, it is virtually impossible to predict — let alone determine — the level of interest rates at the subscriber's retirement age.

The primary benefit of a retirement annuity was that the pension could start at 60. For certain occupations, the retirement fund could begin earlier. Instead of a full pension, one third of the total pension fund could be taken in one lump. It is generally advantageous to take the maximum commutation available. Tax relief has been given on contributions to the pension fund at the highest marginal income tax rate. Premiums paid in a given tax year could be offset against income in that year, and related back to the previous year of assessment. Should there be no profits or earnings in that year, the premium could be related back for a further 12 months.

One of the major disadvantages has been the poor return and dubious performance over long periods of the various retirement annuity plans commercially available. Careful study, and unbiased, professional advice will still be mandatory when selecting a personal pension.

Tax Sheltered Planning

Currently in Britain, the only method available which I consider to be relatively efficient when it comes to tax planning is to utilise pension scheme legislation to the full. While there are many other schemes which purport to offer tax efficiency, the exposure to loss can often be greater than the tax that is likely to be saved.

The essence of a tax shelter is that the Inland Revenue will allow certain tax deductions and credits for money invested in certain areas. The Business Expansion Scheme is one such tax sheltered form of investment. Under most of the propositions permitted under the Business Expansion Scheme, the amount that can be lost is, in my opinion, far greater than the amount of tax that can be saved. Business Expansion Schemes may be tax efficient, but the majority are not efficient as investments. There is the further risk that a Business Expansion Scheme may lose its tax advantages if the company ceases — in the view of the Inland Revenue — to qualify.

Farming is another form of investment which is a tax sheltered investment and perceived to be tax efficient. Income tax legislation and Capital Gains tax legislation treat farming very favourably. Many have been drawn to farming because it is a tax sheltered investment. Those who have been attracted for that reason are now suffering very heavy losses due to the sharp decline in the value of farm land, a decline which I believe will continue. Another factor which will restrict the potential profitability of investing in farms is the importance of the quality of the land farmed. As the European Community changes its support structure, potential profitability — whatever is left — could be severely affected. I would place farm investment in the same category as Business Expansion Schemes. It may be tax efficient, but it is not necessarily an efficient investment.

A further tax sheltered investment is in woodlands. Investors in woodlands have the opportunity to be taxed under different regimes. The choice taken will usually reflect the age and condition of the woodlands in question. It seems that the great majority of tax shelters were born of an inflationary age. During periods of inflation, large capital gains were available from investing in woodlands, farms, etc. The values of many an inflation hedge have now collapsed, and are likely to continue to trend downward, as the deflationary forces build and gather momentum. The value of woodlands, once projected to grow in perpetuity, will suffer accordingly. Like several others, although tax efficient, the lack of investment efficiency could produce losses far exceeding any tax that could be saved in the context of the investment environment of the future.

There has been considerable interest in schemes whereby an individual investor becomes a limited partner in a research and development project. This type of scheme has been heavily promoted in the area of mining exploration and the exploitation of oil and gas fields. There are certain tax advantages to these schemes, but as with the other tax sheltered investments I have referred to, the potential loss far outweighs the potential tax advantage. In the case of oil and gas exploration partnerships, those who have invested in such schemes are still waiting for their wounds to heal. Once again we have an area of tax efficiency that may have suited the inflationary environment of years gone by, but will be totally unsuitable in the years ahead.

Until the Crash of '87, many believed that share prices could and would rise in perpetuity. In a like manner, until the long series of scandals and the defalcation of several Lloyds underwriters, it was perceived that being a Lloyds underwriter was "money for old rope", which could never result in a loss. On the surface, the scheme certainly looked very attractive. As a Lloyds underwriter it was possible to convert income into capital by using the special tax reliefs on the reinvestment of profits. This aspect of the scheme was exceptionally attractive to those with a high earning capacity but limited capital assets. Furthermore, the Lloyds underwriter could receive a treble return on the same capital invested. First, there was the investment income and the capital gains arising from the deposited investment. Secondly, there was a profit arising from the membership of a syndicate — provided that premium income less reinsurance and expenses was more than the claims. Thirdly, there was the investment income and capital gains arising on the premium income.

Essentially, insurance underwriting has always been a high risk business. It always will be. An underwriter's liability is unlimited. If claims are excessive, the individual can be called upon to settle claims to the extent of his entire personal wealth. In other words, being a Lloyds underwriter can put you into bankruptcy. Many have now discovered this unfavourable aspect much to their dismay. . . from personal experience. Here again we have a scheme which is tax efficient, but not necessarily investment efficient, since the risk can heavily outweigh the potential rewards. For an individual who is asset-rich, the assets he would be placing at risk would certainly not justify the return from those assets if pledged to Lloyds. In *The Downwave* I warned of the risks involved in joining a Lloyds syndicate under existing conditions. Those who did not heed that warning are in the main suffering the same fate as the many who refused to believe a stock market crash was possible!

In general, tax sheltered investments do not really provide for the permanent avoidance of tax. In one way or another, a careful study will show that tax sheltered investment does little more than provide for the deferral of tax until a future time — perhaps on retirement, when the individual is in a lower tax bracket, and better able to absorb the level of liability. In the vast majority of tax sheltered investment schemes — both those I have covered and those I have not even touched on — as the venture develops, a greater portion of its expenditure will become non-deductible, and certain tax allowances will gradually diminish. This will have the effect of increasing the taxable income from the venture — of which those participating in the scheme can claim a share — while the cash distributions remain constant. In sum, during the early years of a tax sheltered investment programme, the supposed beneficiary will received deductions for more money than is put into the scheme, but in the later years, he will be taxed on more than he actually receives — which is par for the course in the tax regime of the Gulag.

Utilising Tax Havens

The efficient and cautious businessman will often carry out his business in one country; keep his assets and investments in a second country; and live in a third. There is quite a bit to be said about this approach, considering the unstable nature of the socio-political world in which we live.

It should be recognised that a *tax haven* is totally different from a *tax shelter*. A tax shelter is a tax avoidance plan, peculiar to the laws in the land in which it originated. A tax haven is a foreign country with tax legislation especially designed to attract the formation of branches and subsidiaries of parent companies based in heavily-taxed, industrial nations.

A multi-national corporation has no one citizenship or country of allegiance. By arranging to be incorporated, and subsequently operating, in more than one political jurisdiction, the company becomes a legal entity which is able to do business in whatever country of incorporation offers the most favourable tax concessions *at the time*. The "company" may be owned by a parent in the UK. The "company" can also be owned by a private individual who lives in the UK. Local Governments treat such companies in the same manner as they would any home-grown domestic corporation.

In order to encourage foreigners to set up companies in areas of less than robust economic activity, the governments in question will frequently offer special concessions. These may include complete "tax holidays" that can last as long as 25 years. Other concessions include such attractive incentives as discounts on energy and raw materials, subsidised rentals and land grants, subsidised payrolls for local labour and cash grants. Obviously, the reason governments grant such concessions is to benefit the local population. High rates of unemployment in areas of low economic activity breed unrest and civil disobedience. Prosperity and full employment assist the ruling powers in their efforts to counter low economic activity. The cost of the inducements is relatively inexpensive. Allowing a tax free holiday to a company that would not otherwise be operating in the area leads to a nice equation in which concessions are balanced by the creation of a body of manageable local citizens who can be taxed.

In order to prevent the liquidation of assets and outflow of funds during periods of adverse economic activity, most countries at one time or another have imposed some form of exchange control restricting capital outflows. Aside from the avoidance of taxation in a high tax area, a further incentive offered by the tax havens can be the ability it gives a company to move funds from one country to another, avoiding the debasement of currencies through inflation. Ideally, one must make every effort to preserve the purchasing power of funds, by maintaining those funds in a strong or "hard" currency. The British pound has fallen from a high of $16.48 at the time of the American Civil War to a low of $1.03 in 1985. The US dollar was in a steep decline against most currencies between 1985-1987. The Mexican peso has been plunging faster than the US dollar, as have the currencies of certain South American countries. Sensible corporate treasurers and individuals will usually look to low inflation countries such as Japan, West Germany and Switzerland to hedge the purchasing power of their funds against inflationary debasement. As circumstances dictate, deposits may be shifted from pounds sterling to US dollars, or from US dollars to Swiss francs. Loans are often obtained in a soft currency that is likely to fall in value, to be repaid later in a lesser amount of a hard currency. Many companies still make more bottom-line profit through currency trading than as a result of their nominal business activity.

Transactions of the type mentioned can be carried through only outside the jurisdiction of the currencies involved, when these currencies are subjected to exchange controls. Those with dual nationality and foreign incorporation can accomplish these transactions far more easily than private citizens. Individual citizens are usually bound by national laws making it a criminal offence, as well as a civil offence, to violate fiscal regulations. The laws applicable to dual-nationals and foreign corporations are far more liberal and flexible. For example, if you are a citizen of Mexico you could be imprisoned if you decided to try to purchase property in Japan. But, if you happen to be a British company with a subsidiary in Mexico, there would be nothing whatever to stop that British subsidiary from opening a new factory in Japan, using its foreign earnings — instead of repatriating them to Mexico in devalued pesos.

While the use of a tax haven outside the boundaries of the country of domicile facilitates dealing in multiple currencies, without fear of exchange controls, the principal reason for utilising a tax haven is, of course, to avoid what may become penal taxation. The multi-national corporate structure permits a company to sell profitable services, or manufacture goods within a minimal tax jurisdiction, thus minimising and mitigating the effects of what might otherwise be a penal rate of tax. Let me demonstrate how this could work, with a simple example.

Let's say a certain essential component in your computer costs 2p to manufacture and sells for £1.00. If that particular component is manufactured only in the UK and solely patented in the UK — or any other high tax rate area — the 98p profit will be eroded by the prevailing level of corporation tax, which could be 50% or more. But suppose the component which costs 2p to make is manufactured in a tax free zone such as Panama. If the Panamanian company bills the parent company, the retail price of £1.00 for the component part that cost 2p to manufacture, 98p is retained in the Panamanian company tax-free. Later the proceeds can be moved to a "hard" currency area.

Loan transactions, insurance transactions, shipping, various classes of investment, along with a large variety of high profit margin goods and services, are typically rendered to multi-nationals by offshore corporations and individuals operating offshore. These offshore activities build their own capital. The tax authorities of high tax areas such as Britain, will progressively refine their tax legislation in order to close what they consider to be "loopholes" in their tax legislation. But, as independent advisors are recruited by the authorities to cut down the escape routes available with existing tax legislation, these same advisors will become available in due course to identify new escape routes that have emerged in the existing legislation, while they were busy closing up the old loopholes.

A properly organised tax haven organisation that complies with the laws of the country in which it is established, is as legal from the viewpoint of the country of residence as the interpretation of that country's tax laws permit it to be. In other words, the legal status of a tax haven company, with regard to the taxation rules of the country of residence, is the same as though the company were located in the country of residence. Put another way, a British businessman who uses space in his home for business purposes may run head-on into an Inland Revenue investigation if a disproportionately large area of the home is claimed as an expense against the income of the business or the man himself. This is not a matter of law, but of interpretation. The worst the Inland Revenue investigator can do is disallow all, or part, of what has been claimed as a business expense. On the other hand, if an individual attempts to evade tax by concealing a part of his income — stuffing the cash in his mattress — this becomes an issue of legality. If discovered, the Inland Revenue investigator can file a report that may eventually result in fines and/or imprisonment for the perpetrator. The same principal holds true when attempting to exploit the legislation applicable to tax havens. The responsible individual who makes use of a foreign company should not in any way attempt to establish any practice that could lead to an accusation of tax evasion. The use of a tax haven company must be so organised as to be legally defensible in every respect.

It will certainly be much more difficult for the Inland Revenue to discover what your true earnings are if you are exporting funds out of the country and banking overseas.

The Inland Revenue have made it difficult but not impossible to avoid tax legally, and mitigate your tax liability through the use of offshore tax havens. The mechanics are highly complex. Therefore, competent legal advice is mandatory. But it can still be done. Using proper tax haven planning can radically reduce your taxes and help you maintain a greater degree of financial privacy as well. It will certainly be more difficult for the Inland Revenue to ascertain what your true earnings are if you are exporting your funds out of the country and banking abroad. But, while it may be more difficult for the authorities to acquire the information about you they would like to have under such circumstances, many, many facilities are available to the authorities in high tax countries — especially those in the EEC. If your use of a tax haven involves tax evasion, my best advice to you is, "Go, join your Money". If you're found out, you'll be in big trouble if your feet should ever touch British soil again.

The Great Escape. . . Abandoning the Gulag Anglo-Pedigree

Murphy's Law, which says, "If anything can possibly go wrong it will", is alive and well. Adversity has a way of recurring with unfortunate and increasing regularity. As we move further down the road of the Gulag, murder, robbery, arson, kidnappings, hijackings, civil riots, terrorist incidents and other social disturbances are likely to occur with increasing frequency in a larger number of areas.

Social upheavals will be countered by a proliferation of laws and regulations enacted by the authorities, *supposedly* intended to protect the innocent — but rendering the most innocent, criminal. In some countries, over-legislation almost makes breathing the air and walking on the ground an "offence". It is not necessary for you to become involved in criminal activities to be a lawbreaker, leading to the loss of all your property, and exposure to a prison sentence. If you happen to grow the wrong crops on your farm, you could become a lawbreaker. If you happen to be selling goods at the "wrong" price, or purchasing from the "wrong" source, you could be open to criminal conviction. You may become a lawbreaker by inadvertently causing an environmental impact. If you join a particular group, or hear a certain type of conversation without reporting it to the authorities, you can be charged with conspiracy and locked up. If the conspiracy is linked with terrorism, you can be held for questioning for much longer.

Have you kept up to date with all of the latest advances in medical technology and the laws against drug abuse? If you haven't, you could be running a serious risk. There are various types of medication which your physician may prescribe that fall under the category of "dangerous drugs". You might not be aware of the nature of the medication you are taking, but in the event that you happen to become involved in a traffic accident while under the influence of a variety of medications, you would be liable to be charged with a criminal offence.

If you're like a number of people in our modern society, you must be absolutely fascinated with the capabilities of your personal computer. . . particularly if it's got a modem. You will most certainly want to experiment with the capabilities. . . but, watch it! If you happen to push the wrong buttons, and gain access to someone else's data bank, you could be charged with theft. All of these newly defined "crimes", along with a plethora of inadvertent acts of omission that may also be defined as "crimes", are a growing feature of our modern urban Gulag society which could result in the loss of your freedom and financial disaster through no fault of your own.

Have you stopped to think about your level of immunity to the various matters I've been outlining? Maybe you have. Perhaps, as a pillar of the community, you believe none of what I have said could ever effect you. Maybe you're a banker. Being a banker is a respectable enough profession in most places. . . but not *all* places. If you were a banker in Iran, you would be guilty of a crime punishable by death. When the Ayatollah Khomeini seized power, enforcement of the Islamic ban on money-lending made banking a crime as serious as murder. . . if not more serious. In France, when the banks were nationalised immediately after President Mitterand assumed power with his extreme leftist regime, bankers didn't face a hangman's noose or electric chair. . . merely economic execution. Many French bankers moved out of the country to run their enterprises in the hope that the temporary totalitarian madness would pass. Having been indoctrinated by two centuries of whimsical governments, French bankers quickly diversified. While the nadir of the socialist insanity has now passed, many laws remain on the statute books which make it a criminal offence to commit an act which amounts to nothing more than protecting one's personal assets.

In the years ahead — or even now — might there be a general hostility in your community to people like you? As unemployment rises and crime escalates, those who 'have' will be subjected to increasing intolerance and resentment from the 'have-nots' in the Gulag society. If you are a wealthy person — a property owner, business entrepreneur or employer, you could very easily be labelled as an "exploiter" by those around you. It has happened before during periods of hard times in many places with innumerable variations.

Prejudice and hostility focus the mind when the outlook is bleak. Many people are unwilling to accept their fate in life as a product of their own doing. They will attempt to find scapegoats whom they blame for their plight. It would not be untimely for an individual who shares your politics, religious beliefs, or nationality — or who may have the same colour of skin that you have — to become the victim of persecution and violence. We've seen periods of economic dislocation produce a similar effect many times before.

Perhaps your tax affairs are in apple-pie order. You may possibly have turned every stone to make certain that you have exploited every possible tax advantage available in an absolutely legal way. Yet, the authorities may decide they would like to change the rules in the middle of the game. Tax officials in the UK are notorious as a power accountable only unto themselves. They may exercise their powers in an arbitrary and retroactive manner. Those who are selected for the job of tax inspector are often inclined to be obstreperous, disagreeable tyrants, imbued with envy and resentment constituting an inalienable part of their character. Branches of the British tax regime are empowered to make seizures and confiscations of personal property and assets without trial or the need to refer to the courts. Whenever those powers are exercised, it becomes the responsibility of the taxpayer to prove his innocence. In theory, if the Inland Revenue decided you have earned £2,000,000 last year and would like to have £1,200,000 in tax, they don't have to prove you made that £2,000,000. *You* have to prove you *didn't*: which is no mean feat in terms of the law. Synonymous with the totalitarianism of the Gulag, the powers of the tax authorities reach beyond the law, indifferent to the internationally touted democratic theory — the "presumption of innocence until proven guilty by the due process of the law."

It may seem unlikely now but getting caught in the grist-mill of the Gulag bureaucracy can — like AIDS — be a highly unpredictable affair to which you could become exposed at any time. Problems of the type described, are perceived to be "something that happens to the other guy". . . in another place or another time. . . until they happen to YOU! Accordingly the majority of people will be no more prepared for the Gulag type existence experienced by Germany in the 1920s and 30s than they were for the Crash of '87. Most people never bother to prepare an escape route. They leave themselves with no option when push comes to shove. They just fall!

By now it would not be unreasonable if you have decided simply to abandon the Gulag Anglo-Pedigree. What may be achieved by clinging to the homeland you cherish could easily be offset by the risks you might be taking, depending on your own personal circumstances. For the average Timmy Teabreak, the suggestion of emigration as a means of protecting his wealth and freedom is completely and totally irrelevant. His Gulag mentality is unable to extend beyond the next can of light ale in front of the "Boob Tube", or Saturday's match. His range of movement involves travelling the distance between his bedroom and his place of work where he performs a labour of mindless routine. . . if he's not on the dole! His taxes are deducted at source, and he has no idea whether or not they could be or should be, less. If there is a war, such as the Falklands Campaign, or any other conflict, regardless of what it's about, he will — without the slightest hesitation or objection, pledge his support, and intention to fight, bleed and die for "his country, right or wrong". Timmy Teabreak is the ideal of any government — the proverbial "good, responsible citizen", whom most politicians treat as an expendable, natural resource.

Blind obedience is not one of my virtues. Nor is it one I especially recommend. I personally would not want to be sent into combat, nor would I want a child of mine to be disfigured, mutilated or written off as KIA; all in a cause which, ten years from now, will be perceived as insignificant, petty and unnecessary. I personally feel that most conflicts, laws and regulations, supposedly enacted in the "national interest", cause more problems than they solve, and are tolerable only in the context of a pernicious, pointless pseudo-patriotic orgy of self-sacrifice in which we are expected to participate.

In this world there are, and always have been — and always will be — those who would rather die than renounce their national heritage. "I regret I have but one life to give for my country," were the words of one renowned patriot. People have been burned at the stake for failing to acquiesce in what the Inquisition demanded of them. Joan of Arc was a victim of such idealism. On the other hand, Galileo was more of a pragmatist. In order to be allowed to pursue his ambition, he willingly renounced his belief that the earth revolved around the sun.

During our formative years, we are all taught to believe that our country is the greatest nation in the world. Children in the United States are imbued with this dogma at school. So too were the German youths under Adolf Hitler, the Russians under Josef Stalin and the Chinese coolies under Mao Tse Tung. Without a doubt — at one time — Britain was truly the greatest of all nations, bestowed with an empire that was the admiration of both the East and the West. At one time, a similar position was held by the Roman Empire, the Gupta Empire, the Egyptian Empire, the Byzantine Empire, the Islamic Empire — along with the Empires of Greece and China. We live in a dynamic society which is constantly subject to change. Global leadership changes just as do living standards from one nation to the next.

In recent years, the previously powerful industrialised nations of the West have changed their political ideologies to the point where these nations are now governed by little more than faceless bureaucracies sporting varying degrees of socialist, totalitarian principles. The result has been to create a robot-like citizenry whose actions are totally undeflected by individual responsibility and personal initiative. Even the average worker — for whom the system is supposedly designed — must surely be aware that a system in which the rewards of personal initiative are subject to a level of confiscation which is directly commensurate with those rewards, must be stifling for individual initiative and productivity, leading ultimately to a self-defeating, self-feeding downward spiral of living conditions and personal freedom.

Life, liberty and the pursuit of happiness are the inalienable rights of men. . . not a council house and welfare benefits! I certainly do not advocate the committing of unpatriotic, illegal and immoral acts against the state. At the same time, I cannot encourage unfailing allegiance to a state whose government thrives on the oppression of its citizens to the point of desperation. Governments which attempt to control their citizens in such a way, by appealing to a spirit of jingoism and nationalism, are themselves illegal and immoral. Although unpatriotic, there is certainly nothing illegal or immoral in a person's deciding to abandon a nation where life, liberty, property rights and the pursuit of happiness are restricted. First and foremost, each individual owes an allegiance to himself, his loved ones and those who may depend on him for their well-being, rather than a sterile abstraction known as government, to which he may only be an expendable item — like a dry biro or soiled serviette. In our modern society, the pragmatist must maximise his options and rid himself of unrealistic and unrewarding concepts of red, white or true-blue patriotism which exist only in the abstract. Misled nationalistic ideologies are no longer the subject of academic cocktail party chit-chat; it's a matter of life and death in terms of freedom — physically, financially and psychologically.

Just because you live in a specific country, doesn't mean you have to remain there for the rest of your natural life. A time could come when you may be desperate to leave that country — whether you were born in it or not. A great deal can be gained by achieving flexibility, and not belonging to one country — or being irrevocably tied to any one country. To begin with, by "internationalising" yourself you will have far more freedom of movement now, and your *prospective* freedom of movement is unlikely to be threatened to the same extent as if you were tied to one regime. Limiting your tax exposure is only one aspect of becoming a "foreigner" wherever you may be.

There are many ways you can go about "internationalising" yourself. As a point of departure, "internationalising" your assets is vital. You can also "internationalise" yourself via the purchase of a home in another country. You could also go the full route, either by adopting dual-nationality or by relinquishing your UK citizenship in favour of becoming a citizen of another country. There are many attractive places to live in the world — such as Monaco, Andorra, Jersey, Guernsey, Sark, the Isle of Man, the Bahamas and Cayman Islands. Many of these can be particularly appealing for those who wish to retire, or for those people whose business activities may be out of the country already. Deciding on the methods you should use to "internationalise" yourself is a highly personal undertaking, solely dependent on your existing circumstances and the precise nature of what you wish to accomplish — and are able to accomplish — given existing constraints. I can only offer some broad suggestions and generalities.

Banking Abroad

When the going gets tough, those countries inclined to get tough wind up with exchange controls. Although we haven't seen exchange controls in Britain for quite some time, Britain as a nation has been prone to impose exchange controls. Aside from the possibility of exchange controls, there are many legitimate reasons for keeping some of your wealth outside the UK. Over the centuries scores of individuals have found themselves out of favour with those who assumed power. They have suffered severe financial loss as a result. Jews, Negros, Asians, Protestants and others have borne the brunt of persecution — which extended from the confiscation of their property to the taking of their lives. The survival of many individuals is solely attributable to being able to move their wealth beyond the grasp of a totalitarian government. . . before it was too late. While Britain is currently more tolerant than many other countries occupied by individuals with dissenting views, it is certainly not beyond the realms of possibility that we may ultimately see the financial and social persecution of any who may at some time be deemed "radical" and a threat to the state. Tendencies of this type have a way of developing during periods of economic stress, of the type which is rapidly approaching. It is totally impossible to predict the extent to which the powerful Whitehall bureaucracy will go to achieve what they deem a necessary social conformity and economic stability. By harbouring your funds in another country, you can isolate that part of your wealth from a number of unsavoury possibilities, and achieve freedom from the aforementioned power and influence. The extent of the protection you are afforded will depend where you put your funds, and how you manage to export them.

There are two prerequisites for deciding to which country to export your funds. The first is banking stability. The second is banking secrecy. There is no point in shipping your funds abroad if the end result is going to be a bank failure, or if — by some means — those funds can still be seized by the state which you would prefer to abandon.

Switzerland is the first choice of many who wish to export their funds. Financial secrecy and Swiss banking stability are an outgrowth of the country's long tradition of personal and individual privacy — a tradition that dates back at least as far as feudalism. The legal foundation of Swiss bank secrecy is based on the personal rights established in the Swiss Constitution, the Civil Code and the Code of Obligations, supplemented by provisions of the Criminal Code. In addition, there is the Banking Law of 1934 which was enacted partly in response to the financial crises of the 1930s, but also as a way to inhibit the Nazis' investigations into accounts maintained in Switzerland by German Jewish residents. The Banking Law of 1934 provided for severe penalties for violation of Switzerland's ban on disclosure, making Swiss banking secrecy laws among the toughest anywhere. Yet, there are certain flaws. The Banking Law of 1934 does not include a definition of bank secrecy *per se*. Instead of a narrow legal definition of bank secrecy enshrined in statute, definition is left to custom and practice, and subject to judicial discretion.

Since the body of laws covering secrecy is rather loosely drafted, Swiss banks and their employees generally exercise extraordinary caution, and do not release information unless explicitly required by the judiciary. Moreover, Swiss secrecy laws apply not only to bank-outsider relationships, but also to bank-to-government and bank-to-bank relationships. For example, the mere acknowledgment of the existence of an account is a direct violation of the law, even though it may be confined to employees of two different Swiss banks. Recently, there has been considerable editorial coverage suggesting a relaxation of the independence of the Swiss bankers. From my own observations, this is nothing more than a PR effort on the part of those governments which heavily tax their citizens — principally the UK and the US — and spread these stories designed to discourage anyone considering opening a Swiss bank account. Personally, I have found Swiss bankers to be no less secretive, and no more willing to co-operate with other governments, than they ever were.

Aside from the advantages of secrecy, and a safe haven for funds outside the normal residency of an individual, there are several reasons for banking in Switzerland. The competence and integrity of Swiss bankers, and their standing in the international banking community, are respected the world over. Swiss banks can also provide a wide range of services outside the scope of activities of banks in other areas. Those who bank in Switzerland can place their liquid assets in Swiss francs or other currencies as a hedge against the inflation of the currency of the depositor. Furthermore, there is complete freedom from exchange controls, government regulations and government interference in bank affairs. An added bonus is the virtually unparalleled political stability of Switzerland as a nation.

There are a multitude of ways in which the use of a Swiss bank can mitigate domestic legislation. For example, an American citizen who wishes to avoid the US gift tax on amounts exceeding $10,000, may legally avoid this tax by making that gift abroad, through a Swiss bank. There are many more examples of the manner in which the use of a Swiss bank can help the tax payer *legally* to avoid tax, while placing the tax payer in a stronger bargaining position than if his assets were readily available for sequestration by local authorities. I would now state in no uncertain terms, that Swiss banks will be of no assistance whatever in helping to evade taxes, or break the law. But Swiss banks will be of assistance in helping you reduce the effects of domestic legislation, so that you are not exploited by over-zealous tax authorites.

Another plus for Switzerland lies in the elaborate precautions the country has taken to protect itself against the possibility of a nuclear war. The target has been to provide a modern nuclear fallout shelter for every resident of Switzerland — in cities, towns, villages, and farms even — by the year 2000. Since 1979 Switzerland has spent over $2.5 billion on its shelter programme. That is far more than any other country on a *per capita* basis. All new homes, including vacation chalets, must have fallout shelters. The Government contributes half the cost. A large standing military force, mandatory conscription, and a high level of civil defence preparedness complete the Swiss readiness effort. The object has been to provide Swiss residents with a better-than-average chance of survival in the event of nuclear war, which reinforces Switzerland's image as a safe haven for the funds of foreigners. Of course, if there were a nuclear catastrophe, what would remain of the assets backing Swiss deposits is open to question. On the other hand, in the event of such a disaster, a significantly large number of depositors would probably not be around to collect.

The use of numbered accounts, *Aktiengeseschaften* (companies in which shares are issued), personal holding companies and 'base' companies are a few of the vehicles through which financial transactions can be carried out in complete anonymity. The actual location of Switzerland, with its outstanding transport and communications facilities, adds to the quality of the safe haven it provides for funds. It becomes an easy matter to move funds in and out of the country without attracting undue attention.

Swiss banks may execute transactions on the basis of telephone instructions and — unlike some banks in other areas — can offer a broad range of trust, investment and related services. Swiss accounts can be opened through the post, although the establishment of a relationship beforehand tends to be common, and so advisable. Much of the banking business in Switzerland is in the hands of the "Big Three" — Credit Suisse, Union Bank of Switzerland and the Swiss Bank Corporation. Although there are a number of smaller banks which also have a share of the market. Swiss banks maintain that they do not undertake background checks in cases where questions arise.

But be warned! Banking in Switzerland is not cheap. If it is your intention to stash away a couple of thousand pounds or so outside the UK net — money you might want to keep for a "rainy day" during your European travels — there are better places than Switzerland.

"If you've got £10,000 or £20,000 go to Citibank", one Swiss banker observed. "We can't help you, and you can't help us." While the major Swiss banks say they do not have a formal minimum for opening a numbered account, most will discourage deposits under £25,000. Interest, in any case, is not payable unless the account is well into six figures. So minimum deposits in Swiss accounts tend to be substantial. For example, as of 1984, the minimum deposit at Bank Leu was $10,000. While current accounts bear no interest at all, transaction charges are about double what you would expect to pay in the UK, so are the charges for most banking services in Switzerland. Those deposit accounts that did bear interest during 1984 were paid a mere 3.5% per annum — at a time when rates were more than double that on accounts denominated in currencies other than SFr. The maximum withdrawal on the average account was SFr 20,000 without notice. Larger withdrawals were subject to two months notice. Investment accounts yielded 4% per annum, with the right to withdraw up to SFr 10,000 every six months. Larger withdrawals required six months notice, and were subject to a penalty charge of 1%.

Obviously, exchange rate considerations must be taken into account when comparing the return on accounts, as well as future prospective changes in interest rates and changes in policy. In the mid-1970s, Switzerland imposed severe penalties on foreign account holders in order to discourage capital inflows. At the time, only the first SFr 50,000 of deposits were eligible to earn interest. Accounts in excess of SFr 100,000 incurred a negative interest of 40%. It should also be noted that Swiss deposit accounts are also subject to a withholding tax on interest of 35%. However, there is a rebate of 30% if the account holder is not a Swiss resident. Personally,

I would not recommend maintaining an account in Switzerland in Swiss francs.

During periods of severe, widespread economic dislocation, more people turn to banks outside their country of residence. Switzerland has always been among the most popular. The cost of maintaining a Swiss bank account is likely to increase with any increase in demand. It would therefore be wiser to consider one of the less popular alternatives. Liechtenstein offers interesting possibilities. According to some tax haven experts, by using Liechtenstein you can build a "double wall of secrecy." It is possible to open an account with a Swiss bank, and then have the Swiss bank transfer funds to a foundation, corporation or trust in Liechtenstein, where strict banking privacy is also available. The roles can also be reversed.

A Liechtenstein fiduciary company can establish a *Stiftung* which has the marking of a foundation. The founder of such trust arrangements does not require the traditional founder's rights to control or own the funds, at least officially. Since a Liechtenstein *Stiftung* is a quasi-independent enterprise, carrying its own assets and liabilities, independent of the trustee, privacy is maximised.

Under Liechtenstein Company Law, the *Stiftung* is essentially a family foundation, while the *Anstalt* is similar to a British limited company. Most such forms of corporate structure are openly referred to as "dummy" or "paper" corporations, used to hold or transfer assets while at the same time protecting them from tax liabilities. The *Anstalt* is probably the more popular of the two, and is unique to Liechtenstein. The *Anstalt* is a non-share corporation, enjoying limited liability and subject to an initial capitalisation of SFr 20,000. Once the corporation is formed, the capital can then be invested, invested, or repatriated by the owners at will. The *Anstalt* is able to acquire works of art, rare antiques, or shares in other companies without the identity of the buyer ever being revealed. According to Ian Andersohn, in his book *Making Money*, the *Anstalt* "allows you to move through the financial world invisibly, totally insulated from the hoards of drones who might otherwise seek to be your partner."

The cost of forming the type of Liechtenstein entity which has been described should be in the area of £3,000. Expect to pay about £1,500 for the annual upkeep of the company. Many Liechtenstein companies are formed in Switzerland through Swiss bankers, who arrange the formalities through a Liechtenstein banker or lawyer. These companies are always listed on the Public Register, but not necessarily as the name or names of the beneficial owners of the *Anstalt*. Only the Swiss bankers — and possibly the lawyer in Liechtenstein — know the owner's true identity. The Liechtenstein-Switzerland connection or relationship is often described as the best (and possibly the cheapest) means of securing privacy and anonymity for an international investor.

It must be recognised that the secrecy element is of strictly limited value so far as the UK tax authorities are concerned. You cannot satisfy UK tax legislation simply by paying taxes on the profits made by your Liechtenstein company that are transferred to you in the UK. You will be expected to report to the Inland Revenue any interest you have in a foreign company in addition to that from foreign bank accounts. International investors are boxed-in when it comes to hiding their assets from the UK authorities. Yet, it has been argued that a Liechtenstein discretionary trust can legally escape reporting requirements, as well as UK taxation, on the grounds that the founder of the trust does not acquire the traditional founder's rights to control or own the funds. In consequence, the trust need not be reported as your foreign account, or a foreign interest. Nor need you pay taxes on the profits of the trust.

If the initial objective is merely to conserve wealth rather than establish a tax structure, there are many areas that can fill the bill. There are also some areas which should be avoided. Austria is an exceptionally useful place to store wealth and conduct banking business. There are several account facilities available with unusual features. One such account involves nothing more than a bearer passbook. The identity of the owner is unknown even to the bank. To effect a deposit or withdrawal, one needs only to present the passbook. Obviously, the passbook must always be held in safe keeping!

For the average Briton, the Channel Islands are a useful place in which to conduct business outside the normal net of the UK tax authorities. Telecommunications are good. Trusts established in the Channel Islands provide considerable privacy. Your name does not appear anywhere in the trust documents. However, in the case of a corporation, shareholders' names must be passed on to the Bank of England, which has agreed to keep these names confidential. It is not possible to determine how long this practice will continue. Laws have a habit of changing without notice, and when least expected. At one time, Denmark was a country in which banking business was confidential. Recently, Denmark abandoned confidentiality. The information that Danish banks are obliged to give the tax authorities includes account balances at the end of the year, interest credited during the year, the name and address of the account holder, plus his or her personal registration number. This information must also be provided in respect of foreigners, even though their balances in Denmark, and the interest on them, are free of Danish tax. The extent to which this information will be passed on to foreign countries depends on the tax agreement with the individual country. Confidentiality itself is not a crime, nor is it the root cause of any particular crime. Confidentiality does help to facilitate freedom of movement, wherein the principal value of banking secrecy lies. In this respect — in order adequately to achieve your objectives — my recommendation would be to maintain a proportion of your wealth in non-EEC territories.

Countries that should be avoided are the Nordic countries who are plagued by overt socialism, and offer little in terms of either bank secrecy or sound currency. The same holds true for countries in Southern Europe. Portugal has nationalised its banks and industries. Spain, Italy and Greece have extremely influential Communist parties, representing a perennial threat to the banking systems of these countries. In the event of a global depression, it is fairly certain that large tracts of the banking and industrial complexes could fall under the threat of nationalisation. The countries of Southern Europe are beautiful places to visit and enjoy a holiday, but I definitely wouldn't recommend the keeping of your money in any of them.

The ideal safety area for your funds is to be found in those non-EEC countries which are small, international and lack a fervour to isolate their citizens from natural economic forces through massive welfare programmes, and who, equally, have little desire to save the world by supporting mammoth armies. West Germany is a country where holding funds should be avoided, owing to its dependence on the highly taxed industrialised nations of the West. Its size, its industrial development, its past history, as well as its present military position as a buffer between the US and the USSR, are matched by a banking system that is far too much an integral part of its highly vulnerable industries. Therefore I would not recommend West Germany as a place in which to maintain a foreign bank account.

The French enjoy a long-standing and hard-earned reputation of having citizens who trust neither their politicians nor their currency. Their prudent example should be heeded. The Principality of Monaco shares the prudent attributes of French banking without being subject to the whims of the French Government. Monaco is a constitutional Monarchy presided over by the same family for the past 500 years. Its relationship with France began in 1793. It was granted independence 20 years later.

Monaco is subordinate to France in all matters involving money, exchange controls, banking and customs, along with indirect taxes (notably Value Added Tax) and economic controls. France collects and rebates taxes on a revenue-sharing basis. French nationals who live in Monaco are subject to French taxes and military service. However, foreigners are exempt from taxes. The viability of Monaco as a haven for funds can be gleaned from the statistics, that show bank deposits per Monaco inhabitant averaging $75,000, compared with an average of $3,000 per person in the rest of France. It is clearly in the interests of the French authorities to retain the *status quo* so far as Monaco is concerned, in view of the amount of wealth that is drawn in by the French banking system.

Accounts can be maintained in the currency of the individual depositor's choice, externally, independent of the French system. Most of the major international banking institutions are represented in Monaco — such as Credit Suisse, Societie Generale, Citicorp, Barclays, Chase, etc.

The recommendations I've made so far with regard to the formation of tax efficient foreign corporations and trusts, and the exportation of funds and banking outside your country of residence, represent only the tip of an extremely complicated iceberg. The manner in which an individual may protect his assets by transferring his funds abroad can be as simple as opening a bank account in Jersey, or as complex as forming a series of trusts and corporations involving several bank accounts and establishing a residence if required. The approach to be adopted is directly related to the amount of wealth which requires protecting and the personal circumstances of the individual concerned.

If what I've discussed so far serves no other purpose than to demonstrate the degree of complexity involved, along with the limitations on what can be achieved through forming an international network — while retaining residency in a highly taxed area — then I feel a great deal has been accomplished. What should be quite clear is that the idea of spending £100 or £5,000 for an off-the-shelf tax ruse which will suddenly liberate you from the UK tax code is pure fantasy, and a total waste of money. Unfortunately, international tax planning is an area in which you can easily acquire some very bad, and very costly, advice. There are many tax advisors operating in the field of international tax planning — particularly those with established offices in tax haven areas — that remain in the field even though they have many dissatisfied customers. This is because investors interested in moving along the route of exporting funds and arranging tax havens generally value their privacy, and are therefore unlikely to complain. Even though an individual may fully intend to remain within the law — in the strictest sense — he probably will not want to focus undue attention and trigger off what might prove an extremely expensive contest with the Inland Revenue. As a result, that individual is unlikely to make much of an audible howl when he discovers that the tax plan he paid several thousand pounds for was based on little more than the imagination of the advisor, and fails to provide the certain means of mitigating the tax liability that he thought he was paying for.

There is no shortage of greedy and unscrupulous operators who will attempt to exploit the situation by assuring the client that whatever that client would like is a workable proposition, likely to produce the desired result. In the final analysis, the tax advisor will design a plan which will certainly satisfy the fantasies of the client, but which could also go a long way towards satisfying the tax authorities. In the UK, the Inland Revenue have an extremely effective "Catch-22" clause in the legislation. If the authorities believe that a structure has been created merely for the purpose of avoiding tax — the operative word is *avoiding*. . . not *evading*. . . the tax affairs of the individual can be treated as though the device did not exist. All the client would get from the plan sold to him by his so-called advisor, would be the ability to claim that what he thought he was doing was legal. As a result, the ill-advised client may be able to stay out of prison, but he could still lose part of —or even the *whole* of — his assets in taxes and penalties.

My suggestion is that initially you exploit the simple methods for protecting your assets by sending them abroad. If your tax burden and exposure to the authorities are still unbearable, you should look into the possibility of establishing a more esoteric structure. But, it is essential that you be prepared to spend sufficient funds to obtain an absolute minimum of two opinions. Otherwise, abandon the effort! First, you may wish to employ the services of one of the firms which specialise in international tax planning. They will design a tailor-made plan for you, and execute the transaction. Before allowing the firm to carry out the actual transaction, it is vital for you to obtain a legal opinion from one of the major firms of international lawyers, whom you will hire only to evaluate the plan. If you are to successfully protect your wealth, and mitigate your tax liabilities, this will be achieved only after an extremely careful, legal investigation concentrating on the detail of every aspect of your personal circumstances.

Making that Quantum Leap. . . Joining your Money

I would strongly recommend that everyone living in a highly taxed area such as the UK or the United States has a reasonable amount of his assets offshore. I would make this recommendation without qualification and suggest immediate action should be taken while such action is possible. Waiting too long could result in a missed opportunity. Once you have transferred some of your assets abroad, you may then wish to take a serious look at your overall situation. There may be a strong case for you to join your assets, establishing residence elsewhere. This will depend on your circumstances.

A high income employee of a company may be able to change nationality, move part or full-time to a tax haven, and continue to service his employer. He would then be paid offshore in tax free money provided his chosen place of residence is a tax free area. As soon as your nationality or residence changes, your entire tax complexion changes with it. A tax haven for an individual can be almost any country other than his or her native domicile. Consider the following as an outstanding example:

Many wealthy Frenchmen have adopted UK residence for the purpose of avoiding the high French taxes. Similarly, the Rolling Stones pop group, whose members were all British at the time, adopted French residency in order to escape the high tax levels that prevailed in the UK at the time. This anomaly is caused by the fact that most of the countries which tax their residents heavily exempt foreigners from this taxation provided they reside in the country for less than six months of the year. A "foreigner" is often defined as any person holding a passport from a country other than the one in which he may be physically present for less than six months of the year!

If you are able to achieve "foreigner" status as a UK expatriate, it is possible for you to spend 5½ months sunning yourself on the Côte d'Azur, travel elsewhere for 30 days, and then spend the remaining 5½ months in the UK. Once you achieve this desirable state, you will not be liable for *any* tax, *anywhere*. Furthermore, you will not be subject to currency controls, restrictions on your investments, nor the burdensome and expensive paperwork associated with bureaucratic tax accounting requirements. As a "foreigner" you could be a former Briton who assumed the nationality of anything from an Albanian to a Zambian. I have a client whose funds I have managed for the past six years, who has actually achieved that happy state. His business involves the purchase and sale of yachts and other craft. He spends approximately three months of the year in Florida, five months of the year in the UK and the rest of the year in various countries around the world where his business — or his fancy — take him. He pays no tax anywhere, on anything, other than indirect taxes which are unavoidable.

Adopting the role of a permanent transient may or may not be to your liking. It may or may not suit your personal circumstances. This aspect of exploiting domicility and nationality laws is the extreme of what can be achieved. It is more than likely that you can improve your situation in a less drastic manner, through a change of residence. . . and possibly a change of nationality.

Changing your nationality is probably the safest way of escaping the tax net once and for all, so far as your residence in a high tax area is concerned. In most cases, wealthy individuals who are mobile would be better off changing their nationality from that of a highly taxed country. For reasons that are less than pragmatic, Britons seem far more reluctant to abandon their citizenship than the residents of most other countries. This is probably due to indoctrination during their formative years when most of them are led to believe that being British stands for something that may be regarded as exceptionally moral, and of superior standing. Briton has thieves, rapists, murderers and degenerates just like any other nation. Only individuals can be held as "exceptionally moral and superior standing." Nationality does not automatically guarantee such virtues. Yet many feel that to relinquish British citizenship in favour of another nationality is to renounce all that Britain stands for as a nation. Such a view involves abdication of personal values and individuality in favour of a geographical land mass.

Many feel the "true blue" UK passport is possessed with magical powers which, if thrust in the face of "foreign devils", will drive them away in fearful intimidation — like the Holy Cross held out to Dracula. Perhaps this may have been true at one time. It is no longer true today. In fact, in some areas of the world, holding a British passport can be a liability. There are inhabitants of other lands, along with the government officials of those countries, who feel the same way towards a "Brit", as the average white Anglo-Saxon Southerner in the United States feels toward a negro. Such is the unhappy state of the world in which we live.

The age of British Imperialism is long past. If you happen to get in trouble abroad and show your British passport, you will simply be referred to the British Embassy who will then refer you to a local lawyer. Your British passport will certainly not provide you with any special privileges in a foreign clime. Proof of the fact is provided by the number of Britons now in jail in various parts of the world on drug related offences, or for more obscure reasons which may or may not have any validity. There have been instances where naturalised British subjects holding British passports have been conscripted into the armed forces of their native countries. Greece and Iran provide two recent examples of this. The British authorities in such cases have been powerless to act.

At this stage, it might not be a bad idea to give careful consideration to why you want to retain your British nationality, and what you would lose by changing it. As a British national, you have the right to enter Britain and remain in Britain for as long as you like without asking the permission of any government. As a British national you can hold certain positions in government, and run for an elected office — which you could not do if you abandon your nationality. Finally, you have certain rights against extradition if you happen to commit a crime in a foreign land. Aside from that, legally speaking, your British nationality doesn't entitle you to a great deal more.

The disadvantage of being a British national is that you are subject to all current and future UK taxes, whatever they may be, and wherever they may apply. US citizens are subject to US taxes for their entire lives, no matter where they live in the world. This is not the case in the UK just yet, but I certainly believe the UK tax authorities will ultimately follow the US principle. So long as you retain your British nationality, you could be subject to this heinous legislation, even though you might change your residence. In addition, as a British national you are subject to all British laws and penalities, some of which you might not be subject to as a foreign national.

Those are essentially the advantages and disadvantages of being a British national and holding a British passport. Now let's look at some of the advantages and disadvantages of *not* being a British national. If you're not a British national, the UK authorities are going to treat you as a write-off. No longer will you be under scrutiny when it comes to various elements of UK legislation that apply only to British nationals and British residents. Once you have fully qualified as a non-British national, you will no longer be liable for existing taxes, or whatever taxes are imposed in the future. A further advantage of being a non-British subject is that even though you change your nationality, you will still be entitled to state benefits.

The only really major disadvantage of not being a British subject is that you might be denied entrance to the UK or denied residence here. In addition, you could be liable to be deported at the discretion of the UK authorities. While this may be a distinct disadvantage, the circumstances under which an individual would be deported, or refused entry, are unlikely to apply to an individual who merely wishes to change nationality for the purpose of protecting his assets and future earning power.

Should you decide it might be to your advantage to emigrate and ultimately change your nationality, there are a few things you should be aware of. The gaining of a new nationality is a two-stage process. You must first obtain the right to permanent residence in the country in which you want to live.

Tourist status will not serve your purpose unless you wish to assume the role of a permanent transient. But, even if you assume such a role, you will still have to obtain an alternative nationality.

You will not be able to change your nationality until such time as you have satisfied the residency requirements in the country. The residence qualification for citizenship in other countries varies from country to country, and can be up to six years depending on the country of your choice. Once you have obtained the right to become a citizen of another country, the naturalisation process is then effectively automatic.

There are certain exceptions to the residency requirements which are worthy of consideration. In many countries, people will have a right to citizenship merely by birth, regardless of the nationality of their parents. If you live in the UK and carry a UK passport, but were not born here, you may be entitled to the automatic citizenship of wherever you were born. In international law this is known as *jus solis* — or the law of the soil.

Jus solis is the case in which citizenship of another country is automatic. Automatic permanent residency is more far reaching. Marriage to a national of another country is one of the quickest methods of gaining permanent residency, and subsequent citizenship, of another country. In a few countries — e.g. Australia — it is not even necessary to get married to obtain permanent residency. In Australia all that is necessary is to be betrothed to an Australian national, and permanent residency will be granted.

In Ireland, a passport can be obtained and citizenship subsequently granted, if either the parents or the grandparents of the applicant were born in Ireland. Dual nationality is available, and an Irish passport can be obtained by merely producing the birth certificate of the parents or grandparents, or a letter from the local church verifying the birth place of the parents or grandparents.

In some countries, a permanent resident of that country, or a national of that country, can sponsor close family relatives, who will be able to obtain permanent residency on such sponsorship. In Australia, Canada, New Zealand, the UK and the USA, either a spouse, a descendant or a child, can act as sponsors. Parents can act as sponsors in Australia, Canada, New Zealand and the USA if the child was born elsewhere. There is a restriction to this rule so far as the UK is concerned. Brother and sister can act as sponsors in Australia, New Zealand and the USA, but not in Canada or the UK Policies vary between countries. The Australian Government is actively pursuing a policy of "family reunion". It may only take seven or eight months for your permanent residency to receive official approval.

In some instances, the nature of your employment can qualify you for permanent residency in another country. I have a client who is a dentist. The ruler of one of the Middle Eastern countries decided he needed a dentist on hand permanently. My client was granted permanent residency in the country. In order to qualify for permanent residency in another country by means of your profession or occupation, you will have to find employment in the target country which your prospective employer is unable to fill with local labour. There are some countries that compile a list of skills deemed as in demand. Medical practitioners are invariably high on the list. If you qualify, you'll be granted residency, even without an offer of employment — on the assumption that your skills will enable you to find a place without difficulty.

Some countries will grant residency and eventual citizenship to retired persons who can demonstrate their ability to support themselves indefinitely, and not become a ward of the state. This will usually involve the ownership of a house, and proof of sufficient income to support yourself without having to resort to government welfare programmes. Jersey, Guernsey, Sark, the Isle of Man, the Cayman Islands, Bermuda, Andorra and Monaco fall into this category. There are others, but it is debatable as to whether or not you could remotely consider living in such places.

Several countries will grant you residency and possible citizenship, if you either invest in the country or form a business that creates employment for local nationals. If you invest in a company that is going out of business, thereby preserving existing employment, you may also qualify for residency in certain countries. Those countries which will allow you to obtain residency through the purchase of an existing business, or by setting up a new business, will want you to take an active role in the business. A passive investment will not qualify you, nor will a simple property purchase or property development.

There is a variation on the investment qualification by certain countries. There are countries that will grant you residency and citizenship if you simply make a cash payment to the government treasury, or invest in the country, or both. In a few cases, it all boils down to nothing more than purchasing citizenship. You can become a citizen of Paraguay by merely giving the governement $US 50,000. The cost of becoming a citizen of the Dominican Republic is also $US 50,000, which includes the purchase of a government bond and a home in the Dominican Republic. You can obtain residency and a passport for Bolivia for $US 25,000. But you will not be entitled to citizenship until you have resided in the country for a predetermined period.

If you want to become a citizen of Costa Rica you will have to purchase a property valued in the area of $US 25,000, and also an interest-bearing government bond for about the same amount. You will be granted a passport, but this passport does not entitle you to citizenship. The passport you will be granted initially is known as *pensionada* status. This is a kind of "retirement visa" which comes in the form of a passport allowing the holder to live — but not work — in Costa Rica, and to travel to other countries as a Costa Rican national. In theory, you are required to reside in Costa Rica for at least six months of the year, but in reality, no individual has ever had his *pensionada* status revoked for failure to fulfil this condition for residence.

At the time of writing, the government of Mauritius was planning to offer citizenship in return for the sum of $US 50,000. The $US 50,000 has to be invested in an interest free loan to the Government, repayable over a period of seven years. Repayment is guaranteed by one or more multinational US or European banks.

A new "Citzenship by Registration" programme allows anyone who purchases a ten year no-interest government bond for $US 25,000, along with an additional fee of $US 10,000, to become a Belizian national in about two weeks. It is not necessary to visit the country.

The Ecuadorian Consulate will issue an immigrant visa, and possibly a provisional passport, to any investor who deposits $US 1,000 upon application, and agrees to invest a further $US 24,000 within 90 days of entering Ecuador. The capital may be invested in any industry, farming, or export-oriented business. Citizenship can then be granted at the discretion of the *Ministerio de Relaciones Exteriores*.

If you are of the Jewish faith and wish to emigrate to Israel, obtaining Israeli citizenship is among the simplest methods of acquiring dual-nationality. In certain countries dual citizenship is not allowed. Before you are granted citizenship, it is necessary to surrender your existing citizenship. Israel permits dual citizenship. You will not be required to surrender your present passport on being granted one by Israel. The Israelis also maintain a policy of not reporting your acquisition of citizenship to your parent country. Israel does not tax non-residents or new immigrants, and is liberal in renewing passports abroad every five years.

Israeli citizenship is highly desirable for those who qualify. It is the only non-EEC passport that is nearly the equivalent of an EEC passport. An Israeli is able to work, or live, in most parts of Europe without a visa or work permit. As a stepping stone to acquiring residence and nationality in another country, Israeli citizenship can be useful since Israelis receive special consideration and reduced residency periods in countries such as Spain and Germany. In addition, the USA welcomes large quotas of immigrants from Israel.

But, there are certain disadvantages. Of course, in the event a plane you are travelling on happens to be hi-jacked by some Moslem fanatics, an Israeli passport should guarantee that you'll be among the first to be murdered. Unless it is your intention to acquire military training and combat experience it would be wise — should you be of mitilary age — to check with the Israeli Consulate whether a condition of your citizenship will involve serving in the Israeli Army. I would advise you to obtain a written statement from the authorities to the effect that you won't be conscripted, if it is your wish to obtain Israeli nationality and not be subject to military service.

Now here's a real cutie! In Brazil there is a special rule that prohibits the father of a Brazilian child from ever being extradited from the country under any circumstances. Whether it be tax evasion, fraud, armed robbery or even a murder committed in another country, a man who sires the child of a Brazilian national can under no circumstances be extradited from Brazil, and made to pay for his crime. If a criminal manages to make his way to

Brazil and finds a Brazilian woman who subsequently gives birth to his child, even though he may be a known criminal to the Brazilian authorities, after the waiting period, during which time he will be expected to demonstrate good behaviour, he will then be given Brazilian citizenship.

It is not necessary for the father of the child to be married to the Brazilian mother. The father of a child born in Brazil may even be married to a non-Brazilian. No divorce is necessary. If you have an understanding wife who doesn't object to you copulating with a Brazilian, you have a simple way of obtaining Brazilian nationality. On the other hand, if your wife wouldn't mind having your next child in Brazil, you have another opportunity to acquire Brazilian nationality. Since any child born in Brazil is automatically a Brazilian citizen, if you are the father of that child, regardless of the nationality of the mother, the same rule applies.

Another interesting area where it may not be difficult to assume another nationality is Turkey. Turkish diplomats have sole discretion in granting Turkish nationality. One Turkish ambassador is quoted as stating:

> "Turks have emigrated to all parts of the world; we regard them and all of their descendants as Turks. As a practical matter, anyone who ever came to this office who spoke Turkish and had a Turkish name or some evidence of Turkish ethnic associations would be considered to be a Turk. We are very liberal and flexible about extending the benefits of our passport to those in need of one."

If you have a Turkish sounding name and can speak Turkish, you may qualify for Turkish nationality immediately.

There are over 200 countries where you can apply for nationality with varying degrees of difficulty. Some provide a magnificent life style. Others you wouldn't consider living in for any appreciable period of time. I have merely attempted to provide a broad outline of how you might go about changing residency and nationality in order to achieve a greater degree of freedom and flexibility. Once again, this is an area where you will require detailed advice, geared to your personal circumstances. I would add a word of warning at this point. The nationality business, like the international tax planning business, has no shortage of unscrupulous swindlers who will take your money and provide little in return. When establishing a plan that incorporates a change of nationality, be certain only to deal with escrow agents. The most viable method of incorporating a change of nationality in your plans is to have an advisor assist you with regard to the nationality.

Chapter Thirteen

INVESTING WITHOUT TEARS

Seeking out the highest return without checking the investment's safety
is pretty much like buying the fastest car without looking at the brakes. You
could be in for a real thriller of a ride.

William E. Donoghue

The subject of long term investment can be vastly simplified by reflecting
on the notion that there are basically only three long term investment
strategies flowing from three major conditions of economic activity. The
three major conditions of economic activity I refer to are deflation, inflation
or a period when there is neither.

The most favourable of the three occurs when there is neither inflation
nor deflation. It is only during such periods, with the economy free of the
distortion and dislocations of inflation and deflation, that real wealth can
actually be created. It is during such periods that we find growth in the
labour force, improvements in education, the successful redeployment of
existing technology and the advancement of *new* technologies. Then a sudden
surge in capital investment will combine with all these factors to multiply
the real wealth of our society. The stability of retail and wholesale prices
during such a phase — along with currency stability — makes for more
readily realisable planning, and allows for greater real growth in the Gross
National Product than during any other period of the economic cycle.

The best way for the investor to capitalise on these exceptionally favourable
conditions for economic development is through investment in companies
which contribute to the creation of this real wealth, and in wealth-producing
assets. Companies enjoying a rapid real growth in the goods and services
they produce are the primary beneficiaries. In this type of economic
environment, share prices retain their upward momentum for decades.
Investment in commercial property can also be beneficial if located in a
growth area. Cash, fixed interest investments and what has recently been
defined as "real" assets (residential property, stamps, gold, coins, antiques,
diamonds and other "collectibles") give only a mediocre performance.
compared with the performance of the better opportunities elsewhere. The
last golden era of real growth was during the "upwave" of the 1930s to the
late 1970s. It was during the early 1970s, that a major change took place
in the global economy, when real growth began to be deflected by inflation.

In an inflationary environment, very little real wealth can be created.

Essentially, the investment climate during such a period involves little more than the transfer of wealth. It's like a poker game, where there must be a loser for every winner — or sometimes five losers for one winner — each playing for a finite sum of money in the game.

New wealth, during an inflationary period, is created neither by working hard, nor by saving frugally and investing intelligently. All that happens is that existing wealth passes from those who cannot capitalise on inflation to those who can. With the slowing of real economic growth, and inflation beginning to rise faster and faster, the focus and energy of experienced and intelligent individuals shift from the normal work ethos intended to enlarge the nation's economic pie.

Instead, people will devote their resources and energy simply to grabbing a larger slice of that economic pie — for the minimum contribution. Inflation is the peaceful (and comparatively honest) means by which the wealth and income of the inept investor is transferred to the more astute. At the same time, investment in an inflationary environment can be highly deceptive. Nominal values will usually increase across the board, giving the impression that real wealth is being accumulated. Yet, after allowing for the fall in the purchasing power of the unit of currency, many investors who are convinced that they are increasing their wealth will find they are actually and continuously losers. Investment in any form of property will do well, as will investment in what are currently defined as "real" assets or "collectibles". After adjustment for inflation, the return on stock exchange investment will be relatively poor, compared with the return on what are perceived as "real" assets. The exception is shares in a company able to capitalise on inflation. The performance of cash and cash equivalents during periods of inflation is highly negative, since the purchasing power of money is constantly eroded. Investing in fixed interest securities during a period of rapid inflation is the formula for financial suicide. That is because the purchasing power of the money invested declines along with the underlying value of the securities so long as the inflation persists; and the loss is not in inflation-adjusted terms alone, but in nominal terms also. The investment phenomenon which I have outlined was readily observed from the late 1960s through the late 1970s.

Whereas an economy free from either inflation or deflation permits the creation of real wealth, and an inflationary climate leads merely to the transfer of wealth, in a deflation-prone economy wealth is actually destroyed. Recessions are one product — and one aspect — of the deflationary trend. But it should be borne in mind that these deflationary forces alone can eradicate the lingering and destructive after-effects of inflation. The last traces of the inflationary hangover must be eliminated before real growth can be resumed. Notwithstanding its therapeutic role, recession can be dangerous if the government loses control. Then the recession becomes a thundering depression, frequently made worse by the well-intentioned blunders committed by those in power.

For most individuals, a deflationary environment creates the worst possible climate for investment. With the real wealth of the economy contracting in the course of a long period of depression, most individual investors find they are losing money on whatever assets they happen to hold. There is a significant decline in the value of every kind of property and "real" assets; whether gold, silver, antiques or any other "collectible". Even during this dire phase of economic activity, there are winners. They will be the ones who are invested in the appropriate areas for the deflationary period, and are usually the best placed to exploit to the full the period of real growth following the terminal juncture of the deflationary spiral. During the other two phases of economic activity — the inflationary and the stable — cash equivalents and fixed-interest securities produce nothing but real and opportunity losses. That is to say, they have chosen fixed-interest securities when they would have been better off looking elsewhere. The few investors able to increase both the nominal and the real value of their assets during the deflationary period are those who invested in areas of fixed income and low risk. The investment trends of the late 1920s through the late 1930s produced the kind of deflationary climate in which fixed-interest investors emerge triumphantly as unexpected and unrivalled winners.

Investing into the Upwave

Seldom do we hear a shout from the roof tops announcing the change-over from one economic climate to another. During the fourth quarter of 1979, amber lights were flashing, as the UK authorities and most of the monetary havens of the industrialised nations began to fight inflation in earnest. When the fight against inflation became a controlled depression, the amber lights turned red. The effects of the controlled depression are frighteningly obvious throughout the world. Since the late 1970s, we have seen double-digit unemployment in most developed countries, and particularly in Britain. In all industrialised economies low utilisation of manufacturing capacity has accompanied low or negative corporate profits; especially in Britain. Here de-industrialisation has been chronic, but capacity utilisation still remains low. We have seen extraordinarily high interest rates — both nominal and real — a characteristic of depression. Yet the highest real interest rates have been in Britain. The most conclusive evidence of all, confirming the deflationary nature of the environment, is obviously the plunge in global rates of inflation, a phenomenon we have never experienced since the last period of deflation between the late 1920s and late 1940s. Even Britain, which once seemed a life-member of the double-digit inflation club, has reduced the rate of retail price increases from a massive 26% in the mid-1970s, to just under 4% in 1987. At the same time, UK interest rates too have come tumbling down. During this period of controlled depression, the price of gold fell along with that of other precious metals. So too did the value of stamps, coins, gem stones, diamonds and other "collectibles" previously believed by so many to be capable of rising in perpetuity. Finally, on the 19th October 1987, we had the "shout from the roof tops". . . and the stock market crashed. As I have often said, ". . .a stock market crash is a shout for the hard of hearing". There is absolutely no question about it. We are now in a deflationary phase. The only investors to survive in the period ahead will be those who adopt that one strategy of three which is appropriate to the investment climate we are entering. The Downwave of the economic cycle probably has another five to seven years to run. Then we will embark upon the most benign investment climate of all — the non-inflationary, non-deflationary component of the next Upwave. But those who fail to take immediate steps to preserve, and increase, their capital during the remainder of the Downwave, will simply not have the capital to invest in those areas which will open that once in a lifetime growth potential when the next Upwave begins circa 1995.

Let me make quite clear that Cash is King during a depression. The reason Cash is King is that the amount of cash in the economy steadily declines. Cash becomes a relatively scarce commodity! Many people imagine that in a depression a government can "print money" to cushion the impact of depression, by maintaining a continuous cash flow. Those who think this way do not understand the true nature of a fiat money policy. To begin with, governments do not literally *print* money, so providing some cash. They increase liquidity by making more credit available, using the mechanism of the fractional reserve banking system. So long as the fresh credit is not employed — because people are fearful of borrowing, or getting deeper into debt — there is no further growth in the money supply. Indeed, as people repay their debts, or avoid them through default or bankruptcy, the supply of money actually shrinks. This, you will observe, is in marked contrast to what happens in an inflationary environment. Then we see the supply of money growing as increasing amounts of credit are extended. In a deflationary environment, the amount of credit taken up declines, while the growth of the monetary aggregates becomes negative, as credit is cancelled or unpaid. We can say, therefore, that — so far as monetary aggregates are concerned — deflation is the inverse of inflation.

During the remainder of the controlled depression — which now seems to be getting out of control — simply holding your funds in cash can be more rewarding than you think. Although there will be a risk to certain banking institutions, and other deposit-takers, I still believe there are safe places for you to put your money during the difficult years that lie ahead; places where you will get a positive rate of return, which will be amplified by any increase in the purchasing power of money due to the deflationary pressures that push prices down in nominal terms. To most people, rising prices have been a permanent way of life, and seem likely to continue to be a permanent way of life. Conventional wisdom concentrates on the extent to which prices are likely to rise. Until a few years ago, conventional wisdom also focussed on the extent to which the rate of inflation would increase next year over the current year. If they were truthful about it, very few people believed that inflation *could* halt its rise. Already inflation has fallen significantly. But very few people yet believe that prices too will fall. They *will* fall. . . quite significantly during the remainder of the Downwave. Those who hold cash will enhance their wealth because of that rise in the purchasing power of money due to the fall in prices, plus whatever interest they earn on their capital investments.

If you are getting a return of 7% on funds invested, while prices are falling at an annual rate of 4%, your real rate of return is 11% — of which 4% is tax free! During an inflationary environment, you may get a yield of 15% on your investment. But with inflation running at 16%, say, you wind up with a negative return of 1% while your 15% earnings are fully taxed. There are quite a few hidden benefits in a deflationary environment.

The big question is where you keep your cash! Safety First must be the aim during the depression I see ahead of us. I believe the immediate future is going to be a particularly perilous time for all investors — including the most prudent savers. I really don't want to sound paranoid, but *some* people have been after *other people's* money since the stuff was invented. . . even if it took the form of coloured stones or heads of cattle. In the next few years, with the supply of money decreasing, even more people will be tempted to have a go to get hold of someone else's cash — and they'll be doing so with a vengeance!

No amount of legislation alone will be sufficient to protect your investments. Their safety — of paramount importance in the foreseeable future — will be up to you. For example, take nothing at face-value. Have confidence in your own judgement. Remember. . . any investment which looks *too* good to be true, almost certainly is! Above all bear in mind what your common-sense will tell you. . . if you give it a chance. If, for example, the Backwater Dingbat Building Society is willing to pay you 1% more per annum on your deposit than the Abbey National Building Society, there can be no question about it. Your funds will be at far greater risk deposited with the Backwater Dingbat than with the Abbey National. Likewise, if the Bank of Dork is willing to pay you 2% more for your three-months deposit than Barclays Bank — and give you a ball-point pen! — you can take it that the kind of risks the Bank of Dork is going to have to take to earn that extra 2% will be far greater than any risk that Barclays would be forced into.

As the deflationary forces gather momentum, there will be bankruptcies among the banks and building societies, as there have been in the United States. The Bank for International Settlements (BIS) is well aware that the capital adequacy standards for banks in all 12 member countries are not what they might be. Year by year a growing number of savings and loan institutions and some smaller banks have been going into default in the US. Britain will certainly not remain immune. By attempting to squeeze out that extra 1% of income, you could be risking every penny you possess. Remember, too, that the loose compensation scheme run by the building societies has been replaced by a statutory scheme which offers you far less security. My recommendation is to stay with the biggest and best banks and building societies. No compromise should be considered — not even if the representative (or the Chairman) of the Backwater Dingbat is a second cousin, or a member of your golf club.

Aside from simply holding cash in a bank or a building society, there is a wide range of investments open to you. They involve varying degrees of risk, but still remain compatible with the deflationary scenario we envisage. As well as cash, there are cash equivalents, to which the average investor can gain access by investing in a "money fund". In addition to UK Government Securities and foreign government bonds, there are also corporation bonds, whose quality is almost equivalent to that of government stocks.

Essentially, when you invest in money funds, government securities or bonds, you should have two aims. The first is the preservation of your capital. The second is income. On the surface, neither may seem particularly exciting. The reason is that most people are desperately attracted to the idea that the stock market is a place where you can get rich quick. They fail to appreciate the far greater benefits that can accrue from a program designed to help you get rich *slowly*, but almost certainly *surely*! In their maddening desire to get rich quick, most people fail to appreciate the dynamic power of compound interest. This is understandable when all you're going to get is 5-6% from a savings account, and you're unlikely to reinvest the income. But when you can lock in yields of 10-15% for ten years (or more) on a compound basis, the entire affair must be viewed in a totally different light.

It has been said — with far more truth than humour — that if the Indians who sold Manhattan Island for $24 had placed the $24 in a bank paying the 6% rate of interest prevailing at that time, and if the interest had been added to the principal annually, and both had been reinvested at the subsequent prevailing rates of interest every year since, by 1950 the original $24 would have grown to more than the value of all the real estate in Manhattan today.

Now, let's look at another example, a little closer to real life. A close friend of mine recently purchased a poplar plantation in central France. When he bought it, he calculated that the financial return on a suitably located poplar plantation in that area averaged 8.45% per annum over the past 2,000 years. . . adjusted for inflation. As a conservative investor, he figured that a real rate of return of 8.45% per annum was a pretty good deal. So he bought the plantation. He then carried out a few more calculations. Being in the process of creating a dynasty, it is his intention to keep the plantation in the family, passing it down through the generations. If his descendants continue to replant at an 8.45% average rate of return every year — in other words, "plough back" the assumed yearly return — he reckons that his and all future generations of the family will be financially secure.

After twenty years the value of the enlarged plantation — in constant money — will be five times the original stake. After fifty years, it will be fifty-six times the original stake. And — make sure you're sitting down before you even try to digest the next few numbers — after 100 years the original stake would be multiplied 3,813 times. After 200 years the growth in value would be over 10 million times the initial outlay *in real terms*. Don't forget, "real terms" means *after* any projected rate of inflation has been accounted for. There you have the lessons of not 200, but 2,000 years of history.

Of course, there are certain practical problems inherent in that equation. One is to find sufficient suitable space, were the process to be continued for 200 years. This is one unquantifiable element of the program, which anyone who wishes to try it should consider. Moreover, the dynamic kind of mentality required for such a single-minded program is not encountered every day. Certainly not on Wall Street. But the exercise does illustrate the process by which great fortunes have been amassed. . . perhaps *all* great fortunes.

Financial markets have never offered such *real* rates of return over long periods. Three or four per cent has been more like the norm. But the long waves of expansion and contraction in prices and in economic life have produced variations from the norm, which — when recognised — were capable of building fortunes with very little risk for those of independent thought and farsightedness. In certain types of securities, at certain times, the returns have been even double the 8.45% a poplar plantation could have produced over the past 2,000 years. On some occasions, compound returns available for as long as thirty or forty years were even better than that. At other times, however, real rates of return have been negative for very long periods.

All the evidence suggests that the early 1980s offered a once-in-a-lifetime opportunity to profit from one of the long periods of far above average returns in an investment area that has offered one of the lowest risks — namely, high grade bonds and US government securities.

Investors who bought US government bonds in 1982 could have received a rate of return of 15% per annum without considering the capital gain that accrued between 1982 and 1983. During the summer of 1983, investors in long term US bonds could still have obtained returns of 11.75%. Of course, there was a big boom in bond prices between 1982 and 1986. But there's still plenty to go for at current rates of return. If interest rates happen to move up again, there'll be even more to go for. But don't forget the words of Jesse Livermore, who was probably the greatest market operator the world has ever known: "A man may know what to do and lose money if he doesn't do it quickly enough."

The following table shows you what to expect if you save a constant sum of money each month and reinvest the income through a Government

Securities Unit Trust or by direct investment in high-grade bonds or UK government securities with maturities ranging from 10 to 30 years.

£	10 Years	20 Years	30 Years
	ANNUAL YIELD OF 6%		
10	1,638	4,620	10,045
25	4,097	11,551	25,113
100	16,387	46,204	100,451
200	32,774	92,408	200,902
500	81,939	231,020	502,257
1,000	163,879	462,040	1,004,515
	ANNUAL YIELD OF 10%		
10	2,048	7,593	22,604
25	5,120	18,982	56,510
100	20,484	75,936	226,048
200	40,968	151,872	452,096
500	102,422	379,684	1,130,244
1,000	204,844	759,368	2,260,487
	ANNUAL YIELD OF 15%		
10	2,752	14,972	69,232
25	6,880	37,430	173,080
100	27,521	149,723	692,321
200	55,042	299,446	1,384,642
500	137,605	748,619	3,461,605
1,000	275,217	1,497,239	6,923,210

So far I have demonstrated the effect of investing your money at a fixed rate of interest over a given number of years, reinvesting the income you have received at the same rate. Unfortunately, this theoretical result can be somewhat difficult to achieve. In the first instance, although it may be possible for you to invest at a fixed rate of interest over the next 5, 10 or 20 years by buying a fixed-interest security of the desired maturity, you could have a problem when it came to reinvesting the income at the same rate. Interest rates do move — down as well as up!

Another difficulty arises when it comes to re-investing small parcels of interest. If you are a megamoney operator with £1,000,000 invested, you will have no problem at all investing the £50,000 you receive half-yearly — assuming a yield of 10% on your initial purchases. But, if you're a minnow, with a portfolio of only £10,000 or so, you'll find it difficult to buy additional amounts of your existing holdings in parcels of £500 a time. Aside from anything else, your income would be whittled away by the high dealing costs incurred in purchasing such small amounts.

Again, the effect of compound interest makes an extremely interesting study, demonstrating as it does the potential of any fixed interest investment. But the exercise is essentially a theoretical one. In the real world, it will be the total return on your fixed interest investments — capital and income combined that determines the future profitability of those investments rather than merely the income. Should you acquire your fixed interest investments as interest rates are about to rise, the capital value of your investments will inevitably fall. The extent of your actual loss will depend on the maturities you have selected, and if (and when) you decide to sell. If you sell your investments before the date of maturity when interest rates are rising, your income will be eroded by a capital loss, leaving you with a total return which must be lower than the income received. Should interest rates experience a sufficiently sharp rise, the capital loss could offset every penny of income received. On the other hand, if you make your purchases ahead of a fall in interest rates, your income will be supplemented by the increased capital values, provided you do not hold on to the securities until they mature. This raises the practical point that *no* security once bought should be locked away and forgotten.

That said, the single most important aspect of fixed-interest market investment is the rate of interest. I told you what will happen if interest rates fall, I have also told you what is likely to happen if interest rates rise. But what are interest rates likely to do during the remainder of the downwave and as we move into the upwave? Obviously, the answer to that question will have an important influence on your investment planning. If interest rates are likely to rise, then you would possibly be better off with a money fund or a bank account than with a fixed-interest portfolio. On the other hand, if you have only a money fund or a fixed-interest portfolio and interest rates fall, you will find yourself with a very low return, having completely missed the opportunity of the huge capital gains you could have made in the bond market. While it may be interesting to look at both sides of the bond return equation, it is definitely important to take a position on interest rates, and consider your timing.

As it happens, the interest cycle is one of the most consistent and dependable financial phenomena known to investors. The fact that the interest rate cycle *has* been so reliable and infallible — involving parameters that can be seen to date back several *thousand* years —is probably why so few professionals talk about it, preferring to keep the information to themselves. Just as sure as night follows day, and winter follows fall, interest rates will decline to periodic lows and rise to cyclical peaks. But remember — we are here considering trends, not constructing a detailed time-table. Sometimes the rate of ascent or descent will be slow and gradual, persuading some people that it just "isn't going to happen *this* time round!" A very dangerous assumption for anyone to make! Interest rate moves can also be explosive. Rates moved up quite sharply during 1969-1970. There was another rapid rise during 1973-1975. One of the most explosive moves in interest rates took place during 1981 and 1982.

Until 1982 the frequency of tight money conditions had led to a situation where each successive interest rate peak tended to be higher than the previous one. Moreover the complete cycle of interest rates from peak to trough was becoming progressively shorter. This shortening of the cycle was primarily the effect of an unfolding economic story in the United States and other countries — the tremendous growth of industry in the second half of the century, the great proliferation of government spending, higher standards of living for millions of families — all of which kept inflation going year after year, along with an incessant demand for money and credit. Industry kept on expanding throughout the early 1970s as populations increased. Consumers demanded more and more credit, and still further credit was required for capital expenditure. Consumers have never been interest-rate sensitive, forever willing to pay usurious rates of interest if immediate gratification was offered. It might be they were after a better car, a new home, TV set, video recorder and all the other items that allowed them to live in a manner to which they would have *liked* to become thoroughly accustomed.

During the post-war era since 1945, we've seen a series of business contractions that were relatively short in duration. Industry overexpanded and workers lost their jobs. They then defaulted on their mortgage repayments, and were unable to keep up with their instalment commitments. Mortgages were foreclosed, cars repossessed, televisions, furniture and other goods were carted off in truckloads. The companies whose shares are held by the public are bound to be among those businesses which contracted even before the market for their products declined. Inevitably the price of industrial shares brings the stock market down. When this happens, the demand for money falls. With money no longer so scarce a commodity, the price of borrowing (or lending) money falls and interest rates are cut. Eventually, the process of debt liquidation has spent its force and the whole process starts over again. Interest rates begin sneaking up once more and another peak is reached.

Until the early 1970s, the periods when interest rates fell were much shorter than those when they were climbing. That is because the periods of economic expansion were longer than the periods of contraction. As we now know, this is the normal pattern of the Upwave. It is when the Upwave reaches a terminal stage that the periods of contraction occur with a greater frequency, and the interest rate cycle from peak to trough becomes shorter and shorter, until the entire relationship is reversed. This is what we've witnessed not all that long ago. The recession between 1973 and 1975 was steeper than all of the other recessions since the Upwave began. Between November 1981 and December 1982, during the early years of the Thatcher administration we experienced the shortest fall in interest rates since the 1930s. During the Upwave, in bond *prices* between November 1981 and December 1982, the 14-point upward drive was 50% greater than the average of six complete bull markets in bonds during the 3 decades of the post-war era. At this point, the long-term history of interest rates may serve to illuminate the whole story. The fact that the US is the world's locomotive for interest rates directs our attention to the position there.

The Long-Term Trend in Interest Rates

The history of interest rates in America is highly instructive. Over the past forty-eight years, in America they have been at their lowest ever, as well as their highest. The lowest rate of interest ever recorded in the United States was in about the middle of 1946. During that year, stockbrokers were charging their clients an annual interest rate of 0.75% on the debit balances in their accounts. At the time, if you wanted to buy a home in America, mortgage interest would have been somewhere in the area of 3.75%. Long-term US government bonds were selling on a yield basis of 2.25%. You could buy those bonds on margin with a stake of only 7% of their capital value, and be charged a mere 0.75% on the margin account. Obviously, if interest rates fell a fraction, you would stand to make a quick fortune. That was the extreme low point of interest rates in American history. Since the time of the extreme lows in interest rates we have also experienced the highs — in early 1982, for example.

A few years ago an absolutely fascinating book was published called *The History of Interest Rates*, by Sidney Homer. It contains a record of minimum interest rates in Babylonia, Greece and Rome, between 3,000 BC and AD 350. (Fig 21) While the record keeping may be somewhat suspect, we are given a picture of long-term interest rate activity over a period of extreme statistical significance. Obviously, a record of sequential repetition spanning

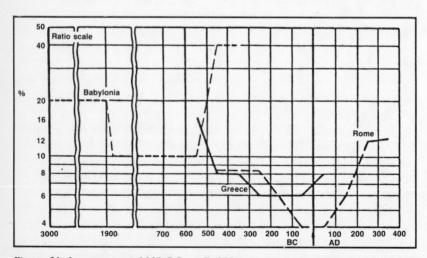

Figure 21: Interest rates 3000 BC - AD 350
  SOURCE: A History of Interest Rates *by Sidney Homer, copyright © 1977.*
  Reprinted by permission of Rutgers State University.

nearly 4,000 years will be more meaningful than interest rate behaviour over the past ten, twenty or thirty years.

It can be seen from this very long picture that interest rates — like trends in property prices — involve long-term cyclical sequences. Within these long-term sequences, parameters of interest rates can be seen. Between 3,000 BC and AD 350, the normative peak in the long-term interest rate cycle was approximately 15%. The normative low for the sequences was approximately 4%. There are a few isolated periods when interest rates moved up into the 20-30% area — but they never remained that high for long. There we have a picture of the trends in interest rates over 3,350 years in Babylon, Egypt, Greece and Rome. When interest rates fell to 4% it would have been reasonable to assume that they had fallen about as far as they were going to. When interest rates rose to 15%, it would be no less reasonable to assume that rates had risen about as far as they were likely to rise.

The trend in interest rates in America for the 170 years from 1800 through 1970 (Fig 22) involves parameters of approximately 8% at peaks and, on average, 3% at troughs. The dots in Figure 23 indicate monthly high or low yields at cyclical turning points in this century. Here we can begin to see some cyclical continuity. From 1862 through 1898, interest rates declined steadily. The falling trend lasted thirty-six years, as did the *bull* market in bonds. From 1898 through 1920, interest rates rose. The rising trend in interest rates lasted twenty-two years — as did the *bear* market in bonds. From 1920 through 1946, interest rates fell. There was a bull market in bonds which lasted for twenty-six years. From 1946 through 1982, interest rates rose. The bear market in bonds lasted thirty-five years. In the early 1980s we begun a new long-term secular down-trend in interest rates, and a secular uptrend in bond markets. What these historical sequences demonstrate is that long-term uptrend is unlikely to be a short-term affair, since the trend in interest rates is nowhere near as volatile as trends in other capital markets.

The period from the 1940s through the early 1980s was an unusual one. The yield on US government securities spanned the range from the lowest interest rates in US history to the highest. The normal parameters for interest rates in America involve 12% at the peaks and 2.5% at the lows — except for temporary trend deviations.

During the period spanning the lows of interest rates in the 1940s and the highs in the early 1980s, the yield on US government bonds moved from a 1946 low of 2.125% to a high of 14.25%. The extreme yield in US government bond prices (exceeding the normal parameters by a significant margin) was responsible for the subsequent tremendous downward drive in yields, and upward push in bond prices. The low in US bond prices was made in the summer of 1981. Between the summer of 1981 and October 1982, bond prices advanced by 38%.

Municipal bonds in the United States did not make their lows until February 1982, to produce a 15% yield. Between February and July of 1982, municipal bond prices rose by 43% to yield just under 9%.

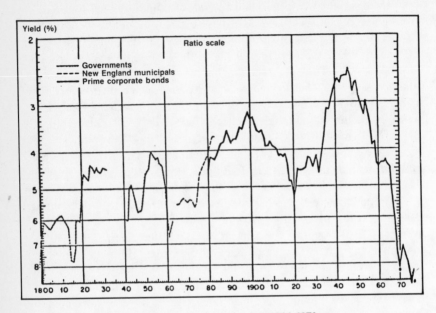

Figure 22: *The trend in interest rates in the US 1800-1970*
Reprinted from Salomon Brothers Inc's Interest Rate Chartbook

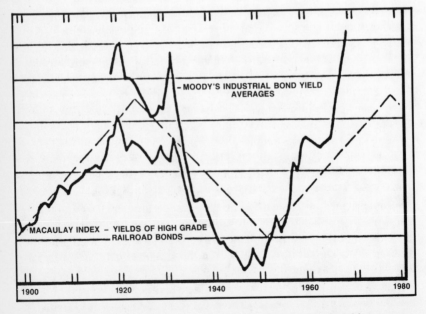

Figure 23: *Kondratieff applied to the Moody's industrial bond yield averages*

The long-term Kondratieff wave cycle involves a fifty-four year average. This involves an Upwave and a Downwave. This has been superimposed on the Moody's industrial bond yield for the corresponding period. (Fig 23) The actual interest rate experience, and the terminal junctures suggested by the periodicity of the long Kondratieff wave, are statistically extremely significant, and could be violated only over several thousand repetitions of history. Since there is a strong relationship between interest rates and inflation, the long-term behaviour of interest rates is coincident with the long-term pattern of price behaviour.

By the mid-1980s, Americans had endured a period of steadily rising interest rates for no less than thirty-six years. People — as a result — have been brainwashed into expecting ever higher interest rates. We've practically come to the point where every individual in the United States is acutely conscious of what banks may be willing to pay for one month-, two month- or three-month deposits virtually on a day-to-day basis. People have never been so aware of interest rates as over the past few years. The general perception has been that interest rates will continue to rise in perpetuity, and any fall in interest rates is merely a temporary aberration. Most people believe that if, for example, economic recovery were to gain momentum and governments were forced to continue to bail out sick companies, demand for money would increase, pushing interest rates up into the stratosphere again. This is the conventional wisdom among investors — amateur and professional alike. One thing we know about conventional wisdom is that it usually reflects the lowest common denominator of intellectual achievement.

The value of these long-term historical trends in interest rates is certainly not that they provide a magic formula. I'm a pragmatist. I don't believe in magic formulae. The value of this study lies in the knowledge that trend persistency in interest rates *does* exist, and it is advisable to take the trouble to utilise the knowledge that can be gained by a study of those characteristics of interest rates which seem to override short-term factors. Several characteristics — apparent in the long-term behaviour pattern of interest rates — can be useful in planning your investment strategy in the years ahead. It can be seen quite clearly that once a long-term interest rate trend had been established in the past, the level of interest rates has moved in that direction for quite an extended period, often for decades. The second important characteristic is that there is a reasonable, normative level for both high and low interest rates. This can be seen over several thousand years of history. The successful investor is the one who buys his investments when they are low and sells them when they are high. The problem for most investors is deciding what is low and what is high. The use of the long-term interest rate pattern spanning nearly 5,000 years goes a long way toward telling us what is low and what is high so far as interest rates are concerned.

A word of warning! I am certainly not suggesting that investors become slaves to these long-term secular trends. When it comes to the shorter-term timing of interest rates, long-term secular trends are not particularly helpful. Indeed, if you are speculating on interest rate trends through the financial futures market, or through fast-moving bond warrants or even "zero" coupon bonds, you can sometimes run the risk of being left sitting through some pretty hairy moves by ignoring deviations in short-term trends.

Awareness of the long-term secular trends is vital, but you should do no more than keep these long-term trends in the back of your mind as one of the tools of judgment. You should certainly not discard the shorter considerations suggested by economics; nor should you ignore the current facts of life. At the same time, never forget that we have been coming out of the greatest change that has taken place in thirty-five years, which is also likely to be the greatest change in interest rates in 5,000 years of recorded history. . . and which also could mean some fantastic opportunities.

In the summer of 1982, we saw a tremendous rise in the value of interest rate-related securities. That sharp rise was only the first in what is likely to be at least two more sudden and sharp drops in interest rates that correspond with at least two more explosive rises in fixed-interest markets. These may not occur immediately. But the good thing about bond investment is that you're not losing money while you're waiting for these explosive rises to occur. You're still getting a reasonable return on your investment, and you know too that if the cycle doesn't give you the capital growth you're looking for, at least the passage of time will! There are guaranteed maturity levels in the bonds you buy which are certainly not available to holders of any other form of investment — such as commodities or equities.

Gaining a true understanding of what Fixed-Interest Securities have to offer (and how all the securities work) is vitally important — particularly since the best move for one investor may not necessarily be the best move for another, whose goals and objectives can be vastly different. Finding the correct path to profit is further complicated by some of the paradoxes inherent in both the UK and US fixed income markets. For example, in the US you can purchase bonds on margin. This means it is necessary only to put up a percentage of the purchase price to buy the bonds. In the case of US government bonds, the margin is 25%. Investors lodge 25% of the purchase price of the bonds with their brokers and borrow the balance of 75%. It costs investors more to deal this way, since there is interest to pay on the borrowed money. This, of course, further amplifies the element of risk.

Fixed-income securities in the UK and the US alike are incredibly diverse. There are literally thousands of issues of different maturities, quality ratings, coupons and structures to choose from. Yet, with few exceptions, all these securities react in the same way to the same major determinant of bond prices — prevailing interest rates. The only difference is the extent of the change an issue is likely to experience, for a given change in interest rates.

Fixed-income securities, generally, are thought by many to be safe, stodgy and conservative. This idea is totally erroneous. By incorporating margin, or seeking highly geared bond issues — such as bond warrants or long dated zero coupon bonds — the action can be much faster than on the currency futures market or the traded option market. The perception that fixed-interest issues are dull and slow-moving is born of ignorance, due to the fact that bond markets have been out of favour for such a long time. In the recent past, equity markets have been saturated with ignorant investors, who have believed that it was the only area where capital gains could be achieved with reasonable speed. Investors believed that equity markets were the markets that really "offer the action" — I would certainly agree. In the years ahead, equity markets are likely to offer plenty of action — downside action. So let's take a look at the alternatives available.

Investing in Cash Equivalents

Fixed-income securities pay interest in one of two ways. The security can be issued with a coupon where the interest is paid periodically, and the principal sum paid at the maturity of the security. This is the method of interest payment with which most investors are familiar. Traditionally, the investor buys his fixed interest security at par (£100). Assuming the bond has say, a 10% coupon and a five year maturity, he will receive 10% per annum, usually at half-yearly intervals. At the end of five years, the £100 he paid will be returned to him.

But there is another way an investor in fixed interest securities can receive his income. This is when the security is issued at a discount from par value, to provide a return that will reflect prevailing interest rates in the absence of any coupon. Let's say the prevailing interest rate is 10%. So you have a choice. You can buy a bond for £100, with a 10% coupon, and collect £10 interest at the end of a year — along with your £100, assuming the bond has a one year maturity. Or, you can buy a bond that has no coupon, at a discount of 10%, and receive par value for the bond at the end of the same year. It's rather like borrowing £90 from John, and offering to pay him £99 at the end of the year, without any promise to pay interest.

The result of the type of transaction I've described is a non-interest bearing certificate. These non-interest bearing certificates are confined to fixed interest securities with a relatively short life. That is to say with maturities of anything from one day to one year. Securities of this type generally fall into the category of what is known as "cash equivalents". The reason for calling them that is that this class of security is usually reserved for financial instruments of the highest quality, readily convertible into cash, at minimal short term risk to the principal. Securities of this kind include UK Treasury Bills, Fine Banks Bills, Fine Trade Bills, Certificates of Deposit, Loans to local authorities, along with a few other non-interest bearing financial instruments. In most cases, these instruments are outside the reach of the average investor, unless he puts his money in a "money fund" or has a friendly bank manager, willing to incorporate his residual funds on a syndicated basis. It's certainly worth asking, since in the period ahead I strongly recommend this class of investment. It should play an integral part of any overall investment strategy, as the risks inherent in our deflationary environment continue to mount.

Fine Bank Bills, Fine Trade Bills, Sterling Certificates of Deposit, Overnight Inter-bank deposits, local authority loans, etc. are handled through the Discount Houses, which represent wholesalers in the money market. In the back pages of the *Financial Times* each day, readers will find such arcane references as:

> "A severe shortage in the London money market developed yesterday. The authorities gave a moderate amount of assistance by buying an equivalent amount of Treasury Bills from the discount houses. There was no official intervention, but in somewhat uneven conditions books were generally balanced."

What you have just read is couched in the language of the discount market — one of the most stable financial institutions of the City of London, respected the world over. The reputation of the London discount houses for efficiency spans more than two centuries. Of all the City institutions with which the Bank of England has a relationship, the discount market receives the most special attention. Essentially, the market run by the discount houses is the mechanism by which the surplus cash floating around the country's monetary system is redistributed. The discount market occupies a crucial position, and its activities can often provide a firm indication of the direction of interest rates and intended monetary policy, along with an indication of the general health and liquidity of the nation. Aside from its role as a general financial intermediary, the discount market also acts as the intermediary between the public and private sectors. Surpluses (or shortages) of cash in the system arise from time to time for a number of reasons. The government — which is in essence the public sector — is continually making payments to, and receiving payments from, the private sector. Government disbursements to the private sector include subsidies to farmers, tax refunds, payments to independent contractors, to suppliers of services required by the government and for the public sector payroll. Government receipts include payments for VAT, income tax, capital gains tax, capital transfer tax, and so forth. On a day-to-day basis, there are always imbalances between revenues and disbursements. The government uses the discount market and the facilities it offers, to redress these temporary imbalances.

The banking system and the corporate sector, usually approached via the banking system, are the source of the discount houses' money. As already mentioned, there are likely to be temporary imbalances between the various sides of the equation — *vis-à-vis* government receipts against government payments. Once the private sector has been brought into the equation, a separate series of imbalances will be introduced. For example, one bank might be short of cash to meet customer withdrawals. Another bank may have a surplus. One bank may have experienced such heavy demand for credit that — for a few hours — the reserve ratio is threatened.

In that instance, the rates on overnight money might soar. Companies and finance houses could find themselves in the same situation, at the same time. As a result, there are occasions when there will be violent fluctuations in the "overnight" money market. Back in 1974, "overnight" money — which the banks use for "window dressing" in order to maintain levels above reserve ratios — was as high as 60% per annum. Of course, the individual bank pays only 1/365th of 60%, since it is unlikely that these "overnight" funds will be required for more than one day by any single bank. During a period of continual tight money market conditions, the lender can expect rates of this nature if he happens to be dealing as a lender of "overnight" money on a day-to-day basis. So, although the same banking institutions may not be paying the 60%, prolonged periods of credit shortage can offer an exceptionally high return to astute dealers. On occasions the discount market will be channelling funds to and fro amounting to some two billion pounds per day.

What the jobber was to the stock-market before Big Bang, discount houses still are to the money market. The discount market has a variety of means, or instruments, by which it can earn more than it pays for the money it receives. An individual depositor on the discount market is, in effect, a member of that market. To illustrate — a company such as ICI may be able to borrow at 1% over Base Rate and have an overdraft facility of £10 billion, of which only £2 billion is taken up. Quite simply, it would pay ICI to utilise its entire overdraft facility if it can earn a clear ¾ of 1% dealing in Fine Bank Bills for one month. Of course, private individuals can also take advantage of money market rates in like manner, provided their situation involves a "positive carry". That is to say, a positive differential between the rate at which they can borrow and the rate which the money market is paying.

There are several money market instruments that can be dealt in with varying advantages. Each day the *Financial Times* lists the various instruments dealt in by the discount houses under "LONDON MONEY RATES".

In effect, the discount market re-lends money to Government on a national and local level, along with a variety of commercial enterprises, by purchasing an assortment of short-term instruments which are listed below. In essence there are four areas in which the discount houses deal. Firstly, there are Treasury Bills which are Government IOUs maturing in ninety-one days after the issue date, and dealt in denominations of £5,000 and £10,000. Treasury Bills are bought and sold at discount below par value and do not carry a coupon. The yield therefore represents the discount to maturity on the face amount of the bill.

A Treasury Bill is the finest of all Bills of Exchange, and is drawn from

London Money Rates.

December 9	Overnight	7 days notice	One Month	Three Months	Six Months	One Year
Interbank Offer	8.75	8.4375	8.5625	8.6875	8.8125	9.0625
Interbank Bid	6.00	8.3125	8.4375	8.5625	8.6875	8.875
Sterling CDs			8.50	8.50	8.625	8.75
Local Authority Deps	8.25	8.25	8.50	8.5625	8.75	8.875
Local Authority Bonds			8.75	8.8125	8.75	8.9375
Discount Mkt Deps	8.25	8.3125	8.375	8.00		
Company Deposits	8.50	8.50	8.625	8.625	8.875	9.0625
Finance House Deposits		8.5625	8.625	8.8125	9.00	
Treasury Bills (Buy)			8.3125	8.125		
Bank Bills (Buy)			8.3125	8.25	8.3125	
Fine Trade Bills (Buy)			8.9375	8.875	8.9375	
Dollar CDs			8.30-8.25	8.00-7.95	8.05-8.00	8.25-8.20
SDR Linked Dep Offer			6.625	6.625	6.625	6.6875
SDR Linked Dep Bid			6.375	6.375	6.375	6.4375
ECU Linked Dep Offer			7.00	7.0625	7.0625	7.1875
ECU Linked Dep Bid			6.875	6.9375	6.9375	7.0625

Treasury Bills (sell); one-month $8^{3}/_{16}$ per cent; three months $8^{1}/_{16}$ per cent; Bank Bills (sell) one-month $8¼$ per cent; three months $8^{7}/_{32}$ per cent; Treasury Bills, Average tender rate of discount 8.0872 p.c ECGD Fixed Rate Sterling Export Finance; Make up day November 30, 1987. Agreed rates for period December 26 to January 25 1988, Scheme I: p.c. Schemes II & III: p.c. Reference rate for period October 1 to November 30 1987. Scheme IV: p.c. Local Authority and Finance Houses seven days' notice, others seven days' fixed. Finance Houses Base Rate 9.5 from December 1, 1987: Bank Deposit Rates for sums at seven days notice per cent. Certificates of Tax Deposit (Series 6); Deposit £100,000 and over held under one month per cent; one-three months per cent; three-six months per cent; six-nine months per cent; nine-twelve months per cent; Under £100,000 per cent from November 24, Deposits withdrawn for cash per cent.

Her Majesty's Treasury pledging the Government's credit. Treasury Bills are also the shortest of all Government securities. At one time, members of the discount market used to get together every week and agree the price they would pay for Treasury Bills. But under present rules, the Bank of England makes a new issue of Treasury Bills each Friday and the discount houses submit a tender to all the bills on offer. The "syndicated tender", as the cartel was euphemistically known, has now been outlawed. Today, each discount house has to decide what it is prepared to offer for the Bills.

A Treasury Bill offers the securest of all homes for money for the period up to three months. It takes the form of negotiable instruments and is instantly resaleable. Rates for Treasury Bills vary not only from day-to-day, but from hour-to-hour; and different discount houses will quote their own rates throughout the day. It should be noted that the difference between the highest and the lowest discount house quote for "T-Bills" is likely to be very small.

The Treasuries of various local authorities (whose rateable value is in excess of certain figures laid down by statute) are empowered to issue their own bills of exchange. Discount houses will deal in these bills in the same manner as they deal in Treasury Bills. The return on Local Authorities Bills is higher than that from Treasury Bills. Bills of Exchange are also issued by local authorities. These are different from Local Authority Deposits, the latter having a coupon in the form of interest. Local Authority Bills of Exchange have no coupon. The yield merely represents a discount on the face amount of the bill.

The discount houses are the most active dealers in short-dated Government securities with up to five years to run to maturity. The houses also deal in local authority debt issues which are similar to short-dated Government securities. The life of these "Local Authority Negotiable Bonds" is usually one year. But it can be two. Local authority debt issue will usually offer the highest yield of all money market instruments. Like short-dated Government securities, the issues carry a coupon, and trade at a discount (or premium) on the face amount, so that their yield is compatible with money market conditions. The Debt issue paper, as most call it, pays a fixed rate of interest. The capital discount value of that paper will rise or fall with prevailing rates of interest, whether it be in the form of Government Securities. Local Authority Bonds or other securities offering a fixed interest return. In recent years we have had securities with a variable rate of interest which have now become known as "floaters", because the rate of interest floats up and down in line with the general level of short term interest rates. This floating rate of interest means that the capital value of the issue will stay much the same.

Discount houses also deal in the market for deposits. These range from the shortest overnight "inter-bank" deposits to longer term deposits with finance houses, local authorities, and companies as well as deposits with the money market itself. Naturally, there is considerable variation between the types of deposit. Rates may be quoted for "call" — meaning that you can get your money back any time you like. Rates are also quoted for "7 days fixed" — which means your money must stay on deposit for 7 days. Rates are also quoted for 7 days notice. This means that in the first instance your funds stay on deposit for two weeks. At any time thereafter, you can reclaim your funds by giving 7 days notice.

Most people are totally unaware of the wide variations in money market rates. In this they are doing themselves a major disservice by readily accepting whatever the local bank is willing to pay. Naturally, the individual bank will offer the best deal it can at any given point in time, but an individual's bank is only one of a number. The deal it offers may be favourable or unfavourable for the customer, dependent on the circumstances of that bank at the time. If a bank has surplus payments, the rate you will receive for your deposit will be relatively low. Discount houses, at the centre of the money market, are in touch with all the banks. The discount house itself will take money on deposit, just as a bank does. But through their contacts with other banks, and with the sophisticated money instruments which have been developed in the market they can usually offer a far more competitive rate than any particular bank. It is up to the individual depositor to try to obtain the highest return available, with the same degree of safety. As one discount house so aptly put it, "You could take pot luck with your bank. . . but it costs no more to dine *à la carte*."

Giving an added sophistication to the money market deposit rates are "Sterling Certificates of Deposit". A negotiable certificate of deposit (or CD, as it is called) *certifies* that a given sum of money is on deposit at a given bank for such-and-such a period at such-and-such a rate of interest. Unlike a normal deposit (where income is payable but the deposit is not negotiable), a CD can be bought and sold. With the CD, of course, goes the right to both the deposit and the interest on it.

This means that as a home for short-term money, the CD has all the advantages of a fixed deposit with a fixed rate of interest plus the fact that it can be sold at any time. Let's say you have funds that you don't think you will need for three months. Suppose you could have purchased from a discount house, a CD with three months to run producing a return of 10%, the highest rate at the time. If all goes according to plan, at the end of three months the CD matures and you collect your capital and interest. On the other hand, if at the end of one month you find you urgently require these funds, the CD can be sold at once at the previous prevailing rate for one month CDs. The same would apply whether you need the money in anything from one day to two months and 29 days. There would be no forfeiture or penalty for taking your money before the maturity day of the CD. This is possible because the discount houses always maintain an active and efficient CD market.

Finally, there are the oldest and traditionally the most stable money market instruments — the commercial bills of exchange, which fall under the category of "Eligible Bank Bills" and "Fine Trade Bills". A bill of exchange is like a post-dated cheque. If someone has given you a cheque post-dated for three months hence, you might be glad to sell it — even at a discount — and get your money now, rather than wait. Basically, a bill is someone's promise to pay a fixed amount at a fixed date in the future. The discount houses actually got their name because they "discount" these bills. . . buying them for cash at a discount on their face value. Until the development of the joint stock banking system, this was the primary method for financing the bulk of all business transactions. This method is at least 2,500 years old. When Glaucus, a citizen of Sparta, failed to meet his obligations on a bill, he and his family were run out of town. They were not allowed back for three generations!

In order to get some idea of how these bills work in practice, let's consider the import of timber from the Baltic. This is a seasonal business, and the importer's cash position varies widely during the year. The exporter in Finland naturally wants to be paid when he parts with the timber. The British importer on the other hand, does not want to pay for the timber until he receives it — and preferably when he's sold it. So, the Finnish exporter

— or more likely his agent in the United Kingdom — draws a bill on the importer payable in, say, three months. That bill can be sold to a discount house, which in turn will either keep it as an investment, or sell it to one of the people with whom they deal for immediate cash.

That type of bill, the simplest kind, drawn by one business on another, is called a Trade Bill. Discount houses purchase millions of pounds worth of Trade Bills, many of them for seasonal businesses. Timber, as we've seen is one — tea, pulp and grain are others. Trade Bills do not necessarily have to finance a shipment, but the principle is that the bill must finance a self-liquidating transaction. That is to say, the transaction which it has financed must have generated the money to meet it when the bill falls due for payment.

With a Fine Trade Bill, a bank may accept liability to provide the funds on behalf of the borrower when the bill falls due. It is as though that post-dated cheque was guaranteed by the bank. Accepting liability on a Fine Trade Bill, which renders it an Eligible Bank Bill, is usually the function of that group of banks known as accepting houses, which are recognised by the Bank of England as such, in the same manner as the discount house deals in Certificates of Deposits that can be bought and sold whenever it is convenient. Obviously a bank guarantee is worth having. It makes the bill more attractive, and reduces the discount that the discount house will require. So the rate of return on "Eligible Bank Bills" is lower than on Fine Trade Bills.

There you have the principal range of money market instruments, and the manner in which they are traded. These instruments, you may have noticed, fall into two categories: those which are interest bearing — reflecting current interest rates in accordance with the coupons payable — and those which are non-interest bearing — where the realisable return is based on the discount at which the instruments are traded. If you are an average investor, you will probably wish to know how you too can gain access to this wonderful market, where rates are so competitive and the instruments of such high quality! Unfortunately, very few private individuals are able to deal with a discount house direct. In the first place, the minimum amount required to deal with a discount house is relatively large. Even though some investors may have the requisite capital available for dealing in the discount market, there is still a prerequisite among members of the money market — the acumen needed to execute money market operations efficiently and successfully.

The minimum an individual would need in order to deal with a discount house — having secured the appropriate introductions — would be £100,000. With £100,000 at your disposal, and earmarked for cash equivalent investment, you may then be able to begin operations with one of the discount houses. But you must be very specific about your actual requirements. It is not the function of a discount house to manage your funds for you or to advise on how your funds should be managed, or in what instruments it would be best for you to invest. Transacting business with one of the discount house market makers is not like dealing with a stockbroker. To begin with, you must be aware of the approximate rates of the various types of money market instruments, and instruct the discount house in the type of instrument you wish to buy or sell, along with the maturities you wish to deal in. The discount house will then quote you rates for the various issues, and execute transactions in accordance with the instructions you give them. It then becomes your responsibility to plan a strategy: whether to sell your CDs, or Fine Trade Bills, before maturity, or present them for collection on the due date.

There are ways in which a private investor can gain indirect access to money market instruments. Several of the larger firms of stockbrokers regularly deal in these markets, and will often act on behalf of clients if instructed to do so — providing the account is large enough. But there could be problems. Let us assume that an individual would want to deal in UK Treasury Bills purely for the safety these securities offer. However, when dealing in UK Treasury Bills through a UK stockbroker, those Bills will be only as safe as the stockbroker himself. Since the stockbroker would not have the full faith and backing of the Treasury, there seems to be little point in dealing in Treasury Bills through a UK stockbroker. The yield on UK Treasury Bills is the lowest on any security because of the implicit safety. There is little point in accepting so poor a return if you cannot avail yourself of the corresponding top level of security.

In the UK there is a range of money funds through which the private investor may obtain money market rates on a managed basis. The funds are usually deposited with a Trustee, in the same way that securities are deposited with a Trustee in the case of a Unit Trust. Here the strength of the money can be no greater than that of the Trustee, or the investment expertise of the management, which may not be quite so prudent as you would like it to be. Therefore, as a method of ensuring safety, I do not believe money funds provide the answer. In general, I would recommend dealing in money market instruments, either through direct access or one of the major clearing banks. I do *not* recommend dealing in money market instruments through a UK stockbroker or through money funds.

Dealing in UK Government Securities

Let us turn to UK Treasury Bills, which are the first call on the obligations of the UK Treasury, and UK Government Securities (or "Gilts"). These are the second call on the Treasury's obligations, reflecting the British Government's absolute commitment to honour the debt the securities represent. No British government in history has ever defaulted on its debt, which makes the gilt-edged market one of the soundest of all for the investor, particularly during a period of domestic and international deflationary strife, when interest rates are likely to fall, and the capital value of UK Government Securities are bound, in that case, to rise.

Traditionally, UK Government Securities were sold to help finance wars. Today the proceeds are used to meet a wide range of UK public expenditure. The UK Gilts market represents by far the most significant source of government debt funding. As debt raised in earlier years falls due for redemption, new issues are released in the form of "tap" stocks, replacing the maturing debt. However, given the continued rise in public debt, there was a steady increase in the number of new issues from 1970-1985. From 1968-1974, the number of new issues averaged about five each year. From 1975-1980, it was in the region of 15. Despite what the Thatcher administration claimed to be its "tight money policy", the number of new issues per annum from 1981-1985 averaged thirty — the highest of any British government. Currently, at the end of 1987, the UK Government Securities market was accounting for approximately 65% of the turnover on the Stock Exchange in London. The UK Government Securities market by then had the third largest government debt market in the world — the largest being the US debt market, with the Tokyo Government debt market coming a close second.

UK Government Securities are issued at fixed interest rates with stated maturity dates, with the exception of the "perpetual" undated securities — War Loan, Consols, "Daltons" and a few others. These securities can be purchased in any amount. The price is normally quoted in terms of £100 nominal. The certificates are all registered in the name of the owner, unlike foreign bonds which are registered either in "Street Name" or "Euroclear". I recommend purchasers of UK Government Securities to have any foreign bonds they purchase registered in their own names, and to take delivery of the securities, rather than leave them in nominees' names with a stockbroker.

On each UK Gilts certificate is shewn the date of maturity and the interest payable to the registered holder. When an interest payment is due on a UK government stock, a cheque is sent directly to the holder of the security or his nominee. Alternatively, the interest may be credited to the holder's bank account. UK Gilts are among the most tax efficient investments. While the interest payable is fully taxable, there is no liability for CGT on purchase or sale.

There are about one hundred conventional UK Government Securities in issue. The interest payable on these ranges from 2½% to 15½%. The maturities extend from one day to over 21 years. The various coupons and maturities have a wide variety of applications which depend on the needs and strategies of the individual investor at the time.

The mainstay of the British Government Securities market, in which the majority of dealings take place, are the "current coupon" conventional issues. Such issues carry a coupon which reflects the prevailing rates for the maturity offered at close to £100. UK Gilts maturing in five years or less are known as "Shorts". Those with a maturity between five and fifteen years are classified as "Mediums". Gilts which mature after fifteen years are dubbed "Longs". Needless to say, with the passage of time, every stock with a given maturity rate will move downwards from the "Longs", through the "Mediums" to finish their days as "Shorts".

All conventional Gilts have a fixed redemption date, although approximately one in five actually has a "split date". These are called "split date" issues, and can be redeemed at any time between the first and last dates, provided the authorities give three months notice of their intention. When the price of a split-date issue is quoted above £100, it is always assumed that the actual maturity date of that issue will be the first date at which it is redeemable. When the price of a split-date issue is below £100, it is assumed that the actual maturity date will be the latter of the two.

UK Government Securities currently trading with coupons considerably above prevailing interest rates are known as "High Coupon" stocks. Those with coupons substantially below prevailing rates are known as "Low Coupon" stocks. As can be envisaged, when interest rates rise, "High Coupon" stocks may become "Current Coupon" Stocks. When interest rates fall, "Current Coupon" stocks may become "Low Coupon" stocks, and "High Coupon" stocks can become "Current Coupon" stocks.

The criterion on which investors should choose the level of the coupon should be a function of the investor's taxable income. For investors who pay no tax (or little tax) and require the highest possible income, "High Coupon" stocks will usually offer the best current return for the range of maturity, as there is no capital gains tax payable on the purchase or sale of UK government stocks. For the same reason, higher rate income tax payers will usually be better served buying "Low Coupon" stocks. Since they trade below par, but mature at par, they offer a guaranteed capital gain over the period to maturity. For investors seeking maximum current income, the current "running yield" is the essential criterion. Investors seeking tax efficient low coupon Gilts should consider the Net Redemption Yield, which represents the return after payment of any income tax due.

Aside from conventional UK Government Securities, there are also "Convertible Stocks". At times these can be very useful in a portfolio geared to a deflationary climate. Convertible Gilts offer the safety of short dated stocks, with the option of conversion into a long dated stock. In this way current rates can be "locked-in" if interest rates fall. Obviously, during periods when the market expects rates to fall, the premium you will pay for the conversion privilege — which is in the price of the stock — will be higher than if the consensus is that interest rates will rise. Furthermore, the premium payable for the conversion feature will become progressively more expensive over time. Convertible UK Government Securities provide investors with an insurance policy, which allows the investor exposure to the long end of the Gilts market if there is a fall in rates, while avoiding the risk and volatility normally associated with conventional "Longs". The cost of this protection is represented by the difference between the yield on the convertible stock and that on a conventional stock of the same maturity. In other words, the yield differential represents the insurance premium. Obviously the narrower the differential, the better the proposition offered by convertible stock. There have been times when the differential has been extremely small. On such occasions, convertible stocks are outstandingly good value. During the deflationary times ahead, you would be well advised to keep a watchful eye on the yield differential between convertible and conventional stocks.

Another variety of conventional Government Securities are the "undated" stocks. In spite of their name, they are not really perpetual. When they were first issued, the UK Government actually did promise to redeem them after certain dates. All these stocks, however, were issued when interest rates were very low. Consider the 2½% Consols, 3% War Loan, 2½% Treasury and 3½% Consols. For the Government to redeem these issues today, would mean paying £100 per bond. Obviously, no British government is likely to wish to redeem 2½% Consols for £100, while they are currently trading in the market for below £30. Should yields ever drop to the level of the coupons on these "undated" issues — or even below — then the UK Treasury might well wish to redeem them. Such a fall in yields today may seem inconceivable. But a fall in the UK inflation rate from 26% to under 4% would also have seemed inconceivable at one time! We live in an environment where reality has continually exceeded the limits of perception. This tendency is likely to continue to an even greater degree during the deflationary years that lie ahead.

The major focal point in the assessment of the relative merits of any British government stock — whether it be conventional, convertible or undated — is the Gross Redemption Yield. In essence, the Gross Redemption Yield represents the combined discounted present-day values of future income payments on top of the proceeds at redemption. Gross Redemption yields are particularly important in the case of high coupon stocks purchased above par (£100). This is because the proceeds received on redemption will be less than was paid for the stock regardless of which direction interest rates have gone. A UK Government Security purchased above par value therefore, produces an unavoidable loss of capital on redemption. From the taxation angle, this capital loss cannot be set off against capital gains made elsewhere.

Essentially, Gross Redemption Yields for a similar range of maturities and corresponding coupons will tend to show only minor variations. These are the result of relative demand and the minor differentials in the stocks. The Gross Redemption Yield on any UK Government Security is calculated on the assumption that the holder does not pay income tax (or corporation tax) on the interest received. This, in the real world, is not the case. But for all practical purposes, calculating a Gross Redemption yield on the theoretical basis is the only way we have of comparing like with like. The logic of this cannot be faulted, when at one end of the tax spectrum stand the gross funds which effectively pay no tax at all, and at the other, the high rate tax payer, who could be losing almost three-quarters of the income from his Gilts holdings in tax.

The Gross Redemption Yields on low coupon Government Securities of corresponding maturities will always be lower than the Gross Redemption Yields on high coupon Gilts. The fact is that we live in a relatively high tax paying society, which discriminates against income while encouraging speculative capital gains. Thanks to the tax treatment of UK Government Securities, low coupon stocks are always going to be in greater demand than the high coupon stocks and therefore will attract a higher premium, and offer a lower yield. High coupon UK stocks will appeal only to a limited number of individuals — those who either pay no tax or a relatively low level of tax — along with a limited range of gross fund investors. These are predominantly UK pension funds which are pleased — and able in tax terms — to benefit from the higher Gross Redemption yields. If you have your own self-administered pension scheme you will fall into the category of gross fund investor, allowing you to take full advantage of the generous yields on the high coupon Government Securities.

It must always be remembered, when it comes to investing in fixed interest securities — whether UK Gilts or other classes of fixed interest security — that what you gain in income you lose in capital gain. During a period of falling interest rates, investors should attempt to maximise the capital gain potential of their fixed interest portfolios, provided this does not lead to excessive risk exposure. Therefore, another feature of the UK Government Securities market, which should be of a major concern to investors, is the "volatility" factor inherent in different classes of UK Government Securities. This is basically the measurement of the potential risk and potential reward attached to a particular class of stock. This factor can simply be defined as the percentage change in the price of any given UK Gilt if the Gross Redemption Yield rises or falls by a given amount. The volatility factor is a function of both the date of maturity and the coupon on the individual security.

First let me demonstrate the coupon element. Take a class of UK Government Securities that matures in 10 years, and is currently yielding 10%. Suppose that the UK Government, in order to prevent the equity market from plunging, slashes rates by 1% this week and — after watching share prices continuing their fall — slashes interest rates by a further 1% next week. The following would be the effect on the capital value of three different UK Gilts: one with a 15% coupon, another with a 10% coupon and the third with a 5% coupon:

| COUPON | PRICE AT VARIOUS YIELDS | | |
	10%	9%	8%
UK Treasury 5% 1997	68.84	73.98	79.61
UK Treasury 10% 1997	100.00	106.50	113.59
UK Treasury 15% 1997	131.15	139.02	147.57

New let's turn the equation around. Let's say we have a situation where the yield curve is perfectly flat and all maturity ranges of UK Government Securities with a 10% coupon yield exactly the same amount — 10%. If interest rates are cut by 2%, and the Gross Redemption yield of the various maturities remain flat, the following would be the effect on the capital value of those UK Government Securities with maturities of 5, 10 and 15 years:

MATURITY	PRICE REQUIRED TO PRODUCE PREVAILING YIELD		
	10%	*9%*	*8½%*
UK Exchequer 10% 1992	100.00	103.96	108.11
UK Exchequer 10% 1997	100.00	106.50	113.59
UK Exchequer 10% 2002	100.00	108.14	117.29

Several conclusions can be drawn from that simple illustration. You can see that UK Government Securities — and all fixed interest securities for that matter — with a corresponding maturity will shew a greater percentage change for a given fall in Gross Redemption Yield in the lower coupon ranges. In other words, the lower the coupon, the greater the change. The higher the coupon, the less the change. At the same time those UK Government Securities with corresponding coupons will be subject to the greatest price changes at the longer end of the maturity spectrum for a given change in Gross Redemption Yield. So the rule is: the longer the maturity, the greater the price change. The shorter the maturity, the smaller the price change — for UK Government Securities with similar coupons.

Other things being equal, the higher the coupon the less important the final redemption proceeds. The longer the life of the stock, the less important is the value of the redemption proceeds, due to the effect of compound interest. Long dated UK Government Securities have a large number of interest payments stretching a considerable way into the future. So the effect of any change in the rate of discount will be magnified many times when applied to later payments. As a result, a variation in Gross Redemption Yield is bound to cause a greater variation in price. Low coupon UK Government Securities — because the greatest proportion of their investment proceeds comes at redemption — tend to behave like longer dated stocks. That is because the present value of the redemption proceeds will be similarly sensitive to the rate of discount compared to stocks with higher coupons.

A high coupon tends to shorten the effective life of a stock, due to the fact that interest payments represent a larger portion of the total return from the holding. Volatility is more a function of effective life than actual maturity. A higher level of yield reduces the value of the final proceeds on redemption relative to the coupon on the stock. Volatility will also vary with the level of yield as well as the maturity. At high yield levels, where coupon payments contribute to a higher proportion of the total return on a stock, "undated" UK Government Securities will take on an effective life which is shorter than that of long-dated stocks. In consequence, "undated" stocks — although deemed "perpetual" — will become less volatile than UK Government Securities with fixed maturities.

With a general working knowledge of the market, and of the individual UK Government Securities available, the investor can employ a variety of strategies in an effort to maximise his total return — or limit his risk — whichever his objective. One approach is simply to accept the "market's" implicit assumption about the future prospects for interest rates and inflation, and then simply adopt an investment strategy compatible with market assumptions. There's only one thing wrong with that approach. It is that markets will always do whatever they have to do to make absolutely certain that most investors are mostly wrong, most of the time!

Another approach is to attempt to outguess the market, and base your decisions on your own projection of the likely course of interest rates, inflation and economic trends. This approach is likely to be the most fruitful. Markets represent the consensus judgment of all those who participate in them, which also reflects the average level of intellectual achievement of the participants. The mere fact that you are reading this book strongly indicates that your level of intellectual achievement is above average. In that case, your efforts to outguess the market are likely to be far more rewarding than those following the consensus judgment of the average — whose intellectual achievement level, I regret to say, experience has taught me to regard as abysmally low.

Let's say that by now you have come to the conclusion that deflation is the path that future economic trends will follow, and that interest rates in the UK are set for an almighty fall. You have two strategies to consider. You can have the courage of your convictions, and adopt an all-out aggressive stance by buying one of the longer dated stocks — such as the UK Treasury 11¾% 2003/2007. Or you might wish to temper your enthusiasm and buy one of the shorter dated stocks which are less volatile — such as the UK Treasury 11¾% 1991. In the case of the longer dated stock, if everything goes awry with your forecast, you might have to wait an awful long time to see your money again. With shorter dated stock, if your forecast turns out to be wrong and interest rates *do* go up instead of down, at least you'll get all your money back in 4 years.

Say you decide to "go for broke" and be aggressive. True, it's pretty difficult to "go for broke" in the UK Government Securities market, but why not kid yourself a bit and have some fun? You buy the UK Treasury 11¾% 2003/2007 at 111, plus the cost of six days accrued interest on the 15th March. The Chancellor of the Exchequer then slashes interest rates in a giveaway budget, and you find that on the 15th of May your UK Treasury 11¾% 2003/2007 stands at 117 28/32, and you don't have to wait for your beard to grow down to your toes in order to get your money back after all.

Now, maybe, Charlie Chicken was looking over your shoulder when you were making your initial calculations, and decided he didn't *want* to be as aggressive as you. Instead, Charlie Chicken decided to buy the UK Treasury 11¾% 1991. When you bought your UK Treasury 11¾%

2002/2007 at 111, plus six days acrrued interest, Charlie Chicken bought the UK Treasury 11¾% 1991 at 103 10/32, plus 18 days accrued interest. When you sold your stock at 117 28/32, Charlie Chicken sold his at only 107 20/32, even though you were both around for the same interest rate tumble.

Because the coupons on both stocks were the same, the accrued interest would be exactly the same for you and Charlie Chicken. But — because you were a swinger and bought the longer dated, more volatile stocks — you made a profit of 6 28/32 while Charlie Chicken came out with no more than 4 10/32 on the shorter dated, less volatile stock. Yet, in both cases, you and Charlie Chicken would have done better than Sammy Nurd who was holding his money in a building society, which lowered the rate he was getting in response to the shenanigans of the Chancellor.

That little exercise is really trifling compared to what you can do if you really want to be a high flier in the fixed-interest market. By incorporating some of the latest financial instruments which the fixed interest markets offer, you can multiply your capital far more rapidly than even the fastest-moving equity markets have been capable of achieving. *You ain't seen nothin' yet* in terms of the profit potential offered by fixed-interest markets. Their profit potential promises to exceed your wildest dreams of avarice, while equity markets plunge and plunge and plunge.

Building a UK Atomic Bond Portfolio

In my opinion, most investors are likely to be better off if they maintain a simple risk avoidance strategy, geared toward capital protection, for the remainder of the deflationary period ahead. They will then be prepared for the tremendous long-term investment opportunities which will present themselves at the terminal juncture of the current contractionary period. At the same time, I am a pragmatist. That means I am fully aware that *most* investors will have neither the patience nor the fortitude to be content with a low risk, relatively stagnant portfolio with limited potential for capital gain for very long. The truth is they crave action!

Glimpsing some form of capital gain potential available somewhere, the average investor is going to be after it! Over the next few years, as the UK equity market spins out the pattern of a bear market, most advisors will be guiding their followers in the direction of equity investment during the many false "new bull markets" that are going to appear like a mirage as the bear market draws to its inevitable conclusion. The market is likely to take far longer, and fall much further to reach its end, than most advisors believe remotely possible. The trouble is they have convinced themselves that they understand the equity market, and will confidently go on recommending equity investment.

Most private investors have convinced themselves that they too understand equity markets. More to the point, they harbour the delusion that they are the only markets where a true capital gain can be made, and instant gratification achieved. The truth is that very few advisors fully understand any market. Not surprisingly, even fewer private investors do. Capital gain potential is solely a function of risk, whether in the equity market, the bond market, or in pork-belly futures. Unlike those in equities, investors in fixed interest securities are able to quantify the risk with a reasonable degree of accuracy — against an unreasonable degree of fantasy when invested in Amalgamated Garbage plc. It is possible to demonstrate that the capital gain potential in fixed income markets equals — if it does not exceed — that in equity markets. If, therefore, I can ween investors away from the dangers that lurk in the unfathomable depths of the equity market in the years ahead, a constructive purpose will have been served. Although I still believe that most investors will not be able to handle the risk factor of anything other than a conservative bond portfolio involving current coupons with short-to-medium term maturities.

Moving one step further down the path of enhancing capital gain potential through the purchase of long-dated, low coupon UK issues, we come to the lowest coupon stock of all, the "zero coupon" issues — a relatively recent financial innovation.

Amplifying Gains with Zero Coupon UK Government Securities

One of the very best possible ways to exploit the full potential of fixed-interest investment through the UK Government Securities market is in zero coupon bonds related to UK Gilts. Zero coupon bonds represent the only investment available at the time of writing where the holder is certain to enjoy the full potential of compound interest, combined with its magical effects! At the same time, in a climate of falling interest rates, holders of zero coupon bonds enjoy a capital gain potential far superior to that with normal government securities, above and beyond the compound interest factor. The worst that can possibly happen if you're the holder of a zero coupon bond is that you double (or treble) your money between the time of purchase and the maturity of the bond, and then have to pay income tax on the proceeds. That, believe me, is the worst case scenario! The *best* case is that interest rates fall sharply and you double or treble your money well in advance of the maturity of the bond. You might then wish to scoop up your profits, paying gains tax on the capital element and income tax on the far lower income portion of your gain. Incorporated in a self-administered pension scheme zero coupon bonds eliminate the tax problem completely. I do not feel there is another available investment to match with the potential of zero coupon bonds as a key constituent of any fixed-interest portfolio.

Unfortunately, availability is the problem. The choice of zero coupon bonds is extremely limited for UK investors. In fact there has been only one series of issues called "zebras" — the acronym for "Zero-coupon Eurosterling Bearer or Registered Accruing Securities." S.G. Warburg & Co. were the house responsible for the £193.2 million issue of British Government Securities sold as a zero coupon bond. In practice, Warburg created a series of separate securities, each entitling the investor to a single payment on maturity. As a consequence, both the principal and interest of the original bond became fully discounted securities.

The Zebras are backed by the following UK Government Securities, of which £100m were purchased. All of them represent "exempt" UK Government Securities:

12¾% UK Treasury 1992
12½% UK Treasury 1993
9% UK Treasury 1994
9% UK Treasury 1992-1996

Seven of the coupons, and four principal corpus's were sold at the full actuarial discount as zero coupon bonds. A few coupons were rolled into the principal amounts for the purpose of increasing the size and liquidity of the individual issues. The Table below sets out the principal amount of each Zebra issue in maturity date order, with the issue price, and initial yields — on both the AIBD and the semi-annual yield basis. All the issues in the following table mature at par (£100). Originally coupon bonds, those coupons which were payable prior to July 1988 were sold off separately, and therefore did not compromise part of the original offering.

Principal Amount Stg Millon	Maturity Date	Issue Price	A.I.B.D. Yield	Semi-Annual Yield
6.5	25.1.88	79.15	11.598	11.280
6.5	25.7.88	75.15	11.489	11.177
6.5	25.1.89	71.40	11.390	11.083
6.5	25.7.90	67.90	11.288	10.986
6.5	25.1.90	64.40	11.279	10.978
6.5	25.7.90	61.05	11.284	10.982
6.5	25.1.91	57.90	11.277	10.976
30.740	25.1.92	53.55	10.781	10.505
32	25.7.93	46.10	10.748	10.474
40	25.1.95	39.70	10.740	10.466
45	22.1.96	36.00	10.707	10.435

The proceeds of the issue total £94.29m while the redemption value amounts to £193.24m. The definitive Zebras are available in either bearer or registered form, in denominations of £1,000 and £10,000. In certain circumstances, the bearer Zebras are exchangeable for registered Zebras and *vice versa*. These zero coupon bonds will have a listing on the London Stock Exchange.

One of the slightly discouraging aspects of the UK fixed-interest market has been the inability of the investor to incorporate any degree of leverage in his fixed interest investment portfolio. Before the issue of the Zebras, only two zero coupon bonds were denominated in sterling — those of Dow Chemical and the Pearson Group. Both issues, incidentally, sold at an exceptionally high premium, in view of their scarcity value, although neither offered the equivalent security — or gearing — of a Zebra.

When Zebras first landed on British soil, there was a plethora of verbiage and hogwash about the issue from the press, often from commentators who knew little of the nature of fixed interest investment and even less on the subject of fully discounted zero-coupon bonds.

For the record, I had been including zero-coupon bonds in my clients' portfolios years before they appeared in Britain! Many of the writers latched on to the opinion given that UK holders of Zebras would continue to be responsible for tax on coupon payments although no coupon payments were received. This was merely an opinion on a hypothetical situation. It has not yet arisen, although zero coupon bonds have been in issue for several years. While such a tax treatment — were it ever to occur — might be deemed detrimental, it would be no more so than the prevailing treatment of fixed interest securities generally in the UK. At the same time, zero coupon bonds have many advantages which completely overshadow the possibility of their being given *normal* tax treatment — which is still debateable:

1. The suggested tax treatment was, in any case, based on a straight-line calculation. This means the investor would actually receive compound interest. In this respect, the treatment suggested would be far more favourable than that applied to traditional UK Gilts or coupon bonds.

2. A Zebra offers the investor an element of gearing in his portfolio. Gearing has a value; and in every other financial market would command a premium.

3. Non-UK investors will have the opportunity to exploit the capital gain potential of the UK Gilts market, while limiting their exposure to Sterling — particularly at the longer end of the market.

4. Investors may lock-in the current yield, and secure a guaranteed reinvestment of dividend payments, ensuring compound interest throughout the period to redemption. This is neither practicable, nor possible, with traditional UK Government Securities — especially for smaller investors.

5. The issue has always been competitively priced, giving a yield comparable to that on most Eurosterling securities of corresponding coupon and maturity, and one which is only slightly less than that from UK Government Securities of similar maturity and coupon.

6. The zero coupon bonds may be bought initially in bearer form, and converted to registered form as and when it appears appropriate to the buyer to make such a conversion.

Owing to the popularity of equities, and the apparent "unattractiveness" of fixed interest investment, zero coupon bonds had a slow start in Britain. I believe this will change in the months and years ahead. As UK investors become increasingly disenchanted with UK equity investment, they are likely to turn to the safety of fixed interest markets as their primary investment medium. In the United States, there has been a considerable amount of attention directed to fixed interest investments ever since the bull market in bonds began in 1982; similarly in the UK, I expect to see a large number of new fixed-interest related instruments. They will include a number of new zero coupon bonds attached to UK Government Securities, and high quality corporate issues, which should be of interest to the investor.

It would be wise therefore, for all investors to become thoroughly familiar with the mechanics of zero coupon bonds, as well as appreciating their potential. At the time of writing, the maturities available stretch no further than 1996. Once zero coupon bonds with maturities stretching to 10, 15, 20 years and beyond are issued, the results that can be achieved will be truly staggering.

What, you may ask, will be the profit potential on zero coupon bonds relative to a given fall in interest rates? The immensely helpful table (Fig. 24) should answer your question, and — at the same time — astound you. The table shews the price of zero coupon bonds given various redemption yields.

Here's how to use the table. Let's say you have a zero coupon bond with nine years to run. (Put your finger on 9.) Now say you want to know what your capital gains potential will be if interest rates fall to 2 per cent. We'll assume that the current yield on a good quality zero coupon bond is 10.5 per cent. At this rate, the price of a nine-year bond is 40.71. If interest rates fall, lowering the yield by 2 per cent to 8.5 per cent, the price that would give you this 8.5 per cent yield will be 47.99. A 2 per cent drop in interest rates would thus give you a capital gain of nearly 20 per cent. But let's go on. . .

Suppose there's a really tremendous fall in rates, similar to that which we saw in the summer of 1982. If interest rates were to drop from 10.5 per cent to, say 5.5 per cent, the price of your zero coupon bond would jump to 61.76, a gain of more than 50 per cent.

Let's take a look then at what happens with some of the longer maturities. As you can see from the table, the price of a zero coupon bond with twenty-eight years to run at a yield of 10.5 per cent will be 6.11. If interest rates fall by 2 per cent (and the yield on the bond shows a corresponding fall), the price will jump to 10.19. That's a gain of nearly 60 per cent for a 2 per cent drop in rates. If by chance there is a dramatic fall in rates, say 5 per cent, the price will jump to 25.51 — and you've made more than four times your money. If that happened to take place over a two-year time frame, you'd pay income tax on two years interest at 10.5 per cent. The remaining 280 per cent gain would attract capital gains tax — and bear in mind you're dealing

Yrs to run	Interest Rates														
	12%	11.5%	11%	10.5%	10%	9.5%	9%	8.5%	8%	7.5%	7%	6.5%	6%	5.5%	5%
29	3.74	4.26	4.85	5.53	6.3	7.19	8.22	9.39	10.73	12.28	14.06	16.1	18.46	21.17	24.29
28	4.19	4.75	5.38	6.11	6.93	7.88	8.95	10.19	11.59	13.2	15.04	17.15	19.56	22.33	25.51
27	4.69	5.29	5.97	6.75	7.63	8.63	9.76	11.05	12.52	14.19	16.09	18.26	20.74	23.56	26.78
26	5.25	5.9	6.63	7.46	8.39	9.45	10.64	11.99	13.52	15.25	17.22	19.45	21.98	24.86	28.12
25	5.88	6.58	7.36	8.24	9.23	10.34	11.6	13.01	14.6	16.4	18.42	20.71	23.3	26.22	29.53
24	6.59	7.34	8.17	9.11	10.15	11.33	12.64	14.12	15.77	17.63	19.71	22.06	24.7	27.67	31.01
23	7.38	8.18	9.07	10.06	11.17	12.4	13.78	15.31	17.03	18.95	21.09	23.49	26.18	29.19	32.56
22	8.26	9.12	10.07	11.12	12.28	13.58	15.02	16.62	18.39	20.37	22.57	25.02	27.75	30.79	34.19
21	9.26	10.17	11.17	12.29	13.51	14.87	16.37	18.03	19.87	21.9	24.15	26.65	29.42	32.49	35.89
20	10.37	11.34	12.4	13.58	14.86	16.28	17.84	19.56	21.45	23.54	25.84	28.38	31.18	34.27	37.69
19	11.61	12.64	13.77	15	16.35	17.83	19.45	21.22	23.17	25.31	27.65	30.22	33.05	36.16	39.57
18	13	14.09	15.28	16.58	17.99	19.52	21.2	23.03	25.02	27.2	29.59	32.19	35.03	38.15	41.55
17	14.56	15.72	16.96	18.32	19.78	21.38	23.11	24.99	27.03	29.25	31.66	34.28	37.14	40.24	43.63
16	16.31	17.52	18.83	20.24	21.76	23.41	25.19	27.11	29.19	31.44	33.87	36.51	39.36	42.46	45.81
15	18.27	19.54	20.9	22.36	23.94	25.63	27.45	29.41	31.52	33.8	36.24	38.88	41.73	44.79	48.1
14	20.46	21.78	23.2	24.71	26.33	28.07	29.92	31.91	34.05	36.33	38.78	41.41	44.23	47.26	50.51
13	22.92	24.29	25.75	27.31	28.97	30.73	32.62	34.63	36.77	39.06	41.5	44.1	46.88	49.86	53.03
12	25.67	27.08	28.58	30.18	31.86	33.65	35.55	37.57	39.71	41.99	44.4	46.97	49.7	52.6	55.68
11	28.75	30.2	31.73	33.34	35.05	36.85	38.75	40.76	42.89	45.13	47.51	50.02	52.68	55.49	58.47
10	32.2	33.67	35.22	36.84	38.55	40.35	42.24	44.23	46.32	48.52	50.83	53.27	55.84	58.54	61.39
9	36.06	37.54	39.09	40.71	42.41	44.18	46.04	47.99	50.02	52.16	54.39	56.74	59.19	61.76	64.46
8	40.39	41.86	43.39	44.99	46.65	48.38	50.19	52.07	54.03	56.07	58.2	60.42	62.74	65.16	67.68
7	45.23	46.67	48.17	49.71	51.32	52.98	54.7	56.49	58.35	60.28	62.27	64.35	66.51	68.74	71.07
6	50.66	52.04	53.46	54.93	56.45	58.01	59.63	61.29	63.02	64.8	66.63	68.53	70.5	72.52	74.62
5	56.74	58.03	59.35	60.7	62.09	63.52	64.99	66.5	68.06	69.66	71.3	72.99	74.73	76.51	78.35
4	63.55	64.7	65.87	67.07	68.3	69.56	70.84	72.16	73.5	74.88	76.29	77.73	79.21	80.72	82.27
3	71.18	72.14	73.12	74.12	75.13	76.17	77.22	78.29	79.38	80.5	81.63	82.78	83.96	85.16	86.38
2	79.72	80.44	81.16	81.9	82.64	83.4	84.17	84.95	85.73	86.53	87.34	88.17	89	89.85	90.7
1	89.29	89.69	90.09	90.5	90.91	91.32	91.74	92.17	92.59	93.02	93.46	93.9	94.34	94.79	95.24

Figure 24: *The price of zero coupon bonds given various redemption yields*

Table prepared by Charles H. Caultas

with the senior security of a company — not the equity. You'll receive this benefit whether or not the profits rise or fall — regardless of the state of the economy and regardless of the outlook for the corporate sector. It should be clear that anyone who prefers to invest in equities while there are these rewards in debt markets, simply has no idea of what investment is about.

As I mentioned, investors who participate in a self-administered pension plan can incorporate zero coupon bonds without incurring any tax liability. The significance of this should not be overlooked. It means that for the first time ever, investors can receive the full benefits of compound interest by investing in fixed-interest markets. The results that can be achieved — even by an investor who confines his activities to relatively low risk issues, with comparatively short maturities — is truly amazing. The investor who bought a Zebra at 36, when issued in 1985, and then holds it until maturity in 1996, will have made approximately 3 times the money he put in. The glittering prospects offered by equity market investment have always seemed highly attractive, due in part to the many vested interests that have timelessly promoted equity investment, and still do. In reality, however, very few investors ever manage to treble their investment stake over an 11-year period — much less succeed in harnessing the dynamic power of compound interest on the longer term maturities.

Partly Paid UK Government Securities

One aspect of fixed interest investment that I personally find more intellectually satisfying than equity market investment, is the ability it gives me to quantify risk. Risk quantification in equity investment is limited to studies based on volatility and financial leverage — which rely more on theory than on fact. When dealing with fixed interest investment we know — beyond any shadow of doubt — precisely what we may expect. We know, for example, that a current coupon, short dated UK Gilt will present far less risk to the investor than a low coupon, long dated Gilt. We also know that a zero coupon bond will offer a greater potential reward, and far greater potential risk than a low coupon UK Gilt with the corresponding maturity. Next on the list of UK Government Securities with an even higher potential reward — and a higher potential risk — come the partly paid UK Securities. Their high risk/high reward characteristic applies particularly within the limited time that the issues are trading in partly paid form.

A partly paid UK Government Security is precisely what the name implies. It is a new issue Gilt for which only part of the full price is paid upon application. The remainder is spread over a given period, in as much as three separate instalments. A partly paid UK Government Security will move *pari passu* with a fully paid government stock of corresponding maturity and coupon. Obviously, by the time the issue in question becomes fully paid, the leverage involved in the exercise has disappeared. As to the risk, we may suppose that an individual purchases more of a partly paid government security — in nominal terms — than he could ever afford to purchase in fully paid form. Then, if there is a fall in the Government Securities market before the issue becomes fully paid, he will suffer a loss equivalent to that on a fully paid issue, and may well be forced to sell before the final pay date.

That's where the risk element comes in. The individual investor may be tempted to splash out on a particular issue because it *is* partly paid, and because he makes the common assumption that the market can move only one way — and that's up! In the present climate, the investor in Britain is constantly being urged to be "enterprising". Besides which, there have been all these splendid privatisation issues, which "everyone" says are so cheap. It was not long after the 1987 stock market crash that newcomers to the game were talking of "getting in on the ground floor", because the opportunity would not occur again. One of the psychological quirks which the tally man has always exploited is that people are frequently prepared to spend far more than they can afford (and borrow to do it) because the goods offered are "such a bargain".

There was a striking example of the way an unwelcome development in the market can rapidly reduce the value — as well as the price — of a partly paid issue. In the case of the ill-fated BP issue, the shares were standing after the crash at around 70 pence. But if you took into account the current price of the existing "old" shares, and the remainder of the issue price outstanding on the "new" shares, the price-tags on the partly-paid shares should have been nearer 23 pence than 70!.

Nevertheless, the fact that there can be a special reward attached to a partly-paid issue should not be overlooked.

The reward element is based on the fact that if the investor guesses right then he will be able to lay his hands on a far bigger number of securities, and so ensure a far bigger profit because the issue *was* partly-paid. A high proportion of "new" investors have, as I said, gained some experience of "partly paid" issues through the UK Government's highly publicised privatisation schemes. Partly paid UK Government Securities operate in precisely the same manner; although it would be unreasonable to expect a fixed interest Government Security to perform anything like the partly paid shares in British Telecom or British Gas. Nevertheless, partly paid UK Gilts will enhance the short-term reward potential of a UK Government Securities portfolio *during a favourable period*. At the same time, the leverage factor will also increase the risk element of the portfolio, thereby threatening capital values under inclement stock market conditions. Partly paid UK Government Securities have three basic advantages for the investor. When it is likely that yields may fall, the buyer is able to lock-in existing yields, before the first sign of a fall, even though he may not have the cash required at that moment to go for a fully paid issue.

A trader (or investor) willing to speculate, and seeking greater leverage on his fixed interest portfolio, can execute a larger position than his cash resources would otherwise permit. The underlying assumption behind the purchase of the partly paid issue is a view that interest rates will fall. If this view subsequently proves correct — the speculator can perpetuate his profit by selling sufficient of the partly paid issue to secure the fully paid issue when the call is due, acting on the further assumption that interest rates are likely to continue falling past the call date.

The mathematics involved in the leverage inherent in a partly paid UK Government Security is fairly easy to understand. Let's say you acquire a £25 paid partly paid UK Government Security in January, with the balance of £75 payable in March. You do so because you want to get the best run for your money between January and March, believing that interest rates will fall. Further, let's assume that this partly paid UK stock is a 10% Exchequer of 1999. Now make one further assumption: that interest rates fall to the extent that a security with a 10% coupon maturing in 1999 will rise by 5 points from January through March. Had you purchased that UK Exchequer 10% 1999 in fully paid form in January, you would have made a capital gain of 5% — the difference between £100 in January and £105 in March. However, the partly paid issue will move *pari passu* with the equivalent fully paid issue by a corresponding £5. So your £25 purchase will have risen to £30 by March, representing a capital gain of 20% — against a 5% gain on the fully paid issue.

But let's change the market climate, thereby turning the equation upside down. In this case, interest rates have risen instead of falling. So the rise in interest rates, prompting a 5 points fall in the value of the fully paid UK Exchequer 10% 1999, gives you a capital loss of 5%. The partly paid issue — which will move *pari passu* with the equivalent fully paid issues — must also experience a fall of 5 points. But this will take the price of the partly paid issue down from £25 to £20.

Your loss will therefore be 20% compared with the 5% suffered on the fully paid issue. Remember — the reward potential of a UK Government Securities portfolio can be enhanced by the inclusion of partly paid issues. But so can the loss potential! In the case of the £25 partly paid issue, the risk/reward factor is multiplied four times. In other words, you will make four times as much profit as you would have made on the fully paid issue under favourable conditions, and you will lose four times as much as you would have done on a fully paid issue given unfavourable conditions. In the case of a £50 partly paid issue, the risk/reward factor will be twice that of a fully paid issue. A £20 partly paid issue will give you a risk/reward factor five times that of the fully paid issue of equivalent coupon and maturity, reckoned as the percentage gain (or loss) on an equivalent amount invested.

Not withstanding what I have just said, it is important to realise that the leverage obtainable on a partly paid UK Government Security is still comparatively low compared to that obtainable on some of the more esoteric vehicles which have recently become available to investors in fixed interest markets.

The Archimedes of UK Government Securities Market. . . Warrants

A famous philosopher once said, "Ninety per cent of everything is garbage." In the field of investment, 99 per cent of everything is garbage. Why? Because we have "gearing". Sophisticated investors have long been familiar with the use of gearing as a way to enhance the profitability of their stock market operations. The basic principles are not new. Nor are the fundamentals so terribly difficult to understand. Archimedes, the great third-century philosopher, is credited with the discovery of gearing or leverage. In the physical sense, leverage is obtained by the use of a bar or rod supported on a fulcrum. Archimedes discovered that a small force applied at a considerable distance from the fulcrum would create a much larger force closer to the fulcrum on the other side. The same idea lies behind leverage or gearing in the financial sense — employing a small amount of capital to do the work of a large amount of capital. . . and applying it at the right point.

Many people are attracted to the equity market because of the various forms of financial gearing it offers, thereby promising a quick profit. These same individuals are often loath to become involved in bond markets because they feel that profits are too slow coming, and the element of financial gearing, and therefore quick profits, is insufficient, if it is not lacking altogether. That may have been true at one time, but it's certainly not the case any longer. We have a whole new ball game in the bond market.

Zero coupon bonds which provide the ultimate in a deep discount display the greatest capital gain potential in the bond market. Since the discount is 100 percent of the return, it would be impossible to increase the gearing when using the deep discount method of bond selection to build a geared bond portfolio. However, there is another instrument which can be used to increase the gearing that much more, and thereby enhance and accelerate the profit potential during a period of falling interest rates. That tool is the bond warrant, a recent additon to the arsenal presently available to the investor, enabling him to maximise his return in the bond market during a period of falling interest rates.

In itself a warrant resembles a long-term traded option. That is to say, it gives the holder the right to purchase an item at a given price over a given period. If the underlying security, or commodity, rises in price, the value of the option will rise. If the underlying security falls in price, the value of the option will fall. In the case of an option, the duration of a contract can vary from weeks to months whereas a warrant will often have several years to run.

In the United States, the exercise price of most warrants attached to a coupon bearing bond is par. One bond warrant allows the holder to purchase $1,000 of bonds. For example, at the issue price of 26, the total cost of exercising the Manufacturers Hanover Trust 14.125 percent 15.5.89 bond warrant worked out at $1,026 per bond. ($1,000 = cost of bond at par + $26 per bond warrant.) With each bond warrant allowing the investor to buy one bond at par, the combination produced a yield of 13.45 percent to maturity on the investment. The exercise price will remain at par. If prevailing yields for that Manufacturers Hanover Trust issue with a 1989 maturity fell to 12 percent, the price of the warrant would have to rise to 91, since a coupon bond with a yield of 14.125 per cent would sell at 109.10 to produce a yield of 12 per cent. If by chance the prevailing yields for this type of issue indicated 10 per cent, the the price of the warrant would rise to 190. A bond with a 14.125 per cent coupon would sell at 119 to yield 10 per cent.

The most highly geared of all bond warrants are those attached to zero coupon bonds, since (as we have seen) zero coupon bonds are the most highly geared of all bonds. However, since we would be dealing with a discounted issue, the exercise price would be relative to the guaranteed yield to maturity at issue. It would rise with the passage of time. That is because the shorter the period of the zero coupon bond, the higher will be the price needed to produce the initial guaranteed yield to maturity.

To take another concrete example, in August 1981, Citicorp issued 200,000 bond warrants. At an exercise price of $422.60 per $1,000, the warrant price of 24 would have produced accrued amortisation to maturity of 13.5 per cent, combining the exercise price of the zero coupon with the price of the warrant. Had interest rates on zero coupon issues fallen, the price of the bond warrant would have risen to compensate for the fall. As it so happens, a fall in the yield to maturity of the zero coupon bond of 1 per cent should produce a theoretical rise to 50 in Citicorp Warrants. If the yield on the zero coupon bonds fell by 2 per cent, this should produce a rise to 77 in Citicorp Warrants. Similarly, a fall in yields of 3 per cent on the zero coupon bonds would produce a rise to 106 in Citicorp Warrants. *These figures may be calculated by combining the cost of the warrant and the exercise price of the warrant to produce a yield compatible with prevailing yields.*

Close followers of the bond markets will know why this example was chosen: because it exemplifies the risk in highly-geared issues. During the summer of 1981 there was a panic in US banking paper. Investment in the debt issues of banks was considered one of the riskiest ventures imaginable. As a result, while several bond warrant issues exploded in price, Citicorp Warrants became literally valueless on 28th August 1981, because the yield on Citicorp zero coupon bonds exceeded the exercise yield of the warrant.

Returning to the UK, we found that when dealing either in a fully paid coupon bond or a zero coupon bond of UK Government quality, it would be virtually impossible to lose all your investment. When dealing in a partly paid UK Government Security, it would also be close to impossible to lose all your investment, because it would take an almighty collapse in UK Government Securities to retrace the entire partly paid portion of a partly paid issue. This is not so in the case of bond warrants. Should the price of the bond be below that of the exercise price of the warrant upon expiry, then you *will* lose your entire investment. In most cases, it would take little more than a fall of 10% in bond prices between the purchase of the warrant and the date it expires for your entire investment to evaporate.

Like the UK zero coupon bond market, the debt warrant market in Britain is still in its infancy. In December 1987, there was one bond warrant exerciseable into the bond of Den Norske Credit Bank, denominated in Sterling. There were two bond warrants exercisable into a UK Government Security issued by Bankers Trust. One was exerciseable into the UK Treasury 10% of 1993; the other into the UK Treasury 10% 1994, which ran until 10th November 1988.

This second bond warrant was issued at a price of £1,850, entitling the holder to purchase £100,000 nominal amount of the UK Treasury 10% 1994 at a price of 108 27/32. At the time of issue, the price of the stock was 105 12/32. Should the price of the Treasury 10% '94 rise to £112.54375 any time before the expiry of the warrant on the 11th November 1988, the holder could at least expect to see a 100% gain — such is the leverage the bond warrant market has to offer. In other words, a 7% gain in the price of the UK Treasury 10% 1994 will produce a 100% gain in the price of the warrant. I would point out that such a gain is no mere prediction. It is a mathematical certainty for reasons which are inherent in the bond warrant market. Remember — a warrant is exerciseable at anytime. So once the Treasury 10% '94 reaches the exercise price (108 27/32), the warrants will move *pari passu* with the stock in question — the UK Treasury 10% 1994. This principal applies to all warrants, whether exerciseable into bonds or equities, provided that the warrants are exerciseable at the discretion of the holder.

Traded Options. . . Make £1 do the work of £1,000

Maybe doubling your money in the course of a year against a 7% gain in the underlying security still isn't enough leverage for you. Maybe you think you can do better by purchasing traded call options in the equity market — always assuming there's a bull market in equities. Since this is highly unlikely over the next two to three years, you'd better forget that idea! Although you may not realise it, you can also purchase traded options on UK Government Securities. The market is thin. The options on offer are limited. But it is another way of adding gearing to a UK Government Securities portfolio with limited risk. Although I am obliged to say that I consider using traded options as involving higher risk than dealing in warrants exerciseable into UK Government Securities. That is because the time parameters are much more limited. Warrants currently exerciseable into UK Government Securities run for as long as a year. Traded options contracts are of much shorter duration. As in the case of warrants, should the price of the bond fall below the striking price of the option when it expires, that option will be worthless, and the investor will have lost his entire investment.

I am going to assume that my readers have some understanding of traded options in general. If not, I would strongly recommend they immediately make their acquaintance. Like all other traded options, the price behaviour of an option on Gilts will reflect the behaviour of the underlying investment. If interest rates fall, the value of the underlying UK Government Security will move the other way. The rise will be amplified by a far greater increase in the price of the traded option. If, on the other hand, interest rates should rise, the price of the underlying UK Government Security must fall. The fall will be matched by a much greater percentage drop in the price of the traded call option. That is because all it gives the holder is the right to buy the underlying security at the striking price of the traded option contract.

At the time of writing two Gilt-edged option contracts are being traded. Given the growing call for fixed interest securities, I expect the number of Gilt-edged options contracts to increase substantially in the years ahead. But, for the time being, all you have is a traded option on the UK Treasury 12% 1995, and the UK Treasury 11¾% 2003/2007. As I explained in my treatise on the UK Government Securities market, those with longer maturities will tend to be more volatile than those with shorter maturities. The traded option contract on the UK Treasury 11¾% 2003/2007 can, therefore, be expected to be much more volatile — offering greater potential reward and correspondingly greater risk — than the traded option for the shorter dated Gilt.

Each traded call option contract entitles the holder to purchases £50,000 nominal of a specific UK Government Security. The exercise prices of the contracts are at 2-points intervals — 102, 104, 106, 108, etc. These two point increments are based on a "clean" exercise price — that is to say without consideration of the accrued interest on the underlying security. Accrued interest is treated separately on a "plus" basis in the case of a call option contract, and on a "minus" basis in the case of a put option contract.

The premiums you have to pay for these options are quoted on the basis of £ per £100 nominal of underlying stock in "points". The points are divided into 32nds. Each point represents 1% of the underlying principal. Therefore, each point quoted as a premium for the traded option contract would be the equivalent of £500 since each contract entitles the buyer to purchase £50,000 nominal of stock. It means that the option premium at £ 1/32 per £100 amounts to £15.625. Therefore, assuming you are quoted a price of 2 5/32 for a traded call option on the Treasury 11¾% 2003/2007, the price you would have to pay per contract would be £1078.125. The calculation is made as follows: $(2 \times £500) + (5 \times £15.625) = £1,078.125$. If the price you are quoted is 2½, the cost per contract may be calculated as follows: (2 × £500) + (16 x £15.625) = £1,250. The prices of the option contracts themselves move in minimum increments of 1/32 of a point.

The option series come on the basis of 3, 6 and 9 months contracts, expiring on the last business day of either February, May, August or November in accordance with the specific series. Positions are limited to 2,500 option contracts in any one series, for any one investor. The market is normally arranged so that there will be a choice of three different expiry dates spaced at three monthly intervals, and a range of no less than three exercise prices at two-point price intervals. Every so often it becomes necessary to change the underlying security, because the passage of time means that a particular UK Government Security is no longer representative of the relevant maturity area. In other words, a long-dated government stock may eventually become a medium-dated one. A short-dated stock may actually be redeemed. The first gilt-edged traded option contracts to be introduced were based on the short-dated Exchequer 10% 1989, which had a four year life when it was introduced on 25th June 1985. This contract no longer exists.

Gilt-edged traded option bargains are dealt with in the same way as UK Government Securities. But they are settled through the London Options Clearing House. This is a subsidiary of the Stock Exchange, serving as the official counterparty to buyer and seller alike. All business in options is transacted for cash settlement the following day. That means a purchaser of options must ensure that the option premium is available to the broker, for payment to the London Options Clearing House, before 10 am the morning after the trade.

There are probably more options strategies than options listed. I prefer the very simple strategy of buying a call option, or a series of call options, solely for the purpose of increasing the leverage of a portfolio. By purchasing warrants exerciseable into UK Government Securities, the investor has the opportunity of participating in the same performance of the underlying securities, but with a far lower capital outlay — and, therefore, a higher percentage capital appreciation on the funds invested. When dealing with traded call options in UK Government Securities, the investor can participate in the performance of the underlying security with an even smaller capital outlay — and a greater percentage return on capital invested — assuming market conditions favour his position.

For example, there have been many occasions when we've seen UK Government Securities rise by as much as 2 points in a day, and five points in a week. As outlined, each point is worth £500 per contract. If the purchaser of one option contract bought at "2", while the Contract was neither "out-of-the-money" nor "in-the-money", finds the UK Government Securities market rising by 2 points on the day, he will have doubled his money in a day! Should he find that the UK Government Securities market has gained five points on the week, he will have made 2½ times his money in that same week. I would remind readers, however, that should they purchase a traded option for "2", and should the UK Government Securities Market fall by 2 points immediately after purchase — and never recover those 2 points before the expiry date — that contract will expire valueless, and the investor will have lost his money.

As I have said, I prefer the simple strategy of purchasing a call option on UK Government Securities for the purpose of enhancing leverage rather than becoming involved in some of the more costly complex strategies. But there is one ploy I would recommend to investors who have a good knowledge of the traded options market, and are reasonably sophisticated. That strategy involves writing call options against an existing UK Government Security with the object of improving the return on the portfolio. Under no circumstances would I recommend writing call options unless they are fully covered by an existing portfolio of underlying UK Government Securities, with maturities and coupons similar to those against which the options contracts are written. Nor, let me say, would I recommend writing traded "put" options.

The reason I recommend writing call options — with the safeguards I mentioned — is the recent increase in the premiums payable for call options on UK Government Securities. While a hike in premiums may not be such good news for the purchasers of such options, it's good news for the writers! Premiums are likely to remain high until there is a much wider choice of UK Government Securities traded option contracts, in view of the defensive character of the market which is likely to continue. There are a few things you should know before writing options against your UK Government Securities portfolio. In general, all writers of options must deposit margin. When writing options on UK Government Securities, the margin you must lodge is 5% of the market value — plus or minus the "in-the-money" or "out-of-the-money" element. Margins are calculated on a daily basis. Let's see how it would work in practice.

Say you have a UK Government Securities 11¾% 1996 in your portfolio. That's close enough to the UK Treasury of 12% 1995 upon which you can write a traded option. There's likely to be very little difference in the price movement of the UK Treasury 11¾% 1996 from that of the UK Treasury 12% 1995 for a given movement in interest rates. You can, therefore, comfortably write a call option on UK Treasury 12% 1995 without undue risk. The worst that can happen is that the UK Treasury 12% 1995 option is exercised and you have to deliver the stock. You will then sell your UK Treasury 11¾% 1996, and buy the UK Treasury 12% 1995 with the proceeds. In the real world, that's unlikely to happen, because options tend to go on being traded until they expire unexercised.

The best thing that can happen to you as an option writer of UK Government Securities traded options is that you keep the entire premium, which happens more often than not. Of course, you'll have a bit of money tied up until the option expires, in which case your opportunity cost should be factored into the exercise. Let's take an example. We'll say you write one contract of the February 112 call on the Treasury 12% 1995, with the price of the underlying security at, say, 108. You will have to put up 5% of the value of the contract, or 5.4 points. Since the underlying security is 4 points "out-of-the-money", that 4 points will be deducted from the margin you would be required to pay. This leaves you with a margin payable of 1.4 points. 1.4 points on £50,000 nominal of underlying security works out at £700. Assuming the price of the contract in the market is 3 points for which you are due to receive £1500 per contract, you will be £800 in pocket — but no more —until the contract expires.

Let us now suppose that by the close of the following day the price of the underlying security has advanced to, say, 109⅜. You will have a margin call, and be required to place additional margin to maintain the minimum. Also, the price of the option will no longer be 4 points "out-of-the-money". It will be only 2⅝ points "out-of-the-money". 5% of 109⅜ works out at 5.468 points. From that will be deducted the "out-of-the-money" element of 2.625 points, leaving you with a net minimum margin of 2.843% on £50,000 nominal of underlying security, against the 1.4% of the nominal value of the underlying security you originally put up. The total liability will be £1,421.50, less the £700 originally lodged as margin. This leaves you with less than £400 in pocket until the option expires. At the same time however, your UK Treasury of 11¾% 1996 is likely to have moved upwards by an amount similar to the rise in the underlying security of the option. So you wouldn't really be losing anything.

I have assumed that all of you out there will have a stockbroker, prepared to allow you to pay the minimum margin. But I should warn you, there is no fixed rule on this. The margin can amount to whatever your stockbroker deems appropriate in your case. Even if your stockbroker thinks you're a ding-dong, who doesn't know what he's doing, he'll still be happy to take your orders. But he will require a higher margin than with a more experienced investor. If anything, the margin you have to pay should give you a good idea of what your stockbroker thinks of your expertise. Money invariably speaks louder than words! Most brokers, most of the time, will make their clients feel that each and every one of them is the reincarnation of Bernard Baruch. But when it comes to margin, it's a different story. The budding Bernard Baruchs will find themselves relegated to the status of investment Neanderthals.

Financial Futures. . . The Market Equivalent of Russian Roulette

The advent of "Big Bang" bought a massive increase in the number of marketmakers in UK Government Securities. This in turn necessitated a substantial increase in the number of UK Government Security related instruments available, to allow the increased number of marketmakers to share in a larger pie, rather than have them all scrambling for a smaller slice of the same pie. In addition to the traded option contracts on UK Government Securities — launched in June 1985, by the London Options Clearing House — the London International Financial Futures Exchange (LIFFE) began to trade in the futures contracts of UK Government Securities.

In the mind of some investors, the derivative instruments of the gilt-edged market, such as financial futures and traded options, are often classed together. There are investors whose actions and activities are very rarely deflected by thought and analysis. In practice as well as theory, the two instruments serve distinctly different purposes, with one of them capable of inflicting considerably more damage than the other. In many cases, the damage that can be inflicted by unrestrained trading in the financial futures market could prove fatal. The difference between a futures contract and a traded option contract is not unlike the difference between your child's doing his sums on an abacus in the front parlour, and performing the same task by counting the pebbles in the middle of the M4 motorway during a peak traffic period.

In recent years, newspapers have continued to print tales about greedy investors, seduced by the huge gains that were widely touted by commodity brokers. Many who indulged in commodity futures trading lost their entire life's savings in a matter of months. A few years back, Prudential-Bache were accused of misleading investors by implying that a certain type of financial future trading strategy was capable of producing a return of 50% per annum. Many lost fortunes, not that Prudential-Bache were to blame. The fault lay with the greed of those investors unwilling to investigate before they invest.

A gilt futures contract, as traded on LIFFE, is a contract to buy (or sell) a fixed quantity of stock at a given price, at a certain point in the future. The cost of the futures contract is the opportunity cost of the cash margin requirement. As such, dealing on the futures market is likely to be far cheaper than dealing in options. But the risks can be appreciably higher. When dealing with an option, your risk is limited to what you have paid for the option. When dealing in a futures contract, your risk theoretically can be the entire value of the contract. You *can* lose many, many, many multiples of what you paid for your contract. Certainly, dealing in financial futures is the quickest way to a fortune in the UK Government Securities market. It is also the quickest way of getting wiped out. It could take no more than a couple of days to accomplish either.

LIFFE offers a range of financial futures contracts including long and short dated gilts, 3-month sterling deposits and long US Treasury bonds. All or any of these instruments may be used by the investor who, in financial terms, is suicidally inclined. It's the kind of investor who would like to increase the leverage of his portfolio for a minimum outlay, while increasing his potential for fiscal annihilation. There is a clear warning in the literature provided by the London Financial Futures Exchange. The nature of futures, it says "is such that potential loss, as well as profit, is unlimited." Even so, it is worthwhile discovering exactly what a futures contact entails — and why it *can* be so lethal.

The UK Government Securities futures contract is a nominal stock with a specified term to maturity at the first day of the relevant delivery month. There is a variety of coupons, with interest payable at half yearly intervals — as on most of the actual securities available on the UK Government Securities market. ·

The nominal value of each contract is £50,000. This price was chosen as being large enough to avoid unwieldy numbers of contracts being traded, but small enough to be acceptable. That meant closely matching exposure to other markets, and staying within the cost considerations of those using LIFFE for serious purposes, as well as those who simply wanted to use the market for speculation.

Contracts are traded for delivery in March, June, September and December. They are traded for five delivery months at any one time. Therefore, as transactions in a new contract begin, the furthest delivery date will be fifteen months into the future. This is your maximum range for play.

Prices on the UK Government Securities futures contract move in "ticks". A "tick" is the value (in pounds and pence) of the smallest movement permitted in each contract, as specified by the London International Financial Futures Exchange. At the time of writing a "tick" was 1/32 of £100 nominal value of the notional stock held. That made it worth £15.625 on one contract of £50,000.

Those who wish to play the financial futures game must put up margin in the same way as those who play the commodities game. The *minimum* margin required by LIFFE is 3% or £1,500 per contract. But, again, the *actual* margin required by a member of the London International Financial Futures Exchange from his client could be higher. If the broker regards you as a Yo-yo, it could be a lot higher. It is more than likely that you *are* a Yo-yo — if you consider playing this market as an inexperienced, small private investor. Even if you're a large, rotund inexperienced private investor, it's safe to assume your margin is going to be far higher than the 3% minimum. The level of your margin will depend on two things: the extent to which you can impress your broker that you have sufficient personal wealth, and his greed for commissions. The greedier the broker, the lower your margin. So if you're determined to get the lowest margin possible, find a greedy broker. It shouldn't be all that difficult!

When dealing in an option contract, you have the right — but not the obligation — to buy or sell a stated nominal amount of stock, at a fixed price, before a prescribed future date — the expiry date of the option. There is a subtle difference when you start dealing in a futures contract. With a futures contract, you have accepted the obligation to take delivery of the item at the specified price, on the specified date. There is no way out — even if the heavens fall! Unless you manage to dispose of the contract to someone else — usually at a loss — before that date. Bearing that in mind, settle down while I show you how the game is played.

Let's say you find yourself a really greedy broker who will actually allow you the minimum margin. Let's also say that you've decided to commit £15,000 to the Financial Futures market. This will enable you to purchase 10 contracts giving you the buying power of £500,000 worth of Gilts. Woweee! You *are* a swinger in the fixed interest market!

Another fine point you should be aware of before you actually give your order is that there are limits. There is a limit to the price movement of 2 points in either direction from the previous working day's official closing (settlement) price on LIFFE. If that limit is breached, there is a cessation in trading. What happens is that — in effect — you're locked in. You can't get out. In no way can you sell your contract until trading starts again. This limit is a protective device made necessary by the fact that players in the Financial Futures market are only required by LIFFE to pay an initial margin equivalent of 3 points. Be warned! Do not for one instant think that it's *you* who are being sheltered from the storm. It's the "house" that's being protected. When a contract trades "limit down", trading stops. The "house" will then send out its margin calls, so that the appropriate — and necessary — margin can be re-established.

Let's now get the ball in motion. You are convinced that interest rates are going to fall. You'll probably be right. They're bound to fall — but not necessarily when you want them to. Boldly, you give the broker your order. He buys 10 contracts. Two minutes after your order has been executed, your contract trades limit down. There have been several occasions when the UK Government Securities market has tumbled by 2 points in a few hours. That "limit down" trade warns you that you're going to have to put up some more margin. The 2 point limit down by the way, means that you've lost 64/32nd's on 10 contracts. Each 1/32, remember, is worth £15.625. You've blown no less than £9,375 in five minutes. Does it make you feel sick? No one's stopping you. Do you want to pull out, and at least get back what's still left of your £15,000? Sorry! You can't. Your contract is "limit down". That means it's not trading. But there's always tomorrow. . . which your broker will tell you is "another day".

Alas, tomorrow could prove even blacker than the day before. The UK Government Securities market could *open* "limit down". It's always possible. If it does, you've blown another £9,375 — in no time at all! Not only has your entire £15,000 gone to money heaven, because you still owe the broker a further £3,750 after two days of play. Even then, it may not yet be over. Until your contract no longer trades "limit down", you're still locked in. You still cannot escape. If your contract happens to trade limit down three, four or five days running, and you're losing close to £10,000 a day, you will no longer be thinking about the market at all. As the man said, in futures "potential loss, as well as profit, is unlimited." Little wonder that you'll be spending most of your time trying to liquidate whatever assets you have left in order to meet your brokerage debts, and consulting your legal advisor on how to escape bankruptcy.

Naturally, there is another side to the coin. Your futures contract could rise just as quickly as the falls I've illustrated. In that case, you'd be gaining £10,000 a day instead of *losing* £10,000 a day. But, considering the infrequency and unlikelihood of such occasions, I do not feel that any further elaboration along these lines is necessary.

When the Road Forks. . . Index-Linked UK Government Securities

After reading about all the wondrous feats you can get up to in the UK Government Securities market, I'll bet you've completely forgotten about the "Gulag Anglo-Pedigree" and the implications for British interest rates! Britain is an inflation-prone economy given to severe monetary excesses. This has been the pattern for decades. Contrary to popular belief, this pattern has become even more deeply etched under the heavy hand of the Thatcher administration, which is nothing other than a more pronounced version of the previous administration — involving a change in style and rhetoric, not policy.

As we move down the 10 years or so of the contractionary Downwave — of which 1987's crashing stock markets were the last visible expression — the deflationary forces have been exerting their pressure on most economies with increasing momentum. . . but not in Britain. Of the 8 major industrialised nations, the rate of inflation projected for Britain by the Economist Intelligence Unit shows Britain as likely to have the second highest. Only Italy is expected to have a higher rate of inflation. However, inflation in Italy has been coming down, while inflation in Britain has been rising. Against a 4.2% average for the OECD countries as a whole — which includes a 7% average for some of the less prosperous members of the group — the rate of inflation for Britain is expected to be 4.7% during 1988 against 1.5% for West Germany, for Japan and for the Netherlands. Exacerbating the inflationary trends in the UK is its projected trade balance. The EIU shows Britain with the second highest projected growth in imports of all major countries, against the slowest growth in exports. Imports are expected to grow by 4.8%, against a lowly 2% increase in exports.

By all indications, Britain is now following the road that led to the ruin of Germany during the 1920s. On the basis of unchanged policies, I expect the 26% inflation rate of the mid-1970s to be exceeded. As we have seen in the past, inflation is the killer of fixed interest markets. During periods of rampant inflation — which I expect to see return to Britain during the 1990s — interest rates will soar and UK Government Securities are likely to be massacred. There will be only one exception — Index-Linked UK Government Securities will provide the only protection that Britons can hope for.

During the remainder of the 1980s and early 1990s, however, I still believe that a portfolio of traditional UK Gilts will serve the British investor more adequately than any other form of UK investment. But the road will fork. When it does, my advice to all British investors will be to hold a portfolio combining very short term UK Treasury Bills and Index-Linked UK Government Securities, to the exclusion of all other investment. Although this advice may seem premature, I feel that investors should become familiar with the Index-Linked UK Government Securities market without delay.

Index-Linked UK Government Securities were conceived as the investor's hedge against inflation, and the economic climate of the early 1980s provided an ideal opportunity for their introduction. On the one hand, a British Government was attempting to convince the electorate of its determination to conquer inflation. The introduction of Index-Linked UK Government Securities was supposed to be proof of this. The majority of sophisticated investors, capable of understanding the concept of Index-Linked UK Government Securities, were unlikely to believe the protestation of the UK politicians. These investors therefore provided a ready market, as they sought protection from the ravages of inflation inflicted on them by so many British Governments.

Index-Linked UK Government Securities provide a low basic coupon of approximately 2.0% to 2.5%, paid semi-annually in the same manner as conventional UK Gilts. The low coupon of the Index-Linked Government Stocks therefore makes them a tax-efficient instrument. Since one object of the Index-Linked Gilts is to provide an income flow which keeps up with the rate of inflation, the coupon is "indexed" to the rate of inflation reflected in the Retail Price Index. So, how's it actually work?

Let's say, you purchase the 2% Index-Linked Government Security of 2006, when the Retail Price Index is standing at 274.1. Should there be a bulge in the rate of inflation over the next year, with the Retail Price Index moving up to 377.1, then your semi-annual interest payment would be boosted accordingly. Your annual interest payment is 2%, so your semi-annual interest payment is 1%. With the rise in the Retail Price Index, your 1% semi-annual payment will be multiplied by 377.1, (the rate of inflation in six months), divided by 274.1 (the level of the index at the time of purchase). The interest payment will now be equivalent to an annual rate of £2.75 for every £100 nominal stock held.

The capital element of the Index-Linked UK Government Security is also indexed to the Retail Prices Index. Once again let's use the 2% Index-Linked 2006 as an example. If the underlying inflation bias in the British economy persists, the move in the Retail Price Index between now and the time the 2% Index-Linked 2006 matures could be quite prodigious. For example, at an inflation rate of 20% per annum, the price of goods and services actually doubles every five years. If in 1986 you purchased a 2% Index-Linked UK Government Security maturing in the year 2006, with the Retail Price Index standing at 274.1, it would not be unrealistic to expect the index to be somewhere in the region of 6,000 by the year 2006; that is, provided the monetary aggregates are allowed to continue growing at the rate in which they have been growing throughout the 1980s.

As I have just said, both the income and the capital element of the Index-Linked stocks are "indexed". Should the Retail Price Index be in the area of 6,000 in 2006, the redemption value for every £100 of the stock held would be 6,000 divided by the base figure of 274.1 which prevailed at the time of purchase. By the year 2006, your £100 of stock would therefore be worth £2,189. Unfortunately, that £2,189 would not buy any more than the £100 you paid for the stock in the first place. Such is the effect of compound inflation! While many people insist that equity market investment is better able to cope with rampant inflation than Index-Linked UK gilts, we don't think so. In all probability many of those who try to make a case for equity investments over gilts are the stockbrokers, who receive twice the amount of commission on equity investment than they do on investments in gilts.

Remember — during a period of rising inflation, Index-Linked gilts have quite a few advantages over equity investment:

1)   Index-Linked gilts offer the promise of a real rate of return. Equity investments do not. Equity investment can easily produce a negative rate of return even though it may give the appearance of booming. As was seen during the German hyperinflation, the German Stock Market Index advanced by 50 billion times its 1924 base date in less than three years. But it still failed to keep up with the German rate of inflation during that period.

2)   Gilts (both Index-Linked and conventional) are free of capital gains tax. Since an unusually high proportion of the returns from Index-Linked gilts come in the form of capital gains rather than income, the after-tax return necessary for an equity protfolio to keep up with a portfolio of Index-Linked Gilts is not likely to be achieved, because all the income on an equity portfolio is subject to tax up to the highest rates, while realised gains are subject to capital gains tax. Thus, the higher the tax rate of the individual, the greater the advantages of a portfolio of Index-Linked stocks during a period of rising inflation.

There is one factor I have not yet dealt with. That is the ability — and willingness — of the UK Government to honour its obligations in full. Everything I have said thus far has been based on the assumption that the authorities *will* honour their obligations to holders of UK government paper. But this has not always been the case in the past nor may it be the case in the future. In fact, the preliminary signs do not speak well for the intentions of a future British government.

One question the holder, or prospective investor, in an Index-Linked UK Government Security must consider is the extent to which the Retail Price Index will continue to represent the true trend of inflation in Britain. Not too long ago, for example, the rise in house prices, and the correspondingly high increase in mortgage payments — both components of the Retail Price Index — promoted the UK authorities to suggest removing these particular components from the Retail Price Index. They claimed it was a "non-representative" component. Since the advent of the Thatcher administration, many economic indices have been altered. The effect of this has been to make the state of the economy — and the nation —appear better than it actually was. Base dates of economic indicators have been changed. Constituents of economic indicators have been withdrawn and replaced by other constituents. In the case of Britain's unemployment calculations, no less than 22 changes have been made during the first 8 years of the Thatcher administration. Obviously, the UK authorities are likely to continue to apply their cosmetic treatment to the economy. As a consequence, the actual rate of inflation may not be what the Retail Price Index suggests it is. If not, the holder of an Index-Linked UK Gilt will not be able to protect the purchasing power of his money to the extent suggested by "indexation".

There is also another more disturbing possibility to be reckoned with. That possibility is exemplified by the fate of those who held UK 5% War Loan in 1932. When Five Per Cent War Loan was issued in 1917, for the purpose of financing World War I, it was in a climate of rising inflation and rising interest rates. It meant that provided inflation continued to rise, and interest rates fell, the authorities could easily repurchase the stock at a discount, effecting a redemption with cheap money. Initially, the stock was rescheduled for repayment in 1947, but that was later changed, and it could be repaid on three months notice any time after June 1, 1929.

The initial plan was a sound one. . . for the Government. But the authorities completely failed to foresee the events that took place over the fifteen years after the stock was issued — namely, the disappearance of inflation, the sharp fall in interest rates and the onset of the Great Depression of the 1930s.

In late 1931 there was another traditional run on the pound — a phenomenon that has been a reasonably regular occurrence for the past 130 years. In just a few months, the pound fell from a dollar rate of US$5.00 to US$3.25. The fall in the value of the pound was a response to the no less frequent practice of the UK authorities, which — when under stress — simply issue fiat money on the assumption that additional liquidity cures all ills. During summer of 1931, the Bank of England, true to current form, began injecting huge amounts of liquidity into the banking system. As a result, interest rates — which normally reflect the relationship of the supply of money to the demand for loans — fell from a level of 5% (where they stood in February 1931) — to 2½% by May 1931. By June 1931, they were 2%. As yields tumbled, investors rushed to nail down the highest returns they could. The price of the existing bonds traded on the London Stock Exchange rocketed upwards. UK Government 2½% Consols jumped 10% in a week, from 65 to 72. However, the Five Per Cent War Loan Bonds remained where they were, at par. This was because they were redeemable at par, on three months notice, anytime after the 1st June 1929.

The original plan of the UK authorities in respect of War Loan had back-fired. The massive issue of 5% War Loan, which they had assumed could be replaced by repurchasing large tranches at a discount — made possible by a rise in interest rates — appeared to be totally impossible in 1932. . . with interest rates at 2%! At the same time, due to the Depression, there was a sharp fall in government revenues, while the interest payments on the huge issue of 5% War Loan — of which over £2 billion remained outstanding — absorbed 40% of all that was being collected from income tax at the time. There was no chance of repaying the bonds in full for cash. The Government simply didn't have the funds. There was also little chance of the Government's being able to continue to finance the interest payments on this bond for any appreciable period, given the extent to which revenue was being drawn away. Nor were the government able to issue any new bonds to refinance the old ones. In order to preserve the impact of the surge in monetary growth, the authorities had to close off the issue of any new government securities to ensure that the increase in the market's borrowing power should be directed only to existing issues, and avoid dilution. So far as the 5% War Loan was concerned, the authorities could follow one path only, the path of deception. The idea was to persuade and coerce, or force if need be, existing holders of 5% War Loan to accept any alternative which would be to the greater good of the nation. . . though not necessarily to the greater good of existing holders of War Loan.

In late June 1932, Chancellor of the Exchequer Neville Chamberlain announced an offer for the conversion of the entire 5% War Loan into a new issue bearing interest at only 3½%, and with no specific maturity. In other words, investors were being asked to part with a stock that was giving them 5% per annum and a full return of capital whenever it was redeemed within the next 15 years. The stock they were being offered in return would pay no more than 3½% per annum and might never be redeemed.

Holders of the 5% War Loan were thus faced with a choice. They could accept the Chancellor's kind offer — or they would be *forced* to accept the Chancellor's offer — like it or not! Initially, in typical government propagandist fashion, the Chancellor exhorted holders of War Loan in the most heart-rending terms that converting to the new issue was a matter of patriotic duty. The government created a War Loan Conversion Publicity Bureau, which launched one of the most ambitious propaganda campaigns of any British Government at any time in history. The idea was to convince the British people in no uncertain terms that it was their duty as citizens to accept the offer. Each day the War Loan Conversion Publicity Bureau published a list of the mighty British institutions that had gladly "done their duty". The "list" was available for all to see, thereby inferring that those who did not appear were "traitors".

During the mid-summer of 1932, Chancellor Chamberlain called on the heads of the major banks to shew a good example to those members of the public reluctant to part with their 5% War Loan. All the major banks agreed, in the full knowledge of the difficulties they might suffer at the hands of the Treasury if they failed to agree. But there was one odd-man-out. That odd-man-out was Reginald McKenna, then chairman of the Midland Bank. Reginald McKenna had been Liberal Chancellor of the Exchequer from 1915-1916, and was, therefore, fully cognisant with the game that the Chancellor of the Exchequer was trying to get members of the public and institutional shareholders to play.

McKenna's refusal to co-operate with Chancellor Neville Chamberlain brought a summons from the Bank of England, where Governor Montagu Norman put further heavy pressure on McKenna, in an effort to secure his co-operation. McKenna again refused to lend the name of the Midland Bank to this coercive strategy, stating it would not be in the interests of the shareholders of the institution whose well-being was in his hands. Of course, McKenna was absolutely correct, both because of the subsequent danger to shareholders and because of his obligations to them. But his integrity was of no avail, while his tenacity probably cost him a peerage. The Bank of England had its way with Reginald McKenna in the end. The irrepressive power of legalised theft was sufficient to persuade the Midland to convert £5 million of the £30 million it held; and the Bank of England agreed to buy out the other £25 million held by the bank and do the conversion on its own — at the expense of taxpayers. While Reginald McKenna felt a strong obligation to Midland Bank shareholders, the Governor of the Bank of England felt no such obligation to the taxpayer.

Following the deal struck with Reginald McKenna, the War Loan Conversion Publicity Bureau was able to announce that all the clearing banks had converted their holdings. It was a shameful case of deliberate deceit by simple omission.

There is certainly one thing the British Government can never be accussed of — and that is underestimating the potential for imbecility on the part of British investors, whether it be in 1932 or 1987. The hoopla and fanfare surrounding the conversion game was — in the same manner as privatisation in the 1980s — a ploy designed to bedazzle and dupe the average holder of 5% War Loan. The propaganda was no less successful than that which launched the massive BP flotation in late 1987 when investors bought the shares, even though the clear downtrend in the market guaranteed them an immediate loss. The campaign for 5% War Loan Conversion was so successful that the Mounted Police had to be called out to control the crowds queueing up to exchange their old certificates for new certificates which also guaranteed an instant loss.

Thanks to all the razzle dazzle, propaganda and appeals to patriotism — along with the fact that anyone who did not formally refuse the offer was deemed to have accepted it — 92½% converted their holdings from 5% War Loan stock — redeemable in 1947 or before — to the 3½% War Loan which was irredeemable. As such, the issue need never — and doubtless never will — be repaid. At the end of the day, it has been estimated that in real terms, those who accepted the government offer in 1932 have subsequently lost more than 99% of their capital.

When it comes to Index-Linked Government Securities, that episode is worth considering. In general, whenever there is an issue of securities, that issue is designed to benefit the government responsible — but rarely, if ever, the purchaser. When 5% War Loan was issued, the government's reasoning was that the issue was bound to fall in value. War always brings inflation, or a debauching of the currency. Whichever side wins the war, the bondholder will be the loser one way or another. But on that unique occasion, following the issue of 5% War Loan, something went wrong. Instead of the bonds falling in value, in line with historical precedent, the bond remained at par value. The baffled authorities then resorted to trickery and deception.

Index-Linked Government Securities were issued by a Government which was ostensibly committed to curbing inflation. If they were successful, the value of the Index-Linked Securities would obviously stay the same, and the authorities would wind up with some cheap financing. But will that happen in reality? Suppose inflation starts to soar again, facing the authorities with the prospect of having to redeem those Index-Linked stocks at several multiples of their face value. In that case, you should not be surprised if the authorities repeat the chicanery of the 1930s. In fact — to be realistic — you should expect it!

The Winners and the Losers Moving into the Upwave

So far I have not identified anything in the way of a major investment in the true sense of the word. The return you are likely to get by following the strategy outlined so far should be adequate — and probably far greater than most investors normally achieve by pursuing most of the "recommended" strategies of a whole galaxy of so-called "advisors". It should be recognised that *my* advice so far has been intended to preserve your capital. Major investment opportunities come later! It is likely that by the end of this decade you will be given the once-in-a-lifetime opportunity to exploit the new upwave, which should be well under way by the turn of the century, when the mind-boggling, technological advances begin to yield results.

In the meantime, you must come to grips with the behaviour pattern that will emerge during the remainder of the downwave. For the plain fact is that a major period of expansion is possible only after a depression has had its purgative effect, which makes the next upwave inevitable. During the depressionary phase — and the period immediately beyond — there will naturally be Winners and Losers; and for the Losers the outcome is bound to be catastrophic. These Losers will fall into several categories — and they are all categories you must avoid. Nevertheless, it will not be that simple, because these categories are likely to appear most attractive to many people, because they cannot grasp the hard fact that the world. . . and the things in it. . . "Ain't what they used to be!"

For example, there was a time when the public had only to open their papers, switch on the TV or be button-holed by their nearest and dearest saloon-bar philosopher to be told, "Buy Now, Pay Later. It's the way to make it!" That may have been wise counsel when inflation was roaring away, but "Fings ain't what they used to be" on this front either. If you're heavily in debt today, you can be certain that you will end up a Loser — having, in many cases, lost your home on the way. So, one of the first things you should do — and today's as good a day as any — is get down to planning your personal finances. Make sure that at the head of your list of priorities you have an entry which says:

REDUCE DEBT BURDEN

The second sad fact is that certain professions and occupations are going to prove more vulnerable than most people think — especially those who belong to them. That is because the contractionary phase will affect some areas more than others. How fast this can happen may be seen from the post-Meltdown fate of some of the leading City market-makers. Even before the SEAQ computers started shuddering, and the rush for the exit began, several City firms had realised that to replace a handful of Gilts jobbers with more than a score of high-powered, highly paid, fabulously equipped market-makers was asking for trouble. But, for various reasons which seemed legitimate at the time, they did so nevertheless. There were some in the City who were equally prepared to allow other aspects of Big Bang, the privatisation craze and the sheer momentum of the long bull market to go to their heads too. The more vulnerable occupations and professions will include fine art and antique dealers, auctioneers, estate agents, restauranteurs, champagne bar proprietors, as well as stockbrokers, commodity dealers and others of that ilk, which the luxury trades were hoping to serve.

If you too happen to be engaged in these professions or occupations, think about changing your job, and learning another trade. Should you feel like owning a cab or driving a milk-waggon, best get ready now. All things considered, driving a taxi or milk cart is a far more respectable occupation than many with a more up-market job description — like Head of Sales Division or Broker. The personality, enterprise and mental agility required in the apparently humbler callings may be very different from what you're used to. But it doesn't mean they are any less demanding. Remember, you will have to "do the knowledge" before you're allowed anywhere near a cab; and you will certainly have to persuade the dairy that you are neither over-educated and over-qualified, nor the kind who'll quit the moment a "proper" job comes along. In any case, there must be several hundred taxi-drivers in the Metropolis alone who are already thinking of giving up the Hackney Carriage trade before it gives them up!

When it comes to investment, there are some areas which should be avoided as diligently as one would avoid AIDS. I am thinking of *objets d'art*, antiques, French wine and other (especially foreign) "collectibles". Beware of local authority loans and anything prefixed by the word "Equity" — starting with the Equity market and market-related investments. These include Equity-linked insurance policies, especially those used in conjunction with an endowment mortgage. Beware also of publications — especially the kind which reach you because your bank, or some other once-discreet establishment, has given its mailing list to the fraternity who offer you everything from instant, total gratification of all four wishes to A CHANCE TO WIN A MAJOR PRIZE! ! !

The disturbing fact that so many level-headed individuals fall victim to the salesman (or sales-harpie), working from a script, should be sufficient to set the alarm-bells jangling. But it isn't — and probably never will be! So beware once more! And be wary too of any investment advisor who steers you in the direction of *any form of trading or speculation*. Steer clear of investment which relies on natural resources, or is related in any way to natural resources. By this I mean not only firms handling and transporting basic raw materials, but manufacturers of agricultural machinery, or suppliers to agriculture and the oil industry. Remember what oil — and building North Sea rigs — was supposed to do for Aberdeen! And what it actually did for the Granite City. As one Aberdonian put it:

> "They came, they saw, they conquered. They were going to make us rich! Then market conditions changed, they went off. . . and we were left with what? Granite Chips with Everything!"

The Iron Rule remains that no investment — no share — can be safe and profitable if the underlying industrial or commercial asset is collapsing. Nor can national or global averages tell us anything about the prospects for a particular enterprise. Except, as I have said, that certain industries and enterprises are bound to be among the Losers.

If you're still nursing an equity portfolio, you're going to find that the really big losses come from shares in companies which were originally boosted by inflation. They are likely to become non-competitive when the bubble deflates. The same degree of caution should be employed over shares bought during the first phase of the stock market collapse, in the latter part of 1987 — when a great number of people were loudly proclaiming, "We've hit bottom!" Also vulnerable are highly-geared companies with a debt-laden balance sheet. Shares in this type of company are likely to fall much faster than the equity market as a whole, even though they may be counted as "Blue Chips". Companies which attract a large following on the grounds that they are "asset rich" must also be avoided. Some analysts — to judge by past experience — will continue doggedly promoting such shares throughout every phase of the bear market. These shares, they claim, are "cheap", because the price is at (or below) "tangible asset value". Unhappily, in the difficult conditions ahead, we must consider what is likely to happen to the value of those tangible assets. (That is something those dogged analysts will tend to shrink from doing; almost as though it would be the acme of bad taste for them to enquire into such matters.)

I have no hesitation in saying that asset values are a poor recommendation, since the value of those assets is likely to fall even more than the company's shares. Although you may find the former lagging the latter until realisation time.

The "safe as houses" concept is likely to prevail for several years yet. But a house is a home, and should be maintained for its utility value; not for any other reason. Above all, do not speculate on your home. If you have accommodation in excess of your requirements, which you are holding on to for investment reasons, my best advice is to sell while you can. Whatever you spend on your home may well enrich your lifestyle, but it will neither enhance your investment prospects, nor improve your solvency potential. There is, above all, one fact which those buying a house as an investment tend to forget — a house has to be maintained. This can be quite expensive, and will not be greatly reduced by the fact that you do not intend to live in it.

In the miscellaneous "highly vulnerable" category, are countries with high external debt denominated in US dollars; international commodity cartels; non-UK government money-market funds; advertising activities, and any business which might be under-capitalised. Investing in almost any area can be injurious to your wealth. But exposure to one of the preceding areas could prove terminal.

Notwithstanding the warning I have given, it should be borne in mind that there will always be a number of businesses and individuals who will survive. It would be absurd to suggest otherwise. Indeed, there will be some who will positively flourish. That was one of the lessons of the 1930s. In my view, the Winners during the next few years will be those who are prudent and cautious, saving and husbanding their cash savings. Businesses operating with the minimum of borrowing should also emerge as Winners. Producers of proprietary brands — where elasticity of demand and competition do not prevent their raising prices when necessary — should be among the more fortunate. So should firms which can raise productivity, contain costs and maintain their profits by means of a higher turnover, avoiding the need to raise prices.

Professions offering the best opportunities in the period ahead will be those in research and development, particularly those in new product development who are capable at the same time of developing a market for their new lines.

Marketing and production people should do well. So should importers of goods where price reductions will produce cost benefits. Those skilled, and qualified, in "business efficiency" and quality control should be in ever increasing demand, as should those in specialist education — whether it be continuing education at business school level for professional people and experienced executives, or teaching trade skills. In general the period ahead will be fruitful for those venture capitalists and entrepreneurs capable of exploiting opportunities pragmatically — when the time is right — without being steered off course by mere wishful thinking.

The biggest winners among the public will be those who hold high-quality, fixed-interest investments; those who adopt a policy of strict family budgeting; and those with low debts, high savings and jobs in a stable area. People who rent their homes, or have variable-rate mortgages, should also do well; as should pensioners and others on fixed incomes. In general, the prospects are good for anyone willing to adopt a prudent, conservative stance, whether in their lives or their investments.

There you have it: a guide to membership of the only two investment communities inside the Gulag. Do, please, bear in mind that if you fail to qualify for the Winners' enclosure, you will automatically find yourself in the overcrowded Losers' compound. You've been shewn how to become a Winner by prudent, cautious investment — and a firm refusal to believe anyone who says that his (or her) dearest wish is to see you rich. There's no need to tell you how to join the Losers — you'll find all the advice you need in the editorial columns as well as in the half-page Ads; to say nothing of the sales literature that pours through your letterbox masquerading as "Objective Counselling" or "Professional Analysis".

At this point, let me wish you well. But not "Good Luck." You're not gambling. . . remember?

Chapter Fourteen

2020 VISION

Now, you may not believe this, but essentially, I'm an optimist. I believe that most of our industrialised society — with the possible exception of Britain — will turn its back on the hyper-inflationary route to the Gulag. Through progressive disinflation and deflation, the coming depression will run its course and our civilisation will emerge triumphant — stronger and with a more certain future than ever before. The potential of the West may not be so great as that of the East, but I truly believe the achievements for the 2½ decades from the mid-1990s through the year 2020 will far exceed anything man on this planet has ever experienced.

The most painful part of the prelude to the next Upwave is likely to be the period 1988 through 1991. Following the trough of the depression — which I judge will take place *circa* 1991, the world economy will probably bump along for a few years. But what follows can already be forecast with a reasonable degree of certainty on the strength of the long-term empirical evidence. The decade of the 1990s is likely to see a boom, just like the boom that followed the Great Depression of the 1930s. On this occasion the momentum of that boom will outstrip anything seen before. It will be such that the technological benefits to mankind are probably beyond our comprehension at this moment, just as the possibility that we might one day succeed in sending a rocket to the moon was beyond the comprehension of those who experienced the 1930s.

A depression, or any major economic contraction, is the direct outcome of the expansion that precedes it. The potential for depression is inherent in the very nature of expansion, especially in the exceptional growth of debts upon which all expansions climb. The realisation of that potential inevitably follows from the resulting rise in real interest rates, the growth in budget deficits across the globe, the over-expansion of productive capacity and the general decline in corporate profitability which is the end result. The effect of a depression is to correct the imbalances in the system that have accumulated during the phase of expansion. Ultimately a level of dis-equilibrium is reached when expansion is no longer possible, and contraction becomes inevitable. As debts becomes self-liquidating through repayment, defalcation, bankruptcy and other means, and while the counter-productive forces of industry weaken, the stage is set for an upsurge of expansion which builds and develops in just the same inexorable self-feeding manner as the Downwave.

The Great Depression of the 1930s and the subsequent recovery, provide a wonderful model of cause and effect which can be of inestimable value in helping us to anticipate the likely events of the 1990s and beyond. It would be unreasonable to expect history to repeat itself with any precision — either in terms of fixed periodicity, repetitive sequences or the virtual duplication of events and circumstances (as I have demonstrated in *The Downwave*) — there has been very little change in the structural repetition in the world's economy over the centuries. This is essentially a function of human behaviour patterns, which have in many ways survived unaltered since primitive man hunted for food with a club, and used the same club to overpower his fellow men.

What does the history of the Great Depression tell us? Most people associate the Great Depression with the "Crash of 1929". So far as the "Crash of 1987" is concerned, most individuals did not associate that "crash" with a possible depression, since there appeared so little evidence that depression might be around the corner. There we may identify two major errors in judgment. The first was the assumption that the "Crash of '29" was a response to the forces of depression that were beginning to mount and were available for all to see. Nothing could be further from the truth. The second error in judgment was the assumption that since no signs of depression accompanied the onset of the "Crash of 1987", that "crash" did not signal a depression.

Long ago the publication of the monumental work by John Kenneth Galbraith, *The Great Crash, 1929* established him as an expert on catastrophes. In his more recent work *Economics in Perspective: A Critical History,* he actually calls into question the title chosen for his previous post-mortem study. Severe though it was, according to Galbraith, the 1929 crash did not hold the potential for disaster that was present in 1987. Like the Titanic, the autumn of 1929 saw the markets take their fatal plunge with style. The best minds pronounced the market as "stale" at the top, and "in need of help" at the bottom.

The true significance and economic consequences of the crash of '29 were not fully appreciated until some time later. Just as the economic message of the "Crash of 1987" is unlikely to be appreciated until the turn of the decade, it was probably not until 1931 that it began to dawn on most people that the sharp recession that had begun several months after the "Crash of 1929" was the start of something very different. It was more than merely a standard business cycle contraction, attended, as some of the others had been, by a financial panic.

Circa 1931, the feelings of most people were those of fear and deep concern. By 1933, when the Great Depression was reaching its nadir, the attitude of people in Europe and the United States was almost universally defeatist. The fantastic growth era of the "Roaring Twenties" was by then no more than a nostalgic memory.

"Everyone we talked to, in the schools, in the universities, would have little vision of what this great country and its resources could do," declared David Kennedy, reminiscing on the state of affairs in the United States trough of the Great Depression. In retrospect, most men of standing are agreed that governments were powerless to prevent a depression, and subsequently pull their individual nations out of the pit once the depression had taken hold. In 1933, David Kennedy was with the Federal Reserve in Washington and was to become Treasury Secretary under David Nixon. Both he and Raymond Moley, Truman's right-hand man, were quite clear that despite all the New Deal programmes in the US and Europe, full recovery from the Great Depression did not come until 1940. "The war got us out of it," said Kennedy, "not New Deal policies".

If we confine ourselves only to the statistical economy — which would be an injustice to human behaviour — there is little evidence to identify the terminal juncture of the Great Depression before 1940. The apparently universal gloom that continued through the late 1930s seems to have been justified. It was certainly shared by those in the highest office of government in both the United States and Europe. Nevertheless few world leaders were prepared to admit to a feeling of desperation before their respective electorates at the time.

What I am referring to are the workings of human psychology rather than statistical economics. For the practical purposes that concern me — and *should* concern you — the universally accepted attitude during the later 1930s was the wrong one, as it usually is. Those who fell victim to the gloom of the masses deprived themselves of some of the greatest business and investment opportunities the world had seen up to that time. Firstly, the worst of the Great Depression was over by late 1932. Furthermore, improvement in the economy was visible in 1933, although most failed to recognise the factors, so imbued were they with the misery and desolation of the earlier years. By 1935, the deflationary forces that ravaged the global economy during the depression year had completed their work. In 1933, the slump in corporate earnings was reversed. By early 1934, there was evidence of a strong uptrend in corporate earnings. Most believed it would be purely temporary, just as they had believed the decline in corporate earnings during 1930 to be temporary.

By the mid-1930s, both commodity prices and retail prices were heading upwards again. Mild inflation had begun to appear. This was dismissed out-of-hand as meaningless, in the same way that the disinflation of the late 1970s was dismissed as meaningless. During the 1970s, the Western world was convinced that inflation was the normal way of life, likely to continue in perpetuity. During the mid-1930s, at the terminal juncture of the down-trend, the majority were convinced that deflation was the normal way of life — and, therefore, would continue in perpetuity! In retrospect — with 2020 vision by hindsight — we can see that the purge in the global economy between 1929 and 1932 was so drastic that the conditions for the ensuing

Upwave had already been laid in three (admittedly not very short) years. Now, let me engage in some 2020 vision. . . but this time with foresight.

Beyond The Downwave and into The Upwave

To face the future requires courage. Courage means acting when you're afraid to act. There is no courage unless you are frightened. But, it is very difficult for any politician in a partisan, take-it-easy, media-dominated consumer society to explain the truth and inform people of the perils that lie ahead, given the multitude of vested interests whose survival is dependent upon repression of the truth. The reason that history repeats itself over and over and over, is because of the apathetic tolerance of deception shared by so many easy-going men and women, who are content to remain oblivious to the lesson of the past. It is, indeed, unfortunate that the masses will neither be shielded from the intense social and financial dislocations that lie ahead, nor will they be given the opportunity of benefiting from the great achievements that also lie ahead. Yet those who face what may be perceived as adversity — decisively, courageously and firmly — are least likely to encounter the full force of that adversity. In the end they will be rewarded beyond their wildest dreams.

When it comes to planning for the future, the structural framework of past experience during the transition from the collapse to early boom of the 1930s — if adjusted to meet contemporary practicalities — will assist in the formulation of new operational guidelines. We must all have a workable plan compatible with the financial, social and economic requirements of the next few years. I will now try to pick up the thread of where I left off in *The Downwave* and attempt to fine-tune the strategy drawn up when I wrote that book five years ago.

In 1982, when I was completing the manuscript, it was my view that sometime between 1982 and 1985 a recession would begin, and that it would lead to a worse business slump than that during the 1979-1982 recession. I wrote that the slump:

> " . . . will be accompanied by a severe panic and it may be such a deep slump that it takes a decade to catch up to the levels of prosperity that were obtained prior to it."

In the original work, I explored the background to the long period of contraction that follows the long period of expansion so that the reader would be able to recognise the essential component of the Downwave which is always characterised by deep depression. As I explained, the Downwave itself began in the early part of the 1970s following the peak in commodity price inflation that had occurred around that period. By the time my book was published, the global economy had experienced the expected post-peak inflation and had passed the terminal juncture of the secondary prosperity. Emerging as it has from the first recession of the contractionary phase of the cycle, it had yet to experience the crisis, panic and deep depression that signal the terminal juncture of the long-wave cycle itself.

I stressed that economic activity associated with the contraction phase of the long-wave cycle would not move downwards in a straight line. Readers were warned to expect several interruptions to the contractionary phase of economic recovery. I also warned that such periods would be treacherously deceptive. Just as in the past, businessmen failed to recognise the vast structural changes in the world economy, treating the period of mediocre economic performance since my book was published as the type of prosperity associated with the economic achievements of the expansionary phase of the cycle. Following the 1979-1982 recession, most thought the world was the same as it had been in the 1950s and 1960s —which is precisely what I had expected. I had said in my book they would be wrong. As the Crash of 1987 has demonstrated, they *were* wrong. In *The Downwave*, I also said that the long-term plans that businessmen were likely to make would be woefully inappropriate. As the events of the years that have passed since my book was published have clearly shewn, the long-term plans that most people have made are going to be woefully inappropriate, and inadequate for the conditions that lie immediately ahead.

It is endemic to the major structural changes that follow the inflation peak that the type of enterprise that prospered under inflation will no longer prosper during a period of disinflation. That was another fact which I pointed out in *The Downwave*. Property development and investment were cited as notable examples. Since 1982, the "collectibles" such as stamps, diamonds, gem stones, gold, silver, etc., have fallen sharply and are no longer viable investments — exactly as I forecast. Although residential property after the 1987 crash was only just about to approach its demise, commerical property rents, prices and levels had yet to approach the euphoric state that characterised the early 1970s — despite the financial inflation that occurred in other areas in previous years.

In *The Downwave*, I focused on the types of businesses that would withstand the contractionary forces, and might even prove profitable during the decade of correction. I also pinpointed those types of investment which would help the individual to protect his capital, and, hopefully, achieve a modest growth.

The period ahead would be one of dramatic changes in the economic, social and cultural environment. I told people they would have to accept and cope with strong shifts in religious beliefs and moral values as well as possibly disturbing changes in social behaviour.

At an investment level, I demonstrated how the investor could cope with the upheaval through the success of the investment policy I followed with the Beckman International Capital Accumulator after *The Downwave* was published. During the three years that followed, the Beckman International Capital Accumulator grew in value by 152% to £50 million, outperforming most unit trusts whose risk profile was appreciably higher. During the final speculative blow-off in the equity market in the UK and elsewhere, the low-risk constituents of the Beckman International Capital Accumulator did not perform as well as the equity list for a little over a year. But after the "Crash of 1987", the Beckman International Capital Accumulator stood at number 4 in its category of fifty comparable funds, outperforming the equity averages by approximately 35%, and outperforming the average Unit Trust by approximately 30%.

On the moral, religious and social front, we saw by the end of 1987 a strong Christian ethic developing among the US electorate, who are sending to Washington people known to subscribe to this Christian ethic. In fact, so dominant has this traditional religious movement become that Peter Jay, in his book *Apocalypse 2000*, cites the possibility that a religious fanatic could be elected to the Presidency of the United States. So far as the morals of our society are concerned, the dreaded AIDS virus has induced a change in sexual mores for those not willing previously to moderate their promiscuous sexual behaviour of their own volition.

I wrote that the period following the publication of my book — which would include the phase of panic and crisis — would produce many fortune-building opportunities. The type of investment climate I was expecting would, I felt, be one in which people who bought bonds on margin, sold short, bought put options, sold naked calls and such, would be able to amass — and compound — profits faster than they had ever dreamed possible in any market. The bull market in bonds that followed publication of *The Downwave* produced precisely the opportunities and rewards I predicted. Those who bought debt warrants — an area which I pioneered in the post-publication period — trebled and quadrupled their money several times over in a few short months during 1986.

At the same time, I purposely avoided elaborating on (and advocating) really high risk strategies. I shall continue to do so. During the worst bear market most can conceive — that of the Great Crash of 1929 — those who chanced their arm and sold short lost fortunes, as did those who were holding on to their shares. The fact is that most people are not able to handle the high level of risk associated with the more refined professional strategies. Most attempts made by amateur investors to ape the professionals have ulimately proved counter-productive — if not disastrous — deflecting the amateur investor's capital assets when he most needs them. The majority who — out of impatience and a desire for instant gratification — attempt these grandstand, speculative plays will lose large chunks of their savings. During the Downwave, with its treacherously deceptive, wild and volatile swings, the principle objective for the individual investor should be to preserve his or her capital — in both nominal and purchasing-power terms. It would be very unwise to attempt a get-rich-quick strategy, because of the many difficulties that are likely to crop up. Apart from that, investors want to preserve their capital, and save their energies for the long, easy bull markets that will follow during the Upwave. During the remainder of the Downwave, most individuals would be well advised to adopt an attitude of acceptance, being content to protect their existing capital. Experience suggests that those who try to get rich slowly but surely. . . probably will! The stock market crash and attendant recession will run its course, however much the unwise, and the innocent, may try to prevent it. Needless to say, if you dissipate your energies and waste your capital by engaging in high-risk, speculative ventures, before the next opportunity for sound, profitable investment presents itself, you will not be in a position to take advantage of it when it finally arrives. That would be a pity, since the business and investment opportunities will be the most rewarding that you are ever likely to see again during the rest of your lifetime.

Most individuals regard the future as nothing more than a continuation of the present moment; their greatest desire being to spend their business and investment lives in a permanent state of post-coital, orgasmic bliss. People seem to forget — or merely ignore — the inescapable lifestyle of their own species. Like birth and death, climax and release, the whole cycle of growth and contraction must be recognized and accepted, if we are to plot a realistic approach to the next stage of evolution.

Western man seems to have been trapped by what could be described as left-brain linear logic. It has become all the more serious since he will frequently *claim* to be employing "left-brain linear logic", when he is actually shewing a cavalier disregard for the rules. For example, you may hear someone say:

"When the weather's cold, I go down with 'flu, and it's cold today! I'm bound to get it."

That sounds as though he's stating categorically that the 'flu will invariably follow the cold. However, when you ask him if this is so, he says:

"No! I merely pointed out that when I've had the 'flu, then it's frequently been cold. And today is a cold day."

It does not matter to those who practise formal logic whether the statement is true or false. All the logician is concerned with is the *validity* of the argument that follows. If the man was arguing that *every time* it was (by an acceptable definition) cold he got the 'flu, then *logically* he could have gone on to say:

"Today is cold. Therefore I shall have 'flu."

But in effect he only said:

"Sometimes when it is cold, I get 'flu. It is cold today. . ."

Therefore, all he could claim — so long as he observed the strict rules of formal logic — is that this *could* be one of the cold days when he WILL get 'flu. Or, to put it formally:

". . . therefore I MAY get the 'flu."

This is not so "off-beam" as you might think. What about the man — or woman — who says:

"Usually when the Chancellor says the prospects for the economy are good, the market stops falling! He said that about the economy only yesterday. . . therefore all the papers say the market is BOUND to recover."

Formal logic requires that had the Chancellor proved right *every* time — rather than *more often than not* — anyone could validly infer that the speech referred to *necessarily* guaranteed that the market would rise. Nevertheless that is precisely what the market may do. . . if enough people are swayed by the Chancellor's speech. Or — put it another way — if the Chancellor has sufficient impact on market sentiment. Logical improprieties are frequently allowed to slip by in our desire to prove, or have proved, what we would like to *see* proved. Lobbyists frequently employ such tactics, quoting what at first glance appear to be challenging facts or unchallengeable statistics. The *Financial Times (Weekend FT, 12/12/87)* provides an admirable example of this approach. In an article on what he saw as "signs of a meeting of minds between conservationists and the World Bank", Christian Tyler wrote:

> "Anyone who has watched the great pillars of smoke towering above the Amazon jungle or gone on hands and knees to count the number of wild life species threatened by a dam, is bound to be pessimistic."

Read carefully, the author is clearly inviting the reader to become pessimistic on the strength of those few lines, without the necessity of watching the pillars of smoke "towering above the Amazonian jungle". It is left to the reader to accept the argument that:

> "A new dam always displaces wild life. It is bad to displace wild life. Therefore all new dams are bad."

Whether it is, in fact, worse to displace wild life than to allow men, their families, their crops and their animals to be deprived of the benefits the dam would bring is not questioned for one moment. For the purpose of the argument it is already assumed that displacing wild life is "bad", and new dams have a "bad" effect by displacing wild life. You and I might well challenge what the author, or the conservationists he is quoting, writes. But that would not concern the logician.

Indeed, the argument could have been set out in very different terms:

> "A new dam is always covered in raspberry jam.
> "Objects so covered are good.
> "Therefore all new dams are good."

You and I might repeat that the whole thing was a piece of nonsense. Raspberry jam, indeed! But the argument set out in those terms is just as acceptable as the first version. Why, you may ask, should it be necessary to go down "on hands and knees" to count the threatened species. To adopt such a posture when assessing the risk to elephant or Bengal tigers would be as absurd as it would be dangerous. But we don't have to be very bright to understand *why* the argument had been set out in that way, and *why* that particular imagery had been chosen.

It stands out even more clearly when we read on:

> "The raw statistics of man's devastation of nature are impressive. Some Indian village women are walking 1400 km a year, the distance from Delhi to Calcutta, to forage for firewood."

Unless we are extraordinarily thick, we can see perfectly well why the example of the Indian village women has been introduced. What does it actually tell us?

> "Some Indian village women. . ."

(Not ALL Indian women, you notice.)

> . . . forage for firewood."

(That means they set off from the village and walk some distance in order to collect wood for the fire.)

That is not in itself all that astonishing. We can watch itinerant agricultural workers in Greece collecting wood for the fire; and throughout North Africa and the Middle East, Bedouin women walk out into what looks like a vast, empty wilderness and come back with huge piles of camelthorn on their backs.

In the case of the Indian village it is stressed that each year these women walk the equivalent of the distance "from Delhi to Calcutta". It's the same kind of measurement as: "if all the economists in the world were six feet tall, and laid end from end. . ."

But let's return to the facts of the case. *Some* Indian village women are "walking 1400 km a year. . . to forage for firewood." That, I calculate, means that they have to walk just under 27 km each week. Allowing them one rest day in seven, they are having to walk just over 4.9 km a day! No further comment is necessary — except to say that it takes more than the simple application of the rules of formal logic to reduce most highly coloured and emotionally loaded arguments to size. Although it will not take us any further.

That is where the dialectic method, introduced by the German philosopher Hegel — and mishandled by the Marxists — comes into its own. Whatever one may think of Marxism (or of Hegel for that matter), the dialectic has two stellar virtues. It recognises change and, over and above that, *explains* change.

Human events are like human organisations. They do not proceed or develop in a straight line, as adherence to linear logic alone might suggest. It would be nonsense to attempt to project (or predict) the future by merely taking a straight line that has been drawn against a time frame and extending it to infinity. True, this is what many a salesman or politician has been known to do. But anyone with practical experience of life knows that you cannot even extend that line for a few *minutes* without making a two-dimensional claim which (as any formal logician will tell you) rests on a familiar fallacy:

Post Hoc. . . the line in the time frame;

Ergo Propter Hoc. . . the extrapolation.

Commonsense, a derivative of social *mores* and experience, tells us that life is punctuated by crises, turning points, changes of direction and — above all — the unexpected. The dialectic accommodates this aspect of life by first of all establishing the *thesis*. For example, that it's a good thing to be a stockbroker. He holds a respected position in society, and earns well. He has to have ability and connections. . . so (being practical souls) we decide to explore the connections. . . clinging firmly to our *thesis* that the best thing to become at this time is a stockbroker. The more we explore the problems and the opportunities, the more it looks as though our original plan has run up against a series of unavoidable obstacles. A new, but contrary set of plans and arguments demand our attention. We are in the second stage of the dialectic — in which we are forced to take into account the *anti-thesis*.

Still holding to our original aims, we seek to measure our thesis against the anti-thesis. . . the *anti-thesis* which has now taken shape. At some stages, we shall have to come to reach a decision. Do we go ahead. . . regardless? Or are we persuaded by the opposing arguments to give up the whole thing? From now on we shall be weighing facts and probabilities, rather than arguments. So Formal Logic will take us no further. But we *must* go further, if we are to resolve the issue. Since we are operating in the real world, we must eventually reach the third and final stage of the dialectic. . . the stage of synthesis.

It does not mean that we shall necessarily be driven to compromise. Indeed, it may be that we make a discovery along the way. . . we stumble across a fresh card to play. . . one we never dreamed would be possible. It could be — to return to our example — that we find the stockbroking profession is overcrowded; and that there are some extremely brilliant young men and women fighting to be aboard. Not so easy after all! Then we remember we have an uncle in a New York firm, which has a London office! As we approach the final stage of synthesis, we shall take this into account. We *shall* become stockbrokers after all. Because we now know we are in a position to play the Joker in the Pack. . . "Our Uncle is Senior Vice-President!"

Clearly the dialectic represents a far more practical *modus operandi* than left-brain linear logic. It allows us to hold to our original plan, while we discover what lies "out there" in the unknown territory we shall have to cross. . . without being driven off course. Adopting the method of the dialectic is to recognise, as John Kenneth Galbraith did, in *The Great Crash*, that:

"The roots of the crash were in the boom that preceded it."

The succession of panics and crashes which have punctuated history — Tulipomania, the South Sea Bubble, the Chicago Property Crash, the Great Depression, the Secondary Banking Panic and the Crash of 1987 — were merely events, momentary spasms marking the terminal juncture of a particular economic period. . . the anti-thesis, you could say, which in the end would lead to a fresh synthesis. The revolving nature of the process makes us realise how absurd it would be to claim that the world today is even within striking distance of the *absolute* terminal experience. We have merely reached the termination of one particular economic period, and the useful life of much of the technology appropriate to that phase. There has been astonishing progress in many fields — especially in scientific discovery and technical application. . . all the way down the century from the electric tramcar through the jet engine and *Sputnik* to the ultimate in manned space exploration. There have been some frightening disasters; along with a hitherto unimaginable improvement in day-to-day living conditions. So much so, that today we call "disaster" what our grandparents would have accepted as a "normal hazard." Yet we still have come nowhere near the pinnacle of man's achievement as we approach the end of the 20th century. There is a glorious 21st century immediately beyond the Downwave.

It is in the nature of mankind, after the period of anti-thesis during the latter part of the 20th century, that evolution will resume its rising path for the three or four decades of the approaching Upwave. Nevertheless, those three to four decades will bear the imprint of the remaining years of the Downwave, as surely as Galbraith realised that the mid-30s crash was rooted in the boom which preceded it. During the years of continuing correction ahead, our economic way of life will change quite markedly. It will be shaped by three major influences: technology, genetic engineering and the service industries. They will deeply influence — if they do not dominate — both the accumulation and distribution of wealth. These factors will also determine the framework for society in general, as well as the investment climate specifically. Therefore, the most important requirement for businessmen and individuals alike will be to prepare psychologically to meet the technology-driven change.

Technology is probably the single most important ingredient in the dynamic of change and development. But technological achievement must be kept focussed and relevant. The questions technology can answer, and the problems it can solve, appear unlimited. The questions technology *should* answer are peculiar to each individual phase of the business cycle. If we are to determine the proper role for technology in our future, we must first ask the right questions. In general people have allowed themselves to be lulled into complacency over the role of technology, making the quite unwarranted assumption that technological advance will solve *all* problems. Others, who have viewed the current pace of technological development, conclude that the stream of new discoveries and developments has ruled out the possibility of recession. They have come to expect far more from technology in the short term than it could possibly deliver. Putting new technology to work calls for extremely large allocations of capital, knowhow and suitably trained manpower. Besides, the time scale of investment of all kinds may run to ten or twenty years. Moreover it may just not be possible for companies to achieve commercial profitability — which is all the public often sees — although an ever wider range of new technology is theoretically available to them.

It should be remembered that many of the apparently new technological options capable of averting depression are no more than spin-offs from old technology. Often they have reached development saturation in terms of their contribution to future economic growth. Currently there are technologies under development which will be the harbingers of the next wave of expansion. But most of them are still on the drawing board, and nowhere near ready for the full commercial exploitation of their as yet unproven potential.

If advancing technology *were* ever capable of reducing the impact of depression there could have been no better time to reduce the ravages of severe economic contraction than during the 1930s. The bulk of all the major inventions, which were to power the tremendous post-war expansion had been firmly in place for quite some time: the automobile from 1887; the airplane from 1903; the automatic telephone exchange from 1891; radio from 1905; the radio telephone from 1906; the vacuum cleaner and also the washing machine from 1907; the tape recorder from 1899; the punched card system — the grand-daddy of the modern computer — had been in place since 1884. In 1929, rocket development first began. Yet, due to the economic circumstances at the time, none of these innovations was able to shew its full potential.

The telephone needed a network before it could be of any real use to the subscriber. But it couldn't create a network until it had already won its subscribers. During the 1930s, the public were concerned with food on their tables, not telephones. Television suffered from a similar chicken and egg problem. It needed a broad programme choice to acquire mass consumers, yet it needed mass consumers to justify a programme choice. Financially speaking, the breakthrough in unit price depended on mass consumption, while mass consumption was directly contingent upon a breakthrough in unit price. In consequence, the exploration of the technologies available during the 1930s was muted by the economic constriction of that period. Global society had to spend ten years in a barren economic wilderness before the commercial exploitation of these and many more innovations was possible.

In any case, what technology is perceived to be capable of achieving, and what it is likely to achieve will probably bear little relationship to each other. There is a considerable hiatus between invention and its exploitation to a point at which the invention makes a significant impact on economic growth. There are so many detours and modifications along the way to the extent that the precise impact on future economic growth is wholly unpredictable during the early development stages of any new technology. Forecasters have demonstrated an absolutely abysmal record, not only at determining the type of economic impact a new technology is likely to have, but also at anticipating the extent to which these innovations are likely to be modified and applied. From the floppy wood and tatty cloth invention of the Wright Brothers in 1903 to the huge metal jumbo jets of the 1970s, capable of carrying hundreds of people faster than the speed of sound, there has been a conceptual gap that very few have ever bridged. It is commonplace that forecasting institutes have rarely — if ever — succeeded in predicting one single major technological innovation. Probably the most basic error lies in ever thinking it was likely that they could.

So, as we look into the future, we might as well do so in the spirit of a game. Face it! Predicting the future is as much fun as any other pastime that you can indulge in — and still keep your clothes on! It's also a game which helps to stretch the mind. For most of the more significant events of the coming Upwave will look highly unlikely, viewed from our present standpoint, at the close of the 1980s. The kind of innovation which most people are capable of conceptualising here and now would not have the necessary impact to power three decades of prosperity. Besides, when there is an almost infinite number of "improbables" — and only a few likely options — we may be certain that most of the developments which will eventually take place will prove to have been on today's list of "improbables". That seems to me a logical certainty. For the purpose of simplicity, the rules of the game we are going to play call for the plain future tense. . . absolutely no conditionals.

The Fifth Wave

Between the start of the Industrial Revolution and today, there have been four major waves of expansion, and three corresponding waves of contraction. Today, at the close of 1987, the infrastructure of the global economy is experiencing the fourth wave of contraction, which will be the precursor to the next long-term expansionary phase. As I outlined in *The Downwave*, a complete long-term cycle of expansion and contraction covers a period of approximately 50-60 years, with the expansionary phase lasting 30-40 years. The periods of contraction, therefore, tend to last 15-20 years. Within this long-term framework, there are periods of recession and recovery, which are the normal functions of the self-correcting nature of the business cycles. These must be considered as inconsequential in terms of the underlying forces of expansion or contraction.

The fifth wave of expansion is likely to start in the early 1990s, continuing through to the year 2020 — and possibly beyond. According to many long-term cyclical theorists whose work has stood the test of time, the propellant for periods of long term expansion is technological innovation. An economy will continue to expand for so long as the technological innovations that powered the expansion are capable of making a positive contribution. When the economic contribution of these new technologies has reached saturation point, a long-term period of contraction ensues until new technologies are introduced. These must be capable of generating a fresh expansion, as did the older technologies which launched the growth phase of the preceding period of expansion.

According to Jay W. Forrester, who was responsible for the development of the Systems Dynamics National Model at the Massachusetts Institute of Technology:

> "There are times during which technical innovation should focus on improving products already developed, and times to prepare daring new products for the future. There are times for technical innovation, and times for managerial innovation. There are times offering opportunities within a corporation, and times imposing threats from outside. There are times for innovation in science and engineering, and times for innovation in society and government.
>
> There seems to be an alternating tide in economic affairs spanning some 45 to 60 years, that determines the climate for innovation. A typical 50-year pattern of long-term economic change includes a decade of depression, 30 years of technological innovation and active capital investment, and finally, ten years of economic uncertainty while the growth forces of the past subside."

If we apply Jay W. Forrester's analysis to our own time, we can equate his 30 years of expansion with the period following World War II. The "ten years of economic uncertainty while the growth forces of the past subside" would clearly be the decade of the 1970s. Since 1980, the global economy has experienced a "controlled depression" which by 1987 was seen to be heading for a "panic phase". . . similar to that of the 1930s. Sometime during the early 1990s, the "decade of depression" will have run its course, and the world will once again be ready for the commercial development of technologies that will herald another 30 years of expansion. It takes no great stretch of the imagination to realise that those who participate in the early stages of this 30 years of expansion will reap the greatest rewards.

Professor Jay W. Forrester sheds considerable light on the technological sequence of the long term pattern of economic behaviour in an article entitled *Changing Economic Patterns* published in *Technology Review* by the MIT. Forrester's computerised study is based on an econometric model containing fifteen industrial sectors — including consumer durables, capital equipment, energy, agriculture, public housing and building construction. Forrester makes it clear that his intention was to construct a model which would be a computer translation of the knowledge people have about the organisation structure and operating policies surrounding their daily activities. Such a model is designed as a role-playing replica of the *real* economy — as opposed to merely the *statistical* economy. The model should behave like the real economy, generating growth, fluctuations, shifts in population between sectors, inflation, deflation, unemployment and other everyday phenomena of the real world which reflect the behaviour of mankind on this planet. Although I have never had much time for econometric models — having had considerable experience in the total inadequacy of most of them — the model developed by Forrester finally comes to grips with the foundation of economic activity. . . the fears, hopes and desires of our species, together with the dynamics of change.

Forrester's model includes three of the major business cycles, the short-term (3 to 7 year) cycle, the medium-term (15 to 25 year) cycle, and the long-term (45 to 60 year) cycle. Forrester believes that the longer-term cycle is the most important in explaining overall economic behaviour and has the most predictive value, particularly in corporate planning. Forrester writes:

> "The long wave manifests itself as a massive expansion of the capital sectors followed by a relatively rapid collapse in their output. It is usually described as a peak of economic activity followed by a 10-year plateau, then a drop into a depression period for about a decade, and a long climb over some 30 years to the next peak. Long wave behaviour seems to account for the great depressions of the 1830s, 1880s and 1930s, and it may be of critical importance in explaining our present economic situation. Forces arising from the long wave seem to explain many present economic cross-currents, raising the spectre of another depression period in the 1980s."

Forrester's computer model, which was used in the famous *The Limits of Growth*, sees the long wave pattern of economic life as a process in which the capital goods sectors grow to a size which cannot be sustained, and ulimately collapse. He traces the dynamics of long wave patterns from the industrial expansion in 1945.

Following the Great Depression and World War II, many industries were ravaged and there was a widespread shortage of capacity. The consumer durables sectors, housing, office buildings, factories, transport systems and schools were also insufficient to meet the growing post-war demand. The need to rebuild the capital stock as quickly as possible meant that the growth in construction rose beyond real long-term requirements. The limits to growth in capital expansion were believed to have been achieved in the mid-1960s, since when tremendous forces to sustain the process of capital accumulation have persisted. This has left an unbalanced economic system, with too much capital equipment and too much debt. Excess capacity in capital equipment has caused the upward trend to falter, while the need to liquidate debt has meant a dismantling of capital plant. The tendencies described by Forrester's model go a long way toward explaining the inexorable de-industrialisation of Britain over the past decade.

In validation of his model, Forrester cites the great technological innovations of the past which have been responsible for the expansionary phase of the long-term economic cycle. Each of the four periods of expansion we've seen since the beginning of the Industrial Revolution can be traced to a technological revolution — steam power in the 1830s, electricity and the evolution of mechanical transport in the 1880s, electronics and plastic in the 1940s. In each case, limits to growth were involved in each of the technological revolutions. Once these limits had been reached a period of burgeoning unemployment combined with industrial contraction and decay presented an inexorable formula for depression, and leading to what Professor Gerhard Mensch termed "technological stalemate". In essence, the basis for the Forrester model is the tendency for technological innovation that leads to increased productive capacity to produce prosperity and a prolonged period of expansion. A technological crisis occurs when productive capacity approaches obsolescence. After that comes the depression during which many new innovations are being developed.

During the development period the environment for technical innovation certainly does not improve. The improvement does not begin during the process of contraction. It begins only at the nadir of contraction. In the major depression that follows the expansionary peak, the climate for innovation remains even more unfavourable than when the global economy was growing. The social structure suffers disarray and profits are low. Those who managed to obtain control during the last stages of the growth period may still be in control. But they will be discouraged. Fundamental research and innovation continue but commercial exploitation remains dormant owing to contracting markets. In any case, the process of wringing the last dregs out of the old technologies has yet to run its course.

Then, like a phoenix rising from the ashes, despair falls away — the door begins to open to reveal a glimpse of a bright new future. Hope springs and flourishes. Rebuilding begins. New technologies emerge. The old technologies are no longer reinforced or re-established. Each major expansion develops around a highly integrated and mutually supportive combination of technologies. For example, energy sources determine the design of factories. Transportation is closely inter-related with the pattern of living. Communications and the pace of business move to the same tempo. Education is geared to the existing technology, and financial institutions become more familiar with the opportunities of the existing technology. When technologies become mature, and established, radical innovations are rejected as impractical. Bankers who have been successful in backing familiar ideas will only accept modest innovation within conventional guidelines. It is only during the early stages of an expansion that new ideas are tried and developed.

The reservoir of new innovations contains over 25 years of stored inventions and accumulated technologies which were not ready, for one reason or another, to be taken off the drawing board during the latter phase of the previous period of expansion. During the early stages of a wave of long-term expansion, new products and new businesses appear in increasing numbers. That is the reason why the early stages of expansion are always the most dynamic and carry the greatest profit potential.

In 1976, Ehud Levy-Pascal, executive of the International Functional Staff

Office of Political Research at the Directorate of Intelligence at the CIA, published a study entitled *An Analysis of the Cyclical Dynamics of Industrialised Countries*. At the time, Levy-Pascal predicted that there were "especially troubled times ahead." Before the sharp fall in the price of oil, Levy-Pascal suggested that energy problems might trigger off the next major downturn. Levy-Pascal also subscribed to the belief in the long-term economic cycle lasting about 50 to 60 years which Forrester, Schumpeter and others had expressed. Adding a further dimension to the placement of technology within the framework of the long-term economic cycle, Levy-Pascal built an economic model incorporating five basic elements or phases.

In the first phase of the Levy-Pascal model, there are one or more major technological innovations ushering in new industries. These innovations give a dramatic uplift to the economy. About 30 years separated the beginning of the first phase from the end of the second. During the third phase, a backwash of economic change revolutionises the system once again. There are major changes occurring in life-styles, individual values and the social system generally. These changes begin among the youth, spreading to parents and the population at large, during a period of severe socio-political disturbance. During the fourth phase of the Levy-Pascal model, politicians eventually embrace policies in keeping with the changes wrought by the new technologies on the economic and social system. A period of relative calm occurs during the transition from the fourth to the final phase. This fifth and final phase involves the stagnation in the economic, social and political spheres as optimism gives way to pessimism. Politically, there is a shift towards conservatism in politics which gets the blame for the dislocation of the fifth phase. We begin the cycle all over again, with a new period of expansion along the lines of the Forrester model. According to Levy-Pascal's timing, the "fifth phase", which began in the early 1970s, is likely to have run its course by the early 1990s. Thereafter, new technological innovations will trigger off another major long-term wave of expansion.

Another economist who has made a major contribution to the explanation of long-wave cyclical behaviour and the role played by innovative technology is Ernest Mandel, whose observations are likely to be particularly helpful when we attempt to anticipate the nature of economic activity beyond the nadir of the depression unfolding during the late 1980s. According to Mandel, technological innovations are bunched together in a counter-cyclical manner during the period of depression separating the antiquated and obsolescent from the new wave of technology which characterises the period of expansion. But, says Mandel, these technologies themselves are not the *cause* of the transition from depression to boom. Mandel believes that the explanation for the major turning points must be sought elsewhere. According to Ernest Mandel, it is the long-term changes in the average rate of profit which are the main cause of business cycle fluctuations, whether of the short, medium or long-term variety. These changes in profitability are fundamental to the capitalist mode of production, but outside the scope of technological considerations.

The upper turning points from boom to depression are seen to be determined largely by endogenous factors, especially the rise in the organic composition of capital (growth of capital intensity). This is not true of those turning points which occur at the nadir of a depression prior to the new wave of expansion. Mandel contends that it takes "exogenous system shocks" of various kinds to lift the system out of a depression before the major expansionary phase can begin.

It would be a mistake to conclude that if the technologies are sufficiently broad and innovative, new technology and innovation automatically lead to a long-wave of expansion. The period from 1930 to 1935 was exceptionally rich in new technology and innovation. Yet aggregate investment in the United States remained relatively stagnant throughout the 1930s, and sustained business expansion did not begin until seven years after the worst of the depression. Although the new technologies which had attracted investment in the United States by the 1940s, were being commercially exploited, Europe had not yet taken off. Indeed, it took until 1948 before the long business expansion in Europe was launched — three years after the end of the Second World War.

There is one thing which can be said about large scale innovation, and said with absolute certainty. It *will* create a long-wave expansion, characteristic of the Upwave of the long-term economic cycle, but only in the context of a simultaneous broadening of the market, along with a rate of economic growth leading to higher employment. Without those supportive factors, large scale innovation may — and usually will — increase unemployment, create greater stagnation in the market for final consumer goods and reduce the overall level of investment.

This is because large scale innovation is bound to disturb the existing balance between the three main factors of production — Land, Labour and Capital; since the commonly accepted theory of production assumes that the level of technology remains constant. Moreover, when we come down to the realities of the everyday world, the decision to purchase and install a new piece of equipment, incorporating what for the firm represents "a higher level of technology", does not take place in a financial or managerial void.

Unless some benefit is likely to result — even if it amounts to no more than compensating for a shortage of certain manpower skills — no firm is likely to spend money and face the upheaval involved merely for the sake of being "more up-to-date". True, a "modern" image may help sell the company's products, just as spending more on research and development may help to push up the price of its shares. But once the decision has been taken to introduce a new and improved computer system, what matters now is the effect it is going to have on the "mix" of production factors. Assuming the firm is not making a move to a fresh site — made possible by the introduction of new technology — the main effect of the change will be on the Capital/Labour balance.

It is impossible to say *what* will be the effect of "modernisation" — and whether it would be a wise decision — until we get down to cases. The circumstances will vary from firm to firm, as well as between different sectors of industry. Let us take the example of a firm manufacturing gear-wheels. There may well be a great deal of new technology, new machines, and new processes which have been available for some time. But the firm has resisted the temptation to scrap existing plant, because the cost of making the change may be too high to justify the investment. The main reason, they will tell you, is that — even with the guarantee of higher productivity — the increased turnover will still be insufficient to cover the additional cost.

On the other hand, a firm in one of the service industries may find it extremely advantageous to introduce the latest technology. The computer which took no more that 350 man/years to produce (thus helping to determine the cost to the company) may well replace 4,000 man/years. It could be that this particular firm may be able to increase its scale of operation to a level at which it will be able (and willing) to absorb every one of the workers displaced when the new system was introduced. However, it may merely be that introduction of the new technology which enabled the firm to retain its existing premises, and continue to operate without having to raise fresh capital.

So long as the Land and Capital factors remain as they are — assuming the new computers are purchased out of savings — the proliferation of new systems is virtually certain to reduce the demand for Labour, without necessarily increasing (or even maintaining) the previous level of economic growth. It should be obvious that the emphasis currently placed on service industries as a foundation for future growth is completely unjustified.

Let us now move on to the social factors responsible for that post-depression period which is conducive to the exploitation of the latest inventions. By now it should have dawned that we should beware of paying too much attention to the warnings uttered from time to time by industrial and City worthies, political leaders, their pop-star supporters and the galaxy of economic "evangelicals" like the CBI and the Institute of Directors. We may well "talk" depression. But we cannot "talk ourselves *into* recession." Growth is not halted, confidence is not shattered by the pessimism of ordinary people — which includes analysts, academics and the business community — when they're not posing for the camera or being quoted "on the record". People become pessimistic when they have to look hard for the signs of growth, with which they have become familiar. They become desperate when they see them evaporating into the mists of uncertainty.

The public grew accustomed to the idea that a rising stock market is indicative of a period of growth and prosperity. If share prices suddenly plunge, and continue falling, an increasing number of the public become more and more pessimistic as they watch their symbol of economic activity declining, along with other familiar signs of prosperity. Sooner or later the public feel they can stomach no more bad news. . . from the market, that is. Eagerly they turn to the latest disaster — almost any disaster —to take their minds off their own worries. It is instructive, as well as fascinating, to look back at the way people in the United States were behaving after the Crash of October 1929. By November 1929, you would have thought the worst was over; just as the public in Britain seemed — and were encouraged — to believe that the 1987 crash had run its course by New Year.

During the last week of November 1929, most US observers believed the crash had become a spent force. Several believed that a full-scale bear market had been compressed into a narrow time frame. Many believed that the unwelcome bears which had come to Wall Street in the Fall, had become completely exhausted in a matter of weeks. By late November '29, the Dow Jones Industrial Average slowly began to rise — on light volume. The rise continued through December. Wall Street entered 1930 with what looked very much like a *subdued* bull market.

Market scare stories had vanished from the front pages of the *New York Times* by mid-November. The front page on New Year's Day 1930 told of the death of 72 children in Scotland. Senator Brookhart of Iowa called for the removal of Secretary of the Treasury Andrew Mellon — on the grounds of his alleged failure to enforce Prohibition effectively. The New York Republicans pledged aid to Governor Roosevelt — for his pension programme. The only piece of stock market related news was Mellon's prediction that 1930 would be a "good year for business".

Among the optimists on the panel of prominent businessmen asked to give their views, was James Farrell of US Steel. He was quoted as saying it was:

> ". . . confidently expected that after the turn of the year operations the steel industry will substantially improve."

Alexander Noyes, the historian, struck what to us must be a familiar note. The Crash was:

> ". . . a reaction from an orgy of reckless speculation."

Treasury Secretary Andrew Mellon pulled no punches. His tone was similar to that of the Thatcher administration when it still spoke of making UK industry "leaner and fitter". "Let the slump liquidate itself", declared Secretary Mellon:

> "Liquidate labour, liquidate stocks, liquidate the farmers, liquidate real estate. . . It will purge the rottenness out of the system. High costs of living and high living will come down. People will work harder, live a more moral life. Values will be adjusted, and enterprising people will pick up the wrecks from less competent people."

Harsh as they may sound today, Andrew Mellon's words appeared reasonable and prudent at the time. By January 1930, it looked as though plungers, gamblers and other disreputable types had lost a lot of money. But the ordinary newspaper readers still seemed to be in good shape. Their brokers were telling them that those who had bought shares when the bull market started in the 1920s were still making a good profit. (Although few individuals were buyers at the start of the bull market almost ten years earlier.) To the average person at that time, the panic was just an exciting event — like the World Cup or the Falklands War. "The Year's Greatest Marvel", wrote *The Times* — neatly sidestepping more urgent topics — was the fact that radio contact had been made with Admiral Byrd at the South Pole.

President Hoover, in his annual message to the American people, referred to the measures already taken and was "convinced that they had re-established confidence." Later he was confident enough to give a definite date for the promised recovery: unemployment would be ended in sixty-days!

For the record, the rally that began on Wall Street on 13th November ended on 17th April 1930. The original Crash of '29 was nothing compared with the devastation which followed until the low point was reached on 5th January 1932. By that time a staggering 86,000 businesses had gone bankrupt, leaving liabilities of $928 million. In 1929, the average family income had been around $2,300. By 1932, it was down below $1,600. In March 1930, there were 513 millionaires — those with a declared income for tax purposes of more than $1 million. Three years later their ranks had been reduced to a pitiful 20!

It is interesting to find that within a few months the public at large — who were eventually to be caught up in the Great Depression — were convinced that the crash had been a phenomenon peculiar to the financial district. Moreover the time lag between the Crash of '29 and the visible signs of deterioration in the real economy left the field wide open for those who appeared to think they could talk the nation *out* of recession.

Maybe we can still remember some of those headlines in the British press shortly before Christmas 1987:

CBI EXPECTS INDUSTRY TO REMAIN BUOYANT (Financial Times)
UK LEADS GROWTH IN EUROPE (The Times)

The pity of it is that most members of the public *want* to be told that things are not *really* that bad! Not surprisingly both the politicians dependent on their votes, and the editors dependent on selling their newspapers. . . in case they lose their advertisers. . . are only too willing to oblige. Meanwhile the markets, which discount the future — rather than the past — pursue their inevitable course. And, as I said, the public grow more and more depressed. There comes a point when markets have fallen for so long, and the public's morale has fallen so far, that a rising stockmarket will not necessarily bring about a renewal of confidence. While markets are discounting the future, most individuals — and some fund managers who should know better — remain hog-tied by the past.

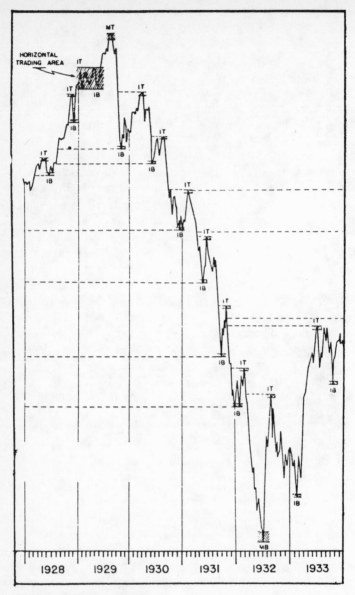

Figure 25: The Wall Street Crash

A rising stock market will instil confidence only if people believe that the recovery can be sustained. Until such time as the public can believe that shares prices will continue to rise, sentiment will remain unchanged. It is Mandel's view that while:

". . .dissymmetry between the turning point of a long boom into long depression and the turning point from a long depression into a long boom has to be emphasised; we believe that the expansionary long waves result from the interaction between multiple, partially autonomous variables, leading to a sudden upsurge of the average rate of profit and a sudden rapid expansion of the world market."

Obviously, World War II and the peace that followed produced the typical "shock" to the system that Mandel saw as mandatory for the exploitation of these innovations and new technology which are the precursor to long-term expansion. On the face of it, similar relationships can be seen during the revolution of 1848, or the flowering of imperialism after 1893. The revolution of 1848 preceded the discoveries of the Californian goldfields. In 1893 came the discovery of the goldfields in the Transvaal. Given the central role played by gold in the world's economic system at the time, this was in both cases a sudden broadening of the global market. Yet, in neither case do we find any evidence to suggest that the expansion which followed was the product of the previous cycles of expanded reproduction. The system, so to speak, was actually catapulted into a broader framework by what Mandel would refer to as a "system shock", necessary for the development of the backbone technologies inherent in a long term expansion.

In other words, what Mandel's observations tell us is that the next Upwave will begin with a "system shock" followed by explosive growth. Precisely what this "system shock" will be, is difficult to determine at this stage. In fact, if it could be determined with any degree of precision, it would cease to be a "system shock". We must therefore "expect the unexpected" at the terminal juncture of the fourth wave of technology, which will coincide with the emerging fifth wave of technology. Investors should be positioned well beforehand. Because if history is to be relied upon, we will be "catapulted" into the next Upwave of expansion. Those already firmly placed to benefit from the catapult effect will experience the greatest benefits in the shortest time.

Tomorrow is no more than yesterday's today. Probably within five years, investors will be moving from the experience of the end of the depressionary era into the beginning of a new wave of expansion, due to last thirty years or more. So far as industry, commerce and the financial community are concerned, five years is like a grain of sand on the beach! Accepting the shortening of the time scale which current technology and a worldwide market have already brought about, unevenness of individual performance, and the day-to-day, month-to-month and year-to-year fluctuations inherent in markets, we must recognise that neither progress nor regression will take the straight line path of linear logic which so gladdens the heart of the statistician and the share pusher. From the 1990s through to the 2020s, we will see some awe-inspiring developments in the key areas of technology. The potential will then be available for all who are willing and able — financially and psychologically — to take full advantage of them.

For years I have been described as a "merchant of doom and gloom". Those who refer to me in those terms probably forget that I was once referred to as a "dreamer", a "perennial optimist". That was when I forecast the benefits likely to be obtained from the exploration and exploitation of North Sea oil, along with the ". . .longest and most glorious bull market in British history". In a short time from now — as I write — I will probably be referred to as a "dreamer" and a "perennial optimist" once again. That will be when I start to prepare investors for that period from the 1990s to the 2020s, which will reward mankind with its most outstanding achievement in the entire history of our planet.

Those committed to Futurology are certainly not all "dreamers", "perennial optimists" or "idealists". Economist Albert T. Sommers, senior fellow and economic counsellor with the hard-headed New York Conference Board, has the task of assisting senior executives and other business leaders in arriving at sound — rather than euphoric or panicky — decisions about their corporations' future planning. These are decisions which are not necessarily based on over-simplistic, straight-line projections of the past into the future. This is true of countless others in high positions in law, banking, accountancy and financial management.

The terminal juncture of the Downwave is about 3 or 5 years away and the terminal juncture of the next Upwave is about 30 years away, in the decade of 2020. To look and plan even ten years ahead much less thirty — may seem to many to be too much like taking an "acid trip", dabbling in witchcraft and black magic, to be taken seriously. I can assure you, I have never been — nor do I intend to become — involved in mind-altering substances. Neither have I had any acquaintance with the occult. Nor is it likely that any of those attending the World Future Society's Conference in New York, in July 1986, were in the grip of drug-induced fantasies or bizarre religious affiliations. The theme, *Future Focus: The Next Fifteen Years* drew speakers like Alvin Toffler of *Future Shock* and *Third Wave* fame. His message did not relate to some vague, hyper-futurist project that would appear in decades to come. It was far more direct and simple. "Mexico" he warned, "was the single most important national-security issue in the United States today." The implications of Alvin Toffler's statement are indeed significant and far-reaching.

Stafford Beer, Professor of Cybernetics at the University of Manchester, produced his "world passport", urging those who attended the conference to apply for one themselves. "World Government" he claimed, "already exists. It has been with us all along. It is the people". There are many elements of the fifth wave that we are entering. These elements span the technological, the political and the sociological. Vast changes in the socio-political environment must also be considered as an aspect, and supportive of the next technological expansion. Referring once again to the observations of Ernest Mandel, one form of "system shock" could well arise from a radical change in the political environment. It was a shock to the system when there was a shift from the Hoover administration to the "New Deal" Administration of President Roosevelt in the 1930s. There are examples throughout history of political upheavals acting as the trigger for a new major wave of expansion. Of course, one must distinguish between a change in policy and a change in rhetoric. Although there has been a radical change in rhetoric since Mrs Thatcher took over from James Callaghan, there has been very little change in policy. Unfortunately for Britain! All Britons have had an extension and amplification of the same type of corrosive socialism that has prevailed in Britain for decades.

At the World Future Society Conference, the Director of the US Federal Emergency Management Agency, Julius W. Becton saw emergency management as a "growth industry". Higher technology created greater potential hazards. Put that together with "more people to get hurt in more places" and we are bound to have more emergencies to cope with. Remember too that the Jay Forrester model calls for three types of innovation during the period of long-term expansion — technological, managerial and political. These may occur simultaneously or in the order mentioned. But there is no particular time sequence laid down, although they are all interdependent. It is clear that the new technologies cannot develop without the managerial developments required to regulate and market the innovations based on these technologies. Neither innovation nor managerial development exist without a major change from the type of political environment associated with a contracting economy. That being so, energetic management will therefore be quintessential in the next phase of long term growth, given the new technologies that will spawn that growth.

Reconceptualising Your Future from the Past

A century ago, when patent attorneys were shutting shop because they thought everything that could be had been invented, a Swedish-born American named John Ericsson launched a new type of battleship off the shores of Brooklyn, New York. As Mr Ericsson's battleship steamed southward toward Hampton Roads — by-passing the jeering clusters of citizenry along the way — popular opinion concerning the vessel's prospects was divided into two distinct camps. Since Ericsson's craft, christened the *Monitor*, was the first ship built with an all-metal hull, many observers — unaware of Archimedes' principle — presumed that the ship would sink at any moment along the route. On the other side of the divide, were the knowledgeable, well versed in the works of Archimedes. They restricted their criticism to the view that since the *Monitor* looked like a cheese box on a raft it must prove impractical in naval and navigational terms. History fails to tell us of a single spectator, among the thousands who watched the *Monitor's* progress, who was primarily interested in the commercial potential of the invention. Casual observers were so accustomed to the idea of ships being built of wood that the notion of an iron hull was as alien as Galileo's suggestion that the earth was round.

On the subject of the future impact of improved communications on the international financial sector, John Heiman, vice chairman of Merril Lynch Capital Markets said, "This means that everybody knew that everybody else knows what's going on at the same time." The result: fiercer and fiercer competition. This in turn implied — according to John Heiman — that the global economy:

" . . . would never be as stable as it was, but it won't necessarily be as unstable as it has been."

He added this provision — that government regulation did not impinge too much on a free flowing financial system. Twelve months later, in July, 1987, the stock markets of the world set out on a course that led to the global collapse in share prices during October and November. It shewed that under modern conditions, and with the speed of modern communications, more can happen in four weeks than in the four previous years. That you may dismiss as a major "local difficulty" — local in that it affected stock markets but not the real economies of the countries concerned. This would be as big a mistake as failing to see the smoke before the whole sheebang goes up in flames. It provides a readily recognisable illustration of the fact that a major change is not confined to the gigantic, visible quantum leap recorded by the history books. Great discoveries, like great disasters, only *appear* to have burst on an astonished world, a product of spontaneous combustion. A cool, calm examination of the relevant circumstances will frequently shew that the disparate elements which combined to produce the fireball had been accumulating and reacting with one another for quite some time. So that the actual conflagration represents no more than the final step in a long, slow process. All the same, the world will probably insist on treating the whole affair as an unexplained miracle — or a world shattering disaster — like the stock market collapse of '87.

The short-range view of John Heiman — which is currently shared by many linear thinkers in his position — belies the longer term capabilities of the communication industry and the benefits it will bring to both the international markets and the global economy in due course. Thanks to the actuarial stability of human nature, the public's reaction to 20th century high speed communications is not all that dissimilar to the 19th century public's reactions to the change over from wooden hulls to plate-iron hulls — disbelieving and curiously disinterested. Britain's Admiral Lord Mountbatten — who was also an electronics engineer — maintained that current capabilities lag so far behind our proven potentialities that we — as a nation — are like a disorganised group of musicians who throw a grand piano down a flight of stairs just to hear the sound of one note. Sadly, this has applied to the communications industry in the 1980s as well as some of the others that are just coming off the drawing board, or are still in the research stage.

The comparatively recent acceleration in the pace of communications, compared with the slow, gradual build up to any major market move is easier to observe — and appreciate — if we are prepared to look back about 4½ centuries to the launch of what was to become the Muscovy Company. Here we had an example of the combination of two of the elements essential for any successful enterprise — what Trevelyan called "the adventurous spirit of the capitalists of the City of London", with the considerable technological advance at that time, which so greatly enhanced what Trevelyan described as "the quality of the new school of sailors and sea-captains."

If we are to arrive at an unfettered and pragmatic view of the future, John Naisbett says we must "reconceptualise" our outlook toward the future. We can learn a great deal from others who successfully "reconceptualised" their approach to changing conditions in the past. We can also learn from those who failed to do so! That's why it is instructive to look back just over 430 summers to that day in May, 1553, when the *Bona Esperanza, Edward Bonaventura* and the *Bona Confidentia* set sail from Deptford to search for the North-East passage to Cathay. The expedition was a success. But reaction was slow among the interested observers. So were the lessons learned. It was years rather than months before the Eastland Company was given its monopoly in the Baltic, and the Turkey Company was established. A further 30 years were to pass before the monarch, by then Elizabeth I, was prepared to grant a charter to "The Governor and Company of Merchants of London trading into the East Indies."

It is just over 300 years since the Hudson's Bay Company was founded. By that time the "Governor and Company of the New River brought from Chadwell and Amwell to London" had been supplying the capital with water for almost 60 years. It was a task the New River Company would perform for almost 3 centuries, until 1904. That was an important and fruitful year! F.S. Kipping discovered silicones. Freud published his *Psychopathology of Everday Life*. The photo-electric cell was developed, and Mr C.S. Rolls became interested in the cars which Mr H. Royce had been manufacturing in the North of England for some time. Royce had, in fact, set up in Manchester in 1884, the year that Hiram S. Maxim developed his recoil-operated "machine" gun and Charles Parsons invented the first practical steam-turbine engine. It was the year Carl Koeller used cocaine as a local anaesthetic, that gold was discovered in the Transvaal, that the United States acquired Pearl Harbour as a Pacific naval base, that accident insurance was introduced into German industry, and the first deep "tube" underground railway was built in London.

A year later, the earliest commercial adding machine was invented by an American called William Burroughs. His fellow countryman, William Stanley invented the transformer. Impure aluminium was extracted by E.H. and A.C. Cowles by electric furnace. Pasteur successfully innoculated a child exposed to rabies. Comte de Charbonnet launched the "artificial silk" industry in France. Russia forbade the sale of Polish land to foreigners. A German engineer developed a light-weight, high-speed petrol engine, and the first electric tram-car took to the rails in Blackpool. All that. . . just over a century ago! With hindsight, it is clear that many of the "modern blessings" we have taken for granted for most of our lives — and those of our parents too — were already coming into use, albeit in a somewhat crude form, while Victoria, Empress of India was still on the throne. But it would still be almost 20 years before man took his first step towards the conquest of the air — on his way to conquer space itself.

Gustave Eiffel had long before completed his tower on the South Bank in Paris. Chicago (the "windy city") had erected the first "sky-scraper" in the world (the 13-storey Tacoma Building), and the first London-Paris telephone line had been opened — just in time to carry the news of the financial panic which gripped both cities! Dewar had liquified oxygen. Tesla developed the one-million volt high-tension induction coil. The building of the Trans-Siberian Railway had commenced, Hermann Dresser had marketed the aspirin, Otto Lilienthal had successfully flown a glider some 2,000 times and W.L. Judson had invented the zip-fastener. Although the world had to wait until just before the Great War of 1914-18 for the first fastener guaranteed to "zip" every time.

A 33-inch refracting telescope had been erected in France, as well as the Flagstaff Observatory in Arizona. Rontgen had discovered X-rays. . . though no one as yet realised the dangers of radiation. King C. Gillette had made his contribution to civilisation by marketing his "safety" razor. The Nobel Prize had been established. Marconi had demonstrated the practical uses of wireless telegraphy on Salisbury Plain, and Antoine Henri Becquerel had observed how radiation from uranium could affect a photographic plate. He also described a little understood phenomenon — "radio-activity". In the year of the Jameson Raid in South Africa, Utah was admitted as a State of the Union, France annexed Madagascar and Samuel P. Langley successfully flew a steam-engined model aircraft. During the next few years, Professor J.J. Thomson discovered the electron, Pierre and Marie Curie discovered radium and polonium, and myxomatosis was recorded for the first time. Pickering found the 9 moons of Saturn. Ramsay discovered xenon, krypton and neon, and Konstantin Tsiolkovalski enunciated the principles of rocket reaction propulsion. The Swiss railways had been nationalised, and in Germany, Rudolph Diesel had demonstrated his "plugless" engine.

Max Planck proposed the quantum theory, the first Zeppelin was built, Benjamin Holt invented the caterpillar tractor, Becquerel discovered the danger to animals of radiation, J.P. Morgan organised the US Steel Corporation, and the Trans-Pacific cable was laid. But that first giant step had still to be taken.

By the end of 1906, the first modern battleship, HMS *Dreadnought* had been launched. So had the *Lusitania*. The Simplon Tunnel had been opened, and Henri Farman was on the point of launching the first successful biplane. Jannsky discovered the four main blood-groups, and Wassermann came up with his test for syphilis. The Channel Tunnel scheme was rejected by Parliament, and the first attempt was made to preserve fruit by freezing.

In 1908, that first great step was taken at last! Wilbur Wright flew an aeroplane for 30 miles in 40 minutes. And at no less than 45 miles an hour! Over the next ten years, the aeroplane was to become an important weapon of war. It was, moreover, to dictate the strategy of the leading nations throughout the 'twenties and 'thirties — striking terror into the hearts of millions as the pundits warned — quite erroneously — that:

THE BOMBER WILL ALWAYS GET THROUGH

There were only twenty years between the signing of the Peace Treaty that ended the First World War and the outbreak of the Second. At the moment of writing this, more than 30 years have passed since Suez, the Six Day War, the death of Stalin. It is almost 20 years since man first set foot on the moon. In a couple more years, we shall be commemorating the 50th anniversary of Germany's invasion of Poland in September 1939. Half a century since the start of Armageddon!

In the thirty years following World War II, a major period of expansion was completed, involving the exploitation of innovations and technology that made the expansion possible. In a few more years we will embark upon another 30 year wave of expansion, involving exploitation and development of new technologies to replace those of the expansion that has now matured, leaving behind a host of innovations, which like the plant and equipment of the period, are now obsolete.

Thirty years represents almost half the life-span of the average individual in the West. In politics, as recent history has shewn, thirty years is just about long enough to introduce a major measure, see it safely installed and running, and then begin fretting that it is no longer working, and deciding to replace it with the latest wonder solution. To take a topical example, the 1944 Education Act, which introduced the three-stream system — Grammar Schools for the academic, Technical Schools for those with aptitude and the desire to learn a trade, and Secondary Modern — for the undistinguished remainder. The system ran until the 1960s when a mere handful of Grammar Schools were saved, a number transformed into Sixth Form Colleges (the equivalent, some claimed, of the American High School) and the vast majority (like the Technical schools) transformed into so-called Comprehensives. This represented the peak of what some have called the "Hamburger Age".

"How untidy," said the Left Wing Prophets of that Age, as they gazed through the butcher's window. There was the customary range of joints and "cuts", steaks and chops — everything, in fact, from steak *filet* to herbal sausages and scrag end of mutton. Then, according to legend, the Philosophers of the New Age had a sudden inspiration! "Why don't we put the whole lot in the mincer and offer the public a really reliable standard product. . . the People's non-sexist, non-racist, Equal Opportunity Educational Hamburger?"

By 1987, after several attempts by Sir Keith Joseph to tinker with the system,

Kenneth Baker, Secretary of State for Education, presented his Great Education Reform Bill to the Commons on Friday, November 20th. Already known by less reverent members of the Whitehall community as GERBIL, the Baker Education Bill — like its companion pieces, the Housing Bill and the Poll Tax Bill — was seen as the first taste of the kind of reforms Mrs Thatcher had in mind for the 1990s. Said Mr Baker, with a happy smile:

> "Parent power is a major force for higher standards. I want to unleash that power."

Standing as we do with the 1990s stretching before us, it would be tempting to assume that Wilbur Wright's heavier-than-air machine merely had to be improved beyond the early aviators' wildest dreams to arrive at *Concorde*. Such a view would be to ignore the discovery and development of new materials, new tools, new techniques which had not even been dreamed of by men like H.G. Wells or Jules Verne. . . or even Leonardo da Vinci. It would be equally wrong, however, to assume that none of the "new" techniques in use in the year 2020 will be improved versions of the tools we have today.

More fascinating are those new techniques, products, and systems which will be based on genuinely new areas of technology which, at the close of the 1980s, can only be seen as possibilities.

Looking at the Upwave from the Downwave

As we watch the markets churn and swirl, and economists muddle and dither, trying to predict economic performance to the tenth decimal place, vast structural changes are taking place beneath the surface in the way we live. They see changes which are also going to effect the way we are *likely* to live. Needless to say, these changes will make a dramatic impact on the long-term pattern of investment — and the type of investments — compatible with the changing environment. Many of these changes are so obscured by the day-to-day ramblings and irrelevant cross-currents inherent in tertiary factors that the true drama of our changing world remains hidden most of the time.

The fact is that investors insist on fighting the battle for financial survival by using the weapons and strategies of the last war. It is not possible to win with so futile an approach. The warriors who have the sense to buy what you may be selling, and sell what you are buying at the early stages of the battle, are few in number. But their skills will more than compensate for the lightness of their forces. David, remember, slew Goliath with technology.

We frequently use history as an aid in forecasting the future. But it has certain limitations. Some aspects of history throw up constant relationships that reappear time and again over the centuries. Other aspects of history are merely random noises that once served to interpret existing conditions. The planner who uses historical precedent as a guide to the future must be able to segregate the constant relationships from the random. The indiscriminate use of historical precedents is not good enough. Especially today, when we are entering an era which will defy many historical precedents. At the same time, this new era will still be governed by long term economic precedents, which are as much a part of life on this planet as sleeping, eating and breathing, and which have transcended the shift from an agrarian to an industrial society. . . and now, to a post-industrial society.

The late Herman Kahn, who was probably the world's most prolific and respected futurist, claimed that the changes that lie ahead will be no less important than the shift we saw 2,000 years ago from an Agricultural Society to an Industrial Society. The philosopher Kierkegaard tells us that all major changes occur by sudden leaps forward, involving "shocks" to the system. I believe the work of both Kierkegaard and Kahn to be among the most sound and far-reaching. At the same time, there are certain signs we can read to anticipate these "shocks".

From our studies of the long waves of economic life on this planet, we find that long periods of growth are the product of new technologies which enable goods to be manufactured more efficiently at lower cost. This common characteristic of economic activity has proved valid both when agriculture was the primary source of activity and when industry was the primary source. We have no doubt this will continue to be so indefinitely.

If we examine the nature of the technology that has spawned the growth phases of the last 200 years, we find mainly static machines replacing labour as the power source for the first long-term period of expansion during the 18th and early 19th century.

The locomotive, and ancillary developments in transportation, spawned the long-term growth phase that began in the 19th century. Developments in the harnessing of electricity and other forms of power were the harbingers of the 20th century growth phase.

A by-product of the cost efficiency that new technologies engender has been the more efficient use of existing natural resources and of primary products. Improved technology has enabled us to extract additional utility value from primary products by means of substitution and natural resource leverage. Emerging technology has made many old technologies redundant. At one time, for example, locomotive transport was the cheapest and most efficient form of transport. This is no longer so. At one time, steam was the most efficient source of power. This too is no longer the case. Let us, therefore, try to see how the new technologies are likely to affect our future — and the *investment patterns* of that future.

Two types of asset invariably compete for your investment favours: real assets and financial assets. Real assets include raw materials, foods, metals, gold, silver, property, antiques, farm land and other items which are essentially *tangible*. Financial assets are the *intangibles*. These include cash, government securities, debt warrants, shares, options, and similar forms of entitlement. Such assets are almost metaphysical by nature. They control the stream of income and capital, yet have little or no intrinsic value. Obviously, if you are to achieve the best return from your investments, with the least possible risk, you must invest only in those assets which are compatible with the prevailing climate. For the long term investor, it is quintessential to determine whether the long-term future is likely to be an inflationary or a deflationary one. It is, incidentally, an established fact that financial assets perform best during periods of deflation, despite many mistaken assertions to the contrary.

This is where technology comes into the picture, since it has an important role to play in determining whether the supply of real assets will increase or decrease. This in turn will be a crucial indication as to whether or not we are headed on a deflationary course — where real assets will fall in value — or an inflationary course — where real assets will rise in value. History shows that long-term periods of expansion have resulted from our ability to use natural resources more economically and more profitably. When we use real assets more economically and more profitably, the demand for real assets should fall, and with it the price. In other words, the technological cycle, at its optimal phase of development, is essentially deflationary.

Let's now look at the mathematics of the new technologies which are likely to emerge following the trough of the period of long-term global contraction which we now appear to have re-entered. Ever since the beginning of the Industrial Revolution, almost all technological progress has resulted in an increase in the supply of real assets. Items which were not considered real assets prior to certain technological innovations became real assets. When the "Spinning Jenny" was first used in the factories of England in 1750, there was a number of primary products that were not considered real assets simply because they had no primary purpose. Technologies produced a primary purpose, and a new range of valuable raw materials was recognised.

At one time, a farmer finding petroleum on his land would abandon it, because to him, it was just a black, slimy mess. But by the time the Industrial Revolution was really getting underway, people who found oil on their land amassed great wealth — as a result of the new technologies that incorporated petroleum in vast quantities. As the Industrial Revolution progressed, an increasing number of new raw materials suddenly acquired a commercial use, pushing up their value. Quite often, the adoption of new materials lowered the value of traditional raw materials, because the new materials often proved to be efficient and cost effective substitutes. Such is the way with new technology! As the years passed, there was an expansion of raw material utilisation, with values spread across a wider range of items than ever in the early days of the Industrial Revolution.

In the '80s, we are now about to enter an entirely fresh era of technology, totally unlike any which emerged in the Industrial Revolution. Ours is a Post-Industrial Society; and for the first time since the 1780s, technologies have managed to maximise the economies of scale in the production process. Those who are profiting the most from today's technological achievements, are not the primary producers — as was the case while the Industrial Revolution was maturing. The current wealth creators are those who build an empire in terms of financial assets, by finding ways to increase value-added, or profit input to the economy, without any appreciable accumulation of real assets.

The way real asset substitution is being employed shews how technology is being applied in the employment of current assets, and the effect on the pricing of basic materials. The micro-processor, incorporating a silicon chip, can be said to use sand as its primary product. Given the amount of sand in the world, it would be ludicrous to expect that micro-circuitry could ever use enough raw material to cause an increase in the price of sand, as would be the case with oil or other less abundant materials. The use of micro-processors has a further advantage: it is energy efficient. The jobs that are currently being done by computer require far less energy, and labour, than was previously required in the days before the advent of computer semi-conductors and micro-circuitry. So here we have an industry taking full advantage of economies of scale to a degree which must affect labour costs and energy costs as the adjustment process continues. An important factor for now on will be the extent to which highly paid staff replace comparatively cheap labour, without increasing overall labour costs — to say nothing of the bargaining power of the new categories of worker.

The silicon chip, which is made from cheap and abundant sand, makes it possible to substitute — through better communications — all sorts of activities involving transportation and considerable movements of men and materials at great expense. A document may now be "sent" across a Continent by modem. This is a substitute for putting the document in the post box, having the postman collect it, and the postal authorities sort it, and then transporting it by aircraft. The amount of time and energy saved through this comparatively simple technology staggers the imagination. Of course, methods and materials used prior to the new technology should now become more plentiful, and therefore less costly. Innovators have yet to scratch the surface of the full range of uses which the silicon chip and micro-processor already offer.

Another reduction in the need for primary products has come from the fibre optics industry. It is possible to transport more messages on a single fibre optic line than would have been possible — using all the lines across the entire world — 50 years ago. Rubber insulated heavy copper cable will no longer be required, and fibre optics require much less maintenance and — also coming from sand — are much cheaper to produce. Before long, the international telephone companies will be among the world's major suppliers of secondary copper, as all the materials currently used in our present inefficient cable systems go for scrap.

One of the more obvious areas where the demand for traditional materials will be reduced drastically is the energy industry. The increasing number of alternative energy sources coming on stream use far less of the primary products than in the past. Ironically, a silicon chip factory in the US was among the first to use co-generation which is now widely used in the US. Co-generation involves the recycling of steam — originally a by-product of the power cycle — which is transmitted back into the power cycle.

Labour, as we have long recognised, is a commodity like any other. The extent to which new technologies will reduce the demand for labour is still not fully appreciated.

As the 20th century draws to a close, markets have been contracting. Competing nations have turned to importing cheap foreign labour to reduce the costs of production. While such a move may lead to greater competitiveness in world markets, it can also breed political unrest in the domestic market. In order to counter the use of cheap labour as a competitive weapon, an increasing number of companies have turned to robotics — the most effective way to compete with those who reduce their production costs through the use of cheap labour. Robots neither complain nor organise against their employer!

The necessary technology is certainly in place for an age of robots. While several of the refinements required for a fully self-sufficient robot are still on the drawing board, the feasibility exists. Robot manufacturers have developed the required hydraulics, automatic vision, micro-circuitry, artificial skin and limbs, sensors and computers. There exists already the capability to store the entire knowledge of the world to date in a housing no bigger than a matchbox. (Assuming that anyone could identify and amass "the entire knowledge of the world!") Scientists claim they have all that is required to construct what would appear to be a fully functional human being with a brain and operational sex organs.

To date, the Japanese are the most advanced in the field of robotics. Initial innovation took place in the US but — consistent with America's current placement in the global supremacy cycle — resources were devoted to other areas of development, so the exploitation of robots did not materialise to any extent. What has taken place in robotics is similar to what happened with micro-processors and television. The Americans took the initiative, but it fell to the Japanese to build a major industry out of their innovations. Here we see a parallel with Britain during the 1930s and 1940s. The British were responsible for most of the major advances in aircraft technology before and during World War II. But it was left to the Americans to develop these innovations into a profitable and viable industry. This was something the British were unable to do, because they had allocated their resources to areas with a higher political priority.

According to James Dines, within the next twenty years the entire computer industry will be "a sub-sector of robotics". The robotics industry, says Dines, will be "the greatest growth industry in the universe". Dines sees robots being used in defence — in charge of automatic weaponry, in outer space exploration — where humans could not survive. He also sees robots on the assembly line, carrying out mundane tasks which would be detrimental to the emotional stability of humans, as well as in a host of applications where human frailty has inhibited greater productivity.

Many technologies that we see as new technologies are really nothing more than spin-offs from old technologies. Computer technology is certainly not new. It dates back to the 1940s. Computers have been streamlined by the inclusion of the micro-processor, but the basic technology remains the same. One of the genuinely new areas of technology which has acquired a commercial application is that of genetic engineering. Genetic engineering involves a variety of techniques allowing biologists to transfer genetic information from one organism to another. In nature, genetic information is constantly being arranged and rearranged, most notably in the process of sexual reproduction. However, in the case of normal sexual reproduction, the genetic outcome is random. By incorporating the techniques of genetic *engineering*, the transfer of genetic *information* can be controlled and directed. In addition, the genetic information can be transferred between quite different organisms. Theoretically, we can take the genetic structure of a rabbit's reproductive capacity and transfer it to a man, giving him the sexual reproductive capacity of the rabbit — if this is desirable. Impotence and sterility may soon be a thing of the past as a result of genetic imprintation.

One of the most actively discussed topics in the field of genetic engineering is that of recombinant DNA research — more commonly known as "gene splicing" or molecular "cloning". According to the discoveries of research scientists, the genetic information of all living organisms is carried by large molecules of DNA. Each DNA molecule is made up of an immense and multifarious number of sub-units. The structure and arrangement of these DNA sub-units serves as a code for all the information required by the organism, and determine — throughout its entire existence — the growth, development and death of the organism. Scientists can now isolate the DNA molecule from the rest of the cell. Then, by cutting out sections of the DNA molecule with awe-inspiring precision, these sections can be joined to other DNA molecules from different organisms and different species. Once the foreign sections of the DNA molecule become a part of the host organism, the host will then be instructed to engage in whatever reproductive process is desired.

Beluga caviar has always been enormously expensive, due to the limited availability of sturgeon eggs. Through the process of genetic engineering, scientists can splice the genes of the sturgeon with those of a host whale. The whale will then produce the eggs marketed as Beluga caviar by the ton.

The potential applications for genetic engineering are legion, spanning many areas of agriculture, medicine and industry. Already a number of companies are investing heavily in genetic engineering. There is a hope that many valuable substances — including Interferon — a cure for AIDS, a vast array of insulins and other hormones may be manufactured more cheaply and efficiently by genetically altered microbes. The DNA which instructs human cells to make insulin has already been transferred and "spliced" into bacteria, which have generated small quantities of insulin. As this process is expanded, much larger quantities of insulin — identical with that produced by humans — will become available.

When the old-fashioned, primitive and inefficient means of sexual reproduction is initiated, the outcome can be a child bearing little resemblance to either of the legal parents. This can be the result of the introduction of a foreign body — such as the personage who delivers milk, groceries, newspapers, or meat — causing considerable confusion, and frequently aggravation. But, more often than not, there is a much simpler explanation. The offspring of the parents may differ considerably in appearance and intellect, owing to the "genetic mixing" of the two parents in the reproductive process. Through discoveries in genetic engineering, and the various techniques which are now available, it is possible to take a single cell from an adult male (or female) and induce it to grow into another fully formed adult. The offspring will, as a result, be a clone of the single parent, and genetically identical.

There are many applications for "cloning" aside from avoiding the suspicions and accusations that arise when two parents with blond hair and blue eyes produce a yellow offspring with black hair and delicately slanted eyes. One of the incentives for developing cloning techniques is the possibility of obtaining a large number of identical offspring. For example, the best dairy cattle might be cloned in the expectation that all the offspring would be equally productive and genetically identical. Of course, the technology could also be applied to cloning humans who have possessed exceptional abilities, which must pose immense ethical and social problems we shall have to learn to cope with. The fact of the matter is that, in the future, all human beings may not be created equal under God! The era of the Immaculate Conception may actually be at hand; and a society of super-humans a genuine possibility, while children may be seen but not had!

This may sound wholly bizarre. But, it would be unwise to allow our inhibited perceptions to limit our anticipation of the future. One trained scientist has actually gone on record to the effect that within twenty years man will have achieved immortality. It has been predicted that the lives of people on this planet could be extended by hundreds of years through various recent developments, such as organ and limb replacement. It is well-known that a function of the ageing process is the inability of body cells to replace dying cells at the same rate they did when we were young. Several breakthroughs have been made in the field of cell regeneration. *Hydro-procaine* — a substance which promotes cell regeneration — is now available in commercial form.

Now a new protein form has been discovered. Called *anzio-genin*, it assists in the production of blood vessels. The application of *anzio-genin*, combined with other advanced technology, could mean that both organ replacement and limb replacement will become outmoded. By the turn of the century, people might well be able to grow new limbs, and manufacture new eyes and ears — within their own organic mechanism — in the way that a tree grows a new branch each season.

As we approach the 21st century, gerontology — the science of ageing — is alive with pre-revolutionary fervour. Signs of a major breakthrough are abundantly evident. The key to extending life expectancy lies in the success of genetic engineering. According to recent scientific evidence, age brings the deterioration of the body's immune system. It is the ability of the immune system to protect us from various potentially fatal diseases that keeps us alive. The disease of AIDS causes a rapid breakdown in the immune system. So no one actually dies from AIDS — people die of the diseases which invade the body as a result of a malfunction in the immune system caused by AIDS. Death comes when the immune system is no longer able to protect the body, and the body self-destructs.

The problem can be traced to a DNA malfunction. As we age, the immune system becomes less efficient because the DNA replacement mechanisms are unable to repair the genetic machinery in the cells as fast as the cells continue to break down with metabolic time. If cellular deterioration could be repaired and cells replaced instantaneously — with 100% efficiency — there *would* be no ageing process. It is a scientific fact that the maximum lifespan of different species, ranging from mice to man, is proportional to their ability to repair injuries to their individual DNA. The relatively extraordinary longevity of man is believed to have evolved as a result of the increase in the levels of DNA repairs and other life maintenance processes. DNA repair is brought about through specific enzymes that examine and identify the type of DNA injury and then deal with it.

Dr. Joan Sonneborn extended the lifespan of a single-celled organism called the *Paramecium* through a relatively simple process following a study of the DNA structure of the *Paramecium*. Initially, the cells were exposed to intense ultraviolet light. The cells were then exposed to a longer wave of ultraviolet light, known scientifically as "black-light". Dr Sonneborn held that the first exposure to ultraviolet light damaged the DNA in the cells, immediately augmenting a natural repair process. Through a mechanism known as "photoreactivation", the second exposure to "black light" eliminated the damage caused by the first exposure. This left the augmented natural repair process free to mend other damage that had built up in the DNA — particularly the damage caused by the natural ageing process.

Methods applicable to human use are now being devised, with the aim of supplementing our existing DNA repair process. The injection of properly altered DNA will act as a vaccine, stimulating the body so that the level of repair enzymes is expanded. Higher organisms — such as our species — possess a reserve repair capacity, which we are rapidly learning to enhance.

Another aspect of the ageing process genetic engineers have been studying is the "genetic clock". This is also a function of the DNA molecule. For many years, it has been recognised that life expectancy can be traced to hereditary tendencies which can be found in the DNA molecule. By manipulating the "genetic clock", aspects of life expectancy attributable to hereditary factors found in the DNA can be neutralised. Life will then be extended accordingly. In addition, similar manipulation and gene splicing can serve to extend life to whatever the normal DNA limitations might be.

Until now, scientists have been struggling to locate the precise position of this "genetic clock". During late 1985, evidence was submitted shewing that the portion of the DNA that affected the "genetic clock" was that proportion which would govern the area at the stem of the brain. Experiments have since been carried out in an attempt to effect life extension in laboratory animals by "genetic clock" manipulation. It is claimed that a major breakthrough is imminent.

It used to be said that the only certainties in life are death and taxes. As we move into the 21st century, however, only one of these may be relied upon, if you subscribe to the ideas of F.M. Esfandiary. He is an author who has taught at the New School for Social Research in New York and the University of California in Los Angeles. Like a few others, he also sees mankind at the brink of "the age of immortality." "Anyone alive in twenty years will be alive in 200 years, and if you're alive in 200 years, you'll be around forever," he told the *New York Times* in 1979. Since then, the progress in life-extensions has been even more remarkable. Esfandiary sees us immortals developing into:

" . . . telehumans. . . whose brains and bodies are at all times connected to other brains, systems and technologies for the sake of instant, direct communications, bypassing the walls, inhibitions and fears that have separated us through the eons."

I'm sure F.M. Esfandiary actually meant what he said in the literal sense. But even taken metaphorically, one can begin to comprehend the elements of immortality for those who have made significant intellectual contributions — and might continue to do so were they not limited by death. One can also contemplate the tele-digitalisation of knowledge in the next few decades, rather than centuries.

A great many new jobs will be created by the digitalisation of all knowledge and information. All individual knowledge will become more and more a question of knowing where to look for information. Translation will be left to computers. Language will never again be a barrier. Computer hardware will be split into two, the portable and the fixed. The former will continue to be based on silicon chips, but the latter will have super-conductive processors of the Josephson junction kind. Lewis Branscom of IBM has gone on record as predicting that the ultimate "pico-processor" might actually be patterned on the DNA molecule that controls the brain.

But far from developing in a human direction, the computer and robot will develop in parallel with the human race. The human brain has two weaknesses: its poor ability to think laterally, and its inability to monitor more than about seven variable factors of a situation at any one time. That is the view of the psychologists. The "artificial intelligence" of computers need not suffer either defect, and can be developed into the area of invention and discovery. In fact, machines will be able to take over the "donkey-work" of technological innovation, freeing the humans to pursue the frontiers of understanding — in particular, the powers of the unconscious mind and the relationship to chemistry to life and to the mind. The wealth of the human unconscious is our answer to the "superintelligent" machine, so feared by many — and usually anthropomorphised into a highly improbable form.

A home computer can be linked by telephone into digitalised libraries and encyclopedias, along with other home computers and those of various service organisations — running the gamut from newspapers to tax lawyers — in a constant on-line, two-way feed. That must transform what would once have been a task demanding our full attention and our intelligence into a routine chore. We would not be all that unlike Esfandiary's telehumans. Once we have liberated the skills and aptitudes now squandered on mundane tasks, and are free to exploit the full capacity of human consciousness. . . and the subconscious, we are on our way to becoming "super-telehumans."

What are the human subconscious and unconscious capable of? Hypnosis has given us some indication. Dr. Lyall Watson (*Lifetide*) recounts an experiment in which a group of students were shown into a room filled with objects of one sort or another, having been instructed to memorise whatever they could in a few minutes. "Before and after" tests showed that hypnosis produced a staggering improvement in the students' observation and memory performance. In one case, however, the difference was small. The experimenter pressed on, and a chance question revealed the most astonishing result. Under hypnosis, the subject was able to recall, without a single fault, the entire contents of the front page of *The Times* of London, which had been lying casually on the table in the room used for the experiment. The newspapers had been so far away that even to read the print was beyond the student's (or anyone else's) capability in the *conscious* state. Think of the amazing powers which could be unleashed — powers which are apparently inherent in each and every one of us. At the moment, we do not fully know what we *don't* know about our human capabilities. But we're learning. . . and learning fast!

In general, before the year 2020, we will have refined the process of gaining teleaccess to digitalised libraries — which will effectively be a vast databank of information, discovery and theory — old and new. This alone should yield amazing dividends in terms of synergy and the avoidance of duplicate thinking. It could bring mankind closer to Teilhard de Chardin's dream of one single mind for all mankind. The digitalised databank — to which all will enjoy free access — will contain every scrap of knowledge gained to date on any given subject. Such an encyclopedia already exists in the field of medicine. Since 1971 it has been on-line at the US National Library of

Medicine, where it is called the *Medical Literature Analytical and Retrieval System* or *MEDLARS*.

Direct access in this way to the world's entire knowledge means that people will be able to unleash the hitherto submerged capacity at the disposal of their inner consciousness, enabling them to make the maximum use of the world's store of knowledge. Unleashing the unconscious will be the focus of training in the schools and universities of the future. The consequences will be awe-inspiring, and certainly far outside our present comprehension. One of the major, traditional impediments to the advance of mankind has not been due — as reformers and pedagogues have maintained — to a simple lack of knowledge. It has rather been the low level of intellectual achievement, which in turn could be due to the way we have deliberately sought to shackle and ignore the unconscious, as though we were afraid to release the powerful forces of which we understand so little.

Happily, we are now entering an era in which we shall not be afraid to think freely and laterally; and in which we shall have the courage to employ the mountain of knowledge which we have for so long been content to *observe from afar*. Once we can overcome our fear-based inhibitions, and release the unknown within us, mankind will have taken its greatest step forward since Aristotle.

To the philosopher and anthropologist, Teilhard de Chardin, the distinguishing characteristic of modern man is that *in him evolution has become conscious*. That does not mean that man can as yet determine his evolutionary future. Or we should be far more deeply concerned than we are over which country rules the world! As we become less emotionally and intellectually dependent on the umbilical cord that still links the leaders and rulers with the ordinary people, those leaders, rulers and politicians will play a gradually decreasing role in our lives until the cord is cut. Unlike our predecessors, we are becoming increasingly alive to the scale and potential of that priceless inheritance — this world of ours — over which we have been given the honour and the good fortune to preside. As Father Teilhard wrote in his masterpiece, *The Phenomenon of Man*:

> "To bring us into existence (the world) has from the beginning juggled miraculously and with too many improbabilities for there to be any risk whatever in committing ourselves further and following it right to the end. If it undertook the task, it is because it can finish it, following the same methods and with the same infallibility with which it began."

Father Teilhard concludes that Israel was the passive recipient of its freedom from ancient Egypt. Lincoln, having freed the slaves in America, would have been the last to claim that emancipation was purely the product of his own — or even the North's — devising. Today we are still doing little more to consummate what was initiated a century ago, than our parents did to achieve the virtual elimination of draft horses in the City of London.

Our first mammalian forebears lived like mice in the woodwork in the world which belonged to the dinosaurs. They lived in much the same way as we do today — as we try to hide from the *dinosaurs* of recession, depression, terrorism, crime and violence. The transcendence of these mammals bears all the earmarks of the power of an idea whose time has come. The concept we have of life itself, is limited by our view of life as it has been during the 20th century. That is to say we are convinced that life will not really change, and that high unemployment will remain as intractable in the future as it has been in the 1980s. This is an even more outdated concept.

A contemporary dinosaur is the fear that improved technology and automation will exert an upward pressure on unemployment — the view held by those with blinkered vision, and an imperfect grasp of historical trends. Despite the intervening peaks and troughs over the past 50 years, one outcome of the rising trend of civilisation over the half-century has been a reduction in the weekly hours of work required to produce a given amount of goods and services. Before 1820, workers were obliged to labour for 60 hours or more a week to provide for their families. During the 18th century, an 80 hour week would have been taken for granted. In those days, it was quite normal for small children to work in the fields, the factories and the mines.

New technology will mean that even greater output will be possible in less than the current 35 hours a week. Weekly hours of work in the 21st century may be expected to fall still further. From the employers' point of view, the fact that more workers will have more specialised facilities at their disposal, means that a higher premium than ever will have to be paid to those will still have to take on the dirtier and more mundane jobs. In essence, however, the wage costs should become less of a problem as fewer hours of work will be required to manufacture the same amount of goods; while higher productivity will boost profits, allowing employers to afford to pay premium wage rates for jobs which will always be labour intensive.

Routine — and still important — chores are already capable of being handed over to the computer and its operator. That means keeping files, setting up appointments, monitoring schedules, book-keeping and accounting, as well as thousands of tasks traditionally carried out by the semi-skilled. The next stage of computer and bio-electronic technology will incorporate a degree of artificial intelligence, coupled to intelligence amplifiers; along with devices capable of being linked to the central nervous system of the operator, thereby raising his (or her) mental powers to awesome dimensions. Replacing people with machines will in many instances produce a faster, easier and more efficient job. Moreover it should benefit the so-called working class, rather than undermine it. This has been the result of many of the emerging technologies which have served to keep living standards on an exponential upward trend for the past 2,000 years. During the 21st century, mankind will take a further step towards individual freedom; and, perhaps even more significantly, one more step away from the old servitude.

Provided all goes well, more and more people will be free to do the things they want to do — and do best. They will tackle the unexpected problem as it arises, and exercise far sounder judgement than possible hitherto — on the basis of a minimum of data. It will be possible because of the average individual's ability to face up to far more complex decisions than ever in the past.

At a practical level, employment in the advanced OECD countries will start to rise during the next decades, following a thundering collapse by the end of the century. The rise, however, will be fragmented, and quite unlike employment trends of the past. The manufacturing sector's share of the workforce will remain comparatively low in the industrialised West. In a way it will be comparable to the shift in employment during the transition from an agriculture-based society to an industry-based one. During the 21st century in the West, we shall be moving from an industry-based society to one characterised by the post-industrial technologies. The developing world will become the "normal" location for industry and manufacture, as the Third World becomes less dependent on natural resources. This will happen because of the new technology which will enable producer-manufacturers to make more efficient use of local resources. For those unable to adapt to the new technologies — which will be available for North and South alike — there will remain a multitude of opportunities in the developing world.

The normal working week, which will give the individual an acceptable standard of living, should be down to around 20 hours. This will revolutionise the lifestyle of the average man and woman, creating vast new markets for the "knowledge" and "leisure" industries. This, in turn, will enhance the productive capacity of the still imperfect human beings whose no more perfect leaders determine the fate of this planet.

As for the consumer boom we may expect during the next period of expansion, it will not be in the West. It will occur in the developing world — from China and the Pacific Basin, to Nigeria and Latin America.

The harnessing of the mighty power of the Chinese workforce, and its direction toward global economic activity, will have an effect like an elephant jumping into a bath! Most people in the West fail to appreciate that China has experienced the greatest economic miracle of the 20th century, which is likely to accelerate in the 21st century. Growing at an amazing 10% per annum, *per capita* income in China passed the 200 dollar mark during the early 1970s, and is still gaining momentum. During the past ten years, the main efforts of the Chinese have been geared towards improving agriculture and providing the population with such necessities of life as food, clothing and education. Exports have been limited, consisting mainly of surplus agricultural production and labour intensive trinkets for the Western consumer. Yet, even this small growth in exports has allowed the Chinese to purchase machines and foreign technology, leaving the country in a strong position to build the infrastructure in preparation for China's industrial revolution. The People's Republic certainly seems ready for full scale industrialisation, and visitors have not been slow in noticing the wide range of instruments, machines and electronic equipment, all of domestic manufacture. It is also evident that a great deal of advanced technology currently available has already been mastered by the Chinese. This can be seen from the launching of satellites and missiles which could never have been done without a vast array of automatic control systems, computers and sophisticated instrumentation.

One of the primary objectives of the current decade — the modernisation and mechanisation of Chinese agriculture — will accelerate the shift of manpower from the primary sector (agriculture) to the secondary sector (manufacturing) in the next few years. Supported by an ample supply of raw materials, China has developed a substantial heavy industrial sector. Its steel output for example, has been growing at the rate of 20% per annum.

Their abundant resources will enable the Chinese to continue with their economic programme. China's coal reserves are equal to those of the US; and Peking's present production, at the end of 1987, reached over 400 million tonnes a year — surpassed only by the US or the USSR. China's oilfields, dismissed as unimportant not so long ago, are now regarded as among the largest and richest in the world — equal to those in the Far East. Today China is self-sufficient in energy and natural resources, those very factors which were primarily responsible for enabling the United States to hold its place as world leader, from the end of the 19th century through the 20th century so far. China, however, enjoys one advantage shared by no other nation on its way up: a huge workforce and an emerging cultural ethic. One in five of the world's population is Chinese, a fact which constitutes a dynamic potential the world would be rash to ignore.

Parallel developments, similar to those in China, are already underway in the Pacific Basin, Nigeria (and some other parts of Africa), as well as South and Central South America. The industrialised nations will share in this boom by way of what might be termed "industrial colonisation". They will achieve a quantum leap during the 1990s, due in part to cheap and more efficient transportation. The OECD countries will supply the capital and manpower. Their growth and development in areas of high technology will be underpinned by the claims they will have staked in the developing countries. Third World debt will become a distant memory. This will come about some time in the 1990s after a purge, followed by amalgamation and securitisation, during the late 1980s and early 1990s.

Meanwhile transportation in the West will be revolutionised by the first successful electric automobiles. This development will owe less to the long expected breakthrough in battery technology, than to the use of microprocessors to control the electricity take-off from the batteries, thereby trebling battery energy conversion in relation to today's forklift truck. Long-distance performance will be made possible by attaching a modular power unit to the urban model, with further modules stacked and ready at convenient points along the highways leading out of town. Although the first electric automobiles were introduced in Britain several years ago — and the famous green Harrods delivery trucks were battery-powered in the early 1900s — their beginning was far from auspicious. Costs were heavy. So was the pressure from the car industry lobby. As the market manufacturers are able to re-tool and apply the wealth of new technology, cheaper and more efficient electric vehicles should become as commonplace as radio, TV, Video — or the ubiquitous microwave oven — by the later 1990s.

There will also be important advances in agriculture. Nitrates — which fail to be used up in the soil, and seep through into the water-supply — will progressively be replaced by nitrogen-fixing algae. Totally new crops will be bio-engineered; and together with protein from carbo-hydrates, they will replace current livestock feed — particularly corn. Never again need there be food shortages, nor — for that matter — an energy shortage or insufficient supplies of any other natural resource. This will end the periodic bursts of price inflation in these commodities. Micro-processor controls will continue to improve utilisation factors across the board for decades to come. When inflation returns in the 2030s and beyond, it will be of an entirely different nature from the past.

In the field of chemical psychiatry, we have already come tantalisingly close to the breakthrough point on being able to identify the chemical basis of memory malfunctions, as well as the various forms of paranoia and phobia. Vasopressin appears to have been successful in providing a dramatic and lasting improvement in memory functions — even restoring the memory of total amnesiacs. Scientists appear to have isolated the chemical responsible for fear of the dark — hence the name, scotophobia. The chemistry of physical pain and pleasure is also becoming a little clearer.

Nowhere has progress been more sensational than in that field of medical technology which includes genetic chemistry and bio-engineering. According to Dr. Robert Wigton, Associate Professor of Medicine at the University of Nebraska, the practising physician today has instant access to a vast amount of diagnostic information. Wigton foresees a day when a doctor need do no more than request a patient's X-ray scan, for a voice-actuated module to produce the X-rays on a screen beside the patient's bed. The physician will then type in all of the data relating to the patient, with his current symptoms, and the module will give an opinion. Since the module will be linked to the master computer containing the most up-to-date discoveries and recommended treatments, the current diagnosis — and prescription — will be arrived at in seconds. Should further tests be needed, they too will be called for. The advice in each case will be backed by the databank containing the world's entire medical knowledge at that time. Cures for cancer and for all known virus diseases could be just around the corner. So could the ability to construct practically any of the so-called building-blocks of life. The wonder lies less in the breakthrough itself then in the vast areas of knowledge that will be opened up.

Just as the databank will reinforce — if not replace — the medical knowledge in the mind of the physician — so robots will become another pair of hands for the physician. During the 21st century, clinics will be equipped with teams of skilled and tireless robots, capable of providing a range of services from emptying bed-pans to assisting with brain surgery. Heart and kidney transplants — brain transplants even — will become routine operations like a tonsillectomy or the removal of a troublesome appendix. What the airplane was to the 20th century, the robot will be to the 21st.

The progress in micro-processing, artifical intelligence and robotics, virtually guarantees that most of the developments that have so far been projected will be achieved sometime during the next decade. The pooling of knowledge, and the teleaccess offered by digitilisation — along with the sophistication in robotics — reinforce the probability that there will be a major, dynamic breakthrough in almost every walk of life. The odds on this happening will be multiplied many times over.

What about man's progress beyond the boundaries of our planet? What could lie in store in that dimension?

In some areas, the time it took to market new developments in automation technology gave cynics an excuse for saying, "It will never happen." Take the case of the development of heavier-than-air craft. No instant take-offs there! Portrayed in Greek legend, invented and re-invented from the Renaissance onwards, the practical man-carrying airplane was not airborne until 1904. Today technological acorns become sturdy oaks in the merest fraction of the time it once took for far simpler industrial developments in the 18th and 19th century. By contrast to the snail's pace development of the aeroplane, Werner von Braun assured the 29-nation man-in-space symposium in Stockholm that developments "immediately ahead" would make our space probings of the previous five years seem:

" . . . as primitive, comparatively speaking, as the first hot air balloon."

On his way back to the US from Stockholm he told the press in Berlin:

"I am determined to fly in one of the spaceships to the moon."

It is conceivable — and well within the realms of possibility — that before the year 2020, the services of a United National Planetary Organisation may have to be set up to replace the pedestrian United Nations Organisation. It is not necessary to seek out members of the space-flight industry to understand why they regard the colonisation of other planets as a serious enterprise. It is as important for them to succeed as it was for Christopher Columbus to win Queen Isabella a sizeable return on the jewels she had pawned. Within the solar system we inhabit, there are a dozen or so planets, and moons of planets, deemed capable of sufficient "re-decoration" to support human life. In place of the rather ponderous two-way economic tensions that business "realists" capitalise on today, we may see twelve intra-galactic economies competing with one another in the not so distant 21st century. Their diverse electoral systems — splintered off from Mother Earth — just as the thirteen North American colonies broke away from England, could well present a more volatile situation. Similar, it might be said, to that enjoyed by the Holy Roman Empire and India when they were each chequer-boarded among alternately competing and co-operating European monarchs and Princely rulers.

Over the centuries we have explored the furthest corners and boundaries of our planet, colonising areas previously deemed uninhabitable; and doing so to the point in some instances of overcrowding. At the end of the 1980s a new territorial imperative lies ahead. As I see it, the Soviet Union will join the other leading nations in contributing to the colonisation of other planets. Both the US and the USSR may well — in the context of developing an impregnable system of defence against nuclear attack — develop laser and other technology to the point at which the arms race will come to a halt. Then the frozen hostility of the Cold War could well begin gradually to thaw, allowing both Washington and Moscow to devote more of the resources of their respective societies to the cause of furthering international co-operation. On the one side we could then see a transformation of their rigidly autocratic regime into something more flexible; and, on the other, a tempering of the absolutes of capitalism with a hint of non-doctrinaire collectivism.

Those who today, with tunnel vision, see nothing ahead but an East/West war of mutual annihilation — with the inevitable destruction of life in all its forms upon this planet — will hopefully come to realise that they are walking in fear of a phantom of their own creation; hiding in the shadows from a dinosaur already on the point of extinction. There is a far greater likelihood of an inter-galactic "Star Wars" type confrontation at some time in the future, than of the dreaded nuclear holocaust on the surface of the earth.

In short, I can see the technology already in place to carry the next Upwave to unprecedented heights — even without the technological development that is as yet unforseeable, and indisputably beyond our current comprehension. Our task now is to determine how we can ensure that we shall be among the first to exploit the vast — and I believe boundless — limits of man's potential.

A Fortune-Seekers Guide to The Upwave

Once upon a time there were five destitute Arabs who set forth across the desert in search of their fortune. After several weeks, while their travels still seemed fruitless, one night as they slept upon the sands a bright light from the heavens suddenly woke them, and an angel appeared.

"I've been watching the five of you" said the angel. "Since your efforts have been unrewarded so far, I'm now prepared to grant each of you one wish so that you can return to your families and abandon your futile quest."

"Praise be to Allah!" exclaimed the first of the Arabs. "All I want is a donkey to take me back to my wife and children."

In an instant, a donkey appeared at his side.

"What a fool", one of the other Arabs muttered under his breath. "He should have asked for much more with his one and only wish. I wish for *ten* donkeys. I can use one of the donkeys to take me back to my wife and children. I'll use the other ten donkeys to provide them with a better living than ever before."

The angel's eye twinkled. Ten donkeys immediately appeared.

After watching the experiences of the first two Arabs, a third Arab cast his wish.

"To Allah all things are possible." said he. "I wish for a caravan with a hundred camels, a hundred donkeys, tents, rugs, food, wine and servants. There will be no need for me to return to my wife and children. My wife and children can join me here on the Oasis over which we will all preside."

The items he had wished for appeared faster than the eye could follow. Suddenly, the Arab saw a weakness in his plan. How ashamed he was to be seen in his tattered clothing when he now presided over such a wealthy domain. But his shame did not last very long. His wish provided for more than he had dreamed of. Deftly, the servants who were part of the wish, dressed him in splendid robes befitting his new status.

The fourth Arab, who was carefully monitoring the progress of his colleagues in their negotiations with the angel, was fully prepared when it came to his turn.

"Make me a king." the fourth Arab commanded.

He lifted his fingers to scratch his louse-ridden scalp. Suddenly he found a golden crown on the spot where there had previously been nothing but an itch! The palace garden over which he was now lord and master stretched out before him almost as far as the eye could see. The turrets of his massive palace reached so high that their pennants were lost in the desert haze.

The fifth Arab, after watching his impoverished companions receiving more and more, concluded that too little was asked by all of them. He decided that he would not merely limit his wish to immediate gratification, but would seek all that the universe could provide.

"Make me Allah!" the fifth Arab ordered of the angel.

Faster than the speed of light, the fifth Arab found himself lying in the hot sun on scorching sand, his body bloody and covered with oozing, leprous sores.

The moral of that story is plain. Those who ask little of life receive little. Those who ask a great deal often receive a great deal. Those who ask for too much — frequently beyond the bounds of what should be realistically expected — often end up with nothing. Investors who always seek safety in markets will receive safety and an adequate return, but little more. Investors who continue to pursue a get-rich-quick strategy — striving for objectives which are totally unrealistic — suffer the financial equivalent of the Arab

on the sands with his leprous sores. For those who are patient and pursue
a strategy of realistic prudence and caution, when it is appropriate to do
so, the Upwave will offer an oasis of opportunity, not seen for sixty years.

The most astute market operators in history made most of their fortunes
by playing the long extended swings in the market; not by switching and
swapping, trading in and out of bull and bear markets or intermediate term
swings in markets. Long haul investment has always proved to be the most
profitable. . . particularly when instigated at major terminal junctures. Over
the past fifty years or so, there have been several important terminal junctures,
but none that offered the type of opportunity presented to investors in 1932
at the depth of the Great Depression. Between 1932 and the 32 years that
followed, no fewer than 360 different companies saw their share price
increase in value by 10,000% and more.

Beginning in 1932, any one could have made a million pounds on a £10,000
investment in a different share in each of the 32 different years that followed.
To do so would have required neither luck nor skill. All that was required
was to pick just one of the hundreds of shares that were in tune with the
emerging technologies of the time, and hang on.

In the classic *1929* by Warren Sloat, during the early summer of 1932
an old-timer on Wall Street is quoted as saying:

> "Anyone who can put his hands on $10,000 to invest in the stock market
> at these prices is a rich man."

Most people at the time likened the comment to the quip, "If we had
some ham we could have some ham and eggs. . . if we had some eggs!"
The reasoning was simple to understand. Very few investors during 1932
— after losing 90% and more of their savings in the market — had $10,000
to invest in Wall Street. In fact, the reason that share prices were so low
was that so few people were willing or able to invest at the time. But there
were those who had heeded the warnings of the late 1920s, liquidated their
holdings prior to the "crash" and preserved that liquidity throughout the
bear market years of the Great Depression. For them, there were fortunes
to be made at their fingertips, just as there will be similar fortunes available
in a few short years for those who act prudently and cautiously as we
approach the terminal juncture of the Downwave, which will be coincident
with the next long-term period of technological expansion.

The basic criteria for investing during the next long-term period of
expansion will be the same as those employed when seeking the fortune
makers of previous periods. The guidelines to be followed are relatively
simple and logical. The hunting grounds I'm about to recommend go as
far back as the time when man's major innovation was fire:

1)   Look for companies that exploit inventions which enable society to
        do things that people have always wanted to do, but could never do
        before. Think of the steam-engine, railroads, the automobile, the
        airplane, television and so forth. Innovations that are going to be

developed will be as dramatic in their impact as those I've just mentioned.

2) Look for companies that are utilising methods, or introducing equipment for doing things we have had to do, but can now do more easily, faster or at less cost than before. But be careful! Computers and robots, although regarded as new technologies, are the fruits of the past. Artificial intelligence is the way of the future.

3) Seek out companies which manufacture equipment dedicated to improving or maintaining existing services, while reducing or eliminating the labour that has hitherto been required to provide such a service. Earlier examples are disposable syringes, sheets in hospitals, disposable nappies, frozen foods and the whole family of photo-copiers.

4) Look for companies that are directing their efforts toward discovering and applying new, cheaper and more efficient sources of energy, in the way oil producers used kerosene to replace whale oil, fuel oil to replace coal, and atomic power to replace all of these. There *will* be an energy source which is likely to be cheaper and more efficient than atomic power.

5) Ecological considerations will be a permanent part of the future. We are just beginning to learn of the potential disaster associated with depleting our resources along with the dangers to health involved in current practices geared towards efficient production. There will be an important role for companies able to do the essential jobs that are currently required, and can do these jobs efficiently with a minimum of ecological damage. An example is the use of sterilised insects for the purpose of pest control rather than chemicals which are harmful to many desirable forms of life — including that of *homo sapiens*.

6) Waste not want not. Garbage can play an important role in your investment programme in the 1990s. I'm not suggesting you invest in garbage. You've probably had more than your fill of investing in garbage during the final stages of the 1980s bull market. Companies that specialise in improved methods, or equipment, for recycling materials — including water — will play a major role in the forward-looking world of the 21st century, by which time the futility of making mountains of waste and oceans of sewage will have been recognised.

7) Have you ever thought how inefficient and antiquated current methods of mass media communication actually are? Can the labour involved in transmitting a newspaper through your letter box every day be justified? Furthermore, is it really necessary to chew up our forests in order to supply you with newsprint that is discarded as waste only a few hours after you receive it. Few items have less value than yesterday's newspaper. But millions of newspapers are printed daily in a form that began in the Dark Ages. We should soon be entering

an Age of Enlightenment, where inefficient methods of this sort are replaced by new and more viable means of communication. In the future, your newspaper may simply be available to you to read on a TV screen, which can also provide you with an instant print-out and retrieval facility, allowing you to preserve the data in your home for many years to come. Companies are already engaged in researching this type of improved mass communication. These companies should be watched closely.

8)   Fire and the wheel have long been regarded as the two inventions that have done more to lift man from the abyss of savagery than any other. As we approach the 21st century, perhaps it would not be unreasonable to conclude that we may have paid homage to fire and the wheel for a bit too long. There is an inherent contradiction in the wheel. The faster it moves, the greater the friction and the stronger the centrifugal force. Speed becomes the product of a geometrical inversion. In order to achieve supersonic speeds in the air, we find a way of leaving the wheel behind. We are moving into an era when supersonic speeds are likely to become as redundant as the speed of a horse. Super-light speed will be the goal of the future. This may be achieved with air cushions on land, or perhaps magnetic forces in space — probably with ideas, methods and equipment as yet undreamed of. Yet, you can be certain there are companies already spending billions on research and the development of methods for transporting people and goods on land without wheels, more cheaply and more efficiently than ever before. Here too you will find the harbingers of the next major wave of expansion involving earnings capabilities as yet untapped.

9)   We are all affected by the weather, probably more than we know. There is no possible way we are ever going to be able to change the effects of weather on the planet, nor can we ever expect to change the weather in the remotely foreseeable future. What we *will* be able to do is predict the weather with far greater accuracy than we have ever done before, while harnessing the tremendously powerful natural forces to our advantage as a spin-off from our ability to predict changes with even greater accuracy. Improving the ability to predict changes in the weather, while quantifying these changes, will bring enormous benefits to mankind. The earth's weather systems are incredibly complex, and the models that describe these systems push today's largest and fastest computers to their very limit. But, during the next decade, technology can be expected to improve exponentially, and our ability to forecast the weather is likely to improve dramatically. The savings in lives will be enormous as will also be the saving in crops, leading to more cost effective food production. High-tech farming could offer a major investment opportunity as large combines

rush to purchase farmland at dirt-cheap prices during the nadir of the rapidly approaching Downwave.

10) For those who do not wish to become involved in the higher technologies, there still remain traditional areas which will provide fortune-making opportunities when the Upwave begins in a few years time. At some point, even the cyclical stocks, such as rubber, chemicals, machinery and construction will improve. For one thing, the companies that survive the depression are likely to have installed massive cost-cutting programmes, and will be entering the next Upwave with a strong balance sheet and a high credit rating. Almost any type of cyclical recovery will increase the earning potential of such companies by several multiples. There are always those generals who are inclined to fight the next battles with the weapons of the last. When a new bull market begins, those investors who are not so far-sighted as they might be, will traditionally move into the shares of those industries that have performed well during earlier bull markets, even though the character of the next major bull market will differ markedly from the one that began in 1975.

Finally, investors should also consider areas of traditional long-term growth where the demography, demand trends, and results of policy changes are compatible with the next Upwave. Specifically, I refer to the auto-industry and the housing industry, where there is likely to be a huge pent-up demand once the next recovery gets underway.

My Upwave Favourites

I have attempted to single out the specific areas which I feel will offer the best investment potential during the bull market that will be the precursor to the next long-term period of expansion — likely to begin in the 1990s. What I am now going to do is give you a "watching list" which includes those companies that I believe are likely to make a significant contribution to the technologies that will be coming off the drawing board, and whose profit potential is likely to rise exponentially with their share price.

First and foremost, I would certainly not recommend you to begin purchasing the shares of any of these companies during the remainder of the coming period of contraction. In most cases, the price of the shares of these companies is likely to move lower. A few may even go bankrupt. Among the list are some heavyweights that are sure to survive. But the big winners are going to be the long shots, which manage to hang on by the skin of their teeth before emerging like a phoenix from the ashes of despair during the approaching Upwave.

I firmly believe the lynch-pin for the future is automation. "Turnkey" CAD/CAM companies will be reserved for the very top of my investment programme, the core group of my investment philosophy. CAD/CAM means computer-aided design/computer-aided manufacturing. The companies involved are cyclical, like the construction companies and engineering companies of previous economic cycles. Just as the construction companies and heavy engineers were front runners during the early stages of previous bull markets, in my view the CAD/CAM companies will be the top performers in the early stages of the next bull market. A major company in this field is COMPUTERVISION, listed on the New York Stock Exchange. INTERGRAPH is another company that deserves careful watching. INTERGRAPH is probably the world's foremost CAD/CAM company. INTERGRAPH is traded on the US Over-the-Counter market.

The aforementioned come in the category of "turnkey" CAD/CAM companies. Of equal importance are the component CAD/CAM companies. GERBER SCIENTIFIC, quoted on the New York Stock Exchange, is the manufacturer of full systems, in addition to components for these systems, for companies that require a more comprehensive service than that offered by the "turnkey" companies. GERBER SCIENTIFIC are major innovators who have incorporated plotter technology that employ knives, lasers and other highly sophisticated tools in order to create the finished product on the factory floor. Watch it! It could be a big winner when the time comes.

Second to the CAD/CAM companies as a major component of the type of investment portfolio I plan to build during the incipient stages of the next Upwave, are companies involved in robotics. Robotic engineering is a classic example of an under-utilised technology that was presented long before it was able to fulfil its ultimate potential. Because robots were unable to carry out the tasks of human beings, they were considered a failure in most applications. But the new breed of robots will be capable of undertaking tasks that previously have been way beyond the capabilities of humans. . . especially when integrated with artificial intelligence.

The growth potential for robots is staggering. Currently the major user of robots is the United States. Yet fewer than 20,000 robots are currently employed in US factories. In the future, the number of robots likely to be employed will equal that of the number of computers that are employed today, running into millions. Many larger companies have incorporated robot manufacturing divisions. I am primarily concerned with those companies whose major activity is robot manufacture. One company I shall be keeping a close eye on in the years ahead is RANSBURG, which is quoted on the American Stock Exchange. RANSBURG is heavily committed to the global sale and distribution of automated welding and spray painting systems for which it has gained an outstanding reputation. RANSBURG is not a direct manufacturer, but comprises part of the robotic service industry.

On the purely manufacturing side I'll be keeping a constant vigil on PRAB ROBOTS. PRAB manufactures both material-handling and arc-welding robots, plus conveyor systems. The products of the company are used by a wide range of industries and have exceptionally advanced heavy duty applications. PRAB is quoted on the US Over-the-Counter market.

Artificial vision is one of the most recent innovations in robot technology, which will aid the efficient application of robots, and expand the areas in which robots can be employed. ROBOTIC VISION SYSTEMS, quoted on the Over-the-Counter Market in the US, is a major manufacturer of artificial vision systems, specialising in three dimensional designs which are used as robot guidance devices in a wide range of demanding applications. The company could be a really big winner, with many high-tech products to sell to companies able to emerge triumphant from the Downwave, and move confidently into the Upwave.

Not quite as "hi-tech" as robotics is the growing field of automatic equipment, which will be the 21st century version of machine tool manufacturers. ACME-CLEVELAND, whose shares are quoted on the New York Stock Exchange, is one of America's principal machine tool manufacturers, and has recently been incorporating computerised control systems. Given the established record of the company in its field, continuing technological progress is likely to place the company in the position of a major pace-maker in factory automation. After all, IBM manufactured scales before deciding in 1932 that it should take a look at "those machines that 'think'". ACME-CLEVELAND could easily be the IBM of the Upwave to come. Another exciting company to watch in the field of factory automation is G&B AUTOMATED EQUIPMENT. The shares of this company are quoted on the Toronto Stock Exchange. The speciality of the company is the design and production of automated equipment for the bonded abrasives industry, a field in which they are already a leader. Although the company is Canadian, they have considerable exposure to international markets, thanks to the specialised nature of their products. Sales to Soviet bloc countries have been extremely impressive. In the Societ bloc, the products of G&B AUTOMATED EQUIPMENT are considered essential technology.

The backbone of any major period of expansion is the manufacturing industry. Only a fool believes otherwise. A back-up to the automated/automatic equipment industry are the manufacturers of automatic material-handling and inventory-control systems. Although I may appear to be scratching the bottom of the barrel in the hi-tech industries, these systems will be an essential aspect of all modern factories in the future. In this area, my watching list consists of two fliers, both of which are listed on the US Over-the-Counter market. They are INTERMEC, a leading supplier of scanners, scanning wands, bar code label printers and other devices which have become standard formats for inventory control. COMPUTER IDENTICS is a maker of scanners, decoders and computerised processors involving an exceptionally wide range of applications in inventory control. On the automatic material-handling side, HARNISCHFEGER, quoted on the New York Stock Exchange, is a prominent feature on my "watching list". HARNISCHFEGER is a major manufacturer of automated warehouses and factory-floor transport equipment. Offering a bit more speculative potential — and higher risk — in the field of automatic material-handling is ENGINEERED SYSTEMS AND DEVELOPMENT, quoted on the

American Stock Exchange. ENGINEERED SYSTEMS AND DEVELOPMENT is a producer of material-handling systems used in distribution centres and a variety of manufacturing applications. The company is also a manufacturer of factory automation systems, including equipment for electronic factories. With ENGINEERED SYSTEMS AND DEVELOPMENT on your "watching list", you get two bites out of the hi-tech apple instead of one!

Process control is the second half of industrial automation. Essentially, automated factory systems are designed for those who manufacture products one-at-a-time. The function of process control is directed toward companies engaged in batch production — paper mills, steel plants, iron foundries, sheet aluminium plants and plastic factories. This type of production requires sensors that monitor a number of production variables — temperature, stress, quality control factors, pressure, density and thickness. One of the leading companies in this field that I will be monitoring is HONEYWELL, listed on the New York Stock Exchange. HONEYWELL is a supplier of control systems to the batch process industry along with a variety of other markets. HONEYWELL is also a manufacturer of advanced computers, and has the capability to supply fully automated systems for the most demanding applications. In view of the comprehensive nature of the company's product line, HONEYWELL has been able to capture an increasing share of the process control market.

A somewhat more specialised manufacturer of process control systems is FOXBORO, whose shares are also quoted on the New York Stock Exchange. FOXBORO's speciality is process control instrumentation, and it is a supplier to a vast array of industries which are steadily improving their efficiency through advancing technology. FOXOBORO's principal expertise has been directed towards closed-loop control system control products. There are two types of loop-control systems at which FOXBORO excels. The open-loop system involves the collection by sensors of data which is then displayed on instrument panels for human evaluation. The closed-loop system involves the collection of data linked to a computer network which automatically makes whatever adjustments are necessary in process control. Millions of dollars are now being spent in the conversion from open-loop to closed-loop systems. FOXBORO maintains 175 offices in 80 different countries, and is placed to take maximum advantage of the potential that exists in this sector of advanced technology. The company's loop control products are frequently used to tie together complete plantwide management systems.

Another company in the process control area whose products span a wide range of applications is TRAUB, quoted on the West German Stock Exchange. TRAUB is one of the world's three leading manufacturers of CNC automatic lathes. Founded in 1938, the company has developed strong Eastern connections over the decades. Whereas business with the East was flat during the first half of the 1980s and most of the company's exports involved the delivery of spare parts for plant previously installed, a dramatic change could develop during the next period of expansion as Eastern manufacturers begin "tooling-up" for the coming boom. TRAUB is a "blue-chip" company, and certainly worth watching.

It must be recognised that the industry groups that will be the forerunners and biggest profit makers for the next period of expansion will be very different from those of previous expansion periods. The technologies will be different, and so will the industries in which the emerging technologies are employed. Many may think the semi-conductor industry is "old hat" — consisting of nothing more than a spin-off from the technology of past decades, whose profit potential has now been exhausted along with the period of expansion that semi-conductors spawned. Well, the industry may be "old hat". Product development is as new as the jet-propelled rocket was in the 1940s. The semi-conductor industry is a cyclical industry. Companies involved in semi-conductor equipment production are likely to be among the leaders when the next long-term major bull market begins.

Back in the 1940s, one of the major areas of expertise in which PERKIN-ELMER was involved was that of production testing. On one occasion, an engineer at PERKIN-ELMER was called upon to produce a report verifying a newly developed servo-motor for a bombsight capable of functioning under all practical conditions. He completed most of the tests, then he ran across the problem of temperature variations for which he needed a temperature chamber. At the time, there were no known temperature chambers in existence. The engineer at PERKIN-ELMER built his own. He used a photographer's strobe light and other adaptations to make 1,000 tests on every servo-motor. Each reading required five minutes. By 1951, the introduction of semi-automatic test equipment by PERKIN-ELMER had cut a two-week programme of this kind down to no more than a half-day's work — capable of being handled by a technician, instead of a graduate engineer. This type of forward thinking and ingenuity encouraged by management has subsequently made PERKIN-ELMER the world's largest supplier of semi-conductor process equipment. It is able to offer the widest range of equipment, along with one-stop shopping for chips. The company makes a wide range of scientific instruments for rapid chemical and physical analysis; optical and electro-optical systems for space and defence programmes; precision electronic components and computers. A distinct advantage that PERKIN-ELMER has over others in the semi-conductor field is their integrated product line in an area where incompatibility of assembly line components has been a constant problem. PERKIN-ELMER is a leader in the design and installation of fully automated production facilities, and should be one of the big hitters of the next period of expansion. The shares of PERKIN-ELMER are quoted on the New York Stock Exchange.

There would be no growth potential in the semi-conductor industry without the computer-aided engineering industry known to the technologically washed as "CAE". CAE systems assist with a great deal of the engineering quintessential to efficient semi-conductor design. Allied to CAE systems is the ASIC industry, which for the technologically unwashed, means the application of specific integrated circuits (or more simply, customised semi-conductors.) I'm watching two companies in this group, and I will be monitoring their progress over the next few years. One is VLSI TECHNOLOGY. The shares are quoted on the Over-the-Counter market in the US. The company produces specialist CAE design tools used in the creation of semi-customised and full-custom chips. SILVAR-LISCO, another company whose shares are quoted on the Over-the-Counter market in the US, is also quite interesting. SILVAR-LISCO is unique among the CAE companies as a software supplier to companies that already have installed CAD/CAM or CAE systems, but require to expand their application packages.

Needless to say, the current "blue chips" are not going to die away into obscurity. Many will be innovating and exploring new areas of technology, and also be among the forerunners in the next wave of expansion, whose shares are capable of demonstrating outstanding potential. I believe the shares of SIEMENS should be considered as a constituent of any portfolio designed to benefit from the next major phase of expansion. SIEMENS and its subsidiaries constitute West Germany's largest electrical enterprise, accounting for about 20% of the electronics and heavy electrical equipment produced in that country. SIEMENS' products include broad groups of electrical items from heavy power equipment to communications and consumer goods.

I am particularly partial toward the prospects for Japan during the next growth period. In Japan there are a host of companies that deserve careful scrutiny, ranging from the giant SONY CORPORATION through MITSUBISHI CHEMICAL, NIPPON ELECTRIC, MITSUI SHIPBUILDING, KAWASAKE STEEL and KANSAI ELECTRIC.

I seem to have neglected the field of research and development in plastics — primarily because most of the firms engaged in this area of future technology are of mega-dimensions. Yet these too should be included among your list of potential winners during the next explosive period of harnessed innovation. My favourites are DOW CHEMICAL, GE PLASTICS, DUPONT, BOEING, BORG-WARNER and SUMITOMO CHEMICALS of Japan.

Getting back to the minnows, two extremely exciting companies were brought to my attention by James Dale Davison and William Rees-Mogg in their superb book, *Panic in the Streets*. They are BIO-TECHNOLOGY GENERAL CORPORATION and CHIRON. Both companies are traded on the Over-the-Counter market in the USA. These companies are the two leaders in a field which is of vital interest to virtually every human being in our civilised society. . . the development and application of bio-technology to life extension. If there was ever a potential winner likely to capture the imagination of the investor in the event of a breakthrough, it's certainly the companies involved in this area of research. Obviously, the potential applications of their research are so far-reaching that a small number of shares in each of these companies — treated as a long-shot speculation — should be in every portfolio when the time is right.

I would now repeat, the list of companies I have recommended are not intended for purchase now, they are suggestions for study when the time seems right. I will be following a number of these companies in my weekly *Investors Bulletin.* I may also be buying some of their shares for the Unit Trust whose investment policy I determine. THE BECKMAN INTERNATIONAL CAPITAL ACCUMULATOR is the only Unit Trust in the entire world that publishes what investments and disinvestments are made — during the week they are made.

Before considering the shares of any of these companies, do your homework and make sure your timing is right. The reward will be well worth the effort.

Epilogue

The preparation of a book of this nature does, of course, involve many months of research, compilation and actual writing. I began during the early autumn of 1986 and essentially completed writing the book with my friend Bob Finigan, formerly of the BBC, in late January 1988.

During that period, developments which have occurred appear to offer even more evidence to shew that the world is moving close to the brink of disaster, and even more rapidly than suggested in the earlier part of this work. Since I began writing the book, we've seen unrestrained monetary growth in Britain which must, indeed, have sown the seeds of chronic inflation, unless overtaken by a devastating deflation neutralising the uncontrolled and reckless behaviour of the British authorities. We've seen the collapse of the US dollar, and the epic October 1987 melt-down across the capital markets of the world. We've also watched the feeble attempts at Westminster and in Whitehall to convince you that they above all are capable of solving the insoluble.

Inevitably, as we reach these final paragraphs, we must concede that the future remains an enigma — with countless variations. I've often told the audience at my lectures, if they would like to view the world in a way that appears less enigmatic — if they wish to get the right answers — they must begin by asking the right questions. Asking the right questions is, indeed, no easy task as we approach the terminal juncture of one era with the next. Because of the success our leaders have been able to achieve in selling the soft option, virtually everyone today is tempted — and willing — to formulate his arguments on the utterly false premise of that soft option. Changing the perceptions of a public that has been brainwashed for decades is a monumental task. In order to be intellectually free and able to ask the right questions it requires all of us to disregard a myriad of false premises which are treated today as sacrosanct.

In *The Downwave*, I attempted to address what I considered then to be the right questions. According to the many hundreds of letters I've received since *The Downwave* was published, it seems I may have helped to change a few misconceptions. The knowledge that I have done that is one of the most emotionally rewarding experiences I have ever had. Since then I have ventured deeper into the abyss of the future in this work, hopefully expanding the horizons I only sensed and touched on before.

Strategically, I have tried to offer a prescription for making money in the disinflationary environment that lies immediately ahead, as well as for successfully exploring all that lies beyond. The prescription is a simple one. Get together some cash from the sale of assets that are incompatible with the type of financial environment immediately ahead. Invest the cash in some long-or intermediate-term bonds — or even in some of the more speculative areas of the fixed interest market. After that, begin formulating a buying programme for shares in companies that are likely to flourish in the long and glorious period of expansion which will follow. And that, in the end, is what's so pleasing about preserving your capital during a period of recession — or even deep depression. There are so many options for the individual who still has money in his pocket when the upturn — and the opportunities — finally arrive.

The end of the depression will usher in a totally new world, offering a cornucopia of opportunities and difficulties. For those who are prepared and have the courage, the possibilities are as exciting as they are enormous, while the success that may be won is likely to be beyond your wildest dreams of avarice. But until that time, your stance should remain one of masterly inactivity.

Don't just *do* something — stand there!

BIBLIOGRAPHY

Alexander, Franz and Staub, Hugo, *The Criminal, the Judge and the Public.* George Allen and Unwin, 1931.

Allen, Gary with Abraham, Larry, *None Dare Call it Conspiracy.* Concord Press, Calif., 1971.

Abraham, Larry, *Conspiracy Peddlers — A Study of the Conspiracy Media in the United States.* (Insider Report).

Bellini, James, *Rule Britannia: A Progress Report for Doomsday 1986.* Johnathan Cape, 1981.

Blythe, Ronald, *The Age of Illusion.* Hamish Hamilton, 1963.

Brittan, Sam, *The Role and Limits of Government.* Temple Smith, 1983.

Cardiff, G.E. and English, J.W., *The Coming Real Estate Crash.* New Rochelle, NY: Arlington House, 1979.

Coakley, Jerry and Harris, Lawrence, *The City of Capital.* Blackwell, 1983.

Cobbett, Donald, *Before the Big Bang.* Milestone Publications, 1986.

Cogan, L. Peter, *The Rhymthmic Cycles of Optimism and Pessimism.* NY, William Frederick Press, 1969.

Dalyell, Tam, *Misrule.* Hamish Hamilton, 1987.

Eringer, Robert, *The Global Manipulators.* Pentacle Books, 1980.

Fest, Joachim, *The Face of the Third Reich (Das Gesicht des Dritten Reiches).* R. Piper, Munich, 1963. Translation pub. Weidenfeld and Nicolson, 1970.

Furth, Charles, *Life Since 1900.* George Allen and Unwin, 1956.

Galbraith, J.K., *The Great Crash, 1954.* The Riverside Press, 1954.
  The Affluent Society, Hamish Hamilton, 1958.
  Money. Andre Deutsch, 1975.

Granville, Joe, *The Warning.*

Greenwood, Walter, *Love on the Dole.* Johnathan Cape, 1933.

Guttman, William and Meehan, Patricia, *The Great Inflation.* Saxon House, 1975.

Hammond, J.L. and Barbara, *The Bleak Age.* Penguin.

Hoggart, Richard, *The Uses of Literacy.* Chatto & Windus, 1957.

Homer, Sidney, *The History of Interest Rates.* Rutgers State University, 1963.

Jay, Douglas, *Sterling.* Sidgwick and Jackson, 1985.

Jay, Peter and Stewart, Michael, *Apocalypse 2000: Economic breakdown and the suicide of democracy, 1989-2000.* Sidwick and Jackson, 1987.

Jenkins, Alan, *The Stock Exchange Story.* Heinemann, for Stock Exchange (Holdings) Ltd, 1973.

Junor, Penny, *Margaret Thatcher.* Sidgwick and Jackson, 1983.

Kahn, Herman, *The Coming Boom.* Hutchinson, 1983.

Keynes, J.M., *How to Pay for the War.* NY, Harcourt Brace Co, 1940.

Kindleberger, Charles B., *The World in Depression 1929-1939.* Penguin Press, Alan Lane, 1973.

Mackay, Charles, *Extraordinary Popular Delusions and Madness of Crowds.* George Harrap, 1956.

Macmillan, Harold and others, *The Next Five Years.* Macmillan, 1935.

Marwick, Arthur, *The Explosion of British Society.* Pan Special.

Mass Observation. Penguin Special, 1939.

Orwell, George, *The Road to Wigan Pier.* Gollancz, 1937.

Animal Farm. 1984.

Packard, Vance, *The Hidden Persuaders.* David McKay, 1957.

Pigou, A.C., *Industrial Fluctuations.* Macmillan, 1927.

Pethwick-Lawrence, P.W., *The Gold Crisis.* Gollancz, 1931.

Plender, John, *That's the Way the Money Goes.* Andre Deutsch, 1982.

Priestley, J.B., *English Journey.* Heinemann and Gollancz, 1934.

Quigley, Prof. Carroll, *Tragedy and Hope: A History of the World in Our Time.* NY, Macmillan, 1966.

Rand, Ayn, *The Fountainhead.* Cassell, 1947.

Rees-Mogg, Sir, *Blood in the Streets.* Sidgwick and Jackson, 1987.

Davidson, William and Dale, James Reid, Margaret, *The Secondary Banking Crisis, 1937-75.* Macmillan, 1982.

Rose, Simon, *Fair Shares.* Comet, 1986.

Rostow, W., *The World Economy.* Macmillan, 1978.

Schumpeter, Joseph, *Business Cycles.* NY, McGraw Hill, 1939.

History of Economic Development. George Allen and Unwin, 1954.

The Theory of Economic Development. Harvard U Press, 1934.
Shirer, William, *The Rise and Fall of the Third Reich.* NY and London, 1960.
Soros, George, *The Alchemy of Finance.* Simon and Schuster, 1987.
Spengler, Oswald, *The Decline of the West.* George Allen and Unwin, 1926.
Thomson, David, *England in the 19th Century, England in the 20th Century.* Penguin, 1950.
Toffler, Alvin, *The Third Wave.* Collins, 1980.
Wapshott, Nicholas and Brock, George, *Thatcher.* Futura, 1983.
Warren, G.F. and Pearson, F.A., *Prices Series.* NY, John Wiley and Sons, 1933.
Wilkinson, Ellen, *The Town That Was Murdered.* Gollancz, 1939.

SELECTED PAPERS AND ARTICLES

Carstairs, G.M., Contribution to *The History of Violence in America,* pp 751-763. Bantam Book, 1969.
Forrester, Jay W., "Changing Economic Patterns", *Technology Review,* Aug/Sept, 1978, pp 47-53.
Hitler, Adolf, *Mein Kampf.* Translated James Murphy, London, 1939 and Boston, 1943 by Ralph Manheim.
Kondratieff, N.D., "The Long Wave of Economic Life", *The Review of Economic Statistics* 17 (6). "Die Langen Wellender Konjunktur", *Archiv fuer Sozialwissenschaft und Sozialpolitik.*
See also: *The Bank Credit Analyst.* May, 1973 pp 27-35; *City Bank Monthly Economic Letter.* January, 1978 — "Kondratieff Invents History" and February, 1978 — "Kuznets Explains History".
Lord O'Brien, *Bank of England Quarterly Bulletin.* June, 1971.
Salomon Bros Inc, *Interest Rate Chartbook.*
Taft, Philip and Ross, Philip, Contribution to *The History of Violence in America,* pp 281-388.

INDEX